8/10 ?

$5.00 ish

HEAVEN'S COMMAND
An Imperial Progress

James Morris

HEAVEN'S COMMAND

An Imperial Progress

A Harvest Book
A Helen and Kurt Wolff Book
Harcourt Brace & Company
San Diego New York London

Requests for permission to make copies
of any part of the work should be mailed to:
Permissions Department, Harcourt Brace & Company,
6277 Sea Harbor Drive, Orlando, Florida 32887-6777.

Library of Congress Cataloging-in-Publication Data
Morris, James, 1926–
Heaven's command.
(A Harvest book)
"A Helen and Kurt Wolff book."
The first volume of the author's trilogy; the subsequent
volumes are: Pax Britannica; Farewell the trumpets.
Includes index.
1. Great Britain—Colonies—History.
2. Great Britain—History—Victoria, 1837–1901.
I. Title.
[DA16.M596   1980]   909'.09'71242   79-24327
ISBN 0-15-640006-5

Printed in the United States of America
H J L M K I

For

HENRY MORRIS

Un-Imperialist

Set in this stormy Northern sea,
  Queen of these restless fields of tide,
England! what shall men say of thee,
  Before whose feet the worlds divide?

OSCAR WILDE

PROLOGUE

The house that is portrayed on the jacket of this work is called Sezincote. It was built in the early years of the nineteenth century for Sir Charles Cockerell, a nabob of the East India Company who had retired to England with a sizeable fortune, and bought a property in Gloucestershire. Cockerell employed as architect his own brother, Samuel Pepys Cockerell, surveyor to East India House, and he in turn was helped by Thomas Daniell the topographical artist, who was an authority on Indian design.

It stands in one of the most intensely English parts of England, on the northern slopes of the Cotswold hills, but it is the most exotically un-English building imaginable. Half-veiled by oaks and elms, lapped by rose-beds and summer-scented lawns, with moor-hens scurrying through the reeds of its lake and all the innocuous English sounds, of laughs and tractors and radio music, sounding through its out-buildings, there stands its copper-sheathed onion dome in marvellous anomaly. Pinnacles attend it, as on a Moghul pleasure-palace, there are high arched mosque-like windows, and deep eaves trace a shadow-line around the roof, as if offering shelter to love-birds and cockatoos. An orange light seems to emanate from the house, its stone facing having been artificially stained to this effect, and in the gardens all about are follies and fancies intended to indulge the nostalgic traveller from the East—Brahman bulls of cast-iron, an Indian bridge across a little nullah, a gay pillared pavilion, a shrine to the sun-god Surya. Contrasted with the solid narrow-windowed mansions of the neighbouring Cotswold gentry, Sezincote is marvellously elated: ostentatious in a way, rather eccentric, but expressing a grand romantic sympathy for the wide horizon and the main chance. It is like a nabob itself, flaunting its gaudy splendours among the horse-squires and wool merchants who stayed at home.

I see it as emblematic of this work about the British Empire because it is, as Bagehot said of royal marriages, a brilliant edition of a more general fact. It illustrates a streak in the English instinct—a taste for things foreign and incongruous, a recurrent yearning to break out of our gentle northern setting, all greens and greys, into more vivid places, where fortunes can be made, outrageous enterprises undertaken, and the restrictive rules of scale and conduct flamboyantly disregarded.

Of course not every Briton ever felt these somewhat immature urges, but repeatedly in the course of British history they have been so forceful, or have been so skilfully exploited, that they have come to direct the policy of the State. I conceive the story of Queen Victoria's empire generally in such terms. I am aware that factors solidly economic or starkly military impelled the power of Victorian Britain across the seas and continents. I know that there is no single explanation for the phenomenon of imperialism, that most European countries felt its compulsion in one degree or another, and that many theorists would consider St Pancras Station, or Keble College, or even the Prudential Insurance Building, to be more properly symbolic of the Victorian empire than Sezincote in the Cotswolds. I am, though, chiefly attracted by the aesthetic of empire: its feel, its look, its human passions, the metaphysics of its power, the sense of it, the intuition—its ships too, and its horsemen, and the dust of its high veld, and its distant trains streaming across the Punjab plain: and paramount for me in this jumble of suggestions is a sense of *alter ego*—as though the British had another people inside themselves, very different from the people that Dickens or Cobden portrayed, who yearned to break out of their sad or prosaic realities, and live more brilliant lives in Xanadu.

Victoria's empire offered a release for such emotions, laced with the hope of profit, the pleasure of authority and the chance of doing good, and much of its history is enlivened by useful enterprise and adventure: but the theme grows heavier as it progresses, an instinct matures into a duty, a duty curdles into a craze, a craze becomes a burden, and the unexpected dénouement to a story of astonishing success is a feeling of relief and emancipation. The idea of empire in the modern sense, which was scarcely formulated at the time my story opens, passed through the whole cycle of acceptance, fashion and decline to be utterly discredited by the time the story ends.

The British Empire, as my own generation knew it in the middle of the twentieth century, was really Queen Victoria's empire, for the older mercantile empire of America, India and the sugar colonies had been something different in kind, remote from the mythology of topee and White Man's Burden upon which we were all reared. I was born in 1926. I was thus just in time to see the schoolroom maps emblazoned pole to pole in the imperial red (large chunks of the Antarctic erroneously suggesting themselves to my childish fancy as thriving colonial settlements); I was in time to witness this immense organism uniting for the last time to fight the greatest war in its history; and I was in time, in 1947, to spend my 21st birthday on a British troop train travelling from Egypt (where the Empire was noticeably not wanted) to Palestine (which the Empire emphatically did not want).

For the next fifteen years or so I found myself vocationally engaged in the dissolution of the empire. At first this experience did not much affect me. I watched with interest as we were driven, step by step, from our strongholds in the east, and took pleasure in meeting the disillusioned sheikhs, kings and sultans who were the last of our imperial protégés. I went to Everest in 1953, and realized without distress that ours was the last of a line of imperial adventures, bred by the discarded public school spirit out of the disbanded Raj. I wrote about post-imperial India, emancipated Singapore, a half-American Canada, a South Africa ruled by Boers, a West Africa ruled by Africans, an Egypt armed by Russia, an Australia defended by America, an abortive West Indian federation, a rebellious Aden, war in Cyprus, prosperity in the Irish Republic, separatism in Rhodesia, Arabism in the Sudan, tribal paramountcy in Kenya. And at the same time I observed a series of world events in which the British presence became perceptibly less apparent, or at least less self-confident. The proprietary sensation with which I had once watched the unfolding of international affairs gave way to a sideline diffidence: where once the great stakes at risk were all my own, by virtue of my passport, now I was only a casual investor.

In many ways Britain was livelier and more interesting than it had been for generations, but it was distinctly smaller, and slighter. On the whole I did not wish it otherwise, but I often wondered what it had felt like to be British before the decline began at all. So my mind turned to that other, lost aesthetic, that dream of empire, which had so seized the imagination of the nation half a century before, and was now so remote. I resolved to write a big, ornate, frank but affectionate work about Victoria's empire, start to finish: an imperial trilogy, a pointillist portrait less of an age than of a conviction, in whose colours I would try to illustrate not only the extraordinary energies of the imperial generations, but also, suggested here and there in shade or brush-stroke, some retrospective emotions of my own.

There is to this approach, I know, an element of escape. It tends to skirt the duller realities, the humdrum at the root. This is, however, a favourite criticism of empire itself—a substitute, its opponents have always said, for the hard truths of national existence. Samuel Cockerell's son Charles, an eminent architect himself, thought that in this respect too Sezincote possessed a quality of paradigm. He turned against the place—it was an expression, he said, of 'our curious penchant for make-believe'. Perhaps it was: but in its rooms, nevertheless, old Sir Charles the nabob happily spent his declining years, dreaming no doubt of blazing Carnatic noondays, or curry suppers beneath the creaking punkahs, and enjoying the benefits of an imperial fortune which, however airy in the fancy, was undeniably solid in the fact.

I am dedicating the volumes of the trilogy separately; but I offer the whole work to ELIZABETH MORRIS, herself a child of Empire, as an expression of my profoundest love, gratitude and admiration.

Trefan, 1973

When Britain first, at Heaven's command,
  Arose from out the azure main,
This was the charter of the land,
  And guardian angels sung the strain:
  'Rule, Britannia, rule the waves;
  Britons never will be slaves.'

JAMES THOMSON

Part One

THE SENTIMENT OF EMPIRE: 1837–1850

Part Two

THE GROWING CONVICTION: 1850–1870

Part Three

THE IMPERIAL OBSESSION: 1870–1897

The Sentiment of Empire
1837–1850

CHAPTER ONE

A Charming Invention

IN October 1837 the Honourable Emily Eden, a witty and accomplished Englishwoman in her forty-first year, was accompanying her brother Lord Auckland, Governor-General of India, on an official progress up-country from Calcutta. Lord Auckland was homesick, but his sister was irrepressibly entertained by everything she saw, and she recorded all her impressions in vivacious letters home. She was anything but innocent or provincial. She was born in Old Palace Yard, within sight of Parliament at Westminster, and had lived always near the centre of English power. Her father had been Postmaster-General and President of the Board of Trade, her eldest sister Eleanor had been the only true love of the younger Pitt, and she herself was an intimate friend of Lord Melbourne the Prime Minister. She was accordingly amused rather than awed by the scale and grandeur of His Excellency's company.

They travelled sometimes by steamer up the rivers which were the principal highways of India, sometimes on camel-back, in palanquins or in elephant howdahs, and they did it with theatrical display. The gubernatorial caravan numbered some 12,000 souls, with hundreds of animals and wagons, and when they stopped for the night a city of tents sprang up, bustling and teeming about Lord Auckland's quarters, with its own bazaars and workshops and stables, its farriers and its wheelwrights, its redcoat sentries, its aides and commissaries, its delegations of local magistrates or doctors or commanding officers, its gaudy emissaries from maharajahs of the country, its rituals of presentation or official entertainment, its camp fires, its hurrying orderlies, its myriad ragged camp followers, its bugle calls at dusk, its smells of spice and woodsmoke and leather and sweat, all under the Union Jack on its great flagstaff beneath the terrific Indian sky. Sometimes it took three days for the cortège to cross a river; the pet dogs of the Europeans wore red coats on the march; when the King of Oudh kindly sent his own cook along to accompany the progress, and Lord Auckland was served a succession of highly spiced pilafs and curries, St Cloup the Governor-General's own chef, who had once been cook to the Prince of Orange, was predictably affronted.

This was the manner of the British in India, where the East India Company had been active for nearly 200 years, first as a trading organization, then as an instrument of supremacy. It was a half-oriental manner, inherited from the Moghuls, intended to over-awe the indigenes and perhaps give the Company's officials a proper sense of their own authority. Miss Eden, who had been in India for two years, and was accustomed to different styles of consequence, found it faintly comic. Her letters show no awareness of majesty. The Governor-General is, after all, only her diffident brother George, pining for a decent inn. His grand officials, advisers and aides are only upper middle class Englishmen, accompanied by gossipy wives, squirmy children and ludicrously cossetted pets. Miss Eden is not moved by the power, or the responsibility, or even the historical continuity represented by their progress. She does not see that vast brown Indian landscape, those half-naked multitudes around them, as a charge upon the English conscience, or a field for high adventure. She sees it all rather as a pageant, and thanks her sister Mary warmly for sending the latest issues of *Pickwick*—which, though it has already appeared in a pirate edition in Calcutta, is fresh and very funny to the Governor-General's entourage. She sees it, in fact, with the eyes of the eighteenth century. She was born in the old century, and her attitudes are Augustan—elegant, fastidious, entertained, urbane. Her England is the England of the younger Pitt; her style is the style of Sheridan, Addison, and the cool amusing ladies of the age of reason.

But on October 30, 1837, she learnt beside the Ganges that the age was ended. The company, which was sailing up-river by barge and steamer, put ashore for the night in pleasant hilly country some 200 miles north of Calcutta. They looked at some convenient ruins in the evening—'very picturesque', Emily thought—gave the spaniel Chance a run, did a little sketching, and received letters from England. These had come by the steamer *Madagascar*, which had left London on her maiden voyage just three months before.[1] Emily read them with delight. She noted her sister's change of address ('I did not know that there was such a place'); and she noted also the accession to the throne of England of Princess Alexandrina Victoria of Kent, 'Drina' to her childhood intimates, 18 years old and rather plump.

So she discovered, beside the holy river, one of history's allegorical events. The world would never be the same again, and in particular Great Britain, whose lethargic plenipotentiary in those parts was her brother George, would acquire a new character. Before Victoria died a very different kind of empire would acknowledge her sovereignty—a brazen, plumed, arrogant and self-righteous empire, ruling its immense possessions not merely by display of force, but with an obsessive conviction of destiny and duty. Out of Victoria's Britain would come a new breed of imperialists, unrecognizable in George Auckland and his leisurely assistants, and so constant would be the flow of British capital abroad, the movement of British migrants, the activities of British merchants, the campaigning of British armies, that by the time Queen Victoria died she would be the mistress of a quarter of the world's inhabitants and nearly a quarter of its land surface.

Miss Eden had no vision of these powers to come. On the contrary, she thought the idea of the little Queen rather touching. It brought a lump to her throat. 'I think', she wrote back to her sister that evening, after telling her about the ruins and the sketching, Chance's run and the quick passage of the *Madagascar*—'I think the young Queen a charming invention'.

2

England in 1837 was a country only half-aware of its luck. It was enduring a period of social turbulence, which the more nervous of the landed classes assumed to be the start of a revolution. The first

---

[1] Perhaps over-straining herself, for only four years later, returning to Calcutta after service in the China Seas, she blew up and sank.

Reform Bill, the Chartist agitation, the Luddites, Peterloo—all were symptoms of change and uncertainty, in a country which was enduring the menopause between an agricultural and an industrial society. The example of the French Revolution was still forceful, and Disraeli's 'two nations' were more than fictional—at least one in ten of the British people were paupers, naked women pulled wagons through mine shafts, poor little children of eight and nine were working twelve-hour days in the dark factories of the north. The traditional English hierarchy seemed threatened at last—doomed, the gloomier patricians thought, since one man in seven now had the vote.[1] The Established Church of England was undermined by non-conformism, agnosticism or worse. The nation's way of life was disrupted by the movement of labour to the towns, and the stylish English cities of the eighteenth century were invested now by tenements and factories: 'at the corner of Wood Street' Wordsworth's Poor Susan habitually paused, to see as in mirage an image of a vanishing England—

> . . . *a single small cottage, a nest like a dove's,*
> *The one only dwelling on earth that she loves.*

The nation was in flux. What the English did not generally realize was that this very flexibility, this clearing of the decks, provided a moment of opportunity unmatched in the history of modern Europe. England had the world at her feet. The very cause of her unrest was her own pre-eminence. Though she still grew 90 per cent of her own food, she was the first industrial nation; and blessed as she was with apparently limitless supplies of coal and iron, during the past fifty years she had so mastered the mechanical arts that she had outstripped all her competitors. The British stood at the threshold of a colossal boom, for they possessed a virtual monopoly of the techniques of steam, which was presently to prove itself the basic energy of the age. In the 1830s their industry was essentially a textile industry, but provided with this marvellous new power they

---

[1] Though the Duke of Wellington as usual got it right, when he assured a jittery fellow-landowner that 'we shall not have a commotion, we shall not have blood, but we shall be plundered by forms of law'.

were soon to manufacture every kind of capital goods—to become, in fact as in phrase, the workshop of the world.

At the same time they had emerged victorious and aglow from the unexampled struggle of the Napoleonic wars, to stand alone among the Powers of Europe. It was ultimately their wealth, their leadership, their power which had defeated Napoleon—they had provided, as Canning had said, the 'animating soul' of the struggle. They had largely dictated the terms of the peace, tempering the revenge of the Germans and Austrians and magnanimously restoring France to the comity of nations. Nelson and Wellington were international heroes—the one nobly dead in his catafalque in St Paul's, the other very much alive as the most tremendous of party politicians. The British fleet was recognized as the ultimate arbiter of the world's affairs. The British Army basked in the reputation it had won at Waterloo. London, with a population of two million, was not only the world's largest city, but also its principal financial exchange, the Rialto of the age.

To liberals everywhere England had replaced Napoleonic France as the hope of mankind. Beethoven in his late years assiduously followed the debates at Westminster, and wrote a respectful set of variations upon Arne's *Rule, Britannia*: Wagner seized upon that stirring melody too, thought its first eight notes expressed the whole character of the British people, and in the year of the Queen's accession wrote an overture based upon it. The romantic legend of Lord Byron shone over Europe still, and the contemporary English taste for tournaments, tales of knightly contest and Arthurian myth was seen as a true reflection of the national chivalry. So perfect were the institutions of England, thought the Abbé de Prat in France, that it must be her destiny to give the world a new aspect; 'To The Glory of the British Nation' cried the obelisk erected by the islanders of Cephalonia in the Adriatic;[1] when the East Indiamen put in for provisions at Johanna in the Comoro Islands, north of Madagascar, the local boatmen used to cry 'Johanna man Englishman, all one brother come, Englishman very good man, drinkee de punch, fire de gun, beatee the French, very good fun!' And though the English gentry might feel insecure in their country houses, unblemished still

[1] Until the occupying Italians meanly chipped the inscription off in 1941.

within the walls of their estates, still to the outside world the island presented a very assurance of stability: a constitutional monarchy of defiant habits and humours, unmoved it seemed by the vagaries of international fortune, safe behind the moat of its Channel, blessed with a stolid, unsoaring, insular certainty of temperament, and passionate chiefly, if we are to go by Turgenev's Anglomaniac Ivan Petrovich, about port wine and underdone roast beef.

3

Alone among the Powers, Britain possessed freedom of action, but her statesmen did not covet the mastery of the world. It was only fifty years since they had lost an empire, in America, and they did not wish to acquire another. Their aim now was a balanced peace, enabling the British people to seek their fortunes wherever they chose without undertaking vast new responsibilities of defence or administration; they accordingly gave back most of the territories their arms had captured during the wars, retaining only a string of bases, Heligoland to Mauritius, which they thought essential to their security at sea.

England had been an overseas Power for nearly 900 years—never since the Norman conquest had the Crown been without possessions across the water. But the idea of empire was suspect in the Britain of the 1830s. It went with foreign despotisms and aggressors, and had long lost the stately pacific meaning that Spenser and Milton had given the word, when they wrote of the Britannick Empire long before. Westminster was called the Imperial Parliament only because it had, since 1800, incorporated the parliament of Ireland, while the State Crown was Imperial only in ancient defiance of the Holy Roman Empire. The eighteenth century British Empire, before the loss of the American colonies, had been a self-contained economic system, protected by tariffs, producing its own raw materials, providing its own markets, shipping its own products in its own vessels. The Corn Laws kept foreign competition to a minimum: the Navigation Acts ensured a British monopoly of trade throughout the empire. Now the economic arguments for such a system seemed to be discredited. The progressive theory now was Free Trade, which would allow the goods of all nations to flow without tariffs and restrictions all over the globe, and seemed to make the possession of colonies obsolete. With Great Britain mistress both of the means of production and the means of distribution, was not the whole world her market-place? Why bother with the expense and worry of colonies? Free Trade was not yet accepted British policy, but already powerful lobbies were pressing for the repeal of the Corn Laws and the Navigation Acts, and deriding the idea of empire. Colonies, said Richard Cobden, 'serve but as gorgeous and ponderous appendages to swell our ostensible grandeur without improving our balance of trade', and if *laissez-faire* was the watchword of the nation's new economic instincts, a suggested slogan for colonial policy was *laissez-aller*.

Memories of the American Revolution, too, helped to sour the notion of empire. A great deal had happened to the world since then, but there were still many Britons alive who had fought against the rebels of the thirteen colonies, or their sons in the war of 1812. The American Revolution had seemed to show that the more successful an overseas settlement, the more certain it was to break away from the Mother Country, and probably set up in rivalry against her. Besides, it had convinced many people that colonialism necessarily led in the end to repression—if not of one's own fellow-countrymen, only striving to be free, then of foreigners in whose affairs the British had no right to meddle. Power corrupted. The British remembered still the trial of Warren Hastings in 1785: though it had ended in acquittal it had served its purpose—to warn the nation against the danger of ambitious satraps, made rich by the spoils of empire and seditious by the temptations of distant authority.

All in all the British were not thinking in imperial terms. They were rich. They were victorious. They were admired. They were not yet short of markets for their industries. They were strategically invulnerable, and they were preoccupied with domestic issues. When the queen was crowned, shortly before her nineteenth birthday, we may be sure she thought little of any possessions beyond the seas. She was the island queen, anointed with the pageantry and ritual evolved by the island people during a thousand years of history— hailed by her island peers, consecrated by her island bishops, cheered through the streets of London by a population which was almost undilutedly English. 'I really cannot say *how* proud I feel to be the Queen of *such* a Nation', she wrote in her journal, and she was unquestionably thinking of the nation of the English, 14 million strong in their 50,000 green square miles. Even the Welsh, the Scots and the Irish were unfamiliar to her then, when the world called her kingdom simply 'England', and only seers could foretell how colossally her responsibilities were to multiply, how wildly the image of her nation would grow, and how different would be the meaning of her royalty before her reign was done. ('Poor little Queen', Carlyle wrote, 'She is at an age at which a girl can hardly be trusted to choose a bonnet for herself; yet a task is laid upon her from which an archangel might shrink.')

4

Far away Lord Auckland laboured: for even now there did exist a British Empire of sorts, an inchoate collection of territories acquired in bits and pieces over the generations, administered partly by the Secretary of State for War and the Colonies, partly by great chartered companies. It was an unsystematic affair, an empire in abeyance, possessing no unity of purpose or sense of whole, and it was characteristic that the only complete register of its affairs was compiled by an enthusiastic amateur, Robert Montgomery Martin, who had travelled in the British possessions and returned to England a dedicated advocate of the colonial system. Martin estimated, soon after the Queen's accession, that the area of the overseas empire was some 2 million square miles, with a population of rather more than 100 million. Some of its possessions were relics of the old eighteenth century empire, some were new settlements of Britons overseas, some were the spoils of recent victory, touched with splendour—as it said above the guardroom door in St George's Square, Valletta, on the newly acquired island of Malta:

Magnae et invictae Britanniae
Melitensium amor et Europae vox
Has insulas confirmat A.D. 1814[1]

[1] *To Great and Unconquered Britain the Love of the Maltese and the Voice of Europe Confirms these Islands.* The inscription is still there, a little battered now.

The grandest of the imperial possessions were in India: there sovereignty had been acquired in stages by the East India Company until by 1837 most of the sub-continent was under British suzerainty, and 50,000 Britons, led by George Auckland, lorded it over more than 90 million Indians. Then there were the West Indian islands, with British Honduras and British Guiana on the American mainland—the sugar colonies, which had for a century and more made a disproportionate contribution to the prosperity of England, but were now rotting in decline. There were the colonies in Canada—Newfoundland, the oldest of them all, Nova Scotia settled largely by loyalists from the United States, French settlements in conquered Quebec, English and Scots in Ontario, and the scattered outposts of the Hudson's Bay Company in the unimaginable wastelands of the west. There were four settlements in Australia, two of them originally penal colonies, and there was Ireland close to home, ruled by the English for seven centuries, and still so primitive that in 1837 the 9,000 people of Tullahobagly, County Donegal, possessed between them ten beds and 93 chairs.

The Cape of Good Hope was British, and so was Singapore, founded by Stamford Raffles twenty years before. There were trading settlements at Penang and Arakan, and Ceylon had been acquired at the Peace of 1815. In Europe the flag flew over Gibraltar, Heligoland, the Ionian Islands in the Adriatic, and Malta—Nelson's 'outerwork to India'. Elsewhere a miscellaneous scatter of islands, strongpoints and trading stations infinitesimally enhanced the grandeur of Mr Martin's statistics—the Falklands and the Seychelles, Mauritius and Gambia, the trading forts of the Gold Coast, Norfolk Island in the South Pacific, St Helena where Napoleon died, Guiana and Fernando Po and Bermuda, defined by one visionary strategist of the day as 'central to the mouths of the Amazon, the Mississippi, the Oronooko, the St Lawrence, and to the innumerable tributary rivers which send their waters through these mighty vomitaries to the ocean'. In all, it was estimated, some 1,200,000 Britons were living overseas, including 56,000 soldiers in the imperial garrisons.

The imperial experience had inevitably left its mark upon the British. The East India nabobs, for example, formed a distinctive sub-society of their own among the British monied classes: often immensely rich, yellowed by their years in Madras or Calcutta, eccentric of habit and authoritarian of style, they filled their houses with ornate mementoes of the east, and lived in a manner assertively different from the ways of their neighbours—more flamboyant, more aloof, and generally less responsible, for though many of them acquired substantial estates upon their retirement from the east, their roots were seldom deep in the countryside. The Caribbean planters, too, many of whom had come home when the abolition of slavery spoiled things in the sugar islands, formed a cohesive group, and the West India Interest provided one of parliament's most persistent lobbies. Many a respected family, from the Barretts of Wimpole Street to the Lascelles of Harewood, owed its dignity to West Indian enterprise; mansions like Stowe and Fonthill were built with sugar money; in the spa societies of Bath, Cheltenham or Tunbridge Wells the planters were instantly recognizable, taking the waters with bronzed cronies from Barbados or Jamaica, and eventually filling a sizeable proportion of wall-space in abbey or parish church.

In London, though the offices of empire hardly showed, the monuments of imperial trade were evident enough. Beyond the Tower the East India and West India docks were thronged with masts and riggings; in the warehouses of the Hudson's Bay Company the beaver pelts and fox skins were piled in their lucrative thousands; in the heart of the City, at the corner of Lime and Leadenhall Streets, stood the headquarters of the East India Company, surmounted by a gigantic Britannia, containing a magnificent library and an Oriental Repository of Indian treasures.[1] In Liverpool, Bristol and Glasgow entire communities had been enriched specifically by the imperial enterprise. These were the home ports of the triangular trade which had, for generations, swopped English manufactured goods for African slaves for American raw materials, making a profit on each transaction. Here the slavers had found their crews, shanghaiing drunkards in the waterside inns of Hotwells or Merseyside, or blackmailing criminals into service. The slaving captains and merchants were still great men there, and the profits of slavery had

[1] Notably Tipu's Tiger, the working model of an Indian tiger eating an Englishman which is still to be shuddered at in the Victoria and Albert Museum.

passed into the civic arteries long before, and nourished other lucrative ventures in their turn.

Here and there throughout the kingdom, too, lesser memorials bore witness to the fact of empire: captured guns from India or Quebec, commemorative plaques to the casualties of tropic wars, personal trophies like the great gates which, high and generally invisible on the mist-shrouded moors of Knock Fyrish in Easter Ross, Sir Hector Munro of Foulis had erected to commemorate the part he played, and the fortune he consolidated, at the capture of Negapatam in 1781. Gatepost pineapples, Hindu cannons in the Tower of London, gilded domes upon a country house, an exotic grave in a country churchyard, an unpronounceable battle honour upon a regimental standard: such small encrustations upon the island fabric were symptoms of the imperial instinct that lay fallow there, momentarily subdued—'the sentiment of Empire', the young Gladstone called it, 'which may be called innate in every Briton'.

And already there were a few citizens who, looking ahead into the Victorian era, thought that the national destiny lay in a more deliberate overseas expansion. There were evangelists who believed in empire as the instrument of Christian duty, and social theorists who believed in emigration as the instrument of enlightened progress, and merchants unconvinced of the advantages of Free Trade, and activists of the West India Interest and the India lobby, and soldiers bored after a decade of peace, and adventurers coveting fresh opportunities of self-advantage. There were fighting patriots, and speculators of exotic preference, and there were even ornamental visionaries, half a century before their time, who conceived a new British Empire framed in symbolism, and endowed with a grand and mystic meaning.

One of these was Robert Martin, who standing back from his immense collection of imperial facts, and contemplating his engravings of colonial seals and charters, concluded that the British Empire of 1837, ramshackle and disregarded though it seemed, would prove to be one of the great accomplishments of history, 'on whose extension and improvement, so far as human judgement can predict, depends the happiness of the world'.[1] Another was J. M.

[1] Martin, who died in 1863, produced his first imperial studies without

Gandy, an able but erratic architect of grandiloquent style. Gandy was already a High Victorian, at the very opening of the Victorian age, and even before the Queen's accession he exhibited at the Royal Academy a design for an Imperial Palace, to be the home and headquarters of the Sovereigns of the British Empire. It was to be a building of overpowering elaboration, domed, pedimented, turreted, colonnaded, upheld by numberless caryatids, ornamented with urns and friezes and mosaic pavements and sunken gardens and ceremonial staircases, and allegorically completed by the marble columns, toppled ignominiously in the forecourt, of earlier and more transient sovereignties.

Fifty years later the Queen might have loved it, for it was only a prophetic expression of national emotions to come: but in 1837 it struck a false note, the Imperial Palace was still-born, and Gandy himself, whose most remarkable monument after all was to be Doric House on Sion Hill in Bath, died unhonoured and unremembered, some say insane.[1]

5

No, in 1837 England seemed to need no empire, and the British people as a whole were not much interested in their colonies. How could one be expected to show an interest in a country like Canada, demanded Lord Melbourne the Prime Minister, where a salmon would not rise to a fly? The Secretary of State for War looked after colonial matters in his less busy moments, and in a back room at the Colonial office in Westminster one might find in effect the embodiment of Britain's imperial authority, shrivelled into the duties of some obscure official—'we know not the name', as the social reformer Charles Buller put it, 'the history or the functions of the individual, into the narrow limits of whose person we find the Mother

---

official help, but turned professional later and became the first Treasurer of the Colony of Hong Kong—a possession he declared to be doomed to failure from the start.

[1] In 1843: he was an associate of Sir John Soane, but seems to have been, says the Dictionary of National Biography, 'of too odd and impracticable a nature to ensure prosperity'.

Country shrunk. . . .' It was as though the kingdom had put the imperial idea deliberately out of mind. As the victorious British proceeded with their experiments of political reform, as the thrilling new railways crept across the island—'the velocity is delightful', reported Charles Greville the diarist, dubiously taking the Liverpool train that year—as the statesmen of England concerned themselves with the settlement of Europe, and the dumpy young Queen timorously submitted to the burdens of her office—'very few have more real good will and more real desire to do what is fit and right than I have'—as Dickens got on with *Oliver Twist* and Landseer started *Dignity and Impudence* and Darwin worked up his notes on the voyage of the *Beagle*—as Cobden stormed on about the Corn Laws, and Charles Barry perfected his designs for the new Houses of Parliament, and the coal-grimed girls dragged their wagons through the stifling mine-shafts, and Gladstone settled down to his treatise on Church and State—as this most fascinating of island states entered upon the thirty-sixth reign of its ancient monarchy, the possession of an overseas empire seemed irrelevant to its wealth, dignity and interest. 'For the fact is, Jardine', wrote a China merchant in London to his colleague in Canton, 'the people appear to be so comfortable in this magnificent country, so entirely satisfied in all their desires, that so long as domestic affairs, including markets, go right, they cannot really be brought to think of us outlanders. . . .'

Miss Eden appeared to put it in perspective. Presently Lord Auckland went into the Punjab to meet the great King of the Sikhs, Ranjit Singh, whose help he required in a war he was about to start. Ranjit, the Lion of the Punjab, was one of the most powerful men in India, and a great ruler of men—half-blind, exceedingly astute, drunk often upon a mixture of opium, raw spirit, meat juice and powdered pearls, perpetually inquisitive, habitually deceptive, the commander of a large and efficient army, the master of a colourful harem of nubile women and graceful painted boys, and the dictator of human affairs between the Indus and the Afghan passes.

Lord Auckland visited this formidable prince in state, giving him seven horses, an elephant and two howitzers as tokens of his esteem, and Ranjit responded with gorgeous pageantries of his own. The issues they discussed were very grave, the decisions they took momentous. Emily, though, watched their transactions with detached amusement, as though they were all no more than Gothick fantasies, or charades. The King of the Sikhs, she thought, looked like a one-eyed mouse with whiskers; and when he entertained the Governor-General at a banquet, illuminated by 42,000 lamps, attended by his fakir Uziz-ed-Din, with his fire-water in a gold carafe, and two bands to play, and the royal children crawling about the floor, and a party of screaming dancing-girls, and an idiot prince, and a long row of turbaned sirdars, and the tyrant slowly sinking into intoxication, and the future of hundreds of thousands of people, the fate of immense territories, all immediately at stake—'still', reported Miss Eden to her sister, 'we all said "what a charming party", just as we should have said formerly at Lady C's or Lady J's'.[1]

[1] Emily Eden died unmarried in 1869, comfortably home in Richmond, a successful novelist, a fashionable hostess, and the author of an entrancing book of Indian letters, *Up The Country*, from which I have drawn these pictures. Her brother George, alas, will appear again in our narrative.

CHAPTER TWO

High and Holy Work

YET almost at once a seminal imperial event occurred: the final manumission of slaves throughout the British possessions. Slavery as such had been abolished in 1834, but for another four years slaves were bound by a system of apprenticeship to their masters, and it was not until August 1, 1838, that the last serfs of empire, nearly all black Africans, were officially emancipated. There were 768,000 of them, not counting those in the hands of native potentates whose bondage lingered longer. This was a fresh start indeed. The old British Empire had been inextricably linked with slavery. Colonies had been built upon the practice, industries depended upon it, and it was only thirty years since British military recruiters, when faced with a shortage of manpower, paid cash for their colonial volunteers. So organic did slavery seem to the shape of the old empire that the eighteenth-century cartographers divided West Africa quite naturally by commodities—the Gold Coast for minerals, the Ivory Coast for elephant tusks, the Slave Coast for human beings. Many British families had numbered their securities in human stock, for to perfectly decent Britons, only a generation before, slavery had seemed part of the divine order. 'To abolish a *status*', thought Boswell, 'which in all ages GOD has sanctioned, and man has continued, would not only be *robbery* to an innumerable class of our fellow-subjects; but it would be extreme cruelty to the African Savages, a portion of whom it . . . introduced into a much happier state of life.' The end of slavery was thus doubly ritual: obsequies for the old empire, consecration for the new.

2

Let us visit, on that day, the little town of Falmouth in northern

Jamaica. It was a pleasant clapboard sort of place, wide straight streets and a lighthouse on the shore, set at the foot of the Cockpit Country on the Atlantic coast of the island. Several great sugar estates dominated the country round about, and Falmouth was the outlet for their merchandise, and the chief shopping and gathering place for their slaves. It was a lively town, made elegant by the colonial British, made exuberant by the expatriate blacks. Clouds softly drifted through the mountain-tops behind: in front the Atlantic breakers frothed and churned. It is true that Jamaica, severely hit by the prospect of emancipation, was in the economic doldrums, but still it was a lovely island, full of gay animation, and mellowed by two centuries of the colonial presence.

The aesthetics, though, were misleading. Jamaica was one of the most important slave colonies—there were 320,000 blacks to some 35,000 whites—and slavery there had been an institution of ruthless power. The shady plantation houses on their hillsides, the picturesque affection of the old retainers, the native merriment, the air of indolent ease, all gave a false impression of magnolia charm and paternalism. In reality the life of the island was based uncompromisingly upon the ownership and exploitation of human beings. Architecturally any of the Falmouth sugar estates graphically illustrated this truth. Take, for instance, Orange Valley, a well-known plantation a few miles north of town. It was built of solid limestone, and displayed an almost ecclesiastical air of conviction. On the hill above stood its Great House, balconied and wide-eaved, lapped by lawns and caressed by creepers. Nearby was the house of the overseer, an English yeoman house, pretty in an unassuming way, as though always conscious of its place at the mansion gates. And all around the central factory area, where the sugar was refined and packed, were the slave-installations—the slots or stables or repair bays in which those human mechanisms were installed, housed and serviced. The refinery had a churchy look, its limestone finely dressed and mortared; the slave hospital was an elegant little structure in the classical mode; the slave quarters were rows and rows of shanties, like rickety garden pavilions, with their vegetable plots behind (slaves were expected to grow their own nourishment) and their gaudy patched washing fluttering upon their clothes-lines. It was a highly functional arrangement: like a ship disposed about its engine-room, the estate was assembled efficiently about its motive-power, the muscle of captive humans.[1]

Orange Valley was clearly built to last, and it looked on the face of it benevolent enough—that gracious house on the hill, that bowered cottage for the overseer, the hospital in whose wards, it seemed, crinolined ladies must surely be soothing with scented hands the brows of grateful fevered blacks. But slavery in the British West Indies was not always like that. A series of exposés had lately revealed that British slave-masters could be as cruel as any Arab traders or Bokhara khan. The English public had read with horrified fascination of ears cut off in punishment, eyes gouged, teeth drawn, hands amputated. Slaves were hung by their arms from trees, nailed by their ears to posts, clamped in steel collars or iron boots. Throughout the British possessions the slave had been utterly at the mercy of his employer—or worse still his employer's wife, who was often more vicious in the refinement of her spite.

Of course there were good owners too, conditions greatly varied in the nineteen British slave colonies, and no doubt evangelical reporters sometimes exaggerated the horrors. But the consensus of evidence was appalling, and it was not surprising that when the final emancipation came at last, on that August day in 1838, the negroes of Falmouth celebrated it with almost hysterical fervour. The pastor of the Baptist Church, the Reverend William Knibb, summoned his congregation for a midnight service of thanksgiving, and the negroes assembled joyously. Mr Knibb was one of the most active non-conformist clergymen on the island, a native of Northamptonshire and a passionate abolitionist, and he carried his faith theatrically, as the blacks preferred. It was very hot that night. The wide lattice windows of the chapel were open, clumsy insects buzzed in the lamp-lights, the congregation was a blaze of primary colours and glistening black, and as the midnight deadline drew near Mr Knibb

[1] Orange Valley is a cattle ranch now, through whose compounds stylish negro cowboys ride. Most of its slave-buildings are in ruins; rats, lizards and a barn owl live in the derelict Great House; but overgrown behind the garden the mausoleum of its founding family, the Jarretts, has monumentally survived the centuries, and is fluttered over by yellow butterflies.

ascended his pulpit with portentous step. 'The hour approaches!' he cried, pointing a quivering finger at the clock upon the wall. 'The time is drawing near! The monster is dying!'—and as the minutes ticked by, and the pastor stood there tense and fiery, and the harmonium played, so the congregation worked itself into a frenzy of excitement and delight, until midnight struck, Knibb cried triumphantly, 'The monster is dead!' and all those negroes leapt to their feet and broke into cheers, songs, shouts, tears and embraces. The slaves were free! They took the symbols of their bondage, chain, whip and iron collar, and buried them for ever in the schoolroom yard, singing a dirge as they did so:

> *Now slavery we lay thy vile form in the dust,*
> *And buried for ever let it there remain!*
> *And rotted and covered with infamy's dust*
> *Be every man-whip and fetter and chain.*[1]

3

Though slavery had been so old an imperial practice, paradoxically its ending did not weaken the idea of empire, but rather gave it new life: for among those who argued that Britain had an imperial mission to fulfil were the prime agents of abolition, the English evangelicals. They were a power in the land. They had infiltrated the Established Church, they had representatives in the highest quarters of government, their most celebrated spokesman, William Wilberforce, was a saint among low churchmen, if a prig among high. The evangelical force—'vital Christianity'—was concerned with every kind of cruelty and injustice. Prison reform, factory conditions, corporal and capital punishment, child labour, cruelty to animals, the treatment of lunatics—all these matters engaged the conscience

[1] Mr Knibb's church was destroyed by a hurricane in 1944, but its present successor, named in his memory, contains a marble panel depicting this scene. In the churchyard is a monument to Knibb 'erected by the Emancipated Slaves, to whose enfranchisement and elevation his indefatigable exertions so largely contributed', and when I went to service there one Sunday morning in 1969 I found his parishioners as merry, kind and passionate as ever.

of the English reformers in the first decades of the nineteenth century. In the imperial context, though, they were concerned most with the welfare of the coloured peoples, and their several institutions became powerful forces of imperial commitment: the Clapham Sect, a humanitarian cult whose members had included a Governor-General of Bengal, a Governor of Sierra Leone, several members of Parliament and a permanent head of the Colonial Office; the African Association, which concerned itself with the exploration of Africa for humanitarian ends, and which was to develop into the Royal Geographical Society; the Aborigines Protection Society, founded in the year of Queen Victoria's accession; or best-known of all, Exeter Hall, not really an institution at all, but a religious meeting hall in the Strand whose name had become synonymous with the entire humanitarian movement.

It was the pressure of this vague but potent guild that gave to the Victorian Empire, in its earliest years, functions of guardianship. Exeter Hall believed that the power of Great Britain should be used to guard the welfare of the backward peoples, to protect them from exploitation, and guide them into the Christian way. The Colonial Office became a stronghold of imperial trusteeship—James Stephen, 'Mr Mother Country', its permanent under-secretary in 1838, was a stalwart of Exeter Hall, while Lord Glenelg, the Colonial Secretary, was hardly less evangelical. Even Lord Melbourne, that worldly old Whig, could hardly disregard so strong a political current, for the evangelicals were skilled propagandists, masters of the pamphlet and the protest march, the petition and the fund-raising needle-party. The House of Commons itself reflected the trend in a motion which, while it did not actually advocate the extension of empire for pious purposes, did call upon all colonial governors and officers to promote the spread of civilization among the Natives everywhere, and 'lead them to the peaceful and voluntary reception of the Christian religion'.

So for many Victorian Englishmen the instinct of empire was first to be rationalized as a call to Christian duty. Lord John Russell, a future Prime Minister, defined the imperial purpose towards the negro people as being 'to encourage religious instruction, let them partake of the blessings of Christianity, preserve order and internal peace, induce the African race to feel that wherever the British flag flies they have a friend and protector, check all oppression, and watch over the impartial administration of the law'. Even the directors of the Hudson's Bay Company, a sufficiently materialist concern, laid it down in standing orders that divine service must be read each Sunday in its remotest Canadian fur posts, for the civilization and instruction of the Red Indians. The statesmen of England had behaved with exemplary modesty and restraint in settling the affairs of the world in 1815, but by 1838 one detects a certain smugness among the islanders, and this superior tone of voice came not, as it would later come, from an arrogant Right, but from a highly moralistic Left. The middle classes, newly enfranchised, were emerging into power: and it was the middle classes who would eventually prove, later in Victoria's reign, the most passionate imperialists of all.

The greatest triumph of the evangelicals was the abolition of slavery. Economically its results had been devastating. Planters were ruined from Antigua to Mauritius.[1] Middlemen of Ashanti, slave captains of Merseyside, overseers of Nassau, found themselves without an occupation. Paupers proliferated in all the slave colonies, squatters defied the land laws, a Select Committee defined the condition of the average Jamaican freedman as *otium cum dignitate*—'idle dignity'—which he fulfilled by working for a few hours two days a week, and going home with a bottle of Bass. Most of the sugar colonies never really recovered. Thousands of Indians had to be shipped to the West Indies to work the estates there, and in Jamaica the authorities were obliged to import German labourers too—dirty and drunk, thought the planters, who were hard to please.[2] In London the West India Association warned that there might be no other course for the Caribbean colonies but to 'appeal to the Crown for a release from their unprofitable allegiance, in order that they may attach themselves to some other country willing to extend to them the protection of a parent State'. In all the British Government had

---

[1] One Jamaica estate that netted £11,000 annually in the 1820s was sold in the 1840s for £1,650, and by the 1850s was said to be worth about £800.

[2] Their descendants survive, around Seaford Town in Westmoreland County, and look today, thanks to a century and a half of in-breeding, whiter than anyone else in Jamaica.

to pay out £20 million in compensation (£8,823 8s 9d of it to the Society for the Propagation of the Gospel, whose *ex officio* members included the Archbishop of York, and whose properties included two plantations in Barbados).

But morally emancipation put the British on a special plane, and set an example for the world. It also gave a fresh impulse to the empire. If so much could be achieved by agitation at home, what might not be done if the moral authority of England were distributed across the earth—to tackle the evils of slavery, ignorance and paganism at source, to teach the simpler peoples the benefits of Steam, Free Trade and Revealed Religion, and to establish not a world empire in the bad Napoleonic sense, but a Moral Empire of loftier intent? So was evolved the chemistry of evangelical imperialism; and since hatred of slavery was its original ingredient, it became the first imperial purpose of Victoria's reign to extend to all parts of the world the convictions of Exeter Hall and Mr Mother Country on what the Americans in their prevaricating bigotry preferred to call the Peculiar Institution.[1]

4

The British could not enforce the abolition of slavery everywhere in the world, but their command of the sea did qualify them to interfere with the movement of slaves from source to customer. In the suppression of piracy the Empire had already assumed a police function. Now its power was harnessed to the evangelical purpose, and for the first thirty years of Victoria's reign the Royal Navy's chief task was the interception of slavers. Legally the anti-slave patrols were international, the American, French and Portuguese navies contributing squadrons: in practice they were almost entirely British, in execution as in concept.

The main slave routes ran out of equatorial Africa east and west. Whether the Africans were destined for emirs of Yemen or planters of Brazil, the conditions of their journeys were equally terrible. Captured in war or slave-raid, by Arabs or fellow-Africans, they

[1] As against the Pernicious Article, which is what the British themselves called the most profitable commodity of their eastern commerce, opium.

stumbled often for hundreds of miles through scrub and forest, chained and yoked with wooden collars, whipped and bullied mercilessly to keep them on their feet. If they were travelling east, they were shipped to Zanzibar, paraded for purchase in the great slave market there, and sold to buyers from Arabia or the further east. If they were going west, they found themselves in stockades or barracoons in the foetid estuaries of the Slave and Ivory coasts, where they were beaten for discipline's sake and put into stock. Here they were in the hands of European renegades and half-castes, who sold them in turn to the slaving captains always cruising off-shore: and so before long they were shipped away on their last journey, by the notorious Middle Passage to Brazil, or (illegally but all too often) to the southern United States. East or west, thousands of slaves died *en route*: on the Atlantic voyage, even as late as the 1840s, probably about a quarter of those embarked.

At first the Royal Navy tried to end the traffic by interception at sea, and a ramshackle squadron of frigates, sloops and gunbrigs, all the Admiralty could spare, pottered up and down the West African coast, or later in and out of Zanzibar, in pursuit of slavers. This was a job the Navy loathed, despite the bounty paid—£5 a head for each liberated slave, or £2 10s if he died before reaching port. The slave-ships were generally faster and better sailers than the elderly war-ships of the patrols, and the Navy's captains were hamstrung by legalism. The West African station, in particular, could be a captain's nightmare. Though there were European trading posts up and down the coast, several of them British, West Africa had no formal frontiers, or even clearly defined sovereignties, and there was scarcely a creek for 2,000 miles that did not sometimes harbour slave-ships. 'Here we are,' wrote one officer of the slave patrol, 'in the most miserable station in the world, attempting the impossible.' The sight of a slave-ship was the signal for the frigate captain to ransack his locker for the necessary regulations, for his action depended upon the slaver's nationality. With some foreign States, Britain had reached full agreement on searches: if a ship had slaves on board, or carried equipment obviously designed for slaving purposes, like shackles, balls and chains, or whips, then she could be seized willy-nilly. With other countries, notably the United States, Britain had not been able to conclude an 'equipment clause'—if slaves were not on board in the flesh, the frigate captain could do nothing. Other States again had no agreement with Britain at all, so that to board a ship might be interpreted in a court of law as an act of war, or piracy.

All this made interception an embarrassing process. Often it was exceedingly difficult to overhaul a suspected slaver in the first place, so that the boarding party was received with caustic condescension. Often the slaver's true nationality was impossible to determine. Most often of all, the unfortunate patrol commander found himself legally impotent, however many pairs of manacles or instruments of torture he found on board, and was laughed overboard by disrespectful Portuguese, or abused by Spaniards. Americans especially could be insufferable. The United States had made slave traffic illegal in 1808, and occasionally contributed a sloop or two to the slave patrols: but slavery itself was still legal in the southern States, the American Ambassador in London was a Virginian, and the Americans had never conceded the Royal Navy's right of search, so that every interception was a diplomatic gamble. American slavers had the best ships, too—especially Baltimore clippers and New York sloops, which were among the fastest vessels afloat, and could easily outmanoeuvre the clumsy broad-beamed brigs of the patrols. One successful American slaver was the schooner *Wanderer*, built as a pleasure-yacht and owned by a Georgia slaving syndicate: she flew the pennant of the New York Yacht Club, and her master once entertained the officers of a Royal Navy frigate to a merry dinner on board, before packing 750 slaves below deck and sailing for home. Another was the barque *Martha Ann*. Given chase in the Atlantic once, this exasperating vessel at first showed no colours, only hoisting the Stars and Stripes after a number of warning shots. Why had she not hoisted colours before? the British officers demanded of her captain, when at last they caught up with the barque, but the American was not abashed. 'I guess,' he languidly replied, 'we were eating our supper.'

5

However hard the Navy tried, the slave trade continued. As the King of Bonny had told the captain of the last English slaver, when they bid a sentimental farewell to each other years before, 'we tink trade no stop, for all we ju-ju men tell we so, for dem say you country no can niber pass God A'mighty'. Every kind of ruse continued to baffle the patrols—false colours, hidden decks, forged papers, mid-ocean transfers. Presently the Navy took to flushing the trade out on shore, and an archetypal imperial action was the destruction, in 1840, of a particularly notorious slave station at the mouth of the Gallinas river, in Sierra Leone. Then as now the estuaries of West Africa were among the nastiest places on earth. Flat, swampy, hot, sprawling, brackish, fly-infested, mosquito-ridden, fringed with gloomy mangroves and monotonous palms, they lay beneath the heartless sun in secretive desolation. Of them all, one of the most detestable was the estuary of the Gallinas.[1] It was hotter and swampier than anywhere, its mangroves gloomier and its swamps more awful, and among its creeks and lagoons, protected by the river bar and the Atlantic surf, a Spanish trader named Pedro Blanco had established a slave mart. Its barracoons, of reed and palm thatch, were scattered among the swamps, invisible from the sea but easily accessible by creeks from the interior. Its warehouses were full of goods for barter, cloths, rum and Cuban tobacco. Blanco himself, who was immensely rich and flamboyantly immoral, lived on an island deep in the swamp, attended by a black seraglio, and on lesser islets all around sentries with telescopes on high lookouts kept watch over the Atlantic.

This was a hideously successful enterprise. Blanco had established an alliance with the chiefs of the surrounding countryside, notably King Siaka of Gallinas, and the coastal tribes acted as his agents, paid in advance for the slaves they could catch inland. A regular trade was established with Cuba, in Portuguese, Brazilian and American slave-ships, and the barracoons were nearly always full of slaves awaiting shipment, sometimes 5,000 at a time. Two or three ships arrived each month at the estuary. Blanco imported his shackles from England, and recruited a staff of Spaniards: King Siaka dined off silver plate.

The Royal Navy knew this place well from a distance, and had

[1] Now renamed the Kerefe, and a popular weekend resort for Freetown sportsmen.

blockaded the estuary for months at a time. But it was independent territory, and until October, 1840, the British could find no excuse to go ashore. Then a black British subject, Mrs Fry Norman of Sierra Leone, was kidnapped by King Siaka's son Manna as security for a debt. 'I have to inform you', Mrs Norman wrote to the debtor, a Mrs Grey of Freetown, 'that Mr Manna has catched me on your account, and is determined to detain me until you come yourself. Between now and night all depends on good or evil heart of Mr Manna. Therefore you will lose no time in coming to my assistance on your account.' But instead of Mrs Grey it was Commander Joseph Denman, R.N., with the armed schooner *Wanderer* and the brigs *Rolla* and *Saracen* who, in an early exertion of the Victorian imperial principle *civis britannicus sum*, arrived wrathful and determined at the bar of the Gallinas.

Denman was the son of a distinguished abolitionist, Lord Chief Justice Denman, and had himself felt passionately about the evils of the slave trade since, as a young lieutenant, he had sailed a captured slaver across the Atlantic with 500 half-dead Africans on board. 'I was forty-six days on that voyage, and altogether four months on board of her, where I witnessed the most dreadful sufferings that human beings could endure.' Denman was aching to settle scores not only with Siaka, but with the Spanish traders too, and he used the plight of poor Mrs Norman as pretext for a double action.

He had no mandate for an attack upon the barracoons—Britain was not at war with the Gallinas chiefs—but he acted Nelsonically, on his own. With three boatloads of blue-jackets he rode the surf, crossed the bar and seized the biggest of the estuary islands. Almost at once, without a shot, the whole iniquitous enterprise collapsed. Hustling as many slaves as they could into canoes, the Spaniards fled up the creeks into the bush. Mrs Norman was triumphantly released. More than a thousand slaves were freed of their chains. All the barracoons and warehouses were burnt. Siaka and the chiefs signed an abject treaty of renunciation, promising to abandon the slave trade altogether, whatever the ju-ju men said, and expel all the slave traders from their territories. The Gallinas trade was extinguished, and the British consul in Havana reported a stream of anxious slave-traders, requesting his advice about future prospects.

Some years later one of Blanco's associates at the Gallinas station, whom the Navy had rescued from his own infuriated captives and shipped away to safety, ungratefully sued Denman for trespass and the seizure of property—a familiar hazard of the slave patrols: but the judges of the Court of Exchequer, who knew the Commander's father well, directed the jury to clear him.

6

This bold little action was a foretaste of imperial manners to come, but its effect was transitory. Though it led to treaties with most of the slave-trading chiefs along the West African coast, they were seldom honoured for long. The legal complexities remained insoluble, and the movement towards Free Trade at home actually encouraged the slave traffic, for it greatly bolstered the economies of slave States like Cuba and Brazil. Though the Royal Navy liberated in all some 150,000 souls, the Atlantic slave traffic did not end until the victory of the North in the American Civil War, twenty years later. As for the Red Sea trade, it continued fitfully much longer still, with illicit shipments of boys to the pederast princelings of Arabia, or allocations of retainers to the Sultan of Muscat. Throughout the first half of the nineteenth century the slave patrol remained one of the Navy's principal chores, a duty as implicit to the fact of British maritime power as guardship duty in Gibraltar, or cruiser service on the West India station.[1]

No less demanding a concern of the imperial evangelists, though, was what to do with the slaves when they were liberated, for of course they could not be returned to barbarism. Fortunately the empire already possessed a haven. In the eighteenth century there had been some 14,000 slaves in Britain itself, scattered in gentlemen's houses throughout the kingdom.[2] When domestic slavery was made

---

[1] Ships of the Royal Navy continued to carry slavery manuals until 1970.

[2] Of whom I cannot forbear to mention 'Jack Black' of Ystumllyn, near my own home in Caernarfonshire. He was the only black man in North Wales, and the local girls adored him: as his biographer austerely observed in 1888, *gwyn y gwel y fran ei chyw*—'the crow sees its young as white'. Jack's gravestone bears the inaccurate but touching epitaph, in Welsh:

illegal in 1772 many of these people, together with ex-slaves from Nova Scotia, became the nucleus of an experiment in humanitarian imperialism—the creation of a new British colony, specifically for liberated negroes, on the coast of West Africa. It was to contribute to the ending of the slave trade everywhere, its sponsors said, by 'civilization, Christianity and the cultivation of the soil'.

The chosen shore had been named by the Spaniards Sierra Leone, for the crouching lion-shape of the hill above its bay, and the capital of the new settlement was called inevitably Freetown, but most of the hamlets upon the peninsula were given names of ineffable British-ness, to stand as texts of enlightenment. There was Wilberforce, there was Buxton, there was Charlotte and there was Regent. Gloucester was down the road from Leicester, and the road from Waterloo to Wellington ran through Hastings, Grafton and Allen Town—all this at a time when the vast mass of Africa had never seen a white man at all, and there was not a single European consul between Freetown on the one shore and Zanzibar on the other. From the very start Sierra Leone, though its population was almost entirely negro, represented an implanted culture: a black British culture, evangelically Christian, conventionally diligent.

The colony made several false starts, for the ex-slaves proved inept colonists at first, and its early years were disturbed. As the wit Sydney Smith observed, there were always two Governors of Sierra Leone, the one who had just arrived, and the one who was just leaving. Among the new settlers there were understandable prejudices against white patronage of any kind: some citizens, after all, believed that the uniforms of the redcoat garrison were dyed with the blood of slaughtered negroes, and that British officers' brains were developed by a potion of boiled African heads. As the years passed, and the neighbouring African peoples infiltrated the colony, and liberated slaves arrived too from the West Indies, and from captured slave-ships, some unsuspected doctrines were grafted up-on the Christian orthodoxies, and distinctly heretical pieties were

India was the land of my birth,
But I was christened in Wales;
This spot, marked by a grey slab,
Is my cold, dark resting place.

pursued in the less respectable quarters of Freetown. Witchcraft was practised when the clergymen were not looking. Secret societies flourished. Streets named for statesmen, governors or eminent men of God found racier local nicknames. Yet Sierra Leone remained above all a Christian settlement upon the African shore, a ward of evangelical imperialism: spires and chapel roofs ornamented the Freetown skyline, and if Saturday nights were rumbustious in the backstreets, Sunday mornings were rich with hymns and self-improvement.

Architecturally the little town was remarkable, for here alone the Georgian style was applied to tropical Africa. Freetown was built to a grid system, partly as an image of European order, partly perhaps to make it easier to police. Some of its streets were surprisingly elegant. They were lined with deep-eaved villas three or four stories high, built of a heavily mortared yellowish sandstone, with white balconies and well-proportioned windows—comfortable, solid-looking houses, pleasantly sited on the slopes of Howe or Trelawny Streets, and made piquant by a certain naïvety of design—a gentle crudeness, which gave them a child-like charm, like rows of dolls' houses in the sunshine. Handsome stone steps led down to the harbour of Freetown, an Anglican cathedral stood predominantly above, and the little capital kept as its fulcrum the handsome oak tree, now the hub of a cross-roads, at whose feet in 1787 the founding fathers of the colony had declared their intentions with a short and low church service.

Freetown society was rich and strange. The founders had been concerned to create an educated African bourgeoisie, to be the governing class of the place, and to perpetuate its Christian origins: the evangelicals were seldom radicals in any modern sense, and generally held strong Whiggish views about property and the continuity of class. Almost at once they founded a place of higher education, Fourah Bay College, which inhabited an imposing building on the hill, and which presently produced an entire social layer of educated Africans—clergyman, lawyers, school-teachers, civil servants. These were the first of the Sierra Leone Creoles, a people destined to play an important part in the development of the British Empire. 'Creole' was a word of many meanings. In the French colonies of America it meant a locally-born European. In Spanish South

American it meant a half-caste predominantly white. In West Africa it meant at first a liberated slave or his descendants, as distinct from a local African: but there it presently came to mean more too, and signified a person who subscribed to the particular Anglo-African culture propagated by Fourah Bay.

The Creoles became an imperial caste. They developed their own Afro-English language, Krio—far more than a pidgin language, but a tongue with its own literature, which sounded indeed like a hazily slurred recording of cultured southern English, but was graced with its own nuances and idioms, and eventually became so divorced from the parent language that scholars translated Shakespearian plays into it.[1] They wore European clothes, conveniently differentiating them from the local tribespeople, whom they tended to despise, and who were either draped in blinding swoops of textile, or almost totally nude. They filled their houses with the orthodox bric-à-brac of the English middle classes, upright pianos and lithographs and portraits of the Queen and framed embroidered samplers. They aimed above all at respectability. We see them, in starched white collars and stifling crinolines, presiding stiffly over public functions, or trailing beneath sunshades to morning service. We see their heavy black features sweating over dog-collars (the first black Anglican bishop was a Creole) or stuffed into red serge jackets (the first black British Army doctor was another) or crowned with judge's wigs, or hung about with stethoscopes, or bespectacled over philosophical treatises. They ran the colony more or less themselves, with intermittent advice from white governors and transient civil servants, and by and large they did it well. One of the earliest coherent plans for self-government in British African colonies was produced by Major Africanus Horton, who had enjoyed a successful

---

[1] For example:

> Paddy dem, country, una all way day
> Nar Rome. Make una all kack una yase.
> Are cam berr Caesar, are nor cam praise am.
> Dem kin member bad way person kin do
> long tem after de person kin don die.
> But plenty tem de good way person do
> kin berr wit im bone dem. . . .

career in the British Army before settling down to a literary and commercial retirement in Horton Hall, Freetown.[1]

Presently, too, the Creoles began to demonstrate talents more specifically their own—throw-backs, so to speak, to the distant times before their redemption. They turned out to be marvellous money-makers. Capitalism sprouted and thrived in Sierra Leone. The paternalist white clerics of Fourah Bay found some of their most promising pupils, steeped in the maxims of Dean Stanley or the examples of William Wilberforce, abruptly blossoming into immensely rich entrepreneurs, landowners or speculators. Dynasties of rich Creoles were founded, and those modest houses of Trelawny Street were often abandoned for more ostentatious mansions and country estates. At the same time the Creoles, while still honouring the principles of the evangelical faith, threw off its gloomier forms. They became a particularly gay and hospitable people. Half-forgotten ancestral rhythms enlivened the cadences of metrical psalms, and the sons of sober bureaucrats discovered in themselves inherited aptitudes for dance and buffoonery.

Sierra Leone still had its ups and downs. Periodic scandals excited the little colony, and heavy-bearded commissions of inquiry occasionally disembarked at Freetown quay to put things straight again. Here as elsewhere, even the most compliant Africans sometimes disappointed their mentors and liberators—as was said by one judicial commission, 'the known Christian moral lesson should be continually impressed on their minds that we must earn our bread with the sweat of our brow'. But the settlement survived, and Freetown itself became the principal base of the Royal Navy on the West African coast—a town where generations of transient Britons, on their way to grimmer places farther south, would be surprised by the gaiety of their welcome, and first discover that there might be some element of fun, after all, in the prospect of a posting to the White Man's grave.[2]

[1] And who was not above giving some sensible advice to white residents in Sierra Leone: 'A strict moral principle is beneficial in the tropics. Agreeable society should always be courted, as it relieves the mind a great deal. The society of real ladies will be found preferable to any other'.

[2] The fun persists, the Afro-English culture having become distinctly

7

So the first monuments of Queen Victoria's empire were monuments of liberty. The fight against slavery at its source would continue throughout the Victorian era, being a prime motive as we shall see of the great mid-century explorations, and it proved a fertile seed of imperial emotion. It was seen as a stake in providence—as Lord John Russell told the House of Commons in 1850, 'it appears to me that if we give up this high and holy work . . . we have no right to expect a continuance of those blessings, which, by God's favour, we have so long enjoyed'. The adventures that were to come, as imperialism itself developed into a kind of faith, and dominion became a national ambition for its own sake, were grounded upon this good old base, erected so long before by the earnest philanthropists of Clapham and Exeter Hall: and when evangelicalism had long lost its dynamism, when a harsher generation was in command, impelled by cruder ends, still the memory of these aspirations tempered the brashness of the British Empire, and sometimes touched the imperial conscience.

---

more Afro in independent Sierra Leone, but Fourah Bay thrives still, the Creoles are still pre-eminent, and there are still sixty-five Christian churches for the 128,000 inhabitants of Freetown. Sierra Leone was the original inspiration for the neighbouring republic of Liberia, settled by freed American slaves, and for the French ex-slave settlement of Libreville, on the Gabon river to the south.

CHAPTER THREE

Sweet Lives

IT was only to be expected that the improving instinct would presently father the interfering impulse, as the evangelical power of Britain pursued new fields of action. It was much easier to reform people if you ruled them, and so the British began, tentatively at first, guardedly, even unwittingly, their long attempt to mould the world in their own image. 'The complete civilization and the real Happiness of Man,' decreed the Aborigines Protection Society, 'can never be secured by any thing less than the diffusion of Christian Principles'; and the diffusion of true Christian Principles could best be achieved by the exertion of British authority.

2

Among the first people to feel the effects were the Afrikaners of South Africa.[1] They were an intensely religious people themselves. A mixture of Dutch, Flemish, German and French Huguenot stock, they had first emigrated to the Cape in the seventeenth century, to farm there under the rule of the Dutch East India Company, and they had established in that delectable country a society altogether their own. They were almost paranoically independent. They wanted to be alone. They asked nothing of government, and offered nothing in return. Bold, bloody-minded, sanctimonious outdoor people, they wanted only freedom to wander where they liked, establish their farms as they pleased, worship their own God and mind their own

[1] Whose generic names I use anachronistically, for convenience. In fact 'Afrikaner' was not much used until the last decades of the century, when it acquired political overtones, while 'Boer' in the 1830s was spelt with a small 'b' and meant simply 'farmer'.

business. With their great creaking ox-wagons and their herds of long-horned cattle, their plump wives in poke bonnets and their rangy dogs behind, they had long ago become indigenous to Africa, and adopted some of its values. The local Hottentots they enslaved, the local bushmen they virtually exterminated, the fierce and magnificent tribes of the African interior they kept at bay by force of arms. The Boers were a very lonely people, but they did not mind. They had virtually cut their ties with Europe, they spoke a bastard Dutch of their own, and they were sufficient unto themselves.

They worshipped a severe Calvinist version of the Christian God. He was a God of absolutes. His commandments were inflexible. He had ordained for ever the hierarchy of the stars and planets, the ordering of the seasons, the place in the world of men and women, beasts and birds. He was a literal God, who had revealed his truths once and for all in the infallible text of the Old Testament. He was a God who had decreed, if only implicitly, that every Boer farmer was his own master, with a right to his own African farm, and absolute leave to exploit the black peoples of the continent as his own conscience allowed.

There were Boers in the Cape peninsula who lived exquisitely, in lovely oak-sheltered towns like Stellenbosch or Paarl, in wide-stoeped homesteads of the wine valleys, or fine old houses, with floors of red tile and furniture of stink-wood, among the gardens of Cape Town. The most Afrikaner of the Afrikaners, though, lived with Jehovah on the Great Karroo, the high dry plateau which lay to the north-east. These were the frontier Boers, the Volk quintessential, who considered themselves an elect within an elect, and embodied all their divine privileges in the conception of *lekker lewe*—'the sweet life', to be lived in lands wide enough to exclude the smoke of the next man's chimney, with a sufficiency of stock, no interference from busybody authority, and obedient black men round the back of the house.

3

In 1815 these grand but disputatious peasants (for like most dogmatists they were always squabbling) had become unlikely subjects of the British Crown. The British had retained the Cape of Good Hope, which they had captured in the wars, as a way-station on the route to India, and they had settled at Cape Town in the easy confidence of victory. They soon established a governing class of English gentry, with a leavening of Dutch burghers left behind by the previous regime. Cape Town became a genial blend of the Dutch and the English Georgian styles, with fragrant gardens running up the slopes of Table Mountain, and avenues of oaks and camphors, and well-proportioned offices of Government arising around the old Dutch castle. Along the coast, too, English settlements took root: Grahamstown, the frontier town, 500 miles to the north-east, elegantly disposed around its garrison church, or Port Elizabeth upon Algoa Bay, guarded by its little stone fort and overlooked by the memorial to its eponymous patroness Elizabeth Donkin—'*to the memory of one of the most perfect of human beings, who has given her name to the town below*'.

India was the reason for the English presence, and India never seemed far away. There were the ships, of course, always swinging around the Cape, or putting into the base at Simonstown for victualling or refurbishment. There was the faintly Indianified manner of English life. And there was a constant shifting society of Britons from India—Hindus, as the Boers called them, as against Kapenaars. Many officers from India spent their leave at the Cape—it did not count as home leave, so that they need not sacrifice their overseas allowances. Some retired to the Cape, a happy compromise between the swelter of India and the mist of England, and some came to recuperate from the fevers of Calcutta and the plains: the spa at Caledon, east of Cape Town, depended almost entirely upon the Indian trade, and was always full of worn-out Collectors, faded memsahibs and debilitated majors of the Bengal Army—who, resting among its springs and rubber-trees, and looking across the gentle plain to the mauve cool mountains beyond, must sometimes have wished they had never set eyes on Malabar or Madras.[1] The Anglo-Indians often brought their own servants with them, and with

[1] The Caledon mineral bath is still there, with the ruined remains of a hotel and one splendid old rubber-tree that must have shaded many an Anglo-Indian in its time.

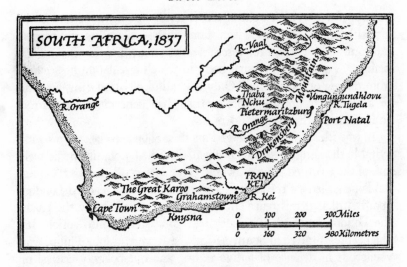

these turbanned or shawled domestics at their heels, browned themselves by the Indian sun they would parade through the esplanade gardens of the Cape, to remind the watching burghers and wondering Hottentots that they were subjects now of a wider sovereignty.

No society could be more alien to the inbred and unimaginative community of the Boers, and almost from the start the British and the Afrikaners distrusted each other. The Boers thought the British stiff-necked, snobbish and interfering, and called them *rooineks*, rednecks.[1] The British thought the Boers ignorant, ungainly and often queer. At first, though, there seemed no conflict of interest. The Boers were essentially pastoralists, landsmen, whose eyes turned instinctively to the open grasslands of the interior. The British were interested in South Africa only as a staging-post to the east, and the little wars which they found themselves obliged to fight against the African tribes along their frontiers were intended only to keep the Cape safe and stable. As late as the 1840s only one surfaced road led out of Cape Town, for strategically the British did not need to extend their authority inland—the smaller and tighter their footholds on the coast, the better. They were not much attracted,

[1] As did the Egyptians a century later—'red-necked blimps of the Brutish Empire'.

53

anyway, by the high veld of the interior: 'a worn-out and emaciated country', John Howison thought it in 1830, 'its mountains, without soil or verdure, resemble skeletons, and its unwatered plains . . . are like an animal body in which circulation has ceased from disease or exhaustion'. Only a handful of wandering artisans or adventurers, mostly Scots or Irish, had penetrated the Karroo to live among the frontier Boers.

It was idealism that changed all this. Sooner or later it was inevitable that English evangelicalism, with its emphasis on the welfare of the coloured peoples, would come into conflict with the dour fundamentalism of the Boers. Disturbing rumours reached London about Afrikaner mistreatment of the Hottentots, and by the 1820s the London Missionary Society had gone sternly into action. Its chief representative in South Africa, the Reverend John Philip, was vociferous in defence of native rights, and outspokenly critical of Afrikaner attitudes. The English newspapers took up the cause, successive English Governments were prodded into action, and before long the more extreme of the Boers began to feel themselves threatened—not in their persons, for from the start they had enjoyed equal rights with Englishmen, but in their way of life.

In 1828 they were horrified to be confronted by an ordinance declaring black men and white to be, 'in the most full and ample manner', equal before the law. In 1833 they were stunned to learn that, by a decision of the English Parliament 4,000 miles away in London, slavery in South Africa was banned. They were told that black people had a right to the possession of land, something which struck at the very roots of the Boer philosophy. They were told that Hottentots had a right to travel where they pleased, without passes. They were warned that they must not take the punishment of Kaffirs into their own hands, as they had with every success for 200 years, but must make a complaint through a magistrate. Their own opinions, they considered, were distorted or disregarded, and wherever they turned they found, in league with the blacks, in conspiracy with the local authorities, influential in London and honoured among the barbarous black chiefs of Kaffirland, the ubiquitous Mr Philip and his clerics, those earnest instruments of the imperial instinct.

All this was too much for the frontier Boers. It seemed to them that not merely the legal or constitutional, but actually the natural order of things was being deliberately disrupted. How was a man to keep order on his farm, if he could not flog a recalcitrant employee? How could the murderous black warriors of the frontier zones, represented by the English missionaries as no more than misunderstood innocents, be kept at bay? How could the divine hierarchy itself be maintained, if Ham was the equal of Shem? The Boers felt betrayed, but worse still, perhaps, they felt despised. So free, so bold, in many ways so generous, now they felt themselves treated as inferiors, half-Europeans, backwoodsmen, by the sanctimonious representatives of the new British order. Unlimited land, cheap obedient labour, security from blacks and whites alike—these were essentials of the *lekker lewe*, and all three the British Empire seemed determined to deny them.

So it came about that in the late years of the 1830s the Boers, the first refugees of Victoria's empire, undertook the hegira of their race, the Great Trek—a mass migration of frontier people, perhaps 10,000 souls, out of the eastern Cape into the unexploited high veld of the interior, where they could pick their own land and be themselves. They were escaping in fact from the modern world, with all its new notions of equality and reason, but on the face of it they were simply trying to get away from the British. They were early victims of that latent British aptitude for interference which was presently to find subjects, and make enemies, from Canada to Bengal.

4

The Boers of the Great Trek—the Voortrekkers, as they were ever after to be known—made for the Orange River, the eastern frontier of the colony. Once across it, they would be free. They moved for the most part independently, in small wagon groups, commanded by craggy elders and guarded by mounted riflemen: but though their exodus was spread over several years, they did move to a general plan. It was based upon the reports of secret reconnaissance parties, and it was propagated among the Volk by word of mouth. They would rendezvous, in their shambled scattered way, at the foot of the

Drakensberg Mountains, in territory claimed only by black Africans, and there they would decide where their final destination was to be. They were very experienced frontiersmen, and they travelled with a loose-limbed expertise. We see their high-wheeled trek wagons plunging through rivers and over ravines, the long ox-teams slipping and rearing, the driver with his immense hide whip cracking above his head, the black servants straining with ropes on the back wheels. We see them camped in laager within the circle of their wagons. The men in their wide-brimmed hats are smoking long pipes beneath awnings, or lie fast asleep upon the ground. The women are imperturbably suckling their children, mending their clothes, or preparing heroic Boer meals of game, eggs and violent coffee. Hens scrabble among the propped rifles and powder horns, a tame gazelle, perhaps, softly wanders among the carts, and in the distance the black men separately squat and gossip beside their fires. It is a truly Biblical scene, and the trekker Boers were searching quite consciously for a Promised Land. They moved in a spirit of revelation, as though pillars of fire were leading them (and one unusually ecstatic group, coming across a verdant spring in the remoter veld, assumed it to be the source of the River Nile, and named it Nilstrom). They were penetrating country almost unknown to white people—up through the scrub of the Karroo into the brilliant immensities of the high veld, which seemed to extend limitlessly into the heart of Africa, which smelt of herbs and heather, and over whose silences the stars hung at night with a clarity unimaginable to the distant philanthropists of Empire.

There were few black people to harass them. The only real opposition came from the warlike Matabele tribe, whom the Boer commandos, loose in the saddle and quick with the elephant gun, smartly defeated in a battle at Vegkop, well over the Orange River, killing 400 warriors and capturing 7,000 cattle. More often the trekkers quarrelled among themselves, for there were all sorts on this epic. Some were rich men, with household possessions piled high in their wagons. Others had nothing but their horses, guns and hands. Few could read or write, fewer still had any experience of administration or leadership, nearly all were people of fractious individuality, exceedingly difficult to control. The story of the Great Trek, for all its poignant grandeur, is a story of endless bickerings, political rivalries and even religious antagonisms. The trekkers mostly travelled in groups of a dozen wagons or so, with ten or twelve fighting men, twenty or thirty black servants and a rag-tag tail of cattle, horses, sheep and goats. It was only in 1834 and 1835 that a sporadic movement of families and friends developed into a migration; and only in 1837 that the main body of the Voortrekkers, some 3,000 men and women, assembled at their rendezvous at Thaba Nchu, at the foot of the Drakensberg on the borders of Basutoland.[1]

Now they began to think of themselves as a State. They were the *Maatschappij*, the Company of Emigrant South Africans, self-constituted in reaction to the British Empire, and from their leaders, so often at each other's throats, they chose a Captain General. Piet Retief at 56 was more sophisticated than most of his contemporaries. He was of Huguenot stock, had grown up in the wine country around Stellenbosch, had lived in Cape Town and was a born wanderer, destined never to settle. He it was who gave the Great Trek its manifesto. Like most such declarations, it was meant to be read between the lines.[2] 'As we desire to stand high in the estimation of our brethren,' it said, 'be it known *inter alia* that we are resolved, wherever we go, that we will uphold the just principle of liberty; but whilst we will take care that no one shall be in a state of slavery, it is our determination to maintain such regulations as may suppress crime and preserve proper relations between master and servant. . . . We will not molest any people, nor deprive them of the smallest property; but, if attacked, we shall consider ourselves fully justified in defending our persons and effects to the utmost of our ability. . . .'

There one hears, perhaps for the first time, the authentic voice of Afrikaner self-justification: the flattened cadences, slightly petulant,

---

[1] Thaba Nchu is some forty miles east of Bloemfontein. The main trekker route roughly followed the present Cape Town to Johannesburg road, crossing the Orange River at Norvalspont. If I seem to treat the Great Trek too romantically, it is perhaps because I cherish, often despite my better judgement, an old admiration for the country Boer, whose dauntless qualities I covet and whose biltong I have shared with grateful pleasure.

[2] And bears a distinct resemblance, in manner as in intention, to Ian Smith's Declaration of Rhodesian Independence, 1965.

with which for a century or more the Boers were to plead their grievances and their cause—a peasant voice, uneducated and unsubtle, but more determined and more courageous than the British would usually suppose. Retief and his colleagues, in their laager beneath the Drakensberg, went on to establish the structure of the State. They determined its name—not New Eden, as had been suggested, but the Free Province of New Holland in South Africa. They adopted a constitution, with a Governor, a Council of Policy and a Court. They decreed that all members of the Volk must take an oath of loyalty: defaulters would be excommunicated, denied civic privileges and perhaps declared Enemies of the People. In a spirit of exaltation only intermittently marred by feuds and jealousies, the great body of the Voortrekkers, in the summer of 1837, thankfully beyond the reach of the British Empire, prepared to seize and settle for ever their Israel in the north.

5

To the south of them lay the coastline of the eastern Cape, now intermittently settled for some 500 miles by British colonists. It is difficult to imagine a society more different from the nomad encampments of the Voortrekkers: yet each was a frontier community in its way, and while the Voortrekkers debate their future with psalms and recriminations away in the empty veld, let us leave them for a while with their impending destiny, and descend the escarpment of the Little Karroo to visit the very British coastal village of Knysna—to point not a moral, as both sides might claim, but only a contrast.

A track led there out of the foothills, dropping through wooded gorges and tortuous passes, between splendid thickets of stinkwood and white pear, to a point where suddenly between the trees one saw a small streak of pure white substance, trapped apparently in a defile among the hills. It looked like a line of snow, or a patch of brilliant white sand, but it was really the Indian Ocean, perpetually foaming between the high looming headlands that were called Knysna Heads. Nowhere on the whole African coast was more exhilarating. The surf was tremendous. The rocks were black and bold.

Gulls swirled in the wind, cormorants dived recklessly into whirl-pools, spray hung on the air, and all day long tides echoed, sucking and reverberating, against the black masses of the headland.

Inside the Heads there lay a lagoon. Around it the British had established a settlement, and had already transplanted to that savage place their own habits and values. The Royal Navy maintained a station at Knysna, but the tone of the hamlet was set by its principal landowner and first citizen, George Rex Esquire, who lived in gentlemanly style in the manor house of Melkhout Kraal. All the scattered farms that looked down upon the Knysna lagoon, black-thatched and white-plastered at the forest's edge, formed part of Mr Rex's estate, and around his presence, and the rent-books of his busy factor, the whole heirarchy of Englishness was assembled upon this distant frontier.

The country was wild—elephants still visited the lagoon shore—but the village was ordered and discreet. Its dust streets were rolled and watered, its houses were neatly thatched, and on a convenient corner stood the St George's Tavern (landlord Tom Horn, lately of Bristol). The social order was self-evident. At the bottom were the coloured labourers, so recently released from slavery. Then came the few local Boers, who talked only a sort of pidgin English, and who lived as woodcutters in the forest, or foremen on the farms. Then there were the small tenant farmers; the captains of the Kynsna-based ships, Scotsmen and Irishmen chiefly and powerful drinkers; the local tradesmen and merchants, the apothecary, the chandlers; and there were the grander gentlemen settlers, the Barringtons, the Duthies, the Nelsons, the Sutherlands, the Bot-terills, or the widow Fauconnier and her children, in whose parlour, in the absence of a church, the Reverend Charles Bull used to take Sunday services, and Captain Duthie, Justice of the Peace, held his periodic courts.

And at the top was Mr Rex, who had personally approved all the original settlers. Rex lived like a polite English gentleman-farmer upon a large scale, but rumour suggested that he was something rather more: and what capped the ineffable Englishness of his village, and made it so unutterably alien to the harsh republicanism of the Voortrek laagers over the mountains, was the fact that, if what one heard was true, the Squire of Knysna was the natural son of George III—Queen Victoria's uncle. Nobody knew for sure, but just the suggestion was enough to ensure for him a feudal respect. Officialdom was fulsome in its gratitude, when Mr Rex erected an obelisk, or donated a site for a parish church. His labourers and artisans were gratified by his every condescension, his tenants were honoured by his briefest visit, curtseys and raised hats followed him down the village street: for this little microcosm of the English way even reproduced that trust in the divine grace of monarchs which was at once the equivalent and the antithesis of the Boer belief in the divine privileges of themselves.

How the Voortrekkers would have loathed it! How smug it would have seemed to them, how patronizing, how impious too! Knysna was a demonstration of all they most resented in the imperial presence: like suburbia to an old-school gypsy, perhaps, or barracks life to a guerrilla.[1]

6

But they were far away from George Rex and his kind. In the flank of the Drakensberg they discussed their next moves. Some decided they would stay where they were, in the country between the Orange and the Vaal rivers. Some thought they would cross the Vaal, to settle in the high grasslands of the Gatstrand and the Witwatersrand. But Piet Retief had his mind upon Natal, the glorious green country on the coast, lush, forested, watered, warm in the bitterest winter, in the summer freshened by breezes off the sea or the high mountains that bounded it inland. In October, 1837, he rode ahead with a party of horsemen and, passing through a pass in the Drakensberg, saw this paradise for the first time: there it lay

---

[1] Whether Rex was really royal, or whether as cynics claimed he sprang from the well-known Rex family of Whitechapel, nobody knows to this day. Modern Knysna romantics believe him to have been the son of George's Quaker mistress Hannah Lightfoot, and fancy they detect Hanoverian profiles in the village even now: but his tombstone in the Melkhout Kraal woods says simply: *In memory of George Rex Esquire, Proprietor and Founder of Knysna, Died 3rd April, 1839.*

below the mountains, green and warm, with palms and bananas, heavenly wild flowers of the tropics, magnificent forests of yellow-wood and tambuti, and far in the distance beyond the downlands and the coastal plain, the blue line of the Indian Ocean. 'The most beautiful land,' wrote Retief, 'I have ever seen in Africa.'

Surely it was Israel. Few Europeans lived in it, and few Africans either, while the British Empire had specifically declined to annex it. Its only suzerain was King Dingaan of the Zulus, and he did not live there himself, but claimed it merely as buffer territory to his Kingdom of Zululand farther north. With this capricious but formidable barbarian Retief, riding down through the foothills with 14 men and four wagons, accordingly opened negotiations.

Dingaan lived in some state. The name of his royal kraal, Umgungundhlovu, meant The Secret Plot of the Elephant, and commemorated Dingaan's assassination of his half-brother Shaka, the greatest of Zulu kings. It was a city of thatched beehive houses above a stream. Behind it the humped wilderness of Zululand stretched away to the north, a terrific empty country of dry hills and green river-beds, speckled only with the villages of the Zulu pastoralists. The nearest European settlement to the east was the Portuguese colony of Delagoa Bay, a thousand miles away: the nearest to the west was Grahamstown, far across the wasteland of the Transkei. The Zulus, a highly organized fighting people, lived in a condition of terrible isolation, having slaughtered most of their nearer neighbours.

The King loved display. He surrounded himself with plump women, jesters and dwarfs. He liked to show off his famous glutton Menyosi, who could eat a whole goat in a single meal. His palace was a great mud hut, its floor rubbed with fat to make it shine, its reed roof beautifully woven, and around it stood hundreds of huts in circular groups: huts for the wives and concubines of the king, huts for the young warriors of the bodyguard, huts for the royal weapons. A large cattle-kraal stood ostentatiously near the palace, the wealth of the Zulus being expressed in cows, and behind it the lazy circling of vultures marked the Hill of Execution, which was littered with human bones and scavenged by hyaenas.

Retief was courteously received. Warriors danced for him,

marvellous in beads and ostrich feathers, with great skin shields brandished high, and plumes bobbing above their heads, and trained red oxen moving in rhythm with their gestures. Dingaan himself, bald, greased and resplendent in red, white and black, welcomed him graciously from his throne at the gate of the cattle kraal. Their talks were brief and to the point. Retief wanted simply to settle his people in the unoccupied territory of Natal, and Dingaan almost immediately concurred. The Boers could settle there, but only if they first performed a service for Dingaan: reclaim from the Basuto chieftain Sikonyela, in the mountains, a number of Zulu cattle he had lately stolen. When they had brought these beasts back to Umgungundhlovu, preferably with Sikonyela too, then the Boers could move into Natal.

Retief was delighted, and the Boers rode back in high spirits to the Voortrekker encampments beside the Drakensberg. The news preceded them, and the Afrikaners, quoting psalms, texts and prophecies, in-spanned at once and hastened impulsively through the passes, helter-skelter down the escarpment into Natal, until there were a thousand wagons, perhaps 4,000 Boers, prematurely encamped around the headwaters of the Tugela within Dingaan's putative territory. There the first citizen was born upon the soil of New Holland, and the Voortrekkers felt that the worst of their hardships were over.

It did not take Retief long to perform his commission. With fifty burghers and ten of Dingaan's Zulus he moved swiftly into the Basuto country, enticed Sikonyela into his camp, kidnapped him and held him prisoner until all the 700 stolen cattle were handed over. A week later Retief set off, with a commando of seventy volunteers and thirty coloured servants, to claim his reward from Dingaan. By now rumours had reached the Voortrekkers that the Zulu king might be less friendly than he seemed. He had been alarmed by the Boer victory at Vegkop—he resented the impetuous entry of the trekkers into Natal—he really had no intention at all of allowing the Boers to settle in his territory—he was blood-crazed and treacherous to the core. ('Who can fight with thee?' his warriors used to intone before him, dancing ferociously for hours at a time. 'No king can fight with thee. They that carry firearms cannot fight with thee.')

But Retief and his men rode boldly back to Umgungundhlovu, and found themselves respectfully welcomed again. There were dances and parades once more. The King talked at length about this and that. Zulu impis marched and counter-marched, beating their war-drums. After three days of mixed entertainment and discussion, Dingaan announced that all was settled, and he signed with his mark a deed granting to the Boers—'the Dutch Emigrant South Africans' —all the land between the Tugela and the Umzimvubu rivers, 'and from the sea to the north as far as the land may be useful and in my possession'. Natal was theirs, 'for their everlasting property'. Retief and his lieutenants, leaving their weapons outside, entered the central kraal to seal the concord with a libation of African beer, while the dancers tossed and whirled in celebration around them, and the drums beat wildly.

They drank: and as they did so Dingaan, rising terribly to his feet in black and feathered splendour, cried '*Bulala ama Tagati!*'— 'Kill the wizards!' Instantly the warriors and the dancers fell upon the Boers. They dragged them to the Hill of Execution, and there, binding their hands and feet with hide thongs, they beat their heads in with clubs and drove wooden spikes, as thick as a man's arm, from their anuses through their chests. Retief was the last to die: they forced him to watch the sufferings of his comrades, and then they cut his heart and liver out, and buried them symbolically beneath the track that led across the river into Natal—'the road of the farmers', as Dingaan contemptuously called it.

7

Down on the coast, though most of the Voortrekkers did not realize it, a British colony of sorts was already established, by the precarious consent of the Zulus. Port Natal had no sanction from London, and Retief had assumed that it would easily be absorbed into the Free Province of New Holland—its only imperial representative was a retired Royal Navy officer, now an Anglican missionary, who had been given powers of magistracy by the Governor of the Cape.

It was a drab little settlement. Except for a couple of stores its buildings were only mud huts, scattered in the coastal scrub. Its citizens were mostly dubious adventurers, half-African of habit—ivory traders or hunters, who dressed in a mixture of European and Zulu dress, who lived with native wives, and who were sometimes honoured as chiefs themselves by their rabble of native and half-caste followers. The Fynn family, for example, who were half-castes themselves, had loyal sub-tribes of their own—Frank Fynn was chief of the iziNkhumbi, Charles governed the iziNgolweni, Henry the Nsimbini. Such people spent half their time in the bush, hunting elephants, trading beads or firearms for hides, meat and ivory, and at home they still lived like nomads, in home-made clothes and boots, surrounded by dogs, skins, guns and carcasses, with miscellaneous Africans wandering in and out, or squatting at their doorways. There was no fort in Port Natal, no policeman, no church: though the Zulus had in theory ceded the little port and its coastline to the Queen of England, they did not regard the cession very seriously, and the Queen herself had doubtless never heard of it.

Captain Gardiner, R.N. (retd.), loyal and devout, had a difficult time of it, for he was not much loved by his disreputable neighbours at the port. Once he had briefly persuaded them to constitute themselves a town—to be named Durban in honour of the Cape Governor, Sir Benjamin D'Urban—and to petition the Government to declare it a British colony: but when this initiative was spurned by London, Gardiner was left without power, without prestige and without assistants. He was rebuffed in all his attempts to bring order to the community, whose members thought him too goody-goody by half, and in the end he gave up, and withdrew disenchanted from Africa to devote himself to good works in Patagonia.[1] The settlers were relieved to see him go: if he was a true representative of British sovereignty, they thought, on the whole they would prefer the authority of the Boers—who, though they might be equally inclined to quote Ezekiel or invoke the Great Incomprehensible Being, at least understood the ethos of the frontier and the veld.

But the news that the Voortrekkers had entered Natal from the north gave to Port Natal a new meaning. In the British view the

---

[1] Where he died of starvation in 1851, the last survivor of a private mission of seven Englishmen landed on Picton Island, off the coast of Tierra del Fuego, to convert the hostile natives to Christianity.

Voortrekkers were renegades from the imperial authority: by the Cape of Good Hope Punishment Act of 1836 the British Empire had claimed jurisdiction over all British subjects south of the 25th parallel—which ran hundreds of miles to the north. Her Majesty's Government were accordingly perturbed to hear that these particular subjects were now stirring up trouble and establishing pretensions among the native peoples so far along the coast. The nearest imperial forces were at Grahamstown, and the notion of such uncouth Calvinists butchering Basutos or subverting honest Zulu kings was profoundly disquieting to Whitehall. So it was that on November 14, 1838, Sir George Napier, Governor of Cape Colony, announced after all the annexation to the British Empire of Port Natal—'in consequence of the disturbed state of the Native tribes in the territories adjacent to that part, arising in a great degree from the unwarranted occupation of parts of those territories by certain emigrants from this colony, being Her Majesty's subjects, and the probabilities that those disturbances will continue and increase'.

Two weeks later a British warship appeared off the little port, and a force of soldiers disembarked. The Union Jack was run up, and a hundred Highlanders of the 72nd Regiment of Foot established themselves in a fort specially erected for the occasion, and naturally named after Queen Victoria.[1]

8

The Boers were bent first on revenge against the blacks. After the massacre at Umgungundhlovu the Zulu regiments, sweeping across Natal, had attacked the scattered Boer encampments on the upper Tugela, killing 500 people, wounding hundreds more, driving off thousands of cattle, and plunging the Volk into chaos. Impis marched here and there, Boer commandos were ambushed, and even Britons found themselves embroiled—a missionary travelling through Natal in March, 1838, met a body of 400 Zulus, bellowing a monotonous war-song, led by a solitary Englishman with an ostrich feather in his

[1] It still stands, and contains in its powder magazine, now a chapel, a Pantheon of Natal's worthies—every one, as it happens, British.

straw hat and an elephant gun covered with a panther skin on his shoulder.

Some of the trekkers decided that this could not be Zion after all, and moved away to the north into the mountains. Many more moved deeper into Natal, some settling in the lee of the mountains, some trekking south-east along the line of the Tugela, some striking for the coast. Now a written constitution was drawn up for the Natal Republic, and a capital was laid out at Pietermaritzburg, some fifty miles north-west of Port Natal. But it remained to settle the score of Umgungundhlovu. In November, just as the 72nd ran up the flag above Durban Bay, Andries Pretorius, one of the most respected and resourceful of the commando leaders, assumed the office of Head Commandant and prepared to fall upon Dingaan. 'O Lord, defer not and do', the elders prayed before his commandos left, 'defer not, for thy name's sake': and in return Pretorius and his men swore that if God gave them victory over Dingaan, they would build a church in His honour to commemorate the day—'we shall observe the day and the date as an anniversary in each year . . . and we shall tell our children that they must take part with us in this for a remembrance even for our posterity.'

So they crossed the Tugela, 400 angry horsemen of God, and rode direct for Umgungundhlovu. On Saturday, December 15, they halted to keep the morrow's Sabbath on the banks of the Ncome River. They set up their laager, they mounted their three guns, and when dawn came on the Sunday they found that squatting silently upon their heels around them, thousands upon thousands in concentric circles, the feathered Zulu warriors waited. 'Do not let us go to them,' said Pretorius, 'let them come to us': and so the sun rose with the Zulus still and silent outside the laager, and the Boers singing solemn hymns within.

When daylight came the Zulus attacked, rattling their assegais against their shields to make a noise like falling rain, and hurling themselves in their hundreds upon the laager. They had scarcely a hope. The Boers, impregnably ensconced behind their wagons, decimated them with rapid fire. For hours the Zulus repeatedly charged, each time they were cruelly repulsed, until at last the Boers sprang from their wagons, let loose their commandos and rode into the impis, shooting the warriors down as they ran, driving them into the river, or slaughtering them as they crouched among the reeds of the river bank. It was like a terrible dream of war. 'Nothing remains in my memory,' wrote one of the Boers afterwards, 'except shouting and tumult and lamentation, and a sea of black faces.' Only three Boers were wounded in the battle, but at least 3,000 Zulus died. They lay on the ground 'like pumpkins on a fertile piece of garden land', and so stained the passing river with crimson that it was called Blood River ever afterwards.

The Boers rode on to Dingaan's kraal elated, but they found it abandoned. Not a soul was there. They plundered it, destroyed what was left, and reverently examining the remains on the Hill of Execution, discovered Piet Retief's knapsack. In it, unharmed, was Dingaan's deed of cession, granting the whole territory of Natal into the possession of the Volk.

9

They built the church they had vowed, in their shanty-capital of Pietermaritzburg, and for ever after they honoured Dingaan's Day as they had sworn.[1] Now the Republic of Natalia was born. A Volksraad met in formal assembly, and for a time the Voortrekkers seemed to have achieved their Promised Land—'I will rejoice, I will divide Shekhem and mete out the valley of Succoth.' Every trekker, it was decreed, was entitled to two farms, and every burgher could take his complaints direct to the elected leaders of the people in the Volksraad. But it was all fruitless. The British Empire, from whose cloying rectitude they had so painfully escaped, could not permit it, and all their sacrifices and hardships, all the horrors of Umgungundhovu and Blood River, came to nothing in the end.

At first the Boers tolerated the presence of the British at Durban,

[1] The church, though it was neglected for nearly a century and was once used as a tea-room, is now restored as the Church of the Vow, while in 1952 Dingaan's Day, December 16, was re-named the Day of the Covenant. Hard-line Afrikaners still resent the participation of English-speaking South Africans in this national festival, and in 1972 Chief Gatsha Buthelezi of the Zulus awkwardly complicated the issue by suggesting that perhaps some Zulus might be invited too.

as Port Natal now called itself. The commander there, Captain Henry Jervis, was concerned chiefly to restore peace to Natal, and he it was who brought Pretorius and Dingaan to terms—unforgiving terms, for Dingaan was forced to withdraw his power far to the north, to the Black Umfulosi River, thus ceding to the Voortrekkers not merely the whole of Natal, but half Zululand too. But once peace was restored and their ascendancy established, the Boers determined that the British must go. They did not recognize the suzerainty of the Crown, they did not need British protection, and they were determined that the Cape Government should not extend its foothold in Natal. They sent Jervis a formal protest at his presence there, recalling in emotive detail the purposes and miseries of their trek—their departure from the Cape 'insulted, ridiculed and degraded', their struggles with barbarian tribes with no knowledge of the Great Incomprehensible, their sufferings at the hands of the murderer Dingaan. Now, they said, they were resolved to be their own masters. If British immigrants landed at Durban they would be treated as enemies of the State, and if they were backed by imperial forces the Natal Republic would go to war.

Unexpectedly the British did withdraw their forces, and it momentarily seemed that the Empire might even recognize the independence of the Republic. But it was only cat and mouse. In September, 1840, the Volksraad wrote to Napier asking that it might 'graciously please Her Majesty to acknowledge and declare us a free and independent people': but even as this disarming prayer reached the imperial authorities in London, so there filtered through to the Colonial Office and the evangelical lobby ugly reports of the Republic's racial policies. It seemed that the Boers still kept slaves, and bullied local chieftains, and in no way honoured the principles of humanitarian imperialism. Besides, the structure of Government, without a Briton at the helm, seemed to be breaking down. Within their Promised Land the trekkers went their own ways incorrigibly. They disregarded their own land laws, they refused to settle where they were told to settle, they squabbled with each other incessantly. Thousands of natives, pouring into Natal to squat on old kraal-sites, threatened security and defeated all efforts to segregate the races. An American trading ship had arrived at Durban and was doing brisk business with the Boers, an intolerable invasion of British mercantile preserves: and perhaps most important of all, coal had been discovered in Natal, and might prove, as was recognized at once in London, 'of the utmost importance to steam navigation in the adjacent seas'.

So when, in December, 1841, the Republic proposed to expel several thousand unwanted blacks into Pondoland to the north, without so much as consulting the King of the Pondos, the Empire intervened again. The Natalians, Sir George Napier warned, were still British subjects whether they liked it or not: and in May, 1842, after a long march overland from the Umgazi River, the forces of the British Army arrived in Durban once more—red-coated, gold-frogged, with a troop of cavalry, and a couple of guns, and wives, and babies, and hundreds of servants, and a gleam of bayonets and a beat of drums, and all the swank, polish and conviction of superiority that the Boers most detested in the British style of life.

10

The British baulking of the Voortrekkers, so languidly but implacably arranged by the distant power of Empire, made the Afrikaner in his heart an enemy for ever. The memory of the Great Trek, its symbols and its sacrifices, Moordspruit the river of death, Weenen the place of weeping, became the central myth of the Afrikaner people, around which they would in future generations preserve their identity and consolidate their attitudes: Blood River, the Church of the Vow, Dingaan's Kraal, even the image of the trek-wagon itself, these would be the tokens of their self-esteem, and of their tribal identity—for in many ways the trekker Boers *were* an African tribe, speaking the same language, of land, cattle, bondage, revenge and primitive divinity, as the Zulus or the Basuto themselves.

They tried once more to preserve their Republic of Natal, for the Boers promptly besieged the troops in Fort Victoria, and nearly starved them out. But once again they were thwarted. A young English settler, Dick King, broke the siege lines at night, and riding non-stop for three days and nights clean across the wild Transkei, alerted the imperial command at Grahamstown. On June 25 the three-masted frigate *Southampton* arrived in Durban Bay, and the Republic was doomed. Within a few years Natal was among the most absolutely British of British colonies, officially defined as 'a centre whence the blessings of civilization and Christianity may be diffused', and the most visionary and unyielding of the Boers, packing their guns and Bibles, had trekked still farther into the interior—over the high Drakensberg, across the Vaal, deep into the territory of the Matabele, to establish high on that bitter plateau the Republic of the Transvaal—so far away this time, in country so sparse and un-enticing, so innocent of advantages, that even the imperial instincts of the British, it seemed, would not again disturb the *lekker lewe* of the burghers.

CHAPTER FOUR

Roots into their Soil

ON the dirt road west of Mirzapur on the Ganges, perhaps 700 miles from Calcutta, there stood the temple of the goddess Kali at Bindhachal. It was a tumultuous and exotic shrine, especially at the end of the rainy season, when supplicants came from all over India to propitiate the goddess. The air was aromatic then with incense and blossom, dust swirled about the temple walls, the tracks were crowded with bullock-carts, wandering cows, beggars and barefoot pilgrims. Night and day goats were sacrificed, their blood spilling down the temple steps, and sometimes one heard the shrieks of devotees, tranced in ecstasy or bloody themselves with flagellation, invoking the blessings of the divinity—Kali the terrible, Kali the blood-goddess, consort of Shiva the destroyer, naked, black and furious, with her sword, her noose, and her bludgeon stuck all about with human skulls—Kali the dark one, with the protruding tongue and the bloodshot eyes, haunter of the burning ground, in whose heart death and terror festered.

This was the holy place of the Thugs, the hereditary fraternity of stranglers, who had for hundreds of years terrorized the travellers of India. Their secret society had branches and adherents from the Indus to Bengal, and they had their own hierarchy, rituals and traditions, and believed that when they strangled strangers on the road, they were strangling in Kali's cause—for Kali herself, when she had strangled the demon Rukt Bij-dana in the dawn of the world, had created two men from the sweat of her brow, and ordered them to strangle, and their posterity after them, all men who were not their kindred.

Thuggee enjoyed the secret protection of rajas and rich men, Muslim as well as Hindu, besides the terrified complicity of the peasantry. It was an ancient secret of India—the mutilated corpse at the bottom of the well, the silent stranger at the door, the unexplained subsidy, the whisper at the cross-roads. At Bindhachal was the priesthood of the cult. There, once a year, the stranglers went to pay their dues to the priests of Kali, and to receive their sacred instructions in return: where they should operate in the following year, what fees they should bring back to the shrine, what rituals they were to perform, if they were to enjoy the protection of the goddess —for if they neglected their obligations, homeless spirits they must become, to linger without hope in the empyrean.

To the British rulers in India, Thuggee had always seemed less than wholesome. 'To pull down Kali's temple at Bundachal and hang her priests would no doubt be the wish of every honest Christian', wrote a contributor to the Calcutta *Literary Gazette* in 1830. But it was the East India Company's traditional policy not to interfere with Indian religious customs. A blind eye was turned, and the rumours and legends of Thuggee inspired in the sahibs and their wives little more than a chill frisson, until in the 1830s the evangelical impulse reached the Indian Empire too, and moved the British not merely to conquer, exploit or consort with their subjects there, but actually to reform them.

2

The gentlemen of the East India Company had not originally intended to govern India, but merely to make money there. This they very effectively did throughout the eighteenth century, ten years' service with John Company often sufficing to set a man up for life in the Shires, see him through a convalescent retirement at Caledon, or even lay the foundations of a Sezincote. Over the course of generations merchant venturing led to military conquest. 'A very old friend of my father's,' wrote William Hickey the diarist, who went to India as a company cadet in 1769, 'presented me with a beautiful cut-and-thrust steel sword, desiring me to cut off a dozen rich fellows' heads with it, and so return a nabob myself to England.' The first forts and factories made way for palaces and barrack blocks—the Company developed from a trading agency to a Government—the

British presence moved inland from the ports to establish an ascendancy over the princes and maharajahs of the interior.

At first the Company, even with its new responsibilities, remained a swashbuckling, showy, amoral kind of service. It bred eccentrics and flamboyants, like old Sir David Ochterlony, for example, British Resident at the Court of the King of Delhi, who used to travel about the country in a carriage and four, huddled in furs, shawls and wraps of gold brocade, and attended by platoons of spearmen, troops of horsemen and, so legend said, thirteen wives each on her own elephant. There were few Englishwomen in India then, the sea passage being so long and dangerous, and the climate so dreadful, so that Englishmen were closer to Indian life than their successors were to be—often with Indian mistresses, generally with Indian friends, and cherishing little sense of racial or religious superiority.[1] They did not wish to change the sub-continent—it would have seemed a preposterous ambition. They treated the native princes with respect and occasional affection, tolerated the religions of the country (they actually administered several thousand Hindu temples), and did their plundering, fighting and trading in a spirit of uncensorious give-and-take. They were for the most part natural conservatives. Often they were men of aesthetic sensibilities too, and responded sensually to all the gaudy seductions of the land.

Their style was urbane. They drank tremendously and lived luxuriously. Prints of the period show the Governor-General bowling through his capital, Calcutta, in a high-wheeled gilded barouche, with foot-grooms running beside and behind, a stately coachman high on his seat, and a dashing escort of cavalrymen kicking up the dust behind. The Bengalis pause to see him pass, with their water-jugs upon their heads, or their burdens laid upon the unpaved street. An ox-wagon awaits his passing. An Indian sentry presents arms. High overhead the kites soar, and perched along the balustrade of Government House, meditatively upon the lion and sphinxes of its triumphal entrance, the adjutant cranes stand statuesque against the sun. An impression of pagan but cultivated ease is given by such a

---

[1] It had been 'jungled out of them', to use a phrase of Emily Eden's.

scene. The Governor-General, though clearly immensely grand, does not seem cut off from his subjects: the relationship looks organic, like that between peasants and gentry in contemporary England, each side knowing each others' faults, and making allowances.

3

But just as in England social relationships began to shift, so in India too, as the new century advanced, the nature of the British Raj changed. In 1813 the Company's trade monopoly with India was abolished, and for the first time English public opinion began to have some direct effect upon British administration in India. 'John Company' was no longer self-sufficient and all-powerful: the British Government held a watching brief, the Crown appointed a Governor-General, and Parliament at Westminster was the ultimate authority of the Raj.

Now the vocabulary of the evangelicals, so familiar already in Africa and the Caribbean, found its way into Anglo-Indian commentaries too. We read of natives awaiting redemption, of Christianity's guiding beacon, of providential guidance and the Supreme Disposer. The Indian territories were allotted by providence to Great Britain, wrote Charles Grant, the evangelical chairman of the Company's Court of Directors, 'not merely that we might draw an annual profit from them, but that we might diffuse among their inhabitants, long sunk in darkness, vice and misery, the light and benign influence of the truth, the blessings of well-regulated society, the improvements and comforts of active industry. . . .' James Stephen wrote of the 'barbarous and obscene rites of Hindoo superstition', and Wilberforce declared the Christian mission in India to be the greatest of all causes. 'Let us endeavour to strike our roots into their soil,' he wrote, 'by the gradual introduction and establishment of our own principles and opinions; of our laws, institutions and manners; above all, as the source of every other improvement, of our religion, and consequently of our morals.'

Our own principles and opinions. Now it became axiomatic that things English were superior to things Indian Britons no longer habitually went out to India in their teens, fresh and receptive: nowadays they generally went in their twenties, and they saw things differently. The old Indian ruling class, which had once worked or fought in equality with the British, was reduced in their eyes to comical or despicable ineptitude, or at most to glittering impotence (for the English always loved a prince, even a heathen one). The eighteenth-century sahibs had respected the Moghul culture, and viewed its decline with a reverent melancholy: their successors mocked and caricatured it—the last of the Moghul Emperors, Bahadur Shah, was left to rot within the walls of the Red Fort at Delhi like a quaint souvenir of the past.

With the first steamers from England there arrived, too, a new generation of Englishwomen, no longer a worldly, amused and tolerant few, but ladies of a more earnest kind, determined to keep their menfolk healthy and orthodox in mind as in flesh. Now a man could spend a family lifetime in India, with municipal responsibilities perhaps, and a prominent customary position in the evening parade through the Maidan. Now there arose a respectable Anglo-Indian community of administrators, merchants and planters, living with their families in genteel circumstances, and decorously attending church on Sundays. The Company had hitherto forbidden the entrance of Christian missionaries to India: now, by Government order, the ban was lifted, and godly apostles swarmed through the Indian possessions. Bishop Heber himself, the author of *From Greenland's Icy Mountains*, assumed the Anglican see of Calcutta, with archdeaconries throughout British India (and one in New South Wales).

The more enlightened the British in India became, the more dreadful India looked. Its ignorance! Its savagery! Its hideous customs of widow-burning, infanticide, religious extortion! Its ludicrous learning and its nonsensical laws! It seemed that God's mysterious ways had denied the Indians, perfectly intelligent though many of them were, the benefits of any true civilization of their own. The old habits of easy-going complicity, suitable enough to a commercial concern, no longer seemed proper to the British of the Raj. Was it not horrible to consider that in Calcutta, only thirty years before, the British had celebrated the Treaty of Amiens by parading with military bands to the temple of Kali herself? Or that in Ceylon, even at the end of the 1830s, they were still shamelessly appropriating to themselves the revenues of the Temple of the Tooth at Kandy? Now, thanks to the illumination of the reformed religion, the way was clearer: India must be Anglicized.

The historian Macaulay, who spent some years in India, argued that this could best be achieved by higher education in the English manner, and in the English language, for 'the literature now extant in that language is of far greater value than all the literature which 300 years ago was extant in all the languages of the earth put together'. Others went further, and in their new-found sense of mission, diligently tried to alter the nature of Indian life. The immense structure of Indian society, which was based upon dizzy complications of caste, religion and land-ownership, was beyond their powers. Nor did they try to abolish the main body of Indian custom, social or legal, which was inextricably enmeshed in Hindu and Muslim belief. They did, however, boldly set out to stifle the most offensive of native customs, however ancient, popular or divinely rooted. They forbade human sacrifice and infanticide. They put down *suttee*, the practice of burning widows, and henceforth, in their treaties with independent princes, insisted on its abolition as a condition of their protection—though the custom was so fundamental to the Hindu moral order that its very name meant, in the Sanskrit, chaste or virtuous.[1] And in a model campaign of evangelical imperialism, combining high moral fervour with advanced organizational skill, they turned their attention to that abomination of Bindhachal, the secret society of stranglers.

[1] And one group of pious Bengalis unsuccessfully appealed to the Privy Council in London against its prohibition. It lingered anyway. In 1927, when the police tried to prosecute a case of *suttee*, one of the vernacular papers could still complain that the British judiciary was 'unfamiliar with Indian social life and outlook, and belonged to another civilization', and isolated widow-burnings were reported even in the 1940s. Human sacrifice was more resilient still. In 1970 a bus conductor and his father in a village near Saharanpur were alleged to have sacrificed a ten-year-old boy to Kali: the crime came to light, it was macabrely said, when villagers felt giddy after eating a sacred *chupatti* distributed by the accused after worshipping the goddess.

4

Their agent of wrath was Captain William Sleeman, who had gone to India in 1809 as a cadet in the Company's Bengal Army. He was a soldier's son, and a figure of Cromwellian integrity—auburn-haired, blue-eyed, with a stubby farmer's face and a fine high forehead. He spoke Arabic, Persian and Urdu, he excelled at the tougher sports, he did not smoke and hardly drank, he read the rationalist philosophers like Locke and Hobbes, and he stayed generally aloof from the womanizing and high jinks that characterized the lives of most young Company officers. In his thirties, Sleeman was seconded to the civil administration, and it was as a magistrate and district officer in central India that he first became interested in the ghastly mystery of the Thugs. Patiently and methodically he learnt all he could about the sect, and so horrified was he by his discoveries that by the 1820s it had become his prime purpose in life to destroy Thuggee, in the practice as in the principle—not merely to prevent its murders and punish its practitioners, but to discredit its tenets too.

The Thugs worked in absolute secrecy according to strictly-enforced rituals. They were highway murderers. Finding a likely group of travellers upon the road, preferably of their own caste, they would infiltrate themselves into their company with ingratiating talk, join them on their journey for a day or two, and then, when the moment seemed ripe, the place suitable and the omens auspicious, fall upon their companions with a well-tried technique of noose-work, knee and grapple, and strangle them from behind with a silken noose. They cut the bodies about with ritual gashes, buried them or threw them down wells, burnt any belongings of no value and ran off with the rest, sometimes taking with them also an especially attractive child or two. Not a trace, of Thug or traveller, was left upon the scene.

By western criminal standards these were motiveless crimes. Any victims would do, and they simply disappeared without trace or apparent cause. If evidence of Thuggee ever came to light, most Indian peasants were far too frightened to reveal it, and in the ordinary courts of law Thugs were nearly always acquitted; for the stranglers were migratory and all-knowing, might take their revenge anywhere, and were the servants of Kali herself, who lived on blood. The Thugs were active all over India between November and May, the travelling season, and were at their most murderous in Bhopal and Bhilsa, in central India, where Sleeman estimated that the odds against a citizen's safe passage in the months of Thuggee were almost two to one. In 1812 it was reckoned that 40,000 people were killed by the Thugs each year; in three months of 1831 one gang murdered 108 people; many individual practitioners had strangled, during a lifetime in the guild, a thousand victims with their own hands.

The Thugs had their own hierarchy and forms of initiation, and their own secret language, which, like the Romany of the gypsies, enabled them to express hidden meanings in the presence of strangers. Its words, though Hindustani in form, were mostly peculiar to itself, and its meanings were sinister. *Bisul purna*, for instance, was a clumsy strangling; *jywaloo* was a victim left for dead but found to be alive; *khuruk* was the noise made by the pickaxe when digging a grave. The *rumal* was the yellow silk handkerchief, tied around a silver rupee, with which the stranglers killed. The *pola* was the secret sign left by one Thug for another. The *gobba* was the round communal grave of Thuggee, in which the victim corpses were packed around a central core of earth, to prevent the jackals exhuming them, or the corpses themselves, as Sleeman once put it, 'emitting that effluvia which often leads to their discovery'.

Thuggee was strictly hereditary. A boy-child was initiated stage by stage into the full horror of the craft—as a scout first, then as a grave-digger, then as assistant murderer, and finally, if he could show the necessary attributes of steel and ferocity, as a qualified *bhurtote* or strangler, an aristocrat among Thugs. A boy's first murder was an occasion for rejoicing, like a rite of puberty or circumcision, and elaborate ceremonials attended the sacred pickaxe which every thug gang carried—*kussee*, the holy emblem of the craft, which was a tooth from the mouth of Kali, and without which no strangling could be sanctified. After every murder the Thugs sacramentally ate a morsel of consecrated sugar, and this coarse yellow *goor*, they

believed, irrevocably altered them. 'The *goor* . . . changes our
nature. It would change the nature of a horse. Let any man once
taste of the *goor* and he will be a Thug, though he know all the trades
and have all the wealth in the world.'

The British had known about the Thugs for many years. As
early as 1673, John Fryer had reported the awful bravado of a
young Thug who, tied up for hanging, 'boasted, that though he were
not yet Fourteen Years of Age, he had killed his fifteen men'. But
generally the British, like the indigenes, preferred not to see, or at
least to convict: in 1827, when three Thugs turned informer and four
more were charged with murder, the British circuit judge not only
dismissed the case, but sentenced the informers to five years for giving false evidence, their sentence to be preceded by five days spent
riding backwards on donkeys round and round the city of Jubbulpore. It was not until 1830 that a new Governor-General, the
reformist Whig Lord William Bentinck, appointed Sleeman Superintendent for the Suppression of Thugs, gave him fifty mounted irregulars and forty sepoy infantrymen, and set him loose in an area twice
as large as England, Scotland and Wales put together to destroy what
Sleeman himself called 'the most dreadful and extraordinary secret
society in the history of the human race'.

The evangelical mission could be merciless itself, in the knowledge of its rectitude, and civil liberties got short shrift in Sleeman's
Thug-hunt. He operated from headquarters at Saugor, a drab and
dirty town set on a forbidding lake in the heart of the Thug country. His campaign depended upon the use of informers—'approvers',
as they were called then—convicted Thugs whose lives were spared
in return for information and help in the field. The informers themselves, though they might not die, never regained their liberty—
'like tigers', it was said, 'their thirst for blood is never to be ap-
peased'—and captured Thugs were removed from the ordinary processes of law, and tried by a Special Commissioner. Those who were
sentenced to seven years' imprisonment or more had branded upon
their backs and shoulders the words 'Convicted Thug' in the
vernacular—'a deviation from the Regulations fully warranted
by the crime of Thuggism, which justly places those who practised it beyond the pale of social justice'. Later they were

tattooed with the single word 'Thug' neatly on their lower eyelids.

5

Sleeman worked with a relentless urgency. He had a Cause. 'I glory in it,' he wrote, 'and ever shall do.' With a few assistants fired by his zeal, with his wild troop of horsemen, turbanned, sashed and sabred, relentlessly he tracked down every clue and brainwashed every captive: and 'ever at the stirrup of . . . the Thug-hunting Englishman', he wrote, 'went one or two apostate members of their own murderous guild'. Every thread of information was passed to his headquarters at Saugor, until he had built up a detailed intelligence file on everything to do with the history, the symbolisms, the customs and the techniques of Thuggee, linked to a ten-foot map more detailed than India had ever known.

In ones and twos at first, later in scores, the Thugs were brought chained and hangdog into his courtyard, to be registered, interrogated, and locked up in the gloomy castellated prison which overlooked the lake. They were, to judge by drawings of the time, distinguished-looking men, mustachio'd more often than bearded, wearing turbans, white sashed dhotis over pantaloons, and sandals with curled toes. Sometimes the relatives of innocent victims passed by them in the yard, to identify exhumed corpses, or claim the possessions of murdered relatives. Inside Sleeman's offices, day after day for years, the painstaking questioning and interpretation of evidence proceeded. Once caught, a Thug suspect seldom returned to the world: condemned upon the evidence of his own comrades, he very soon found himself branded on the back and shoulders, thrown into jail at Saugor or Jubbulpore, or summarily hanged.

Sleeman found Thugs everywhere. He winkled them out from village and from castle. Some were senior officials in the service of Indian princes: one experienced strangler was spotted drilling the soldiers of the Ruler of Holkar in the courtyard of His Highness's palace. Some were the trusted servants of Europeans: the most important of all Sleeman's captives, the great Thug leader Feringheea of Gwalior, had been an intelligence agent in the employ of Sir

David Ochterlony. Several Thugs had spent half a lifetime in the service of the East India Company's armed forces, and one caught by Sleeman's irregulars was a well-trusted police informant on other varieties of crime. Sleeman also hounded down the bankers and patrons of Thuggee—'capitalists of murder', as he splendidly called them—and by the end of 1833 the Special Commissioner was able to report to Bentinck that 'the final extirpation of these enemies to mankind cannot be far distant, and will afford the noblest trophy to adorn His Lordship's return to his native country'.

This was the first systematic attempt to deal with organized crime in India—something quite new in Indian history. Yet even more effective than all the forensic and administrative skill, so characteristic of the new age, was the moral zeal behind it. The power of Sleeman's Christian conviction proved far stronger than the power of the Thugs' fraternal oath. Informers were obtained in surprising numbers, and once within the range of Sleeman's steady blue eyes, not to speak of those fierce horsemen in the lines outside, they talked freely and fluently—sometimes even engagingly.

'I am a Thug,' ran the confession of one eminent assassin, 'my father and grandfather were Thugs, and I have Thugged with many. Let the government employ me and I will do its work.' Each Thug-hunting posse, with its attendant apostates ready for betrayal, was a triumphant confirmation of Christian superiority over the forces of evil and ignorance. The Thugs themselves recognized this spiritual ascendancy. They had always believed their own powers to be supernatural. They worked to auguries and omens, and they were in occult partnership with their kin of the animal world, the tiger— 'those who escaped the tigers fell into the hands of the Thugs', reminisced a famous strangler of Oudh, 'and those who escaped the Thugs were devoured by the tigers'. Yet even these arcane advantages, it seemed, were not enough to withstand the *iqbal* or auspice of the British. It was so powerful, one Thug assured Sleeman, that 'before the sound of your drums sorcerers, witches and demons take flight. How can Thuggee stand?' The powerful patrons of Thuggee, too, prudently recognized this force: Dhunraj Seth, for instance, a rich banker of Omrautee who had invested deeply in Thug enterprises, now directed his funds into a securer field—the

East India Company's monopoly of the opium trade with China.
Sleeman was not surprised. He was a true son of his times. Fascinated though he was by the intricacies of Indian religion, he trusted
in the omnipotence of western right and reason. We have verbatim
records of his conversations with captured Thugs, and from them
we can hear him, muffled but still indefatigable across the years,
deliberately pitting his own convictions against the superstititions
of his captives. Once or twice he seems to falter. One persuasive
prisoner, who had admitted to 931 murders by his own hand, tried
to convince Sleeman that the pleasures of Thuggee were merely akin
to, though distinctly superior to, the pleasures of big-game hunting,
to which Sleeman was himself addicted. 'For you, sahib, have but the
instincts of the wild beasts to overcome, whereas the Thug has to
subdue the suspicions and fears of intelligent men and women, often
heavily armed and guarded. . . . Can you not imagine the pleasure
of overcoming such protection during days of travel in their company, the joy of seeing suspicion change to friendship, until that
wonderful moment arrives when the *rumal* completes the *shikar*—
this soft *rumal*, which has ended the life of hundreds? Remorse,
sahib? Never! Joy and elation, often!'

In any case, Thugs habitually insisted, they did not kill irrespon-
sibly, like common murderers—God was in effect the strangler,
and God allowed them the profits of their trade. Mere thieving they
despised. 'A thief is a contemptible being, but a Thug—rides his
horse—wears his dagger—shows a front! Thieving? Never! Never!
If a banker's treasure were before me, and entrusted to my care,
though in hunger and dying I would spurn to steal. But let a banker
go on a journey and I would certainly murder him.' Thuggee was
holy work. God was the killer.

'Then by whose killing,' asked Sleeman once, perhaps a little
anxiously, 'have all the Thugs who have been hanged at Saugor and
Jubbulpore been killed?'

'God's, of course.'

'And there is but one God?'

'One God above all Gods.'

'And if that one God above all Gods supports us we shall succeed?'

'We see that God is assisting you, and that Devi has withdrawn her protection on account of our transgressions. We have sadly neglected her worship. God only knows how it will end.'

There was a nagging sense of incompleteness to such an exchange. Sleeman had to work hard to convince himself that his methods were fair, however unimpeachable his cause, and once, having lately learnt of the existence of yet another Thug gang, 300 strong, he was plunged into self-mortification. 'What a sad but faithful picture of our ruined nature does this present! Three hundred sons of fallen Adam leaguing themselves together for the purpose of *murder*! Are we by nature in the sight of God better than they? Certainly not . . . we are all—even you, gentle reader—in the sight of God as those 300 Thugs. As it is written, there is none righteous, no not *one*!'

6

By 1841 the cult had been virtually exterminated.[1] Several thousand Thugs had been tried, hundreds had been hanged, many were imprisoned or transported to the penal settlements of the Andaman Islands. The less terrible of them were sent to a trade school within the prison at Jubbulpore, where they learnt such useful crafts as carpet-making, cloth-weaving, carpentry and brick-laying. As the assassins lost their lust for blood, Sleeman built a walled village near the jail, where their wives and families lived. Later still the prisoners moved in there too, and until late in the Victorian era curious Anglo-Indians used to visit them as they aged, to gain a horrible thrill from their glimpses over the wall, and imagine all the terrors of noose, dismemberment and burial which had given the old reprobates such holy pleasure long before.

Almost to the end the campaign had found its opponents among the British themselves, for there were still men who believed such practices as Thuggee to be the prerogative of the Indian condition, and who doubted if reformist zeal could properly be applied to such

[1] Though the office of Superintendent of Thuggee survived until 1904, and until the 1940s at least the office of the Intelligence Bureau at Simla was popularly known as Thagi Daftar—Thug Office.

a people. As Sir Thomas Munro, one of the most celebrated of Anglo-Indian administrators, had said long before: 'I have no faith in the modern doctrine of the improvement of the Hindus, or of any other people. When I read, as I sometimes do, of a measure by which a large province had been suddenly improved, or a race of semi-barbarians civilized almost to Quakerism, I throw away the book'. Thuggee was an Indian tradition: what was more, it was a religious custom, and even Macaulay did not believe in trying to wean the Indians from their religions.

So Sleeman was not without his critics. Some were old-school administrators who believed in the principle of non-interference— 'do nothing', as it used to be said, 'have nothing done and let nobody do anything'. Others were legalists who objected to his authoritarian methods. Others again, especially British Residents at the courts of independent Indian princes, thought he behaved unconstitutionally. The Resident at Gwalior, for example, opposed the Thug-hunters so resolutely that Gwalior became a Thug sanctuary, and after murder expeditions, so Sleeman maintained, stranglers could return there with as much safety as an Englishman to his inn. The Resident at Bharatpore was no less hostile: he was astonished to learn, he wrote to the Governor-General, that in the hunt for Thugs the end justified the means, 'a doctrine which I had erroneously supposed to have been long since exploded alike from morals and politics'.

But these were eighteenth-century voices, arguing against the times. Sleeman's campaign against the Thugs exactly fitted the developing ethos of Empire, even to its element of righteous ruthlessness. Charles Grant had expressed it perfectly. 'We cannot avoid recognizing in the people of Hindustan,' he had written, 'a race of men lamentably degenerate and base; retaining but a feeble sense of moral obligation; yet obstinate in their disregard of what they know to be right, governed by malevolent and licentious passions, strongly exemplifying the effects produced on society by a great and general corruption of manners'. No class of Hindu, clearly, was more degenerate and base than the fraternity of Thugs, or was governed by more malevolent and licentious passions; their practices offended against a universal moral law which, the evangelical imperialists argued, stood above religious faiths, and which it was the first duty of Empire to uphold.

7

As for Sleeman, he bore no grudge against the Thugs, remorselessly though he had hunted them for so many years. He was a generous soul, he was no prig or chauvinist, and his satisfaction appears to have been purely ideological. He had proved the *iqbal* of Victoria's Empire, and deepened its roots in India. On New Year's Day, 1833, he set out on an official tour of his territories, carried in a palanquin, wearing his gold-faced tunic and his feathered cocked hat, preceded by an elephant and escorted as usual by sepoys and cavalrymen. With him went his wife Amelie, the daughter of a French sugar-planter in Mauritius. Mrs Sleeman was far gone in pregnancy, and what with the jolting of the palanquin and the nightly exertions of setting up camp (for they travelled less sumptuously than the Edens), on the sixth day out from Saugor she was seized with labour pains.

They pitched camp as soon as possible, in a grove of lime and peepul trees beside the way, and there in the shade a boy was born. It was an apposite *accouchement*. As Sleeman well knew, the grove had been notorious for generations as a haunt of Thugs—a *bele*, a place of strangulation. In that place, over several centuries, scores, perhaps hundreds of innocents had felt the Thug knee in the small of the back, the Thug breathing behind the head, and the soft silken pull of the *rumal* around the neck. A Thug baby born in such a murder-place would be considered unclean, and would pass his contamination down the family line, but Sleeman knew better. He was a man of the imperial enlightenment, and he, his wife and the baby boy all lived happily ever after.[1]

[1] Or at least for another twenty years, until he died with Amelie at his side—a Major-General, British Resident at the Court of Oudh, recommended for a knighthood, of a heart attack off the coast of Ceylon, on his way home after forty-six years in India to the land of just and old renown.

CHAPTER FIVE

Laws of War

FORCE was ever the fuel of empires, though, and inevitably Victoria's was very soon at war. The first Victorian punitive expedition was mounted in November, 1837, just six months after the Queen's accession, and for the rest of the century her dominions were seldom at peace. Waterloo and Trafalgar had left Britain with the power to prevent any further global conflict for a century, but the Pax Britannica itself, the peace of Empire, was maintained only by incessant small campaigns. 'The great principles of morality,' the good Lord Glenelg once declared, 'are of immutable and universal obligation, and from them are deduced the laws of war. . . . Whether we contend with a civilized or barbarous enemy, the gratuitous aggravation of the horrors of war on the plea of vengeance or retribution, or on any similar grounds, is alike indefensible.' Few educated Englishmen would dissent in principle: in practice, by the nature of empire, Queen Victoria's wars did not always lack their gratuitous aggravations, and in the scale of the imperial motives the philanthropic was nicely balanced by the belligerent. War came naturally enough to the British, after so much experience of it, and empire offered them a more or less perpetual battle-field.

2

There were two main imperial armies. The first was the British Army proper, with its headquarters at the Horse Guards in London. In 1838 it was about 100,000 strong, divided into three guards' regiments, eight cavalry regiments, thirteen infantry regiments of the line, eight regiments of artillery and an incipient corps of engineers. Rather more than half of it was normally stationed abroad, and there were garrisons and contingents scattered across the globe from Tasmania, where the Army guarded the convict settlements, to Jamaica, where a force buried deep in the queer hill-country called the Cockpit, high above Falmouth, kept watch upon those refractory aboriginals, the Maroons. As a social institution the Army had scarcely changed since Marlborough's day. Its officers, many of them rich men of fashion, bought their commissions still, and did not generally find their duties onerous: training was minimal, and the average officer had plenty of time to spend on field sports, horse-breeding, or living it up in town. As for the rank and file, they remained Wellington's scum of the earth, so astonishingly redeemable by discipline and dangers shared. They enlisted for twenty-one years, and a large proportion of them were Irish Catholics, supplemented by recruits from all the simpler regions of Britain—the Scottish Highlands, the West Country, mid-Wales—and by an assortment of riff-raff and pseudonymous rogues.

Professionally the Army had not much progressed since Waterloo. Tactics were still based upon the square and the thin red line, training was still a matter of rigid regulation inflexibly enforced. Marksmanship was hit-and-miss: if a soldier hit the target once in three or four attempts, he was considered a good shot. Parade orders were still those of the eighteenth century—'The battalion will change front by the wheel and countermarch of subdivisions round the centre—Close up the supernumerary ranks—Right sub-divisions right about face, the whole right wheel—Quick *March!*' The grand bewhiskered sergeants of 1815 were still the Army's core in 1839, and the soldiers went to war in the same long greatcoats, thick scarlet uniforms, shakos and whited bandoliers.

The Army lived ritualistically. Flags, guns and traditions were holy to it, and loyalty to one's regiment was the emotional keynote of the service. When a soldier was sentenced to death he was paraded blindfolded before his own regiment, made to kneel upon his own coffin, and, while the band played the Dead March from *Saul,* shot there and then. An elephant who refused to pull a gun to one Indian battle was formally court-martialled, and sentenced to receive twenty-five lashes of a chain administered by a fellow-elephant.[1]

[1] Though the British never liked using elephants in war—they suffered from footsores, and their ear-drums were vulnerable to the crack of rifle-fire.

Ceremony and display was immensely important to the British military ethos, and this taste for splendour was carried over to the Empire, and became an imperial technique too.

The other imperial army was a very different force. Since the seventeenth century the East India Company—'John Company'— had maintained its own armed forces. By 1839 this army was divided into three Presidency forces, raised by the three administrative divisions of British India, Bengal, Madras and Bombay, the general commanding the Bengal Army being normally the senior officer of all. It was a force unique in the history of Asia. Though raised and paid by the Company, it was in effect at the disposal of the Crown, and formed a mercenary army bigger by far than the Queen's own forces. There were a few regiments of European infantry, recruited mostly from Ireland or among the drifters and adventurers always at a loose end in British India, but most of the other ranks were Indian: sepoy infantrymen of all races and religions, wearing uniforms that looked more British than Asiatic, drilled to British methods, grouped in numbered regiments in the British style: colourful troopers of irregular horse, raised on a personal or family basis by individual British officers—like the celebrated Skinner's Horse, 'the Yellow Boys', raised by the half-caste James Skinner, and run as a kind of club.

The commissioned officers of this curious force were all British, educated at the Company's own military academy at Addiscombe in Surrey, where they took a two-year course in military subjects, Hindustani, mathematics and mechanics. They did not buy their commissions (though a boy could be nominated for one by a grandee of the Company) and promotion was generally by merit. The long hot years in India inevitably took their toll; many officers deteriorated before their time, or succumbed to debauch and gluttony, and the glamour of it all masked many flaws and deficiencies. Even so, John Company's Army was a formidable machine—experienced, professional, and at some 250,000 men larger than any European army except Russia's.

The two imperial armies did not greatly care for one another. Their styles were different, and the contrasts jarred. The Indian armies had abolished flogging in 1835; the British Army flogged

AFGHANISTAN, 1838

so readily that troops in the Queen's regiments were nicknamed 'bloody-backs'. The British private soldier generally soldiered *faute de mieux*: the sepoy generally came from a military caste, proud of his hereditary calling and much respected for it. British Army officers were often terrific swells, Indian Army officers were mostly middle-class career men. Contact between the armies, which frequently served side by side, was polite but not often enthusiastic: British Army officers did not much like working under the command of Company generals, and Company soldiers resented the fact that many of the best local appointments, like that of C-in-C, Bengal Army, were reserved for Queen's officers.

But between them they were extremely powerful, and the story of Victoria's Empire, as it unfolded during the next half-century, weaved itself around their joint existence, and often followed their trumpets.

3

The first big Victorian war was precipitated by Emily Eden's brother George. In the 1830s most of the British possessions could be considered invulnerable. The Royal Navy made them so. There was a long land frontier, it was true, between Canada and the United States, but 10 million Americans with their minds on other things did not then pose any serious threat to the stability of the Empire: on the contrary, the Royal Navy was their own first line of defence, and the only real guarantor of their Monroe Doctrine. As for the scattered islands and remoter settlements of the Empire, they were either so awful as to be scarcely worth coveting, or accessible only by courtesy of the British fleet.

The one exception was India, where during the past half century British power had been extending steadily towards the north. Here the British must defend a land frontier 2,000 miles long. No fore-seeable threat arose from the decadent Chinese Empire in the north-east.[1] To the north-west, however, stood Russia, whose strength was uncertain, whose intentions were always mysterious, and whose empire in Asia had grown as fast as Britain's. In theory at least the most vulnerable corner of the British Empire was the top left corner of India, and there lay the home ground of the Great Game, which was to share courts with the Eastern Question for much of the nineteenth century. At one time or another Turkey, Persia, Egypt and the Balkans were all considered by British strategists to be the Key to India, but the classic Great Game was played in the mountain kingdom of Afghanistan, and there more than anywhere the British repeatedly scented danger. Immediately to the north of it the Russian Empire lay, probing towards Bokhara and Khiva; immediately to the south lay the British Empire, whose influence extended, thanks to a treaty with Ranjit Singh the Sikh, to the line of the Indus river. Between the two the Afghan kingdom stood glowering and secretive, inhabited by some of the most warlike

[1] When the British acquired Hong Kong in 1841, indeed, in the course of a trade war against the Chinese, one commentator likened the new colony to 'a notch cut in China as a woodsman notches a tree, to mark it for felling at a convenient opportunity'.

peoples on the face of the earth, and veiled always in intrigue. It was little-known to Europeans, except by disrepute. Its capital, Kabul, lay deep within the mountains at 6,000 feet, clustered at the foot of a mediaeval citadel, the Bala Hissar, on a desolate gravel plain: a foxy, evasive kind of city, riddled with xenophobia and conspiracy, and living it seemed always on its nerves. All around were unmapped, bald and inhospitable highlands, pierced by narrow ravines and deep river-beds, traversed only by rough tracks. The kingdom made its living by plunder and agriculture, for the Muslim Afghans thought trade an ignoble occupation, and left it to foreigners. The general character of the people was at once savagely independent and desperately unpredictable. The Afghans could be lively, humorous, courageous, even warm-hearted: but they could also be bigoted, sly, and murderous. They were uncompromisingly picturesque. The women were enveloped head to foot in the white cylinder of the *burkha*, with only a mesh at the eyes to demonstrate the human presence within. The men wore huge turbans, or satin caps with gold brocade crowns, with leather boots buttoned up to the calf, huge sheepskin cloaks over their shoulders, and shirts with wide sleeves for the concealment of daggers or poison phials.

The Afghans were not only implacably chauvinist, they also fought incessantly among themselves, for they were split into great tribal divisions—the Durranis, the Ghilzais, the Barakzais—and sub-divided multitudinously into clans—Hazarahs, Tajiks, Sadozais, Khaibaris, Afridis—not to speak of innumerable Pathan groupings on the southern border, and Tartars and Uzbegs in the north. All these groups had their own characteristics, their own traditions and their own loyalties, and they made Afghanistan extraordinarily difficult for a foreigner to understand, and almost impossible to govern. There had been eight changes of royal dynasty in the past half-century, deposed monarchs generally being murdered, but sometimes only blinded.

The British wished, on the whole, to preserve the independence of this unnerving State, as a buffer against Russian pretensions. In the 1830s, however, they had doubts. The Amir Shah Shuja-ul-Mulk, one of the flabbier of Afghanistan's generally gristly kings, had been deposed thirty years before and had been in exile ever since, first as an enforced guest of Ranjit Singh, then as a pensioner of the British in India. It was now rumoured that his successor, the virile Dost Mohammed, might be plotting an association with the Russians. There were whispers of Russian missions, subventions, arms supplies, and at the same time the Russians were known to be backing the Persian army which was, in a desultory sort of way, besieging the Afghan fortress of Herat in the west. These were misty, contradictory reports, but in 1837 a British agent, Alexander Burnes, went to Kabul ostensibly on a commercial mission, and confirmed that there really was a Russian mission in the city. Just what the Russians were up to, nobody knew:[1] but they were evidently up to something in the far north-west.

4

Lord Auckland, a weak, diligent and ordinary man, was perturbed. It took six months to get an answer from London, so the problem was all his. Burnes had recommended that the Dost, for all his flirtations with the Russians, should be regarded as a potential ally rather than a likely enemy. Auckland and his advisers in Calcutta determined otherwise. Dost Mohammed, they decreed, must be removed from office in the interests of imperial security, and the aged and compliant Shah Shuja restored to his throne in Kabul. In October, 1838, Auckland accordingly published, from his retreat at Simla in the Himalayan foothills, a manifesto of intent. The Governor-General felt the importance, it said, of taking immediate measures to arrest the rapid progress of foreign intrigue and aggression towards the imperial territories. Since Dost Mohammed and his supporters had proved themselves 'ill-fitted . . . to be useful allies to the British Government', the British proposed to restore to the throne of Kabul the exiled and rightful king, who would 'enter Afghanistan surrounded by his own troops, and will be supported against foreign interference and factious opposition by a British army; and when once he shall be secured in power, and the inde-

[1] Intelligence was limited, since no Briton in India understood their language.

pendence and integrity of Afghanistan established, the British army will be withdrawn'.

This was a dishonest proclamation. Far from being ill-fitted as an ally, Dost Mohammed was conceded by everyone who met him to be infinitely superior to Shah Shuja, and his subjection to Russian influence was at best uncertain. There was no sign that the Afghans wanted Shah Shuja back, and still less evidence that they would welcome a British army to protect him. The Perso-Russian siege of Herat presently failed anyway. From the start the Afghan enterprise was distrusted by many Britons at home. Lord Palmerston, Foreign Secretary in Lord Melbourne's Whig Government, was convinced that the Russian threat was real and urgent, but the Court of Directors of the East India Company, when details of the invasion plan reached them in London, were horrified. The Duke of Wellington thought the difficulties would start when the military successes ended, and the Press, in London as in Calcutta, attacked the manifesto for its distortions and sophistries. In Parliament angry members demanded publication of the relevant documents: Palmerston obliged them, first cutting out, however, all the good things Burnes had reported about Dost Mohammed.

But Lord Auckland, in the way of undetermined men, was determined. He had made up his mind for once, and he would stand by his resolution. The British armies would enter Afghanistan early in 1839, and the Great Game would be settled once and for all. Besides, Lord Auckland thought, it would be an opportunity for Ranjit Singh the Sikh to demonstrate the reality of his new alliance with the British, by contributing a large proportion of the forces required: an opportunity of which, in the event, he wisely took no step to avail himself.

5

Some 9,500 Crown and Company troops, with 6,000 men under the febrile command of Shah Shuja, formed the Army of the Indus, the principal invasion force for Afghanistan. Before it went to war it was ceremonially paraded, by courtesy of Ranjit Singh, at Ferozepore on the Sutlej river, south-east of Lahore. Ranjit came down from his capital for the occasion, and Lord Auckland, as we already know, travelled there with his sister Emily and his caravan of 12,000. The meeting between the two leaders was less than majestic, for their two lines of elephants collided and Ranjit fell flat on his face in front of two British nine-pounders—and the evening's entertainments were less than decorous, for Ranjit presented a cabaret of dancing girls and bawdy buffoons, and drank too much—but the purely military functions were stately and impressive, and on December 10, 1838, the Army of the Indus moved off from the parade ground for its war against the Afghans.

Wars went slowly then, and the army took a circuitous route. Shah Shuja wished to take the opportunity of subduing some unruly Amirs of Sind, to the west, whose allegiance he claimed—a commission easily performed, for the unfortunate Amirs were told by the British commander that 'neither the ready power to crush and annihilate them, nor the will to fall into action, were wanting if it appeared requisite, however remotely, for the safety of the British Empire'. The winter had gone, and the spring had arrived with its promise of flooded streams and heat-haze, before the troops crossed the Indus River and marched up the mountain valleys towards Quetta, Kandahar and Kabul. For the first time since the days of Alexander the Great, it was said, the 'flags of a civilized nation' flew across the Indus.

The soldiers' progress was laborious, for behind them in an apparently endless stream there stumbled some 38,000 camp followers and 30,000 camels. The army was to live off the country, but took with it nevertheless thirty days' rations of grain, and enough sheep and cattle for ten weeks' meat. It also carried an astonishing supply of inessentials. Two hundred and sixty camels, it was said, were needed to carry the personal gear of the commanding general and his staff. One brigadier needed sixty. One regiment required two just for its Manila cigars. There were tons of soap, gallons of wine, crates of jam, crockery, linen, potted meats. Each officer was allowed a minimum of ten domestic servants—most had many more—not counting the grooms for his camels and the six bearers he needed if he took a palanquin.

Every regiment had 600 stretcher-bearers. Every platoon of every regiment had its water-carriers, its saddlers, its blacksmiths, its cobblers, its tailors, its laundry-men, and there were the men who polished brasses, and the men who put up tents, and the cooks, the orderlies, the stable-boys—together with all their wives, and all their children, and often aunts, uncles or grandparents—and troops of prostitutes from half India, with fiddlers, dancing-girls, fortune-tellers, metal-workers, wood-gatherers—with herdsmen to look after the cattle, sheep and goats, and butchers to slaughter them—and there were carts and wagons by the thousand, palanquins, drays, chargers, ponies, dogs—and so all this great multitude stumbled away to war, each corps with its band playing, a regiment of Queen's cavalry, two of Company cavalry, nine regiments of infantry, engineers, gunners, Shah Shuja's 6,000 hopeful sepoys and those splendid prancing banditti, the Yellow Boys. A mighty dust hung in the air behind them, as a sign that the Raj was marching.

6

As a military operation the invasion was a qualified success. The army presently ran short of supplies, as its lines of communication grew more tenuous, and it was repeatedly harassed by the Afghan marksmen of the passes. Its intelligence proved faulty, too, perhaps because it had no intelligence department. But Ghazni, the first place to offer formal resistance, was taken by storm in a neat little *coup d'armes*, and when Afghan forces consequently fell back in confusion, the Dost himself, refusing British terms of 'honourable asylum' in India, fled north to take refuge with the crazy Nasrullah Khan, Amir of Bokhara, who promptly locked him up. Organized opposition seemed to be at an end, and on August 6, 1839, Shah Shuja, supported by the full panoply of British imperial power, entered Kabul to re-assume his throne.

Aesthetically the King's return was fine. A scramble of low mud buildings and roofed bazaars, dominated by the powerful silhouette of the Bala Hissar, Kabul was just the place for pageantry, and the King cut a sufficiently imposing figure. His coronet unfortunately no longer bore the diamond called the Koh-i-Nor, Light of the Universe, for that well-known gem had long before been extracted by Ranjit Singh as a fee for his hospitality, but in other respects the restored ruler of Afghanistan adequately looked the part. He was a good-looking man, dark of skin and stoutly built, with his luxuriant beard dyed black, and he was gorgeously dressed that day, and scintillated with jewelry, and rode a white charger accoutred in gold. Beside him rode the representatives of the British Empire, wearing the cocked hats, ostrich feathers and blue gold-laced trousers of the diplomatic uniform, and behind him the soldiers of the Raj, dusted down and fattened up after their year's march from Ferozepore, demonstrated in simple terms the power behind his throne.

The Kabulis, it is true, watched the King ride by in sullen silence. They paid more attention to the British diplomatists than to Shah Shuja, and very few citizens showed him any royal respect at all. But the old man was childishly pleased to be back in his palace (though everything, he said, seemed *smaller* than it used to be), and his British bodyguard, firing him a royal salute and offering him their insincere congratulations, for they all despised him, left him there with his own soldiers and returned to their camp. 'I trust,' said General Keane the commanding officer in his dispatch to Lord Auckland next day, 'that we have thus accomplished all the objects which your Lordship had in contemplation, when you planned and formed the Army of the Indus, and the expedition into Afghanistan': but he did not really think so, for he expressed his thoughts very differently in a private letter to a friend. 'Mark my words,' he said then, 'it will not be long before there is here some signal catastrophe.'

7

Much of the army was now sent back to India, and General Keane went with it, leaving a division of infantry, a regiment of cavalry and an artillery battery. The Russians had vanished from Kabul, and the capital in its baleful edgy way was apparently docile. The British settled in. Their chief representatives were an Ulsterman and a Scot—Sir William Macnaghten, 'Envoy and Minister at the Court of Shah Soojahool-Moolk', and Sir Alexander Burnes, unexpectedly back in Kabul as British Resident. These were now the real rulers of Afghanistan, the puppet-masters.

Macnaghten had never been there before. He was 44, but looked much older—an Indian civil administrator, bespectacled, habitually top-hatted, with a dignified presence and plenty of ambition: '*our Lord Palmerston*', Emily Eden called him, perhaps a little cattily. He was a great linguist, and though his talents were mostly of the bureaucratic kind, his manner could be pedantic, his views were often fatuous and his appearance was, in that anomalous setting, sometimes a little comic, still he had courage and was honest—if not always with himself, at least with others. Burnes was a more elusive character. A kinsman of Burns the poet, he had begun life in the Company's armies, but in his twenties had made a famous series of journeys in Central Asia, penetrating as far as Bokhara and the Caspian. He was lionized in England, where they called him Bokhara Burnes, and William IV had once summoned him to Brighton Pavilion and made him talk for an hour and a half about his amazing adventures. It was Burnes' reports from Kabul, during his mission there in 1837, that had turned Auckland's mind to the idea of invasion: though he had admired the Dost, still he prudently adjusted his views to the Governor-General's policies, and had accordingly been knighted shortly before the war began. He was still only 34, a wistful-looking man with a long nose, a sparse moustache and pouches under his big brown eyes.

Although the Dost was still alive, and there were signs that most of the Afghan tribal chiefs would never pledge allegiance to Shuja, the British set out to enjoy themselves in Kabul. The 16th Lancers had unfortunately taken their foxhounds back to India with them, but there were many other pleasures available. The climate in the autumn was pleasant, the natives, if undemonstrative, seemed friendly enough, and there was little work to do. They built a racetrack, and skated on frozen ponds, and played cricket in the dust, even persuading a few Kabulis to take up the game. They learnt to enjoy the wrestling matches and cock-fights that the Afghans loved, and they organized amateur dramatics. In the early mornings they went for rides over the hills: in the evenings they listened to band concerts; in the night, very often, they comforted themselves with seductive girls of Kabul. One or two married Afghans.[1] Others, be-

[1] Notably Colonel Robert Warburton, who married a niece of the Dost, and

fore very long, were joined by their wives and children from India. There was no shortage of food now, and the officers entertained each other lavishly. Burnes used to give weekly dinner parties at his house in the city, with champagnes, sherries, clarets, liqueurs, hermetically sealed salmon and Scottish hotch-potch ('veritable hotch-potch, all the way frae Aberdeen').

So safe did the British feel that presently the Army was moved out of Kabul proper, leaving the Shah protected only by his own levies in the Bala Hissar. Now the whole force was concentrated in a big cantonment on the low damp plain to the east, within sight of the citadel but about a mile from the city's edge. It was a disturbing spot. The Kabul River ran across the plain, slate-grey and shaly, and between the camp and the city there were orchards and gardens, intersected by irrigation channels. In the spring the view could be beautiful enough, with the pinks and whites of the orchard blossoms, the shine of the water, the clutter of the bazaars and houses beyond, and the silhouette of the great fortress rising in tiers upon its hillock as a centre-piece to the scene. But all around the plain lay arid hills, one ridge beyond another, featureless and bare: and on their brown slopes stood here and there, relics of the centuries of Afghan feuding, small fortress-towers, some crumbled, some recently patched up, which gave to the whole place an ominous watchful air, as though even when one was thinking home-thoughts on the river bank, or hacking back to camp through the apple-orchards, one was never altogether unobserved.[1]

Here the Kabul Army ensconced itself, with all its camels and camp followers, all its appurtenance of stable, canteen, bazaar and married quarter. There were garrisons too at Kandahar and Ghazni to the

---

whose son Sir Robert Warburton, half British, half Afghan, was to be the most celebrated frontier administrator of British India—'uncrowned King of the Khyber'.

[1] A sensation that lingers even now. The plain has scarcely changed, and from the ridge to the east of the Bala Hissar, on one of those heavy hot mornings that contribute so powerfully to the flavour of Kabul, it is all too easy to imagine the isolation of the cantonment far below, and even to trace its outline in the dust. Kabulis well remember where it stood, for the war is a key event in Afghan national history.

west, and at Jalalabad to the east, and in the field columns were always on the move, and Macnaghten's political officers were ubiquitous. The British hoped that by a combination of display, bribery and coercion all the factions of Afghanistan could be persuaded into cooperation, but they never succeeded. Some groups of the community gave no trouble. Others, particularly the Muslim fanatics called Ghazis, and the Ghilzai tribe which controlled the main mountain passes into India, had to be repeatedly subdued by punitive expeditions, fun for the officers and good experience for the troops. Generally the political officers were treated with wary respect: but in the south at Kelat the half-naked and terribly emaciated corpse of Lieutenant Loveday was found chained to a camel-pannier, while over the border to the north Colonel Charles Stoddart, on a more advanced mission of intelligence, was thrown by the mad Nasrullah into a deep pit full of bones, decomposing matter and especially bred reptiles.[1]

Yet Macnaghten and Burnes felt sanguine. In his comfortable gardened Residency in the heart of the city, down the road from the Bala Hissar, Burnes had little to do but quite enjoyed himself—'I lead a very pleasant life, and if rotundity and heartiness be proofs of health, I have them'. Macnaghten, whose wife presided graciously over the social life of the cantonment, lived no less contentedly in the Mission Residence upon the plain. 'All things considered,' he thought, 'the perfect tranquillity of the country is to my mind perfectly miraculous. Already our presence has been infinitely beneficial in allaying animosities and pointing out abuses. . . . We are gradually placing matters on a firm and satisfactory basis . . . the country is perfectly quiet from Dan to Beersheba.'

There remained the Dost, who in the summer of 1839 escaped from Bokhara and re-entered Afghanistan with a force of Uzbegs. For a time he did seem to threaten Macnaghten's tranquillity—'I am like a wooden spoon', he had said, 'you may throw me hither and thither, but I shall not be hurt'. But this worry was surprisingly soon removed. In the cool of the evening of November 4, 1840,

---

[1] From which, professing Islam, he was presently removed and beheaded, together with Captain Arthur Conolly, author of the phrase 'the Great Game', who had been sent to Bokhara to negotiate his release.

Macnaghten was taking an evening ride with his assistant George Lawrence, through the gardens near his Mission. They were approached by two Afghan horsemen. One stopped at a distance, the other came close and asked Lawrence 'if that was the Lord Sahib'. Told that it was the British Envoy, the Afghan seized Macnaghten's bridle and cried that 'the Amir was there'. 'What Amir?' asked Macnaghten, taken aback. 'Who? Who? Where?' 'Dost Mohammed Khan', he was told: and presently the second horseman approached, and the Dost himself, dismounting, pressed the Envoy's hand to his forehead and his lips, and offered his sword in token of surrender.

The Dost was a striking man, and he behaved with a dashing dignity—'Every effort was made to soothe the Ameer's feelings,' we are told, 'and he soon became serene and cheerful.' After ten days he was sent away to exile in India, escorted by a troop of horse artillery and two regiments of infantry, and warmed by the admiration of his enemies.[1] His departure seemed to set the seal upon the Afghan adventure, and before very long, it was thought, the British might return to India too, leaving Shah Shuja with his 6,000 soldiers to look after his own destinies.

8

Yet just as there lingered over the cantonment some suggestion of disquiet, so presently more sensitive minds in the occupying army were troubled by forebodings. The story of the war against the Afghans is full of omens and dark prophecies. 'A signal catastrophe', General Keane had forecast, and many of the soldiers, with their vulnerable lines of communication through the Ghilzai passes, sometimes felt a chill breath of isolation. William Nott, one of the most outspoken of the generals, wrote: 'Unless several regiments be quickly sent, not a man will be left to note the fall of his comrades'. Colin Mackenzie, one of the most perceptive of the majors,[2] wrote:

[1] Admiration long felt in England, too. My copy of his biography, by Mohan Lal, was given in 1861 as a leaving present to one of his boys by Lionel Garnett, when a housemaster at Eton. It was dedicated to Queen Victoria.

[2] Who was later to be a general himself, and went on to discover the marvel-

'Our gallant fellows in Afghanistan must be reinforced or *they will all perish.*' In Kabul Major Hamlet Wade, watching a ceremonial review of the 44th Regiment, suddenly saw the passing troops not as a parade at all, but as a funeral procession—'What put such a thought in my head, I know not'. At Jalalabad, 150 miles to the east, Colonel Dennie of the 13th Light Infantry had an even more explicit vision. 'You will see,' he observed one day, 'you will see: not a soul will reach here from Kabul except one man, who will come to tell us the rest are destroyed.'

A sense of uneasiness spread. As a ruler Shah Shuja was a poor substitute for the incisive Dost, surrounding himself with doddering and petulant advisers, and becoming ever more querulous himself. The British officers, though they made many friends in Kabul, made many secret enemies too, by their free and easy behaviour with the women—who, frustrated as they often were by their husbands' pederastic preferences, were dangerously ready to oblige. Private soldiers were increasingly insulted and molested in the streets of the city. The keener professionals were concerned about the state of the cantonment: badly sited on the open plain, impossible to defend, with the main commissariat store actually outside the perimeter defences—'a disgrace', as one young artilleryman wrote, 'to our military skill and judgement'.

Now rumours began to nag, of new plots among the Ghilzais, of a threatened rebellion in the north, of Persian intrigue in the west; and the army in its cantonment, after a year in the tense and oppressive atmosphere of Kabul, showed the early signs of communal neurosis—petty quarrels and rivalries, snobbishness, touchiness. 'The whole country is as quiet as one of our Indian chiefships,' wrote Macnaghten ever more resolutely, but fewer believed him now. 'The Envoy is trying to deceive himself,' wrote the formidable Lady Sale, whose husband General Bob had been having a tough time with the Ghilzais, 'into an assurance that the country is in a quiescent state,' while in London the Duke of Wellington was not deluded by the Envoy's dispatches. It was impossible to read them,

---

lous sculptures of Amaravati—which, after lying for fifty years in the stables of East India House, are now among the treasures of the Victoria and Albert Museum.

he said, 'without being sensible of the precarious and dangerous position of our affairs in Central Asia'.

Into this disturbing setting there hobbled, in April 1841, a new Commander-in-Chief—literally hobbled, for Major-General William Elphinstone was not merely, as one of his senior subordinates wrote, 'the most incompetent soldier that was to be found among the officers of the requisite rank', he was also so crippled by gout and other unidentified infirmities that he could hardly walk. Elphinstone was a delightful man, but hopeless. Everybody liked him—he was an old friend of Auckland and his sisters—but nobody thought him the slightest use as a general. Patrician, kind, beautifully mannered and nearly 60, he had last seen action at Waterloo, and though the son of an East India Company family, spoke not a word of Hindustani or any other oriental language. Why this gentle sick old gentleman should have been commanding an army in Afghanistan is difficult to imagine, when he might have been happily retired in England cherishing his memories, his Commandership of the Bath and his knighthood in the Order of St Anne of Austria: and indeed he apparently found it difficult to explain to himself, for he strenuously denied his fitness for the job—'done up', he said of himself, 'done up in body and mind'.

The rougher of the senior officers treated the implausible newcomer with frank contempt, and he seems to have viewed the situation despairingly from the start. Even his rheumy eye observed the dangers of the cantonment, and he was anxious in his invalid way about the Kabul army's direct line of communication with India— through the passes to Jalalabad to the east, and thence through the Khyber to Peshawar and the Indus. 'If anything occurs,' he said vaguely once to one of his officers, 'for God's sake clear the passes quickly, that I may get away.' One senses that even in this incompetent's mind, as the army loitered through its second year of the Afghan enterprise, a mood of premonition impended, an instinct that the inner forces of Afghanistan were assembling, out of sight and understanding, against the foreigners on the plain.

So they were. At dawn on November 2, 1841, a mob arrived at the gates of Burnes' Residency in Kabul, shouting abuse and screaming for the Resident's blood. Telling his guards to hold their fire,

Burnes walked on to his balcony with his assistant, William Broadfoot, and his own brother Charles. He tried to appeal for order, but was shouted down. Shooting broke out and Broadfoot, after picking off six of the Afghans in the garden below, was shot dead through the heart.[1] The mob was now all around the Residency, the stables were burning, and a stranger appeared inside the house, urging the Burnes brothers to follow him quickly outside. They inexplicably trusted him, and throwing Afghan robes around their shoulders, followed him through the door into the chaotic garden. At once their guide shouted 'Look, friends! This is Sekunder Burnes!' —and the Afghans fell upon the brothers with their knives, and very quickly hacked them both to pieces.

9

'My dear Sir William,' wrote the General to the Envoy later that day, 'since you have left me I have been considering what can be done tomorrow. Our dilemma is a difficult one . . . to march into the town, it seems, we should only have to come back again . . . we must see what the morning brings, and then decide what can be done.'

For partly by design, more by combustion, the riot in the Kabul had now become a rising. The Kabulis had first assumed that, the British Resident having been murdered and the British Residency burnt to the ground, the British Army would come marching up the road to exact a terrible revenge. All that happened, though, was the arrival of a modest infantry force to give the King some extra protection within the Bala Hissar. Encouraged by this feeble reponse, thousands of Afghans in and around the city broke into open revolt, and within a few days the Kabul region was in a state of war, and the British were in effect besieged within their cantonment.

General Elphinstone continued to consider what could be done tomorrow, but never did decide. He had fallen off his horse on the morning of the riot, and had never felt well again. His conferences of

[1] A year to the day before, his brother James had been killed in a skirmish against the Afghans: four years later his brother George was killed in action against the Sikhs. They came from Kirkwall in Orkney.

war were painful to experience, the old general vacillating, wondering, changing his mind, and frequently embarking upon detailed reminiscences of the Peninsular War. Even his choice of phrase was lugubrious. 'It behoves us to look to the consequences of failure'—'Our case is not yet desperate, I do not mean to impress that'—'I was unlucky in not understanding the state of things'. Since he seemed to have no opinion of his own, everybody else offered him theirs, subalterns to brigadiers. Some thought they should leave the cantonment and move into the Bala Hissar *en masse*. Some thought they should abandon Kabul altogether, and retreat to Jalalabad. Some thought they should seek out the leaders of the insurrection, and negotiate terms.

Each day more Afghans joined the rising, until a guerilla army of several thousand artisans and tradesmen swarmed around the cantonment, becoming bolder by the hour. It was a raggle-taggle army, by the standards of the victors of Waterloo who watched it apprehensively from their fortifications, but it was both skilful and determined: it had its own cavalry, its long-muzzled *jezails* easily outranged the British muskets, and its marksmanship was horribly exact. Soon the road between the cantonment and the city was blocked; worse still, the Afghans had seized the commissariat fort, plundered it, burnt it, and thus deprived the British of nearly all their stores. All this in full sight of the cantonment, within whose perimeter the decrepit general rambled on, and the private soldiers kicked their heels in half-mutinous despair—'Why, Lord, sir', complained Elphinstone to Macnaghten one day, after reviewing some of his soldiers, 'when I said to them "Eyes right", they all looked the other way'.

They made a couple of sorties. Both failed ignominiously, the British infantry running away, and this was their last attempt at offensive action. They were beaten almost without a blow. Food was running short, winter was setting in, the troops were demoralized, the camp-followers were panic-stricken, the political officers were baffled or discredited, the commanding officer was all too often prostrate, the British Resident was dead. All the Afghans now seemed to be in arms against the British, and by the end of November Macnaghten had decided to negotiate a settlement.

10

At this climactic moment there arrived upon the scene a formidable Afghan leader—Akhbar Khan, the Dost's son, who had been in exile in Turkestan, and who now returned to Kabul with a force of Uzbegs at his heels. With this fierce, sly but attractive potentate Macnaghten now opened negotiations. Arranging to meet him on the banks of the Kabul River on December 11th, the Envoy offered him the draft of a treaty of submission, couched in the most abject terms. The presence of the army in Afghanistan, it said, was apparently displeasing to the great majority of the Afghan nation; and since the only object of its presence there was the integrity, happiness and welfare of the Afghans, there was no point in its remaining. Macnaghten offered to evacuate the country at once, lock, stock and barrel, giving Shah Shuja the choice of going with them or remaining in Kabul, and promising to return Dost Mohammed to his country as soon as the army had safely passed through the Khyber on the road to India. In return, the Envoy suggested, the Afghans would guarantee the safe conduct of the British, and would immediately send provisions into the cantonment to keep them alive enough to march.

The Afghans understandably accepted. They must have been astonished. It was agreed that the Kabul garrison would march in three days' time: but in the meantime Macnaghten, who had just been appointed Governor of Bombay, and faintly hoped still to extract some credit from Kabul, embarked upon a subtler course of conduct. There arrived in the cantonment on the following evening an unexpected messenger from Akhbar. Captain 'Gentleman Jim' Skinner, a member of the celebrated Anglo-Indian fighting family, had not been seen since the start of the uprising, when he had been caught in Kabul: it transpired now that he had been befriended by Akhbar, and he came with a secret additional proposal from the prince. It was this: that he and Macnaghten should deceive the other Afghan leaders with a hidden compact. Shah Shuja would remain upon his throne; Akhbar would be his Vizier, and would receive a large fee from the British Government, and a pension for life; the British could stay in the country for another eight months, and then leave apparently of their own free will. Face would be saved. Honour would be restored. Macnaghten would be Governor of Bombay. The original purpose of the invasion would be achieved.

Bringing such a message, remarked Gentleman Jim, was like being loaded with combustibles, but the distraught Macnaghten snatched at the offer, and signed a statement in Persian to say so. Nothing, in a country so hideously entangled with double-cross, could have been more dangerous. Several people warned the Envoy of treachery, and suggested that it might all be a plot. 'A plot!' Macnaghten cried—'a plot! let me alone for that—trust me for that!' Anyway, as he told George Lawrence, it was worth the risk. 'The life I have led for the last six weeks you, Lawrence, know well; and rather than be disgraced and live it over again, I would risk a hundred deaths. Success will save our honour, and more than make up for all risks.'

So two days before Christmas, 1841, Sir William Macnaghten, with three British officers and a small detachment of Indian cavalry, rode out of camp once more to meet Akhbar Khan. They took with them a lovely Arab mare, as a present for the prince. There was snow on the ground, and they found Akhbar, with a group of chiefs and a hovering crowd of Ghazis, awaiting them some 360 yards from the cantonment. A carpet had been laid on the snow, and upon it Akhbar and Macnaghten, greeting each other courteously, sat down together. Akhbar spoke first. Was Macnaghten, he asked, ready to put into effect the proposition of the previous night? Why not? Macnaghten replied: and instantly Akhbar cried, 'Seize them! Seize them!', and the chiefs and onlookers fell upon the Englishmen to screams and imprecations from the Ghazis all around. Macnaghten's Indian escort turned and fled. The three staff officers, almost before they knew what was happening, were bundled pillion on to horses and galloped away through the murderous Ghazis. One fell and was killed immediately. The other two were imprisoned in a nearby fort. Behind them, as they were swept away, they just had time to see the Envoy, his face ashen, being dragged head first down a snowy slope. 'For God's sake!' they heard him cry in Persian, before they were out of earshot, and Macnaghten disappeared for ever.

It is probable that Akhbar himself shot Macnaghten in the confusion, and that the maddened Ghazis then cut him to pieces with their knives. Later that day the imprisoned officers saw a dismembered hand bobbing up and down outside the bars of their window, and learnt that it was Macnaghten's. 'Look well,' the Ghazis screamed at them, 'yours will soon be the same!' Though they did not know it, the Envoy's head, deprived at last of top hat and spectacles, was already being paraded through the streets of the capital, while the rest of his corpse was suspended from a meat-hook in the great bazaar.

11

Even now the Afghans expected reprisals, but the British had lost all fight. All they wanted was escape. Far from unleashing his troops furiously upon the city, General Elphinstone, now further debilitated by a wound in the buttock, merely re-opened negotiations, as though Her Majesty's Envoy and Plenipotentiary had never been murdered at all. This time there was no subterfuge. The Afghans dictated the terms, the British accepted them. The Army was to leave immediately, handing over hostages for the return of the Dost, together with all its treasure and almost all its guns. The Afghans in return promised to provide 'an escort of trustworthy persons' to see the British Army, 26 years after Waterloo, safely through the passes to the Indian frontier. Nobody believed them. It was Christmas Day, but the signing of the agreement gave no comfort to the British, who were now terrified, bitterly cold and very hungry—the only food the private soldiers got that day was a little flour with melted ghee. As the shivering army packed up its possessions, rumours of treachery haunted the camp. The eighteen chiefs who had signed the agreement, it was said, had secretly sworn to destroy the whole force, and all its followers. Lady Sale, diligently writing up her diary on Boxing Day, said she had been told that the chiefs meant to capture all the women and kill every man except one: and opening by chance a copy of Campbell's poems, she found the stanza:

Few, few shall part, where many meet!
The snow shall be their winding sheet,
And every turf beneath their feet
Shall be a soldier's sepulchre.

On January 6, 1842, the army began its retreat, the most terrible in the history of British arms, and the completion of a tragedy whose 'awful completeness', as the historian Sir John Kaye was to write, was unexampled in the history of the world. To reach the safety of the British garrison at Jalalabad, the force had to travel through ninety miles of desolate mountain country, deep in snow, held in fief by the predatory Ghilzais, and now additionally infested with Ghazis too. The cold was terrible, and the march began in confusion. In all some 16,500 souls struggled out of the cantonment: about 700 Europeans, 3,800 Indian soldiers, the rest camp followers and their families. More than a thousand horses went with them, together with bullocks to pull the carts, camels, mules and ponies. Most of the European women and children travelled in camel-panniers: the camp-followers straggled along behind as best they could, frightened, bewildered, littered with babies, and cooking-pots, and all the voluminous half-fastened baskets, boxes and bundles that poor Indians carried on the march.

The moment the last soldiers of the rearguard left the cantonment gates, the mob poured in to plunder and destroy: and hovering always on the fringe of the column, sometimes sending peremptory messages to the general, sometimes coming close, sometimes disappearing, the chiefs of the Afghans predatorily rode. The retreat was a misery from the first step. As the troops marched in tolerable order along the snow-covered track across the plain, the camp followers in their thousands milled all about the column, turning the march into a muddled rout, pushing their way frantically towards the front, shouting and jostling, separating platoon from platoon, soldiers from their officers. Sometimes troops of Ghazi horsemen dashed among them, slashing with their sabres and galloping off with loot: the rearguard lost fifty men almost before it had left the lines.

So it was obvious from the start that the Afghan assurances meant nothing. If the escort of chiefs was capable of keeping off the Ghazis and Ghalzais, it had no intention of doing so: this would be cat and mouse to the end. Within an hour or two many of the soldiers were frost-bitten, while hundreds of the Indian bearers threw down their loads in despair and ran away into the wilderness. Before it had left the valley the army was virtually without food, fuel, shelter or ammunition, and behind it left a trail of dead and dying people, like a track of litter after a grisly holiday—some wide-eyed and insensible, some pleading to be put out of their misery, some stabbed about with knives, for the fun of it, by the Afghan children who swarmed through the mêlée. When the British camped for the first night, only six miles from the city, they looked back to see the night sky red and flickering with the flames of the burning cantonment: and when the rearguard arrived in the small hours, exhausted from its running day-long battle, and its soldiers shouted in the darkness, 'Where's the 54th? Where's the 6th?', they found the camp in a state of nightmare chaos, men and women dying all around from hunger and exposure, and were told everywhere, as they looked for their units, that 'no one knew anything about it'.

12

The retreat lasted just a week. During the first three days the way led through a series of precipitous passes, most of them 5,000 feet high and all deep in snow, and day by day the struggling mass of the British and their dependents grew smaller and weaker. They were never left at peace. Now and then they saw their escort chiefs, cloaked upon their horses upon distant knolls, or awaiting their arrival at the head of a pass, and sometimes Akhbar himself appeared with a demand for hostages, a gloating recrimination, or ever less convincing assurances of goodwill. Every day the harassment grew more brazen, until every gully seemed to hide an ambush of horsemen, and there were marksmen on every ridge.

Terrible scenes were enacted in the snows. We see Lieutenant Melville of the 54th Native Infantry, speared and stabbed in back and head, crawling after the column on his hands and knees. We see Dr Cardew of the medical service, fearfully wounded, tied to the last gun and left beside the road to die, while his soldiers mumble their goodbyes to him. We see Mrs Boyd and her son Hugh, aged four, tumbled out of their panniers as the camel that carries them is hit by a bullet and crumples slowly, groaning, to its knees in the snow. In the middle of the carnage, the hunger, the cold, the terror, we see an Indian deserter from the Mission guard, blindfold and ragged, shot on the spot by a firing squad.

On the fourth day Akhbar sent a message to Elphinstone suggesting that the English women should be handed over to his care. Eleven women and their children, including Lady Sale and Lady Macnaghten, were handed over to the care of the Afghans, together oddly enough with several of their husbands: they were taken away to a little fort in the hills, and fed that night on mutton and rice. By then the fighting strength of the army was down to 300 British infantry, about 480 sepoys, and 170 cavalrymen, most of them frostbitten, many snow-blind, many more without weapons or ammunition. They had passed through the first of the great passes, and there were seventy miles to go.

By the end of the fifth day the last of the sepoys were dead or missing, and no baggage was left at all. For miles the track was thick with the corpses of the camp-followers. Perhaps 12,000 people had died since they left Kabul, only a few thousand Indians survived, and the only people fighting back were the men of the 44th Regiment and the 5th Light Cavalry. They had passed through the second and third of the passes, and were fifty miles from Jalalabad.

On the sixth and seventh days the survivors struggled through the worst of all the ravines, the Jugdulluk, an allegorically gloomy defile, where the winding track passed between immense impending crags, and only a few scraggly holly oaks broke through the snow. Here the Afghans had blocked the way with a barrier of prickly ilex, six feet high. The soldiers fell upon it with their bare hands, while a fury of fire was poured at them from the ridges on either side, and Ghilzai horsemen galloped mercilessly among them—scrabbling frantically away with their frost-bitten fingers, dying in their hundreds, until at last a gap was made in the barricade and there was a mad rush of horsemen and foot-soldiers through it, the horses rearing, the shots flying, crazed soldiers sometimes shooting at their friends, and into the confusion the Afghans falling with their knives and long swords to leave the snow stained with blood, mashed about with footfalls, and littered with red-coat bodies.

By the eighth day the army had no commander. Summoned to a conference at Akhbar's camp, Elphinstone had been held there as a hostage, and his soldiers never saw him again. But by now there was virtually no army either: only some twenty officers and forty-five British soldiers had survived the slaughter in the Jugdulluk. At a hamlet called Gandamack they found themselves surrounded by Afghans and called to a parley—a handful of emaciated, exhausted and mostly unarmed Britons, with Captain Souter of the 44th wearing the regimental colours wound about his waist. It was a trick. The soldiers were slaughtered, only half a dozen being taken prisoner. The only survivors of the army now, apart from a few wandering sepoys, were fourteen horsemen, who, by-passing Gandamack, had galloped desperately towards Jalalabad—twenty miles away.

By the ninth day only six survived—three captains, a lieutenant and two army doctors, one of whom, Dr Brydon, had already lost his horse, and had been given a pony by a wounded subahdar of the native infantry—'take my horse', the Indian had said, 'and God send you may get to Jalalabad in safety'. At Futtehabad, sixteen miles from Jalalabad, the officers found themselves kindly welcomed by the villagers, who offered them food, and urged them to rest for a while: two of them were murdered there and then, three more were killed as they fled the place.

13

So there remained, on January 13, 1842, only one survivor of the Kabul army—Surgeon Brydon, Army Medical Corps, galloping desperately over the last few miles to Jalalabad, Afghans all around him like flies, throwing stones at him, swinging sabres, reducing him in the end to the hilt of his broken sword, which he threw in a horseman's face. And quite suddenly, in the early afternoon, Brydon found himself all alone. The Afghans had faded away. There was nobody to be seen. Not a sound broke the cold air. He plodded on through the snow exhausted, leaning on the pony's neck, and presently he saw in the distance the high mud walls of Jalalabad, with the Union Jack flying above. He took his forage cap from his head and feebly waved. The fortress gates opened; a group of officers ran out to greet him; and so the retreat from Kabul, and the first of Queen Victoria's imperial wars, came to its grand and terrible end.

'Did I not say so?' said Colonel Dennie, who was watching from the walls. 'Here comes the messenger'.[1]

[1] The British returned to Kabul within the year, spoiling Sir John Kaye's awful completeness, but blowing up the great bazaar as a reminder of their displeasure, and subduing the Afghans until the next Anglo-Afghan war, forty years later. Shah Shuja was soon murdered, of course, and Akhbar died in 1847, supposedly of poison: but Dost Mohammed was returned to his throne after all, and proved himself, as we shall later see, a true friend to the British Empire. The Great Game soon revived, and provided perennial alarums and arguments for the rest of the century. Lord Auckland, who wrote of the catastrophe that 'the whole thing was unintelligible to me', became First Lord of the Admiralty and died a bachelor in 1848. Poor Elphinstone died in the hands of Akhbar, who sent his body to Jalalabad, respectfully wrapped in aromatic blankets and attended by the general's valet. Dr Brydon we shall meet again: his pony was last heard of by Mr Eric Linklater the novelist who, when he wished to replace a damaged iron fence upon his estate in Cromarty, was told that it had been bent during an unsuccessful jump by Dr Brydon's famous pony, and had been left unrepaired in memorial ever since —a pleasant but unconvincing fantasy, Mr Linklater tells me, for Brydon did not return from India until 1860, when the pony would have been about 20 years old.

As for the retreat from Kabul, though largely forgotten in Britain it is vividly remembered in Afghanistan: when in 1960 I followed the army's route from Kabul to Jalalabad with an Afghan companion, we found many people ready to point out the sites of the tragedy, and recall family exploits. I asked one patriarch what would happen now, if a foreign army invaded the country. 'The same', he hissed between the last of his teeth.

CHAPTER SIX

Merchant Venturing

ON the other side of the world, on a summer day in those same 1840s, there sits around a polished oak table a group of men so far removed from the world of Akhbar and Elphinstone, so indifferent we may suppose to the aims of evangelical imperialism, that they might be living in another century, or another civilization. Yet they represent an imperial dynamic no less potent than strategy or philanthropy: profit.

There are ten men in the room, with a secretary in attendance, and they are sitting around the table as in a board room. They look a grave but weather-beaten lot, like businessmen hardened, and most of their faces are of a gaunt Scottish cast. The room is comfortably dignified. A log fire burns, and on a side-table are the minutes of previous meetings, in large leather-bound volumes, with quill pens, and bottles of ink, and sand-blotters. The hours pass in earnest deliberation, expert and hard-headed, and the talk is of trade percentages, available stocks, staff promotions, distribution problems. Scratch, scratch goes the pen of the secretary, page after page across the foolscap, and at the end of the session the ten men file up to sign their names and ranks at the bottom of the page, in steady unostentatious hands, before following their chairman through the door into the corridor outside—down which, when the door is opened, a fragrance of wine and roast victuals comfortably drifts.

They are in an elegant white house upon a creek. It is made of painted clapboard, and it has wide shuttered windows, a belfry over the adjoining warehouse, gardens and outhouses behind: all around thickets of trees run darkly to the creek, and to the wide islet-speckled lake which lies below. It looks an urbane and cosy place— a well-stocked, warm, carefully cherished place, where men can do their business in a civilized way, with pleasure in each other's company, and plenty to eat and drink.

These are the Governor-in-Chief, the Chief Factors and the Chief Traders of the Northern Department of Rupert's Land of the Honourable Company of Adventurers of England Trading Into Hudson's Bay, and they are meeting for their annual council meeting at the trading settlement called Norway House, which lies on the shore of Playgreen Lake in largely uninhabited, mostly unexplored, and almost inconceivably remote forest country 1,500 miles west of Montreal. They have come there by boat and canoe from the far corners of the Canadian wilderness: and Sir George Simpson, their formidable little chairman, has arrived in a canoe so splendidly accoutred, so gorgeously manned, that his immense journey through the forests has been almost a royal progress.

2

Trade and Empire had always gone together—had once, indeed, seemed virtually synonymous. That trade necessarily followed the flag was an often specious theory not yet formulated, but since the earliest days of British overseas settlement, the chance of fortune had been a prime motive of expansion. The bartering white man on the alien shore was an original archetype of empire: beads, skins, gunpowder, cowrie shells, calicos, rum and slaves were staples of English glory. Trade had first taken the British to India, and though the lost colonies of America were profit-seeking enterprises of a different kind, still the old 18th century empire had been frankly a commercial structure.

The tradition of the English merchant venturers was born in the sixteenth century, when Edward VI gave a Royal Charter to a company formed by some 100 English gentlemen, and three ladies, called 'The Mysterie and Companie of the Merchants Adventurers for the discoverie of Regions, Dominions, Islands and places unknown'. This concern, later the Muscovy Company, set the pattern for all the chartered companies that were to follow. It was formed with royal approval to perform, at a profit to itself, some service to the State—which in those days had few ships and little cash of its own. It was specifically a trading company, but it was incidentally an instrument of policy—the three little ships of its first expedition failed in their attempts to find a northern route to Cathay, but instead the company opened up trade with Russia, founded the first British trading stations or 'factories' in foreign territory, and learnt a great deal about the geography of Central Asia. The Muscovy Company never aspired to foreign dominion, but in establishing diplomatic contacts, in assembling intelligence, in exploration and in the establishment of trade routes, its merchants were in effect doing the work of the State.

By the early decades of Victoria's reign two great exemplars of this tradition survived, and were now assuming a new role in national affairs. The relationship between trade and dominion was becoming more complex. As Disraeli said of that traditional colonial commodity, sugar, all considerations now mingled in it: 'not merely commercial, but imperial, philanthropic, religious; confounding and crossing each other, and confusing the legislature and the nation lost in a maze of conflicting interests and contending emotions'. On the one hand were those, like Cobden, Bright and the economists of the Manchester School, who believed that the advent of free trade would make empire altogether obsolete: even Disraeli himself, presently to become the most eloquent of imperialists, thought in the 1830s that colonies were 'millstones around our necks'. On the other hand were those who saw Britain's new worldwide supremacy as an unequalled opportunity of profit. The British had just satisfactorily concluded a small war intended only to persuade the Chinese that the continuing importation of opium from British India would be to everyone's advantage, and the financiers of the City of London were beginning to see that the scattered possessions of empire, so many of them acquired as trophies of war, might be as useful to trade as they were to strategy.

The Chartered Companies reflected this transient uncertainty, and stood recognizably betwixt and between. The East India Company no longer had mercantile functions at all. In 1833 it had surrendered its monopoly of the India and China trades, except only in opium, and it was now a kind of sovereign agency, administering its Indian possessions on behalf of the Crown, and only incidentally paying its stockholders their guaranteed 10 per cent dividend. Its governing Court of Directors was subject to an official Board of Control, and with its own civil service, its own fleets and armies, its own military academy and its own administrative college, it was not exactly a company any more, nor exactly a ministry, nor quite a Power, but rather, as Macaulay said of it, 'the strangest of all governments, designed for the strangest of all empires' (and properly exemplified, perhaps, by the cart-loads of jewelry, silks and ceremonial weapons which, presented to the Governor-General of India on any tour, must scrupulously be handed over to the Company's accountants when His Excellency returned to Calcutta).

The other Chartered Company of Queen Victoria's empire was the Company of Adventurers of England Trading Into Hudson's Bay, whose factors we have observed leaving their council chamber for dinner (smoked buffalo tongues, moose noses, beaver tails, wild duck, trout, whitefish and venison—though discipline being, as a contemporary observer recalled, 'very strict in those days', sherry and old port was all they drank).

3

Canada in 1845 was almost all empty. There were busy settlements in the east, along the St Lawrence River, in the maritime provinces and around the eastern shores of the Great Lakes, but most of the vast territory to the west was inhabited only by scattered Indian tribes, Eskimos, wandering trappers and isolated traders. In theory the whole country was British. Since the end of the French wars Canada had formed one of the weirder of the Crown's dependencies, peopled, where it was peopled at all, mostly by Frenchmen, American loyalists and dispossessed Highlanders. The eastern settlements had been grouped into five separate colonies. The whole of the rest of the country, from the Great Lakes in the east to Vancouver Island in the west, from the American frontier to well over the Arctic Circle, was the domain of the Company of Adventurers: all the land draining into Hudson Bay was actually their property, and everywhere else they held the exclusive right to trade.

The Company was founded in 1670, when Charles II granted

Prince Rupert and a group of associates the right to be the 'true and absolute Lordes and Proprietors' of the territory, most of it never seen by Europeans, 'in whatsoever latitude they shall bee that lye within the entrance of the Streightes commonly called Hudson's Streightes'. Not only were they granted a trading monopoly within this vast region, Rupert's land, but they were to hold possession of it all 'in free and common socage, on the same terms as the Manor of East Greenwich', paying the Crown two elks and two black beavers whenever the King should enter the territories—which must have seemed to the Adventurers, in 1670, a sufficiently improbable contingency.

Fur was the principal object, and for the next 150 years the Company's agents lived lives of gruesome hardship to confirm their lien upon the Canadian fauna. They fought wars with the French. They built fortresses. They established trading posts of nightmare isolation. They explored, by canoe and on snowshoe, the limitless creeks and lakes of the interior. They sailed their little ships 7,000 miles each year, from Gravesend to Hudson Bay and back again, to load up with the skins of foxes, bears, martens, otters and above all beavers. In the 1780s the company was challenged by a fierce group of interlopers, mostly Scots and French-Canadian, called the North West Company—Nor'-Westers for short—who defied the Charter and fought the company with guile and virulence, corrupting the local Indians with rum or slaughtering them with gunfire, undercutting Company prices, sometimes burning Company posts: but after thirty years of competition the Adventurers, failing to obliterate these piratical newcomers, amalgamated with them instead, and absorbed many of their qualities. In 1821 Parliament extended the Company's trading rights to cover all the western Canadian regions discovered since Charles II's day; within Rupert's land itself the Adventurers were in quasi-sovereign possession of some $1\frac{1}{2}$ million square miles of territory, unquestionably the largest slab of real estate ever controlled by a board of directors.

4

So when the Factors of the Northern Department assembled at

Norway House for their annual council, it was an occasion full of consequence. From Lac la Pluie and Saskatchewan, Mackenzie River and Athabasca, Peace River, Isle à la Crosse, Red River, York Factory on the shores of the Bay itself, the great Company canoes converged upon Playgreen Lake. Indians and half-breeds rowed them. From each stern flew the Company flag, bearing the Union Jack and the letters H.B.C., and magisterially amidships sat the Company officer, bearded or mutton-chopped, with his wide hat rammed on his head and his Scottish face impassive—as the free-and-easy crew, in gay kerchiefs or speckled headbands, smoking clay pipes and slung all about with mugs and sheath-knives, sang wild French songs of the *voyageurs*, or exchanged bawdy witticisms in the patois of the west.

Hundreds of lesser travellers, too, converged upon Norway House in June, for this was the great clearing-session of the year's work, when prices were fixed, routes mapped, and agreement reached on what the Minute Book formally described as Arrangements. There were traders from half Canada, who came there in bark canoes, or in the big York boats, evolved by the Company's own boatmen, whose square-sailed silhouettes, with their steersmen standing aft like gondoliers, were by now the familiars of the Canadian west. There were Indians out of the forest, whose tepees were clumped among the trees around the post, and whose canoes scudded busily up and down the creek. There were half-breeds and their families, most of them crossed Iroquois with French, with some who claimed MacTavish, Frazer or Mackenzie blood: tough brown people, whose language was a queer singing mixture of French and Indian dialects, and who knew more about travel by canoe, with all the incidental expertise of portage and woodcraft, than anyone else in Canada. All this colourful crew hung about the landing-stage of Norway House, to cheer and shout and fire off feux-de-joie as the big canoes splashed in one by one, to the blowing of bugles, the handshaking of Scotsmen, the volatile embraces of reunited *voyageurs* and the ceremonial greetings of Indians.

The annual climax came when George Simpson himself, the Governor-in-Chief, made his own spectacular arrival, direct from Hudson's Bay House at Lachine, 1,500 miles away on the St Lawrence River above Montreal. This was a dramatic moment always.

The blast of a bugle preceded him around the point, and as the crowd swarmed down to the waterfront, and the Norway House officials straightened their cravats and assumed their beaver hats, nobly into sight there swept the gubernatorial canoe, bigger and grander than anyone else's, with a brighter ensign at its stern, more stalwart half-breeds at its paddles, and an altogether matchless air of importance.

Sir George was a stickler for appearances. His crew had gone ashore an hour or two before, to smarten themselves up and make their vessel shipshape, and now the equipage looked very splendid, with its faultless sweep of line, the gaudy decorations of its prow, its vermilion painted paddles and the lovely disciplined sweep of its motion across the water. In the prow stood the bearded half-breed guide, clad in leather, and sometimes the *royageurs* burst into song as with a flourish of colour and panache little George Simpson, the Governor-in-Chief, bolt upright in a tall black hat and a sober suit, swept flamboyantly into Norway House.

For eight days, nine in the morning to five at night, Sir George conferred with his Chief Factors and Traders of the North, John Rowand, Donald Ross, Nicol Finlayson, John Edward Harriott, William Sinclair, Paul Fraser, William Mactavish, Edward M. Hopkins from West Ham and George Deschambeault the Canadian —for in those days a Briton was still a Briton, but a Canadian was probably French.

5

These were the rulers of the West, and patently paramount among them was Simpson, 'the Little Emperor', whose taste for swank and consequence gave to their gatherings such a sense of grand occasion. An illegitimate child of modest parents, Simpson had been raised in the manse by his grandfather, minister of the parish of Avoch on the Moray Firth. He went to work for his rich uncle Geddes, a sugar-broker in London, and twelve years later emerged abruptly into history, confident, ambitious and vain, as Governor-in-Chief of H.B.C.—just when the Company, by absorbing the Nor'-Westers, was reaching the climax of its opportunities.

He was a short, thick, fair-haired, blue-eyed man, now about fifty, who swam daily in the coldest weather, and was one of the hardiest and swiftest of wilderness travellers—'built upon the Egyptian model', as a contemporary wrote of him, 'or like one of those short square massy pillars one sees in old country churches'. He had run the whole gamut of the Canadian experience. He had gone for days without food sometimes, and at other times had gorged himself with a true trapper's gusto—with eleven others, he once recorded with satisfaction, he had eaten three ducks and twenty-two geese at a single session. He knew all about drunken Indians, gloomy Hebrideans, mutinous *voyageurs*. He had swum icy rivers, waded through swamps, sledged or snow-shoed for weeks at a time, and had explored for himself much of the immense new territory recently opened up in the far west. He went around the world once, and had the journey recorded by a ghost-writer in two self-conscious volumes.

Simpson was a lusty fellow, like many another Company man. He father several children by half-breed women, but in 1830 he had pensioned off his last 'bit of brown' and married a cousin, Frances Simpson, aged 18, whom he immediately took by canoe from Montreal to Hudson Bay, starting each morning before dawn, often travelling till well after dark, frequently soaked to the skin in weather which was almost freezing, sleeping on rocks, sand or damp earth, and attended only by gentlemen 'not exactly calculated', as poor Frances recorded in her diary, 'to shine in polished Society'.[1]

This alarming little man was the local dictator of the Company, maintaining from his agreeable house at Lachine an iron grip upon all its affairs. He was a disciplinarian of the Scottish school, regarding a man's private and public life, his personal and his professional character, as integrates of a whole, and thus subject equally to the supervision of his employer. When he first went to Canada he was described as 'one of the most pleasant little men I ever met with', but over the years his image changed. Now he was 'the crafty fox Sir George', 'an intriguing courtier', master of 'stratagems in bows and smiles', a despot and a martinet. He kept an almost in-

---

[1] She bore him two sons and three daughters, all the same, before dying aged 41 in 1853. Other ladies gave him at least three sons and three daughters.

quisitorial record of the Company's chief employees, meticulously analysed in a pocket notebook. Its judgements were stringent. 'Manages Indians and Servants very well . . . but is rather hippish and fanciful in regard to ailments.' 'Lavish of his own means, extravagant and irregular in business, and his honesty is very questionable.' 'A sly, sneaking, plausible fellow who lies habitually, full of low cunning, suspicion and intrigue.' 'Would be a Radical in any Country under any Government and under any circumstances.'

By 1845 he had achieved complete mastery in Canada, and he had turned the annual council meetings at York Factory or Norway House into mere formalities of assent. 'You are dependent', wrote one Company officer, 'upon the goodwill and caprice of one man . . . it is his foible to exact not only strict obedience, but deference to the point of humility.' Another disgruntled colleague, recently exiled to an unpromising outpost called Chimo in Ungava, went further still: 'In no colony subject to the British Crown is there to be found an authority so despotic as is at this day exercised in the mercantile colony of Rupert's Land; an authority combining the despotism of military rule with the strict surveillance and parsimony of the avaricious trader. From Labrador to Nootka Sound the unchecked, uncontrolled will of a single individual gives law to the land.'

This was the remarkable man, shrewd, bland, rich, tough, cynical, whose personality dominated those wastelands of the west, and whose presence brought such pageantry to Norway House—where, as the same bitter victim expressed it, 'the sham Council is held, and everything connected with the business of the interior arranged'.

6

Commercially the Company, after a long lean period when beaver hats went out of fashion, had flourished since the amalgamation with the Nor-Westers. This was not, like the East India Company, a mere front or shadow of a business concern. This was still a working company, unimpeded by Government interference, which possessed capital stock and paid dividends. It was a profit-sharing enterprise: two-fifths of its profits, split into eighty-five shares, were paid to its own officials in the field. The rest went to some 200 shareholders or 'proprietors', and they were paid dividends that never, during Simpson's ascendancy, fell below 10 per cent, and sometimes rose as high as 25 per cent.

Technically the headquarters of the Company was Hudson's Bay House, in Fenchurch Street in the City of London, but by 1848 the Northern Department, which covered most of the uncultivated Canadian west, was the dominant force. The Company was primarily a collection and distribution agency. It collected furs, it distributed manufactured goods like blankets, ironwork, firearms and hard liquor.[1] The whole of the north-west was like a great watershed for its trade, and down multitudinous rivers and inlets, over thousands of portages, the annual brigades of York boats carried their cargoes of fur to the collection point at York Factory on the Bay. This was a township in itself, gathered around the big clap-board building of the Factory, with its huge flagpole of Norway pine, its belfry tower and its palisaded compound. Here were the warehouses, the repair shops, the coopers' yards, living quarters for officials and servants, boatyards, food stores. Here the accountancy of the trade was done, and here the Company ships, each year when the ice broke, collected their cargoes and discharged their trade goods. In summer, when the brigades came down the Hayes River from the interior, the foreshore at York blazed with hundreds of camp fires, and the place was boisterous with drink and fisticuffs. In winter, when the ice came over the Bay, the woods behind were muffled in snow, and the opaque winter light of the north fell like a veil over the landscape, then the Great House was shuttered and barricaded, and the Company officials shut themselves in with oil-lamps and beaver rugs to await the spring.

All over the hinterland, west and south, isolated trading posts represented both the acumen and the authority of the Honourable Company. In the wildest and remotest parts of Canada, in the bitterest weeks of winter, one would find the Company store with its

[1] Which was supplemented by illicit whiskey from across the American frontier, commonly made of one part of raw alcohol to three parts of water, coloured with tea or plug tobacco, and flavoured with ginger, red pepper and black molasses.

flag flying, its stock of simple goods, its half-breed storekeeper or even perhaps its unexcitable Scot with his Bible, his Shakespeare and his *Ivanhoe*. In the larger posts Chief Factors or Chief Traders presided, and everywhere the hierarchy was strict. Chief Traders deferred to Chief Factors. Juniors were respectful to seniors. Promotion was by ability, and generally went to Scots of dogged resolution and craft, Englishmen being too carefree, Frenchmen too foreign. Accountancy was strict. Storekeeping was thorough. It was an organization solid, experienced and stubborn.

Yet it inspired among its employees a truly romantic sense of loyalty. Son followed father into its service, and whole communities of northern Scotland thought of themselves as Company folk. Men and women passed their entire lives within its orbit. Jessy Ross, for example, whose father sat at Sir George's right hand at the Council table, was born at York Factory, married a Company man, spent most of her life in Company trading posts, and was to die at Norway House. Simpson himself was followed into the Company's employ by two illegitimate sons and three cousins, and over on the Pacific coast 'Big John' McLoughlin, the celebrated Chief Factor of Vancouver, had among his underlings three sons and a son-in-law.

For there was to life in the Company's service a northern beauty that captured the imagination of the most unlikely participants. This was a wild tremendous country, like a vaster Scotland perhaps, where the emptiness had a desert allure. The light was haunting and the air electric, and even the terrible cold had its own compensations. Hudson's Bay House at Lachine, looking out upon all the bustle of its wharves and warehouses upon the Lachine Canal, sometimes blazed with winter festival, when the Governor gave one of his famous parties, and the traders and their wives arrived merrily by sledge in beaver hats and poke bonnets, when the newest timorous arrival from Britain was jollied along with hot punch and badinage, and the Company's current crop of children was entertained by old Sir George at his most disarming:

Come, call out your sleighs, and away let us run
To the Hudson's Bay House, for an evening of fun.
For Sir George has agreed, with his blandest of smiles,

That the children shall wake all the echoes for miles.
See, from Upper and Lower Lachine how they pour,
While a sleigh from the Square dashes up to the door,
How little hearts pound, and small feet trip about,
And Mammas are well pleased—'tis the Children's own rout!

There was excitement of a different kind to the loneliness of the trading posts, buried in their woods beside their creeks. The isolation, of course, could be fearfully depressing: no neighbours but Indians and crude *voyageurs*, nothing to read but Scott and Holy Writ, no visitors but the odd taciturn trapper, the dour inspecting official, or the fur brigades when they swept by once a year. The insects were terrible, too: blackflies, buffalo gnats, deerflies, mooseflies, klegs, no see-ums, creepin' fire and ubiquitous, unspeakable mosquitoes.[1] But there were lovely spring flowers to see, low on the ground when the snow cleared, and bears, beavers and foxes to watch, and through the aromatic forests the creeks ran with a wonderful blue-green sheen, gleaming through the undergrowth as though the whole land were resting upon a sheet of coloured glass. In the older stations, too, Rupert House, Cumberland House, Norway House, York Factory, there survived some of the antique splendour of the Honourable Company, which could still fire the pride of Company men, and gave to their life's adventure an extra dimension of dignity. At the mouth of the Churchill River, for instance, on the Bay itself, there stood on a low protruding spit the ramparts of Prince of Wales Fort, founded in 1732, captured by the French in 1782, restored to the British after the wars, and still one of the grandest works of masonry in North America.

It was a great square structure of dressed granite, with curtain walling and loopholes for 42 guns. Inside was a yard, with living quarters and lookouts. Outside one could see, beautifully carved above its main gate, the graffiti of the craftsmen who had come to this end of the world to build it long before, with the masonic

---

[1] Who are said to inhabit the Canadian north in an incidence of 5 million to the acre: a naked man would be sucked dry of all his blood in 3½ hours, and even the caribou, some theorists believe, are driven to their migrations by the insect bites.

symbols of their craft. It was not in itself a very beautiful building, but its evocations were thrilling. It spoke still of old adventures, wars and profits, the beginnings of expeditions, the end of long voyages, and often the Company men from the new post up-river would clamber over its walls and look out across the bay from its ramparts. In the spring it could be lovely up there, but in the winter it was terrific. Then one could walk across the frozen ice to the fortress, and to the north there was nothing but ice, congealed in its last waves of autumn, with the grey clouds of the arctic above it, and a mystic northern radiance. Ravens, ptarmigans and snow-geese flew across the muskeg behind. Occasionally a wolf howled. Sometimes one saw a polar bear, far out on the ice, or the motionless forms of seals: and sometimes from behind the headland a team of Eskimo hunters would slide out with their dogs and sledges, whips lashing, ice-crystals flying, and their voices echoed across the ice as they grew small in the distance, and hung upon the silence behind them.

7

This was empire-building, but of a shallow and infertile kind. It was, in the words of one British merchant, the 'patient, thrifty, dexterous assiduity of private and untrammelled enterprise'. It is true that the presence of the Company prevented the horrible Indian wars that occurred on the American side of the frontier, and under its auspices something was done to improve the social standards of the tribes: it was at Norway House that the Reverend James Evans, a Wesleyan missionary, first devised an alphabet for the Cree language, printing parts of the Bible on birch bark with ink made of fish oil and soot, and type cut from tea-chests.[1] But patriotism played a secondary part in it, the elevation of the natives was only incidentally considered, and the flag that flew so bravely across Canada bore always the qualifying characters H.B.C. The Adventurers dabbled in agriculture, but only as a means of self-benefit—one function of their

[1] The alphabet is still used, but poor Mr Evans was wrongly accused of living immorally among his Crees, and disappeared ignominiously from the imperial annals, failing even to find a place among the 167 Evanses listed in the *Dictionary of Welsh Biography*.

subsidiary the Puget Sound Agricultural Company was to raise cereals for the Russian colonists in Alaska.[1] The Company did not want to see the west settled or developed. It would be bad for the fur trade. It would pervert the local Indians, or lead to wars against them. Doubtless it would in time force the Company out of its monopoly—'where the axe of the settler rang', it was said, 'there the trapper must certainly disappear'. The Scotsmen who set the tone of the Company, and thus of the British presence in western Canada, were not the colonizing type: the senior men were traders *par excellence*, and the rank-and-file were mostly simple Scotsmen, from the dispossessed sheepfolds or the austere northern isles, with little gift for arable farming and a fragile sense of domesticity—'close, prudent, quiet people', as an unsympathetic observer wrote of them, 'strictly faithful to their employers and sordidly avaricious'. The Company did not publicize the existence of good agricultural land in its domains. The Pacific coast, its spokesmen maintained, was quite unfit for colonization, while the terrible frosts, the uncontrollable floods and the periodic plagues of grass-hoppers obviously made the great plains of Manitoba and Saskatchewan perfectly useless too.

By the 1840s, nevertheless, there was pressure from eastern Canada to open up the west for colonization. To the south the Americans were pursuing their own manifest destiny boldly across the prairies, and the eastern Canadians wanted the same freedom to expand—besides, they were afraid that if they did not move into that tempting vacuum, the Americans would. Since 1811 there had in fact been one isolated European colony in the heart of the Canadian west. It stood at the confluence of the Red River and the Assiniboine, two of the chief thoroughfares of central Canada. There an idealistic young peer, Lord Selkirk, had planted a colony of Scotsmen and Irishmen, on a land grant of 116,000 square miles allowed him by the Company—of which, as it happened, he was a substantial stockholder.[2] Their progress had been fitful. They were inept settlers

---

[1] Such firm friends of the Honourable Company that their trading agreement operated without problems throughout the Crimean War.

[2] Besides being a landowner over the frontier in the United States. It was the Selkirk estate in Scotland that was raided by the privateer John Paul

anyway, and they had faced the hostility not only of the Nor'-Westers, but worse still of the Metis, the half-caste hunters and *voyageurs* of the area, than whom no class of person could be less in rapport with Gaelic-speaking Presbyterian pastoralists. The Metis depended, like the traders, upon the wilderness of Canada. They roamed the prairie in search of buffalo and the creeks in pursuit of beaver, and they felt the presence of the settlers, with their crudely ploughed fields and their council meetings, to be a threat to their entire manner of life. In 1816 they had killed twenty-one of the settlers, and though by 1845 the settlers lived more securely under Company administration, and had established a picturesque rural community along the river, still they were like grit in the prairie machine—inorganic deposits in that country of hunters, toughs and nomads.

8

But the Red River colony was a portent. Isolated though the settlement was, cut off from the eastern colonies by almost impenetrable wilderness, it showed what might be done. The line of little houses along the twin rivers, the stone church of St Andrews in whose porch, on winter Sunday mornings, the snowshoes of the parisioners were neatly piled, the blunt stone farmhouses which, year by year, extended ever farther into the prairie—all these more truly forecast Canada's future than the passage of the Company canoes up and down the river, or the whoopee of the Metis on their ponies. At home in England the trend of empire was against the Company. The radical imperialists wanted all Canada open to settlement. The evangelists wanted every valley exalted. The financial community resented the tight-lipped and privileged manner of the Company—'like a commercial tomb', somebody said, 'closed with the key of death to all except a favoured few. . . .' Even Lord

---

Jones in 1778, in the first American foray into Europe: Selkirk, then a child, had been roughly treated by the American seamen, perhaps because Jones, who was born in those parts, believed himself to be the unacknowledged heir to the earldom.

Palmerston thought commerce was not enough in itself as a justification of empire—it should lead 'civilization with one hand and peace with the other, to render mankind happier, wiser, better'.

New notions of imperial purpose were challenging the old, and in 1857 the conflict was to find expression in a Parliamentary Inquiry. The Government of Canada, newly self-governing, had proposed that the west should now be opened for settlement, and all the more progressive expansionists took advantage of the occasion. Though nobody perhaps quite realized it, it was the end of an era, for though the idea of Chartered Companies was to be revived later in the century, never again would a private company rule such immense possessions so frankly in the interests of profit. The Select Committee thus had an inquest air: in the 550 pages of its printed report almost every aspect of imperial duty was considered in the anachronistic context of a charter from Charles II. On race, for example: was the Company good to the natives? ('I saw nothing but the utmost kindness to the Indians and fairness in dealing.') On religion: was it a patron of Christian apostolism? (Twenty Anglican clergymen worked within the Company territories.) On development: was it a patron of technical progress? ('A monopoly is no advance to any civilization.') Most appositely of all, on colonization: did Sir George Simpson still consider that no portion of the territory was still fit for settlement, and if so how did he account for the passage in his well-known travel book *Journey Round the World,* volume I, page 55, in which he declares Red River to produce extraordinary crops, plump and heavy wheat, quantities of grain of all kinds, beef, mutton, pork, butter, cheese, and wool in abundance? ('I there referred to merely a few small alluvial points occupied by the Scotch farmers.')[1]

The Committee's conclusions were not draconian, but were to

[1] Simpson must have cursed that ghost-writer, especially when his book asked of one Canadian river, in a passage sadistically quoted by the Committee: 'Is it too much for the age of philanthropy to discern through the vista of futurity this noble stream, connecting as it does the fertile shores of two spacious lakes, with the crowded steamboats on its bosom and populous towns on its borders?' Gladstone, who was a member of the Committee, commented in his autobiography that the Little Emperor 'in answering our questions had to call in the aid of incessant coughing'.

prove conclusive all the same. Though the Company of Adventurers was left paramount in the west for another thirteen years, still it was recognized that the Canadian people had a higher claim to the country. The Factors and Traders were not yet dispossessed of their heritage, and Sir George Simpson, prevaricating though some committee members thought him, was spared to die, full of years, honour and hard cash, still Governor-in-Chief, in his house at Lachine in 1860:[1] but the days of such late nabobs were numbered all the same, and as the members of the Select Committee appended their signatures to the report, they were really signing the epitaph of all the merchant venturers of England, piped with vermilion paddles through the tundras of the west, or familiarly smoking their hookahs on silken divans with the descendants of Aurungzebe or the Great Moghul. As Lord Valentia had once observed, welcoming the construction of a new Government House in India, the British Empire ought no longer to be governed by 'a sordid mercantile spirit'. It should be ruled 'with the ideas of a Prince, not with those of a retail-dealer in muslins and indigos'.

9

We are looking ahead. No epitaphs seemed imminent at Norway House that summer day, and no assembly could look less like a convention of retail drapers than the Factors and Traders gathered there. The Little Emperor was still in his prime—'head of the most extended Dominions in the known world', as he was described once at a State dinner in Norway, 'the Emperor of Russia, the Queen of England and the President of the United States excepted.' The Company prospered and was free. Confidently, around their polished table, they discussed next year's Arrangements. They arranged furloughs, and new appointments, and pemmican supplies for the establishment on the Pelly River. They arranged rations for the summer brigades, supplies of birch bark for canoe building, a going rate in the west for the Mexican silver dollar. They resolved that missionaries might be sold provisions at 50 per cent advance on the inventory prices, that paws should not be cut off the pelts of martens

[1] Of apoplexy, like many another empire-builder: he is buried at Montreal.

(it reduced their value in London by 'upwards of ten per cent'), that 2,500 pairs of tracking shoes and 500 buffalo tongues should be sent to Norway House from the Saskatchewan district, that Mr Roderick Mackenzie should be appointed an apprentice postmaster at a salary of £20 per annum, and that the quota of beaver skins to be sent to England in the autumn shipment should not exceed 18,000 skins.

When, eight days later, the company dispersed, back to the Athabaska and the Mackenzie, English River and Lac la Pluie, north to the Bay or over the Rockies to the Pacific slopes, when the Governor's bugle sounded for the last time across the lake, and Norway House returned to its ledgers and routine, no doubt it seemed that these Arrangements would survive more or less for ever. And in a way they would: the merchant venturers might disappear from the conduct of empire, but the profit motive never did.[1]

[1] And the Honourable Company itself, now purely a trading company, is selling bras and toothpaste to this day across the counters of Norway House—which, when I was there in 1969, looked as white and busy as ever, with the motor-canoes of the Crees racing up and down that creek, amphibian aircraft landing on the lake, and parked in the gardens behind the store a snow-tractor emblazoned with the armorial bearings of the Adventurers, beavers in quarters, fox sejant proper, elks supporting, and the date of the original Royal Charter, 1670.

CHAPTER SEVEN

White Settlers

IN November 1846 the Governor of Nova Scotia, Sir John Harvey, received a fateful instruction from Lord Grey, the Colonial Secretary in Lord John Russell's Whig Government at home. Harvey's territory was one of the five British colonies on the mainland of Canada, on the eastern flank of the Little Emperor's country. It was a pleasant region of Scottish flavour, given an elegant veneer by the hundreds of loyalist families who had moved there after the American Revolution, bringing with them their fastidious tastes in architecture and their inherited sense of independence.

Since 1819 Nova Scotia had elected its own legislature, and politically its capital, the seaport of Halifax, was unexpectedly sophisticated. Political parties slandered each other, newspapers thundered, debates went on all night. Province House, where the Assembly met, was so much the most impressive building in the colony that country people came hundreds of miles to look at it, and inside it the legislators—farmers, merchants, sea captains— honoured all the forms of British parliamentary procedure. 'It was like looking at Westminster through the wrong end of a telescope', wrote Charles Dickens, who attended the State opening in 1842. 'The Governor delivered the Speech from the Throne. The military band outside struck up *God Save The Queen* with great vigour; the people shouted; the Ins rubbed their hands; the Outs shook their heads; the Government party said there was never such a good speech; the Opposition declared there was never such a bad one; and in short everything went on and promised to go on just as it does at home.'

But it was not really quite like Westminster. For one thing the total population of the colony was only about 100,000, and for another, though the Halifax Assembly dutifully honoured the parliamentary traditions, it had no ultimate responsibility at all. Its arguments were impotent. Its decisions could be vetoed without question by the Governor, who governed with the help of a Council nominated entirely by himself, and was accountable only to London. Constitutionally the Canadian colonies were in more or less the condition of the American possessions before the Revolution, and they were well aware of the parallels. In both Upper and Lower Canada—the first predominantly British, the second predominantly French—there had actually been small rebellions.[1] Everywhere else there was growing agitation against domination from England—'Resolved', said a motion presented to the Quebec Assembly in 1834, 'that this House is nowise disposed to admit the excellence of the present Constitution of Canada'. In Nova Scotia there had been no violence, but the Reform Party of the little colony fought incessantly for responsible government. 'We seek for nothing more than British subjects are entitled to,' they said, 'but we will be content with nothing less.'

All this was ominously reminiscent of 1775, and 'American notions of liberty' was a pejorative phrase much used by conservative Englishmen when they discussed Canadian affairs. The British did not know how best to react. They were chary of exerting what Canning long before called 'the transcendental power of Parliament' over all British possessions—'an arcanum of empire, which ought to be kept back within the penetralia of the constitution'. On the other hand they were reluctant to let colonies go simply by default. In 1838 Lord Melbourne's Whig Government had been concerned enough about the discontent in Canada to send a special emissary as Captain-General, High Commissioner and Governor-in-Chief of all the colonies there. Their choice was at first sight strange: Lord Lambton, first Earl of Durham, was one of the most splendid swells of his time, and the man who had given a distinctly undemocratic *bon mot* to the language in his youthful assertion that anyone should be able to 'jog along on £40,000 a year'. He was a quarrelsome and

---

[1] Directed in Lower Canada against a soldier-Governor of the old school, Sir Francis Bond Head, who had allegedly been knighted by William IV for his skill in throwing a lassoo.

difficult aristocrat, almost excessively handsome—just the man, one might suppose, to drive the discontented Canadian reformers to their own Tea Parties and Continental Congresses.

Appearances, however, were deceptive. 'Radical Jack' Lambton, 'The Angry Boy', was a man of progress himself, an active supporter of the 1832 Reform Bill at home, and an advocate of colonial reform too. He believed that the idea of Empire need not be stagnant, but could be reanimated by bold innovations—'the experiment of keeping colonies', he thought, 'and of governing them well, ought at least to have a trial'. Durham went out to Canada in terrific state, several ships being required to transfer his effects. He soon restored order there, and was nicknamed The Dictator only half in fun: but he saw as his real task the discovery of a formula to keep Canada, and all such white colonies of the Crown, loyal to the British Empire. As one of the Canadian discontents himself said, he was 'the first statesman to avow a belief in the possibility of a permanent connection between the colonies and the Mother Country'.

Now, eight years later, the consequences of his mission were still impatiently awaited all over the Empire, for to many it seemed that the future of the white settlement colonies was the key to the survival of the Empire itself: and nowhere were reforms awaited more eagerly than among the legislators of Halifax, into whose session Charles Dickens, wrapping himself against the brilliant January cold, had found his way during his single day ashore in Nova Scotia ('the day uncommonly fine; the air bracing and healthful; the whole aspect of the town cheerful, thriving, and industrious').

2

In 1846 there were five main groups of white settlers in the overseas empire. In Canada there were perhaps 1½ million Europeans, about half of them French-speaking. In the Caribbean a dozen islands were inhabited by some 70,000 Europeans. In Australia five convict settlements had matured into communities with their own legislatures. In New Zealand there were infant colonies on both islands. In South Africa perhaps 20,000 Britons co-habited with twice as many Afrikaners.

Many people in England still thought it might be wise to be rid of these possessions while the going was good—sooner or later they were sure to be a nuisance. Others, drawing similar conclusions from different premises, and comparing the generally torpid state of Canada, for example, with the vivacity of the United States, thought it only fair to the colonies to release them from their imperial bonds. On the other hand evangelicals thought the colonists should be kept under imperial control for the sake of the Indians, Negroes and aboriginals they might otherwise be tempted to oppress, and strategists argued that if Britain did not control these far-flung territories, rival Powers might seize command of the oceans. Finally there were the visionaries who called themselves the Colonial Reformers, who believed that systematic colonization was not merely an opportunity, but a duty: these were the hungry forties, the home population had grown by a half in thirty years, and the right thing for England was the migration of whole communities, to found their own British dependencies elsewhere in the world.

Whatever their views, almost everyone interested in the Empire realized that the existing half-cock system could not last, for in the end any true-born Englishman, wherever he lived in the world, would surely demand the right to run his own affairs. As it was, none of the infant overseas settlements were truly self-governing. Many had their own Assemblies—some, like those of the Bahamas or Bermuda, 200 years old, and constitutionally identical with the assemblies of the lost American colonies. Their powers, however, were equally limited everywhere. Sir John Harvey and his colleagues could ignore all their resolutions if they wished, and very often did. The white settlers of the Empire, full British citizens though they were, were unrepresented in Parliament at Westminster: yet in the last resort it was the will of that very different legislature, so many thousands of miles away across the waters, that decreed the way they lived.

3

Some of the white settlements were already quite urbane. Some were very raw. One in an interesting transitional condition was the colony of New South Wales. This had begun as a penal settlement, and it was only in 1840 that the transportation of convicts there had been suspended: yet in many ways its capital, Sydney, was already a paradigm of the white overseas empire—uncertain yet assertive, crude-genteel, possessed of a certain latent power but racked with inferiority complexes, half loyal, half abusive to the Mother Country far away. New South Wales considered itself absolutely British. In a colony still inhabited chiefly by ex-convicts and their children, there was no thought of national independence—its citizens were, as a sad couplet said,

> *True patriots all, for be it understood,*
> *We left our country for our country's good.*

The separate colonies of the Australian mainland—New South Wales, Victoria, South Australia, West Australia—were isolated from each other by immense tracts of hideously unexplored country, and could communicate only by sea.[1] Nevertheless already the country had acquired a certain bold allure of its own. British soldiers in India committed offences in the deliberate hope of transportation there, prison governors in the colonies complained that the quality of transported criminals was not low enough, while the children of the original convicts were growing up with all the dash and dubious merits of a frontier society.[2]

Architecturally Sydney was surprisingly impressive, for a city that had been in existence scarcely more than half a century. As the great three-master from England sailed carefully between the headlands of Port Jackson, then as now one of the supreme moments of travel, to discover the glorious sheltered harbour within, with its islands and wooded coves sprawling languid under the sun—as the stranger approached this celebrated and notorious place,

---

[1] Australia never was annexed as an entity, but when 'a gentleman attached to the French Government' once asked the Colonial Secretary, Lord John Russell, how much of it was British, 'I answered him "the whole", and with that answer he went away'.

[2] 'The ancient profession of picking pockets,' as Sydney Smith once wrote, 'will certainly not become more discreditable from the knowledge that it may eventually lead to the possession of a farm of a thousand acres on the River Hawkesbury.'

populated first by thieves, murderers, whores and paupers, he saw before him not a dismal penitentiary, but a prosperous and not unattractive seaport of some 30,000 inhabitants, set pleasantly on a green peninsula, and busy with the masts and riggings of many ships. A steam ferry puffed back and forwards across the harbour, and among the trees on the outskirts of the town, looking across the water, were isolated villas and cottages on the foreshore, like pleasure pavilions in a great water-garden.

A church steeple dominated the town, from the highest point upon its promontory, and there were cannon gleaming on the rampart of a fort, and many wooden windmills on the ridge above, and presently the traveller still apprehensive about the nature of the place would be comforted to see the brand new palace of the Governor, commodiously built of stone, as the local guide-book said, 'somewhat in the Elizabethan style, but not exactly'.[1] All around it lay a green expanse of botanic garden, splashed with orange-flower and bougainvillaea, stocked with the figs, sugar-canes and bamboos of Empire as well as the quinces and apples of home. It was really very encouraging: and when one stepped ashore, into the broad straight streets of the town, familiar British sights and sounds were everywhere. The Lord Nelson Hotel looked snugly inviting, men of the good old British regiments stood guard at the barracks, the Eclipse stage coach clattered across the cobbles with the mail for Parramatta just as it might run out of Charing Cross on the Oxford road. With all this, as one gratified newcomer wrote, there seemed to be every sign of sobriety, 'as much respect shown to the Sabbath . . . as even in Edinburgh, which is acknowledged to be, in this respect, the most exemplary town in the world'.

Sydney had an official manner, for it had been mostly laid out by Governor Lachlan Macquarie, a major-general and a man of taste, who had found it in what he called a state of 'infantile imbecility', a muddle of lanes, shambled huts and unpainted barracks, and turned it into this handsome white town, hedged with geraniums and

---

[1] It was by Edward Blore (1787–1879) who had already become famous as the architect of Sir Walter Scott's new Gothic house at Abbotsford, and who gave the finishing touches to Nash's Buckingham Palace. He never visited the site, but his Government House is still there.

speckled with orchards. The Governor was fortunate to find among his convicts a gifted architect, Francis Greenway, a bankrupt Gloucestershire builder who had forged a credit note and been transported for fourteen years' penal servitude. Greenway had grown up in the knowledge of Regency Clifton and Bath, and Macquarie had plucked him from the chain-gang to give a similar dignity to Sydney. Though the Governor's plans for a truly imperial capital, on a Roman scale, mostly came to nothing, still Greenway was so successful that he was presently granted an absolute pardon and became for a few years the official Government architect—dying in poverty all the same, for he was a quarrelsome and incorrigible man, in 1837.

So the little city had been elevated by a number of good Regency buildings, an excellent simple church, the biggest barrack block in the overseas Empire, and one or two well-proportioned terraces of private houses, shady with verandahs, magnolias and lush Moreton Bay fig trees, whose fruit lay upon the city pavements squashy beneath one's feet. Well-connected as our traveller doubtless was, or we would not be in his company, soon he found himself inside one of those agreeable residences, or in one of the suburban villas, perhaps, which soon spread out to the south, or in the quarter made newly fashionable by the steamboat service to the north side of the harbour. In these districts he would discover that the social consciousness of Sydney was already acute. There was a distinct Sydney gentry, descended not of course from convict stock but from soldiers, merchants, officials and successful 'squatters' or sheep-graziers. Families like the Wentworths, the Macleays or the Macarthurs were already fearfully snobbish, and had long since apotheosized their own fairly ordinary origins into legends of patrician privilege. 'Personal history is at a discount,' as one new arrival reported in 1843, 'and good memories and inquisitive minds are particularly disliked. . . .' Such residents, however, loved to greet the *right sort* of visitor from England, and to demonstrate that even in Australia, my dear, some of us know what breeding means.

There were Sydneysiders already noticeably peevish at any suggestions of provinciality, who would have you know that the *very* latest novels were to be found at the circulating library, and that in their experience Rickard's Fashionable Repository was quite the equal of anything in Bond Street. Many more, though, assiduously aped all things English, fluttered ingratiatingly about the Governor's family or the officers of the garrison, and would never dream of wearing a dress from Rickard's so-called Fashionable Repository, preferring to import all their clothes direct from London. As a contemporary satirist wrote of them:

> *No bar sinister leaves a smutch on*
> *The ermine pure of their escutcheon!*
> *Belgravian swells, whose manners show*
> *They once had bloomed in Rotten Row!*
> *And now, transplanted here, to pass*
> *For an Australian upper-class!*

There was a lot of money about in Sydney. Our visitor might well find himself received by an ex-convict footman, waited upon by an ex-convict butler, lit by gas-light, fed upon excellent roast beef, oysters, warm wine and melted butter, entertained by over-jewelled young beauties, and driven home to his lodgings in a crested carriage by a liveried coachman.

But if he dismissed his driver at the door, and took a turn before bed to work the claret off, he would find another Sydney down the road. After that first euphoric surprise, everybody was struck by the contrasts of this strange town. 'My first feeling,' reported Charles Darwin in 1836, landing fresh from Galápagos, 'was to congratulate myself that I was born an Englishman: but upon seeing more of the town afterwards . . . my admiration fell a little.' It was hardly surprising. Most of the Sydneysiders were very rough people indeed, criminals, convict families, or men of that wandering raffish kind who found their way in those days to all the seaports of the colonial world, deserters, fugitives, off-season whalers or sealers, to pick up a living along the waterfront, or linger rootless in the slums. The proletariat of any port was tough enough then, and the proletariat of Sydney was perhaps the toughest of all.

Between the posh streets of the little town, tucked away behind the mansions and the public offices, were Sydney's notorious slums. Here lived the flotsam of the old penal settlement, in shacks and tenements dropping away through the hilly district called the Rocks to the sleazy quarters around the quays, where the haphazard huts built by the convicts long before were now doss-houses and bordels. Goats wandered at large among these back streets of Sydney, and the drains ran uncontrolled from the front door of one hovel to the back door of the one below. This was a Sydney sprung direct from the hulks and prisons of Britain—'sent and transported', as the judicial formula ran, 'to some Place beyond the Seas'. Its inhabitants were bred to the lash, the chain-gang, the stocks and the punishment cell—in the mid-1830s some 6,000 floggings were inflicted in New South Wales every year, mostly for petty misdemeanours. If they were brutal or dissolute when they left England, they were far worse now: one local judge observed that sometimes the entire business of New South Wales seemed to be the commission of crime, 'as if the whole colony are continuously in motion towards the several Courts of Justice'. Aborigines wandered drunken and dispossessed along the waterfront of Sydney, and some of the most terrible people alive brooded in the Rocks or waited in the alleys after dark.

In the great cities of England, the presence of such a ghastly underworld could go almost unnoticed to the stranger: in this small town it could not be escaped for long. In the centre of the lovely harbour, in full view of the botanical gardens, the old convict punishment centre of Fort Denison—'Pinchgut Island'—stood as an inescapable grey reminder, on the sunniest day, at the blithest picnic, of Sydney's harsh *raison d'être*. Some of the richest citizens of the town were emancipated convicts themselves, and for years the two chief political factions were the Patriotic Association, the mouthpiece of the emancipists, and the Exclusionists, the 'Pure Merinos', who thought all transported persons should be excluded from the franchise. A young Briton arriving in Sydney in the 1840s found that half the influential citizens to whom he carried letters of introduction would have nothing to do with the other half—'if you visit one', the bank manager warned him, 'you cannot visit the other'. Probably the richest woman in the place was Mrs Mary Reibey, who had been transported to Sydney aged 13 for stealing a horse in Staffordshire, had married a ship's officer, and so prospered in her widowhood

as an independent merchant that she now owned several houses in
Sydney, several farms and a couple of ships.[1]

A tradition of brutality and corruption inevitably tainted Sydney.
Even those Sydneysiders who claimed descent from Army officers,
settled in Australia at the end of their service, were sometimes
the grandchildren of crime—many officers had made themselves
fortunes by the illegal sale of rum and use of convict labour. Life was
cheap, sensibilities were numb. We read of the popular Rat Pit in
Pitt Street, where all sorts of animals were pitted against each other
in gory combat, and of dogs and goats mercilessly baited in the
streets. A visitor in 1838, watching a fight between bulldogs in a
tavern on Brickfield Hill, saw one dog-owner chop the two back
legs off his animal just to demonstrate its fighting spirit, and Sydney
butchers habitually skinned or plucked poultry while the creatures
were still alive—easier to do, they used to say in the market, while
the carcass was limp.

In this mixed ambiance, cruelty in idyll, luxury beside squalor,
Sydney was growing up and throwing off its penal past. In some ways
it was already like a new industrial town of the English Midlands,
only more intense. Its setting was far more beautiful, its public
buildings were more handsome, and its sense of opportunism was
fiercer than anything in Birmingham or Stoke; the ostentation of its
nouveaux-riches was even more preposterous, and from top to bottom of its society ran that flaw of ruthless crudity. In an age of developing materialism it was a city that could hardly fail, and when in
a few years gold was discovered in New South Wales, Sydney was
transformed in a flash from town to metropolis, and built itself a
handsome Royal Exchange, and a University.

The citizens of this settlement were already chafing under colonial control. They might admire the urbanity of the men sent from
London to supervise their affairs, but they certainly did not feel
themselves inferior, or incapable of self-government. As the *Centen-
nial Magazine* remarked of Governor Sir Charles Fitzroy, second son
of the third Duke of Grafton, who was sent out specifically to cope
with constitutional demands, 'Fitzroy was about as fitting a man, in

[1] She died in 1855, a well-known Sydney *grande dame*, and one of her grand-
sons became Premier of Tasmania.

every respect, as could have been picked out of the entire English nation to be sent abroad to misgovern a colony, and to corrupt its morals by his evil example. A vulgar voluptuary and systematic Sybarite, prurient, unprincipled, utterly destitute of intellectual force, he could neither govern the colony, nor his household, nor himself. He lived only for the gratification of his own base passions'.[1]

4

Not every settlement was so outspoken, or so coarse-grained. A very different kind of society was established towards the end of the 1840s on the south island of New Zealand, near the spot where the Waimakariri River enters the Pacific. This was the principle demonstration of the theories of Edward Gibbon Wakefield, the most remarkable of the Colonial Reformers. The son of an intellectual father, Wakefield was a true original, a political theorist of brilliance, a character of disastrous impetuosity. He looked, according to contemporary portraits, rather puzzled or blotched by life, but he was really a man of violent resolution. He ran away with an heiress when he was 20, and at 26 went to prison for falsely inducing an immensely rich schoolgirl to marry him at Gretna Green—he needed her money, it was said, to get into Parliament.

In later life he devoted all his gifts and energies to the cause of overseas settlement, which he presented to the public in altogether new ways. For him emigration from Britain was not a passive expedient, but an active enterprise. He believed in systematic voluntary

[1] The Sydney of the 1840s can still, with difficulty, be traced. A few of those grand terraces survive—Lower Fort Street, for instance, which stands demurely in the shadow of the Harbour Bridge—and so does the Lord Nelson. The Rocks have mostly been cleaned up, and with the harbour quarter are about to be fallen upon by enlightened developers. The botanical gardens are as lovely as ever. Below Government House stands the former Empire's most startling architectural *tour-de-force*, the winged Sydney Opera House. Macquarie's plans for a truly monumental city, which embraced a castle and a huge piazza with a cathedral in it, are represented most piquantly by the Conservatorium of Music—erected as stables for a new Government House (to be based upon Thornbury Castle in Gloucestershire, 'only bolder') which was never even started.

colonization, not only to reduce the pressure of population in England, but also to create healthy, well-balanced, loyal new societies in the colonies. This should be accomplished, he thought, by striking a proper balance between capital, labour and land. If land in a new colony was too cheap there was no labour, and no capital investment to develop the country, but if land prices were kept reasonably high then a complete society could be transferred from the Mother Country to any distant dependency. The money received for the land itself would be used to finance the migration, so that the whole process, called in the language of imperial economics 'the Doctrine of Sufficient Price', would be self-financing and self-perpetuating.

Wakefield planned no Sydneys. He wanted close-knit, compact settlements of respectable citizens, mostly of the middle-classes—no extravagant younger sons, no emancipated forgers, no footloose ruffians or discharged libidinous seamen. On soil that was British but mostly virgin new social experiments could be undertaken— each colony would be 'an immense nursery, to see what may be done for society'. Emigrant groups would include not only farmers, industrialists and labourers, but professional men of all sorts too, singers and milliners, printers and chemists—'and at least one good Political Economist at each settlement'.

A hopeful field for such experiments was New Zealand, the most distant of all the possessions of the Crown, which had been acquired in 1840 specifically to keep it *decent*. Since Captain Cook had circumnavigated the islands in 1769, New Zealand had been plagued by European adventurers of all sorts. Its able and cannibalistic indigenes, the Maoris, had been corrupted with rum and gunpowder, so that the tribesmen had slaughtered each other in their tens of thousands, and had eaten Europeans by the hundred, and on many parts of the coast doubtful white settlements were lodged—deserters, whalers, escaped convicts, speculators, sheepherders, a sprinkling of missionaries and a few *pakeha Maoris*—Europeans who lived Maori style, body tattoos and all. Darwin, in 1835, thought the white New Zealanders 'the very refuse of society', and five years later the British Government stepped in to stop the rot (and incidentally to forestall the French). They acquired sovereignty over the whole country by a formal treaty with a number of Maori chiefs—being determined to prevent, they said, that 'process of war and spoliation, under which uncivilized Tribes have invariably disappeared as often as they have been brought into the immediate vicinity of Emigrants from the Nations of Christendom'. The Treaty of Waitangi guaranteed the Maori chiefs, in the name of Te Kuini Wikitoria, 'full, exclusive and undisputed possession of their lands and estates', and though this assurance was soon whittled away, still the original British intentions towards New Zealand were generally benevolent.[1]

So it was that in 1843 the colony of Canterbury was conceived. It was one of several Wakefieldian settlements founded in New Zealand, and was one of two that were deliberately denominational, like the earlier Utopias of the United States. The Otago colony was Church of Scotland, and Dunedin, its capital, was to remain Scottish to its core for ever. The Canterbury settlement was Anglican—High Anglican at that, for the Oxford Movement was reaching its tapestried apogee in England, and the Canterbury Association, founded to promote the colony, was richly Tractarian. Wakefield himself had no religion, but he was prepared to use any instrument to achieve his ends—he approached the Chief Rabbi once.

His lieutenant in the Canterbury Association, John Godley, was an Anglo-Irish Anglican Tory, Harrow and Oxford, and between them they attracted to the Association's support a wide circle of High Church bigwigs. Many of them were, like Godley, graduates of Christ Church, Oxford, and therefore bishops. Two were archbishops. There were several peers and fifteen members of Parliament. Behind this formidable façade Wakefield himself, denied a public role because of his early indiscretions, industriously and powerfully laboured, consulted at every stage, visited at his Reigate cottage by successions of MPs, and even invited to nominate a bishop for the new settlement. *The Times* was attracted to the cause by all this consequence, and in 1849 the Association was given a royal charter. The Canterbury Pilgrims, as they romantically called themselves, primed by a course of lectures on New Zealand, and confirmed in their

[1] 130 years later the Maoris are still disputing the Treaty of Waitangi, which scarcely kept them in full possession of their ancestral rights, but they have achieved positions of great power in the State, and are probably the most thoroughly assimilated of all the old Empire's indigenous subjects.

resolve by an immensely grand farewell dinner, sailed for the Antipodes literally with the blessing of the Establishment, for their leaders had visited Canterbury specifically to receive it.

Four ships sailed, direct from London, carrying 775 well-behaved pioneers. They were separated of course into cabin, intermediate and steerage classes, and the richer emigrants, like Mr and Mrs James Fitzgerald, who sailed in the *Charlotte Jane* (730 tons), paid £42 for a stateroom in the stern, half the width of the ship, for which they provided their own purpose-made furniture. The first party disembarked upon the uninhabited shore of what is now called Lyttleton Harbour—a dramatic meandering fjord, overlooked by the high bluffs of the Banks peninsula, with the snow-peaks of the Alps shining celestially in the distance. They were met by His Excellency the Governor and his lordship the Bishop of New Zealand, the one an inclination of ostrich plumes, the other an agitation of surplices, and when they had laboured up the steep track to the ridge above the harbour, they looked down in wonder upon the site of their chief settlement on the other side—a swampy treeless place beside the sea, harmless but unstimulating, where advance parties of surveyors and engineers were already at work with teams of Maori labourers.

They had brought with them an organ, a church bell, some prefabricated houses, a printing press and a reference library of 2,000 volumes given them by Christ Church, Oxford. Though the exclusively Anglican membership of the colony was already regrettably diluted, still they soon had a thriving Church of England settlement upon that flaccid shore. Its leaders hoped that it would be 'a centre from which arts and morals should be spread throughout the southern world', and they proposed that in the very heart of it there should stand a High Anglican centre of faith and education, part college, part cathedral, to be paid for in the Wakefieldian spirit largely out of land sales. Since the model for this institution was to be Godley's own *alma mater*, and since so many of the wealthier settlers had been educated there too, they accordingly called the capital of their new colony Christchurch.

There were few Maoris in that part of New Zealand, so the Pilgrims wrote on a clean slate. They constituted from the start, as

Wakefield wished, a working cross-section of the English community —'a complete slice of England', so *The Times* said, 'cut from top to bottom'. The original intention to supply a nobleman and a bishop as spiritual and temporal heads of the colony unfortunately languished when no nobleman could be persuaded to emigrate and the bishop changed his mind after a month in the settlement: but they made a start with the church, the school and the library, they painfully worked out details of land tenure, grazing rights, Church endowments and squatting privileges, and they presently settled into a reasonably ordered and prosperous routine. It was all very English. Transplanted oaks and plane trees flourished, and in their branches chirped and procreated the skylarks, blackbirds, sparrows, greenfinches, yellow-hammers, magpies, plovers and starlings misguidedly brought from home.

It was not, however, much like the society Wakefield had envisaged. Few of his theories worked in New Zealand. Educated men would not go there, capitalists would not risk their capital there, poor men could neither buy land nor find jobs. Human nature betrayed the Doctrine of Sufficient Price. Wakefield had described the Canterbury pioneers as 'not merely a nice, but a choice society of English people': but not all of them were nice in the long run, rascals arrived among the regular communicants, and many of the more fastidious Pilgrims (who called themselves 'colonists', as against the steerage class 'emigrants') soon returned disillusioned to England.

The Canterbury plain was essentially grazing country, fine for sheep-farming, unprofitable for arable: but half the settlers had no capital to buy sheep, so they let grazing rights to less respectable kinds of New Zealander, or hired Australian stock-men whose devotion to the Thirty-Nine Articles was uncertain. Many more turned to sheep-farming themselves, and moved to the great sheep-runs beyond the settlement, where they soon lost any pretensions to gentility, and lived like wild free peasants, grazing their animals over the wide hummocky plains, and through the damp valleys of the foothills.

Even Christchurch itself began to lose some of its decorum, and showed signs of the rough colonialism Wakefield so despised. He had always hated the idea of 'New People', claiming an equality that was 'against nature and truth—an equality which, to keep the balance always even, rewards the mean rather than the great, and gives more honour to the vile than to the noble. . . .' Yet a New People the Canterbury Pilgrims presently became, not so New as the Sydneysiders indeed, but still a long way from the discreet hierarchy that the peers and prelates of the Association had foreseen. The simpler settlers, wrote an observer in 1853, soon became 'mightily republican'—distinctly insolent, too, so a French visitor thought. They seemed to change almost as soon as they set foot in the Antipodes, straighter of posture, better of dress, plumper of figure, and no longer feeling it necessary, it appears, to refer to gentlemen as 'Mr' or touch their hats to ladies. As a cheerful Scot wrote of the process:

> *When to New Zealand first I came,*
> *Poor and duddy, poor and duddy,*
> *When to New Zealand first I came,*
> *It was a happy day, sirs.*
>
> *At my dour cheeks there's bread and cheese,*
> *I work or no', just as I please,*
> *I'm fairly settled at my ease,*
> *And that's the way o't noo, sirs.*

The truth was that settlement colonies were essentially for poor men. Educated people would find nothing in a place like New Zealand, except escape from personal troubles at home, and the ideals of the Colonial Reformers mostly faded in time. 'No person who has ever enjoyed a life in England would, I think, profess to *prefer* a colonial life', wrote E. B. Fitton in 1856, and for ever afterwards most educated Englishmen found New Zealand, though kind and beautiful, fundamentally a bore. Still, though Christchurch grew more egalitarian and less Tractarian over the years, it remained by colonial standards always a conservative city: its Cathedral arose as ordained among the plane trees, its Christ's College became a university, its Christchurch Club became alarmingly exclusive, and there were always citizens to recall, referring to rectory water-colours upon the drawing-room wall, or indecipherable sepias of tennis-parties in family albums, that their forebears were those Mr Wakefield really had in mind, when he spoke of choiceness.[1]

5

Such were two of the Empire's white settlement colonies. They had this in common, with each other as with most of the British communities abroad, that they thought very highly of themselves. Most of their settlers were, by English standards, plain uncomplicated people—'bare-minded', Bagehot was to call them—but they were less than modest in their attitudes. 'The people of this Colony,' wrote an English official in Tasmania in the 1840s, 'very much resemble the Americans in their presumption, ignorance, arrogance and conceit. They believe they are the most remarkable men on the Globe, and that their Island "whips all Creation".'

It was not surprising that most of them had long been pressing for responsible Government. The Canterbury Pilgrims did so almost the moment they landed, Godley himself maintaining that he would rather be ruled by a tyrant on the spot than by a board of archangels 3,000 miles away, and some of the most passionate advocates of self-rule in Australia were men recently emancipated from the particular frustrations of Her Majesty's prisons. In the Canadian colonies, in South Africa, even in the decaying Caribbean islands, self-rule was vociferously and sometimes scurrilously demanded. Successive British Governments, remembering 1775, and not at all sure what would be best for the colonists, for the subject natives or for Britain herself, muffled the issue and marked time: but in 1838 Lord Melbourne had placed the problem on the lap of Radical Jack, and presently received in response the Durham Report.

Durham himself had been recalled from Canada because he exceeded his constitutional powers in dealing with the leaders of a rebellion, but his report was among the most important documents in the whole history of the Empire. It formulated a new relationship

[1] The last of all the Pilgrims, the Reverend Frederick Brittan, who had disembarked at Lyttleton in 1850, died in 1945, after seventy-four years as a priest in the diocese of Christchurch.

between London and the white colonies, and thus shaped the pattern of the Victorian Empire as a whole. Durham was an imaginative man, and he took with him on his Canadian mission the ubiquitous Wakefield and another well-known Colonial Reformer, Charles Buller. The Report was presented to Parliament in February 1839 (but much of it had already been leaked to *The Times*, perhaps by Wakefield). It was in effect an endorsement of the fundamental Wakefieldian thesis—that the colonies should be cherished as extensions of English society, and therefore competent to govern their own affairs. Not everyone admired it. Lord Brougham the law reformer observed to Macaulay that its matter came from a swindler (Wakefield), its style from a coxcomb (Buller), while 'the Dictator furnished only six letters, D-U-R-H-A-M'. Much of it was concerned only with the more immediate object of Durham's mission, the settlement of differences between French and English Canada. But it became a charter for British colonial development, a fresh start after the disasters of half a century before. The Durham Report advocated nearly complete self-government for the advanced white colonies, with only foreign relations, constitution-making, overseas trade and the disposal of public lands left in the authority of Westminster. Colonial governors would no longer be local autocrats, but would be responsible directly to the elected legislature of the colony, and thus no more able to decree the course of local events than was the Queen herself in London.

Radical Jack never saw it implemented, for he died in 1840, aged 48: but its genius was soon recognized, and in his own home country, between Durham and Sunderland, they built in 1844 a proper memorial to its meaning—a many-columned Doric temple, proud, high and lonely on Penshaw moor.[1]

6

It was because of this now celebrated report that Sir John Harvey of Nova Scotia, not the most distinguished of Colonial Governors, not

---

[1] Still, to my mind, the greatest of all the lapidary memorials of the British Empire, and marvellous to see on a misty morning from the Newcastle road, when it looks like a last monument to the Empire itself.

indeed remembered for anything else at all, received his instructions from London that November day in 1846. The publication of the Durham Report had caused excitement throughout the Empire, the Colonial Reformers hailing it as the start of a new era, the evangelists wondering if it would mean abandoning the heathen to colonial brutalism, the petty grandees of Nassau or Toronto fearing it might mean the end of their happy hegemonies. For years nothing came of it. Successive British Governments, Whig and Tory, doubted whether it was practicable as a programme for colonial progress. Could responsible Government be anything but independent Government? Would it not mean the end of the white settlement Empire anyway? Would abandonment be more profitable? Would it be better to wait and see?

But in 1846 Lord John Russell's Government came into office. Its Colonial Secretary was Lord Grey, Durham's brother-in-law, and among his advisers was Charles Buller. Now at last the Report was accepted as imperial policy, and the ideas of the Colonial Reformers were vindicated. In November Sir John Harvey received his dispatch from home. 'I have to . . . instruct you,' it said, 'to abstain from changing your Executive Council until it shall have become perfectly clear that they are unable, with such fair support from yourself as they have a right to expect, to carry on the government of the province satisfactorily and command the confidence of the Legislature. . . . It cannot too distinctly be acknowledged that it is neither possible nor desirable to carry on the government of any of the British provinces in North America in opposition to the wishes of the inhabitants.'

In this historic instruction, the first of its kind in imperial history, the British formally recognized that the Victorian Empire was to be different in kind from the settlement empire of the eighteenth century. Its overseas Britons were to be trusted not to break away from the Crown, but to adhere to it in liberty, and to live in the British way without coercion, as they would at home. The doctrine was formulated that an Englishman took with him to the colonies 'as much of law and liberty as the nature of things would bear'. Within twenty years all the bigger white settlements would have responsible Government, only the plantation colonies of the West

Indies continuing with their quaint old constitutions, and would become in most respects sovereign nations, distant diagrams or figures of Britain, honouring the Queen independently and at a distance. Here is the oath of allegiance sworn by the parliamentarians of Tasmania, then called Van Diemen's Land, when the first self-governing assembly met in Hobart:

I do seriously promise and swear, That I will be faithful and bear true Allegiance to Her Majesty Queen Victoria, as lawful Sovereign of the United Kingdom of Great Britain and Ireland, and of this Colony of Van Dieman's Land, dependent on and belonging to the said United Kingdom; and that I will defend Her to the utmost of my Power against all traitorous Conspiracies or Attempts whatever which shall be made against Her Person, Crown and Dignity; and that I will do my utmost Endeavour to disclose and make known to Her Majesty, Her Heirs and Successors, all Treasons and traitorous Conspiracies and Attempts which I shall know to be against Her or any of them; and all this I do swear without any Equivocation, mental Evasion, or secret Reservation, and renouncing all Pardons and Dispensations from any Person or Persons whatever to the contrary. SO HELP ME GOD!

The new nations overseas would prove the most durable, and the most noble, of the imperial achievements, as the American Ralph Waldo Emerson realized: 'I have noted the reserve of power in the English temperament. In the island, they never let out all the length of all the reins, there is no Berserkir rage, no abandonment or ecstasy of will or intellect. . . . But who would see the uncoiling of that tremendous spring, the explosion of their well-husbanded forces, must follow the swarms which, pouring now for two hundred years from the British islands, have sailed, and rode, and traded, and planted, through all climates . . . carrying the Saxon seed, with its instinct for liberty and law, for arts and for thought—acquiring under some skies a more electric energy than the native air allows—to the conquest of the globe'.

Sir John Harvey was not at first pleased by the prospect. He had no faith in responsible government for colonials, had trouble enough already with the Nova Scotians, and recognized in the Durham Report irritating echoes of local agitations. He obeyed his orders nevertheless. When, at the next election, the Nova Scotia Reformers returned a handsome majority, and Sir John's nominated Ministers were obliged to resign, instead of naming another Government of his own he did what constitutional figureheads must, and called upon the Opposition to form a Government. Now everything really did go on, as Dickens had prematurely judged, 'just as it does at home'.

CHAPTER EIGHT

An Act of God

IN the county of Cork in south-west Ireland lay the village of
Schull, which took its name from a monkly school, *scoil* in the
Gaelic, long since vanished and forgotten. It was only a straggle of
mud cabins and shanties along the waterfront, treeless hills behind,
in front a bleak and complicated inlet from the sea called Roaring
Water Bay. There was a little church near the shore, and a Catholic
chapel, and down at the quay the sinister black curraghs of the
fishermen, black leather over wood frames, were drawn up like
gleaming eels on the shingle. There was no city for many miles, only
the hangdog town of Skibbereen—'Skib' for short—on the road to
the east: over all hung the watery green-gold light of western Ireland
—which, with its scoured and limpid glow, was not unlike that radiance we imagined from the ramparts of Fort Prince of Wales on
Hudson Bay.

Into this melancholy settlement, in February 1847, there sailed
Her Majesty's Steam Sloop *Scourge* (Commander Caffyn). She tied
up at the quay below the church, and her captain went ashore: and
the report he later made upon what he found there is one of the most
horrific of all imperial documents. Schull was in a state of nightmare.
The weather was bitter, the village was half derelict, and most of
the people were in the last stages of starvation. Some were like
living skeletons, some had weirdly swollen stomachs or distended
limbs. Here and there corpses lay upon the ground, half-eaten by
rats, or gnawed at by starving dogs: elsewhere putrifying masses of
flesh had been thrown into shallow pits. In one hut Commander
Caffyn found a group of seven people crouched silent beside a peat
fire, while from an adjacent room came the screams of a woman,
lying like a pile of bones upon her bed, dementedly demanding food.

There were children with jaws so distended that they could not speak, men with bodies swollen to twice their normal size, babies with arms like little sticks, men with the blotched blackened skins of scurvy, boys whose heads of hair were reduced to patches, but upon whose faces a downy growth had eerily appeared, making them look, attenuated as they were and often silent with hunger, like poor enervated apes.

2

The captain was sickened but not surprised, for this was the Great Irish Famine, another catalytic episode in the history of Victoria's Empire, and all over Ireland that year such horrors were commonplace. The famine was caused by a disease which had destroyed the potato crop throughout the island, and had in a few months reduced a population of exceptional stalwart health to the brink of extermination.

The Irish peasantry lived almost entirely upon the potato, eating in ordinary times the staggering average of 14 lb a day per head, and this vegetable, boiled, stewed, served in soups, made into bread, gave them all the sustenance they needed, and so supplied them with vitamins and calories that they were among the biggest people in Europe. 'There are some things too serious for joking,' an old Irish saying had it, 'and one of them is the potato.' Crops had often failed before, and at any time there were Irishmen near the starvation level, but the Great Famine was exceptional because it was so widespread and because it lasted for several years: the crop failed partially in 1845, wholly in 1846, wholly again in 1848. The disease, which came from America and had appeared patchily in England and on the continent, was dramatically sudden in effect. Overnight an entire crop could be blighted, the leaves black, the stem brittle, and in a few days a promising potato field might be reduced to a mess of rotting vegetation. Even potatoes which seemed healthy when dug presently began to rot: and the peasants, who habitually stored potatoes for the winter season in shallow pits, found that not only their growing crops, but their stores of provision too, were utterly devastated at a blow.

With famine came disease. Typhus and relapsing fever spread throughout Ireland, ravaging bodies debilitated already by hunger, filth and vermin. Dysentery became epidemic, the ground around the cabins at Schull being blotched with its tell-tale clots of blood. Scurvy was everywhere. Viruses of all kinds were carried from town to town, door to door, by the wolfish half-starved beggars who roamed the countryside. The island was in despair. Perhaps never before, at least since the Middle Ages, had a corner of Europe been so horribly devastated. The hospitals, the workhouses, the prisons were packed with starving destitutes, and Caffyn, like most visitors to the ravaged west, found himself surrounded by crowds of half-mad, half-dead people, often nearly naked, desperate with hunger and disease—'in a few minutes', wrote one visitor to Skibbereen, 'I was surrounded by at least twenty such phantoms, such frightful spectres as no words can describe. Their demoniac yells are still ringing in my ears, and their horrible images are fixed upon my brain'. The workhouse admittance sheets for the period are pitifully classified—'Sickly and lame', 'Sickly and cripple, very dirty', 'Occupation begging, very dirty'. In Skibbereen workhouse half the children admitted soon died—'from diarrhoea', reported the doctor, 'acting on an exhausted condition'.

So dependent were the Irish upon the potato, by force of habit as by economic circumstance, that they had scarcely tried any other food—such grain as they grew they could not eat, because they used it to pay their rents. Now they were reduced to roots, weeds and berries. 'I confess myself unmanned', wrote one sensitive Welsh observer, 'by the intensity and extent of the suffering I witnessed, especially among the women and little children, crowds of whom were to be seen scattered over the turnip fields like a flock of famishing crows, devouring raw turnips, mothers half naked, shivering in the snow and sleet, uttering exclamations of despair while their children were screaming with hunger. I am a match for anything else I may meet with here, but this I cannot stand.' There were reports of dying people eaten alive by dogs: in Kenmare the parish priest entered a cottage to find a live man lying in bed with his dead wife and two dead children, while nearby a cat ate the body of a third child.

Probably a million people died in the Great Famine—most of them from the diseases of malnutrition. The population of Ireland was recorded in 1841 as 8 million, and the island was among the most densely populated parts of Europe. By 1851 death and migration had reduced it to 6½ million, and wide areas of countryside stood derelict and abandoned. All over Ireland, from poor Schull and delirious Skibbereen to the once prosperous farmsteads of Ulster, there arose the Irish mourning cry—that terrible keening wail, that howl of women's voices, to the grave chanting of verses and clapping of hands, with which this people greeted the advent of death.

3

'Am I,' Mr Michael Shaughnessy, a barrister, asked himself incredulously, surveying these ghastly scenes in 1848, 'am I in . . . a part of the British Empire?' He was. Ireland was the nearest overseas possession of the Crown, and excepting only lesser islands of the British seas, the oldest too. It had been a British possession for 700 years, since Henry II had first sent his armies across the Irish Sea, and settled his Anglo-Norman knights within the fertile enclave of the Pale. Since then successive 'plantations' of Scotsmen and Englishmen had been settled there, and a governing class of Anglo-Irish Protestants had come into being, but still the island was never subdued or Anglicized. It remained an intensely foreign place. The Irish peasantry was passionately but primitively Catholic, still speaking the ancient Gaelic tongue, and honouring in the folk-memory all the saints, kings, heroes, poets and jesters of their own Celtic tradition —a lyric tradition, expressed long before in an airy and fanciful love of nature and of liberty:

> *A little bird*
> *Has let a piping from the tip*
> *Of his shining yellow beak—*
> *The blackbird from the yellow-leaved tree*
> *Has flung his whistle over Loch Laigh.*

Time and again the Irish had rebelled against the English. Always the English had beaten them down. The Irish gentry had been virtually extinguished, the Irish proletariat was powerless.

The last big Irish rebellion had been in 1798, when Wolfe Tone's rebel forces, helped by French troops and money, had been ferociously defeated by an England preoccupied with her wars against Napoleon. This tragedy, which was scored on every Irish patriot's mind, had been almost immediately followed by a gesture called the Act of Union. A legislative act imposed by the English Parliament, this was intended as a fresh start to the relationship. It was to make the two countries one. Ireland's own Parliament, a body of Protestant gentlemen dealing only with Irish domestic affairs, was to be abolished, and instead the Protestant voters of Ireland would send 100 members of their own to speak for the island at Westminster. But it only exacerbated the ancient quarrel, for not only was it, in Irish eyes, another national humiliation, but it did not even bring the island prosperity. The powerful English manufacturers presently demolished what little Irish industry there was. Wages sank, and even the demand for Irish foodstuffs declined. The Irish were now not only enslaved, as they saw it, they were also poverty-stricken as never before. Their overcrowded island, which they loved with an atavistic zeal, could not support them, and they were left baffled and embittered.

Much of the land was owned by landlords in England, and though the two countries were now officially one, and Westminster was known as the Imperial Parliament in consequence, the peasant in Ireland possessed none of the security enjoyed by English labourers. A smallholder in England had rights of tenancy by law, and a general assurance of decency by custom. A smallholder in Ireland had no security whatever. He was simply permitted, by a man he had often never met, through a generally contemptuous and usually alien agent, the use of a small plot of land. He generally paid his rent in grain, using the rest of the land to grow his own potatoes. He had to provide his own cabin, his own fences, his own water: but if, by the sweat of his own hands, he succeeded in making some improvement on the property—as likely as not, that is, converting a barren patch of heath into productive land—if, after no matter how many years of family toil or sacrifice, he had increased the value of the holding, then there was nothing in the world to stop the landlord putting up the rent, and evicting him if he could not pay. Often he had no lease at all, and could be thrown out without more ado: if he had a lease, it was not difficult to find a pretext for anulling it.

The more cruelly the peasant was exploited, the more his family grew: until the catastrophe of the Great Famine, the Irish population was growing faster than any other in Europe. Irish people married young—what was the point of waiting?—and bred prolifically. As a result, the poverty of their circumstances was infinitely depressing; many Irish families, even at the best of times, knew little more of the great world than tribesmen in Afghanistan or Crees at Norway House. Dublin itself, architecturally one of the most prepossessing cities in the Empire, was pestilent and filthy: in the hot weather its elegant streets and lovely squares stank horribly, and in the winter a characteristic sight was that of the poor vagrants huddling against the 'Hot Wall' of Jameson's Brewery in Bow Street, where a little warmth seeped through from the boilers inside.[1] The average country dwelling was a one-roomed mud cabin, often without windows, with a thatched roof and a pile of manure outside the door. In the bleak west, where little English was spoken, there were people living in burrows in the bog, and people who had never seen a tree. In Galway, as a correspondent of *The Times* discovered in 1846, there were peasants so vague about the meaning of money that they were known to pawn it, getting 10s for a £1 note, or 15s for a gold guinea. There never was, the Anglo-Irish Duke of Wellington once said, such a country. 'Now that I have seen Ireland,' wrote the German traveller Kohl, 'it seems to me that the poorest among the Letts, the Esthonians and the Finlanders, lead a life of comparative comfort.'

The English at home disliked the Irish almost on principle. Working people resented them because they offered a reservoir of cheap labour, educated people despised them as half-savage—'that wild, reckless, indolent, uncertain and superstitious race', as the young Disraeli once called them in *The Times*.[2] Yet observers who

[1] As it still does.
[2] Superstitious certainly. 'Do you believe in fairies?' 'I do not, but they're there.'

met the Irish in Ireland gained a different impression. The Irish were certainly stubborn and unco-operative, but there was a dignity to them, different in kind from the homelier assurance of the English countryman, which sprang directly from their pride of race, nation and religion. Their courtesy was gentlemanly, their hospitality almost universal, and they were very sprightly. For all its monotony, their diet had made them a handsome and energetic people, and they loved dancing, drinking, racing, and all convivial, hell-for-leather activities. Their impetuous tempers, which could quickly flame into violence and treachery, easily sprang into gaiety too, and they enjoyed (though they could not often indulge it) a gypsy taste for colour and flamboyance.

4

In the early 1840s, before the Famine, this intelligent and un-appeasable people had been in a reckless condition once again. A movement to repeal the Act of Union, as the first step towards independence, had become a national passion. Ireland was never short of prophets, and the spokesman of the 1840s was Daniel O'Connell —'Swaggering Dan'—the first Catholic mayor of Dublin since the Reformation. O'Connell was the most famous man in Ireland, the most beloved and the most hated. With his round pudgy face, his curly hair and the satirical smile at the corners of his mouth, he looked almost a caricature of an Irishman, and perennially Irish too were his political methods. He was a fastidious rabble-rouser, a man who stood in pictorial attitudes, a wit, a caustic sophist, who could combine instant sarcasm with a rumpled benevolence, and was once described by Disraeli as being a more terrible enemy of England than Napoleon himself.

The Irish adored him. They loved his subtle invective—it was O'Connell who called Sir Robert Peel's smile 'the silver plate on the lid of a coffin'—and his popular image was best expressed in a drawing which showed him wrapped in a fur-collared coat, with his top-hat breezily on the back of his head, and on his face a Gorgonzola expression of ironic goodwill. He was called 'The Liberator', and his vast demonstrations were conducted with absolute order. A quarter of a million people gathered in 1843 to hear him speak on the hill of Tara in County Meath, the legendary seat of the Irish kings—the dramatic mass of the hill was entirely covered, summit to foot, with the vast silent crowd and its fluttering banners. It was said to be the largest assembly ever gathered in Ireland, and when the crowd dispersed to its vehicles after the meeting, the horseback marshals found that not a thing had been stolen, nor a fence damaged.

Under such leadership the Irish were united as never before in support of Repeal, but they did not want to break away from the Crown. The appeal of the old Gaelic culture had not yet been harnessed to political purposes, and the links with England seemed to most people too old and too complex to be broken. Thousands of poor Irish families, every year, crossed the Irish Sea to look for work in Liverpool or London. Perhaps a majority of the enlisted soldiers of the British Army were Irish Catholics—*St Patrick's Day* was the most familiar of all the Army's marching songs. The new railway lines in England were being built largely by Irish navvies. The Repealers did not think in terms of armed insurrection, either, for they thought that in the end the sheer weight of Irish opinion would be enough to end the Union.

The English were nervous nonetheless, and took no chances. They imprisoned O'Connell once, in 1843. They proscribed his monster meetings. They packed troops into Ireland. When a Repeal meeting was organized at Clontarf outside Dublin, where Brian Boru had repelled the Norse invaders in the eleventh century, they used guns, warships and thousands of soldiers to prevent it. A pattern of coercion was emerging, and it seemed to Irish fatalists that for all the irrepressible patriotism of the people, Ireland was getting less Irish every year:

> *O Paddy dear an' did ye hear the news that's goin' round?*
> *The shamrock is by law forbid to grow on Irish ground!*

Such was the state of Ireland on the eve of the Great Famine: overcrowded, discontented, lively, oppressed, politically inflamed. Nearly every observer forecast catastrophe, without often being specific. If it was not a catastrophe of one kind, it would certainly be of another.

5

In castles, Anglican rectories, pleasant country houses and Georgian terraces throughout the island were scattered the Anglo-Irish, the rulers of the Protestant Ascendancy. Though some of their families had been there for centuries, they were strangers in the land. They honoured a separate religion, they spoke a separate language, they lived in a manner inconceivably remote from the slums of Dublin or the mud huts of the west, and they viewed O'Connell and his kind not as patriots, but as traitors. To them Ireland was irrevocably, organically, part of the United Kingdom, alien but their own, and by ordinary English standards they had become half-foreign themselves: 'bold, queer-looking people', is how Jane Austen once described an Anglo-Irish family.

Some of the Anglo-Irish were immensely rich, with vast estates and the authority of local princes. Some were habitually insolvent. Whatever their circumstances, they formed an occupying caste. Their head was the Lord Lieutenant of Ireland, living in his castle in Dublin as representative of the Queen. Their church was the Church of Ireland, with bishops of gentlemanly stock and choirs well-trained to the harmonies of Handel or S. S. Wesley. Their young men frequently went off to take commissions in the British Army, which was officered by the Anglo-Irish as largely as it was manned by the Irish Catholics, or to join the East India Company—the very first famine relief fund was subscribed in Calcutta. Those who stayed at home provided virtually the whole professional stratum of Irish life, besides controlling what Irish industries and businesses remained, and creating almost everything that was visually beautiful (for while the ancient Irish folk-crafts languished, the English brought to the particular washed air of Ireland, at once sparkling and imprecise, the meticulous charm of London's Georgian style).

They lived in enclave. Consider Kilkenny, a small market town some seventy-five miles south-west of Dublin. Just as in a city like Madras the English lived aloofly in their own quarter, with the Indians out of sight in 'Black Town',[1] so in a town like Kilkenny

[1] Until, that is, it was renamed George Town in honour of King George V.

rulers and ruled were clearly segregated. At one end of the town stood the castle of the Dukes of Ormonde, hereditary butlers to the Crown of England. In its great hall, in 1366, had been enacted the Statutes of Kilkenny, forbidding the Anglo-Irish intimate contact with the indigenous Gaels, and thus setting the style of the apartheid which has split Ireland ever since. It stood immensely above the River Nore, full of treasures, all towers, gateways, monumental stables, with a private theatre and a fine Parade where the garrison paraded on festive days to pay tribute to the Duke. Not far away was the Anglican cathedral of St Canice, once a Catholic see, now plastered all over with honorifics of the Ormondes, trophies of Anglo-Irish gallantry and other reminders of changed times. Down by the river was the Protestant school of Kilkenny College, where Swift, Congreve and Bishop Berkeley had all been educated: in the upper town were the comfortable terraces where the Anglo-Irish doctors, lawyers and army officers lived, the respectable stores where their wives shopped, the comfortable old Club House Hotel where their sons roistered. Shabby and unpainted amidst this trim consequence, the remains of old Ireland lingered in poor monastery wall or neglected church: and across the river at the lower end of the town, well away from Castle, Parade, Club House and Cathedral, was the quarter called Irishtown, where the natives of the place resided hugger-mugger.[1]

Or take a place like Mallow. This little town in County Cork was a spa. It had been adopted by the Anglo-Irish at the end of the previous century, and in the 1840s it was still one of the more fashionable Irish towns, at whose upstairs bay windows visitors from all over the island sat behind their fans to watch the gay world go by. Mallow too had its castle, in a park at the end of town with a herd of rare white deer, but its civic imagery was of a different kind. If Kilkenny stood for the power of the Anglo-Irish, Mallow represented the boyish, engaging qualities of this contradictory people. Here, in

[1] The Irish began their reconquest of Kilkenny in 1857, when a new Catholic cathedral was completed not far from the castle: but to this day the lower town is called Irishtown, Kilkenny College rather wanly survives (it went on to educate Beatty of Jutland), and the Club House Hotel is pungently embellished with Anglo-Irish mementos.

an atmosphere of well-bred high jinks, they indulged their passions for gambling and horseplay. Here members of the club known as the Rakes of Mallow indefatigably debauched themselves, and members of the oldest hunt in Ireland, the 'Dashing Duhallows', tried to kill themselves several times a week in season. The real centre of Mallow was the pump room of the spa. This was a little half-timbered house built in a mock-rustic manner in a dingle beside a canal, and it stood there on the Fermoy road like a heartless laugh: for it was like a parody of the real country cabins in which, only a mile or two along the same road, the starving peasants lived with their pigs and their piles of excrement. Around this dainty structure the life of Mallow revolved: the evening whist-parties, the race meetings on the banks of the Blackwater, the starlight dinners, the scandals, the drunken quarrels maudlinly resolved, and all that witty, unreal *joie de vivre* which kept the Ascendancy energetically insulated from the terrible truths around it.[1]

For though the Anglo-Irish often loved their subject Catholics, and were often excellent landlords to them, they seldom understood them except on a level of benevolent badinage. They responded easily to the comic and gregarious side of the Irish, and the Irish obliged them with japes and blarney. But they seldom recognized the strength of the Irish identity. It was not that the Protestants of the Ascendancy were unkinder, or more insensitive, than other peoples. It was simply the force of history. They had been raised as the children of a superior culture, deposited among an illiterate peonage who honoured a debased religion and talked a useless archaic tongue: and of course the more they looked upon the Irish in this way, the more true their illusion became. Centuries of oppression had made the Irish tortuous and unreliable, now fawningly obsequious, now rising in vicious rebellion, and it was undeniably true that they seldom lived up to the standards of fairness and restraint expected of an Englishman.

So a gulf lay between the peoples. They met in the centre, where

[1] The Mallow spa house is still there, its half-timbering plastered over, there are still bay windows on the first floors of Main Street, the white deer survive in the castle park and the Duhallows are as dashing as ever: but a clock tower in the Tudor style stands on the site of the Rakes' club house.

Protestant and Catholic middle-classes co-existed, but Catholics seldom penetrated the ballrooms of Viceregal society in Dublin, while Protestants slumming it in the taverns of the Irish felt themselves intruders. It was rare indeed that an Anglo-Irish family mingled on genuinely equal terms with the local Gaels. One that tried was the family of St Georges, who lived at Tyrone House on the Galway coast, looking across to the Connemara Mountains. The younger St Georges had, so to speak, gone native. They liked the local girls, took to the company of local farmers, and gradually became absorbed in the environment. Politically this may have been far-sighted, but socially it was a disaster. Their gaunt mansion on its bluff above the sea had been one of the gayest houses in Galway, its invitations eagerly accepted, its lights ablaze across the bay on summer evenings. By the 1830s, as the St Georges began their metamorphosis into Irishness, it was beginning to look forlorn, without the spanking jaunting-carts drawn up at its door, or the tea-parties on its lawns: and before long, so inexorable were the unwritten laws of the English occupation, Tyrone House would be altogether deserted, its lovely gardens overgrown and its high silhouette windowless against the sky.[1]

6

The best of the Anglo-Irish behaved admirably during the famine, setting up soup kitchens, foregoing rents, visiting the sick and the dying, and frequently dying themselves from infection. 'It will be consoling to her Ladyship to learn', Lady Gore-Booth of Drumcliffe, County Sligo, was told by her parish priest, 'that the humble prayers of God's humble creatures were offered every night in every home for the spiritual and temporal welfare of every member of her Ladyship's family.' The great houses were besieged by poor people begging food or work, and some of the landowners started ambitious relief schemes of their own. At Birr in King's County, for example, the third Lord Rosse suspended work on his telescope, the biggest in

---

[1] Still, I remarked to a passing farmer one day in 1970, it would make a fine house even now—what a place for a ball. 'Oh', the Irishman picturesquely replied ,'wouldn't you say it was too late for that kind of fandango?'

the world, which lay black and tremendous on stone piers in the middle of his demesne, to supervise the digging of a moat around the estate, a project which, though it was planned on orthodox military lines and perhaps had a cautionary intent, nevertheless gave work to hundreds of poor labourers.[1] Where the relationship was good before the catastrophe, it seems to have been strengthened: we find one landlord warmly thanking his destitute tenants for helping him through *his* troubles by the prompt payment of rents. Some members of the Ascendancy felt themselves, in this universal emergency, closer to the Irish than they had ever been before, and it was generally admitted that Anglican clergymen proved more effective shepherds to this errant flock than most of the Catholic priests.

But clearly this was a crisis beyond the capacities of Ireland. It was left to the imperial Power, at a time when imperial duties were still hazily conceived, to save the Irish from extermination. Ideologically the British were ill-equipped for the task. In their eyes Ireland was a hybrid sort of possession, neither quite a colony nor quite a region of the Mother Country. They were astonishingly ignorant about it: Whitehall knew more about the economic situation of India than of Ireland. Politically individualism was the fashionable doctrine, and economically laissez-faire was all the rage —in the matter of famine as in all else, the less the State interfered, the better. Sir Robert Peel, who was the Tory Prime Minister during the first months of the famine, did buy £100,000 worth of Indian corn and meal in the United States, with which he hoped to prevent Irish food prices soaring: but everyone knew that he was using the issue to force through the final repeal of the Corn Laws, the supreme triumph of Free Trade, and his more virulent opponents actually disbelieved in the existence of the famine. His Government fell in 1846, and the Whigs who took over, under the dwarfish and canny Lord John Russell, were even more resolute Individualists. Abetted and advised by the devout Free Trader Charles Trevelyan, permanent head of the Treasury, the British

[1] The moat remains, a Lord Rosse still lives in the castle, and the Giant Telescope, through which the stars of the Owl Nebula were first resolved, may still be seen rusted on its piers in the demesne. King's County, however, is now called Offaly, unfortunately I think.

Government decided that if the potato crop failed again the imperial Power would interfere no more in the natural progress of affairs, would import no more food, but would leave the control of the disaster to the forces of private enterprise.

This was the negation of empire, whether empire of the old commercialist kind, which depended upon Government protection, or of the new idealist kind, which relied upon Government support. But the educated classes of England, indignant though they were about slave conditions in Jamaica, or even the unjust harassment of innocent Afghan tribesmen, were inured to miseries nearer home. The poor were always with them—'wretched, defrauded, oppressed, crushed human nature', wrote an American observer of England in 1845, 'lying in bleeding fragments all over the face of society'. London, the greatest of all capitals, was also among the most heartless; the new factory towns of the English Midlands and North were places of unrelieved ugliness and exploitation; it did not often lie upon the English conscience that only 60 miles away across St George's Strait there lay beneath the authority of the Crown the saddest country in Europe.

So throughout 1846 and 1847 Ireland was left to find its own solutions. There was no Government relief, no Government buying of food, and the costs of public works, the only form of relief, was borne entirely by the local rates. Butter, milk and eggs were still exported from Ireland, for it would be economically improper to interfere with the natural flow of commerce, and soldiers convoyed them to the seaports, in case the populace rebelled against this organic process. The Irish peasant, it was officially decreed, must buy his own food on the free market, and the Irish landlords (whom the Whigs blamed for the disaster, for they were nothing if not impartial) must foot the bill.

But the Irish economy was not geared to such demands. In normal times Ireland hardly imported anything, least of all food: there were very few import merchants, and only rudimentary systems of distribution. The orthodox principles of supply and demand simply did not work in such a country at such a time. There were few middle-class committee people to organize relief. The stiff upper lip, the spirit of self-help, the gift of cooperative efficiency, all were lacking from the Irish ethos. So desperate was the situation, so impoverished were many of the landlords themselves by now, so cruel was the winter of 1847, that by the end of the year nearly half a million men had no work at all, and when the free enterprise system did begin to work, and food trickled in from England, hardly anybody could afford to buy it. Now the peasants were deprived even of the nettles, the roots, the blackberries they foraged for in summer, and in some places there was nothing to eat at all but seaweed.

There was an official change of heart in the first months of 1848, when an Ireland gripped in snow and starvation seemed almost beyond redemption. The Government decided that against all its principles, and against the solemn convictions of Her Majesty's Treasury, direct relief must be supplied. Commissariat officers were summoned from distant parts of the Empire—Canada, the West Indies, the Mediterranean—to help dole it out, and a dramatic gesture symbolized the decision. The chief bastion of the Whig Progressives in London was the Reform Club, a splendid Renaissance palace in Pall Mall. The chef of this prestigious club was Alexis Soyer from Paris, one of the most famous cooks in the world, and in February 1848 he was officially invited to go to Dublin to superintend the distribution of Government soups. He had himself devised a recipe for a nourishing broth which would cost only $\frac{3}{4}$d a quart: a $\frac{1}{4}$ lb leg of beef, 2 oz of dripping, 2 onions, $\frac{1}{2}$ lb of flour, $\frac{1}{2}$ lb of pearl barley, 3 oz of salt and $\frac{1}{2}$ oz of brown sugar, to 2 gallons of water. This tenuous mixture was dispensed from a building very like a cattle-shed, erected outside the Royal Barracks in Dublin, with a hundred bowls set at long tables and supplied with chained spoons. In the starving went by one door, to eat their broth and leave at the other end: and when a bell rang, in came another hundred, until, when the system was working at its smoothest, M. Soyer from the Reform Club was feeding 8,750 Irishmen a bowl of soup a day.

But it was too late. Ireland was crippled, and the imperial Government never was able to master the catastrophe. The British had not yet had much experience of natural calamities in their possessions—they had never felt it their responsibility to deal with the endemic famines of India. Nor had they yet learnt to apply the new technology to the imperial mission. The great famine was an Act of God, as the insurers insisted, and neither the Government, nor the land-lords, nor even perhaps the peasants, improvident though they were, could properly be blamed for it. It was everybody's fault, and nobody's: but what it chiefly demonstrated, in our historical con-text, was the incompleteness of the imperial purpose. England's sense of imperial duty was still intermittent, and shared only by a minority: the Empire had no pride of cause or mission yet, and no conviction of destiny.

7

In the middle of it all O'Connell, aged and demoralized, died at Genoa. They brought his body home to Ireland, and laid it in state beneath a black catafalque in the Dublin Pro-Cathedral (only the Protestants, who constituted some ten per cent of the Dublin popu-lation, had a *full* cathedral—two of them, in fact). Priests stood in attendance, and Dubliners poured in night and day, pale and black, to light their votive candles and weep beside the coffin.

But The Liberator had long been past his prime, and in his old age there had arisen a new and more militant body of Irish protest—Young Ireland. This was a very different movement. Led by William Smith O'Brien, a Protestant landlord descended from Brian Boru him-self, it had intellectual leanings, published its own newspapers, and numbered in its ranks men who actually hated England and all she stood for, and were ready to die upon her bayonets. Its most active leaders had cataclysmic visions of sweeping the British into the sea, out of the ravaged island once and for all—'a kind of sacred wrath', one of its leaders, Joseph Mitchel, called it, and Fintan Lalor, another, saw the famine itself as the key to revolution. 'Unmuzzle the wild dog', he instructed the people in sinister metaphor. 'There is one at this moment in every cabin throughout the land, nearly fit to be untied—*and he will be savager by and by*.'

It was 1848, the year of revolution throughout Europe, and in Ireland these men believed their time too was near. On a wave of fearful idealism the leaders of Young Ireland, at this abysmal mo-ment of their country's history, launched themselves into armed rebellion. They were frank about their intentions. This was to be a holy war, and a fight to the death. It was a cause, they said, cleansed of the tricks and corruptions of politics, a cause for 'the young, the gallant and the good'. But in Ireland then the young, the gallant and the good were mostly near starvation, and were interested less in political independence than in physical survival. The Young Irelanders found themselves revolutionaries without a revolution. The Catholic clergy would not help—the Pope himself, in a Rescript, instructed the Irish priests to 'apply themselves to watch over the spiritual interests of the people, and in no way to mix themselves up with worldly affairs'. Attempts to arouse the exhausted Irish public fizzled dismally, and by the summer the Young Irelanders, having made their seditious purposes plain to the world, found themselves with no arms, few supporters, and less than £1,000 in the bank.

The British for their part were almost over-prepared for them. Alarmed by the revolutions sweeping across Europe, and by the near-revolution of the Chartists at home, they assumed a general rising to be imminent—a servile war is what the Lord Lieutenant, Lord Clarendon, foresaw, like the slave rebellions of earlier empires. Habeas Corpus was suspended, and troops were encamped on the outskirts of every major town. O'Brien and Mitchel were arrested and charged with sedition. O'Brien was acquitted by a jury that included three Catholics, and was unable to agree: Mitchel was sentenced, by a unanimous Protestant jury, to fourteen years' transportation, and was whisked away within an hour of the verdict, chained in a warship on his way to Bermuda.

The surviving leaders shakily proceeded with their plans. At the end of July Smith O'Brien toured the country districts, but was greeted with apathy almost everywhere. At Enniscorthy he was told the people were not ready. At Wexford they were cowed by the presence of British warships off-shore. At Kilkenny he found that owing to a misprint his followers numbered not 17,000, as he had been led to expect, but only 1,700. At Cashel, the ancient and spectacular shrine of Munster, where the cathedral and its attendant castle clustered high on a craggy rock above the plain—at Cashel, where if anywhere the spirit of Irish independence should have blazed, O'Brien found no Young Irelanders at all. Only at Mullinahone, in northern Tipperary, did the disheartened revolutionary find a rebellious potential. There they rang the chapel bells for him, and several thousand men assembled with pikes, forks and a few guns. Most of them had come only in hope of food, and when they were told that they would have to forage for themselves during the campaign, nearly all went home: but for O'Brien the die was cast. He marched his force northwards to the village of Ballingarry, in Limerick: and it was there on July 30 that the Young Ireland revolution of 1848, the most pathetic in the long history of Irish risings against the English, reached its poignant dénouement.

When O'Brien paraded his followers outside the village he found he had some 40 armed men, 20 with guns, 18 with pikes, together with an unarmed rabble of about 80 men and women. The scene sounds heartrendingly Irish. Ballingarry was the very model of a Limerick village, a small cluster of mud houses grouped around a road junction, sloping slightly on the face of a hill, and looking across green but stony country to the wide plain of the Mague below. Its inhabitants were mostly starving, and sat huddled in shawls and rags on stools outside their huts, or hung around the tavern listless and emaciated. Its roads were unpaved and dusty, and above it rose the stark volcanic mound called Knockfeerina, with a cairn on the top, and a Giant's Cave in its flank, and the charisma of Irish legend all about.

Here in a field, marked off with stones and boulders, the ragged army prepared for battle. At its head, on horseback, was the patrician O'Brien, a tall and sombre figure, with wistful child-like eyes, a Roman nose and a broad honourable brow; beside him was his chief lieutenant, Terence McManus from Liverpool, tall too but cast in a stagier Irish mould, with his loud laugh and his irresponsible swagger; behind them in tattered ranks was as sad a force as even Ireland had known, clutching its sticks and stones and shotguns, pitiably thin, utterly ignorant, but sustained, one can only suppose, by some truly noble urge or desperate grievance. These were the eighty Irishmen preparing to take on the British Empire, as their country sank into despair around them: but they were denied even a tragic finish, and the revolution ended ridiculously.

Even as the force paraded, news arrived that a body of police was on the way. The rebels threw up a barricade, ready to defend Ballingarry, and gunmen, pikemen and stone-throwers were poised in readiness. The villagers gathered at a prudent distance to watch. When about thirty policemen came marching down the road, and saw the barricade ahead of them, and this raggle-taggle crowd all about, they lost their nerve, broke ranks, and ran for the nearest house. It belonged to the Widow McCormack, and was a pleasant four-square farmhouse on the crest of an adjacent rise, with a walled cabbage patch in front, a yard behind, and a little thicket of trees to protect it against the wind. Mrs McCormack, as it happened, was on her way into Ballingarry, leaving at home her five or six young children, so without formality the policemen, clutching their muskets and helmets, precipitously dived into the house, closed the doors behind them, and barricading the windows with Mrs McCormack's mattresses, disappeared from view.

Off the rebels went hot-foot and hilarious in pursuit, breathless up the steep bumpy slope, leaving Ballingarry out of sight behind them. McManus dashed headlong into the yard, and seizing a bale of hay laid it against the back door and set fire to it. The others threw themselves on the ground and awaited events: and at this moment the Widow McCormack, having learnt on her way to the village that her house was about to become a historic site, tearfully appeared upon the scene, understandably anxious about her children. She seems to have moved the courtly O'Brien, for he told McManus to burn no more hay, and with a couple of others went boldly around to the front of the house, opened the garden gate, and walked up to the front door beneath the muzzles of the policemen's guns. There was silence. O'Brien climbed on to a window-sill, watched breathlessly by the rebels behind him and the policemen in front, put his hand through the open window over the piled mattresses, and shook hands with the flabbergasted constable inside. 'We do not want your lives,' he grandly said, 'only your arms.'

But now the rebels crouching below the garden walls began throwing stones at the house. The nervous police replied with a volley of musket fire. One rebel was killed, another severely wounded, and almost before the constables had time to reload, the entire revolutionary force, under fire at last, faded away from the Widow

McCormack's farm, to hide in outbuildings or declivities round about, or slink away in their rags to cabins in the village. O'Brien, pausing only to declare that an O'Brien never turned his back on an enemy, retreated nonetheless on horseback, and in half an hour the revolution was over. Mrs McCormack, returning to her home, found that the children had not been harmed, and set about clearing up the mess.[1]

8

Ten years earlier it might have ended differently, but the poor Irish had lost their spirit. Famine had broken them, and few had heart for protest or self-assertion. An instinct now seized this tragic people to leave Ireland for ever, and start afresh in some less cursed land. It was as though, after centuries of hopeless struggle, the fire had died in them. Never was a people further from the ecstasy of revolution. Instead in their hundreds of thousands the Irish survivors made for the ports, with their poor bundles of possessions and their children heavy on the hand. This was something quite new to Ireland. Unlike the English and the Scots, the Irish had never been wanderers. They had no instinct for the exotic: perhaps they were exotic enough in themselves. They loved their country with a mystic attachment, and the free English-speaking communities scattered across the world, familiar though they were with Cockney or Glaswegian, seldom heard the brogue.

Now something cracked. The island lay desolate, and if any Irishmen hoped for a true union with England, that prospect had vanished for ever. The contrast was cruel, between the rich and powerful kingdom on one side of the Irish Sea, just getting into the stride of universal supremacy, and the shattered sister isle so close

[1] Her house stands today just as it was, above its door the inscription *Remember 48*, and is often visited by thesis writers from America. Its occupants in 1970, Mr and Mrs Daniel Morris, kindly showed me a pistol supposed to have belonged to O'Brien—who was sentenced to be hanged, drawn and quartered, but was transported to Tasmania instead, and having been unconditionally pardoned, returned to Ireland to die a free man in 1864. His brother Lucius became the 13th Baron Inchiquin, and the O'Briens were never revolutionaries again.

and yet so unutterably estranged. In these conditions the Act of Union was clearly no more than an act of dominance, and far from exciting the sympathy of the English, the Great Famine had merely sharpened their exasperation. 'The great evil with which we have to contend,' wrote Charles Trevelyan, 'is not the physical evil of the famine, but the moral evil of the selfish, perverse and turbulent character of the people.' The Irish were so *hopeless*, so absolutely dependent upon the leadership and organization of others. They fought each other for relief foods, they stubbornly resisted any change of diet, they stole and cheated and lied in the midst of tragedy. And after all the British had done for them, even then they had, in the depths of their ingratitude, mounted the revolution of 1848—itself, in its mixture of self-delusion and ineptitude, a typically Irish operation. Russell himself summed up the public attitude thus: 'We have subscribed, worked, visited, clothed, for the Irish, millions of money, years of debate, etc, etc, etc. The only return is rebellion and calumny. Let us not grant, lend, clothe, etc, any more, and see what that will do'.[1]

The island seemed doomed, governed by rulers who despised it, and plagued too by self-doubt and even self-contempt. In the years immediately after the Great Famine about a million Irish people decided to start again elsewhere, or were shipped off by landlords only anxious to be rid of them ('I have got rid of crime and distress,' said Mr Spaight of Derry Castle, Tipperary, 'for £3 10s a head,' while Sir Robert Gore Booth, whose family was so humbly prayed for by their tenants in County Sligo, responded by shovelling three shiploads of them off to America). Most of them wanted to go to the United States, the old enemy of the British Empire, where hearts beat, they had been told, to an Irish rhythm. 'The Irishman looks on America,' wrote the litterateur Colley Grattan, 'as the refuge of his race. . . . The shores of England are farther off in his heart's geography than those of Massachusetts or New York.' In those days, though, America did not offer unlimited immigration, so most of the refugees went first to Canada.

[1] A classic English view of the Irish problem. It is remarkable how many of the more sympathetic officials in Ireland during the famine had names like Wynne, Griffith or Jones.

The journey there was only an extension of the Irish nightmare: first the long trudge across Ireland to the sea, in parties often of five or six hundred half-starved travellers, to board steamers in Sligo or Cork, or to be crammed on to schooners and sloops in lesser havens like Ballina, Killala or Tralee: then the miseries of the passage, often *via* Liverpool, in conditions akin to those on the Middle Passage of the slavers, in ships often unsound, with heartless and frequently incompetent crews, packed aboard without enough food or water, sometimes without any lavatories at all, and often infected with typhus: and finally the landing on the other side, unwanted still as they all too often discovered, and greeted only by overworked health officers and resentful immigration men.

9

Let us end this, the saddest chapter of the whole imperial story, with a glimpse of the arrival of the Irish in their New World, at the quarantine station of Grosse Isle in the St Lawrence river below Quebec. The river there is very beautiful, about a mile wide, streaked with long low islands, and backed by the genial elevation of the Laurentian hills—in summer as green and inviting as Burgundy, in winter all white. The colours are bright and clear, and the farms of the French Canadians are speckled prosperously along both banks of the river. To the west the stream broadens majestically towards the open sea, and in the early morning sun the islands are inverted in mirage, and seem to hang there suspended between sky and water. The air is very still, and life on the river banks moves gently and simply.

But Grosse Isle is tragically busy. It is a longish humped island almost in midstream, thinly wooded, and littered with the huts of the quarantine station. For several weeks the Irish immigrant ships have been arriving infected with fever, and ship after ship has been detained below Grosse Isle. Far down towards the sea the vessels are waiting, thirty or forty of them, shabby battered ships for the most part, lying there lifeless in the stream. The air is foul about them. All around their moorings, and around the island too, the water is thick with scum, floating rubbish, barrels and old rags: and through this muck a stream of small boats passes from ship to shore, loaded with scarecrow complements of men and women, some dying, some already dead. Some boats are loaded only with corpses, wrapped in canvas or nailed in crude coffins: on the island people can be seen painfully stumbling, even crawling, towards the huts. Some feebly call for help, food or water. Some cannot move or speak at all, and when they are lifted out of the boats, simply lie there on the beach.

This is the landfall of the promised land. Through the scummy water, in and among the anchored ships, one small steamer industriously chugs, picking up those immigrants who have been passed as healthy by the doctors, and are being allowed up to Montreal and a new life. The passengers who crowd its rails look almost as ill as those feebly lying on the island shore, or watching from the decks of the anchored ships: but on the prow of this small vessel, as she navigates a course through the sickness and the despair, an Irish fiddler merrily plays an Irish tune, and a few dancers foot a jig in the sunshine.[1]

[1] Grosse Isle is now an animal quarantine station, and is normally closed to visitors, though there is a suggestive view of it from Montmagny on the southern bank. The fever sheds still stand, and a monument commemorates the Irish who died on the island. 'In this secluded spot,' says its inscription, 'lie the mortal remains of 5,424 persons who flying from Pestilence and Famine in Ireland in the year 1847 found in America but a Grave.'

CHAPTER NINE

'What a Fine Man!'

NEVER again would the British shirk their imperial duties so shamefully as they did in Ireland, but even so empire remained largely a matter of impulse. The ideas and initiatives of men in the field governed its growth as potently as did the policies of Governments or the theories of economists, and many a stroke of imperial history depended originally upon a quirk of individual character, or the mood of a moment. In the Far East the adventurer James Brooke, son of an East India Company civil servant, had intervened so effectively in the affairs of Sarawak that he was now Rajah of the island. In the Indian Ocean the Scottish entrepreneur John Clunies-Ross morosely ruled the Cocos Islands, living (so Darwin reported) in 'a large barn-like house open at both ends', and hoping (so he said himself) that his exertions 'may in time become productive of some considerable accession to the commerce of the British Empire, and contribute to the extension of her population, her language, and her true glory and grandeur'.

Especially did character count in India, the most dazzling and extraordinary of the imperial possessions, where old habits died hard. The sense of Christian mission, as we have seen, was now having its impact upon the Raj, but generally through the agency of individual consciences—without a Sleeman the Thugs would still have been at large, without a Bentinck *suttee* might still be legal. There was still room in British India for grand characters and impetuous decisions: and nowhere was the power of individualism more decisive than in the warlike expansions by which the British, in the late 1840s, extended their sovereignty into the independent territories of the north-west—first Sind, then the Punjab. The whole style of these adventures was set by the personalities of individual

Britons, of whom one of their own number observed with characteristic frankness, when asked to account for the success of their system, 'it is not our system, it is our men': so before the Indian Empire reaches its institutional maturity later in the century, let us introduce ourselves to a few of the more remarkable Anglo-Indian imperialists of the time—bearing in mind that if they had ever heard of such a category of person, they would certainly be astonished to find it applied to themselves.

2

First Charles Napier, the conqueror of Sind. We see him in his late prime, for this, his first and only major command in war, came to him late in life—at 60, when he had almost given up hope of generalship in battle, and was resigned to an unexciting retirement. He is not an easy person to miss. A man of middle height, he has a most peculiar face: hook-nosed, glaring-eyed, with long white side-whiskers and small steel-rimmed spectacles of his own design—'a beak like an eagle', Thackerary thought, 'a beard like a Cashmere goat'. He wears a queer helmet, also self-devised, with a long flap hanging down behind; and though he is scarcely a stalwart figure, looking a little scrunched or scrawny, still his bearing is imposing and his eye strangely commanding. He is an odd spectacle indeed, and his oddity is calculated: he used to say his enemies never harmed him because they were too taken aback by his strangeness, and he once appeared at an enormously ceremonial dinner in his honour wearing a frock-coat, buff corduroy breeches, and an English hunting-cap peaked in front, swathed in white cotton behind—when he sat down at the end of his speech the band struck up 'The King of the Cannibal Islands'.

Napier came of a brilliant Scots family whose name is inescapable in the annals of the Victorian empire. His father was a famously handsome and exceptionally cultivated soldier; his mother was said by Horace Walpole to be 'more beautiful than you can conceive'; his three brothers all achieved eminence; his cousins, forebears and descendants commanded armies, ships, garrisons or colonies from one end of the empire to the other. But his immediate family was not rich, and though he grew up among the opulent Anglo-Irish of County Kildare, and was the grandson of a Duke, and a first cousin of Charles James Fox, still he went to the local village school, and never forgot the meaning of poverty. 'The poor are like slow sailing vessels,' he wrote in middle age, 'they are deeply laden with the heavy cargo of poverty.' In 1839, when he was already a general, he was living with his wife and daughter above a butcher's shop in Nottingham, having nothing but his pay. When he arrived in India to command a division, he claimed, all he possessed in the world was £2.

Though he was a soldier from the start, being commissioned at the age of eleven, a bluff empathy endeared him to people far outside the normal military range of acquaintance. He was a kind man. When, in 1839, he found himself defending northern England against the threat of a Chartist rebellion, his sympathies were largely with the poor victims of industrialization—'God forgive me', he said of the employers, 'but sometimes they tempt me to wish that they and their mills were burnt together'. He gave up blood sports because he found 'no pleasure in killing little animals', and when after his death they erected a statue of him in Trafalgar Square 'the most numerous contributors', as its inscription said, were private soldiers.

Napier's early career was one of breathless hazard. He was wounded six times and had two horses killed under him in the Peninsular war, commanded the attack on Little Hampton in Virgina in the war of 1812, stormed Cambrai during the 100 Days, was shipwrecked in Ostend Harbour in 1815, and in 1822, scarred all over and precociously experienced, became Resident of Cephalonia in the Ionian Islands, then under British sovereignty. Almost at once he acquired his own philosophy of empire, which he succinctly defined as 'a good thrashing first and great kindness afterwards'.

His attitudes to subject peoples were conditioned first to last by his memories of Ireland, and all his life we find him using Irish images and comparisons. 'Look at unhappy Ireland!' he cried from the other end of Europe, 'How feeble is a system of iniquity! How weak is injustice!' He had a soft spot for the anomalies, castaways and crooked corners of Irishness: soon after he had been awarded the Order of the

Bath, a general campaign medal was issued to the army he commanded—'*Now*,' he wrote to the Governor-General of India, '*I can meet Corporal Tim Kelly and Delaney without a blush!*' It was he who, in 1845, commissioned the young Richard Burton to investigate the homosexual bordels of Karachi: not only was he interested professionally, because of the bearing of pederasty upon the British catastrophe in Kabul three years before, but he also had, as Burton phrased it admiringly in a footnote to his *Arabian Nights*, 'a curiosity as to their workings'.

In the imperial context all this added up to a quixotic but generally benevolent bloody-mindedness. Napier was congenitally opposed to higher authority, to orthodoxy, and to anyone who ventured to disagree with him: on the other hand he was unshakeably addicted to commonsense, to fairness, to unquestioning responsibility and to anyone who helped him. He was a prickly, gesticulative, arrogant man, full of acidulous wit—'if it had no vent', he once told his mother, 'my death would ensue from undelivered jokes' —and he identified himself emotionally with his simpler subjects, be they Greeks, Irishmen or Baluchis. He had two children by a Greek mistress in the Ionians, and named one of them Cephalonia after his island ward—when he sailed for home their mother first decided to keep them, then changed her mind and pushed them in a small boat towards his departing ship: Napier, though he later married two virtuous English widows in succession, cherished them lovingly all his life.

He believed strongly in the merits of British power. When an apparently respectable foreigner once arrived illegally in Cephalonia, Napier breezily swept aside the immigration laws and stood guarantor for the stranger himself. It was unlikely, he said, that the man would misbehave himself in an island policed by 500 Connaught Rangers. To make the point clear, Napier pointed out the magnificent colonel of the Connaughts, striding by outside his window, and observed that one would be foolish indeed to provoke the wrath of such a soldier. 'By the lord, yes,' said the foreigner, 'you speak truly. I would not like to be in his way if he was angry: what a fine man!'

3

This was the essence of Napier's imperialism: a bold disrespect for unnecessary fuss, a staunch faith in the effect of British authority, a robust belief in force of character. All these principles he took with him to India for the great triumph of his life, the conquest of Sind in 1843.

It was not altogether apparent that Sind, a barren brown territory straddling the central reaches of the Indus, ought properly to be conquered; but its potential importance was obvious, and once the British had navigated the river, as a local sage once remarked, 'Sind has gone'. So it proved. The British first undertook to protect the Amirs of Sind, not a very estimable collection of princes, against the Sikhs to the north—'the two contracting parties bind themselves never to look with the eye of covetousness upon the possessions of each other': but later George Auckland's successor Lord Ellenborough, wishing to expunge the memory of the Afghan War with a touch of glory on the plains, decided that whatever the treaty said, Sind must be annexed—'like a bully', it was said at the time, 'who has been kicked in the streets and goes home to beat his wife in revenge'.

Nearly everybody disapproved of this venture, from Peel, Wellington and Gladstone in England to most of the British administrators on the spot. Charles Napier, the general appointed to command it, did not care a rap. He felt only a vehement contempt for most politicians, most civil servants, most bigwigs of the East India Company and all the Amirs of Sind. He had no difficulty in taking the country, once the Amirs had been provoked into war, and his brother William, the distinguished historian of the Peninsular campaigns, left a celebrated description of his principal battle: 'Guarding their heads with large dark shields [the Sind troops] shook their sharp swords, gleaming in the sun, and their shouts rolled like peals of thunder as with frantic might and gestures they dashed against the front of the 22nd. But, with shrieks as wild and fierce, and hearts as big and strong, the British soldiers met them with the queen of weapons, and laid their foremost warriors wallowing in blood. . . .' Briskly exiling the aggrieved potentates, relieved of poverty at last by picking up prize money of £60,000, setting up his headquarters in the walled city of Hyderabad upon the Indus, Napier proceeded to rule the country absolutely by his own lights, and at a salary of £15,000 a year. *Punch* suggested that he had reported the conquest in one wry pun—'*Peccavi!*'[1]—assuming that the old swashbuckler, with his principles of human liberty, might feel some pang of remorse. But it was not so. The annexation was characteristically defined by Napier, in advance, as 'a very advantageous, useful, humane piece of rascality'. He allowed that it was a consequence of the British aggression in Afghanistan, but then someone always suffered from injustice in the end. In this case it would be the Amirs of Sind, 'and on a crew more deserving to bear it hardly could it alight'. The Amirs were, he concluded, tyrannical, drunken, debauched, cheating, intriguing and altogether contemptible.

But he was concerned as always for the welfare of the common people of the country, and considered himself the sole judge of their needs. Suttee, pleaded the Brahmans of Sind, now faced for the first time with reform, was an immemorial custom. '*My nation also has a custom. When men burn women alive, we hang them. Let us all act according to national customs!*' Wife-killing was perfectly legitimate, it was pleaded for a convicted murderer, if the wife had angered the husband. '*Well, I'm angry. Why shouldn't I kill him?*' By such abrupt and soldierly methods Napier established the British province of Sind, and made of it a territory quite different from those governed by the civilians of John Company. He created the port of Karachi, he encouraged navigation on the Indus, he foresaw the possibilities of irrigation in the north. He was at once an early prototype of the paternal autocrat later to become so familiar a figure of the Raj, and a late exponent of eighteenth century idiosyncrasy. It may be said, in fact, that an imperial tradition had been born thirty years before when this good, self-opinionated man, facing the Chartist leaders at a moment when England seemed on the edge of revolution, had declared his principles to the angry working-men before him. He supported sympathetically, he said, everything they stood for: but if they ever provoked riot and disorder in pursuit of those honourable ends, by God, he would shoot them all.

[1] 'I have sinned', in Latin, as *Punch* readers did not then need to be told.

4

Next the British power, with some false starts and more than one humiliation, pushed northwards up the Indus into the Punjab. This rich and fertile country, 'the land of the seven rivers', had been for many years under the domination of the Sikhs—that formidable religio-militarist nation, bound by the seven self-disciplinary rules of their religion, whose most celebrated ruler, Ranjit Singh, we encountered in the first chapter of this book. Having raised the Sikhs to a pinnacle of power, Ranjit had died in 1839, reputedly worth £12m, and drunkenly magnificent to the last. His successors were less masterful, squabbled dangerously among themselves, and in 1845 conveniently gave the British a pretext for intervention by sending an army across the imperial frontier. War followed, the British suffering some ignominious reverses, and enjoying some knockabout affrays, before their inevitable final victory ('a stand-up gentlemanlike battle', is how General Sir Harry Smith described the battle of Aliwal in 1846). After a period of indirect rule, and some further bouts of fighting, the Empire annexed the Punjab in 1849.

These were experimental days of empire. Just as Napier had established a new kind of Government in Sind, so an *ad hoc* administrative machine was devised for the Punjab. It too was personal, autocratic, military, but it was a much more earnest instrument of dominance; in the Punjab the Empire moved a stage further towards providential duty, the destiny of race, and the other lofty abstractions of late Victorian imperialism. At the head of the Government was a board of three members, and this absolute tribune made its principles of Government absolutely clear. Justice, for instance, would be 'plainly dealt out to a simple people', avoiding all technicality, circumlocution, and obscurity, with accessible courts of law in which every man might plead his own cause, and be confronted face to face with his opponents. Bureaucracy would be kept stylishly in check: 'with good Officers rules are almost superfluous, with bad Officers they are almost ineffective.' There would naturally be, the board publicly admitted, some enmity against such 'powerful and humane' conquerors, but the mass of people would advance in material prosperity and moral elevation. Promptness, accessibility, brevity and kindliness were the best engines of government, and the board set itself out to be 'considerate and kind, not expecting too much from ignorant people', and 'to make no change, unless certain of decided improvement'.

A commission of some 80 young Company men imposed these disciplines upon the mixed Sikh, Muslim and Hindu population of the Punjab. Some were soldiers, seconded to political jobs, some were civilians. They formed an ideological shock-force, dedicated, energetic, cohesive, progressive, which fell upon the conquered country like a reforming cadre, examining all its institutions, assessing all its possibilities, and impressing the personality of the Empire upon every last peasant in every corner of the land. They codified the law. They reconstituted the coinage. They ended banditry. They built roads and canals. In four years they established a complete new system of Government to control every facet of public life in a country the size of France. The men of the Punjab School, we are told, worked ten to fourteen hours a day. They had no leave unless they were sick, and they prided themselves upon their membership of a *corps d'élite*, whose new order of Government would be its own memorial.

But the style of the whole operation, its air of Puritan complacency and superiority, was set by two brothers: John and Henry Lawrence, the dominant members of the board. They often quarrelled, and they differed greatly in character, but they were both men of instinctive power. They were like prophets, inspired by divine messages to acts of profound generosity or uninhibited ferocity: or perhaps like Wagnerian figures of fable, for they were burning people, romantics of an almost fanatic kind, full of zeal, certainty and purpose. Emily Eden might have thought them slightly preposterous, and Charles Napier, who became commander-in-chief of the armies in the Punjab, predictably detested them both.

5

The Lawrences were the sixth and eighth sons of an Anglo-Irish soldier. A third brother, George, was one of the staff officers who escaped when Macnaghten was murdered at Kabul: he was deputy commissioner of Peshawar under his brothers' authority, became a general and wrote a book that set a fashion in Anglo-Indian titles —*Forty-Three Years in India*.[1] The Lawrence boys had followed their father around the world, school to school, station to station— Henry was born in cantonment in Ceylon, John in barracks in York-shire—and had enjoyed a mixed but broadening upbringing. 'I was flogged once every day of my life at school,' John Lawrence said, 'except one—and then I was flogged twice.' One went to the East India Company's civilian college at Haileybury, the other to its military academy at Addiscombe, and they sailed for India in the 1820s—at a time when the British political mission there was scarcely conceived, let alone defined, and a young man might feel, like William Hickey before him, that he was embarking upon a career with no higher purpose than pleasure and good money.

Not the Lawrences. Both were intensely religious young men, Bible-readers, workers. They were High Victorians before their time, and took their life and labours seriously—Henry, almost as soon as he arrived in India, joined a coterie of like-minded officers who prayed and meditated communally at a house cryptically called Fairy Hall, Dum Dum. Step by step they rose, the one in the military service of the Company, the other in the political. Henry, when stationed in Nepal, married a clergyman's daughter—the first white woman ever seen in Katmandu—and after serving in the first Burma War, the Afghan war, and the war against the Sikhs, became Resident in Lahore. John married a parson's daughter too, and steadily ascended the hierarchy of the civil service, by way of Paniput and Gurgaon, Etawah and Kurnaul, to be Collector of Delhi. So the two brothers, their temperamental differences wider now but their capacity for passionate purpose still equal, were united again upon the Board of Administration of the newly annexed Punjab. Henry was the Presi-dent, John the administrative genius. They differed incessantly, chiefly on the technical details of Government, sometimes simply on issues of outlook or priority. Once they were actually estranged.

[1] The most famous of the *genre* was *Forty-One Years in India*, by Field-Mar-shal Lord Roberts of Kandahar, but as a professional in the field my own favourite is George Aberigh-Mackay's *Twenty-One Days in India* (1882).

But their partnership was formidable, and was to set its mark upon the Punjab for a century to come.

In the Punjab they reached their prime. Henry was the weaker, softer, more irritating, more cultivated of the two. He was also perhaps the more priggish, and one senses in him a certain Fairy Hall quality of ingratiation. He was a marvellous looking man, like a great sage—'Sir Henry looked to Heaven and stroked his beard', wrote an Indian commentator of him, 'and then he knew what to do'. There is one picture of him which shows him immersed in the contemplation of a family portrait, sitting very upright in his chair, and gazing with a disturbing intensity at the picture: his high cheek-bones, his big nose, the lined and sunken aspect of his face, give him an ascetic, almost Arab look. In another painting he is seen sitting cross-legged before the throne of the ruler of Udaipur. He wears a little peaked hat like a railwayman's cap, and is seated in an attitude of almost jejune respect before the immensely condescending and far more magnificently whiskered prince: but even so, surrounded as he is by jewelled, feathered, turbaned and sword-girt magnificos of the court, it is Lawrence's rigid and fibred figure that catches the eye, and makes one realize at a glance who is the real power at that Durbar.

Henry had little time for niggling matters of cost or method. His was the big picture. 'Settle the country,' he used to instruct his subordinates simply, 'make the people happy, and take care there are no rows.' He had a taste for the company of Indian princes—cross-legged at the Rajah's feet was an apposite pose—but he had an imperious temper, too, unfortunately tinged with moodiness. Lord Dalhousie, the Governor-General, found him more and more tiresome as the years passed, but those who worked more closely with him, and who were able to balance the grandeur against the irritations, are said to have loved him greatly. He had a warm heart and a tongue more reckless than malicious. He was usually ready to apologize. His scale was grand, and when he died the four British soldiers who were his pall-bearers kissed the forehead of his corpse, one by one, in respectful farewell.

John Lawrence grew into something different—a brusquer, angrier, more inflexible and formidable man, earthier of values and bolder of action. When Henry left the Punjab in 1853 he handed over

the Presidency to John, and said in a parting letter: 'If you preserve
the peace of the country and make the people happy, high and low, I
shall have no regrets that I vacated the field for you. . . . I think
we are doubly bound to treat them kindly *because they are down*'.
John's immediate reply was harsher. 'I will give every man a fair
hearing, and will endeavour to give every man his due. More than
this no one should expect.' There is nothing gentle to John Lawrence's face. It is almost brutal in its strength and dignity—heavy-
jawed and thick-necked, with frowning eyes and a high forehead, a
military moustache, a sober hair-cut and an unlaughing, incorruptible mouth. He looks like one of those over-informed progressives
whose inflexible convictions wither the small talk at frivolous dinner-
parties. It is a modern style of face, and John Lawrence was an early
imperial technocrat. He was logical, ruthless and efficient. He
thought in terms of cost and effect, not worrying too much about
cause, and he worked to an unremitting rhythm, night and day, even
phrasing his public proclamations in thumping antiphony, half Old
Testament, half steam-hammer.

Only the rashest Indians crossed swords with this vehement
Cromwellian, but he made many enemies among his own people.
'More like a navvy than a gentleman', wrote one fastidious colleague,
and many more resented his addictions to living rough, ostentatiously working all hours and 'getting the best out of people'. He
was an early exponent of the team spirit, reactions to which have
formed a dividing line among educated Englishmen ever since. John
Lawrence called himself 'an old bullock for work', once claiming that
he had not had a day's rest for nearly sixteen years, and by the expression of such attitudes, another colleague wrote, 'he effectually
prevented anyone from being comfortable'. He was excellent at
money-matters, and skilfully transformed the financial situation of
the Punjab: but it was money in the principle, or in the account
book, that concerned him, and he never coveted it for himself, or
responded to the allure of eastern fortunes. After the Sikh wars the
Koh-i-Nor, seized by Ranjit Singh from poor Shah Shuja, was
seized in turn by the East India Company, and was given to John
Lawrence for safe keeping, wrapped up in a small box. By his own
account he popped it into a waistcoat pocket and forgot all about it,

and when Queen Victoria happened to inquire about it six weeks later, had to ask his servant if he had come across it. The servant did recall finding 'a bit of glass' in one of his suits, and so it was sent to England on the paddle-frigate *Medusa*, guarded by soldiers in an iron casket, to be added to the Crown Jewels in the Tower of London.[1]

John Lawrence was later to become an archetypical mid-Victorian hero. He grew paunchy in his later years, and developed heavy dewlaps, but the British public made him a semi-deity, and erected statues in his honour—'it will seem almost blasphemy,' wrote one of his less adulatory subordinates, 'to say a word against him'. The Punjab School of Imperial Government, of which he was the real creator, was the pride of the Indian Empire for generations to come: he himself lived to become the Queen's Viceroy in India, and died in 1879 a peer of the realm, the father of 10 children and a director of the North British Insurance Company.

6

The young men of the Punjab were often inspired for life by the examples of the Lawrences. Personal government was their creed, and they were always on the move among their peasantry, accessible to all, presiding over improvised courts of law, living on chapattis or rice and talking always in the vernacular. Many of them were early practitioners of that imperial ideal, muscular Christianity, which was given its impetus by Dr Arnold and his co-educators of the public schools, and given its name by Disraeli. They believed that they were personally performing God's will, like prefects acting for the headmaster, as they disciplined sluggish villagers, or punctured the self-esteem of headmen: Herbert Edwardes, aged 30, felt inspired to translate the feeling into a comprehensive new legal code for the ribesmen of the Bannu valley—he wrote it in Persian, and in eight-

---

[1] I pass on the anecdote for what it is worth, not believing a word of it, but the Koh-i-Noor may still be seen at the Tower, set in the crown made for the coronation of Queen Elizabeth, consort of George VI, in 1937. It weighed 186 carats when Shah Shuja owned it, but was recut in London to a weight of 106 carats.

een clauses it dealt conclusively with most varieties of human dispute, infanticide to land claims.

In temperament the Punjab men widely varied. At one end of the emotional scale let us consider John Nicholson, who was to become a fable in his lifetime. Even more strikingly than John Lawrence, Nicholson was a modernist. He established his ascendancy over people, whether Indian or European, by the blaze of a fervour that seemed the very latest thing. He was only 35 when he died, as the youngest general in the British service, yet his epitaphs were those of a great national figure. 'I have never seen anyone like him,' recalled Field-Marshal Lord Roberts in *Forty-One Years in India*, 'he was the beau-ideal of a soldier and a gentleman.' 'I never saw another like him,' said Herbert Edwardes, 'and never expect to do so.' 'The idol of all soldiers', thought Field-Marshal Lord Gough. 'His name cowed whole provinces', said Lord Dalhousie the Governor-General. 'The memory of his deeds,' said John Lawrence, 'will never perish so long as British rule endures.' He was compared on his death-bed to 'a noble oak riven by a thunderbolt', and a contemporary Indian is supposed to have said of him that 'you could hear the ring of his horse's hoofs from Attock to the Khyber'.

All this in his thirties, at a time when the British services, military or civilian, were not short of striking characters. Nicholson was yet another Anglo-Irishman. His father, a lapsed Quaker who practised as a physician in Dublin, died when he was a child, and he was brought up by his mother, who apparently remembered him with glazed awe. At three, she said, she observed him laying about him with a knotted handkerchief at some invisible enemy—'trying to get a blow at the Devil', the infant explained, 'for he wants me to be bad'. This unnerving piety guided him through life, and lost him many friends: for he was given to tracts and sanctimonious aphorisms, and one of his earliest achievements was to reform the moral tone of the English community in Kashmir, where scandalous things went on beside the lakes—his successors there, we are told, 'found the moral atmosphere much purified'.

But he was a fighter. 'You may rely on this, my Lord,' Dalhousie was told one day, 'that if ever there is a desperate deed to be done in India, John Nicholson is the man to do it.' Part of his fascination was purely physical. He was a big man, 6' 2", heavily built, with large dark-grey eyes, a full mouth, and an expression of contemplative assurance. People thought he looked like a bigger Disraeli, and there was something Jewish to the style of his face. In other ways he seems to us the very model of the conventional Victorian hero—manly, as the word was, but sensitive, noble, firm: 'grand and simple', Roberts called him. Even now, when tastes have changed and Victorian preferences often seem sickly or even comic, one can see between the lines of the lithographs how compelling his presence must have been. He looks utterly *sure*. You might not confide in him your innermost secret, especially if you were planning a holiday in Kashmir, but you would certainly trust him with your life.[1]

Like so many of his contemporaries, Nicholson first saw action in the Afghan War; he spent some months as a prisoner of the Afghans, and on his way back to India after his release discovered the body of his own younger brother, Alexander, naked and mutilated in the Khyber. He made a name for himself in the Sikh wars, and so came as one of the Lawrences' protégés to the Punjab. There, among the fierce untameable Sikhs, he established so absolute an ascendancy in his own district that people actually deified him. He had first acquired a myth of sanctity after the battle of Gujerat in 1849, when entirely on his own responsibility he had released all the Sikh prisoners, telling them to go home quietly. This mercy in victory so impressed them that they believed him to be more than human (and certainly it was not how they would have behaved themselves). A brotherhood calling itself the Nikkulseynites declared him to be a reincarnation of Brahma, and fakirs dedicated themselves to his honour, and had themselves flogged in reverent penance. When he died two holy men killed themselves, and the cult of the Nikkulseynites long survived him, and was intermittently re-discovered by historians and anthropologists until the end of the century.

Yet he treated Indians tyrannically, submitting his conduct to no arbitration but his own—or God's, which was the same thing in

[1] I would, anyway, but not perhaps Mr Michael Edwardes, who described Nicholson in his book *Bound to Exile* (1969) as 'a violent, manic figure, a homosexual bully, an extreme egotist who was pleased to affect a laconic indifference to danger'.

practice. In Bannu, when a potentate spat contemptuously at his feet, Nicholson made him lick up the spittle, and then had him kicked out of the camp. Elsewhere he had the beard shaved off an imam who ventured to scowl at him. He flogged miscreants without compunction, and publicly displayed the corpses of convicted criminals. 'There is not a man in the hills,' one Punjabi chief is alleged to have testified, 'who does not shiver in his pyjamas when he hears Nicholson's name mentioned.'

Still, an essential quality of the Victorian hero was tenderness, a feminine sensibility to set off the courage and command, and this too Nicholson assiduously displayed. Though he believed in rough and instant justice, was a terrible tiger-hunter and a famous guerilla leader, still he possessed a sentimental streak, and indulged himself frequently in protracted misunderstandings and reconciliations. He was a hero-worshipper, like so many of his time, and though he was an incoherent writer and an almost inaudible speaker, his friendships were urgent. Later analysts would say they were unconsciously homosexual, but they doubtless sprang from just the same earnestness and desire for fulfilment that made him so dedicated a man of action.

We shall see later how he died: for another extreme of temperament let us turn from him to one of his closest friends in the Punjab. William Hodson was the most dashing and ruthless of all the Punjabi men, and his name was to enter the vocabulary of arms. In spirit a survivor from the old days of the East India freebooters, Hodson was a soldier through and through, but unlike most of his colleagues, he was bred to the humanities. He was the son of a canon of Lichfield, was at Rugby under Arnold, took a degree at Cambridge and was a man of wide reading. He loved Shakespeare, and this was natural, for he was Hotspur brought to life. He enjoyed war for war's sake, fought it with superb panache, and was one of the greatest British leaders of irregular troops. He was a blue-eyed, blond English gentleman, and like many another, he was flawed—as though the type were too perfect, the ensemble too balanced to be true. He was the sort of man who is commonly called fearless, a quality that so often masks some inner atrophy, and in his unquenchable hunger for physical conflict one senses an uncertainty of spirit. We are told that in battle, heedlessly slashing with his sabre or galloping pell-mell towards the enemy lines, his face was habitually wreathed in smiles: in a sword-fight he laughed out loud, and sometimes encouraged his opponent like a fencing-master—'Come along now, make me sweat for it! You call yourself a swordsman? Try again, try again!'

Hodson had, so his contemporary J. W. Kaye said, 'the fierce courage of the tiger unsubdued by any feelings of human compassion'. He had a taste for subterfuge, too, and despite his canonical background and improving friendships, was not guided by any very evident code of morals. He was a born *condottiere*, or perhaps a secret policeman, and among the wild irregular horsemen of his own regiment, Hodson's Horse, we see him abandoned to all the delights of brigandage—fair-haired and bright-eyed among those swarthy mercenaries, swathed himself in the loose gaudy draperies of the Punjabi horseman, scimitar at his side, jack-booted, lean and tense—an Englishman gone feral, and totally acclimatized to the fierce culture of the country. There is to his presence, as there is to all those Englishmen who relinquished themselves so absolutely to India, something strained, even a little pathetic: Hodson was presently to be accused of manipulating the mess accounts (a charge never finally resolved), and the final act of his life, as we shall presently see, was one of theatrical and even paranoiac cruelty.

7

These were terrific people—not all terrifically good, but terrifically forceful, commanding, convincing. They seemed bound to win, and their success was self-generating, until a soldier like Nicholson went into action armoured against all odds, and an administrator like Lawrence could recognize no alternatives. They spanned a changing era in the history of Britain in India, and that time of transition was coming to an end.

With Sind and the Punjab under the flag, the British had almost completed their long conquest of India. In the east their flank was secured by the annexation of the idyllic kingdom of Burma. In the north Dost Mohammed, now a direct neighbour of the British Empire, was proving himself a good friend after all. In the west the armies of the Company, in the last of all their frontier wars, farcically invaded Persia with a show of power which, while it made very little difference to the Persians, and was largely concerned with the alleged sexual indiscretions of the British Minister in Teheran, did consolidate British supremacy in the Persian Gulf. Within India a new political theory, the 'doctrine of lapse', empowered the Raj to acquire Indian States whose rulers died without an heir, and very soon placed under British rule a number of ancient principalities never previously heard of. Finally Lord Dalhousie, in a parting coup at the end of his Governor-Generalship, forcibly annexed the great central State of Oudh—for as Dalhousie reasoned, the 'British Government would be guilty in the sight of God and men if it were any longer to aid in sustaining by its countenance an administration fraught with suffering to millions'.

So the pattern of sovereignty was established once and for all. Half India was still ostensibly under the control of its own princes, hundreds of them, ranging from millionaire rajahs to petty village chieftains: but none of them was really competent to act without the approval of the Raj, and the British were the true rulers of the entire sub-continent, Khyber to Irrawaddy. Another era was ending. Soon personal imperialism of the Punjabi kind would be no more than a legend, or a smoking-room hazard, and the Napiers and the Hodsons, the prophets and the *condottieri* would give way to more ordinary successors. But though in one sense they were survivors, in another they were precursors. If they had one quality in common, it was conviction—whatever their motives, they had no doubts: and before long the British Empire itself would act not merely by haphazard instinct, by that unconscious imperial sentiment which Gladstone had recognized as innate to the nation, but by a growing conviction of the right to rule.

PART TWO

The Growing Conviction
1850–1870

CHAPTER TEN

Grooves of Change

LONG before imperialism became a national cause, a popular enthusiasm or even an electoral issue, it occurred to some Britons that they might be a kind of master race. This was not because of their dominions across the world, nor because they believed in any biological superiority, nor that they were yet persuaded of a divine injunction to be great, but because they were so patently the titans of technology. England was the workshop and the laboratory of the world: the British began to feel, as they gazed upon their blast furnaces and rushing railways, their steamships and their cast-iron bridges, their presses and mills and mechanical looms and iron ploughs, that they possessed in themselves some Promethean fire. They began to think that with technology they could achieve anything, even spiritual regeneration. 'Forward, forward,' cried Lord Tennyson, who thought railway trains ran in slots—'Let the great world spin for ever down the ringing grooves of change!'

Through the shadow of the globe we sweep into the younger day;
Better fifty years of Europe than a cycle of Cathay.

Constable had represented the English genius in terms of hay wains and cathedral spires: Turner now interpreted it apocalyptically in thrilling visions of steam, speed and power. As the railways, the couriers of all this excitement, spread with astonishing rapidity across England, a buoyant sense of optimism went with them: the worst miseries of industrialization were apparently over, the threat of social revolution seemed to have passed, British skill and science was ready to usher mankind into a golden age. *Dulce et decorum est,* said the monument in St James's Church, Sydney, commemorating John

Gilbert, an ornithologist speared to death by aboriginals in 1845, *pro scientia mori.*[1]

This exalted enthusiasm was particularly marked at the very head of the Empire. Prince Albert, Queen Victoria's handsome consort from Saxe-Coburg, fervently believed that this was the age of redemption. Nature was about to be conquered: the first barriers of evil were down. With his eager interest in everything modern, useful or mechanical, Albert was himself a very image of technical enlightenment, while his wife the Queen, in the full flush of a happy marriage, was imperially explicit about the situation. 'We are capable,' she wrote in her diary on April 29, 1851, 'of doing anything.'

2

For in that year the British deliberately symbolized this sense of hope and power in the Great Exhibition, the first of the modern international fairs, which was honestly designed to honour the achievements of all nations, but was to be remembered chiefly as a magnificent celebration of Victoria's Britain. Nothing could better represent the British instinct of easy, almost airy possession, the sensation that Britannia could now control the elements themselves, than the palace which Joseph Paxton built for the occasion in Hyde Park. For a few months this building, more truly than the Houses of Parliament or even Westminster Abbey, was the focus of British pride: wherever they were in the Empire, in places like Burma where no train had yet been seen, or in Australia where they had yet to experience a telegraph wire, Britons read of the Crystal Palace with self-congratulatory wonder. It really was, as the Queen wrote, 'one of the wonders of the world, which we English may indeed be proud of'.

Punch called it the Crystal Palace, and there had never been a structure like it before. It was the allegorical marriage of art, technique and something very like faith—something more than sense could scan, thought *The Times*. Paxton was not an engineer, still less an architect: he was a former head gardener to the Duke of

[1] 'It is sweet and proper to die for science', an up-dating of Horace's tag about dying for one's country.

Devonshire, and he based his exhibition building upon the lily house he had built at Chatsworth to house *Victoria Regia*, a gigantic species of water-lily recently introduced from an otherwise little-appreciated corner of the Empire, British Guiana.

The Crystal Palace was made entirely of glass and iron, except for the wooden vaulted roof of the central crossing—an afterthought, added to the design to save chopping down three great Hyde Park elms. It was all light and right angles. A few people, among them the Astronomer Royal, said it would fall down when the wind blew, or that its iron would expand disastrously in the heat, and a well-known opponent of the whole exhibition, Colonel Sibthorp, MP for Lincoln, declared it to be the dearest wish of his heart that it *would* fall down: but this was a confident age, the Building Committee of the exhibition bravely accepted its design, and in seven months 2,200 English and Irish workmen erected it.

> *As though 'twere by a wizard's rod* (wrote Thackeray)
> *A blazing arch of lucid glass*
> *Leaps like a fountain from the grass*
>   *To meet the sun!*

There it stood against the glorious green of a London summer, opened with fanfares and parade by Queen Victoria and her enlightened prince ('the *greatest* day in our history, the *most beautiful* and *imposing* and *touching* spectacle ever seen'). Its nineteen acres of interior space were decorated by the exuberant Welshman Owen Jones, who thought that primary colours were a mark of a great civilization, but who relieved early apprehensions, we are told, by toning down his original effects. The décor was stunning nevertheless, and suggested to *The Times* reporter the day of the Last Judgement, not perhaps what Mr Jones intended. Three times as long as St Paul's Cathedral, the Crystal Palace consisted basically of a single hall, 1,800 feet long, with an open vista from one end to the other. There were parallel halls, and balconies, and a wide cross-hall, and a high splashing fountain in the very middle of it all; and everywhere in this vast glassy space, bright with reds, yellows and light blues, were statues, pavilions, allegorical tableaux, show cases, chandeliers, wrought iron gates, vast suspended clocks—bays for all the thirty-four participating nations, a Mediaeval Court, a Hall of the Zollverein—steam engines actually working, model bridges, elaborate claret jugs, meritorious toast racks, tasteful asparagus tongs, toilette glasses decorated with squirrels or sea-nymphs, papier mâché trays worked in gold and pearls in the German Gothic style, and Daniel Gooch's glorious broad-gauge locomotive *Lord of the Isles*, all green and polished brass, brand-new from the Swindon railway works.

Ceaselessly through this astonishing museum strolled the visitors, 6,063,986 in less than five months: proud Cockneys with their streamers and balloons; foreigners in queer cloaks, turbans and tarbooshes ('their bearded visages,' said *The Times* mischievously, 'conjuring up all the horrors of Free Trade'); Thomas Love Peacock several days running; a Chinese sea-captain who appeared at the opening ceremony and was assumed to be the representative of the Chinese Emperor, quietly submitting to every honour; Charles Dickens, who went twice, and thought it all too much for him; the Queen herself, who went *many* times, and thought it quite wonderful, and felt *proud* and *happy* there. The whole interior scene was one of bright and complex vivacity, and adding a green complication to the whole, visible from almost every corner of the building, were the delicate silhouettes of the indoor elms.

From outside the scene was calmer, and grander. The Crystal Palace was built parallel with Kensington Gore, on the south side of Hyde Park, between Queen's Drive and Rotten Row. Though it was large, its proportions were so elegant, and it was so long for its height, that it looked like a great summer-house in the park. On any fine day little groups of sight-seers sat merrily clumped about the green, skirts and picnic baskets spread around them, and when the Queen was there one morning she met all the parishioners of three Kent and Surrey parishes walking two by two through the grounds, 'the men in smock frocks, with their wives looking so nice'. Behind them the building lay resplendent. The glass glittered. The flags flew. From chimneys here and there steam escaped in small white plumes, with a smudge of smoke from the detached boiler-house. To many the Crystal Palace looked like a contemporary cathedral, and the exhibition organizers, half-recognizing the sanctity of steam and engine-oil, pulleys and machine-tools, defined it in ecclesiastical terms—the great hall was called its nave, the cross-hall its transept.

'It is a noble object,' as Sir Robert Peel had observed, 'to test by actual experiment to which extent the ingenuity and skill of the nations of the earth has corresponded to the intentions of their Creator', but once again the Queen herself put it more spaciously: 'The progress of the human race resulting from the labour of all men ought to be the final object of the exertion of each individual. In promoting this end we are carrying out the will of the Great and Blessed God. This latter motto is Albert's own.'

3

The exhibits of the Great Exhibition included such unmistakably imperial items as a Bushman's blanket from Cape Town, a gold ring inscribed with the emblems of the Ionian Septinsular Union, hats made of cabbage-tree leaves by Australian convicts, a dress such as worn by the women soldiers of the King of Dahomey, a preserved pig from Dublin and the Koh-i-Noor.

This was proper, for already the possession of the Empire effectively contributed to the material progress of the British. 'Rome,' said the prospectus of the Zoological Society of London, founded by Sir Stamford Raffles the imperialist and Sir Humphry Davy the chemist, 'at the period of her greatest splendour, brought savage monsters from every quarter of the world then known . . . it will become Britain to offer another, and a very different series of exhibitions to the population of her metropolis; namely, animals brought from every part of the globe to be applied either to some useful purpose, or as objects of some scientific research'. And savage monsters were the least of it. Almost every branch of science or industry benefited, if only indirectly, from the imperial experience.

British textile manufacturers, for instance, learnt all they could from the techniques of Indian dyeing—and so mastered them that in a very short time they had virtually destroyed the Indian cotton industry. British iron-masters became, thanks largely to imperial needs, early specialists in pre-fabrication: as early as 1815 an iron bridge by John Rennie, the builder of Waterloo Bridge in London, was shipped out to Lucknow ready-made, by order of the King of Oudh.[1] British marine cartographers were preeminent because of imperial demands, the survey ships of the Royal Navy operating virtually without rivals in every ocean. British anthropologists were able to investigate the cranium sizes of Australian aborigines, or the folk-lore of the Naga hill tribes, as a matter of imperial right. British geographers had access to an unprecedented flow of material from explorers and administrators in distant fields. From every climate the geologists and zoologists of Britain received specimens of plants, crops, rocks and unsuspected mammals, sent home to London, as often as not, by the hosts of enthusiastic amateurs who stalked the outback, the veldt or the Himalayan foothills with their guns, bottles and sample cases.

And conversely, science and industry had their profound impact upon the Empire itself—upon the very idea of empire, indeed, for it was now in mid-century that the advance of technique seemed to give a new logic to overseas dominion. Suddenly the world seemed smaller, more manageable, and the notion of a political unity scattered across all the seas, and through all the continents, seemed to make new sense. Fourteen years earlier the visionary engineer Isambard Kingdom Brunel had dramatically foreshadowed this conception. In the year of the Queen's accession he had launched his paddle-steamer *Great Western* specifically as a floating extension of his railway from London to Bristol, destined to carry the island energies out of the island altogether, across the Atlantic to the new worlds on the other side. Now, in the 1850s, steam and iron could carry the imperial momentum clear across the world.

4

From the first British overseas settlement until Victoria's day, nothing had greatly changed in the way people travelled about the Empire (except perhaps in Newfoundland, where the construction of roads had done away with Newfoundland dogs as a means of trac-

---

[1] It still stands, among the most important Rennie structures extant, and was to come in useful during the Indian Mutiny of 1857.

tion). In 1837 it still took three days to travel from London to the very nearest of the overseas territories, Ireland—by Royal Mail coach to Holyhead, by packet boat to Kingstown. It took at least a month to get to Halifax, six months to Bombay, eight months to Sydney. Within India the Grand Trunk Road carried just the same traffic as it did when the Moghuls built it, and travellers from Calcutta to Peshawar went by barge to Benares, a month's journey, by horse or carriage to Meerut, and finally by palanquin to Peshawar, travelling at night preceded by torch-bearers with torches of flaming rags. Within Canada, as we have seen, people travelled only by canoe, sledge and snowshoe. Within South Africa people travelled, like the Voortrekkers, in wagons drawn sometimes by teams of a dozen oxen. Within Australia hardly anybody travelled at all.

Earlier generations of imperial soldiers and administrators had grown accustomed to immense journeys as important phases in a man's life, and sometimes indeed the journey lasted longer than its purpose: Ensign Garnet Wolseley took eight months to reach the second Burmese war, was wounded on his second day in action, and was immediately sent home again. Lasting friendships and enmities were made in the course of the imperial journeys, and prudent men carefully prepared for them. Lord Saltoun, sailing to his command in the China War of 1839, took care to enlist a staff officer who played the cello, Captain Hope Grant of the 9th Lancers, to accompany his own violin on the 164-day voyage to the Yangtze;[1] we read often of officers teaching themselves languages *en voyage*, working out the entire strategy of a forthcoming war, or undertaking some fundamental reform of morals—'you should endeavour to improve your manners on the passage,' John Nicholson told his young brother Alexander, whom he was so soon to find castrated in the Khyber, 'as without good manners you can never advance yourself'. Cadets who embarked as timid youths at Chatham or Portsmouth emerged at the other end, after several months cooped up with their bored and frustrated soldiers, experienced leaders of men.

[1] Grant took a piano, too. He had learnt to play the cello at school in Switzerland, and published some compositions for the instrument. When, some years later, he was posted to Simla, it took ninety-three servants to carry his equipment, military and musical, into the hills.

Steam was to change all this with dramatic suddenness, and radically altered the relationship between Britain and her Empire. Macaulay, who returned from Calcutta just before the first steamships sailed on the India run, instantly recognized their ideological power—the truncation of distance, he thought, was one of the greatest of civilizing forces. By 1840 the Cunard steamer *Unicorn* was sailing to Halifax in sixteen days from Liverpool, by 1843 Miss Eden was receiving her instalments of *Pickwick* in six weeks from London, by 1850 passengers were travelling from London to Holyhead in a day and a night. Now men were able to take home leave several times in their imperial careers, or go home for medical treatment or convalescence. Wives and families went out to the imperial possessions, totally altering the flavour of eastern empire. Administrators or commanders were transferred easily from one colony to another, and the writing of dispatches became a rather less entertaining process, when one could expect a tart response from the Secretary of State within a matter of weeks. In Canada the first paddle-steamers penetrated the rivers of the west, often finding it so difficult to cross their uncharted sandbars that they had to be jerked over by winches mounted on spars—'grass-hopping', the river-men called it. In India a pressure group called the New Bengal Steamer Fund pressed for better steamship services with a poignant list of advantages: 'The shortening by one half the lengthened and heart-rending distance which separates the Husband, the Wife, the Parent and the Child, thus maintaining in continually renewed vigour the best affections of the Heart, in affording the means for a more rapid inter-change of commercial communications by which the interests of both countries cannot but be greatly promoted, and last things though not least in opening wide the door for the introduction of European Science, Morality and Religion into the heart of India'.

And most of all the railways, those supremely British artifacts, gave to the Empire a new and elevating sense of purpose. Imperial activists well realized their meaning. As early as the 1830s Lord Durham had foreseen that the railway would eventually be the instrument of Canadian unity, and Charles Trevelyan had prophecied that in India it would 'stimulate the whole machinery of society'. By the 1850s Lord Dalhousie, Governor-General of India, envisaged a continent transformed by the railways—politically, by a new fusion of peoples and religions, economically by easy access from the interior to the ports, strategically by a new ability to rush armies from province to province, frontier to frontier. Victoria's empire, as it evolved in the second half of the century, was essentially an empire of steam: and as the frontier roads were to the Romans, so the extending tracks of the steam railways were to the imperial British.

Many of the Empire's grandest monuments were railway works. There was Robert Stephenson's tubular Victoria Bridge across the St Lawrence at Montreal, when completed in 1859 one of the great bridges of the world: 24 iron tubes, each 16 feet wide by 20 feet high, linked together to make a passage $1\frac{3}{4}$ miles long, and supported by 24 piers across the great river—'one of the chief lions of Montreal', as Baedeker quaintly described it. There were the immense echoing railway termini which, in every great city of the British Empire, were soon to stand beside the Anglican Cathedrals as outward signs of an inner faith, sometimes like eastern fortresses, sometimes like Gothic palaces, frequently more imposing than the offices of Government and often magnificently embellished with brasswork, symbolic emblems and polished mahogany. There were railways whose very tracks looked like bonds of Empire—the tremendous Canadian Pacific, snaking with trestle bridge and dramatic tunnel from ocean to ocean, or Stephenson's line across the Suez desert, connecting the steamboats of Red Sea and Mediterranean, or the mountain lines which wound their laborious way, with chuffs and clankings echoing down the wooded valleys, into the frontier hills of the Himalaya. Or, later in the century, there was the grotesque and gigantic Lansdowne Bridge over the Indus River in Sind—which, with its towering complex cantilevers, its dense mesh of pillars, struts and guys, its battlemented gatehouses and its rumbling double track for trains and road traffic, was to remain among the most unforgettable sights of the Raj.[1]

[1] Most of the great lines and stations remain as busy as ever, though often shabbier. The Montreal Bridge was replaced in 1898, only its piers surviving; the Lansdowne Bridge still stands, though the North Western Railway now crosses the river by a new steel arch bridge a few hundred feet downstream.

All over the Empire, in the 1850s, the railway-builders were at work. The first Indian line, from Bombay to Thana, was laid in the year of the Great Exhibition. The line from Dublin to Cork had just been completed. New lines were under way in Canada, Australia and South Africa, and before long the engineers would be laying rails in imperial territories as improbable as Bermuda (20 miles long from tip to tip) or Malta (area 94 square miles). The spectacle of the steam locomotive puffing brass-bound and aglow across steppe, prairie or scorched veld was to remain one of the perennial inspirations of the imperial mission, and was readily adopted by the Church of England too as a figure of salvationary progress:

> *The line to heaven by Christ was made*
> *With heavenly truth the Rails are laid*
> *From Earth to Heaven the Line extends*
> *To Life Eternal where it ends.*
>
> *God's Word is the first Engineer*
> *It points the way to Heaven so clear,*
> *Through tunnels dark and dreary here*
> *It does the way to Glory steer.*[1]

5

The Empire's liveliest entrepreneur of progress was Lieutenant Thomas Waghorn of the Overland Route. Waghorn was an impecunious young naval officer who early realized, like Napoleon, that the best way from Europe to India was not *via* Persia or Afghanistan, but *via* Egypt. He seized upon the advent of steam to prove the point, and became a kind of familiar of the route to India. Convinced that a practicable overland link could be made across the Isthmus of Suez, to connect steamers in the Mediterranean with steamers in the Red Sea, he argued the case so incessantly, travelled so impetuously from London to Egypt, Egypt to India, to Gibraltar and Malta, Jeddah and Alexandria, Aden and Bombay, that everybody remotely

---

[1] Passengers wishing to study this prospectus more closely may do so on a tombstone in the south porch of Ely Cathedral—'*if you'll repent and turn from sin, The Train will stop and take you in*'.

concerned with the India traffic knew of him. In London they thought him half-cracked. In Egypt Ferdinand de Lesseps, the great French engineer, recognized a fellow-spirit in him, and later erected a monument to the man who 'alone, without any help, by a long series of labours and heroic efforts, demonstrated and determined . . . the communication between the East and the West'.

Waghorn had been placed on the Navy's unemployed list at the end of the French wars, had sailed as a merchant officer on the Indian routes, and later became a river pilot on the Hooghly. Accustomed there to piloting sailing ships from England that had taken anything up to a year on the route around the Cape, he threw up his job, like a convert to some sacred cause, to spend all his life agitating for a steamer route *via* Egypt. Steamers already sailed to Alexandria from London, but the price of coal in the Red Sea was prohibitive, the journey across the Isthmus of Suez was thought to be dangerous, and anyway ships had always gone the other way. Waghorn argued, he pleaded, he wrote memorials, he buttonholed great men, he even did a demonstration journey for the Government—an experiment incompletely successful, for he was reduced to sailing from Suez to Jeddah in an open boat without a compass and with a crew of mutinous Arabs. Repeatedly rebuffed by authority, Waghorn went on to establish his own unofficial service, in direct competition with the companies on the Cape route. He acted as his own manager, his own constructional engineer, commissariat officer and often courier, and so he brought into being Waghorn's Overland Route—'not only without official recommendation', as he wrote himself, 'but with a sort of stigma on my sanity'.

It was a *tour de force* of free enterprise. Like so many other worthies of Empire, Waghorn stood 6' 2" in his socks, and had a frank, appealing face, tinged with an understandable tristesse. He may not have been able to impress Authority in Britain, but he was very persuasive elsewhere, and he presently won over to his cause the formidable Mohammed Ali, Viceroy of Egypt under the firman of the Sultan of Turkey. A picture by David Roberts shows him modestly sitting, between the British Consul and the artist, on a divan in the Viceroy's palace at Alexandria, while the Pasha smokes a hookah and listens to his plans, a secretary sits cross-legged on the floor taking notes, and in the harbour behind a solitary small steamer, almost lost among the heavy riggings and huge drooping ensigns of the three-masters, subtly suggests developments to come. By 1839 Waghorn had won over the East India Company, too, and had become their deputy agent in Egypt, and finally, when the British Government extended its own mail service from Falmouth to Alexandria, Waghorn became the official enterpreneur of express mails between England and Egypt—'care of Mr Waghorn', said the superscription on letters sent *via* the Suez route.

To achieve all this he organized an elaborate transit service between Alexandria and Suez. In the earlier years of the Overland Route passengers travelled by horse-drawn barge down a canal, dug by Mohammed Ali's forced labour, from Alexandria to the Nile. There they transferred ten at a time to a tiny steamboat, the *Jack o'Lantern*, which paddled spasmodically upriver to Cairo, sometimes breaking down, frequently running aground, and infested with cockroaches, rats, flies and fleas. At Cairo the travellers waited at Shepheard's Hotel, recently founded to cater for the Overland Route, until a semaphore signal relayed across the desert announced the arrival of the India steamer at Suez: they were then jolted and sweated at breakneck speed in specially designed closed vans to the Red Sea, stopping on the way at a series of fly-blown but tolerably well-equipped rest houses. It was not a pleasant journey, but it was worth while, for it cut the journey to India by several weeks. By 1847, when it had passed out of Waghorn's hands into the control of the Peninsular and Oriental Steamship Company, some 3,000 people crossed the Isthmus annually, and the organization maintained 4 canal steamers, 46 desert carriages, 440 horses and 3,500 camels (many of them employed in carrying coal from the Mediterranean, where it was relatively cheap, to the Red Sea, where it was still ruinously expensive).

Waghorn's official reward was a small pension and a grant of £1,500 which went instantly to his creditors. He died in 1850, protesting to the end, but his vision was its own fulfilment: he had seen what technique could do for empire. By the 1840s the fortnightly group of British travellers had become a regular part of the Cairo scene, with their little pale babies, their ayahs, their attendant

dragomans and their turbanned retainers. 'O my country,' cried
Thackeray in admiration, having seen Waghorn in action during
an eastern journey of his own, 'O Waghorn! *Hae tibi erunt artes*.[1]
When I go to the Pyramids I will sacrifice in your name, and pour
out libations of bitter ale and Harvey Sauce in your honour.'[2]

6

There was a marked difference in taste between the engineering
exhibits at the Crystal Palace and the lapis-lazuli trays, the pearl-
studded vases and the imitation Gothic sofas. The trains, bridges
and ships of the day, like the Crystal Palace itself, were nobly
clean of line—decorated often with gilding, figureheads or flourish,
but still functional in a convinced and stylish way. In the overseas
empire, too, now presenting in some of its aspects a blurred mirror-
image of Britain herself, new means of communication were the
most stylish emblems of the imperial purpose.

Let us look, for example, at an imperial road. Along the southern
coast of Africa, between Cape Town and Port Elizabeth, the British
had by now thickly settled in the rocky coastal plain since called the
Garden Route, east and west of Knysna. This was a delectable
country, its plains lying complacently between a glorious surf-
washed shore and the mountain barrier of the Little Karroo. It was
frequented by no ferocious tribes or dogmatic Boers, plagued by no
extremes of heat, cold, drought or flood, and was watered by rivers
which, rushing out of the iron-flecked uplands, streamed towards
the sea the colour of white wine. But until the middle of the century
it was exceedingly difficult to reach by land. Wagons simply pushed
a way through thick and tangled foliage, or were heaved agonizingly
over wild rocky passes, just as they had been pushed and heaved

---

[1] 'Let these be thine arts', from Virgil's invocation to Rome to 'bear
dominion over the nations and impose the law of peace.'

[2] The scheduled steamship services from England to India, begun thanks
largely to Waghorn in 1842, ended in 1970, when the P and O liner *Chusan*
(24,000 tons) made the last run to Bombay—

> *But still the wild wind wakes off Gardafui,*
> *And hearts turn eastward with the P and O.*

since the Europeans had first passed that way at the end of the previous century.

In 1849 they opened a new road to circumvent the worst of these hazards, naming it after John Montagu, the Colonial Secretary in Cape Town. This was a most accomplished artifact of empire. It was a toll road, and dues were paid at a polygonal toll-house of beautifully dressed granite, standing on the edge of an uninhabited escarpment, but fit for a nobleman's lodge. The road wound carefully through the foothills by exquisitely calculated gradients, its bends never abrupt, its camber always gentle. Fine stone walls protected its curves, its stone culverts were meticulously mortared, and now and then it crossed, by way of a strong unobtrusive bridge, one of those rushing torrents of hock. Through that untamed landscape it ran like a coiling thread of rational judgement: and at the far end of the escarpment, easing itself past the second toll-house into a direct conclusion, it deposited the imperial traveller in the oak-lined village of George, where English inns awaited him with chops and ale, and Archdeacon Welby's rectory might have been transported, roses, chintz and all, from some well-heeled parish of the shires.[1]

Or take the Rideau Canal at Ottawa. This was an ambitious imperial venture of the 1830s, built at the expense of the imperial Government to provide a new water-route to the West, by-passing the rapids of the St Lawrence River. It was a demanding project. Between Kingston and Ottawa there stood a ridge of high ground, and it was necessary to build thirty-three locks to take vessels up it, and another fourteen to take them down to Lake Ontario on the other side. The work was supervised by a colonel of the Royal Engineers, the principal distributors of technique throughout the Empire (though only their officers were called Engineers, the other ranks being Sappers and Miners still). It took five years to build, and for the rest of the century was to take a steady flow of steamboats and barges between the Great Lakes and the St Lawrence.

[1] Though it has been supplanted by a bigger road, one may still drive the length of the Montagu Pass, from Oudtshoorn to George, and the shade of those old culverts provides some of the pleasantest picnic sites in Africa. George itself was described by Trollope as 'the prettiest village in the world', and it is still very agreeable.

Nine of its locks were built adjacent to one another in a ladder immediately above the Ottawa River—in the very centre of the new capital, and beside the wooded bluff upon which they would present-ly erect the Parliament building of Canada. This was a splendid sight—a grand solution to an engineering problem, and a handsome object in itself. The river widened there into a basin, and upon it, between its thickly wooded banks, steamboats busily chugged and huge rafts of tree trunks, loosely lashed together, came floating down from the forest country to the west. There were mills on the south-ern shore, and all around them huge masses of timber untidily floated, prodded here and there by men with poles, or nudged about by boats. It was a very Canadian scene, suggestive of wild black woods not so far away, trappers and *voyageurs* and Indian para-mours: but in regimental contrast the locks of the canal marched uniformly up the hill above the river. They looked at once disci-plined and urbane, even perhaps a little snobbish, as they carried their little steamboats stage by stage away from that brash colonial tumble at the bottom. The Rideau Canal was specifically an imperial project, conceived it is said by the Duke of Wellington himself, intended largely for imperial military traffic: and its address was distinctly imperial too, as though it would never allow a steamboat in its charge to go native.[1]

Here is another memorable product of the imperial technology. We stand upon the Grand Trunk Road in India, the principal strategic highway of the sub-continent, which runs direct from Calcutta, through Delhi and Lahore, to Peshawar in the Punjab; and along its dusty tree-lined length, hovered over by crows, rutted by wagons, supervised by guard towers like a Roman way, we hear above the distant chatter of women at their washing, and the laughter of children playing in the stream, muffled upon the air a noble snorting. The labourers pause upon their hoes. The women suspend their scrubs. The naked children scramble up the bank to the road. The passing ox-wagons hastily swerve aside, and even the spanking tonga of the passing memsahib, trotting down to

---

[1] The Rideau Canal still functions, though only for pleasure craft nowa-days, and the Bytown Museum beside its locks in Ottawa, one of the oldest buildings in the capital, is the original storehouse of the canal-builders.

cantonment in Rawalpindi, apprehensively hesitates. Stand back. Adjust your dust-veils. It is time for the passage of the Government Steam Train, on its way to Attock on the Indus.

With smoke and sparks streaming from its bulbous funnel, here it comes at ten miles an hour along the wide straight road. On the driving platform of its three-wheeled traction engine, surrounded mysteriously by wheels, valves and levers, sit the European engineer and his assistant, one in a topee, one in a soft black cap, with bright kerchiefs around their necks, and expressions of resolute professionalism. There is a cyclopean light on the front of the engine, and its wheels are vast, solid and clad in rubber. Majestically clanking and puffing it approaches us, and now we see the turbanned Sikh fireman sitting with his piles of logs in the tender, and behind him the long line of the train—two-wheeled carts alternating with high four-wheeled wagons, like English hay-wains, and far at the back, wobbling slightly on its passage and raising a cloud of dust, a closed passenger carriage thickly covered, inside and out, with white robed travellers—standing on the couplings, hanging to the doors, crouched precarious upon the roof.

The great machine passes us. The engineer courteously removes his hat. The fireman grins, bows repeatedly and murmurs inaudible respects. The carts and wagons rumble by. The crowded passengers at the back stare down at us expressionless but superior, as though they have been admitted to some higher existence. With a stately hoot of its steam-whistle the Government Steam Train, unquestionably steering a way to Glory, ponderously but imperially disappears.[1]

7

Botany gave style to the empire, too, and was one of the oldest of the imperial enthusiasms. From the earliest days of British expansion navigators, explorers and settlers had been concerned to collect rare

---

[1] Its creator was R. E. B. Crompton, then an ensign in the Royal Engineers, who went on to become a celebrated electrical engineer and an originator of the tank, while its engine was designed by R. W. Thomson, later to invent the pneumatic tyre.

plants, transfer cuttings, experiment with the smoking of rolled-up leaves or the eating of hitherto unsuspected tubers. Since 1841 Kew Gardens, Queen Charlotte's delicious belvedere beside the Thames outside London, had been a State institution, where all available botanical knowledge was considered, sifted and turned into green delight or sustenance; and by the middle of the century Kew had its derivatives or ancillaries in most of the British possessions—part pleasure-places, part scientific laboratories, with their learned keepers and their catalogues, experimenting, classifying, and sending a copious flow of samples, products or memoranda back to the central clearing-house at home. One important outpost in this chain of research was Jamaica, and a visitor to that island making a tour of its botanical gardens might be deluded into supposing that the British Empire was already a cohesive, centralized organization. Each of the three island gardens, each in a different climatic zone, played its own particular part in research, with its own specialities, its own methods, and its own team of diligent scientific gentlemen.

In the old garden at Bath near the northern coast, the second oldest in the western hemisphere, the mid-Victorian visitor would see a collection of plants chosen for their medical value, and for 'qualities useful of the arts'—jujubes, that is, sago palms, camphor, litchi, tea plants, trees producing dyes, resin, or cabinetwoods. The little dark rectangle of the gardens, all fronds and shadows, was overlooked suitably by a small Anglican church, and contained specimens of the akee plant, first brought to Jamaica in a slave ship and now luxuriant all over the island, and the breadfruit brought from Tahiti by Captain Bligh, now a staple diet of the Jamaicans, and many thriving descendants of a cargo of rare plants captured by Admiral Rodney from a French warship during the wars—mangoes, cinnamon, oriental ebony, pandanus.

On then to Castleton, a far grander institution on the banks of the rushing Wag River, towered over by palms and wooded hills in the centre of the island, and stocked originally with 400 specimens direct from Kew. This was one of the great tropical gardens of the world, a truly Victorian establishment, with no hint of serendipity to its arrangements, but rather an ordered and deliberate magnificence. Here, where the rainfall was 100 inches a year, bananas experimentally thrived, bamboos sprouted by the river, and the visitor could inspect teak trees from the newly acquired regions of Burma, figs and resinous guncardies from India, or mouse palms from British Guiana. Ferns dripped, orchids, climbers and stranglers twined themselves among the wild pines, queer birds croaked, black gardeners padded about with machetes, and in a green clearing among the woods there soared regally above the lily ponds a group of marvellous palms, fit for an imperial greenhouse, or for incarceration within the transept of the Crystal Palace.

And so to Cinchona, Jamaica's high altitude garden, perched at about 5,000 feet on a ridge in the Blue Mountains—high above the heat haze of the coast, accessible only by rough tracks, with a landscape of stubbly hills and deep ravines stretching all around it, and the rich green of its own presence like an allegory in the wild. This, though one of the loveliest places imaginable, was no frivolous retreat either. It was established originally for the cultivation of quinine, an imperial specific.[1] They experimented with Assam tea up there too, and a gardener came out from Kew to plant European vegetables and flowers for the Kingston market, in the hope that one day the entire eastern part of the island might become one huge vegetable garden, revivifying the dying economy of the sugar-cane.

Here one could feel a sense of imperial purpose almost as absolute, if rather less disconcerting, than the furies of those young men in the Punjab. How usefully instructive, to be guided through the Cinchona vegetables by Mr Nock direct from Kew! How truly civilized, to see Mr Fawcett hard at work upon his Flora of Jamaica in his elegant Great House among the buddleias! How gratifying to know, as one looks out through the dark pinewoods to the deep valleys beyond, that one day all this beautiful island, liberated from bondage by British evangelism, will be made green, smiling and content by British science![2]

---

[1] Hence its name. The Countess of Cinchon was a seventeenth century Spanish lady of Peru who was cured of an ailment by an alkaloid medicine derived from the bark of an Andean tree. The tree took her name and was anglicized as quinine.

[2] The economic ambitions of Cinchona were never quite fulfilled, but all three gardens thrive to this day—if not as scientific enterprises, at least as

8

Quinine they badly needed, for if there was one aspect of applied science that seems, in retrospect, inadequate to the imperial needs, it was medicine. Here is Mr J. J. Cole, a surgeon with the British forces during the Sikh wars, on the recently discovered anaesthetic chloroform: 'The practical surgeon views it in the hands of the military medical officer as a highly pernicious agent, which unquestionably it is. . . . In time of war, on the field of battle, on the bloody plain, or in the field hospital, it should not be found. . . . That it renders the poor patient unconscious cannot be doubted. But what is pain? It is one of the most powerful, one of the most salutary *stimulants* known'.

In England the principles of hygiene, as of modern surgery, were slowly being grasped, but the British knew hardly anything about the more exotic diseases of their overseas possessions, and often seemed to live as unhealthily as they possibly could. Since they generally believed fervently in the medicinal qualities of claret, they drank it ferociously—not perhaps quite as lavishly as they had in the heyday of John Company, when three bottles a day was normal for a man, and a bottle an evening quite customary for a healthy woman, but only because self-indulgence of that kind had gone out of fashion. The clothes they wore bore no relation to climatic conditions, but merely copied, a year or two late, the current London or Paris fashions. The water they drank was generally untreated, the food they ate was prepared out of sight by unwashed employees.[1] The average age of those many Britons already buried in the imperial cemeteries was pitiably young: this was partly because so many died in battle, but chiefly because medical science was not yet geared to the progress of empire.

---

public parks. Cinchona is still accessible only by foot, Castleton's splendours now have a decayed allure, and at Bath Lord Rodney's original pandanus is still alive.

[1] Though the Anglo-Indian nickname for the staple of their cuisine, 'Sudden Death', referred not to the consumer but to the chicken, usually killed a few minutes before dinner.

Nobody knew the origins of malaria, yellow fever, typhus, cholera or typhoid—which was common in London itself, and presently killed the Prince Consort. Nobody indeed could distinguish malaria from yellow fever, and they were lumped together under the generic diagnosis Malignant Fever, and variously thought to be contagious, to be induced by inebriation, to emanate from the effluvia of ships' bilges, or to strike indiscriminately out of the noxious tropical air.[1] One well-known imperial hypochondriac, Judge Roger Yelverton of the Bahamas, insisted that malaria in Nassau was caused by the storage of coal for the Imperial Lighthouse Tender, and when an anonymous modernist called this nonsense in the columns of the *Nassau Guardian*, he imprisoned the newspaper's editor for refusing to reveal the writer's name.[2]

The treatments proposed for all these complaints ranged from the lunatic to the merely excruciating. Military surgeons were, like Mr Code, often draconian in their mercies, and the fashionable quacks of Calcutta or the Cape shamelessly exploited their patients' miseries and their own ignorance. Cholera, for instance, which was supposed to come from eating fish and meat at the same time, or from vaporous germ-clouds constantly drifting above the landscape, was often treated by the application of a red-hot ring to the patient's navel, causing, so the doctors convincingly explained, 'a revolution in the intestines'. Malaria was often treated by bleeding—if no surgeon was at hand somebody would open a vein with a pocket-knife—and scurvy sores were soothed with poultices made of soggy sea-biscuits. Panaceas of every kind flooded the market. The explorer James Grant's medicine chest, when he went to Central Africa in the 1860s, contained Brown's blistering tissue, lunar caustic, citric acid, julap, camomel, rhubarb, colocynth, laudanum, Dover's powders, emetic essence of ginger and something called simply Blue Pill. General Gordon used to swear by Werburgh's Tincture, which would 'make a sack of sawdust sweat'. As for seasickness, the basic imperial complaint (after alcoholism, perhaps),

[1] Hence the name *mal aria*, first adopted by Britons on the Grand Tour in Italy.
[2] This preposterous case went to the Privy Council, and became an important precedent in disputes concerning the freedom of the colonial press.

a thousand useless remedies were authoritatively prescribed: arrow-root, pork, drinking sea water, opium, plasters on the stomach, ice-bags on the spine, or the use of the Bessemer Saloon, a cabin suspended amidships and intended to ignore the oscillations of the hull —'there is no reason now,' declared Messrs Lorimer and Co. of London, advertising their infallible Cocaine Lozenges, 'why the most timid should not thoroughly enjoy the tossing of the billows like true Britons'.

One has only to read the memoirs of the Victorian adventurers to realize the horrors of imperial life and travel in those days. The explorer John Speke, in Africa in 1857, suffered from something called Kichyoma-chyoma, 'the little irons', which entailed agonizing inner pains, ghastly deliria, epileptic spasms, making a barking noise and moving the mouth 'in a peculiar chopping motion . . . with lips protruding'. In the same year the thousand men on board the troopship *Transit*, stranded on a bare and blazing coral reef in the Java Sea, kept up their strength on a diet of chopped baboons cooked in a stew of salt pork and beans—each hoping, so a survivor recorded, that somebody else was eating the baboons. Time and again we read of imperial travellers amputating their own limbs, or lying blind or paralysed for weeks at a time. In the cantonment at Kabul in 1841 Lieutenant Colin Mackenzie found his right arm gripped by the teeth of a mad bulldog—'his jaws reeking with blood and foam, his mouth wide open, his tongue swollen and hanging out, and his eyes flashing a sort of lurid fire'. He held the creature at arm's length and throttled it with his left hand.

Plagued with such discomforts themselves, the British had little time to concern themselves with the ailments of their subject races: not for another fifty years would there be any systematic attempt to distribute the discoveries of medical science throughout the imperial peoples. Survival of the rulers was the first necessity, and just how precarious survival could be was shown by the mortality returns which, from time to time, reached the Colonial Office from its distant stations. There was a terrible death-rate in all the tropical dependencies. In the late 1850s, of every thousand soldiers and their wives stationed in Bengal, sixty-four men and forty-four women died in an average year. During twenty months in Hong Kong, the 59th

Regiment buried 180 of its soldiers. As late as 1873, of 130 British soldiers on the Gold Coast, only twenty-two were fit for duty. Many died of tuberculosis, that scourge of the Victorians, many of dysentery, apoplexy, hepatitis or pneumonia. But the most telling statistics were sometimes to be found at the bottom of the list, after the more normal causes of death: *Suicide, Suffered the Penalty of the Law*, or worst of all, *Worn Out &c.*

9

As the century passed, and the flow of the steamships thickened, and the great railways crossed the continents one by one, so the charisma of technique faded rather, and the British saw their command of steam, iron, steel and electricity less as an instrument of redemption than an engine of command. (So did their subject peoples: the Ashanti of West Africa thought the Empire's telegraph wires to be an infallible war fetish, and strung their own cords from tree to tree in emulation.) In the 1850s, however, science was still an abstraction of holy beauty, and the Crystal Palace, though of course it was a tacit declaration of British material strength, stood too in the public mind for the universal benevolence of British aims. Whatever made Britain richer or stronger, like the acquisition of Sind, say, or a monopoly of the Canadian fur trade, made the world a happier and Godlier place:[1] every new steamship, every additional Government Steam Train transported to some newly-amazed corner of the world, or some hitherto unjustly neglected society, demonstrated the benefits of the British example.

> *Uplift a thousand voices full and sweet,*
> *In this wide hall with earth's invention stored,*
> *And praise the invisible universal Lord,*
> *Who lets once more in peace the nations meet,*
> *Where Science, Art and Labour have outpour'd*
> *Their myriad horns of plenty at our feet.*

[1] Palmerston said of Hudson's Bay Company that its functions should be to strip the local quadrupeds of their furs, and keep the local bipeds off their liquor.

So Tennyson wrote in his *Ode Sung at the Opening of the International Exhibition*, and as this sense of divine potential was the inspiration of the exhibition itself, so it was at that moment the temper of Victoria's scientifically-developing Empire. The profits of the great show were used to buy eighty-seven acres of land in South Kensington, and upon this estate there arose a complex of scientific and artistic institutions—the Science Museum, the Victoria and Albert Museum, the Natural History Museum, the Geological Museum, colleges of science, mining engineering, music, art. And when in later years they erected a memorial to Prince Albert, whose solemn enthusiasm so permeated the Great Exhibition of 1851, they portrayed him holding upon his knee, beneath his high sculptured canopy overlooking Kensington Gore, not as it happened a copy of the Holy Scriptures, but its virtual synonym, an Exhibition Catalogue.[1]

[1] Several other relics of the Exhibition survive in 1973. The Crystal Palace itself, transferred in enlarged form to Sydenham in 1852, was burnt to the ground in 1936, an event which, though I had never been within a hundred miles of the building, and had no very clear idea what it was, mysteriously impressed my childish imagination. However the wrought iron gates which divided the north transept of the original structure now divide Kensington Gardens from Hyde Park, to the east of the Albert Memorial, while the Model Dwelling House for Working People erected under the Prince Consort's supervision near Knightsbridge Barracks is still in use as a park superintendent's office in Kennington Park, near the Oval. The Royal Commission for the 1851 Exhibition still exists, and by prudent husbandry of its 1851 surplus has been financing scholarships in the arts and sciences ever since.

CHAPTER ELEVEN

The Epic of the Race

Hence the royal ladies looked through their grilled windows to see

HIGH above the Jumna River at Delhi, towering over the bazaars and alleys of the walled city, there stood the fortress-palace of the Moghul Emperors. Clad in decorations of gold, silver and precious stones, this had once been the most magnificent palace of the East, the envy of rulers from Persia to China, a mile and a half around, walled in red sandstone, sited with all the expert advice of astrologers, magicians and strategists. This was Qila-i-Mubarak, the Fortunate Citadel, Qila-Mualla, the Exalted Fort, approached through the high vaulted arcade of the Chata Chauk, where the royal bands played five times daily in the Royal Drum House, and the ambassadors of the nations prostrated themselves in the Diwan-i-Am before the Shadow of God.

Here the royal ladies looked through their grilled windows to see the Stream of Paradise rippling through its marble chute, here Aurungzeb worshipped in the copper-domed mosque of the Moti Masjid, here in the Golden Tower above the river the Emperor on ceremonial occasions greeted his people far below, and here in the Diwan-i-Khas was the very crucible of the Moghul Empire, white marble ceilinged in silver, with water running through its central conduit, and on its dais the Peacock Throne itself, inlaid with thousands of sapphires, rubies, emeralds and pearls, guarded by jewelled peacocks and a parrot carved from a single emerald. The Red Fort was one of the great masterpieces of mediaeval Muslim art. *If there be a Paradise on earth*, said the famous inscription above its Diwan-i-Khas, *it is here, it is here, it is here.*

2

In 1857 there still lived in this marvellous place the last of the Moghul monarchs, Bahadur Shah Zafar. By now the palace was only a parody of its own splendours. With the crumbled mass of its red sandstone, with its audience chambers stripped of their glories and the overgrown lawns of its Life Bestowing Gardens, it was like a relic from some dimly remembered, half-legendary golden age. Yet Bahadur, a powerless pensioner of the British, was still the titular King of Delhi. The British preferred it so. When they found it legally or tactically convenient, they could refer to him as the embodiment of traditional power, or claim to be acting as his constitutional successors. Their representatives visited him with formal respect, entering his presence barefoot or with socks over their boots, and until the 1850s presenting a ceremonial bag of gold, the *nazar*, in tribute to the Ruler of the Universe. Bahadur, who was very old, accordingly lived in a phantom consequence. He was an eastern monarch of the old kind, frail but dignified. His face was fine-drawn and long-nosed, he was bearded to the waist like a king in a Persian miniature; he wandered about his palace leaning on a long staff.

He was a poet, a scholar, a valetudinarian, and believed himself to possess magic powers.[1] He distributed charms and shadowy privileges. By his authority a royal bulletin was issued each day, reporting events inside the sorry court as might be chronicled the affairs of a Jehangir—or a Victoria. He was surrounded still by swarms of servants, and attended by many wives and unnumbered children, and at the Lahore Gate his personal bodyguard, 200 strong, was quartered under its British commander. To many millions of people, especially Muslims, he was still the true ruler of India: and it was as a ruler that he bore himself still, conscious of his heritage and deeply resentful of the changing world outside. 'A melancholy red-stone notion of life', Emily Eden had called it.

Bahadur lived altogether at the mercy of the British. They paid him a subsidy of £200,000 a year, but they had effectually removed the centre of Indian life from his court to their own capital at Calcutta. They did not even bother to keep European troops in Delhi, so unimportant a backwater had it become, and it was administered as a provincial city like any other. Sometimes they thought Bahadur

---

[1] For instance he thought, wrongly as it proved, that in time of necessity he could turn himself into a house-fly.

should be removed too, to somewhere less historically suggestive, but for the time being they let him stay. They had, after all, made it clear that upon his death the imperial title must lapse, so that in a sense he was already no more than a ghost or a memory, an emperor in the mind.

3

Early on the morning of May 11, 1857, this monarch *soi-disant* was sitting in his private apartments overlooking the river when he heard the noise of a crowd shouting and jostling in the dusty space below, where petitioners habitually appeared to offer their pleas, and jugglers or dancing bears sometimes performed for the royal entertainment. It was Ramadan, the Muslim month of fast, when tempers were always testy, and the combination of heat, hunger, exhaustion and religious zeal was traditionally the begetter of riots.

The old king sent for the commander of his guard, Captain Douglas, who stepped out to a balcony to stop the disturbance. There below him, between the palace and the broad sluggish sweep of the Jumna, were hundreds of Indian soldiers, some on horseback, some on foot, in the grey jackets and shakoes of the Company service, dusty from a long journey, their horses lathered, waving their swords and calling for Bahadur. Douglas shouted to them to move away, for they were disturbing the king, and after a time they went: but an hour or two later the noise began again, fiercer and louder this time, and shots rang out beyond the palace walls. There were angry shouts, a fire crackled somewhere, women screamed, hoofs clattered, and suddenly there burst into the royal precincts a rabble of cavalrymen, firing *feux-de-joie* and shouting exultantly. Behind them a noisy mob of sepoys and ruffians from the bazaar, scarlet and white and dirty grey, poured into the palace. Some ran upstairs to Douglas's quarters, and finding him there with two other Englishmen and two Englishwomen, murdered them all. The others swarmed through the palace, brandishing their swords, singing, or simply lying down exhausted on their palliasses in the Hall of Audience.

The terrified old king retreated farther and farther into the re-

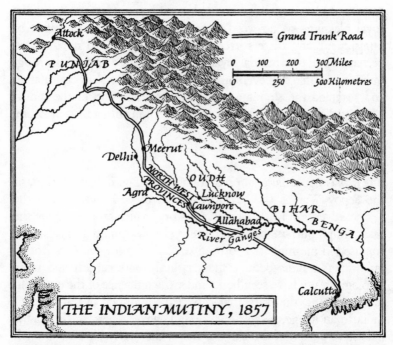

THE INDIAN MUTINY, 1857

cesses of his private quarters, but presently the leaders of the mob found him. Far from harming him, they prostrated themselves at his feet. They were rebelling, they said, not against the Moghul monarchy, but against the rule of the English, and they asked him as Light of the World to assume the revolutionary command. Bahadur did not know what to do. He was surrounded by advisers—Hasan Ansari his spiritual guide, Hakim Ahsanullah his physician, Ghulam Abbas his lawyer, his sons Moghul, Khair Sultan, Abu Bakr. He was not a man for quick decisions. He was old, he said, and infirm. He was no more than a pensioner. While he prevaricated, a messenger was posted to the British Lieutenant-Governor at Agra, forty miles away, in the hope that the Raj might resolve the issue by sending a rescue force: but as the hours passed and nobody came, as the mutineers dossed down in the palace, and their leaders pressed for an answer—as the sounds of looting and burning came from the city, with random musket-fire, and explosions, and hysterical laughter—as the princes whispered in one ear, and Ghulam Abbas in another, and the soldiers stumbled in one by one bareheaded to receive the royal blessing—as no word came from the British of comfort or punishment, and there stirred in the king's poor old mind, elated perhaps by all that martial loyalty, some inherited pride of the Moghuls—some time that evening, after dark, Bahadur Shah capitulated, and assumed the supreme and symbolic leadership of the Indian Mutiny. At midnight his soldiers greeted him with a 21-gun salute.

4

But it was not a national revolution at all. The Indian Mutiny, or the Sepoy War as the Victorians often called it, was one of the decisive events of British imperial history, which set a seal upon the manner and purpose of the Empire: yet it was limited in scale and confused in meaning. It had been smouldering for years, as British intentions in India became more radical, more earnest and more ideological. We have seen how, under the influence of the evangelical movement, the British conceived the ambition of re-moulding India to an image of their own design; now we see, in the fragile indecisive person of the King of Delhi, the inevitable reaction. All the conquests and conflicts of two centuries had led at last to this: in 1857 it was finally to be decided which were the stronger, the muddled loyalties and traditions of India, or the new dynamic of Victoria's Britain.

The British had made many enemies in India by their developing dogmatism—what Sir James Outram, one of the more sympathetic of their administrators, called 'the crusading, improving spirit of the past twenty-five years'. There were enemies of course among the princes, so many of whom had been humiliated, and who had been especially incensed by Dalhousie's doctrine of lapse. There were enemies among the Brahmins, whose supremacy of caste depended upon a series of shibboleths and assumptions now being systematically discredited. Religious leaders resented the advent of Christian missionaries, and the arrogant assertion by men like Nicholson and the Lawrences that Christianity contained the only truth. Ordinary people of all sorts rankled under the growing exclusivity of the British, fostered partly by better communications and the arrival of that archetypal snob, the memsahib. Colder and colder the rulers were withdrawing into their cantonments and clubs, to clamp themselves within a round of amateur theatricals, pig-sticking, gossip and professional ambition which shut them off from Indian life outside, and made them more and more contemptuous of it: by 1852, when the young Frederick Roberts reached India, one of the sights of Allahabad was the last of the hookah-smoking Englishmen, once familiar figures of Anglo-Indian life—he had a servant called his *hookah-bardar* just to look after the pipe.

That the British were powerful everyone knew. Their *iqbal* was formidable. But there were signs that they were not infallible. Kabul in 1842 had not been forgotten, and rumours were now reaching India of British reverses in the Crimean War, which had broken out in 1854.[1] The British were ludicrously thin on the Indian ground—in 1857 there were 34,000 European soldiers to 257,000 Indians—and they depended for their security, as any percipient native could see, upon the Indians themselves, represented by the sepoys of the Company armies. Out of this ground-swell of disillusion, signs and portents bubbled. Prophecies were recalled, legends resuscitated, secret messages circulated, and there were whispers of conspiracy.

Among the sepoys there were already special reasons for disaffection. In earlier times a sense of brotherly trust had characterized the regiments, and a family spirit bound British officers and Indian soldiers alike. Now many of the officers had wives and children in India, and they found it easier to live the sort of life they might lead at home in England, to the exclusion of their men. Though many officers would still swear blindly by their soldiers, and stand by them in any emergency, many of the sepoys felt a less absolute loyalty to their commanders. The rapport had faltered, and the British knew far less than they thought about the feelings of their Indian troops.

[1] How merciful was the Great Ruler of all worlds, wrote General Sir Garnet Wolseley in retrospect, to end the Crimean War before allowing the Indian Mutiny to begin—'we should have manfully faced the double misfortune, but it must have very seriously strained our resources'. As it was, many regiments came direct from one campaign to the other, feeling less than grateful, one may imagine, to the Great Ruler.

In particular they were out of touch with movements within the Bengal Army.

Most of the Company sepoys were Hindus, for the three armies were all based in predominantly Hindu areas. The men of the Madras and Bombay armies were drawn from all classes and many regions, but the Bengal army was more homogeneous. Not only were its sepoys mostly of high caste, but they nearly all came from three particular regions, notably the recently-annexed kingdom of Oudh. Men like the Lawrences early saw the dangers inherent to this sytem. The Bengal sepoys were clannish, caste-ridden and susceptible. John Lawrence thought they should be supplemented by Sikhs and Muslims. General J. B. Hearsey, commanding the Presidency Division of Bengal, believed the army should set about recruiting Christians from the Middle East, Malaya, China, or even South America—'but they must be Christians, and then TRUST can be reposed in them'.

Yet in the officers' messes of the Bengal army there was little unease. Most officers refused to believe reports of subversion, and retained the affectionate trust in their men that was a British military tradition.

5

The new Enfield rifle, with which the Company armies were about to be re-equipped, used greased cartridges which must be bitten open to release their powder. Half the grease was animal tallow, and it was thickly smeared on the cartridges. Early in 1857 the rumour ran through the Bengal sepoy regiments that the grease was made partly from pigs, abominable to Muslims, and partly from cows, sacred to Hindus. This was a device, it was whispered, by which the British meant to defile the sepoy, or break his caste. Deprived of his own religion, he would be more or less forcibly converted to Christianity and used as cannon-fodder wherever the British needed him.

These rumours had reached the Government at Calcutta as early as January, 1857. Mutinies were not unknown in the Indian armies, and action was prompt. The factory-greased cartridges, it was ordered, were to be used only by European troops, and the sepoys were to grease their own with beeswax and vegetable oil. But it was too late. By now the sepoys had convinced themselves that the cartridge-grease was only one of a series of perfidies. At the end of March a young soldier of the 34th Native Infantry, Mangal Pande, stationed at Barrackpore under General Hearsey's command, ran amok and shot at his European sergeant-major on the parade-ground. The Adjutant at once mounted his horse and galloped to the scene, but Pande shot the horse beneath him, and as the Englishman disentangled himself from the harness, fell upon him with a sword and severely wounded him. There then arrived on the parade ground, as in some tragic pageant, General Hearsey himself, mounted on his charger and accompanied not only by his two sons, but by the en-tire garrison guard—all advancing, sternfaced and indomitable, upon the confused young sepoy. The general rode directly towards him, a son on either flank, and Pande stood with his musket loaded ready to fire. 'There was a shot,' reported the young Frederick Roberts, who was there, 'the whistle of a bullet, and a man fell to the ground—but not the General! It was the fanatic sepoy himself, who at the last moment had discharged the contents of the musket into his own breast.'

Poor Pande did not die at once, surviving to be hanged in public, but his name went into the English language: 'Pandy' became the British Army's nickname first for a mutineer of 1857, and later for the Indian soldier in general. His regiment was disbanded, its fate being publicly proclaimed at every military station in India, but the effect was not what the British intended. The 34th achieved a kind of martyrdom among the sepoys, and within a few weeks there occurred the next act of what seems in hindsight an inexorable tragedy. At Meerut, north of Delhi, eighty-five troopers of the 3rd Light Cavalry refused to obey orders. They were court-martialled, sentenced to ten years' hard labour each, and publicly degraded at a parade of the whole Meerut garrison. This was done with ritual solemnity. The garrison was drawn up in ranks around the parade ground. Commanding the scene was a regiment of European soldiers, ready for any trouble, and a battery of artillery with loaded guns. The mutineers were paraded under a guard of riflemen. Their sentences were read aloud, their uniforms were stripped from them, and on to the parade ground advanced the smiths and armourers, with hammers, shackles and chains. In a terrible silence the garrison, at attention, watched while the chains were riveted on. Sometimes a prisoner cried aloud for mercy. Sometimes there was a mutter in the sepoy ranks. It took more than an hour, and when at last the parade was dismissed, the prisoners marched off to their cells and the regiments returned to their quarters, a heavy sense of sorrow hung over the camp. Veteran sepoys wept in shock and despair, and at least one of the English subalterns, the future General Sir Hugh Gough, 'was weak enough almost to share their sorrow'.[1]

It was Sunday next day, May 10, 1857 and all seemed quiet in Meerut. Rumours reached the British officers of restlessness in the town bazaars, and there appeared to be a shortage of domestic servants in the cantonment that day, but morning and afternoon passed peacefully, and in the evening the European soldiers polished their boots, brasses and badges as usual for church parade. Then without warning, soon after five o'clock, Meerut exploded. Suddenly through the cantonment armed sepoys were furiously running, shooting, looting, dancing, leaping about in frenzy, setting fire to huts and bungalows, galloping crazily through the lines, breaking into the magazines, deliriously releasing the men of the 3rd Cavalry from their shackles and chains. A mob from the bazaars followed them, augmented by convicts freed from the city prisons, and policemen off-duty. Many of the sepoys tried to protect the officers and their families, but the crowd swept through the cantonment like a whirlwind, murdering Europeans and Indians alike, and leaving the whole camp ablaze, with clouds of black smoke hanging on the evening sky. The ground was littered with corpses, some horribly hacked about, with smashed furniture, with weapons and charred clothing and piles of ash.

In a frenzy of passion and fear the mutinous cavalrymen galloped

---

[1] He was one of the few British officers to fear the worst, and perhaps his instinct was hereditary: his great-uncle was Lord Gough, conqueror of the Sikhs, his father was a Bengal civil servant, his elder brother was an officer of the 8th Bengal Cavalry, and he himself was to spend forty more years in the Indian Army, before dying in 1909 as Keeper of the Crown Jewels.

out of Meerut into the night, in scattered groups. Some still wore their high feathered shakoes and their cross-belted scarlet jackets: some had got out of their uniforms and thrown away their weapons. After them hastened hundreds of infantrymen, in field grey. All assumed, as their passions cooled, that the British dragoons stationed at Meerut would soon be after them, but when they left the blaze of the cantonment behind, and hurried away down the Delhi road, they unexpectedly left the noise and the excitement behind them too, and were presently passing through silent sleeping villages. Nobody followed them. It was a bright moonlit night, and most of the horsemen rode to Delhi almost without stopping.

By eight o'clock next morning the first of them crossed the Bridge of Boats across the Jumna, within sight of the Red Fort: and pausing to kill a passing Englishman, out on his morning exercise, and setting fire to the toll-house at the lower end of the bridge, almost before the King of Delhi had finished his breakfast they had arrived at the dusty space below the walls of the palace, and were calling for Bahadur Shah.

6

The Mutiny was a muddle. It had no coherent strategy and no enunciated purpose, and what symbolic leadership it had came from Delhi. There most of the Europeans were quickly slaughtered. Whole families died. All the compositors of a newspaper were killed as a matter of principle, and nine British officers in the arsenal blew it and themselves up when ordered to surrender 'in the King's name'. The few survivors fled the city, some to be murdered in the countryside, some to reach safety in Agra or Meerut; and so Delhi became once more, at least in pretension, the capital of a Moghul Empire.

The king's heart was scarcely in the revolution, and he consoled himself by writing melancholy verses in his garden, but around him the forms of an administration were erected, and he was obliged to act the emperor. Proclamations were issued in his name, regiments urged to mutiny under his royal aegis—'large rewards and high rank will be conferred by the King of Kings, the Centre of Prosperity, the King of Delhi'. A ruling council was constituted, six elected soldiers to look after military matters, four civilians as public administrators. A Commander-in-Chief was appointed, and all the princes were made generals. The king processed through the city streets on his elephant, and in his name food was requisitioned for the troops, and city bankers were persuaded to pay them.

But it was all a sham. The king did not trust the sepoys, and they soon lost their respect for him. They camped all over his beloved gardens, treated him as they pleased and ignored his diffident requests. Thousands more mutineers poured into Delhi over the weeks, sometimes marching over the bridge of boats with bands playing and flags flying, but the city remained in disorder. Shops were looted, homes were stripped, drunken Indian officers roistered through the streets. Business was at a standstill. The neighbouring countryside was ravaged by bandits and robbers. In the heart of the chaos, within his red-walled fortress, Bahadur sat helpless and despondent. His treasury was empty, and around him his self-appointed ministers and generals ineffectively bickered. They had ruined, he said, a kingdom that had lasted for five centuries. Sometimes he threatened to abdicate, or to kill himself, or to retire to Mecca for ever. But they kept him there upon his shadow-throne, and almost the only solace he found was in his ever gloomier verse—

*Clothed in my burial sheet I shall spend
My remaining days in the seclusion of some garden.*[1]

This was the nearest the Indian mutineers had to a command centre, an organization, or even an objective. For the rest the rebellion, which spread murderously from station to station throughout northern India, burnt sporadically and haphazardly. Most of the princes and maharajahs stayed cautiously aloof, and there were no senior Indian officers to direct operations. The only common purpose was to get rid of the British Raj, and there were no concerted plans for a replacement. By the middle of June, 1857, the British had lost their authority in most of the central provinces, a slab of country

---

[1] Though as a poet he generally was, so *The Times* correspondent W. H. Russell reported severely to his readers, 'rather erotic and warm in his choice of subject'.

extending from the borders of Rajasthan in the west to Bihar in the east. Everywhere else, though, they remained in command, and they demonstrated soon enough that it was only a matter of time before the rebellion was put down.

But from within the mutinous region terrible reports emerged. Whole communities had vanished. It was like a cauldron in the middle of India, and to the British in the other provinces, and even more to the British at home, life in the war zone seemed to have collapsed into incomprehensible nightmare. Two places only, besides Delhi, impressed their condition upon the horrified world—Lucknow the capital of Oudh, Cawnpore on the Ganges: and the names of these two Indian cities, hitherto so obscure, were now to become engraved for ever in the imperial memory.

7

Bahadur and his family apart, the only eminent Indian prince openly to throw in his lot with the mutineers was the titular heir to another ancient dynasty, subdued by the British long before, but still proud of race and origin. If the King of Delhi offered a cause of loyalty chiefly to the Muslims of India, Nana Sahib of Cawnpore, the adopted son of the last of the Mahratta rulers, was the closest the Hindus had to an emperor. To his people he was the Peshwa, successor to all the Mahratta glories, but to the British he was only the Maharajah of Bithur, a small town on the Ganges some ten miles above Cawnpore; for he was living in exile, and was denied all dignities like royal salutes, seals, or ceremonial gifts. The British kept a jealous watch upon him, as the possible fulcrum of a Mahratta revival, and he could not travel without their permission, or even appear in public without an Englishman at his side.

They liked him, though. He was not a very striking man, fattish, middle-ageing, sallow. But he was hospitable and generous, was fond of animals, and frequently entertained the officers of the Cawnpore garrison in his somewhat eccentric palace, half opulence, half gimcrack, beside the river at Bithur. It was true that he was known to cherish a grudge against the East India Company, who refused to pay him a royal pension, and it was noticeable that he would never accept the garrison's hospitality in return for his own. But the British did not resent these symptoms of wounded pride. They rather enjoyed his company, relished rumours of his unorthodox sex life, and trusted him far enough to let him visit all the military stations upon the Grand Trunk Road, and to mingle freely with the officers of the garrisons.

Cawnpore, a town of some 150,000 people, was one of the most important of those stations. Here the Grand Trunk Road was crossed by the road from Jhansi to Lucknow, and here too was one of the principal crossings of the Ganges. There was a sizeable British community in the town, and a garrison of four sepoy regiments with a European artillery battery. The news of the Meerut rising reached Cawnpore on May 14, 1857, but for a week nothing much happened. Only a vague premonition ran through the cantonment—'something indefinite and alarming overshadowed the minds of all'. Nobody seriously thought the last of the Mahrattas would ally himself with the last of the Moghuls, and anyway the garrison was commanded by the highly respected Sir Hugh Wheeler, whose wife was Indian, and who had been fighting battles in India on and off for half a century. Still, Indians and Europeans eyed each other guardedly, the gunners kept their guns well-greased, and Wheeler's agents in the town kept a steady stream of intelligence flowing into headquarters.

The general decided that while he would do nothing so rash as to disarm his sepoys, he would at least prepare a refuge for the British community in case the worst occurred. He chose two hospital barracks on the edge of the cantonment. He did not think mutineers would actually dare to attack the place, when the crunch came, so he did not fortify it very strongly, merely throwing two low earthworks around the buildings; and he felt sure that help would soon come from elsewhere anyway, so he did not overstock it with provisions (happily accepting, though, the regimental messes' cheerful contributions of wine and beer).

Presently Nana Sahib, who was allowed to maintain a small bodyguard of cavalrymen and elephants at Bithur, approached his friends in the garrison and asked if he could help. Would the English ladies, for example, care to take refuge with him at Bithur? Or could he and his men help to keep things quiet in Cawnpore? The general preferred the second offer to the first. One of his problems was the defence of his treasury, which lay awkwardly, like the commissariat at Kabul, well outside the cantonment lines. Perhaps, he suggested, His Highness would care to reinforce the sepoy guard there with some of his own men? Nana Sahib agreed at once, moved into Cawnpore with 500 men and a couple of ceremonial guns, and settled in a bungalow between the treasury and the magazine. General Wheeler was delighted—he was proud of his Indian sympathies. 'It is my good fortune in the present crisis,' he reported to the Governor-General, 'that I am well known to the whole Native Army as one who, although strict, has ever been just and considerate to them. . . . Pardon, my Lord, this apparent egotism. I state the fact solely as accounting for my success in preserving tranquillity at a place like Cawnpore.'

Poor Wheeler! His success was illusory, and brief. On June 3, his informers told him that a rising was imminent, and all the women, children and non-combatants made for the new entrenchments. Almost at once, as if in response, the sepoys rioted, firing their pistols at nothing in particular, setting fire to buildings, and then, ignoring the Europeans crouched within their flimsy fortifications, rushing off helter-skelter towards the Treasury. They had no trouble with the Nana's soldiers, and loading the treasure into carts, and grabbing the munitions from the magazine in passing, and releasing all the convicts from the town gaol, and setting fire to all the documents in the public record office, off they set in motley triumph up the Grand Trunk Road to Delhi.

Now the Nana showed his colours. Nobody knows whether he had been in league with the sepoy leaders from the start, whether they impressed him into the cause, or he incited them. It used to be suggested that he was the spider behind the whole web of the Indian Mutiny, and that his visits to military stations were intelligence missions. Whatever the truth, less than 20 miles along the Delhi road the mutinous sepoys halted and returned to Cawnpore, where they apparently placed themselves under the Nana's command: and next day Wheeler received a letter from the Nana himself warning the British quixotically that he was about to attack their entrenchment. The European officers hurried into the refuge; guns were primed and sandbags strengthened; at noon on June 6, 1857, the first round fell into the hospital barracks, and the siege of Cawnpore began.

This pathetic action was to enter the mythology of the Empire. In the mid-Victorian era womanhood was elevated to a mystic plane of immunity, and the vision of European women and their children violated or murdered by mutinous ruffians touched atavistic chords of fury. In contemporary pictures the siege of Cawnpore, which was to have a lurid ending, was painted in appallingly lurid colours. Every sepoy is black, wild-eyed and blood-stained; every English mother is young, timid, spotless, terrified, and clutches to her breast a baby still immaculately pantalooned. It was above all the killing of women and children that horrified the public, when news of the Mutiny reached England: and of all the fearful tales of the rising, the story of Cawnpore was the most often and perhaps the most enjoyably retold.

Wheeler's entrenchment was in open ground about half a mile from the Ganges—a treeless place without a flicker of green, where black birds of prey circled always overhead, and the dry dust got into everything. Here the British were besieged for eighteen days. There were about a thousand of them, including 300 women and children. The two buildings were small single-story blocks with verandahs, and the arrangements (wrote Kaye, historian of the Mutiny as he was of the Afghan War) 'violated all the decencies and proprieties of life, and shocked the modesty of . . . womanly nature'. Indeed all the feminist elements necessary to such a Victorian drama were present at Cawnpore. Several babies were born during the siege. There was a wedding. Children played among the guns, mothers pathetically kept up their journals. Stockings and lingerie were commandeered to provide wadding for damaged guns ('the gentlewomen of Cawnpore', as Kaye says, 'gave up perhaps the most cherished components of their feminine attire to improve the ordnance . . .').

But though it read like a parody in contemporary accounts, it was all too real. There was plenty of ammunition, but the commissariat supply was eccentric, and in the first days of the siege one saw private soldiers drinking champagne with their tinned herrings, or rum with their puddings. Later everyone got a single meal a day, of split peas and flour, sometimes supplemented by horsemeat ('though some ladies could not reconcile themselves', we are told, 'to this unaccustomed fare'). The sepoys never stormed the position, but they kept up a constant fire of musketry and artillery, night and day, so that the British never got any rest, were always at their guns, and were forced to make constant sorties to keep the enemy at a distance. Every day there were more casualties, and as the tension increased, the food ran short, the bombardment relentlessly continued and the sun blazed mercilessly on, several people went mad. Every drop of water had to be fetched from a well outside the entrenchment, and man after man was shot getting it. Another well was used for the disposal of corpses: the dead were laid in rows upon the verandahs, and when night fell they were dragged away from the steps, feet first.

The temperature rose sometimes to 138 degrees Fahrenheit, the guns were too hot to touch, and several men died of sunstroke. On June 12 the thatched roof of one of the barracks caught fire, and the building was burnt to ashes, through which the men of the 42nd Regiment raked with their bayonets, hoping to find their campaign medals: all the medical supplies were lost in the blaze, and the survivors were forced to draw in their defences, and huddle in the single building left. Poor Wheeler was now distraught. 'We want aid, aid, aid!' he wrote in a message smuggled across the river to the British garrison at Lucknow. 'Surely we are not to die like rats in a cage?' When his own son Godfrey was killed—'Here a round shot came and killed young Wheeler', recorded a graffito, 'his brains and hair are scattered on the wall'—the old general was broken, and lay on his mattress all day long in tears.

By now the place was full of half-starved children, sick and wounded women, men blinded, insane, or helplessly apathetic. 'June 17th', recorded one young Englishwoman's diary, 'Aunt Lilly died. June 18th. Uncle Willy died. June 22nd . . . George died. July 9th. Alice died. July 12th. Mamma died'.[1] Yet on June 23 the most determined rebel assault was beaten off, and after thirteen days

[1] And she died herself on July 15.

of siege there was reached a kind of stale-mate. The sepoys were too timid to take the place by storm, but too impatient to starve it into submission. On June 25 a solitary Eurasian woman, barefoot, with a baby in her arms, appeared on the flat ground before the entrenchments, holding a flag of truce. They carried her half-fainting over the rampart, and she presented an envelope ceremoniously addressed to 'The Subjects of Her Most Gracious Majesty, Queen Victoria'.

The Nana was offering terms. 'All those who are in no way connected with the acts of Lord Dalhousie', his unsigned message ran, 'and are willing to lay down their arms, shall receive a safe passage to Allahabad'—100 miles away, and the first downstream city still held by the British. After a day of discussion with his officers, Wheeler accepted the offer, insisting only that his soldiers keep their side-arms, with 60 rounds of ammunition apiece. There were parleys on the flat ground before the entrenchment; the guns were handed over; and at dawn on June 27 the evacuation began.

Sixteen painted elephants, eight palanquins and a train of bullock-carts, with sullen mahouts and insolent drivers, took the sick and wounded out of the camp, down a shallow wooded gulley towards the river. Behind them straggled the walking survivors, rifles on their shoulders, scraps of baggage in their hands, ragged, dirty and silent. Most of the sepoys who swarmed around them treated them with contempt or contumely: others asked kindly after old friends or former officers. Crowds of sightseers followed too, but a few hundred yards before the river, where the track crossed a stream by a wooden bridge, they were all stopped. Only the British and their guards were allowed to proceed, the macabre procession of elephants, carts, palanquins and exhausted soldiers proceeding heavily in the heat towards the waterfront.

On a bluff beside the river there stood a small white temple, attended by a tumble of thatched huts, through whose purlieus dogs and geese wandered, and monkeys bounded. Below it was the *ghat* at which the Hindu faithful performed their ablutions in the holy river. Only a narrow gap in the bluff, sprinkled with trees, gave access to the water's edge. As they stumbled down to the waterfront, the British could not see far either up or down the river, but lying off-shore in front of them they discovered some forty high-sterned river boats, thatched like floating haystacks, with their crews waiting impassively on deck. There was no jetty at the *ghat*. The fit men were made to wade into the stream, carrying their wives, children and wounded—a forlorn emaciated company, many of them bandaged or splinted, some carried out on stretchers, some clutching raggety bundles of possessions. Bewildered and terrified, watched by the silent boatmen and the sepoys leaning on their muskets on the shore, they scrambled dripping and bedraggled aboard the boats, nine or ten souls to each craft. The last people to embark, Major Vibart and his family, were seen aboard with every courtesy by sepoys who had been in Vibart's regiment, and who insisted on carrying his bags.

On a platform before the little temple sat the Nana's representative, a functionary of the court at Bithur, keenly watching events below, and cheerfully crowded around the bridge over the gulley behind, peering through the gap like spectators at a sporting contest, hundreds of sightseers waited to see the last humiliation of the Raj. As soon as Vibart was aboard something ominous happened: instead of pushing off, all the boatmen jumped overboard and hastily waded ashore. Pandemonium followed. The British opened fire on the boatmen, and simultaneously the troopers who had so politely escorted the Vibarts aboard opened fire upon the boats. In a moment there poured into the stationary flotilla, from guns hidden on both banks of the river, a heavy fire of grape-shot and musketballs. The British were overwhelmed. Soon the thatch of the boats was aflame, and the river was littered with corpses, and threshed with desperate survivors. Women crouched in the water up to their necks, babies floated helplessly downstream, men tried desperately to shove the boats into midstream and get away. Indian cavalrymen splashed about the shallows, slashing at survivors with their sabres, and the few people who managed to get ashore were either bayonetted then and there, or seized and whisked away beyond the gulley. Only one boat escaped, rudderless and oarless, and after nightmare adventures on stream and on land—chased through the night by maddened sepoys—besieged in a burning temple—without food, weapons, maps—at last two English officers and two Irish privates, all stark naked, swam ashore in friendly territory to tell the story of Cawnpore.[1]

Nobody else lived. Every man was killed. Every surviving woman and child was taken to a house called the Bibighar, the House of Women, a mud flat-roofed building beside the Ganges canal which a British officer had built for his Indian mistress long before. On the afternoon of July 15 several men, some of them butchers by trade, entered the Bibighar with sabres and long knives, and murdered them all. The limbs, heads and trunks of the dismembered dead were carried to a nearby well, and almost filled its 50-foot shaft.[2]

8

The other sacramental episode of the Indian Mutiny was the siege of Lucknow. This city, annexed by the Raj only in the previous year, was naturally full of dissidents—deposed princes, soldiers of the disbanded royal army, dispossessed stipendiaries, and a vast number of citizens who, far from welcoming the new enlightenment, missed the delinquent old days of cheap opium and corruptible officials. The British, who had a low opinion of Oudh traditional life, ensconced themselves in a grand towered Residency and used as an ammunition store the Kadam Rasul, a building particularly sacred to

[1] The last of them, General Sir Mowbray Thomson, survived until 1917 and was the most reliable eye-witness of the tragedy. Who opened fire first, the British or the Indians, and whether the Nana deliberately planned the massacre, we shall never know.

[2] It is all remembered in Cawnpore (nowadays spelt Kanpur). The fatal ghat, where the temple still stands on its bluff, is still called Massacre Ghat, and on the site of Wheeler's entrenchment there is a huge and awful memorial church, with a slab commemorating the '15 officers, 448 men, 3 officers' wives, 43 soldiers' wives and 55 children' who died. The massacre well, however, in the centre of the modern city, has sensibly been obliterated by the Indians since their independence, the British having covered it with a mourning angel of white marble. I wish I could say that a hush of elegy still hung over Cawnpore, but in fact it is a flourishing textile city, and in 1971 I was shown around its grim historical sites in a spirit of distinctly cheerful detachment. As for the Nana, he disappeared into myth, and nobody knows when or how he died.

the Muslims of Oudh because it contained a stone impression of the Prophet's footprint.

But the Chief Commissioner was Henry Lawrence, fresh from the Punjab, and he seemed to have things well in hand, pursuing a careful mean between conciliation and firmness, and assuming plenary powers as commander of the military forces in Lucknow as well as head of the civil government. Lawrence thought he knew his Indians, and believed in trusting them as long as possible: 'until we treat Natives, and especially Native soldiers, as having much the same feelings, the same ambitions, the same perceptions of ability and imbecility as ourselves, we shall never be safe'. The mutiny had flared quickly throughout Oudh, and by the middle of June only Lucknow itself remained in British control: but though Lawrence was not well, he exuded his habitual kindly confidence, personally supervising the military arrangements, and sometimes going into the city incognito to see how the wind was blowing.

He had decided that the garrison, with the entire British community, should be concentrated within the Residency compound. This elaborate complex of buildings stood among flowered lawns in the very centre of Lucknow. To the north flowed the river Gumti, to the east was the huge tumbled pile of the Farhat Bakhsh, 'the Delight-Giver', the palace of the kings of Oudh. Closely around the compound walls straggled the native city, a foetid maze of alleys and bazaars, and towering over its gardens stood the Residency itself, a tall and ugly thing, from whose upper stories one could survey the whole expanse of the city, its towers, domes and minarets rising splendidly from the squalor at their feet. Within the thirty-three acres of the compound there were sixteen separate buildings— bungalows, stables, barracks, orderly rooms—and all this enclave, surrounded by mud ramparts, Lawrence now turned into a fortress. Trenches were dug, palisades erected, booby-traps set, wire entanglements laid. Artillery batteries were posted around the perimeter, and within the buildings the Residency staff prepared themselves for a siege. By the time the mutiny broke out in Lucknow, towards the end of June, the entire European population of the place, including a garrison of some 1,700 men, was entrenched within the compound.

Soon everyone in England would know the topography of this place, and remember its names—the Baillie Gate, the Redan Battery, Sago's Garrison, Grant's Bastion. Anglo-Indian life was encapsulated there, grand ladies of the Company establishment to clerks and shopkeepers who were only just acceptable as Britons at all. There were merchants of several foreign nationalities, too, and many loyal Indian sepoys who had voluntarily joined the garrison—half the defending force was Indian—and several important political prisoners, including two princes of the royal house at Delhi. Tightly within their thirty-three acres this heterogeneous company huddled for safety, beneath the god-like authority of the Resident: beyond the walls the whole of Oudh was soon in hostile hands, and every house overlooking the ramparts had its quota of snipers and archers.

Almost the first casualty was Lawrence himself. A howitzer shell fell in his room, and when through the smoke and dust somebody call 'Sir Henry! Are you hurt?' there came after a short pause the faint but decisive reply: 'I am killed'. He lived in fact for two days more, giving detailed instructions to his successor about the defence of the garrison, and was buried quietly in the Residency graveyard beneath his own epitaph—'Here Lies Henry Lawrence, Who Tried To Do His Duty'. Without him the British sank into fatalism. The heat now was ferocious, the bombardment was unremitting, and one could hardly move a foot in the open without a sniper's shot from over the walls. One by one the buildings toppled, until the whole compound was a sort of wreck. Food ran short. The air stank of carrion and excrement. Many of the women lived in cellars, where they were plagued by mice and rats, and often fell into gloomy fits of foreboding. 'In the evening, Mrs Inglis went to see Mrs Cooper, and found Mrs Martin sitting with her. They all had a consultation as to what they would consider best to be done in case the enemy were to get in, and whether it would be right to put an end to ourselves if they did so, to save ourselves from the horrors we should have to endure. Some of the ladies keep laudanum and prussic acid always near them'. (But Mrs Case and Mrs Inglis agreed that they should merely prepare themselves for death, leaving the rest 'in the hands of Him who knows what is best for us'.)

Many of the Indian sepoys now deserted, and by July, 1858, the British were losing an average of ten men a day killed and wounded—among the wounded, after gallant service from the first day of the siege, was Dr Brydon, whom we last saw slumped on his pony outside Jalalabad twenty years before.[1] Sometimes rumours reached them of help on the way, and on August 15 a message arrived from the British. 'We march tomorrow for Lucknow,' it said. 'We shall push on as speedily as possible. We hope to reach you in four days at furthest'. And it added in Greek script, in case of interception: 'You must aid us in every way, even to cutting your way out if we cannot force our way in. We are only a small force.' This was cold comfort for the defenders, now reduced to 350 European soldiers and some 300 sepoys. They were harassed by constant mining operations under the ramparts—sometimes mines exploded well within the compound, and twice the ramparts themselves were temporarily breached. There were 200 women to care for, with 230 children, and 120 sick and wounded, and the rebels now had 18-pounder guns within 150 yards of the walls. The compound was a shambles.

Still, four days was not too long to wait. Not everybody behaved well at Lucknow: we hear of people hoarding food, stealing, standing upon seniority. For the most part, though, the British in the shattered Residency stuck to the principles of their age and culture, even in this extremity. Not only did they read their Bibles assiduously, attend church service regularly, and even entertain each other to formal meals, but they lived according to the strictest tenets of supply and demand, such as their compatriots had tried so disastrously to enforce on the other side of the world in Ireland. Food was bought from traders at current market rates, which were by the nature of things astronomical, and Sir Henry Lawrence's possessions were actually sold at auction within his ruined house, fetching very satisfactory prices.

The four days came and went. A week passed, and a month. It was not until September 23, after 90 days of siege, that the defenders heard gunfire on the other side of the city, and two days later there

[1] He survived this calamity too, dying comfortably on his estate in Scotland 15 years later.

burst into the compound a column of Highlanders, ragged, un-shaven, kilted and furiously warlike, under the joint command of two remarkable generals, Henry Havelock and James Outram. Outram was an urbane old India hand, who had spent his youth in wars against Indians and Afghans, had put down sundry lesser insurrections, and had been Napier's political officer in Sind. Since then he had emerged victorious from the footling Persian War of 1856, and here he was a Grand Commander of the Order of the Bath, gazetted to succeed Lawrence as Chief Commissioner for Oudh. He was the senior officer with the relieving force, but he had generously, or perhaps cautiously, conceded the operational command to the second general, a very different manner of soldier. Havelock was a veteran of the Queen's army, a home-spun fighting commander. He had fought in practically every Indian battle during the past forty years, he had read all the military manuals, he had a blazing eye and a stubborn chin, and he had been converted many years before to a dogmatic Baptist creed. He believed absolutely in every word of the Bible, especially the bloodthirsty parts: for as Kaye innocently observed of him, 'he was thoroughly persuaded in his own mind that war was righteous and carnage beautiful'. This was his first general command, all the same, and with these tremendous convictions to inspire him, and with the blood-maddened Highlanders at his heels, and the sophisticated Sir James always considerate at his elbow, he was just the man for the job. The Highlanders, overjoyed to find any survivors at all inside the Residency, bayonetted a few loyal sepoys in error as they entered, and played the bagpipes all night long in triumph.

But no sooner had the relieving force lifted the siege, than they were besieged themselves. There were only a thousand of them, many of them wounded, all exhausted. They were in scarcely better shape than the people they had come to rescue, and within the compound their presence soon proved to be more a curse than a blessing. By now conditions were desperate. People were eating sparrows, and smoking dried tea or chopped straw. The surgeons had run out of chloroform and performed operations in public among the beds. Dysentery and scurvy were rife, and so were lice—most of the soldiers had shaved their heads bald, heightening the nightmare flavour of the experience. No building was much more than a shell—everything riddled with balls like smallpox, as the garrison chaplain put it—and into the ruins there now poured the torrential rains of the monsoon, dripping into every shelter, and clouding everything in a damp hot haze. All the time the rebel sappers mined beneath the compound, and one could often hear the clink of pick-axes far below one's feet: the rebels drove twenty mines under the compound, the British drove twenty-one counter-mines, and there were sometimes macabre battles between the sappers far in the clammy underground. Through it all the Union Jack flew from the Residency tower, defiant among its ruins in the heart of the hostile city.

At the end of October word filtered in that a second relieving force, under General Colin Campbell, was approaching from the north, and so there stepped into the limelight a hero of Lucknow soon to become legendary. Henry Kavanagh was an Irishman, ginger-haired and very large, who had worked for the Post Office department, and had made his name within the compound by his intrepid behaviour in the mines, where he spent night after night with loaded pistol awaiting the arrival of rebel sappers, and sometimes shooting them through the narrowing wall that separated their respective galleries. He now volunteered to find his way through the enemy lines, make contact with Campbell, and guide the relieving force into the Residency. Heavily blacked with lamp-oil, disguised in turban, orange silk jacket and pyjama trousers, and accompanied by an Indian guide whose heroism was to be less devoutly remembered by posterity, Kavanagh swam the river, bluffed his way through the rebel check-posts, and met a British picket: eight days later he returned to the Residency, dressed this time in a cotton quilted tunic, corduroy breeches, thigh length jackboots and a pith helmet, to conduct Havelock and Outram triumphantly through the shattered slums to Campbell. As the three generals met, Campbell's soldiers raised a cheer, and Havelock, at the moment of his glory, greeted them Napoleonically. 'Soldiers', he stentoriously cried, 'I am happy to see you!' (And a formidable lot they must have looked—Sikh cavalry in tangled draperies, English infantry in slate-grey, turbanned Punjabis, plumed and tartaned Highlanders, and the 9th Lancers, one of the smartest cavalry regiments in Europe, with white turbans twisted around their forage-caps).[1]

This time the relieving force did not join the garrison within the compound, but merely kept Lucknow quiet to allow the withdrawal of the survivors. First came the women and children, on the night of November 18, through the ruins of the riverside palaces to the British lines—some in wagons, some in litters, some walking. They moved under constant fire, helped and jollied along by soldiers or by the sailors of Campbell's naval brigade. Sometimes they were ushered into trenches, sometimes they passed through a camouflage of canvas screens. With them went all the crown jewels of the kings of Oudh, together with some £250,000 worth of treasure from the British Residency.

Next, at midnight on November 22, the old garrison marched out, breaking step to avoid arousing the suspicions of the rebels: and finally the rearguard, a few hundred gunners and Highlanders, crept past the Baillie Gate to join the army outside the city, leaving their camp-fires burning in the deserted ruins of the Residency. The siege of Lucknow was over. By dawn next day a procession six miles long, of soldiers, bullock-carts, litters, elephants, horsemen, sepoys and camp followers was crossing the silent plain towards Cawnpore—the babies crying now and then, the pipes intermittently playing, the tired grave generals in their palanquins, and all about them the great cloud of dust that marked the passage of armies, friendly or hostile, defeated or victorious, across the face of India.[2]

---

[1] The 9th, with whom I had the pleasure of serving nearly a century later, so distinguished themselves in the Mutiny that they ever afterwards called themselves the Delhi Spearmen: 14 of their officers and men won V.C.s in the campaign, including Private Goat.

[2] Havelock died almost at the moment of success, and was promptly beatified by his fellow-fundamentalists—soon after his death a kind of Holy Tablet was issued in his name, each commandment opening with the dread words HAVELOCK SPEAKS . . . (and he says, for example, that Whatever A Man's Professional Calling, He Ought to Aim Evangelically At Doing Good). Outram, 'the Bayard of India', died in 1863, and is one of the few British administrators still commemorated by a statue on the Maidan at Calcutta: there is also an effigy of him on the Thames Embankment, puzzling

9

These were the epics of an event which was itself to be called, by the Anglo-Indian historian Sir Charles Crosthwaite, 'the epic of the Race'. The rising grumbled on, in guerilla skirmish and punitive hunt, until the summer of 1859, but long before then the British had resumed their command of the sub-continent, and the myth of the Mutiny was permanently established in the Victorian folk-lore. It had never spread beyond the Ganges valley, nor had the other Company armies joined the Bengal sepoys. The Punjab had remained quiet under the masterly John Lawrence. Dost Mohammed had not taken advantage of the times to invade India and repossess the Peshawar country the Afghans claimed as their own. Despite their faulty intelligence and inept staff-work, the British had dealt efficiently with the rising, and the conduct of their armies did much to restore the British military reputation after the failures of the Crimea. The Indians were never to rise in arms against the Raj again, and far from weakening the imperial confidence of the British, on a conscious level at least the Mutiny hardened and coarsened it.

It brought out the worst in many of them. Even the heroines of the Lucknow siege, when they were relieved at last, came stumbling out with bags of rupees in their arms, and did nothing but grumble —'not one of them said a gracious word to the soldiers who had saved them', one officer recorded, 'a fact which my men remarked upon'. Even that gentle cellist Hope Grant of the 9th Lancers, now a general and a knight, entering a Hindu temple at the ancient city of Ajoudia, contemptuously kicked over the sacred image of the monkey-god inside, 'to the horror', as he complacently recorded, 'of the dirty fat priests about, who had worshipped, or pretended to worship it, since they were boys'. In general the British fought at least as savagely as the Indians, and in the aftermath of the tragedy

---

to that overwhelming majority of Londoners who have never heard of him. The ruins of the Residency, which were to be immortalized by Tennyson in heroic verse, are preserved to this day by the Indian Government, with diligent respect.

the worst national streaks of intolerance and chauvinism showed themselves: the restraining authority of Lord Canning, the new Governor-General, merely brought him the contemptuous epithet 'Clemency' Canning. The British saw the war as a straight fight between good and evil, and the savageries of the rebels, though they could hardly be exaggerated, were shamelessly exploited. Contemporary accounts are rich in gloating detail—every sepoy a crazed barbarian, every Englishwoman raped before mutilation. In memoir after memoir the Indians are pictured as faithless and brutal ingrates—'niggers', as they were now often called, who were animated by no normal instincts of mercy and kindness, and showed no sign that they might ever, even in God's infinite mercy, be capable of redemption.

It was in an Old Testament mood that the Christian public of England now looked out to the smoking desolation of northern India. *The Times* demanded death for every mutineer in India: 'every tree and gable-end in the place should have its burden in the shape of a mutineer's carcass'. The Duke of Cambridge, Commander-in-Chief of the British Army, proclaimed the nation's support for 'all who have the manliness to inflict the punishment'. The atrocities committed by the mutineers, declared Lord Palmerston, were 'such as to be imagined and perpetrated only by demons sallying forth from the lowest depths of hell'. When every gibbet was red with blood, declared a speaker at the Oxford Union, when the ground in front of every cannon was strewn with rags and flesh and shattered bone, 'then talk of mercy. Then you may find some to listen'.

And the revenge was terrible enough. Indians called it 'the Devil's Wind'. 'No maudlin clemency', wrote an eye-witness of the recapture of Cawnpore, 'was to mark the fall of the city', and it is probably true that no British Army in history has been so inflamed with furious passion as were the Queen's regiments in India then. 'Cawnpore! Cawnpore!' they used to shout, as they stormed another rebel position with their merciless bayonets, slashing and spiking, taking no prisoners, and going on to burn, hang and sometimes disembowel. Officers were as maddened as their men. When the British found the charnel house of the Bibighar, they made their captives lick the caked blood from its floor before hanging them, and afterwards arranged guided tours of the premises for regiments passing through. Whole villages were burnt and all their inhabitants hanged. Passers-by who ventured to turn their backs upon a punitive column were often shot for insolence. Looting was indiscriminate and unchecked —'the men are wild with fury and lust of gold', reported an eye-witness at Lucknow, '—literally drunk with plunder . . . faces black with powder; cross-belts specked with blood; coats stuffed out with all sorts of valuables'.

The British armies swept across the country in a kind of fever—we read of a force marching sixty miles in twenty-four hours in the middle of May, of three officers galloping non-stop for thirty miles to an action, of 130 miles covered in sixteen hours by relays of horses, galloping all the way. Most of the regiments came to look like wild insurrectionists themselves: their spanking uniforms were long worn out, and officers and men alike wore what they pleased—tweed coats, turbans, cloaks, making them all seem, stripped of order's livery, beyond order's authority too. One well-known field artillery unit, whose harnesses, we are told, seemed to be held together with pieces of string, was commanded by a major in a fez and a Turkish cloak, tied around the waist with rope, and marshalled by a battery sergeant-major in a coat made from the green baize of a billiard table. 'The gentlemen must be very savage', an Indian law-yer of Cawnpore noted apprehensively in his diary, and when the warship *Pearl* sailed up the Hooghly to Calcutta and fired a cere-monial salute, the crews of the country boats jumped overboard in terror, and the crowds on the quay fled for their lives, assuming it to be a signal for the destruction of the city.

When, after the end of the fighting, inquiries were held, court-martials conducted, and sentences legally passed, condemned muti-neers were lashed to the muzzles of guns and blown to pieces to the beat of drums. The cruelty of the British matched the cruelty of the Indians, and both sides fought equally from the heart. Though many Englishman soon looked back to their revengeful passions with re-morse, still the relationship between rulers and ruled never re-turned to its old pragmatism, Indians and British accepting the best and worst in each other as transient phenomena of history. After 1857 the Raj regarded itself as a ruling enclave, different in kind from its brown heathen subjects—an institution rather than a community, whose best intentions and most useful works were, for ever after, to be tinged ineradicably with distrust, disapproval or superiority. And as we shall presently discover, the emotions of the Mutiny found their echoes all over the British Empire, permanently affecting its attitudes, and leaving scars and superstitions that were never quite healed or exorcised.

10

For a last picture of this most horrible of imperial wars, let us return to Delhi, where the tottering old king, still writing his melancholy lyrics among the sprawling sepoys in his garden, remained the figurehead of the rising. His reluctant return to authority was brief. Long before the end of the mutiny, even before the relief of Lucknow, John Lawrence had formed a flying column in the Punjab, British and Sikh, and had sent it storming down the Grand Trunk Road to the relief of Delhi. John Nicholson commanded it, and leading his own regiment of Sikh irregular horsemen, fiercer and leaner than ever, was William Hodson. Such a combination of the righteous and the predatory could hardly lose. 'Where have we failed when we acted vigorously?' Lawrence rhetorically demanded, dispatching his young men to the rescue of the Raj. 'Where have we succeeded when guided by timid counsels?' The Punjab Movable Column, clattering at twenty-seven miles a day down the great road, fell upon Delhi with irresistible spirit, and in a week of street fighting recaptured the city, Nicholson entering the pantheon of empire, as was almost pre-ordained, by dying in the hour of victory at the Kashmir Gate.[1]

The British found the Red Fort abandoned. Only a few dour and fatalist sentries remained at their posts, asking for no quarter, and getting none. Anybody else found in the building was killed too as a matter of course, and that night the British commander ordered his dinner to be served among the exquisite arabesques of the Diwan-i-Khas. There was no sign of the King, but presently intelligence arrived that he was hiding with a ragged mass of followers in the tomb of his sixteenth-century predecessor Humayun, a vast

[1] Where his tomb remains, in a garden across the road.

mausoleum, domed and minareted, which lay within its own gardens some miles east of the palace—almost a town in itself, court opening into court, and one of the noblest Moghul monuments in Delhi.

The intelligence chief of the Delhi force was Hodson, and to him fell the task of arresting the King of Delhi. Since we last met him in the Punjab Hodson had been accused of unjust treatment of native princes, and had been pronounced unfit for political office. He was more than ever a bitter and resentful man, his ferocity sharpened, his taste for vengeance heightened, his contempt for Indians sourer than ever. He was nevertheless given carte blanche to deal with the royal family as he thought fit, except that he must spare the life of the king, whom the British proposed to try for treason.

Off to the tomb of Humayun Hodson rode, with fifty of his own wild troopers, slashed about with cummerbunds and sabres, bearded, turbanned, booted, like a savage praetorian guard of the Raj—galloping heedless through the crowds of refugees who poured out of Delhi with their carts and bullock-wagons, and who cringed into the gutters as this terrible squadron swept by. The force halted in the open square outside the gate of the shrine, and sending an emissary inside to demand Bahadur's surrender, Hodson awaited the supreme moment of his life. One can almost see him now in the great dusty square, half an Englishman, half a Sikh, dusty, lithe, ardent, dressed in the haphazard flamboyance dear to irregular cavalrymen down the centuries, the son of the Archdeacon of Lichfield awaiting the submission of the last of the Moghuls. A small crowd had gathered in the morning heat, waiting there silent and expectant around the horsemen, and presently there emerged from the shrine a palanquin, born by four servants. Inside lay Bahadur, gaunt and exhausted, his long beard straggled upon his chest.

Hodson promised him his life, with the proviso that if any attempt were made to rescue the king on the way back to Delhi, Bahadur would be shot like a dog. Then the little procession moved off along the road to the city, the crowd following silently behind, and gradually thinning out as they approached the British sentries at the Lahore Gate. The city was almost deserted. Through the Chandni Chouk bazaar they passed in silence, the troopers reining in their horses: and at the Red Fort Hodson handed over to the civil power the Light of the World, who was promptly locked up in a dingy little house within the walls—where, sitting cross-legged upon a verandah, listlessly cooled by frayed peacock-feather fans, and sometimes shrieked at by harridan wives from behind their shabby screens, he offered for many months one of the favourite sight-seeing experiences of Delhi.

Next day Hodson went back to the tomb of Humayun to arrest two of the royal princes still sheltering there. To them he promised nothing. On the way back to Delhi he ordered them out of their cart, had them stripped to their loincloths, and borrowing a carbine from one of his soldiers, shot them both dead with his own hand. Watched by a vast crowd of Indians, he took the bodies into the city and had them thrown upon the ground in front of the police station: and there they remained until, their stink becoming unbearable, they were buried in the cause of sanitation.[1]

[1] Hodson himself was killed during the relief of Lucknow in 1858: his estate was valued at £170, not counting the horses, and his regiment survived the Raj as the 10th Bengal Lancers (Hodson's Horse). The King of Delhi was tried in his own Diwan-i-Khas for rebellion and complicity in murder: described by prosecuting counsel as a 'shrivelled impersonation of malignity', he was sentenced to life imprisonment and exiled with his nagging wives to Rangoon, where he died in 1862.

CHAPTER TWELVE

Pan and Mr Gladstone

SWEPT away with the carnage of the Indian Mutiny were the last dilettante deposits of England's eighteenth century empire. There had been a pagan, or at least agnostic charm to that old sovereignty—short on convictions, rich in gusto and a sense of fun— but there would be little that was airy or entertaining to the new empire emerging from the shambles of Lucknow and Cawnpore. It knew its values now, stern, efficient and improving, and it recognized as its principal duty the imposition of British standards upon the black, brown and yellow peoples. The Mutiny had demonstrated indeed that not all the coloured peoples were capable of spiritual redemption, as had earlier been supposed, but at worst the British could always concentrate on material regeneration—the enforcement of law and order, the distribution of scientific progress and the lubrication of trade.

2

Almost the first possession to feel the impact of these certainties was, as it happened, the most allegorically pagan of them all. Since the end of the French wars the seven Ionian Islands had been ruled by the British. Tossed from the Venetian Empire to the French, and momentarily to the Turks and the Russians, in 1815 they had been made a British Protectorate. The British had wanted them because of their strategic position. Not only did they stand on the fringe of Islam—just across the Corfu Channel the Muslim world began, in the high mysterious hills of Turkish Albania—but they also covered the entrance to the Adriatic Sea, and stood protectively beside imperial routes to the east.[1] Corfu, the principal island of the group, was fortified as a naval base, while the other islands of the archipelago each received its small imperial garrison. British administrators, mostly Army officers, established a government for the islands, and a constitution was devised which, while satisfying some of the forms of liberal enlightenment, in fact left every jot of power satisfactorily in imperial hands. The flag of the Septinsular Union included the colours of all the constituent islands, but dominantly in the middle was the British royal standard.

For half a century the Ionians remained a military station and a popular place of resort. A succession of notable individualists sailed out from Britain to rule the islands, giving the Union a peculiar distinction in the annals of Empire. They were men often cast in the older imperial mould, honouring values of a lost magnificence and working in lordly disregard of cable or Parliamentary motion. For such men the Ionian Islands, one of which was Homer's Ithaca, offered a vividly figurative background. Theirs was an age much influenced by Byron's version of classical romanticism, and they often found themselves symbolically at home among the gods, shrines and legends of the Hellenic world, as they moved from gaol inspection to road works, petty session to pay parade, through the wine-dark sea.

3

In October 1858 a British naval cutter, bright as buttons and heavily ensigned, sailed up the narrow channel to Gaios, on the island of Paxos a few miles from Corfu: past the little island of the Madonna, where British redcoats now lived in the barracks the Venetians had built; past the British Residency on the waterfront, gabled, arched, balconied and terraced in a kind of Venetian Georgian; until, its sailors handily jumping ashore with their boathooks, it moored alongside the minuscule piazza of Gaios. This was as pretty a Greek island square as one could wish—copybook Ionian, scrubbed and whitewashed, with a terraced hillside rising above, and the little side-streets of the town winding invitingly out of sight. In the

[1] Upon which they eventually became a staging-post, when in 1928 Imperial Airways made Corfu a stop-over on its London-Cairo flights.

centre stood a church, with seats outside for meditative clerics; on the corner was a tavern, with chairs for policemen and fisherfolk to sit back-to-front upon. In this square, legend said, Antony and Cleopatra dined on the night before the battle of Actium, and clustered there that morning was a distinctly theatrical committee of dignitaries. The British Resident was there, in the cocked hat and epaulettes of his office; and the officers of the little garrison; and all the local aristocracy, part Greek, part Venetian, swarthy and pomaded; and grandest of all, the heavily bearded Greek Orthodox Bishop of Paxos, in his full canonicals of high black hat, episcopal staff and dangling silver cross.

The gangplank was thrown ashore, and from the cutter there emerged, eyes ablaze with interest and resolution, William Ewart Gladstone, aged 48, already one of the most famous of Englishmen, and now visiting Paxos as Special Commissioner to the Ionian Islands. He had been sent by the Prime Minister, Benjamin Disraeli, to report upon the future of the islands—whether they should remain British, as the British would clearly prefer, or whether they should unite with the newly independent Greece, as most of the islanders apparently now wished. Out of office himself, a passionate philhellene and a distinguished Homeric scholar, Gladstone had arrived in Corfu on board HMS *Terrible*, had been saluted with guns, had inspected guards of honour and done all kinds of things not normally to his taste: and though the British in the islands almost universally detested him, and the Greeks generally disappointed him by not being sufficiently Homeric, still he had enjoyed himself, visiting six of the seven islands and making several learned and incomprehensible speeches in the Assembly at Corfu.

Now, at the end of the year, he had come to Paxos, the representative of the mightiest of empires visiting one of its least significant wards. Among the British administrators of the Septinsular Union, that old spirit of swashbuckle tenuously survived even now, and Gladstone came among them like an emissary of a new and graver order. His very purpose there was unprecedented, for this was the first time Victoria's empire had seriously considered a voluntary abdication of sovereignty. Off the gangplank stepped Mr Gladstone, forward stepped the Lord Bishop of Paxos, and there occurred the best-known moment in the whole history of the British in the Ionians.

Mr Gladstone took the bishop's hand and reverently kissed it, remaining with his head silently bowed expecting to be blessed. The Bishop was taken aback. He did not know what to do. He had certainly never blessed an Anglican statesman before, and was perhaps unsure whether it would be liturgically proper. There was an awkward pause. The Resident of Paxos, the commander of the garrison and other Britons watched with amusement from the side-lines—having indeed, as one of them wrote, 'considerable difficulty in maintaining the gravity befitting so solemn an occasion'. The Bishop hesitated; the statesman waited; and then, reaching opposite decisions at the same instant, the one bent down to bestow his blessing, the other straightened himself to stand.

They collided: and the barely perceptible laugh that arose from the British bystanders was a last laugh from the old empire—a chuckle from the adventurers and the nabobs, the freelance rulers of Punjab or Sarawak, the fur traders of Norway House, the heedless Anglo-Irish and the plantation princes of Jamaica.

4

Before we progress ourselves into the High Victorian, let us spend a few pages in the Ionians, for they were in many ways the most delectable of all the imperial islands. For most of their time in the Ionians the British remained absolute autocrats.[1] There was a Senate and a Legislative Assembly in Corfu, and perfunctory gestures of democracy were made in all the other islands—from north to south Paxos, Levkas, Ithaca, Cephalonia, Zante and the distant Kythera, south of the Morea. Real power, though, was firmly in the hands of the British Residents, and of their superior officer the Lord High Commissioner in Corfu, whose salary in the 1830s was the

[1] In breach, one would suppose, of the Treaty of Paris, which engaged them to set up a 'free and independent State' in the islands under British protection: but as one early administrator observed, they had not fought revolutionary France merely to encourage the same 'wild and speculative doctrines' elsewhere in the world.

same as that of the President of the United States, or $\frac{1}{23}$rd of the entire Ionian public revenue, and who was known as 'the Lord High' to the respectful, 'the Lord Mighty' to the impertinent, '*il Lordo Alto*' to the Italianate Ionian gentry, and to the Greek peasants as the Harmost, the ancient title of Spartan colonial governors. At first the islanders did not much care, having an immense respect for the nation that had defeated Napoleon. Later the loyalty faltered, and the general feeling became overwhelmingly in favour of union with Greece—'*Enosis*'.

The British slightly liberalized the system with a new constitution in 1848, but mostly continued to think that they knew best. Few of them spoke Greek or Italian, the twin languages of the Ionians, and they ruled with a bluff disregard of local aspirations—'keeping all classes', as D. T. Ansted wrote in an angry critique, 'in the condition of children, so that they are not much more fitted to conduct their own affairs now than they were half a century ago'. There was no malice to this despotism. The British did not wish to oppress the inhabitants, they just wanted no trouble. As usual they built good roads, laid on fresh drinking-water, and made useful objects like lighthouses, lock-ups and lunatic asylums. They improved the quality of justice. They relieved the condition of the Jews, who had been confined to ghettos in the Venetian way. They kept order, most of the time, in a region that was traditionally among the most turbulent in the Mediterranean (though since no local man would do the job for them, they were obliged to hire an executioner from Albania, who used to arrive from across the Corfu Channel wearing a parti-coloured costume like a jester, and a face mask). They also introduced the potato, which old-school Greek Orthodox clerics promptly denounced as the original Eve's apple.

But few of them thought much of Ulysses' successors. 'The constant use of garlic,' wrote one administrator, 'and the rare use of soap, impress an Englishman very disagreeably,' while another observed that the modern Greek habit of reducing everything to pecuniary standards 'makes Homer, Plato and Co. creditors for a large capital.' The Orthodox religion of the islanders would surely make them, if the pinch ever came, pro-Russian, and in the meantime they never seemed to go to sleep. 'Oh *what* have I done,' one

Englishman was overheard groaning to himself on his balcony one night, vainly trying to sleep through the shattering street noises below, 'what *have* I done that Her Majesty should banish me to this vile and abominable place?'

So they ran their petty bailiwicks with a tight-lipped self-reliance, as they might have organized Madrasis or Baluchis long before. It was a source not so much of chagrin as of astonishment to them that the Ionians were prepared to exchange the security of imperial rule for the hideous uncertainties of *Enosis*: or as Lord Kirkwall phrased it, 'it is of course mortifying to the pride of Englishmen that the Ionians should prefer to be united to poor, weak and distracted Greece, to remaining under the protection of strong, wealthy and well-governed England'. The Ionians were a lively and intelligent people, but their temper was more Levantine than Attic, and to Britons of the day they must have cried out for firm and incorruptible command.

5

Some remarkable imperialists had done their time in the Ionians during the half century, and their memories were by no means forgotten in Mr Gladstone's day. Charles Napier, for instance, had left an ineradicable mark upon Cephalonia, one of the rowdiest of the islands. He adored the place. 'Cephalonia is never out of my mind or my heart', he wrote years later. 'They say *first* love is the truest, and Cephalonia is mine.' Nor was he speaking figuratively, for his illegitimate descendants still lived on the island, having inherited a small plot of land he had acquired in Argostoli. At a time when most of his colleagues despised the islanders, Napier stood stoutly by them. 'I like their fun, their good humour, their paddy ways, for they are very like Irishmen.' He learnt Greek and Italian, he made many local friends, and he governed the island with the help of the best of the local gentry (the others reminded him of the worst sort of Irish absentee landlord), fiercely resenting all outside interference. Napier scoffed at constitutional advance, but worked like a slave building highways, founding schools, dredging harbours, planting forests, conveying water, starting experimental farms and repressing corruption.

All over Cephalonia his artifacts remained. There was his neat little stone lighthouse on the Argostoli point, designed for him by his friend John Kennedy, a neighbour in County Limerick (cost exclusive of lantern £117). There was his handsome prison building, to the very latest circular design, on the quayside at Listori. His water conduits still supplied the people of Argostoli, and everywhere the influence of his idiosyncrasies survived. Since his day the British had put down several awkward insurrections in Cephalonia, but they never abandoned the style he bequeathed to them there. In the little British cemetery at Argostoli, over the harbour causeway, was buried a Captain John Parker, who had been murdered during an affray in 1849. Parker's little dog, having failed to drive off his assailants, stayed gamely beside his master's body, attacking anyone who approached: and when they buried the young officer, upon the top of his tomb the British, in a truly Naperian touch, placed an admiring effigy of his pet—crouching, bristly and always awake.[1]

6

In the 1820s Lord Guilford had come to the Ionians. He had hit upon the idea of founding a university there, for he was a devoted hellenist, rich, and was shocked that modern young Greeks had no university to go to at all. He thought first of establishing it on Ithaca, the home of Ulysses himself, but unfortunately that island was virtually inaccessible, practically waterless and almost uninhabited, so he plumped for Corfu instead. It was a good second best. Not only was it the Corcyra of the ancients, but it was also the place where Lord Guilford himself, in 1791, had been received into the Greek Orthodox Church. For this civilized man, Eton and Christ Church, and a son of the Lord North who had lost the American empire, was a genuine cosmopolitan. De Quincey once called him 'a semi-delirious

---

[1] It crouches there still, among the wild garlic of the overgrown cemetery, though chipped and headless from earthquake and vandalism. Many of Napier's works, notably his model prison, were destroyed in the Ionian earthquake of 1953, but Mr Kennedy's lighthouse has been rebuilt more or less to his original design, the water conduits still flow, and Napier himself is generously commemorated in the admirable little museum at Argostoli.

Lord', but he spoke six languages, wrote poems in classical Greek, and was a Fellow of the Royal Society. He had been the first British Governor of Ceylon, a post he found uncomfortably beyond even his varied capacities, and ever since the British acquisition of the Ionians he had devoted his energies to the idea of the university.

It was founded in 1824, with Guilford as its President. He lavished upon it books, scientific equipment, manuscripts and works of art, and for a time it really was the prime centre of higher learning in the Greek-speaking world. For a generation nearly all the doctors, lawyers, academics and senior civil servants of the Greek kingdom were its alumni. It had faculties of theology, jurisprudence, philosophy and medicine, a library of 25,000 volumes and a worthy collection of antiquities. Its students wore brightly coloured tunics, like ancient Greeks, with red leather buskins to the knee, while the enthusiastic earl, who generally lived on campus, wore his purple robe and gold headband on all occasions, and was often to be seen attending dinner parties disguised in effect as Sophocles or Plato.

The British at Corfu were vastly amused by this eccentric scholar—'very pleasant', Napier called him, 'addressing every person in a different language, and always in that which the person addressed did not understand': and though by 1858 there were seldom more than twenty students to each faculty of his foundation, most young Ionians now going to Athens for their higher education, still the Corfiotes had never forgotten him, maintaining a flattering statue of him, *sub fusc*, in a garden off the esplanade.

7

Less happily remembered was 'King Tom' Maitland, in death as in life the bane of the Corfiote liberals. He was the first Lord High Commissioner, and it was he who devised the original constitution, and set the authoritarian style of the Protectorate. He had created 'a liveried Senate and a sham Assembly', complained one group of Ionian liberals in a memorandum to London, 'to jingle the bells of liberty as they danced in the fetters of slavery'. He had even adopted the Venetian anti-treason measure called High Police, instinct with all the secrecies of the Ten, which enabled him legally to do almost anything to almost anybody. Joseph Hume the English radical had called his government 'more odious than the tyranny of Turkey or Persia . . . a disgrace to England'.

Maitland was a breezy and bibulous old Highlander, rough of tongue and uncouth of habit, a famous valetudinarian, very dirty, very rude, very queer and at heart very kind. 'Who the devil are you?' was the first thing he said, when he met one of his subordinates for the first time. 'I hope you're not such a damned scoundrel as your predecessor.' He once entered the assembly of Septinsular Senators, who met at that time in his drawing-room, wearing only a shirt, a red nightcap and slippers, and after taking a supercilious look at the assembled politicians, expostulated in his loud Scottish voice 'Damn them! Tell them all to go to hell!'—and went back to bed. When he died during a visit to Malta, so the diarist Private Wheeler recorded, the Corfiotes gave him a sort of vicarious funeral, with a coffin before the altar in the church of St Mark's, thousands of candles and dirges sung all day: while the soldiers of the garrison 'drank a glass in memory of King Tom, got as drunk as lords and went to bed happy as princes'.

King Tom's memory was all over Corfu, to the embarrassment one imagines of that stately liberal, Mr Gladstone. He was a friend of John Nash the architect, and though he thought 'gratuitous education the greatest of all humbugs', nevertheless had a taste for good design. He laid out the handsome esplanade beside the sea, at once a parade ground, a promenade, a sports field and an arena for imperial ceremonials. He built the porticoed hall of the Legislative Assembly. Above all he built the palace of St Michael and St George, one of the two official residences of the Lord High Commissioners.[1] This was a majestic affair—embellished with the seven emblems of the Protectorate, attended by guard rooms and belvederes, vaguely classical in style, distinctly imperial in manner, and built of Maltese sandstone by especially imported Maltese craftsmen.[2] Gardens surrounded it, with palms, cypresses and orange trees—'our awnges',

[1] The other was a few miles down the Corfu coast, and in this house, now called Mon Repos, was born Prince Philip of Greece, who was to be consort to Queen Elizabeth II of England.

[2] Who proliferated in Corfu, and whose descendants live there still.

as one Lady High used to call them, according to Edward Lear—and there was a large ornamental pool in front, and a triumphal arch with Britannia in a barque.

The opening of this building had been a marvellously jolly occasion, still remembered nostalgically by elderly Corfiotes. There were boxing and wrestling matches in the great square outside, and inter-island athletic contests made dazzling with local costumes. Outside the palace a stream of competitors tried all day to climb a 40-foot greased pole to grab the pigskin of wine, the goat, the lamb or the doubloon suspended from the top. Greek horsemen galloped around the square, plucking rings from lines, brigandish Albanians wrestled, and at the concluding tournament all the competitors were in antique dress or local costume. No wonder King Tom, whatever his political offences, seems to have commanded a certain affection among his subjects: for when he died they erected an elegant Ionian rotunda in his honour, with his name all around it in the vernacular—*ΘΩΜΑ ΜΑΙΤΛΑΝΔ ΟΥ ΜΕΓΕΛΗΣ ΒΡΕΤΑΝΝΙΑΣ*— *Thomas Maitland of Great Britain*, just as he would have wished it.[1]

8

In the prime of the Septinsular Union the Ionians had been a favourite port of call for well-heeled British tourists. With their heavenly spring climate and their picturesque peasantry, their incomparable views of sea and mountain shore—with the mass of Albania looming so thrillingly across the water, and the fireflies wavering in the dark moat of the Corfu fortress—with their scents of sage and orange blossom and wild flowers, the dappled shade of their great olive groves, the limpid blue of their coves—with the Paxiots casting flies from cliffs to catch swallows, and the Corfiotes processing with the embalmed body of St Spyridon, and the Zantean watchmen alert in their elevated branch-houses among the vineyards—with the Greek wind curling the Ionian waves, the flying caiques of the

---

[1] The rotunda survives, together with the old garrison church and the esplanade. The palace became the Corfu residence of the kings of Greece, and today, in the unavoidable absence of royalty, is mostly shut up. Even now King Tom is retrospectively loathed by the Corfu intelligentsia.

treacherous island waterways, the old Venetian hugger-mugger towns and the sacred sites of Homeric legend—with all these pleasures actually supervised by the British flag, the Ionians were perhaps the most inviting possessions of the entire Empire.

Moreover they were obligingly situated on the flank of the Grand Tour, enabling British philhellenes, surfeited with the ouzos and moussakas of their addiction, to drop off for a week or two of claret and mutton chops. Lord High Commissioners were plagued by well-connected visitors with letters of introduction and classical educations, and sometimes tremendous grandees put into harbour in their yachts, to hobnob with the admiral and set society a'blush. Turnock's Royal Hotel was a fashionable rendezvous, and 'an English house' came to mean a house with a bathroom, suitable for letting to milords.[1]

Byron, who once thought of buying Ithaca, spent some weeks on Cephalonia on his way to Missolonghi: emissaries from all parts of Greece came to visit him there, and he became so attached to Charles Napier as to mention him on his deathbed.[2] Albert Edward, the Prince of Wales, also visited Cephalonia. He gave a dinner party on his yacht in the harbour of Argostoli, and throughout the evening the bands of his six attendant warships played in turn, plus one on shore. The young Disraeli sailed into Corfu once, with his disreputable friend James Clay, and strutted around the island dressed as a Greek pirate, in a blood-red shirt, red slippers and a blue striped jacket. Edward Lear came several times—he was offered a job as director of an art school in Corfu, but thought it a 'very small tittle-tattle place' where the British lived 'very sklombitiously'. Lord Cochrane, the Scottish commander of the Greek revolutionary navy, often sailed glamorously into port for sustenance or entertainment —he had already been thrown out of the Royal Navy and the House of Commons for alleged corruption, had commanded the infant fleets of Chile and Brazil, was reported to be earning a vast

---

[1] It still did, Mr Lawrence Durrell tells us in his *Prospero's Cell*, at least into the 1930s.

[2] His house, at Metaxata, was destroyed in the 1953 earthquake, but there is still a sort of pergola called 'Byron's Ivy', and a Byron's Rock upon which, so local sages maintain, he used to sit and write masterpieces.

salary from the Greek insurgent government, and was all in all a very dashing fellow.

Not all of them were much excited by the heroic elements of the place. When the poet Aubrey de Vere visited the islands in the 1840s he drew the attention of one fellow-countryman to the great white rock on Levkas from which in legend the poetess Sappho hurled herself to her death in the Ionian Sea. 'Yes,' the Englishman replied, 'I have heard it was the scene of a distressful accident.'

9

As a military station the Ionians retained their eighteenth-century manner to the end. In the early years the Ionian Army, as the garrison was called, included many soldiers who had commuted some punishment into a long-service engagement (later they were posted to a special regiment in Sierra Leone), but many well-known British regiments also did a tour of duty in the islands. The officers and their wives loved it, contemptuous though they generally were of the Greeks. We see them in old pictures serenely promenading the esplanade at Corfu with swagger-sticks and parasols, while at the beauty spot called Pelleka, so Ansted sourly suggested, 'large deposits of oyster shells and broken champagne bottles will clearly indicate to future generations the important uses and sacred character of the place'. The more boisterous officers loved to gallop over Corfu on perilous paper-chases, or shoot wildfowl on the great lake of Buteinto. The more cultivated relished its classical associations. RICARDUS EDMUNDUS SCOTT, said a pedantic tombstone in the Corfu cemetery, PRAEFECTUS ARTIFICUM BORUM MILITARIUM VERNACULE QUI ROYAL ENGINEERS DICINTUR.[1]

The private soldiers generally seem to have been drunk. They used to drink, Private Wheeler said, 'until they could put their

---

[1] 'Richard Edmund Scott, Prefect of the Corps of Military Works, Called in the Vernacular Royal Engineers'. Lafcadio Hearn, the writer on Japan, was born in the Ionians, where his father was a military surgeon, and named after the island of Levkas. So was Edith Somerville, of the Anglo-Irish literary partnership Somerville and Ross: her father was Colonel Thomas Somerville of the 3rd Buffs.

fingers in their throats and dabble in it'. They were allowed to buy liquor only in designated grog-shops, called canteens, whose proprietors served them dreadful concoctions of dregs and tailings. The men accepted the stuff fatalistically—it was one of the very few imperial stations where wine was the normal soldiers' booze. 'Damn all canteens', they used to say, according to one contemporary observer, 'come on though, bloody *cattivo*, no goodo the vino, you son of a bitch—give us another touch'—and so they would spend their evenings, drinking and cursing and laughing, until at last, penniless, sick and blind drunk, they staggered vomiting home to barracks. When a reforming officer once angrily overturned a barrel of hooch in the gutter, the soldiers rushed out of the canteen and scooped it up with their mugs.

Still, the military aesthetic was always powerful in the British Ionians. When Edward Lear was looking out of his window one day a regiment of foot came marching by, and their colonel saluted him so smartly that Mr Lear, 'not liking to make a formillier nod in presence of the hole harmy', saluted back and got paint all over his whiskers.

10

In earlier years the British mixed freely and on equal terms with the islanders, and local leaders were loaded with favours. The Order of St Michael and St George, later to become the general order of chivalry, was founded specifically to award services to the Crown in Malta and the Ionians—a powerful instrument of supremacy, King Tom its inventor and first Grand Master thought, 'and certainly the cheapest that we can make use of in these parts'. The first knights of the Order, later to embrace a thousand Sir Reginalds and Sir Georges, all had names like Sir Platos or Sir Athanasius.[1] Just as in eighteenth-century India the English had sometimes gone in official procession to Hindu temples, so in the Ionians the British played statutory parts in both Greek Orthodox and Roman Catholic

[1] The Order still possesses an assembly chamber in the Palace of St Michael and St George, and visiting Knights and Commanders are sometimes to be seen inside it, giving thanks to King Tom.

ceremonies. The commanding general, with his staff and corps commanders, carried huge candles in the Orthodox Passion procession: four British colonels held a silken canopy over the officiating priest in the Catholic procession, preceded by a file of infants dressed as cherubim: and when the patron saint of Corfu, St Spyridon, was removed from his sepulchre each year and placed upright before the high altar in his church, the British national anthem was played, and British soldiers stood guard around him, cheerfully accepting gratuities from devotees who wished to kiss the holy feet.

Sometimes Englishmen married islanders, and some English families settled for good in the islands.[1] A thin but recognizable veneer of English manners had been laid upon the archipelago. They ate apple chutney on Corfu, and drank ginger beer out of stone bottles, and measured in yards and pints. They enthusiastically played cricket, with minor adjustments to the rules and terminology. 'How's That?' was not only an appeal, but also a verdict of Out, full toss was called *Bombada*, bowled was *apo xila*. Teams from the British Army or the Royal Navy often played the Byron Cricket Club on the gravel pitch in front of the palace, and cricket crowds of unfamiliar vitality greeted the events of the game with groans, wild cheers and transient brawls. A character called ὁ Λόρδος, The Lord, in tail-coat and top-hat, had even found his way into the immemorial Karaghiosis cycle of puppet-plays, where his behaviour was ineffably imperial.[2]

Travellers were liable to find that only the paper money issued by the Ionian Bank, the British-owned bank of the islands, was acceptable in hotels: but anyone would accept the splendid coinage, perhaps the most truly imperial currency of the British Empire, which showed Britannia on one side and the Lion of St Mark on the other. In the bandstand on the promenade, ornately reminiscent of Brighton or Scarborough, military bands played pleasant airs on

[1] Like the Tooles, for instance, wine merchants of Cephalonia, who thrived there from the 1830s to the 1930s, or the Crowes or Sargints who were still to be found on Zakynthos until the 1950s.

[2] He appears in it to this day, just as cricket is still played on the gravel pitch, and one can still buy apple chutney (though the yards and pints went out in 1960).

summer evenings: and here as everywhere there was a polished class of indigenes which, easily adapting itself to historical circumstance, had become in many ways more English than the English themselves, and certainly more to the manner of St Michael and St George.

11

Such a possession, so redolent still of earlier, easier times, was clearly an anachronism in the new empire of the 1850s. It was true that the strategists argued incessantly for the retention of the Ionians. Giving them up, it was said, would be 'the open and definite renunciation of the mastery of the Mediterranean', and when in 1858 the British Government wanted to test the efficiency of a new strategic cable, it was to Corfu that a trial message was sent—one word, Charles Greville the diarist heard from Lord Derby, to which a reply came back in six seconds ('I would not have believed this on any other authority').

Mr Gladstone himself, though accepting the need for political reform in the islands, did not grasp the force of the *enosis* movement. His mission was complicated anyway by the untoward publication, in the London *Daily News*, of some highly confidential dispatches from Corfu, and all in all he was not a great success as Special Commissioner to the Ionians. He irritated the British by wanting to change things at all, he disappointed the islanders by declining to recommend instant union with Greece, he embarrassed his best friends by arranging for the recall of the current 'Lord High' and inexplicably assuming the office himself. After only three months he went home to England, where he presently crossed to the Liberal benches and became Lord Palmerston's Chancellor.

So it was not until 1864 that the British eventually left the Ionians, blowing up the Corfu fortifications to prevent their use by an enemy (or a friend, as the islanders not unreasonably complained), and keeping an eye open for any other island territory—Cyprus for example—which might serve as a strategic substitute. But Gladstone's very presence on the Paxos quay was really an act of foreclosure. His earnest mid-Victorian figure in that setting, among the shades of those rumbustious pro-consuls, was like a last inspection of the old order. And there was in fact, as the renowned Homeric scholar doubtless knew, a deeper symbolism to his arrival at Paxos. Nineteen centuries before, during the reign of Tiberius, a ship from Egypt had been sailing past this very island, bound for Italy, when Thamus its master heard a voice from the shore. 'Thamus! Thamus!' it cried. '*Pan magus tethneeke!*'—'Great Pan is dead!' Whereupon, we are told, 'there were such piteous outcries and dreadful shrieking as hath not been the like . . . at that time all Oracles surceased, and enchanted Spirits that were wont to delude the people henceforth held their peace'.

Christian commentators assumed that this had been the moment of the Crucifixion, when the false gods of the ancients died: others pined still, perhaps, even in 1858, for those enchanted Spirits, bathed in fire and dressed in bright colours.

CHAPTER THIRTEEN

The Imperial Style

IN 1861 work began on the construction of a new headquarters for the British Empire. In one of the grandest sites in Europe, between Whitehall and St James' Park in the heart of Westminster, Lord Palmerston's Whig Government authorized the construction of a great new building to house the India Office, the Foreign Office and the Colonial Office. It was a true palace in the Italian Renaissance manner, magisterially sited, richly ornamented, columned, balustraded, with an open courtyard decorated with majolica friezes, innumerable statues and symbolic medallions, and a chimney piece inherited directly from the old East India House in Leadenhall Street, itself now demolished. It was a building recognizably descended from the sea-empires of Venice and Genoa, and through them from the classical imperialisms of old: but at its north-west corner, overlooking St James's Park, architectural purists were dismayed to find a curious square-topped tower, oddly out of style, placed asymmetrically at the corner of the structure, and strangely linked to it by another distinctly un-classical feature, a rounded corner.

This was a touch of the picturesque, and as such it was more proper to its subject than its critics knew. The designer of the new building was Sir George Gilbert Scott, one of the most celebrated architects of the Victorian era, and a principal exponent of the Gothic Revival. The High Gothic style, of which the greatest example in London was the new Palace of Westminster, completed in 1860, was to prove in the end the most truly imperial of British architectural idioms: touched up often with exotic embellishments, domes, pagoda tops or Hindu motifs, it was presently to commemorate the British presence everywhere from Hong Kong to Ottawa, and was adapted to every kind of structure, cathedral to engine-shed.

It was in this quintessentially Victorian style, long since out-grown its mediaeval origins in technique and elaboration, that Scott himself wished to build the entire imperial headquarters. He en-visaged upon that splendid site a fantasy of pinnacles, mansard roofs, gargoyles, tall red-brick chimneys and lavish quirks of orna-ment. Deposited there next door to Downing Street, towering over the domed Horse Guards, the Banqueting Hall and Adam's ex-quisite Admiralty Screen, it would have transformed the character of Westminster, imposing the Gothic as the predominant official style, and thus by association establishing London as an imperial capital above all else.

To a Tory Government it might have been welcome: Gothic was well established as the Tory style of architecture, just as imperial-ism would later be a Tory speciality of politics. Lord Palmerston, however, brusquely rejected the plan. His ideas of empire were es-sentially classical ideas—*civis romanus sum* was the analogy he had majestically offered, when the imprisonment of the Portuguese-naturalized Gibraltaran sea-captain Don Pacifico had nearly led to war with Greece a few years before. Scott offered a Byzantine modi-fication of his scheme, which Palmerston predictably characterized as 'a regular mongrel affair', but reluctantly acquiesced in the end, and immersing himself in a new set of source-books and examples, provided the classical *palazzo* Lord Palmerston demanded.

He allowed himself, though, that one Gothic compensation on the corner; and far more than the sumptuous central courtyard of the building, or its laborious scholarship of spandrel or pilaster, the unexpected tower above the lake was to represent to posterity the spirit of mid-Victorian Empire.[1]

2

For the Empire was taking a Gothic turn. Its style, in life as in art,

---

[1] Though Scott was not allowed to crown it, as he wished, with four gigantic female figures, one of them Britannia; other parts of his Gothic design, however, he was able to adopt for his later masterpiece, St Pancras Hotel.

was becoming more elaborate, more assertive, more utterly itself—
as Blake had written, the classical forms were mathematical, but
Gothic forms had *Life*. Let us view, in illustration, two architectural
compositions of the Raj in India, one an inheritance of earlier years,
one a mid-Victorian creation, and see how differently they reflect
the imperial aspirations of their day.

One's first view of the city of Calcutta, as one sailed up the
Hooghly through the shoals and mudbanks of the Ganges Delta,
was essentially *gracious*. This was deliberate. No more than a slat-
ternly collection of hovels until the British settled there, Calcutta
remained even now largely an eighteenth-century city, and faithfully represented the spirit of an older empire. To the right there
stood Fort William, a powerful heap of ramparts and barracks, with
the spire of its garrison church protruding above the walls, to proclaim the Christian presence, and the green space of the Maidan
all around to provide a clear field of fire. On the left there extended in
happy contrast the leafy expanse of the Botanical Gardens, green-
houses gleaming through the banyans, to remind the traveller that
this Empire was concerned not only with power, but with science
and beauty too. There were wharves all along the southern bank,
lined with three-masters and hung about by country craft, and
immediately in front, as the river bent northwards, there stood the
mass of the central city, grouped in stylish esplanade at right angles
to the stream.

It was a white city, plastered white, peeling in many places and
patched with damp, but still to the eyes of a newcomer ethereal
against the Indian sky. Around its buildings, as the century progressed, the untidy straggle of an Indian city grew, but earlier
Victorian visitors to Calcutta nearly all commented upon its white
elegance. They called it the City of Palaces, partly because its buildings were so grand, but partly because, in the pilastered classicism
of its predominant style, it suggested a dream-like evocation of
Rome or Greece. This was intentional too. As they emerged from
the free-for-all eighteenth century, the British in India had been
concerned to represent themselves as enlightened despots, and they
saw their eastern settlements, as the American colonists had seen
Ithaca or Syracuse, as nuclei of classical ideals and virtues. By and

large the architecture stuck to classical rules—Doric for masculine, warlike buildings, Corinthian for pleasure—and if the detailing of these edifices was imperfect, only irritating purists fresh from home complained about their proportions.

There was the great palace built by Lord Wellesley, brother to the Duke of Wellington, with its great sweep of porte-cochère, its vast colonnade, the white tropic birds poised upon the urns that crowned its balustrade, and the sentries all scarlet and white beside its gates. There was the Town Hall, double-columned in Tuscan Doric, and the Greek Doric Mint, with its portico a half-size copy of the Temple of Minerva at Athens, and the church of St John's with its façade a facsimile of St Martin-in-the-Field's in London;[1] and all down Mission Row, and along the Chowringhee edge of the Maidan, and far away down Garden Reach towards the sea, the immense stucco mansions of the merchants and traders stood opulently in the sun—not in squares or terraces, as they would be in London, but each in its own wide compound, like a Roman villa.

This was a retrospective scene, as though the British were recalling a golden age of antiquity, and trying in a gentlemanly way to recreate it in their oriental empire. That the stucco was often peeling and the masonry flimsy, that the great drawing-rooms of those mansions were frequently half-furnished and echoing, did not detract from the illusion: there was an element of theatre to the City of Palaces, insubstantial like a stage set, which many travellers thought proper to so resplendent a showplace. Besides, implicit to the neoclassic outlook was an element of romantic melancholy, and if more sophisticated visitors could not always admire these buildings as examples of the best constructional techniques, at least one could cherish them as ruins of the future.

But later in the century a very different aesthetic governed the architects of the Raj, who were by then mostly officers of the Royal Engineers, and responded professionally to the imperial sentiments fashionable in their day. Now the British were concerned to express

---

[1] Whose pattern, published by James Gibbs in his *Book of Architecture*, was reproduced not only in India, but in South Africa, Canada and Australia too: perhaps the last example was the Dutch Reformed Church at Cradock in South Africa, completed in 1867 nearly 150 years after the original conception.

not the classic purity of their standards, but their detached omnipotence. The mid-Victorian buildings of empire were nothing if not assured. In the vast vaulted roofs of railway stations they displayed the technical command of empire; in the derivative spires of cathedrals, or the daunting mahogany halls of Government Houses, they tried to demonstrate its inner calm: and nothing illustrated the Empire's sense of divine hierarchy more revealingly than the hill-station, a uniquely British contribution to the cultures of the east.

Hill-stations were never thought of by the Moghul rulers of India, who preferred retreats of more languid purpose. They were a device of the mid-Victorian British, pining for the briskness of the north. Until the imperial armies penetrated the Himalayan foothills, in the 1820s and 1830s, the hills were almost unknown to Europeans. Up there the British could start from scratch, and in the high enclaves of the hill-stations, narrowly set upon their terraced ridges, the Britishness of Empire could find its most intense expression—for at Simla, Darjeeling or Mussoorie the gentlefolk of the Raj, celestially withdrawn from the Indian millions on the plains below, lived for a few months in the year entirely for themselves. Such Indians as were present were there as feudatories, servants or dependents, and the emotions of the British, all too often inhibited in the stifling heat of the lowlands, vividly flowered in the mountain brilliance above.

Darjeeling, say, must have seemed a vision of release when the jaded memsahib or exhausted Collector took the last bend out of the deodars and saw it standing there above. Behind it the stupendous Himalaya rose; away to the south the foothills tumbled in terrace and fold towards the plains; yet theatrical though the setting was, instantly the eye was drawn to the modest centre of the stage. Your hill-station was scarcely more than a village, and was ludicrously dwarfed by the scale of the country, but it had the startling impact of an intruder. It was defiantly, gloriously out of place—a figure of despotic privilege.

Where there should be an eaved white temple with prayer flags up there, a Gothic steeple rose instead, with a weathercock on top, and the white blobs of tombstones in the yard behind. Where one might expect the palace of Mir or Maharajah, a hotel in the East-bourne manner stood, wicker chairs upon its terrace, awnings above its windows. There were military-looking buildings here and there, and genteel half-timbered villas disposed above rustic steps, and along the top of the ridge there ran a wide paved esplanade, with a bandstand, a fountain in a public garden, and benches, as on a promenade at home, surveying the Himalayan prospect.

In decreasing consequence down the ridge to the south, the rest of the town obsequiously fell: lesser hotels, pensions and Eurasian sorts of villa, a clutter of bazaars, an open-air market, a square at the bottom where the rickshaws waited. Socially it was a vertical con-struction—posh and British on the summit, mixed half-way down, utterly indigenous in the lowest layers. Visually it was a neatly hatched compression of planes. The horizontals were the buildings in their tiers; the verticals were the tall thin trees which stood every-where like cypresses in Italy, and were matched by the tower of St Andrew's at the top; the diagonals were the slopes of the hills themselves, which framed the town, and by intersecting behind it accentuated the meshed and intricate texture of the scene. The hill-stations were mostly built by military engineers, and if their indi-vidual buildings were generally undistinguished and sometimes repellent, their civic patterns were rather handsome. Bath, itself the echo of an earlier empire, was familiar to many an imperial soldier, and in Darjeeling's simple but elegant plan we perhaps see innocent derivations of Lansdowne and Great Pulteney.

Yet it was not the shape of the town that was exciting, and cer-tainly not its architecture, but the suggestion it gave of concentrated force. For all its respectable trappings it looked a fierce, perhaps a vicious kind of place. It was all in movement. Even from a distance one could see the urgent jostle of its bazaars, the bright crowds hastening arm in arm along the Mall, or clattering hilariously about on mountain ponies. The air was full of sparkle; hoots, shouts, axes, hammers, bugles or even bagpipes sounded; sometimes the sun flashed brilliantly off a window, or a flag fluttered red white and blue through a chink in the buildings.

It was an insignificant, in some ways a preposterous little settle-ment, but it was more truly a symptom of absolute power than the

City of Palaces had ever been. It was the belvedere of a ruling race, obedient to no precedent, subject to no qualm, from whose terraces as from some divine gazebo the British could look down from the cool heights to the expanses of their unimaginable empire below.[1]

3

All over the Empire this trend towards the aloof and the grandiloquent was apparent. Government Houses, for example, became very grand indeed, however minuscule their colonies: for as a perceptive official memorandum put it, 'the keeping up of an outward appearance of power will in many instances save the necessity of resort into the actual exercise of it'. The one at Hamilton in Bermuda had a Medici air: it was supposed indeed to have been originally designed for erection outside Florence, and stood among great groves of cedar-trees, crab-grass lawns and banana orchards as if a prince were indeed its occupant, instead of (more often than not) a superannuated and not very successful general. The one at Nassau in the Bahamas, on the other hand, aspired more towards Chatsworth or Woburn in manner, and actually had deer in its park, while the one at Hobart in Tasmania, set with turrets and flagstaffs against the mass of Mount Wellington, looked suggestively like Balmoral.[2]

Even the white settler colonies progressed with astonishing speed from the homely to the pretentious. Some lovely buildings had been erected out there in the earlier years of the century. There were the delectable country houses of Tasmania, built to a square simple Georgian of finely-dressed stone: rectory sort of buildings, Gainsborough buildings, with their big sash windows, their whitewashed dairies, the lovely oaks and elms transplanted with them from the English countryside, their verandahs incongruously roofed with corrugated iron, their tall chimneys aromatic with eucalyptus smoke. Or there were the stone farmhouses built by British settlers in the

---

[1] Darjeeling remains much as it was, and the hill-towns of India, half-heartedly copied elsewhere, were to prove, I think, the only truly original socio-architectural conception of the British Empire—unless you count the bungalow.

[2] And had a ghost which, perpetually wandering its corridors, moaned down the years an enigmatic message: '*It's a quarter past eleven*'.

flank of the Little Karroo, along the coast from Cape Town—buildings so strong, so organic, so deep-shaded by trees and cosy with dry-stone walling, so exquisitely set in their hill-sides, that they might have been lifted stone by stone from Radnor or Brecknock, together with their pigs, sheep and leather buckets.[1] And the handsomest small market towns of East Anglia could offer no happier architectural ensemble than the public square at St George's in Bermuda, which was seventeenth century in origin, but had been discreetly embellished and preserved throughout the heyday of the sugar colonies: an authentic hole-in-corner English square, opening at one side to the harbour, and cluttered all about with wood-framed shuttered houses, open staircases and tall white chimneys—two comfortable old pubs, and the town pillory, and poking quaintly above the houses the tower of St Peter's, 300 years old already, in whose shady churchyard the negroes sprawled and gossiped among the tombs sealed with whitewash, and from whose belfry on Sundays mellowed English bells summoned the expatriates to worship.

But this modesty of scale and demeanour had not survived. The early settlers knew their place in the comparative order of things, but your mid-century Australian or Canadian was limitless of pretension. The cities of the new British nations were urgently grandiose: ugly often, like Toronto, heavy sometimes like Melbourne and Auckland, but never diffident and seldom mean. Even the cramped terrace houses of Sydney, sprawling in their white thousands over the hills of Paddington or Balmain, possessed a certain air of ease, with their wrought-iron balconies and their voluptuous magnolias, while in fast-rising suburbs from Victoria to Ontario the new rich of the British Empire, flourishing on wool or diamonds, railway boom or ostrich feather fashions, built themselves mansions in the full amplitude of the Gothic orthodoxy.

Such new buildings offered no ideological lessons. They were no longer a projection of ideals, like the great white houses along

[1] When I was looking at these buildings in 1970 I stopped for tea at the Kruis Valley Tea Rooms. I was given home-made brown bread, butter and strawberry jam, and ventured to strum through some of the music I found on the piano—*Smilin' Through*, and Henry Hall's Selection of Love Songs. The Empire dies hard in nooks and crannies.

Garden Reach at Calcutta, nor was there to them any suggestion of fantasy or transience. They expressed, like Darjeeling, more pride than purpose. We are here, they seemed to say, on top of the world: as though the dream of empire, scarcely yet formulated, had already in a sense been fulfilled. The Anglo-Indian bungalow had begun life modestly and racily as a Europeanized Bengali cottage—a stationary tent, as one Englishman suggested in 1801: but by the middle of the century it had become, with its wide verandahs, its gauze screens, its elaborate cooling devices and the servants thronged and squabbling through its out-buildings, more like a rich man's retreat.

4

For if some of the gaiety was leaving the Empire now, so was much of the easy amateurism. In art especially a new professionalism was apparent. The British Empire had never been short of artists: every possession, every campaign, had been meticulously recorded in a hundred sketch-books. There had always been professionals in the field, men like the Daniells or Zoffany who followed the flag specifically in search of subjects or commissions: but more notably, there had been an inexhaustible number of amateurs. Many were soldiers, especially engineers, who had learnt the elements of sketching as part of their military training, and whose pictures were touched up for them, or corrected, by professionals at home. Many were officers' wives, among whose lady-like accomplishments water-colour painting was almost obligatory.

So the earlier years of Victoria's empire were richly recorded. Often the pictures were fearfully inaccurate, sometimes as a result of the professional touching-up, sometimes because of lack of skill, sometimes because the artist over-responded to his stimuli, and saw the giant carved figures of the Elephanta Caves, say, or the rapids of the Winnipeg River, even bigger or more tumultuous than they really were. These distortions were, however, guileless. They were part of the prevailing dilettante charm, like the harmless exaggeration of a raconteur, or a memory that grows brighter with the years. By the 1850s a different kind of distortion was appearing. Now for the first time we see imperialist art. In the popular history books hack professionals portrayed the scenes of the Mutiny in a spirit of vicious caricature, while the generals or pro-consuls whose pictures appeared in the magazines began to look more than mortal. An unearthly aura seems to surround the imperial heroes in these commissioned portraits, and they stand in god-like poses on their hillocks, or battlements, or Parliamentary terraces, holding foam-flecked chargers, maps or Order Papers: their faces are invariably grim, they are often romantically cloaked or furred, and they seem to be looking out across veld or S.W.1. towards imperial hazards yet to be defied.

Even in the flesh, one sometimes feels, the imperial activists now moved pictorially. We read of an incident, for instance, during the siege of Lucknow, when the Nepali prince Jung Bahadur visited General Colin Campbell in his tent outside the city. A guard of kilted Highlanders greeted him, pipers stalked up and down, the guns of battle rumbled and shook the ground as the two men talked, and in the middle of the durbar, impeccably timed, a tall and handsome British officer, glamorous in fighting gear, entered the tent to report the capture of one of the main enemy strongholds—'very little loss on our side, about 500 of the enemy killed!' Or consider the British entry into Peking during the China War of 1856, when Lord Elgin arrived to express the Queen's displeasure at the obstructive behaviour of the Chinese. Three miles up the highway to the House of Ceremonies the British majestically marched—General Sir Robert Napier in the van, Lord Elgin in a sumptuous sedan chair with another horseback general at his side, then 400 marching soldiers, and 100 sailors, and two bands—through the symbolic gates of the hall, through the ornamental gardens, up the cobbled way—and when, near the Grand Entrance, Prince Kung, attended by 500 mandarins, closed his hands before his face in submissive greeting, 'Lord Elgin', we are told, 'returned him a proud contemptuous look, and merely bowed slightly, which must have made the blood run cold in the poor Prince's veins'.

5

One man with a dream, at pleasure,
Shall go forth and conquer a crown;

The Imperial Style

And three with a new song's measure
Can trample a kingdom down. . . .

Yet the dream did not, by and large, much inspire the writers of
England. They could not ignore the imperial crescendo, of course,
and many had imperial connections of their own. Captain Marryat
captured the Akyab Peninsula in the first Burmese War. Fanny
Burney's brother was first Resident of Arakan. Thomas Love Peacock worked at East India House. Thackeray was born in India. One
of Dickens' sons was in the Canadian police, another was buried in
Calcutta. Sometimes they portrayed imperial characters incidentally, as Thackeray immortalized the nabobs in the person of Colonel
Newcome, and Dickens lampooned the evangelical imperialists in
Mrs Jellyby. Carlyle, Ruskin, Matthew Arnold, all wrote around the
imperial theme at one time or another, and by the nature of his
office Tennyson, Poet Laureate through the High Victorian years,
intermittently celebrated the Queen's imperial dignity—

> *. . . Statesmen at her council met*
> *Who knew the seasons when to take*
> *Occasion by the hand, and make*
> *The bounds of freedom wider yet.*

> *By shaping some august decree*
> *Which kept her throne unshaken still,*
> *Broad-based upon her people's will,*
> *And compassed by the inviolate sea.*[1]

The best novels about imperial life were written by practitioners on
the spot (most of the worst, too, especially those that made up the
vast and painful corpus of Anglo-Indian romance). Meadows Taylor,
for instance, was an Anglo-Indian whose book *Confessions of a Thug*
was a memorable fictional reportage of the Sleeman campaign: while
Marcus Clarke's *For the Term of His Natural Life*, which first exposed

---

[1] Though Tennyson was not so obvious a choice for Laureate as one might
suppose—'there are three or four authors of nearly equal merit', wrote Lord
John Russell to the Queen in 1850, 'such as Henry Taylor, Sheridan Knowles,
Professor Wilson, and Mr Tennyson, who are qualified for the office'.

the horrors of the Tasmanian convict settlements, approached the stature of epic.[1]

But the giants of the day did not respond to the fact of British ascendancy in the world, the establishment of new Britains overseas, or the hardening imperial arrogance of the nation. No great literature came out of the Mutiny, one of the most extraordinary events in human history; nobody wrote the sagas of the imperial families, generation succeeding generation on the distant frontiers; to English men of letters the imperial story was only ancillary to greater themes at home, and even the wistful imperial tragedies of time, distance or disillusion, did not seem the stuff of art.

6

Only the lapidary monuments of the Raj sometimes suggested this fragile sense of waste. Occasionally a tomb itself revealed it, like the little Ionic temple which, high above Grand Harbour at Malta, honoured the memory of Sir Alexander Ball, the first Governor—built of Malta's soft golden stone, shaded by palms and hibiscuses, and looking so cool, so white, so small and poignant in that setting that it might have been a monument to homesickness itself. More often it was the inscription upon the tombs that could move the susceptible traveller. Comic sometimes, pathetic very often, sometimes pompous, sometimes innocent, they were like a communal text of the great adventure, chiselled on granite, sandstone or marble across half the world.

They could be caustic, like this tribute to a Governor of Bermuda:

To enumerate the many rare Virtues which shone united in the Governor of that little Spot were to tell how many great Talents and excellent Endowments are wanting in some, whom the Capriciousness of Fortune Exposes in a more elevated and Conspicuous station.

They could be melancholy, like this plaint from West Africa:

By foreign hands thy dying lips were closed,
By foreign hands thy decent limbs composed,

[1] And seems to me distinctly akin, in style and intent as in material, to the revelatory novels of post-Stalinist Russia.

The Imperial Style

By foreign hands thy humble grace adorned,
By strangers honoured and by strangers mourned.

Often, especially after about 1850, they expressed with a stunning blandness the evangelical fatalism of the day, like that favourite epitaph for babies dying in the miseries of a tropic confinement or infancy—*The Lord gave and the Lord hath taken away, Blessed be the name of the Lord.* This is the motto that Battery Sergeant Major J. Evans, Royal Artillery, chose for the grave of his little daughter, Minnie, aged 4½, buried at Malta in 1874: I'M GONE TO JESUS. WILL YOU COME!! And when they erected a memorial church upon the site of the entrenchment at Cawnpore, to honour the Britons so hideously slaughtered at the Ghat or in the Bibighar, they placed upon its wall a definitive text of imperial Christianity: *The sufferings of the present time are not worthy to be compared with all the glory which shall be revealed to us.*

Sometimes epitaphs successfully translated the bravado of the imperial way—*Abruptly Terminated by Assassins,* as it said succinctly of somebody's life on a brass in Lahore Cathedral. At Multan, for instance, the epitaph of two young administrators whose assassination in 1848 led to the final annexation of the Punjab began with the romantic declaration:

On this, the farthest frontier of the British Indian Empire,
which their deaths extended,
lie the remains of

PETER VANS AGNEW		WILLIAM ANDERSON
of the	and	Lieut. 1st Bombay
Bengal Civil Service		Fusilier Regt.

And hardly less vibrant was the tributary verse to General Sir Charles Fraser, V.C., in the Royal Garrison Church at Aldershot:

Wounded, helpless, sick, dismounted,
Charlie Fraser, well I knew
Come the worst I might have counted
Faithfully on you.[1]

[1] The regimental spirit is perhaps less advisedly evoked in a neighbouring memorial, whose subject is said to have died 'from the effects of a wound

The nearest to literary grandeur among the imperial epitaphs, perhaps, was achieved by Macaulay, who wrote the tribute to Lord William Bentinck inscribed upon his statue on the Maidan at Calcutta:

Who, placed at the head of a great Empire, never laid aside the simplicity and moderation of a private citizen. . . . Who infused into oriental despotism the spirit of British freedom. . . . Who never forgot that the end of Government is the welfare of the governed. . . . Who abolished cruel rites. . . . Who effaced humiliating distinctions. . . . Whose constant study it was to elevate the moral and intellectual character of the nation committed to his charge. . . .

And undoubtedly it was Walter Savage Landor, in the most famous imperial epitaph of all, who came nearest to capturing the frail sense of disillusion that haunted the British Empire even in its prime. Rose Aylmer was an almost legendary young Anglo-Welsh beauty with whom Landor had fallen in love at sight one day in the Swansea Circulating Library. She had been staying with an aunt in India, had died of dysentery, and had been buried in the Park Street Cemetery in Calcutta, itself an imperial city of the dead, laid out in avenues of domes, obelisks and classical temples like an architectural display. Upon her tomb was inscribed the elegy which almost alone, among all the hundreds of thousands of imperial epitaphs, catches the heartbreaking loss of life and love which was so often the price of dominion:

> *Ah, what avails the sceptred race!*
> *Ah, what the form divine!*
> *What every virtue, every grace!*
> *Rose Aylmer, all were thine.*
>
> *Rose Aylmer, whom these wakeful eyes*
> *May weep, but never see,*
> *A night of memories and sighs*
> *I consecrate to thee.*

received in action with the regiment at El Teb, the re-opening of which was caused by over-exertion at the regimental athletic sports'.

She was 20 when she died so squalidly in Bengal—from eating too much fruit, we are told—and the poet survived her for sixty-four years.

7

Let us end with the humblest of literary forms, the graffito. Every empire left its scratches. The Spanish conquistadores carved their names in exquisite calligraphy on desert rocks in New Mexico. The Romans cut theirs sacrilegiously upon the Colossi of Memnos. The British left the same such homely souvenirs across the world, wherever a ship put in, a company halted on the march, or an idle sentry doodled with his bayonet point in the night. At Muscat in the Persian Gulf, where the British claimed misty powers of suzerainty, a tall bluff above the harbour was daubed all over with the names of British warships, piquantly flaunted up there beside the fortress that represented the lost empire of the Portuguese. On the walls of the water catchment tank at English Harbour, in Antigua, Nelson himself had scratched the name of his ship, HMS *Borealis*, and the remains of his own name could still be seen, it was said, among the myriad Robinsons, Thomases and Williamses carved there in the limestone. On the ruins of Persepolis in Persia, that grand fragment of an older empire, generations of British imperialists had shamelessly carved their signatures: wandering diplomats and intelligence agents, soldiers scouting the approaches to India, unexplained adventurers, scholars taking the long road home. And in the Red Fort at Delhi, where the British Army now maintained a garrison of its own, many a redcoat had by now scratched his initials, his regiment and the homesick date upon Bahadur's soft sandstone. Slightly sweaty we may imagine such a young man there, in his thick serge and white-crusted webbing, his rifle propped against the wall, his helmet pushed to the back of his head, his tongue protruding slightly in concentration beneath his moustache: the bul-buls sing in the garden trees, a distant clamour sounds from the bazaar, a desultory murmur of Indian voices rises from some shadowy arch beneath his watchtower—until he hears the orderly sergeant approaching, with a stertorous clatter up the winding stone staircase, and hastily returning his bayonet to his scabbard, tilting his topee correctly above his eyes, he stands ready with his back to the parapet, in case those new-scratched letters in the old stone, with half a heart and a sweetheart's crooked initials, should show up in the moonlight and betray him.[1]

[1] All these graffiti may still be seen by the indefatigable aficionado of Empire, and most of the epitaphs too, though I have taken some anachronistic liberties in their selection, are still legible—even Bentinck's, for his statue is one of those that remain on the Maidan at Calcutta. Perhaps I may be allowed to add one more for its own sake—that of Lieutenant Christopher Hyland of the 62nd Regt., who died in Bermuda in 1837 and is buried beneath the sly backhander, devised perhaps by his mess-mates:

> *Alas, he is not lost,*
> *But is gone before.*

CHAPTER FOURTEEN

Illustrious for the Nile

O N September 16, 1864, the spa of Bath in Somerset awoke in a
state of half-illicit anticipation. Long past its prime as a
fashionable resort, its prevailing tone was set now by retired military men and colonial administrators, and the walls of its ancient
abbey were crowded with memorials to the imperial departed—as
was said of them,

> *These walls, so full of monument and bust,*
> *Show how Bath's waters serve to lay the dust.*

Bath's glorious Georgian squares and crescents, which made it one
of the handsomest cities in Europe, were mostly peeled and shabby:
the old place had subsided into provincial respectability, and had
acquired a name for seedy dullness that was to persist for another
century.

But September 1864 was a gala month there. The British Association for the Advancement of Science, founded thirty years before to
foster public interest in the sciences, was holding its annual conference in the city. Savants and enthusiasts had arrived from all over
the kingdom, and at a moment when applied science had reached an
apogee of esteem, all educated eyes were turned to the proceedings
in Somerset. The London newspapers carried long daily accounts;
the *Bath Chronicle* had imported forty typesetters from the capital to
produce a daily newspaper reporting nothing else. The celebrated
squares, parades and terraces of the city were alive with the comings
and goings of the great, and the *Chronicle's* social reporters[1] could
scarcely keep up with the soirées, the concerts, the balls and the private dinner parties—over whose tables, between whose quadrilles,

---

[1] Who continued until 1939 to record the arrival of hotel guests in Bath.

eminent men of science argued the possibilities of a fifth dimension, or discussed the anthropological characteristics of the Lapps Public interest had never been so great, and the attendance was a record: 1,630 members and associates had applied for tickets, and that did not count, of course, foreigners or ladies.

For the general public the greatest scientific excitement of the day was exploration. The urge to open up the world was inextricably linked with the gathering emotions of Empire, and anything to do with foreign discovery aroused an avid interest. The Royal Geographical Society, a force in the land, held its own annual conference as Section E (Geography and Ethnology) of the British Association, and down at Bath the real lions of the month were the celebrities returned from exotic parts. Henry Bates the Amazon naturalist was there, and Bishop Colenso of Zululand, and J. M. Stuart, the first man to cross Australia from south to north, who was visibly and satisfyingly shattered by his terrible journey two years before. Dr Livingstone of Africa was staying in appropriate splendour at No. 13, The Circus, one of the finest houses in Bath, attended wherever he went by adulatory crowds; and present too, though less easily recognized, were influential figures on the fringe of the exploratory saga, like Sir William Armstrong of Newcastle, whose patented rifled guns kept the world, in a manner of speaking, safe for British adventure. Bath that September, in fact, was like an analogue of the imperial momentum itself—the zest, the hero-worship, the covert rivalries, the fascination of distant places and sensational goings-on, not least the sanctimony—for as Dr Livingstone told the Mayor's welcoming banquet at the Guildhall, British discoveries were never selfishly hoarded, but were 'communicated to the world, and being known to the whole world were prevented from being lost'.

Even by these stimulating standards the 16th was a special day. Among the celebrities in the city were the two most controversial figures of African exploration, Richard Burton and John Hanning Speke. They were enemies. Together they had, in 1856, gone to Africa to search for the source of the White Nile, the supreme prize of exploration. Speke claimed to have found the source, during a solitary sortie. Burton doubted it, and the resultant quarrel had become public property. The antagonists were theatrically contrasted. Speke, the scion of a well-known Somerset family, was an upstanding young Victorian gentleman of the middle rank, a sports-man to his finger-tips, boyish and well-spoken, his eyes frank, his ears slightly cauliflowered. Unmarried at 37, he was a local hero: his family home, Jordans, was only forty miles away, and he had relatives on the outskirts of Bath itself. Burton, on the other hand, could hardly have been more alien to the spa. He was the very antithesis of Victorian decorum. His eyes flamed, his black mous-taches drooped, he had a profound knowledge of oriental porno-graphy and was reputed to have done dreadful things in many remote corners of the world. He had made a famous journey in disguise to the forbidden places of Mecca, and had been the first European to penetrate the scarcely less alarming city of Harar in Ethiopia. A true scholar and a marvellous linguist—he had translated the Portuguese poet Camoens—Burton had recently married a hare-brained, fanatic but doting Catholic, Isabel Arundell, and he lived in a more or less constant condition of fury.

These two men had not met since their return from Africa in 1859, but the newspapers and learned journals had reverberated with their differences. The insults and innuendoes had grown more vicious each year, and as a climax to it all the Royal Geographical Society had arranged a formal confrontation between them, to be held in public at 3 pm on the 16th as part of Section E's proceedings. It was the prospect of this meeting that so excited Bath that morn-ing Anything, it was thought, might happen—*The Times* called it a gladiatorial exhibition. While Speke might be expected to behave with a certain Somerset restraint, the daemonic Burton was capable of any enormity, and with Livingstone himself tipped as a probable referee, the meeting promised the combined allures of a sporting contest, a scientific debate and an evangelical demonstration.

2

The compelling fascination of the Nile had exerted itself upon empires long before the British. Through the centuries historians, geographers and romantics had propounded theories about its source, which had acquired in turn a fabulous, an intellectual and a

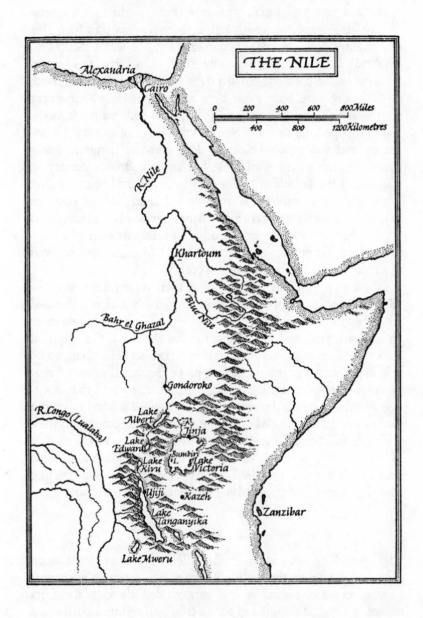

THE NILE

Alexandria
Cairo

0   200   400   600   800 Miles
0   400   800   1200 Kilometres

R. Nile

Khartoum

Bahr el Ghazal

Blue Nile

Gondoroko

R. Congo (Lualaba)

Lake Albert

Jinja

Lake Edward

Bumbiri I.

Lake Kivu

Lake Victoria

Ujiji

Kazeh

Zanzibar

Lake Tanganyika

Lake Mweru

strategic meaning. The river was said to spring from 'fountains' deep in the African interior, from a range of snow-capped peaks, from a system of great lakes, or from Ptolemy's Mountains of the Moon in Ethiopia. The source of the Blue Nile had been identified by James Bruce the Scot in 1770, but the greater stream, the White Nile, remained as total a mystery as ever. Nobody knew where it came from. It was a superb enigma, and as the British responded to their imperial destiny, as the public began to acquire its proprietorial interest in the other side of the horizon, as the London strategists evolved the theory that control of Egypt was essential to the security of British India, so the conundrum of the Nile became almost a national obsession. The British regarded it as a challenge specific to themselves, its solution as the greatest prize awaiting any British adventurer of the nineteenth century: and the tremendous journeys of the explorers in inner Africa, lasting years at a time, chronicled with mysterious rumour and consummated with best-sellers, provided for twenty years a running excitement for the people.

Burton and Speke had been the first to make the attempt. By 1858 most of Africa was imperfectly understood. Kilimanjaro and Kenya had been seen. Much of the Niger had been navigated. The Kalahari was penetrated. The mythical Timbuctoo had been reached at last, and had proved a dreary fraud. The time was right, the pundits of the R.G.S. had decided, for a determined attempt to reach the fountains of the Nile: so they commissioned Burton and Speke, both officers of the Indian Army, to make the attempt from the east coast—the most direct route, it was assumed, and one whose lower course had been well established by generations of Arab slavers bringing their captives for shipment at Zanzibar. The two soldiers had already been in Africa together, on a disastrous expedition in Somaliland four years before. Burton, at 37, was famous for his journey to Mecca: Speke was 31, unknown but ambitious.

One would have thought them incompatible from the start— Burton the rootless Anglo-Irish intellectual, bored by blood sports and picking up languages like stones from the ground, Speke the quintessential English sportsman, 'a right good, jolly, resolute fellow' who seldom read a book—the one believing that the extension of Christianity was a prime purpose of exploration, the other almost alone among public figures of his time in thinking that Islam could do better.

In February 1858 they together became, nevertheless, the first Europeans to set eyes on Lake Tanganyika, which Burton thought might be the Nile's source: but it appeared to lie too low, and had no apparent outlet. Exhausted and sick—Speke was almost blind with trachoma, Burton half-paralysed by malaria—they returned to recuperate at the slave-trading settlement of Kazeh, which stood at a cross-roads of the slave routes.[1] There the acquaintance was further strained, Burton delighting in the company of the unprincipled Arab grandees of the place, Speke, one feels, suspecting them of vices even worse than slaving. So Burton was only too pleased when Speke, his eyesight recovered, proposed to make a solitary reconnaissance to the north, leaving Burton to work up his notes and get his strength back. They had heard of another, larger body of water, Ukerewe or the Northern Lake, three weeks' journey away. Might this not be the source of the Nile? Burton was not very interested, but early in June Speke set off on mule-back, with twenty porters and thirty armed guards, determined to find out.

So the controversy began. Twenty-five days later, on August 3, 1858, Speke became the first European to reach what is now Lake Victoria Nyanza. It is easy to imagine why the experience had for him a revelatory quality. Set among rolling scrubby downland, interspersed with forests of dark green—speckled with little islands, haunted by ibis in the daytime and fireflies at night—splashed with gay tropic colours of mango, orchid and wavering bird, and rippled always by a warm African breeze, the lake was a marvellous surprise. Some 250 miles long, only a little smaller than Scotland, it was really an inland sea, and in that country seemed spectacularly anomalous, like an error of creation, or at least an afterthought.

Speke was later to become a favourite victim of Freudian amateurs, and certainly his reactions to this grand vision invite analysis. The names he chose for his discoveries were revealing in themselves. The hillock he stood upon he called Somerset, the creek at his feet he called Jordans, the lake he called Victoria for the queen—

[1] It is now called Tabora, and is a railway junction on the line from Dar-es-Salaam to Lake Tanganyika.

herself, we are imaginatively told, a dream-synonym for his mother. And he went on to reach a dramatic intuitive conclusion. He flatly decided, without further evidence, that this was the source of the Nile. He explored no further. He spent only three days on the lake. He saw no river outlet. Yet he *knew*, for certain, that this was the beginning of the White Nile, and he hurried excitedly back to Kazeh to tell Burton.

His reception there was caustic. 'It was,' Burton recorded drily, 'an inspiration perhaps . . . the fortunate discoverer's conviction was strong; his reasons were weak.' A local worthy had told Speke that Lake Victoria probably extended to the end of the world. 'Strongly impressed by this statistical information,' Burton commented in his best pedagogic style, 'my companion therefore planned the northern limit about four to five degrees north lat.' It was not that Burton dismissed Victoria as the main source of the Nile. It was Speke's irrational certainty that infuriated him, coupled no doubt with a nagging feeling that he had missed his own chance of glory by staying behind.

Like husband and wife at the end of a long day, they found they could not mention the subject without bicker, and so they returned laboriously and unhappily to the coast, sick, exhausted and tired of each other—they had been in each other's company for nearly three years. When they reached Aden it was agreed that Speke should go on to England at once, and that Burton should follow a little later, when he was stronger. According to Burton, the parting was self-consciously cordial. 'I shall hurry up, Jack,' Burton said, 'as soon as I can,' and Speke is alleged to have replied: 'Goodbye, old fellow; you may be quite sure I shall not go up to the Royal Geographical Society until you come to the fore and we appear together. Make your mind quite easy about that.'

But when Burton reached England, only two weeks later, Speke's 'discovery of the Nile's source' was already one of the excitements of London. Speke had reported to the R.G.S. the very first day after his arrival, and was presently commissioned to take his own expedition back to Africa to confirm his conclusions. Burton arrived home almost disregarded—'a mere skeleton', Isabel recorded, 'with brown-yellow skin hanging in bags, his eyes protruding, and his lips drawn away from his teeth'. He must have been worth seeing, but nobody took much notice of him—the ground was, he said, 'completely cut from under my feet'. The two men never spoke to each other again, and Burton never returned to the Nile.

3

But Speke went back with a very different companion, James Augustus Grant of the Indian Army, who worshipped Speke with a spaniel devotion, and who would never dream of contradicting him: a gentleman through and through, as was said of him, the son of a Scottish minister, an ardent big game hunter, a gallant campaigner in the Indian Mutiny, huge of build, unquenchably modest of demeanour—'that old creature Grant', General Gordon was to write of him years later, 'who for 17 or 18 years has traded on his wonderful walk'.

Their journey this time led them through the three queer kingdoms of Uganda—Bunyoro, Buganda, Karagwe—which lay along the western shore of Lake Victoria, and had never been visited by white men before: the many queens of Karagwe were fed entirely on milk, and were so fat that they could only grovel seductively on the floor, the King of Buganda walked in a stiff tiptoe way meant to simulate a lion's prowl, and had burnt alive some sixty of his own brothers, and when Speke once went for a drink with the Queen-Mother, he found her on all fours drinking beer out of a trough. Escaping with difficulty from these peculiar hosts, Speke and Grant set off once more to the north, and once again, by instinct, accident or design, Speke was alone when he reached Jinja, on the northern shore of the great lake, and saw at last, with his own eyes, the Nile falling over its rim in cataract and rainbow.

The river banks there were covered with thick jungle, and coming upstream Speke could not see the lake until he was quite close to it. Then, as he crossed a fold in the ground, suddenly the falls were there: beyond them lay the vast green-blue expanse of the lake, and the water tumbled over its edge like a bath overflowing, splashing and rushing to the rapids below, where fish leapt in thousands through the spray, where crocodiles and hippopotami lay in the shallows, where every rock was crowned by its slim black fishermen, and the whole air glistened with the shine of the spray.[1] This time Speke had no qualms when he returned to camp. He felt himself absolutely vindicated, and Grant agreed. 'Inform Sir Roderick Murchison,' they cabled home as soon as they could, 'that all is well . . . and that the Nile is settled.'

But it was not. When Speke and Grant stumbled into the southern Egyptian outpost of Gondoroko, after two and a half years in the field, they found an unexpected Englishman hurrying to greet them: a big, jolly, bewhiskered personage, his eyes full of fun and confidence, who advanced upon the exhausted explorers like a vision of Christmas to come. This was Samuel Baker, son of a prosperous shipowner, who had knocked about the world from Ceylon to the Danube, and had now come to Africa with his beautiful young Hungarian wife to rescue Speke and Grant, if they need rescuing, and to do some exploring on his own. Baker decided that, since it was now clear that the Nile *did* emerge from Lake Victoria Nyanza, he would try to discover if there were any other source. Speke and Grant had not followed the whole course of the Nile, on their way northwards from Victoria: they had taken a big short cut, and there was evidence that in the loop of the river they did not see some additional supply of water entered the stream. There must exist, the Bakers thought, another lake: and so, armed with Speke's own map, they marched boldly off to find it.

They had a frightful journey. All their baggage horses died, they were laid low with fever, their porters mutinied, savages attacked them with poisoned arrows. The King of Bunyoro demanded Mrs Baker as a hostage, offering one of his own virgins in exchange, until Baker drew his pistol and threatened to shoot him there and then, and Mrs Baker, rising terribly from her seat, hurled at the monarch a tirade in Arabic, of which he understood not one word. It was a proper Victorian adventure. The hero was stalwart, and British. The heroine, though foreign-born, was beautiful and brave—'not a

---

[1] The falls have been obliterated by the construction of the Owen Falls power station downstream, and there is a golf course on the lakeshore near the Nile effluent: a club rule allows the removal of a ball by hand if it lands in a hippopotamus footprint.

screamer', as her husband put it. The savages were savage. The elephants screamed 'like railway engines'. When the explorers could not jolly man or nature into compliance, they used a touch of healthy British persuasion, like a cocked gun or an upper-cut to the jaw, and they entered every hazard, recorded every spectacle, with an enthusiastic diligence worthy of Prince Albert himself (who had died, as it happened, soon after their departure from London).

On March 14, 1864, Baker spurred his ox up a hill on a fine spring morning, and looking down a steep granite cliff at his feet, saw the lake they were looking for. It was like a sea of quicksilver, he thought, bounded far in the distance by blue mountains, and glittering in the sun. 'England had won the source of the Nile! Long before I reached this spot, I had arranged to give three cheers with all our men in English style in honour of this discovery, but now . . . I felt too serious to vent my feelings in vain cheers for victory, and I sincerely thanked God for having guided and supported us through all dangers to the good end. As an imperishable memorial of one loved and mourned by our gracious Queen and deplored by every Englishman' (Baker ambiguously adds) 'I called this great lake "The Albert Nyanza"'—and so the White Nile acquired, in both its branches, an imperial pedigree.[1]

4

The twin reservoirs of the river were thus identified, but even so the Nile was not settled. During Baker's absence the controversy between Burton and Speke had reached its climax, with public opinion veering now towards Burton's view that the true source of the Nile was much farther south, in the vicinity of Lake Tanganyika. Neither Victoria nor Albert had yet been circumnavigated: it was possible that Tanganyika and Albert were in fact linked by a river, or that another big river flowed into Victoria. For by now the search for the true source was becoming a little farcical, and the hunt was being pursued or argued from lake to feeder, feeder to tributary, tributary to spring, to locate the very farthest point from which the principal flow of the river could be said to issue—a river which, though in its

[1] Imperishable too, it seems: even the Russian atlases still call them Lakes Victoria and Albert.

last thousand miles it receives no tributary at all, in the first thousand miles is fed by dozens of streams, lakes and ancillary watersheds. The mid-Victorians believed in ultimate truths. Bruce had discovered the actual group of springs from which the Blue Nile issued. His successors were determined to pinpoint the exact damp origin of the White.

In 1865, the R.G.S. accordingly turned to an elder statesman among explorers, David Livingstone, and commissioned him to settle the issue. At 52 this marvellous and maddening Scot stood in a different class from all his colleagues. He was the Christian hero, in an age when the cult of the hero, particularly one both holy and remote, was in the ascendant. The son of a modest tea-merchant, with a medical degree from Glasgow, he had gone to Africa as a medical missionary, but was famous for his great exploratory journeys— across the Kalahari, down the Zambesi, through the basin of the Nyasa. He had done more than anyone to expose the continuing evils of the African slave trade, and he had established relations with the African peoples different in kind from those of other explorers and missionaries. Idiosyncratic though he was, quarrelsome, stubborn, conceited, he had a magic gift. People of unexpected kinds responded to him, and those who did not detest him loved him devotedly.[1]

Livingstone's prestige was enormous—Florence Nightingale called him the greatest man of his generation. Though in fact his life had been largely a life of failure, personal and professional, still he was one of the most famous men on earth, idolized by the public and respected by the scientific community. He would be the perfect arbiter of the Nile dispute, in the field as in the debating chamber: so at the beginning of 1865 Murchison invited him, on behalf of the R.G.S., to return to Africa to solve 'a question of intense geographical interest . . . namely the watershed or watersheds of South Africa'. Did Lake Tanganyika empty itself to the north? And if so, could the river that flowed out of it possibly be the Nile?

[1] As the Dictionary of National Biography records in a celebrated passage: 'Livingstone got off his riding-ox, and in spite of his weak health presented a six-barrelled revolver at the chief's stomach. This prompt action at once converted him into a friend'.

It was Livingstone's last and greatest adventure, and it was purely secular, unless one argued that British supremacy in geographic science would be best for the natives in the long run. On the whole Livingstone supported Burton's theories. He thought the true beginning of the Nile would prove to be a river that arose south-west of Tanganyika, called by the Africans Lualaba. This might itself be the Nile, he thought, or alternatively, Albert and Tanganyika might form part of a central chain of lakes, through all of which the Nile flowed. In April 1866, he set off from Zanzibar to find out, accompanied by no Europeans, but by four old African friends, Chuma, Susi, Amoda and Wikatani. Before he reached Lake Tanganyika a terrible calamity occurred. He lost his medicine chest. 'I felt,' he wrote, 'as if I had now received the sentence of death.' Certainly from that moment nothing went right. Delayed by tribal wars, constantly sick, losing his teeth one by one, no more, he said, than 'a ruckle of bones', he pushed slowly on to the eastern shore of Tanganyika, reaching the Arab slavers' village of Ujiji very near death.

He had hoped to find supplies there, but they had all been looted, and there was no mail for him either. He was almost beaten by these disappointments, and spent six whole months at Ujiji trying to regain his strength. Then he moved painfully westward once more. Months and years passed in his wanderings, 1869 into 1870, and then into 1871, and still he looked for the Lualaba. By now hardly anyone would help him. He had never disguised his enmity to the Arab slave-traders of the interior, while the local Africans were too terrified of the slavers to come near him. Even his own porters deserted. He could get no reply to the messages he sent to Zanzibar. His shoulder, torn by a lion years before, was giving him great pain, he was half-starved and had practically lost hope. When at last, after five years in the field, he reached the banks of the Lualaba, nobody would row him down the river to see which way it turned in its flow, or whether it really could be the Nile.

So he limped back to Ujiji and threw himself upon the mercy of the Arabs, hoping somehow or other, one day, to continue his quest. There he lay sick, penniless and exhausted, lost to the world, utterly out of touch with Europe, his mission a failure, his whereabouts one of the mysteries of the age: and there on November 10, 1871, Henry

Stanley of the *New York Herald*, advancing into his camp beneath the Stars and Stripes, with his caravan of porters loaded with bales of food, tents, expensive equipment and ingenious accessories to African travel, walked through the wondering crowd of Arabs, took off his hat, and uttered one of the epic texts of the Victorian age, as sacred to the faithful as it was comic to the irreverent: '*Dr Livingstone, I presume?*'

' "Yes", he said with a kind smile, lifting his cap slightly.'

5

Stanley was a Welshman. Born John Rowlands at Denbigh in 1841, he had run away from the workhouse at St Asaph, and shipped as a cabin-boy for the United States. There he was adopted by a kindly cotton-broker, Mr Stanley of New Orleans. After fighting on both sides in the civil war (he was never a man of strong convictions) Stanley had taken to journalism, becoming the best-known special correspondent of the *New York Herald*. Having distinguished himself in reporting a small war in Abyssinia, Stanley had been given an agreeable roaming commission. 'Go to Jerusalem, Constantinople, the Crimea, the Caspian Sea, through Persia as far as India. After that you can start looking round for Livingstone. If he is dead bring back every possible proof of his death.'

Stanley had done as he was told. He had travelled through the Holy Land, had scratched his graffito upon the walls of Persepolis, had reported on imperial India, and in January 1871 had arrived at Zanzibar, tough, 30 years old and very bumptious, on the last stage of his mission. He knew nothing about Africa, or about exploration, but he was a hard-bitten, ambitious, able and healthy young newspaperman, ready to do anything for a good story. Finding Dr Livingstone would be an incomparable scoop, to use the word just coming into vogue in American newspaper offices. He had plenty of money, so he bought all the best gear and hired all the most reliable porters: but he took no chances, in the way of his trade, and told nobody in Zanzibar the purpose of his journey. If anyone asked him where he was going, he simply said 'To Africa'.

He followed the now familiar route west, along the tracks of

Burton, Speke, Grant, the slave caravans, and on the way he repeatedly heard rumours of a European living on the shore of Lake Tanganyika—an old wan man with grey moustaches—a man walking, wearing American suiting and a cap—a white man at a place called Urua—finally, as he approached the lake, an old sick man with hair upon his face, who had come from a very far country, and was living at Ujiji. Stanley's excitement was transferred professionally to the pages of his book *How I Found Livingstone*. 'Hurrah! This is Livingstone! He must be Livingstone! He *can* be no other!' As they approached Ujiji he ordered Old Glory unfurled (though he thought of himself still as British, he was an American citizen), and soon he was surrounded by hundreds of negroes and Arabs from the village, shouting '*Tambo, bwana, Tambo!*'—'Welcome!'

Down they all went into Ujiji, and there in the distance on the verandah of his hut they saw Livingstone. 'I see the doctor, sir', said one of Stanley's Africans. 'Oh, what an old man! He has got a white beard!' As for Stanley himself, 'what would I not have given for a bit of friendly wilderness, where, unseen, I might vent my joy in some mad feat, such as idiotically biting my hand, turning a somersault, or slashing at trees, in order to allay those exciting feelings, that were well-nigh uncontrollable'. He did control them, however, not wishing to 'detract from the dignity of a white man appearing in such extraordinary circumstances', and so gave his folk-phrase to the language—'Dr Livingstone, I presume'.

Livingstone, it seemed, did not in the least wish to be rescued. Now that fresh supplies were at hand, he wanted only to complete his task. Stanley had other duties to perform, and taking Livingstone's precious journals with him, and bidding an affectionate and respectful goodbye to the old man, in March 1872 he left for the coast to sublimate his scoop—which very rightly made him celebrated throughout the world. From Zanzibar he sent back to Livingstone a team of porters, and in August the doctor set out once more on his travels. He had been reprieved, he thought, in order to crown his life with the supreme African discovery. 'No one will cut me out after this exploration has been accomplished, and may the good Lord of all help me to show myself His stout-hearted servant, an honour to my children, and perhaps, to my country and race. . . .'

By now he had some doubts about his own theory, fearing that the Lualaba might prove to be not the Nile, but the Congo, but he laboured on nevertheless—week after week, mile after mile, his body growing frailer with dysentery and exhaustion, his journal more despondent. 'Weary! Weary!' he writes one day. 'I am ill with bowels, having eaten nothing for eight days.' 'Inwardly I feel tired.' 'Rain, rain, rain.' 'The water was cold, and so was the wind.' 'Wet, wet, wet.' 'A dreary wet morning, and no food that we know of near.' 'This trip has made my hair all grey.' 'I am pale, and weak from bleeding profusely.' 'I am excessively weak, and but for the donkey could not move a hundred yards.' 'Tried to ride, but was forced to lie down.' The bold inked handwriting of the journal degenerates into faint and indistinct pencil: and the last entry of all, April 27, 1873, says: 'Knocked up quite and remain—recover—sent to buy milch goats. We are on the banks of the Milimamo'.

On April 30, 1873, Livingstone called for Susi and asked him how far it was to the Lualaba. Three days, he was told. He murmured 'Oh, dear, dear', and dozed off. Next morning they found him dead, kneeling by the side of his bed, his head buried in his hands upon the pillow, as if in prayer.

6

So it happened after all that the mystery of the Nile was solved not by one of your Indian Army gentlemen, nor by a rich game-hunter, nor even a saintly missionary, but by the brashest, least-educated and most successful explorer of them all. Now 34, Stanley was suspect in England. People thought him a charlatan, a fortune-hunter, an exhibitionist. He was disliked for his humble origins, his American citizenship, his Welsh showiness, his trade and his thick skin, and because he made few gestures towards higher motives.

Methodically and expertly, nevertheless, this formidable man planned a new expedition to Africa, this time jointly for the *Herald* of New York and the *Daily Telegraph* of London. First he would circumnavigate Victoria. Then he would circumnavigate Tanganyika. Finally he would sail down the Lualaba wherever it went. Thus he would, in one immense and dramatic journey, solve the problem of the Nile and make clear the shape of Central Africa. And everything he set out to do, he did. With his three young English toughs, his five English dogs, his 350 porters, his eight tons of stores and his 40-foot wooden boat the *Lady Alice*, out he went from Zanzibar once again. It was a truly imperial journey. If Africans opposed you, you shot them down. If you could not keep up, you died. Reaching Victoria Nyanza in April 1875, Stanley sailed round the whole lake and thus proved that Victoria was a single sheet of water, and that no big river flowed into it. Next, pausing only to massacre some natives on the island of Bumbiri, who had been rude to him, off he went to Lake Tanganyika, and launching the *Lady Alice* with dispatch, in a few weeks he had circumnavigated that too, and proved that it had no outlet that could qualify as a Nile source.

There remained the enigmatic Lualaba, which flowed no man knew where, and which still might prove to be the headwaters of the Nile. Two of Stanley's three Englishmen were dead by now, and Stanley himself had no notion where the voyage would take him, whether he would land up in Egypt or on the Atlantic coast, or would merely be disgorged into one or other of the lakes. But indomitably they launched the *Lady Alice* and paddled away downstream. It was the most sensational journey of all. The river led them through every kind of African hazard—fearful cataracts, cannibal assaults, portages through python-infested forests, running battles with savages in war-canoes, hunger, sickness, treacherous guides and the eerie threat of war-drums in the wilderness. Stanley's last English companion was drowned. Stanley himself was given up for dead when the *Lady Alice* was swept away in a river turbulence. But on January 20, 1877, he took an altitude reading, and found that they were 1,511 feet above sea level—some 14 feet below the level of the Nile at Gondoroko, where Speke and Grant had met the Bakers fifteen years before. So he knew that the Lualaba was not the Nile but the Congo, and that it was taking them not northward to the Mediterranean, but westward to the Atlantic Ocean.

Thus, though it was to be another seven months before Stanley's exhausted expedition arrived at the estuary of the Congo on the Atlantic shore, that day the Nile was settled.

7

Speke was right, Burton was wrong: but before we leave this, the central saga of exploration in the imperial age, and the beginning of the 'scramble for Africa' which was to give a new style to imperialism, let us go back to Bath again, in 1864, and take our leave of the original antagonists. Burton and his wife had characteristically put up at a hotel near the railway station, but Speke stayed no less typically with his cousin, George Fuller, at his agreeable country house Neston Park about ten miles from Bath. They saw each other for the first time since 1859 at a preliminary meeting in the Mineral Water Hospital on September 15, the day before the scheduled debate. It was a moment charged with unexpected pathos, if we are to believe Isabel Burton's account. The two men did not speak, but their eyes met. 'I shall never forget his face', wrote Isabel of Speke. 'It was full of sorrow, and yearning, and perplexity. Then he seemed turned to stone.' After a while, she reported, he began to fidget, and exclaiming half aloud, 'Oh, I cannot stand this any longer', got up from his seat. 'Shall you want your chair again, sir?' asked a man standing behind. 'May I have it? Shall you come back?' 'I hope not', Speke said, and left the hall.

So at least Mrs Burton described it. Certainly Speke left, and following the habit of a lifetime drove out to Neston to let off steam with an afternoon's shooting. By 2.30, we are told, he and his cousin, with a gamekeeper, were out in the fields looking for partridges. Neston stood on an outcrop of the Cotswolds, and they were shooting across a stony, bare and bleak countryside, where the autumn light was often moist and misty, and the air dank. It was native ground for Speke. Not only were those fields his cousin's property, but in a house nearby lived his own elder brother William. Speke had, in fact, hurried from Section E home to his roots—away from the word-splitting and the hypotheticals back to the rough, where a chap was not stifled by science or twisted by recriminations, but could breathe freely among his own kind, in good country air with a gun under his arm.

At about four o'clock, as the three men crossed a field near the

Bath road, a shot sounded. Speke was at that moment climbing a drystone wall two or three feet high, and the others looked around to see him falling off it. They ran to the spot, and found him bleeding profusely from the chest. He was conscious, and asked them not to move him: but by the time Fuller had got hold of a doctor and returned to the scene, Speke had died where he fell, watched by the helpless keeper. His body was taken to his brother's house, and an inquest was convened for the following morning, the very day of the great debate.

When the news was announced to the expectant Section E next day, even Burton was stunned for a moment. Unable, he said, to speak himself, he asked Murchison to read a statement on his behalf, expressing his 'sincere admiration of Speke's character and enterprise', despite their differences of opinion. Within a few moments, though, he had recovered sufficiently to read a paper he happened to have with him about the current state of Dahomey in West Africa, with particular and detailed reference to the habit of human sacrifice. We are not told how the audience reacted to this ghoulish alternative, but the *Chronicle* did report in the same issue both Speke's announced intention of returning to Africa 'to spread the blessings of Christianity', and Burton's heretical conclusion on Dahomey—'under these circumstances it is pleasing to remark the gradual but sure advance of El Islam, the perfect cure of the disorders that rule the land'.

'Captain Speke came to à bad end,' Burton wrote to a friend four days later, 'but no one knows anything about it.' In Somerset nevertheless he was given the farewell appropriate to a hero and a favourite son. Muffled bells tolled all day in Taunton, the county town, and Murchison, Livingstone and Grant all went to the funeral in the family church at Dowlish Wake—Grant indeed momentarily descending into the vault with the coffin, carrying a wreath of laurel leaves and everlasting white flowers and sobbing sobs that were 'audible all over the sacred building'. Speke's father was granted the right to augment the family arms with 'the supporters following; that is to say, on the dexter side a Crocodile, and on the sinister side a Hippopotamus'.

But how he died was always to remain obscure. 'The charitable say he shot himself', Burton wrote, 'the uncharitable that I shot him'. Murder by Burton is certainly a tempting hypothesis, and there is an undeniably persuasive frisson to the vision of the great pornographer, cloaked and Satanic, skulking in the lee of the death-wall that September afternoon. But Burton was not really the murdering kind—he loved to shock, not to kill. It was Speke who was truly the man of violence. He it was who, confronted by emotional crises, relieved them by going out and shooting something, and though the local inquest dutifully returned a verdict of accidental death, metaphorically touching its cap to Squire Fuller, still there were many besides Burton to assume, in September 1864, that what he chose to shoot that particular day was himself.[1]

8

Burton lived for another twenty-five years. He never went exploring again, and doubtless regretted to the end of his life the day he allowed Speke to go off to the northern lake without him. But he made his fortune with the first unexpurgated translation of the *Arabian Nights*, and after a lifetime of furious controversy, fluctuation, scholarship and adventure, died in 1890 famous and a Knight of the Bath—notorious to the end among the orthodox, looking in old age as magnificently sinister as ever, and idolized still by the faithful fatuous Isabel, who took the posthumous precaution of burning most of his journals and many unpublished manuscripts.

For his tomb Isabel erected, in the Catholic cemetery of Mortlake, London, an Arab tent all made of marble, fitted up as a chapel inside, with room for two coffins and real camel-bells that tinkled when the door was opened. On a slab upon its wall was a poem by Justin Huntly McCarthy:

> *Oh, last and noblest of the errant knights,*
> *The English soldier and the Arab Shiek* (sic),
> *Oh, Singer of the East who loved so well*

[1] A memorial obelisk still stands on the site of the tragedy, unsuspected by the passing motorists a hundred yards away on the Bath-Yeovil road. Its inscription admits of no doubt: *Here the distinguished and enterprising African traveller, Captain John Hanning Speke, Lost his life in the accidental explosion of his gun, September 15, 1864.*

The Growing Conviction

The deathless wonder of the Arabian Nights,
Who touched Camoens' lute and still would seek
Ever new deeds until the end, farewell.[1]

But Speke was buried with a more imperial romance. Deep in the green silence of the Somerset countryside, among thatch and apple orchards, stood the church of St Andrew at Dowlish Wake, the sanctuary of the Spekes. Spekes were everywhere inside. There were Speke memorial windows. There were Speke commemorative plaques. There was a Speke vault, and a Speke chapel, and a monument to a Speke who had died with John Nicholson at the storming of Delhi. And in the heart of it, John Hanning Speke himself presided in stately life-size bust, bearded and masterly, above the big black marble sarcophagus that contained his remains—ornamented by laurel leaves, embellished with gun, sword and sextant, and supported as the College of Heralds had decreed, by a Crocodile dexter and a large Hippopotamus sinister.[2]

So Speke won in the end. A family man to the last, an English gentleman of the rooted kind, his half-suppressed, half-ashamed romanticism sustained him in death as it impelled him in life, as in a wider sense it impelled the great Empire itself. Once Henry Stanley from St Asaph workhouse had established the truth of that tragic intuition on the shore of the northern lake, nobody could dispute Speke's right to the proud Latin epitaph upon his tomb: A NILO PRAECLARUS—*Illustrious For the Nile.*

[1] The tent is still there, chipped and forlorn, directly opposite the headquarters of the East Sheen Scout Group—if you stand in Worple Street beside the railway track you may see its pyramidical mock-draperies protruding over the cemetery wall. A tired rose-bush stands before it, and Isabel has long since been re-united with Richard inside.

[2] Everything at St Andrew's is just the same, except for the addition of later Speke generations, and there are still Spekes about in Somerset, and Fullers at Neston Park.

CHAPTER FIFTEEN

Governor Eyre

EMPIRE was not yet a popular enthusiasm. The British public was still half-illiterate, imperialism was seldom an electoral issue, and there was nothing gaudy or flamboyant yet to the idea of imperial dominion. Grave authority was the keynote of the British Empire in the fifties and sixties, and the piety of the old reformers had become institutionalized. Here is one Colonial Secretary's formula for the elevation of the backward peoples: 'The policy which I believe to be best adapted to promote civilization is that of raising the revenue required for the support of those institutions which distinguish a civilized from a barbarous society, by such taxes as may tend the most to render a mere subsistence difficult to be obtained without exertion. . . .' At the same time the old liberalism of the Colonial Office itself, though still alive and active, was acquiring a coarsening dogmatism too, a trace of arrogance and contempt, which one can trace to the terrible disillusionments of the Mutiny.

These processes were sadly illustrated in the life story of Edward John Eyre, the equivocal hero of this chapter.

2

Eyre, whose father was vicar of Hornsea and Long Riston in Yorkshire, was born in 1815, and at 17 had emigrated alone to Australia, whose empty immensities strangely suited him. Apprenticed to a sheep farmer, he became an explorer, and was the first white man to travel along the Great Australian Bight, the desolate and empty southern coastline of the continent. His expedition was one of the most terrible in the annals of adventure. Setting out with his white overseer Baxter and three aborigines, Wylie, Joey and Yarry, in the New Year of 1841, he reached the settlement of Albany, a thousand miles to the east, in July. In those six months every kind of calamity occurred, and fearful episodes of the journey had entered the Australian folklore—the moment when Joey and Yarry shot Baxter dead and decamped with almost all the stores—the nightmare hours of hazed heat through which the renegades shadowed Eyre and Wylie eerily at a distance through the bush—the ghastly days and nights of thirst, when they lived by mopping up the morning dew—the eagle stew they gorged upon one day, the penguin Wylie ate upon a beach, skin and all. At Lucky Bay, half-way along the coast, a traumatic moment occurred, for when he was very nearly dead, Eyre discovered a French whaler moored off-shore, and was offered a passage to Albany: but a fanatic energy drove him on, he would not abandon his journey, and after twelve days he set off implacably once again, alone with the patient Wylie, for the last few hundred miles through rainstorms and misery to King George's Sound.

He made several other famous Australian journeys, sometimes with herds of sheep, and seems to have felt an unexplained affinity for the aborigines, those shadow-characters of the never-never. He treated them with a kindness rare among Australian pioneers, and presently became an exceptionally humane Protector of Aborigines on the Murray River—'it is a lamentable thing', he once wrote, 'to think that the progress and prosperity of one race should conduce to the downfall and decay of another'. In Australia he was always remembered as a benevolent hero, and there was a Mount Eyre named for him, and an Eyre Peninsula, and a salt lake as big as Cyprus.

In New Zealand his reputation was less straightforward. In 1846 he was appointed Lieutenant-Governor there, and again showed a particular empathy for the natives: his marriage at Auckland in 1850 was a double ceremony with a Maori couple. In other ways, though, something blighted seems now to have emerged in his character, as though the Australian wasteland had drained him of warmth and colour. He quarrelled incessantly, haggled about his salary, showed a preposterous fondness for gold braid and consequence while sanctimoniously refusing to receive social calls on Sundays. His superior officer, the Governor, finally declined to answer his endless litigious letters, and deprived him of all official responsibilities. Eyre left the colony in 1853 for a post in the West Indies, leaving a memory behind him still courageous (there was an Eyre Peak in Otago), but petulant and obstinate too.

A hero in Australia; a prosy squabbler in New Zealand; it was in the Caribbean that Edward Eyre, in his fifty-first year, achieved the most unexpected of his reputations. For there as Governor of Jamaica, in the year 1865, he became known as a murderer.

3

Conditions in Jamaica had not greatly changed since that day in 1838 when Mr Knibb had watched the hands of the clock turn in his church at Falmouth. The colony was still half-destitute, never having recovered from the shock of emancipation, and was also suffering from high prices because of the American Civil War. Many of the old estates were abandoned now, or run by the listless and corrupt agents of absentee landlords. The negroes, who were mostly reluctant to work for wages, coveted the lands thus left idle, and often squatted on them; the whites preserved a colour bar more rigidly than ever, living lavishly but often in debt surrounded by servants in their Great Houses. The colony was fearfully run down. Roads were impassable, bridges were broken, plantations had reverted to bush. Kingston, the commercial centre, was full of filth and vice, and violent crime was common everywhere. In the inaccessible interior of the island a British garrison kept perpetual watch upon the Maroons, an inner nation of ex-slaves who had never been subdued by the British, but lived indignantly autonomous in treaty relationship with the Empire. Jamaica was riddled with queer religious revivals, Christian, pagan and sometimes a combination of the two; it was embittered by racial grievance; and it was periodically ravaged by epidemics of cholera and smallpox—the stink of Kingston was said to be detectable several miles out at sea.

Above all the shadow of slavery fell across the island still, darkening the demagoguery of the agitators and the revivalists. Some negroes still thought emancipation had given them a statutory right to the ownership of land. Others were easily persuaded that the whites were preparing to make slaves of them again. The pattern of life had not much changed, for all the fact of freedom, and the Great Houses were still figures of absolute white supremacy, their myriad servants merely managing to be, so Trollope found in 1858, servile and insolent at the same time.

The capital of Jamaica was Spanish Town, a dingy little metropolis in the southern plain, redeemed only by a few fairly dilapidated colonial houses, a small dignified cathedral and the buildings of Government. 'Stricken with eternal death', Trollope thought it. Its centre was an imposing eighteenth century square, deliberately designed to exalt the fact of British power. Dominating it on the north side was a memorial to Admiral Rodney, created by the London sculptor John Bacon and erected in 1783 to honour the victory of The Saints, which saved Jamaica from the French: flanked by captured cannon, ornamented with banners, unicorns, tritons and sculptured battle-scenes, the Admiral stood dressed as a Roman grandee pointing his baton imperiously into the square, and had a small hole in his back which was really the mark of some joist or pulley, but was taken by simpler citizens to represent the bullet-hole that killed him.[1] To Rodney's right was the Governor's Palace, King's House, monumentally pillared. To his left was the Assembly Hall, the home of the Jamaican legislature.

The colony was still governed under one of the old pre-1787 constitutions, unreformed by the Durham Report. The Assembly was elected, was responsible for most of the island's internal affairs, and was composed largely of coloured men. But the electorate was infinitesimal—about one in every 200 citizens, the qualification being a sizeable land ownership—and the members represented above all the interests of the planters and businessmen. Though they were divided upon party lines, and squabbled and intrigued, in cabals and caucuses, along the best Parliamentary lines, they were generally united in opposition to the Governor and his nominated council, and they were backed off-stage by the high-spirited and irresponsible elite of the white landed gentry, often the fifth generation of English settlers in the island. The Governor in his palace represented the traditionally moderate authority of London: the

[1] He died in his bed in Hanover Square.

Assembly members across the square spoke for the Great Houses of Jamaica, or the graft-ridden commerce of Kingston: and over the intervening garden executive and legislature metaphorically and sometimes physically (for one could easily see from window to window) glared.

Into this arena of resentment stepped E. J. Eyre, in the summer of 1862.

4

The whites were afraid of a general negro insurrection. They remembered always the example of Haiti, whose declaration of independence in 1804 had been celebrated with a massacre of all the white inhabitants. There were rumours of smuggled arms, seditious meetings, the drilling of armed negroes in the mountains. Revivalist preachers, sometimes no more than Christianized Obeah men, were thought to be drumming up discontent—in particular the ministers of a sect called the Native Baptists, who had gained the support of the Baptist Missionary Society in England. The negroes, though pathetically loyal to the person of Queen Victoria, certainly distrusted British justice in Jamaica, and resented the colony's high taxes, and they were thought by the whites to be capable of any enormity. A half-caste minister of the Native Baptists, William Gordon, was their most articulate leader, and was represented to Eyre as a prime mover of sedition: he was a man of property and a member of the Assembly, was prone to inflammatory racialist speeches, and had quarreled so violently with his white fellow-magistrates in his home parish, St Thomas-in-the-East, that he had been removed from office.

All this was happening at a particularly sensitive moment of imperial history. It was only seven years since the end of the Mutiny, and even in the distant Caribbean memories of its massacres and revenges were still horribly vivid. All over the Empire racial attitudes had hardened, and by now probably a majority of educated Britons had come to sympathize with Carlyle, who once described the emancipated West Indian negroes as 'our beautiful black darlings . . . sitting yonder with their beautiful muzzles up to the ears in pumpkins, imbibing sweet pulps and juices . . . while the sugar-crops rot around them uncut, because labour cannot be hired, so cheap are the pumpkins'.

Certainly Eyre, a stiffly orthodox Anglican, believed that the Jamaican negro was his own worst enemy. The real cause of discontent, he reported to the Colonial Office after a few months as Governor, was 'the incorrigible indolence, apathy and improvidence of all ages, and the degraded and immoral social existence which they all but universally lead'. When a negro petition was sent to the Queen asking for economic help, it was answered on Eyre's advice by an unctuous proclamation presented to the public as 'The Queen's Letter'. It was by their own industry and prudence that the negroes must improve their conditions, said this repellant exhortation; 'Her Majesty will regard with interest and satisfaction their advancement through their own merits and efforts'.

Eyre very soon made an enemy of Gordon. By now the Governor had matured into an inflexible man, prone to self-pity, and he was in no mood to be defied by a population of immoral and indolent peasants. He doubtless felt secure not only in the assurance of his own rectitude, but also in assuming that all the authority of the post-Mutiny Empire would stand beside him, if he dealt severely with black subversion. One day in August 1865 a small deputation of negroes plodded into the square at Spanish Town. They had walked some forty-five miles from the hill country of St Thomas-in-the-East, the other side of Kingston, and they wished to lay before the Governor the grievances of their community. They presented themselves at the palace door, above whose portico the flambeaux flared, and through whose portals there presently appeared, one supposes, some lofty and liveried attendant. The petitioners explained themselves and waited: but presently the servant returned to say that His Excellency would not receive them, so back they walked into the mountains again.

5

The leader of the delegation was Paul Bogle of Stony Gut, a settlement in the mountains north of Morant Bay. Bogle was a prosperous farmer, an ordained deacon of the Native Baptist Church, and a protégé of Gordon. His smallholding at Stony Gut was buried in-accessibly in the southern flanks of the Blue Mountains, approach-able only by a maze of steep little lanes. Around it dense woods grew, often dripping and aromatic, for the rainfall there was heavy, and there was no town nearer than Morant Bay, twenty miles away on the coast.

At Stony Gut, in the autumn of 1865, a religio-military cult thrived. The settlement consisted of a house, a yard, and a heavily-built chapel which served also as a fort: and there Bogle assembled several hundred militant black supporters determined to right their wrongs by force. Armed with machetes, pikes and bludgeons, they drilled assiduously among the woods, sang their hymns discordantly in the chapel, administered their own justice, swore death to the white men, marched and counter-marched among the forest trees, blew their conch shells, played their fifes and beat their drums—insulated there secretly among the woodlands, so that only the neighbouring villagers could hear their arcane preparations. They were very simple men, concerned chiefly with local grievances, and inspired as much perhaps by their gimcrack brand of Christianity as by any coherent political philosophy. They were, however, in touch with militants elsewhere in the island. 'Blow your shells,' ran one of their almost incantatory recruiting letters, 'roule your drums! house to house; take out every man; march them down to Stony Gut; any that you find take them in the way; take them down with their arms; war is at my black skin, war is at hand. . . . Cheer, men! Cheer in heart! . . . When you do come to Stony Gut . . . blow your shells and tell what place you is from before entered.'

Bogle was already at odds with the white magistrates who repre-sented law and order at Morant Bay, and one day in October 1865 a squad of negro policemen was sent up to Stony Gut to arrest him, and twenty-eight of his followers, for sedition. Bogle's men promptly beat them up and threw them out, except for three who were tem-porarily taken prisoner and made to swear, upon pain of death, to 'join their colour'. Two days later the little army, waving its weapons, shouting its pious slogans and trumpeting its conchs, set off itself for Morant Bay to attack the citadel of white reaction in the parish of St Thomas-in-the-East, the Court House.

Down they marched, down the winding track through the mountains, fortified by their own concoction of rum and gunpowder, and keeping their spirits up too with the music of drum and fife. Once there were rumours of a Government force coming to meet them, and they hid for a time in the bush: but friends joined them as they passed, villagers ran flatteringly out to watch them, and as they entered the little town of Morant Bay, clustered on a bluff above the sea, a large crowd assembled to the beat of the drum, pressing around those motley militants—who, waving their pikes and cutlasses still, shouting and singing and blowing their horns, marched along the modest main street of the town and burst into the square before the Court House.

The scale of the ensuing tragedy was very small, no more than a flicker of the imperial drama. The Court House was a trim and authoritarian little building up a double flight of steps. Chickens scrabbled among the outhouses on the left of the square, and the Anglican church stood to the right. Behind the Court House, among a huddle of indeterminate administrative buildings, a cannon looked out to sea. Symmetrical, confined and rather pretty, the square was just the place for violent action, especially in the tetchy and humid afternoon of a Caribbean October day.

The magistrates were in session inside the Court House, but Morant Bay had been warned of Bogle's approach, and a line of red-coated Volunteers was drawn up at the end of the square. They fired a single volley, dispersing the sightseers but having little effect upon the rebels, before they were assaulted by a shower of stones and bottles, and swept aside with bludgeons, machetes and even a fish-spear. Before long the Court House was on fire. The magistrates were forced from room to room until at last they made a break for it, stumbling out of the burning building to run the gauntlet of the mob, hide in backstreets, seek shelter in neighbouring houses, or lie low in the bush. Most of them were caught. Some were chopped to pieces with machetes, some were bludgeoned to death, one had his throat cut and his mouth wrenched open with a stick. In all seventeen whites were killed and thirty-one wounded (and one black man was murdered too—he was said to have 'a black skin and a white heart').

The rioters were exuberant. They left the burning building and the shambled square, and went off to release the prisoners in the town gaol: since they were not rebelling against Queen Victoria, they said, they would respect her property, and the convicts were told to discard their prison uniforms. Then off they went again up the long winding track to Stony Gut, blowing their horns triumphantly now, dusty, bloodstained and ecstatic. They had harmed no women or children in Morant Bay; they had done very little looting; they had carefully spared the two white doctors of the town; but they undoubtedly saw themselves as the advance guard of a negro crusade, its purpose a little vague but its spirit truly evangelical. When they reached the clearing in the forest, they filed into the fortress-chapel for a religious service. It was three o'clock in the morning, and the scene must have been weird—all those black exalted peasants, sweating from the day's bloodshed and emotion, kneeling in the lamplight in their silent fastness. Bogle himself addressed the congregation, as its pastor and commander, and gave humble thanks that 'God had succeeded him in this work'.[1]

6

Eyre interpreted the divine intention otherwise, for the news from Morant Bay raised some terrible questions. Was this the start of the threatened insurrection? Was it part of a general conspiracy? The Governor very properly took no chances. Martial law was declared throughout the county of Surrey, the eastern third of Jamaica, except in Kingston itself: and the regular troops of the Crown, about 600 strong, were swiftly mobilized to contain the rising. They occupied the coastal towns of Surrey, and closed the passes through the mountains to the north. In addition the Maroons, who stayed loyal to their British treaty, supplied some 300 formidable if unorthodox soldiers, while the frigate *Wolverine* and the gunboat *Onyx* ferried troops, provided landing parties and maintained communications between Kingston and Morant Bay.

[1] Morant Bay has scarcely changed, and still has an ominous air on a blazing afternoon, suggesting to me one of those eerily deserted shantytowns through which the gunfighters of the westerns menacingly approach each other in the silence.

It was rainy weather, and the campaigning was tough. In the hill country, its hot jungly terrain intersected by deep ravines, tracks were often washed away by a single torrential storm. At best they were deep in mud or blocked by landslides. One can imagine the opinions of the soldiery in 1865, loaded down with pack and musket, stacked up with extra rations of beef and rum, hacking and cursing their way from valley to valley, village to village, sometimes for days at a time without taking their boots off. Many were veterans of the Mutiny, and by and large they were not of a liberal temper. When they came to a negro village, they burnt it. When they challenged a black man on the march, they flogged him if he stopped, shot him if he ran.

No revengeful Queen's battalion in Oudh or Rajputana behaved more ferociously than these embittered soldiers. 'Hole is doing splendid service', reported the Deputy Adjutant General to his superior, 'shooting every black man who cannot account for himself (sixty on the line of march).' 'I must tell you,' wrote a private soldier to his parents in Hampshire, 'that I never see such a site before as we are taking them prisoners by a hundred per day—we saved them for the next morning to have some sport with them. We tied them up to a Tree and give them 100 lashes, and afterwards put a shot into their heads.' One captured rebel was used as a rifle target, the firing party shooting him at 400 yards. A servant of Bogle's was tied to an officer's stirrup and made to divulge the names of rebel conspirators—'a revolver now and then to his head causes us thoroughly to understand each other'. A woman at Stony Gut was flogged to make her reveal Bogle's whereabouts: she got twenty-five lashes first, another twenty-five a quarter of an hour later, another twenty-five half an hour later still, and was then left all night with a rope round her neck as an earnest of things to come.

Down in Morant Bay, courts martial quickly disposed of prisoners. They were held under the aegis of the Provost Marshal, who had fought in the charge of the Light Brigade, had won a Victoria Cross, and was probably not quite sane—a year later he killed himself. Negroes were flogged for neglecting to remove their hats in his presence or answering back. One man was hanged because he ground his teeth. The court martial members were junior army and navy officers, and they handed down death sentences with a merciless panache—the condemned men being hanged symbolically from the ruined courthouse arch (generally by sailors, for as the president of the court once observed, 'they are handier with ropes than soldiers are'). All in all, retribution was terrible in Surrey County. Martial law continued in force for its maximum legal period, thirty days, and 439 negroes were shot or hanged. Some 600 more were flogged, mostly without trial, and about 1,000 dwelling-places were destroyed. The rebellion was suppressed absolutely. No resistance was offered after the first few days, the rest of Jamaica remained peaceful, and the soldiers were perfectly frank about their punitive measures, evidently assuming that nobody who mattered would object.

Bogle himself was soon caught. They gave him the distinction of hanging him from the yard-arm of the *Wolverine*, lying in Morant Bay: and his settlement at Stony Gut was razed to the ground, farmhouse, chapel and all, leaving only a jumbled pile of stones over which the green ground-foliage soon encroached.[1]

7

Eyre assumed that Gordon was the real force behind the rebellion, and put out a warrant for his arrest. Four days later he gave himself up at the military headquarters in Kingston. This placed the Governor in a quandary, for there was no martial law in Kingston. A trial there would be a protracted and messy affair, embroiled in politics, religion and every manner of local side-issue. Besides, Gordon had not been near St Thomas-in-the-East during the troubles: the evidence for his complicity was largely circumstantial, and in Kingston, before a properly appointed court of the Queen's Justices, he might well be acquitted.

[1] It may still be found, well away from the road in the damp forest, and Bogle himself has been half-deified in Jamaica, even his pock-marked face ('very ferocious looking', a contemporary reporter thought, 'the very type of the fiend') being selectively immortalized upon bank notes. In 1970 I met his surviving great-grandson, at Lyssons on the coast, and asked him what kind of person the rebel had been when not on the path of black power—kind, fierce, majestic, simple? 'He was a lovely man', the present Mr Bogle said.

But Eyre was perfectly certain of the man's moral, if not his legal guilt, and in this he was probably right. Gordon often talked freely of insurrection—he had publicly called the Governor 'an animal . . . voracious for cruelty and power'—he had encouraged Bogle in his activities at Stony Gut—he was a sworn enemy of the magistrates at Morant Bay. There is even evidence that he was in touch with the black Government of Haiti. Eyre was determined that no quibbles of legalism would save this villain from his deserts: he had clearly made up his mind that the man must hang, and applied to the task his stubborn will and his lonely sense of duty.

He decided to take Gordon to Morant Bay, and have him tried there by court martial. He must have known that this was illegal, but he presumably supposed that the end would justify the means. Nobody, after all, had been blamed for far graver irregularities during the suppression of the Mutiny: Hodson had gone unpunished for the murder of the princes, was even hero-worshipped for it—'I cannot help being pleased', he had written, 'with the warm congratulations I receive on all sides for my success in destroying the enemies of our race'. Together, then, Eyre and Gordon embarked upon the hard-working *Wolverine* and sailed out of Kingston Harbour—out into the bay where, looking back towards the island, captor and captive could see the mysterious mass of the Blue Mountains rising range upon range above the filthy city, sheltering in their thick bush and high dark forests all the secret resentments of the blacks.

They were like figures in a morality play, the two passengers: both religious and indeed self-righteous men, both deeply committed to causes: one representing, if at many removes, the autocratic certainty of empire, the other expressing, if incoherently, the lost pride of primitive sovereignty. A storm allegorically blew up, too, as they sailed along the coast, and kept them tossing and miserable outside Morant Bay. When they disembarked upon the little quay, they both looked distressed. Eyre was a tall thin man, narrow-chested, dry-looking, heavily bearded and powerfully nosed, his movements oddly awkward, the look in his eye introspective but improving. Gordon, led ashore by guards, looked paradoxically kindred. He too had a desiccated air, if we can judge by his photograph, his face too lacked warmth or humour, his mouth was set forbiddingly, as in caricatures of hell-fire evangelists, and his steel-rimmed spectacles look in the pictures as though they might ominously glint.

Gordon was led ashore through a crowd of sailors. They abused him as he passed, and behaved as though they would happily tear him limb from limb. The British sailor was a rough diamond in the 1850s, and the language used that day, thought one eye-witness, was 'hardly the thing to put to paper'. *'Would you like a taste of the cat, you old bastard?' 'By Jesus, you'll catch it!' 'Set the bloody dogs on him!' 'You won't be long here, you old windbag, we'll soon string you up!'* Gordon winced to each epithet, and Governor Eyre the vicar's son, we may reasonably surmise, preferred not to hear.

Gordon's judges were two naval lieutenants and an ensign of the West India Regiment. The principal charge was high treason. Most of the evidence presented was, by formal legal standards, inadmissible. The trial lasted six hours. The sentence was inevitably death. 'General Nelson has just been kind enough to inform me,' Gordon wrote to his wife, 'that the court-martial . . . has ordered me to be hung, and that the sentence is to be executed in an hour hence: so that I shall be gone from this world of sin and sorrow.' It was a grey overcast September morning; the clouds hung heavily over the hills; they took him up the steps of the Court House, bound his hands and feet, and hanged him from the arch.

Governor Eyre, having delivered his charge to judgement, did not wait for the execution, but returned to his palace in Spanish Town. There the news of Gordon's death was brought to him. In a very real sense it was his own death too. For the rest of his life he was haunted by the fact of that court-martial in Morant Bay, which ended his career as absolutely and almost as squalidly as if he had himself dangled, noosed and pinioned, from the arch of the Court House door.

8

He lived in some splendour in King's House. In those days it was the finest Government House in the West Indies, and pictures of its entrance hall show it terrifically dignified, with doric columns and chandeliers and galleries and enormous royal portraits. Nelson and Rodney were both received there: so was Captain Bligh, when he arrived with his cargo of breadfruit trees from the Pacific (only to find that the West Indians preferred the plantain anyway).

Among its gilded splendours Eyre brooded in anxious isolation, as he waited for official reaction to his measures. He was an early victim of an imperial dilemma that would grow more perplexing as the years passed—the conflict between means and ends. The British had often acted cruelly, in pursuit of what they honestly believed to be their civilizing mission, but in the old days of slow communications and instant responsibility, the public at home had often been unaware of it, or at least remained indifferent. Now the whole blaze of public scrutiny could be directed in a matter of days upon the actions of a distant and harassed pro-consul, and to some people at home the very Empire itself, forcibly held together by the Power whose prerogative it was to teach the nations how to live, seemed a contradiction in moral terms.

Eyre was hailed by the whites of Jamaica, and by many of the blacks too, as the saviour of the colony. Without doubt many European lives were saved by the severity of his action, and possibly a general rebellion really was averted. At the same time Eyre took advantage of the situation to win once and for all the perennial battle between Governor and settlers. As soon as the rebellion was over he summoned the Assembly and persuaded its members, after two centuries of fiercely defended independence, to abdicate their powers to the Colonial Office—tacit recognition that the plantation empire was dead, that the whips and chains of slavery really must be buried, and that the relationship between black and white had moved into another phase.

But the means he employed to these good ends were truly ferocious—1,400 lives for 17, thousands of innocent people humiliated, thousands more made homeless, the law flouted, human rights abused. It is true that Eyre could not know of the excesses of the troops in the field, and the fact that the Jamaica rebels were black was probably irrelevant to his excesses: but his manipulation of justice was unforgivable, and his whole conduct seemed to express a contempt for simple people that jarred oddly against his treatment of the aborigines in his youth. He was like a man trapped between convictions: not a savage man, but impelled into savagery; not a racial bigot, but obliged to act like one; not even a strong man really, but forced into strength by that very same streak of stubbornness which, long before at Lucky Bay, had sent him off once more on the last 600 miles to Albany.

9

When the news of Eyre's actions broke in England, there was a furore. Hodson's action outside the Tomb of Humayun may have been popular in India at the time, but Kaye tells us that in England 'I have never heard a man express a word of approval'. So it was with Eyre. In Kingston he may, for a moment, have had the white community at his feet: in London he was excoriated. 'TWELVE MILES OF DEAD BODIES', said the newspaper headlines, and a Commission of Inquiry was soon sent out to Jamaica. It found Eyre skilful, prompt and vigorous in his immediate reactions to the rebellion, but thought his use of martial law excessive, and condemned the severity of his punishments. The Governor was removed from his post, and in August 1866 he returned to England—where he at once found himself the hapless central figure in a *cause célèbre*.

The philanthropic lobbies of England, whose front or chapter was still Exeter Hall, believed that mere dismissal from Office was quite insufficient punishment for a man like Eyre—'Old 'Angsman', as the people called him. A body called the Jamaica Committee was established to bring him more properly to book, and numbered among its members John Stuart Mill, Charles Darwin, Thomas Huxley, a number of nonconformist tycoons, many academics and clergymen, and Thomas Hughes of *Tom Brown's School Days*. Its leaders resolved to prosecute Eyre privately for nothing less than the murder of William Gordon. In opposition to them was founded the Eyre Defence Committee, supported most prominently by men of imagination: Carlyle, Ruskin, Dickens, Tennyson, Charles Kingsley, backed by 71 peers, 20 members of Parliament, 40 generals, 26 admirals and 400 clergymen, mostly Anglican.

The controversy raged on and off for two years, and passions ran high. Families were divided, friendships broken. Charges of hypocrisy, stupidity, racialism and wrong-headedness flew between the partisans. There was a debate in Parliament, funds were raised, pamphlets furiously printed, and in the wider world the charges against Eyre were seen as charges against the Empire itself. 'What do you say to the Nigger insurrection on Jamaica,' wrote Friedrich Engels to Karl Marx, 'and the brutalities of the English?' 'The Jamaican story,' Marx replied, 'is characteristic of the beastliness of the "true Englishman".' Motives varied wildly in this protracted controversy, and language was unrestrained: Eyre was 'the personification of wrong', 'the saviour of society in the West Indies', 'a murderer whose hands were red with blood', 'a brave, gentle, chivalrous and clear man', 'The Martyr', 'The Monster', '"Angsman Eyre". Three times it went as far as the courts, but Eyre was cleared each time.

10

Through it all the ex-Governor maintained an aloof and dignified silence. Once he appeared at a banquet. Once he defended himself in court—with a single speech four sentences long. For the rest he said nothing, wrote nothing, seldom appearing in public, never arguing his case or answering his detractors. When the affair died at last he was left without a job and with a reputation as equivocal as any in England. The Government of the day gave him a pension in the end, as a retired Colonial Governor, but he never got another appointment, and lived the last years of his life in silent seclusion in Devon.

He seems to have been a passionless sort of man, inaccessible, as self-sufficient in his last years as he was when we first hear of his peculiarly disheartening sort of heroism, labouring across the Australian wastelands in search of nothing whatsoever. He makes a pathetic figure of Empire—so unloved, so intractable, so hemmed in by the restrictions of his age and background, and in the end so self-destructive. In old age he took a lease on Walreddon Manor, some five miles out of Tavistock on the edge of Dartmoor. He chose the house unquestionably for its remoteness. He wanted to be forgotten, and to forget. Walredden was a stern stone manor house, mediaeval in origins, Tudor and Queen Anne in architecture, which lay above sloping lawns near the River Tavy. It was a secretive house. Reached by tortuous high-hedged lanes, sloshed about in winter by running water from over-flowing ditches, it made a perfect last retreat for E. J. Eyre.

He lived there very privately, almost anonymously, with his wife and two of his children. The household staff knew nothing of his tragic and tumultuous past, and called him 'General Eyre', perhaps supposing him to be just another of those retired imperial soldiers who abounded in the West Country. A certain stir was caused in Devon when he died, and unsuspecting neighbours realized that the old gentleman of Walredden had been Hangman Eyre of Jamaica: but it was many years since the event, and the passions had long subsided. They buried him in the churchyard at Whitchurch, within sight of the moor, beneath a cross of grey granite. On the plinth it said: *'Edward John Eyre, Australian Explorer and Governor of Jamaica. He did his duty in that state of life, into which it pleased God to call him'*. The cross was tall, but the churchyard was full of high Cornish and Celtic crosses, some slightly toppled with age, and was interspersed with slender trees: and on a winter day all those white and grey verticals, in dense perspective towards the distant moors, looked rather like the sad silver gum-trees of the Outback.

CHAPTER SIXTEEN

'Ain't the Pentateuch Queer?'

THE conviction of Empire was increasingly reinforced by a sense of duty, and became heavily veneered with religiosity. The Victorians were *believers*. They believed in their Christian Master, in their providential destiny, in their servants of steam and steel, in themselves and their systems, and not least in their Empire. As the mysteries of life were unfolded to them, explicitly in the triumphs of applied science, opaquely in intellectual conceptions like the Survival of the Fittest, so their own particular place in the divine scheme seemed ever more specific: they were called to be the great improvers, and the instrument of their mission was empire.

This was a complex illusion. At one level it was purely Christian trust, unquestioning—'Truly there is a God in Heaven!' exclaimed the Reverend Richard Taylor when the ship *Sobraon*, escaping unscathed from Wellington Harbour after the New Zealand earthquake of 1848, immediately ran aground on a rock through an error of navigation, drowning sixty people. The mission stations which, throughout the second half of the century, sprang up throughout the tropical possessions, were manned by and large by militants with no doubts—this was a Christian Empire, and it was the imperial duty to spread the Christian word among its heathen subjects. By 1850 the Christian missionaries could claim to have converted 20,000 Indians, at least 10,000 Africans, almost all the Maoris of New Zealand and virtually the entire population of Fiji. Fighting Christians established the Missionary Road, the chief exploratory route into central Africa from the south, and all over the Empire aggressive scholars were at work translating the sacred texts of Christianity into exotic tongues: the Cree for Jesus was Γ ხ ∩, the Fijian Christ was *Karisito*, and the pygmies were taught to write the holy name, in very large letters, KRISTO YESU.[1]

The administrators of Empire, too, and very often its conquerors, were generally practising Christians: the new public schools at which so many of them were educated were invariably Church of England foundations, with parson-headmasters. God directed all imperial affairs, as Charles Trevelyan the head of the Treasury realized, when he observed how hard it was for the poor people of Ireland, in their ignorance, to be 'deprived of knowing that they are suffering from an affliction of God's providence'. Explorers like Speke or Grant saw themselves as God's scouts—even Stanley turned evangelist in 1875, and converted the King of Uganda and all his court to Christianity. Generals like Havelock and Nicholson slaughtered their enemies in the absolute certainty of a biblical mandate (though General Hope Grant was horrified, during the Indian Mutiny, to think that the British might be 'sending their victims into eternity to answer for a life possibly mis-spent') and most of the imperial heroes were identified in the public mind with the Christianness of Empire—not simply humanitarianism, not Burke's sense of trusteeship, but a Christian militancy, a ruling faith, whose Defender on earth was the Queen herself, and whose supreme commander needed no identification. Every aspect of Empire was an aspect of Christ: imperial technique would certainly convert the Africans to Christianity in the end, the novelist Trollope assured himself, inspecting a South African mine—'when I have looked down into the mine and seen three or four thousand of them at work . . . I have felt that I was looking at three or four thousand growing Christians'.

2

Yet the deeper religious convictions of the British Empire were more muddled and ambiguous than they appeared. To the public at home

[1] Not that such catechism training was always successful. The Hau Hau cult of New Zealand, though partly biblical in its beliefs, included among its rituals the sacrifice of Anglican clergymen.

the Christian mission of empire might seem clear-cut and inescapable, but it often looked less evident in the field. Old traditions died hard, in climates less bracing and disciplinary than those of England itself, and the Christian vocation of imperialism was sometimes blurred. The temple-bells rang seductively from the pagodas of Moulmein. There was a gaudy fascination to the rituals of Benares. Among the miseries of Africa the solace of Islam, faith of the slave-traders, was often more soothing than evangelical pioneers were ready to admit. And not infrequently, pursued in torrid and innocent corners of empire, the Christian faith came to seem less an instrument of salvation than a means of power—in the South Seas, for example, the Reverend Shirley Baker so interpreted his divine mission that he became the virtual dictator of Tonga, devoutly manipulating the revenues of Church and State alike, besides enforcing sumptuary laws so pious that a woman could be fined for failing to wear a pinafore in her own kitchen.

To the mid-Victorians the greatest of Christian heroes was Livingstone, who had once said that if his explorations led to the ending of the slave trade in Africa, 'I shall regard that as a greater matter by far than the discovery of all the sources of the Nile put together'. Livingstone gave coherence to the notion of Christianity and Commerce in partnership, and his sometimes wild ideas about Christian colonization in Africa powerfully inflamed the later course of empire. He was a true believer, and when he died his own black servants, recognizing the power of his character, themselves brought his body home to that shrine of all things grand and good, the imperial capital. Through 1,500 miles of bush those simple Africans carried him, strapped in a cylinder of bark and calico within a sail-cloth hammock—Susi, Chuma, Amoda and some sixty others, from Chitambo's village near Bangweolo in nearly a year's laborious travel to the coast opposite Zanzibar. The Royal Navy took the embalmed body home to England, a special train met the ship at Southampton, and to the mourning of the nation the hero was buried in the supreme imperial sanctuary, Westminster Abbey, in the centre of the nave before the choir. 'Brought by faithful hands over land and sea,' read the inscription they placed upon his tomb, 'here rests David Livingstone, missionary, traveller, philanthropist . . . for

30 years his life was spent in an unwearied effort to evangelize the native races, to explore the undiscovered secrets, to abolish the desolating slave trade, of Central Africa. . . .'

Could anyone personify more exactly the assurance of the imperial mission? Yet here is a conversation between this towering Christian and his absolute antithesis in the imperial hierarchy, a befeathered pagan rain-doctor of the Bakwain tribe in central Africa—the very class of man, one might suppose, for whose enlightenment Victoria's Empire existed. Did the rain-doctor really believe, asked Livingstone, that he could command the clouds to drop rain? Christians believed that only God could do that.

Rain-doctor: 'We both believe the very same thing. It is God that makes the rain, but I pray to him by means of these medicines.'

Livingstone: 'But we are distinctly told in the parting words of our Saviour that we can pray to God acceptably in his name alone, and not by means of medicines.'

Rain-doctor: 'Truly! but God told *us* differently. He made black men first, and he did not love us, as he did the white men. He made you beautiful, and he gave you clothing, and guns, and gunpowder . . . towards us he had no heart . . . (but) God has given us one little thing, which you know nothing of. He has given us the knowledge of certain medicines by which we can make rain. We do not dispute those things which you possess, though we are ignorant of them. You ought not to despise our little knowledge, which you are ignorant of.'

Livingstone: 'I don't despise what I am ignorant of; I only think you are mistaken in saying that you have medicines which can influence the rain at all.'

Rain-doctor: 'That's just the way people speak when they talk on a subject of which they have no knowledge.'

Livingstone: 'God alone can command the clouds. Only try and wait patiently: God will give us rain without your medicines.'

Rain-doctor: 'Well, I always thought white men were wise until this morning. Whoever thought of making trial of starvation? Is death pleasant, then?'

This dialogue was recorded by Livingstone himself, and it does not appear to indicate any absolute conviction of Christian superiority—the pagan seems to have won the exchange, if not in theology at least in logic. The truth was that the Christian mission of Empire was often blunted at the tip. The Godhead that seemed so choate at home burgeoned into disquieting patterns, doubts and distortions among the alien subject cultures, and while some of these manifestations were patently misguided, and could never stand up to the scrutiny of an Oxford mind, others remained to nag at the convictions of the imperialists, and sometimes confuse the imperial issues.

In particular the issue of an official religion confused both the rulers and the subjects of the British Empire, and even engaged the anxieties of the Queen herself. Nobody was sure whether there was such a thing, whether this was truly a Christian empire, or merely an empire mostly run by Christians. There was certainly a State church at home, but this did not necessarily mean that the Anglican Church was the established religion of the Empire too, and out of the consequent perplexity there swirled a seminal imperial controversy.

Not only did the British Empire guarantee religious tolerance, within the limits of humanity, to all its millions of Hindu, Muslim, Buddhist, animist or pagan subjects: it was also schismatical at the top. Its rulers might generally be Christians, but they were Christians of many colours. Bishops indeed followed the flag, and by the middle of the nineteenth-century there were Anglican sees throughout the imperial possessions, but so did all manner of Wesleyan, Baptist, even Roman Catholic ministers of religion. Anomalies abounded. The aborigines of Australia found a Spanish Benedictine monastery implanted at New Norcia as early as 1846, while in Newfoundland, one of the oldest British possessions, local politics were frankly based upon the antipathies between Protestants and Catholics. During the Irish Famine it was an edict from Her Majesty's Privy Council which proclaimed that the Dearth and Scarcity Prayer should be read after the third collect ('. . . and grant that the scarcity and dearth, which we do now most justly suffer for our iniquity, may through thy goodness be mercifully turned into cheapness and plenty. . . .'): yet Maynooth, the greatest of the Irish Catholic seminaries, was founded with British Government funds.[1]

When the Anglican Bishop of Jamaica visited his flock in the Bahamas, he was habitually greeted at Nassau by a military guard of honour and a salute of nine guns: yet the true imperial status of the Church of England remained uncertain. Were its bishops public servants, like Governors or commanders-in-chief, or were they independent men of God, like Baptist ministers or rain-doctors? Was their church part of the imperial system as a whole, or was it only a series of settler churches? Was Queen Victoria Defender of the Faith only in the United Kingdom, or everywhere in her imperial possessions?

3

The central figure of this tortuous controversy became, in the 1860s and 1870s, John William Colenso, Bishop of Natal, whom we briefly glimpsed as a distinguished imperial visitor to the British Association meeting at Bath in 1864. Colenso (whose name was Cornish, though his more xenophobic enemies thought it distinctly unsuitable for an Anglican prelate) was an ecclesiastical maverick. He was not at all one of your Trollopian Victorian clergymen, except perhaps in a taste for disputation, having been born the son of a minor civil servant, and started life as an assistant to the Reverend Mr Grubb, who ran a school at Dartmouth in Devon. Clever both at mathematics and logic, he won scholarships to Cambridge, and became in turn a prosperous country vicar, a well-known mathematical author, and finally Bishop of the remote and newly established see of Natal, with his cathedral at Pietermaritzburg on the edge of Zululand—established by the Boers, it will be remembered, as capital of their Natal Republic.

There he became a force in the land. The British of Natal, no less than the Boers, profoundly feared and distrusted the formidable Zulus to the north, a people still of military tastes and ferocious tendencies.

---

[1] Astutely: at its foundation its priests were instructed by the Vatican to show loyalty to the British Crown 'at all times and places', and throughout the 19th century they remained staunch supporters of the imperial Establishment.

Colenso, on the other hand, much admired them, and bravely stood up for their interests. The fighting Zulu ethos suited him. Gleaming Zulu princes were his friends, eager Zulu pupils were constantly at his country house, Bishopstowe, where the bush ran away empty and exciting towards the open veld, and framed between the young trees of his garden stood the flat-topped local Table Mountain, which the bishop liked to call his 'altar' (he owned properties on its slopes).[1] He compiled a Zulu grammar and a Zulu-English dictionary. He wrote text-books for Zulu youths about geography, history and astronomy. He translated into Zulu the whole of the New Testament and several books of the Old. He loved to be called *Sobantu*—'father of the people'.

These sympathies hardly endeared him to British officialdom, still less to the coarser-grained settlers of Natal, and he gained the reputation of a nigger-lover—not of the unctuous evangelical sort, whom the settlers despised, but in a more dangerous kind. Still, he had good friends among the more intelligent Europeans as well as the Africans, was engrossed in his studies of the Zulu culture, and lived comfortably with his view, his garden and his Zulu pupils at Bishopstowe. His name might now be forgotten were it not for a different heresy: his gradually fostered suspicion, while a colonial bishop of the Established Church, that every word of the Bible was not after all literally true. That every word of the Bible *was* literally true had been one of the expansionist principles of the Empire, and in Africa it had gained added force: for the British increasingly agreed with the Boers that Holy Writ gave them specific authority over the black peoples of the continent—hewers of wood, as Joshua conveniently defined them, and drawers of water.

Both as scholar and as priest Colenso appeared to doubt this divine right. He was anxious, of course, to convert the Africans to Christianity, but he did not wish to erode their own culture. He allowed converts to live their own way—in particular polygamously, without the degrading preliminary divorces which more rigid evangelists demanded. His very intimacy with the heathen Zulus

[1] The trees are big now, and the house was burnt down years ago, but the view from the farm that stands upon its site remains unchanged, and Colenso's cherished garden is still full of tangled charm.

seemed to smack of heresy, and his concern for their traditions flew in the face of the imperial conviction. Inevitably his attitudes brought him into conflict with the Establishment, both secular and spiritual.

In 1861 he was busy translating the book of Genesis into Zulu, and the more he worked at it, the more unorthodox his reactions became. He was confronted on every page, as he later said, by the question, 'Is all that true?' 'My heart answered in the words of the Prophet, "shall a man speak lies in the name of the Lord? I dare not do so".' From doubting the literal truth of the words of Genesis, he went on to question the authorship of the entire Pentateuch, the first five books of the Old Testament. Much of their content, he decided, was not historical at all: much more was really centuries newer than was thought. Then he discovered that the Mosaic law never existed before the captivity in Babylon, and that the book of Deuteronomy was a fake, and that the books of Chronicles were falsified for the aggrandisement of priests and Levites. All these shattering doubts he freely made public, and the public responded by assuming that his long apprenticeship with the Zulus had half paganized him. As a contemporary limerick suggested,

> *A bishop there was of Natal*
> *Who took a Zulu for a pal,*
> *Said the Kaffir, 'Look 'ere,*
> *Ain't the Pentateuch queer?'*
> *And converted My Lord of Natal.*

Like thunder upon his head came the reaction. Ripostes poured from the presses in Britain as in Africa, committees demanded his resignation, *Punch* had Archbishop Longley, the Primate of All England, writing to Colenso in severe iambics:

> *My dear Colenso,*
> *   With regret,*
> *We hierarchs in conclave met,*
> *Beg you, you disturbing writer,*
> *To take off your colonial mitre.*
> *This course we press upon you strongly*
> *Believe me, yours most truly,*
> *   Longley.*

In Cape Town Bishop Robert Gray, the Metropolitan of British South Africa, announced his intention of charging Colenso with heresy. He believed himself to have absolute jurisdiction over his subordinate bishops: his powers, he said, exceeded even those of the civil courts, and there could be no appeal against his decisions. Convening a court in the unfinished cathedral at Cape Town, in December 1863 he publicly deposed the Bishop of Natal from his see, and presently went on to excommunicate him too.

Colenso was undismayed. He refused to recognize the powers of Bishop Gray, and did not attend the court. The Church was part of the constitution of England, he argued, but not of South Africa, and Gray was no more entitled to charge him than he was to charge Bishop Gray. He appealed to the Crown, and in 1865 the Privy Council decided in his favour. The Crown, it decreed, 'had no power to constitute a bishopric in a colony which had its own independent legislature'. The Church of England was not a part of the constitution in any colonial settlement, and its ministers were merely members of a voluntary association, without legal power or immunity. Bishop Gray's metropolitan authority was therefore spurious, and his punishment of Colenso null and void.

These proceedings were as excitedly followed in Victorian England as had been the affair of Governor Eyre, and the reports of the hearings, which fill a volume of 400 pages, make curious reading. The gravamen of the charge against Colenso was 'erroneous teaching'—refusing to believe in the eternity of future punishment, or maintaining that 'our blessed Lord was ignorant and in error upon the subject of the authorship and age of different portions of the Pentateuch'. More relevant politically was the suggestion that he believed in the universal equality of man. It is as much an imperial as a religious anxiety that we sense in the Dean of Cape Town's rhetorical address for the prosecution. All men, Colenso was alleged to think, stood upon the same level before God. There was no difference between them, and the whole of mankind was the recipient of God's grace in the gospels. 'My lords, let me call your attention to that word recipient. That is to say, as he explains it, regeneration, a death unto sin and a new birth unto righteousness, belongs to us from our birth hour, that is by man, by nature. . . .

And further, he distinctly implies that all men, as men, have the Holy Spirit. Now, my lords, when opinions such as these are met with, the question naturally comes—what, then, is the good of being a Christian?'

Or, the Dean might have added, of having an Empire?[1] When the Privy Council restored Colenso to his see, its councillors were declaring in effect that there was no such thing as an imperial church, and gradually the various colonial churches were dis-established. Bishop Gray flatly refused to accept the Council's decision. Colenso, he said, had been 'handed over to the power of the Evil One', and had no place in a House of God. The mission bodies in Natal withdrew their support and their funds from Colenso, and there was an unsuccessful attempt to block his stipend from England. The first General Synod of the Anglican Church assembled in London specifically to debate the problem,[2] and the newspapers celebrated the affair with learned editorials and clerical cartoons. The more insistently the law in England declared Colenso still to be the rightful Bishop of Natal, the more Bishop Gray determined that he was no such thing, and in 1869 he made the final gesture of colonial defiance, and consecrated his own rival bishop to the see.

Farcical scenes ensued. Colenso, returning from London to his little cathedral of St Peter, was theatrically anathemized by his own Dean at Sunday morning service. The Cape Town sentence was read aloud before the congregation, and the Dean added to it the rider that what the Church bound on earth was bound in heaven too. 'That sentence stands ratified in the presence of Almighty God', he assured the Bishop. 'Depart! Go away from the House of God!' The cathedral doors were locked, its harmonium was silenced, its bells were immobilized, its plate removed, and when the rival Bishop

---

[1] As an Afrikaner academic explained to me a century later, 'you must realize that we are divided into our separate races, black, brown and white, *according to our degree of original sin*'—the ultimate rationalization, I thought, of the imperial idea.

[2] It was celebrated by W. S. Gilbert in *The Bishop of Rum-ti-Foo*:
> *From east and south the holy clan*
> *Of bishops gathered, to a man:*
> *To Synod, called Pan-Anglican;*
> *In flocking crowds they came.*

McCrorie arrived in state from Cape Town, a rival new cathedral was hastily built for him, and dedicated to St Saviour.

For years the schism rocked the little town, and made it far more famous for the presence of Colenso than for the memory of its old Boer heroes. Each bishop had his own fanatic following: when they met each other they did not speak, and when McCrorie once inadvertently bowed to Colenso, he excused himself with the apology that 'my feelings as a gentleman overcame my feeling as a Christian'. Colenso became a martyr to some, a traitor to others—snubbed by civic dignitaries, adored by doting congregations, the subject of innumerable sermons, debates, scholarly papers, theological exchanges, insulting diatribes and maidenly odes. Through it all he maintained his friendship with the Zulus, even during years when the British Empire was actually at war with them, and when he died in 1883, the most celebrated of all imperial churchmen, they laid him under the altar of his own little cathedral beneath the single word *Sobantu*.[1]

4

These imperial disputes were comprehensible only to the elect, and so were many of the Empire's lesser mysticisms: for by now, as the Queen's reign approached its voluptuous climax, the Empire itself had become a kind of faith. Not many of the subject peoples shared this concept in its full and hazy glory, nor many foreigners either: but the British came to believe in it fervently, and propagated it with such zeal that the sacramental nature of the British Empire, all its panoply of pomp and power, its constantly reiterated declarations of duty, its belief in its own infallibility, its ritual air of amplitude and dedication, itself became in the last decades of Victoria's century one of the ruling factors of the world.

An increasingly sacrosanct article of this faith was the monarchy —'commonly hidden like a mystery', as Walter Bagehot had said of it, 'sometimes paraded like a pageant'. Queen Victoria had not, of

[1] His following, calling itself the Church of England in South Africa, survives to this day despite the opposition of the Cape Town hierarchy, and has its own Bishop.

course, always been a semi-sacred figure. She was an interesting curiosity to Emily Eden; she was subject to scurrilous criticism throughout the first half of her reign; she was highly unpopular when, upon the death of her dear Albert, she withdrew weeded into privacy. But now, as she came into her own as a person, so she assumed too the mantle of imperial fulfilment. It was Benjamin Disraeli, during his second and greater Premiership, who achieved this apotheosis. Himself a romancer, an adventurer, a Jew, an exotic, he inspired Victoria with the vision of imperial splendour, diamond-starred, universal, upheld by elephants, emus and giraffes, attended by turbanned lancers and respectful aborigines. It was upon Disraeli's inspiration that Victoria was proclaimed Empress of India, a sublimation prosaically achieved by a far from unanimous vote in the House of Commons, but rapturously received by the Queen. An Empress she was by Act of Parliament, and as an Empress she bore herself ever after. She signed herself VRI with satisfaction, she loved to have Indians around her court, and she became to the aficionados of Empire far more than a mere constitutional monarch, but a vital item of dogma.

This was a novel kind of religion for the English. Not since the days of Elizabeth I had they revered a monarch so, or responded with such devotion to the spirit of kingship, and it was especially in the imperial context that Victoria achieved this charisma. The Empire gave her the eponym Great White Queen, endowing her with a legendary force not unlike Moby Dick's, and it was the Empire which made of her an unorthodox Earth-Mother, ample, experienced, kindly, wise, to whose serge skirts the heathen or ignorant might cling in sanctuary, and beneath whose stern admonishment tyrants and rebels alike might reform themselves.

The Queen's symbolism was accepted as magic in many different ways. The English themselves, with their well-known taste for the arcane, were still half-bemused by hereditary notions of divine right, now extended to embrace British sovereignty as a whole. Many of the rituals of empire, conducted wherever the British served or settled, were like libations to an unseen but ever-present divinity—Toasting the Queen, in the hot hush of the regimental mess, while the punkahs creaked heavily above the candles, and on the sudden silence the buzz of the crickets sounded—mounting the Queen's Guard, with all the formalistic stamping and shouting which was the liturgy of the British Army—praying for the Queen's Majesty— saluting the Queen's statue—issuing commands, in the depths of the forest or the icy expanses of the Arctic, in the Queen's Name—even curtseying in one's best rose-strewn hat to the Queen's Governor, who might not be very godlike in himself, but was by virtue of his office anointed with a divine unguent.

Simpler subjects of the Empire believed the Queen to be wonder-working in a more literal way, and worshipped her at shrines. Notables of Sind, on ceremonial occasions, bowed low before her portrait, which was veiled from the eyes of lesser citizens, and offertories of many kinds reached her from afar—wild beasts, ivory caskets, thrones of buffalo hide, or the bag of flour which, in 1849, came to her from the first water-mill ever to be owned by Maoris. For twenty-five years after the death of her chief representative in Bombay, Sir Robert Grant, the sepoy guards at Government House at Poona presented arms to any cat leaving the palace after dark, it being understood that His Excellency's soul, and thus Her Majesty's authority, had transmigrated felinely. Even the estranged Irish received the Queen with reverence, when she visited Dublin soon after the Great Famine, and the Sioux and Cree of the Canadian wilderness hailed her as the White Mother, the ultimate squaw, hitherto personified chiefly by mountain peaks, particularly imposing pine-trees, or spectral bison. In India the Queen was seen as the direct spiritual successor of the Moghuls, and of royal houses more ancient still, and there her elevation to Empresshood was celebrated with a Durbar that was a very Mass of the imperial rite, in which all the principal acolytes were princes themselves.

This occasion figures in every Anglo-Indian memoir of the period, and was the model for several royal durbars to come, at which the oblational nature of the Raj was re-affirmed from reign to reign. Queen Victoria did not attend herself—she never went out of Europe—but so powerful was her presence by proxy that for years afterwards Indians claimed to have seen her there. The Durbar symbolically marked the end of the Moghul dynasty, poor Bahadur having died at last in his eighty-eighth year: the conquerors from

Persia were to be succeeded in the continuum of Indian royalty by the benevolent tyrants from England. To impress this providential process upon the minds of the Indian princes, themselves eager practitioners of the royalty cult, there was mounted upon the plains of Delhi, within sight of the Red Fort, the most flamboyant pageant even India had ever seen. Its focus was the Queen's viceroy, Lord Lytton the poet, and it was Lytton himself who decreed its style, encouraged by the romantic Disraeli far away. It was to be a pseudo-feudal, pseudo-religious ceremony. The princes of India were paying homage to their supreme prince, Kaisar-i-Hind, Victoria RI, and they were to do so in all the splendour of their lesser princeships. The taste for the mediaeval had died out in England, but it triumphantly survived in India, that last resort of magnificence, and Lord Lytton saw the Durbar in chivalric terms.

For each attendant princeling an escutcheon was devised, and these were distributed reverently among the feudatories. One by one the princes were taken before the Viceroy, escorted by cavalry officers and saluted by guns, and placed before a full-length portrait of Her Imperial Majesty. The satin banner was brought in by kilted Highlanders, and the Viceroy presented it with the spoken text: 'I present Your Highness with this banner as a personal gift from Her Majesty the Queen in commemoration of her assumption of the title of Empress of India. Her Majesty trusts that it may never be unfurled without reminding you not only of the close union between the throne of England and your loyal and princely house, but also of the earnest desire of the paramount power to see your dynasty strong, prosperous and permanent'. Then a crimson ribbon was placed around the prince's neck, with a gold medal of the Queen's head, and the Viceroy intoned: 'I further decorate you, by command of Her Majesty. May this medal be long worn by yourself, and long kept as an heirloom in your family in remembrance of the auspicious date it bears'.

Then around the durbar ground the heraldics improbably fluttered, while all the British Lieutenant-Governors, curates of the Crown, stood in attendance beneath their own ceremonial ensigns. Some of the princes had brought their own pipe bands, troops of colourful retainers, or elephants, and they were dressed themselves in stupendous fineries. Battalions of infantry stood on parade around the durbar ground, and squadrons of cavalry pawed and snorted, and trumpets blew, and guns fired, and in the centre of it all, upon a dais of gilded ironwork, dressed in flags, red and golden cloths, shields, arms, banners, with the imperial crown on a red velvet cushion—at the centre of it all Lord Lytton resplendently represented the Empress, if not corporeally, for he was a tall thin man, at least in the abstraction of royalty.

Some European witnesses thought it all rather tawdry, and others were uncomfortably reminded of the Communion service in the Book of Common Prayer ('a full, perfect, and sufficient sacrifice, oblation, and satisfaction, for the sins of the whole world'). Among Indians it was a great success. 'O Mother,' said one loyal address, adeptly catching the spirit of the occasion, 'O beloved, residing in the Palace of London, the descendants of the great Emperor of Delhi are burnt in the fire of your might. Surely today angels will sing your Majesty's glory in the heavenly regions.'[1]

5

In the British Army the imperial ju-ju was woven into those talismans of pride, the regimental standards. In former times the standard had been carried into battle to provide a prominent rallying-point for the regiment: the ceremony of Trooping the Colour was a drill exercise of this practical function. Through most of Victoria's century the standards were still taken into action, but by now their exhibition was purely symbolic. Like fetishes of Africa, they embodied in themselves the spirit of loyalty, of sacrifice, of comradeship which lay at the root of the British military system, and thus of the imperial momentum.

The soldiers' devotion to their colours was almost fanatic. Men would happily die for them (though in the Afghan War of 1839

[1] Rival god-kings did sometimes arise among the subject peoples, but they seldom maintained their challenge for long, the natives generally preferring the distant allure of the Great White Queen. The most endearing of the rebel divinities was Te Whero Potatau, who was hailed by the Maoris as a Messianic king, but who protested himself that he was only a snail.

Captain Souter, who had wound the colours of the 44th Regiment prominently around his waist, found his life spared by the Afghans because they thought he must be an officer of special importance, worth a useful ransom). We read of officers braving the most frightful hazards of assegai, jezail or dismemberment in the cause of the colours, and when at last a regiment's standards were due for retirement, worn out themselves by these adventures, or outliving a disbanded formation, nobody would dream of burning them, or taking them as souvenirs: instead they were carried in solemn parade to the regimental church—where, hung high above the memorial chapel, and slowly disintegrating into spindrift down the years, they remained for ever in cobweb sanctity, like the bones of saints and martyrs in foreign countries.[1]

Guns were holy too, for reasons still more obvious. It was a disgrace to abandon any piece of equipment on the field of battle, but to abandon a gun was apostasy. It was an artillery officer's ultimate ignominy, in fiction a favourite short-story device, in fact a permanent blot on a man's record. Innumerable tales of imperial heroism were attached to the guns—saving them, spiking them, manning them to the death. Nothing more shocked Elphinstone's gamer officers in Kabul than his limp agreement to hand over the ordnance to the Afghans, and nothing more distressed the officers and loyal sepoys of the Indian Army, in the flood of cautionary measures that followed the Mutiny, than their deprivation of artillery. More properly, perhaps, even than the honoured standards, the guns were a depository of the imperial faith: for they were machines as well as weapons, oiled and burnished with mid-Victorian diligence, and it was no coincidence that the Royal Artillery, bound as it were by vows to its gun-carriages and breech-blocks, was to remain into the twentieth century the most professional corps of the British armed forces.

---

[1] A moving example still extant is the Queen's Colour of the 1st Battalion, 24th Regiment (South Wales Borderers) which hangs in Brecon Cathedral. Two officers were cut to pieces by Zulus trying to save this standard after the Battle of Isandhlwana in 1879. It was found after their deaths, embellished by the Queen with a wreath of silver immortelles, and carried by the battalion for another fifty-four years.

6

All this may seem dangerously close to war-worship, but Englishmen found it easy enough to reconcile their imperial imagery with a pre-Raphaelite vision of Christianity—the Gun beside the Light— as Cecil Spring-Rice demonstrated in the second verse of his famous patriotic hymn, *I Vow To Thee My Country*:

> *And there's another country, I've heard of long ago,*
> *Most dear to them that love her, most great to them that know;*
> *We may not count her armies, we may not see her King;*
> *Her fortress is a faithful heart, her pride is suffering;*
> *And soul by soul and silently her shining bounds increase,*
> *And her ways are ways of gentleness, and all her paths are peace.*

When all is said, the nearest thing the Empire had to a religion of its own, as cohesive as Catholicism or Islam, was the rite of the Anglican Church, diffused in such mysterious ways across the world. By now there were cathedrals in St Helena, Hobart, Grahamstown and Hong Kong. The Bishop of Gibraltar's see extended from Portugal to the Caspian,[1] the Bishop of Newfoundland was also Bishop of Bermuda, and the black Bishop of Sierra Leone had recently ended the worship of the monitor lizard in the Niger delta. St Paul's Cathedral, Calcutta, took five hours to dedicate—'for ever hereafter dedicated and consecrated', the officiating Bishop said it was, 'by this our definitive sentence of final decree which we make pronounce and promulge in these writings, saving and reserving unto us and our successors Bishops of Calcutta all ordinary and Episcopal Jurisdictions rights and privileges'. Bishop Colenso may have seemed a lost heretic to his Metropolitan in Cape Town, but to his Zulu disciples he was undoubtedly a high priest of the imperial conviction, and wherever the British flag flew in the world, Anglicanism was generally accepted as the outward form of its inner grace.

In Dublin the great men of the Ascendancy bowed to the Queen's Viceroy as he entered his pew in the grim old cathedral of St Patrick, where the war memorials commemorated many a death in the im-

[1] And he lived in Malta.

perial cause, and the congregation optimistically sang Hymn 303 in the Church of Ireland hymnal—*Lift thy banners, Church of Erin, to thine ancient faith we cling*. In Malta the sailors marched for church parade to the cool shuttered cathedral built at the express desire of Queen Adelaide on the shores of the Grand Harbour—a temple of the English way, from whose forecourt after Matins the captains could look out to their warships lying at anchor below, at whose altar commanders' wives and bank managers' ladies devotedly arranged the flowers, in whose front pews the Governor shared equal precedence with the Admiral Commanding, and through whose louvred windows the fine old English hymns rang lustily across the lanes of Valetta (where the Papist Maltese superstitiously crossed themselves before their images, and those ratings excused church parade that day loitered in the Gut waiting for the brothels to open).

In Madras the soldiers, the civil servants, the box-wallahs and their wives crowded stiff-collared and muslined into the garrison church of St Mary's, within Fort St George, whose very walls breathed the antique glamour of the Raj: there were baptized the three daughters of Job Charnock, founder of Calcutta, by the Hindu mistress he had rescued from the suttee pyre—there Clive was married, and the Duke of Wellington worshipped, and eight Governors lay buried—the Princess of Tanjore had presented the altar rails, the altar piece was captured from the French at Pondicherry, and the church itself, so tradition said, had been designed not by an architect at all, but by Edward Fowle, Master Gunner of the Fort. And far away in the east the Sunday congregation crowded into the white cathedral of St Andrew's above the Padang at Singapore—white in Anglican purity, white beside the fretted peeling presence of the city around, white against the rusty coasters lying in the roads, white for Raffles who had founded the city, and who hoped the Empire would be remembered always in 'characters of light'—white with the linen suits of the merchants in their pews, and the vestments of the clergy beyond the lectern—white for the Great White Queen, the improving zeal of Empire, the blank pages of ledgers yet to be completed, or perhaps for the uniforms of the toiling convicts who, only twenty years before under the direction of the Royal Engineers, had created that holy building in the heat.

In any of these great churches, any Sunday morning, the empire builders assemble in their hierarchy, Europeans in the front pews, Africans, or Indians, or Chinese, or plain aborigines behind: and Lady Dicehurt envies Mrs Duncebury her pearls, and young Tom Morris sniggers at Mrs Timbury's hat, and down they all kneel in familiar discipline, two or three hundred gathered together in the name of Empire, while the chaplain's Oxford English echoes among the memorials: and when the time comes the choir, rising to its feet with a swishing of starched surplices and a faint emanation of gum-drops, launches into one of the full-throated anthems of Anglicanism—Wesley's *Wilderness*, Mendelssohn's *Oh for the Wings*, or best of all, if it is nearly Christmas time in Melbourne or Toronto, Crotch's

> *Lo, Star-led Chiefs,*
> *Assyrian Odours bring*

—a work which, with its magic ensemble of the exotic, the homely, the reverent, the funny, the lyrical and the mysterious, truly sings the ethos of Empire.[1]

---

[1] Though impious choristers had their own version of it—*Lo, Startled Chefs/Assyrian Sodas Bring*—just as younger Canadian churchgoers preferred to venerate the Twelve Opossums.

CHAPTER SEVENTEEN

The Humiliation of the Metis

THE British were now exporting to their dominions a kind of package civilization, offered in competition with the local product, and backed by powerful service arrangements. Sometimes this was conscious policy: Sir George Grey, Lord Melbourne's Under-Secretary for the Colonies, had long before recommended the deliberate destruction of tribal systems everywhere in the Empire, and their replacement by societies of agricultural small-holders. Sometimes it was a matter of economic strategy: Manchester, for example, had virtually demolished the Indian textile industry, the basis of Indian folk-craft and a mainstay of traditional Indian life.[1] More often, though, it was instinctive, or even incidental, and was seen by the British, if they saw it all, simply as an aspect of historical determinism.

The indigenous cultures reacted variously to this assault. Some, like the Hindu and Muslim civilizations of India, yielded but did not break, treating the western culture as a transient phenomenon.[2] Some, like the Burmese, simply took no notice. The aborigines of Australia faded away uncomprehending. The Irish fitfully but furiously resisted. And there was one culture at least which, while its followers understood very well how powerful was the imperial challenge, threw everything into a last spasm of resistance, determined to do or die in defence of its own ways. This was the back-

---

[1] While making shameless use of its designs: Forbes Watson, who assembled a pioneer collection of Indian handloom fabrics in the interests of art and scholarship, was actually subsidized by the Lancashire manufacturers in the interests of profit.

[2] As late as 1969, so the anthropologist Sol Tax reported, the North American Indians seemed to be 'waiting for us to go away'.

wood culture of the Metis, into whose prairie fastness of Western Canada the power of the British Empire, in the later years of the 1860s, complacently and inexorably advanced.

2

We have already encountered these striking half-breeds, paddling Governor Simpson's canoe flamboyantly to Norway House, or guiding the snowshoe traders of the Honourable Company through forest trails of Rupert's Land. They remained, 20 years later, still a bold, free people, semi-nomadic—hunters, trappers, boatmen, guides, traders. They were a handsome and hospitable lot, with their rich strains of Indian, French and Scottish blood, and though they were given to heavy drinking and protracted roistering, most of them were devout Roman Catholics. In earlier years the Hudson's Bay Company had generally approved of them. They made useful employees, they helped to keep unwanted settlers out, and they were valuable intermediaries with the full-blooded Indians. Most of the Metis were illiterate. They spoke a patois of their own, a mixture of antique French, Cree or Chippewa, English, and prairie terms of their own devising: and all their values, too, were mixed—half wild, half settled, half European, half Indian. They were a sensitive, proud, but troubled people, not quite sure where they stood in the world and its history.

By the 1860s the greatest Metis concentration was in the region of what is now Manitoba, in the heart of the Great Plains. Their chief market centre was Pembina, across the frontier in the United States, but their true homeland was the Canadian country to the north, along the banks of the Red and Assiniboine rivers, where some 6,000 of them still lived in a gaudy and heroic life-style. There they formed a relatively compact and recognizable community, hunting the dwindling buffalo herds in exciting horseback sweeps, and farming in the old French manner with strips of land running down to the river banks. They believed themselves to have inalienable rights in the country, to be its true masters if not actually its owners. They preserved a sense of brotherhood, and with their priests and their elected leaders, their bright clothes, their dashing songs and their long adventurous memories, were able to sustain an inbred and truculent culture not quite like any other.

But it was in this very region, on the banks of the Red River, that the Hudson's Bay Company had permitted the one permanent European settlement within their territories of the west. We have already seen how uncertain were the origins of this remote colony. At one time its survival had seemed unlikely, but it had persevered, put down roots, and eventually thrived. In the 1860s it was still theoretically governed by the Company, but had hardened into a self-reliant frontier community, each for himself and all for progress. By now about 2,000 Europeans lived in the Red River colony— mostly Scottish by origin still, but with admixtures of Englishmen and Americans. No less than the Metis, they were proud of their own accomplishments, and fiercely egalitarian. When Henry Hind, a well-known Cambridge geologist, called at one Red River farm in the course of a scientific journey, he was invited to sit down for lunch. The table was laid for one. 'Where's my plate?' promptly demanded Mr Gowler, the master of the house. 'Oh John,' his wife cried, 'you would not think of sitting at table with a gentleman?' 'Give me a chair and a plate!' retorted the pioneer. 'Am I not a gentleman too? Is not this my house, and these my victuals? Give me a plate!'

Red River was the only sizeable settlement in central Canada. To the west of it the open prairie extended to the Rockies. To the east lay an appalling barrier of forest, quagmire, lake and rocky outcrop, smothering northern Ontario, and so impenetrable that the only really practicable route to Red River from Ottawa or Toronto lay south of the frontier, *via* Chicago and St Paul. The settlement was rough-and-ready, but not unattractive. Its nucleus was the Company post called Fort Garry, a fortified compound at the confluence of the two rivers. This was the centre of Red River life. Here the traders brought their pelts and their produce, the courts sat, the administration had its offices. The rooms were painted in garish reds, yellows and oranges, to break the monotony of the endless blues, whites and greens outside, and life around the fort, too, was always full of colour. In summer flotillas of canoes were drawn up on the river bank outside, and from the gate convoys of Red River carts, drawn by horses or oxen, set off into the prairie barked about by dogs—carts designed specifically for the prairie, whose high wooden wheels made, as they turned on their ungreased wooden axles, a high screeching noise, nerve-racking and distinctive, which became to most visitors the unforgettable theme of Red River. In winter horse-drawn sledges galloped in and out, their passengers swathed in furs and bright striped blankets, or long trains of dog-teams arrived over the snow from outlying settlements—St Andrew, Little Britain, or Old England. Indians and Metis crowded around the stores and the purchase offices, huddled hangdog outside the courtroom door, or plodded in with piles of skins or horned elk-heads on their shoulders.

Around the fort was a little clutter of log houses, shops and ware-houses. A handsome stern-wheeler puffed up and down the river, and along its banks, for ten or twenty miles, there extended the homesteads of the English-speaking farmers, with their stout granite houses, their churches and their gardens, comfortably above the water. An air of rural contentment hung about these country parts, tinged with nostalgia—there could hardly be a more homesick church than the Anglican church of St Andrew's, peaceful beside the river, with its imported English trees doing well in the churchyard, its authentic English smells of church must and hassock (though the hassocks were made of buffalo hide), its notices of church functions pinned in the little stone porch, its cosy rectory muslin-curtained around the corner, and even the skylarks which, especially brought from the Old Country, often soared and sang in the cold empyrean.

But through this analogue of the imperial order swirled and swaggered the Metis—improvident, merry, drunk, quick-witted, cherishing little love for the Company and its traditions, and no loyalty to the misty congeries of British colonies known as Canada. They mostly lived along the banks of the Assiniboine, and there they had their own Catholic basilica of St Boniface, with a bishop and a school. The Metis had repeatedly clashed with authority in the Red River, chiefly because of the Company's trading policies. They were fierce free enterprisers, and they had many friends and relatives across the American frontier. In particular they looked for profit and pleasure to the thriving American city of St Paul, 400 miles to the south, where trade was free and liquor ran more freely than the Company ever allowed. The Metis of Red River were like running fire in a warm haystack, and they often exploded into violence. To the Anglo-Saxon settlers they were dangerous and volatile aliens, not to be trusted with guns, spirits or women: and the Metis, for their part, often egged on by French Canadians, by Americans, by Irishmen, and other inveterate enemies of the British Empire, viewed the settlers with implacable distrust.

In 1867 the four most populous colonies of British North America, Quebec, Ontario, Nova Scotia and New Brunswick, confederated themselves into the Dominion of Canada, a self-governing possession of the Crown, under the leadership of Sir John Macdonald— 'Old Tomorrow', as the Indians called him. Two years later the Hudson's Bay Company surrendered to the new Government all its political and territorial rights, and the whole of the west became part of the confederation. All at once Canada became a nation, coast to coast, and the politicians, the financiers, the engineers and the surveyors began planning a railroad which, by linking the Atlantic and the Pacific shores, would make the whole enormous territory an exploitable British whole, proof against the expansionist tendencies of the Americans to the south.

The Metis were not forewarned of these developments. Nobody asked their opinions. They merely learnt, in 1869, that henceforth the Red River area would be governed by an altogether new authority, appointed from Ottawa and doubtless dedicated to the extension of British civilization throughout the spaces of the west.

3

The first suggestion of resistance to this change occurred in the autumn of 1869, shortly before the transfer of authority. The Canadians had already decided that the Red River settlement must be reinforced by good Anglo-Saxon stock from Ontario, to act as a base for the opening of the whole west, to keep out the Americans, and to balance the influence of the French Canadians and their Catholic missions. A military survey party was sent to Fort Garry to choose the best sites for new settlement, and was instructed to use the Ontario system of settlement survey—square blocks, that is, instead of the linear system of 'river lots' traditional throughout French-speaking Canada. The Metis were fiercely resentful. They well understood the implications of the survey. They knew that it meant the influx of large numbers of diligent Canadian farmers, to turn the whole prairie into a grain factory, and put an end to the buffalo hunting and the easy-going Metis life.

The surveyors had been told to keep well clear of the river-side lots, to avoid trouble with the Metis, but they were hazy about the existing property system, and one team trespassed upon the grazing land of a Metis farm some two miles from Fort Garry. The farmer violently objected, and ran off to get help: and presently the disconcerted Canadians saw, striding menacingly across the land, a group of young Metis bravos. There were fifteen or sixteen of them, unarmed but belligerent, dressed in the usual Metis gear of skins and fringed leathers, and looking distinctly unfriendly: lithe slim-waisted young men, different in physique, in temperament, in language, in values, in origins and in manner from the stolid soldiers—who, pausing with their surveyor's chain in their hands, incomprehendingly awaited their arrival.

Their leader was a stocky, white-skinned man in his late twenties, with curly hair and dark eyes: and while his companions stared silently at the surveyors, this man walked up to their chain, and in a gesture of theatrical affront, placed his foot upon it. 'You go no farther', he said. The country south of the Assiniboine was the country of the Metis, and no survey would be allowed. 'You go no farther'. The surveyors argued, the Metis were inflexible, and the soldiers, baffled, outnumbered and probably rather scared, gave up the attempt and returned to camp.

So Canada learnt of the existence of Louis Riel, an archetypal resistance leader of the British Empire. His father, half-French, half-Indian, was himself a well-known Metis activist: his mother was a Frenchwoman, daughter of the first white woman in the north-west. Riel was thus as genuinely rooted to the soil as a Metis could be: to his one-eighth Indian blood had been added a heritage of pioneers and ardent Catholics, and he had been educated at a seminary in Montreal, and politically indoctrinated during a stay at St Paul.

He was a passionate patriot, emotional, volatile, often naïve, and was to prove one of the most poignant figures of the imperial story, moving through the pages of Canadian history in a mist of tears. He was like a child. Quick to temper or to forgive, vain, oddly guileless, his touchiness was partly a sense of racial humiliation. His religion was mystic. The British never knew where they stood with him, and we too are left disturbed by his memory, not sure whether he is hero, charlatan or madman. William Butler, one of the most sensitive British Army officers of his generation, met Riel at Fort Garry and thought him preposterous but compelling—'a sharp, restless, intelligent eye, a square-cut massive forehead overhung by a mass of long and thickly clustering hair, and marked with well-cut eye-brows—altogether a remarkable-looking face, all the more so, perhaps, because it was to be seen in a land where such things are rare sights'.

4

The first Lieutenant-Governor of the North-West Territories, William MacDougall, left Ottawa well ahead of time to travel to Fort Garry *via* St Paul. He was known to be an inflexible Scottish Canadian businessman with no taste for half-castes or Catholics, and under Riel's fervent leadership the Metis determined they would have nothing of him. They raised a para-military force of their own, strictly disciplined, well-organized, and prudently sworn to drink no alcohol, and when MacDougall arrived with his staff at the Canadian frontier, he found no loyal reception committee with flags and testimonials. Instead he was handed, the moment he stepped on to the soil of the new province, a brusque decree. 'Monsieur,' it said, 'Le Comité National des Metis de la Rivière Rouge intime à Monsieur McDougall l'ordre de ne pas entrer sur le Territoire du Nord-Ouest sans une permission spéciale de ce Comité.'

This blunt instruction took MacDougall aback. He was not legally Lieutenant-Governor yet, as the transfer of authority was not yet complete, so to the entertained delight of the Americans he did what he was told, and withdrew huffy and bewildered to rented quarters at Pembina. In the meantime Riel rode into Fort Garry with a hundred horsemen, and seized authority from the Company. He and his people, he announced, were not rebels. They were not disloyal to the British Crown. They merely wanted to negotiate with the Canadian Government their own terms for entry into the new confederation. Riel summoned a convention, half English-speaking, half French, to meet at the fort, and when a group of settlers showed signs of resistance, he promptly imprisoned seventy of them inside.

Now Red River was in a constitutional limbo. Its *de jure* Government was still the Company, its *de facto* ruler was Riel, and to complicate the issue further the Canadian Government decided to postpone the transfer of power until things had quietened down at Red River. Unfortunately they omitted to tell the unfortunate MacDougall of this decision, and when the original date for the transfer arrived, December 1, 1869, though still on the wrong side of the frontier he drew up a proclamation in the Queen's name. Headed 'Victoria, by the Grace of God, of the United Kingdom of Great Britain and Ireland, Queen', it announced that 'our trusty and well-beloved William MacDougall' was given governmental authority over the territory from that day.

This was a fraudulent text, not even having the authority of Ottawa, let alone London, and not as it happened being true: but that night MacDougall, with seven companions and two pointer dogs, crossed the Canadian frontier in carriages after dark, evaded the Metis patrols, and drove to a deserted Hudson's Bay post two miles inside British territory. It was nearly midnight when they arrived, and a blizzard was blowing, but there in the driving snow, with full if chill solemnity, a Union Jack was unfurled in the darkness: and by guttering candle-light, shielded by his companions from the wind, and grimly holding the parchment in mittened hands, the debilitated politician read aloud his spurious decree. There was not a soul to hear, except for his own aides and animals, and when the ceremony was over the eight men clambered into their carriages, and followed by the despondent pointers, clattered and slithered through the snow ruts back to the United States.

News of this silly ritual soon reached Riel, but he dismissed it as illegal. Red River, he said, now had no official Government at all.

'A people, when it has no Government, is free to adopt one form of Government in preference to another, to give or to refuse allegiance to that which is proposed.' So the Metis established a regime of their own, 'and hold it to be the only and lawful authority now in existence in Rupert's Land and the North West, which claims the obedience and respect of the people'. A new flag was raised above Fort Garry, a fleur de lys and a shamrock on a white ground, and an official newspaper appeared, *The New Nation*. Riel seized the monies held by the Company at Fort Garry, and on December 27, 1870, was elected President of the Provisional Government of Rupert's Land and the North-West (an honorific which made him, in theory at least, ruler of the largest republic in the world).

So the Metis, instinctively throwing everything into the ring, became masters of Red River. They had done it by force but without bloodshed, and their legal case was, if scarcely foolproof, at least arguable. At the end of the year MacDougall, recognizing a *fait accompli*, quit Pembina to the catcalls of the American frontiersmen, and returned ignominiously to Ottawa.

5

In London the Imperial Government viewed these events with a remote patrician calm. Lord Granville, Colonial Secretary in Gladstone's Liberal Government, was no imperialist, and he urged restraint upon Ottawa. 'The Queen has heard,' he cabled the Canadian Prime Minister, 'with surprise and regret that certain misguided persons have bonded together to oppose by force the entry of the future Lieutenant Governor into Her Majesty's settlements on Red River. Her Majesty does not distrust the loyalty of Her subjects in these settlements, and can only ascribe to misunderstanding or misrepresentation their opposition to a change which is plainly for their advantage. She relies on your Government for using every effort to explain whatever is misunderstood, to ascertain the wants and to conciliate the goodwill of the Red River settlers. But meantime she authorizes you to signify to them the sorrow and displeasure with which she views their unreasonable and lawless proceedings. . . .'

The Governor-General of Canada was Sir John Young, who had

previously been Lord High Commissioner in the Ionians, and knew all about fractious un-Britons. He used the Queen's message as the basis of a proclamation, promising that if the Metis obeyed and dispersed, no action would be taken against them: but the mood in Ottawa, itself hardly more than a lumber village above its river, was scarcely conciliatory. To orthodox Canadians Riel's rebellion was only symptomatic of Canada's deep inner stresses: they saw it as French, Catholic, reactionary and probably treasonable. It flew in the face of progress. It was a gesture from the ignorant past. Within a few months of Confederation, it seemed, the young Dominion had a separatist movement on its hands, and from a quarter even the prescient Lord Durham could never have foreseen.

So the agitated Ottawa politicians were relieved when help came from an unexpected quarter—Hudson's Bay Company, the traditional enemy of western settlement. The Company was adroitly modifying its public image. Sir George Simpson was dead and gone, the monopoly was abolished, and the Honourable Company, handsomely compensated with land grants for its loss of sovereignty, was busily preparing itself a new future in retail trade and land development. Donald Smith, Simpson's successor as chief representative in Montreal, was a Company Factor of the new school, and he soon saw the possibilities of the Red River imbroglio. He offered the Government the loyal cooperation of all his officers to 'restore and maintain order throughout the territory', and humbly suggested that he might himself go to Fort Garry as Special Commissioner, charged with investigating the situation, explaining things to the Metis, and taking such steps 'as may seem most proper for effecting the peaceable transfer of the country'.

Smith was as figurative to one side of the dispute as Riel was to the other. As Lord Strathcona he was presently to be the prime begetter of the Canadian Pacific Railway, which was largely built on Company land, and which more than any other agency distributed the imperial civilization across the Canadian west. He was an immigrant from Scotland, the son of a Moray tradesman, who had risen from the ranks in the Company's service, and had grown rich by his canny manipulation of the stock market—not least by buying shares in his own company, of which he presently became chief shareholder.

His colleagues among the factors thought this process smacked of corruption, and all his life Smith was attended by a detectable aura of double-dealing: but he was a strong, courageous man, charmless, ambitious, ill-educated, without many principles but admirably resourceful. He was 50 years old when, two days after Christmas, 1870, he arrived by sleigh at Fort Garry to put matters straight with the reactionary primitives of the prairies.

He knew that a settlement at Red River would be a great personal triumph, perhaps the first step in a political career: and Riel too recognized that his arrival at Fort Garry turned the issue into something like a trial of personalities, the self-controlled scheming Scot versus the passionate and unstable half-breed. For this duel of semi-heroes a public assembly was summoned, in a field near the fort: and from all over the settlement the people came by sledge or snowshoe to pass their judgement. The temperature was 20 degrees below zero, the snow was deep, but more than a thousand people gathered there, and stood huddled and frosty in their heavy furs, when a ragged salute from the Metis riflemen announced the arrival of President Riel of the Provisional Republic and Mr Smith from Montreal.

They mounted the platform, the meeting was called to order, and the two men faced their audience: Smith as speaker, to present Ottawa's case, Riel as translator to interpret it. The cold was terrible. All over the field little fires were lighted, fed by small boys with wood, and the listeners crouched silently over them as hour by hour, translated phrase by phrase, Smith talked. It took all day, and next day, still translated by Riel himself, Smith continued his argument. This time his appeal was personal, even emotional. He was, he said, not associated with MacDougall. He only wanted to be useful. He was an independent Scot, married to a wife from Rupert's Land itself, interested only in the well-being of the Red River settlement, and even willing to resign from the Company if it would help.

Gradually, to Riel's chagrin, Smith won the people over. He assured them that all their civil and religious rights would stand, that their existing properties would be respected, and that all Red River people, whatever their race, would enjoy exactly the same status as British subjects in any other part of the Dominion. Finally he invited the convention to send its own delegates to Ottawa, to confirm all this for themselves, and 'to explain the wants and wishes of the Red River people, as well as to discuss and arrange for the representation of the country in Parliament'. The meeting broke up to cheers, an astonishing triumph for Smith, and for a moment it seemed that the rebellion was peacefully over, and that the Metis would come to terms with the British Empire.

6

But at this moment blood was shed. Riel's prisoners were still held inside the fort, and now a posse of Canadian settlers, with a few Indians, gathered outside the town to assault the fort and release them. They took as hostage a young Metis. He escaped, and in doing so killed a local Scotsman: the infuriated Canadians pursued him, caught him, and killed him in return. Advancing with blood up through the snow towards the fort, the Canadians were greeted by a conciliatory message from Riel, announcing that he had already released the prisoners. He urged the settlers to support the Provisional Government, and signed his message 'Your humble, poor, fair and confident public servant'.

The Canadians were mollified by this appeal, and began to disperse to their several homesteads: but as one group passed the main gate of the fort a group of Metis horsemen suddenly emerged, surrounded them, herded them into the courtyard and locked them up. Two weeks later, when Smith had returned with his good news to Ottawa, one of them was taken from his cell and charged with having taken up arms against the Provisional Government. He was Thomas Scott, a half-caste Irish Protestant with a long record of enmity to the Metis, and it did not take the *ad hoc* court long to find him guilty. A firing squad well-primed with liquor shot him in the snow outside the walls of the fort, watched by a crowd of citizens.

This savage and deliberate act infuriated public opinion in Ottawa, but at first Riel himself did not seem to realize its gravity. 'We must make Canada respect us', he merely said, and settled down to show that the Metis were capable of running the affairs of the colony. Trade was resumed. A new code of laws was published. Money circulated, and daily life returned to normal. In Washington the State Department, fondly imagining the detachment of the whole north-west from the British Empire, seriously considered recognizing the Provisional Government as an independent State. Riel ran up the Union Jack beside his Metis ensign, and two Red River delegates left for Ottawa, as arranged by Smith, carrying a firm but moderate List of Rights.

There, too, it seemed at first that bygones were to be bygones. Most of their demands were met. A new province would be established with its capital at Fort Garry, and 1,400,000 acres of it would be reserved for ever for the Metis. There would be separate schools, guaranteeing the security of the French language, and all existing titles and occupancies would be respected. The new province would be called Manitoba—'a very euphonious word', the Dominion Parliament was told, meaning 'The God That Speaks'. It was true that an imperial armed force would be sent to Fort Garry, to take over security duties from the Metis militia: but this was really intended, Riel's delegates were told confidentially, to appease the angry Ontarians.

Riel had apparently triumphed. The Metis were satisfied with the agreement. Their way of life had been saved, and though the Manitoba Act made no mention of an amnesty, still the delegates had been repeatedly assured that one would be arranged, and that the events of the past few months would be forgiven and forgotten. Subject to such an amnesty, the Provisional Government accepted the terms, and Manitoba came into being on July 15, 1870. The Metis forces were dispersed from Fort Garry, and the Dominion Government agreed that Riel should remain in charge until the arrival of a new Governor. 'I congratulate the people of the North-West,' he told the members of his Assembly, in his stilted formal English, 'upon the happy issue of their undertaking. I congratulate them on having trust enough in the Crown of England to believe that ultimately they would obtain their rights. . . . Let us still pursue the work in which we have lately been engaged . . . the cultivation of peace and friendship, and doing what can be done to convince these people that we never designed to wrong them. . . .'

Riel certainly contemplated his own part in the affair with sincere pride, and years afterwards, when his glory was gone and he looked back upon these events from a nadir of despair, he remembered them only with pride. 'I know,' he said, 'that through the grace of God I am the founder of Manitoba.'

7

His trust in the Crown of England was not altogether misplaced. The Canadians in Ottawa had been repeatedly restrained or prodded in the liberal direction by cables from London, and the British Government had agreed to the dispatch of an armed force to Red River only in the understanding that the troops would have no 'co-ercive' mission. Riel underestimated, though, the force of the imperial conviction. This was a sovereignty approaching the peak of its confidence, unlikely to permit a semi-literate Papist half-caste to impose his own terms upon the course of progress. Reason might urge restraint upon the imperial activists: instinct egged them on.

Of course the British Empire had neither forgotten nor forgiven the death of Thomas Scott, now elevated to martyrdom by patriots far away: and though the delegates had been expressly assured in Ottawa that Riel should remain in office until the arrival of the new Governor, and though Riel had actually prepared an address of welcome for him, and planned a guard of honour to receive him, still it was not really part of the imperial design to recognize this alien rebel as an interim ruler. The promised amnesty was never legally promulgated, and the armed force being sent to the west as a 'benevolent constabulary' thought of itself from the start as a punitive expedition, and much relished the prospect of an affray in Manitoba. As one of its officers wrote, it was a dull period for the fighting soldier. 'There was not a shadow of war in the North, the South, the East or the West. There was not even a Bashote in South Africa, a Beloochie in Schinde, a Bhootea, a Burmese, or any other of the many "eeses" or "eas" forming the great colonial empire of Britain who seemed capable of kicking up the semblance of a row.'

Only Louis Riel in Fort Garry. The commander of the force dispatched to Manitoba was perhaps the most promising young officer of the British Empire, and probably the most cock-sure—Colonel Garnet Joseph Wolseley, quarter-master general in Canada, veteran of campaigns in Burma, the Crimea, India and China, and author of that well-known manual of military conduct, *The Soldier's Pocket-Book*.[1] He was 37 in 1870, and he saw things clearly in terms of right and wrong: he was almost always right, his opponents almost invariably wrong. A fervent Anglo-Irish Protestant himself, with an inherited antipathy towards Catholics, he considered himself God's soldier always, and approached the innumerable battles of his imperial career with a courage formidably buttressed by piety. Wolseley was one of the few intellectual soldiers of his day. He was intensely interested in theories of war, and was as ambitious professionally as he was socially thrusting.

The Red River expedition was his first independent command, and he was ready to make the most of it. He saw the rising as an attempt by the resentful French Canadians, robbed of their sovereignty in Canada by British arms, to block the westward advance of the Empire with a French-speaking Catholic province of their own. Riel was no more than a 'noisy idler', the dupe of the 'clever, cunning, unscrupulous' Catholic bishop at Red River, and the whole affair was a conspiracy between French clerics in the field and French-Canadian wire-pullers in Ottawa. It was Wolseley's job, as he saw it, to extinguish this subversion by force, and to humiliate its leaders.

Fortunately for this clever soldier, the little campaign posed problems of a peculiar and challenging kind. Washington refused to allow the troops passage through American territory, so instead of taking a comfortable train to St Paul Wolseley had to plan a route from the Great Lakes across hundreds of miles of almost impassable

[1] Which he took with him on all his campaigns, together with the Bible, Shakespeare, *The Imitation of Christ*, the Book of Common Prayer and the Meditations of Marcus Aurelius, an old favourite of imperialists. On page 285 of his lengthy memoirs, Wolseley rashly suggests that his wide military experience may have made him bumptious. *'Clearly'*, comments an astringent contemporary scrawl in the margin of my copy.

forest territory to Lake Winnipeg and Red River. Many people thought it could never be done. Wolseley very competently did it.

His force might have been specifically recruited for the punishment of Catholics and French-Canadians. His intelligence officer, William Butler, was an Anglo-Irish Protestant. The kernel of his force was a battalion of the King's Royal Rifle Corps, stationed then at Halifax in Nova Scotia, and everyone's idea of professional redcoats. Most of his other soldiers were Ontario militia-men, many of them avid Canadian expansionists, many more Orangemen, and nearly all congenitally anti-French and pro-Empire:

> *Let them blow till they are blue and I'll throw up my hat*
> *And give my life for England's flag—*
> *You can bet your boots on that!*
> *The flag that's waved a thousand years,*
> *You can bet your boots on that!*

'Most of us felt,' wrote Wolseley, 'we had to settle accounts quickly with Riel, who had murdered the Englishman, Mr Scott.' Invigorated by this sense of cause and of imperial brotherhood, the expedition was rapidly fitted out and organized, and set out by rail and steamer to Thunder Bay, on the western shore of Lake Superior.

From there it was some 660 miles to Fort Garry and Riel. A rough road had been hacked out for the first forty-five miles, to the remote and lovely Shebandowan Lake, deep in the forests: from there Wolseley planned to take his force by water, through the hidden mesh of rivers, across the water-maze called Lake of the Woods, into Lake Winnipeg and thence down Red River to the fort. In all military history, he loved to say, no such operation had ever been contemplated before. It would entail not only skilful boatmanship and navigation, but also an infinity of laborious portages. Wolseley had no proper maps, and most of his soldiers had never set foot in a canoe before.

Everything was geared to boatloads, for no supplies at all could be obtained between Thunder Bay and Red River. The boats themselves were specially designed, each to carry eight or nine soldiers and two or three *voyageurs*, together with supplies for sixty days—salt pork, beans, flour, biscuit, salt, tea, sugar and 'preserved potatoes'. Each boat also carried tents, ammunition, cooking gear, blankets, and American axes—the standard Army issue being, so Wolseley said, 'so ancient in type that it might have come down to us from Saxon times'. They took nets to catch fish, six-pounders to blast fortifications, tools to mend boats, and Captain Redvers Buller, another rising young regular officer, to be quartermaster general. What would happen to them all if the Metis chose to mount a guerilla war against them, or incited the forest Indians to oppose the expedition, even the confident Wolseley could not foresee, but at least he had the logistics well in hand, and in May 1870, off the expedition set into the wilderness—the Empire on the march once more.

Wolseley was to talk about it for the rest of his life, so powerful an impact did it make upon his imagination. The professional friendships he made during the Red River expedition were to form the basis of his celebrated Wolseley Ring, the most influential cabal of the late Victorian army, which we shall repeatedly encounter later in our story. The techniques he learnt he was to use again, as we shall presently see, in a more famous venture far away. He remembered always the romance and strangeness of the campaign. 'For Fort Garry!' shouted the soldiers as they pushed off from the shore of Lake Shebandowan, and out they paddled across the still blue water, boat after boat crammed to the gunwales, their oars dipping, their big lug-sails bravely spread, their rifles stacked in the stern and their colourful *voyageurs* crouched forward. 'It brought to my mind the stories read in boyhood of how wild bands of fierce Norse freebooters set out from some secluded bay in quest of plunder and adventure.'

The journey took ninety-six days, some of it in torrential rain, most of it tormented by blackflies and mosquitoes. Sometimes the boats were all together, sometimes 150 miles separated the first from the last. Sometimes the force scudded across calm water, smoking pipes and singing—

> *Come boys, cheer us! We'll have a song in spite of our position*
> *To help us in our labours on this glorious Expedition!*
> *Jolly boys, jolly boys,*
> *Hurrah for the boats and the roads, jolly boys!*

Sometimes they spent entire days heaving their boats over miles of portage. They wound their way through the dark complexities of the Lake of the Woods. They leapt breakneck through the rapids of the Winnipeg River, the soldiers huddled beneath the gunwales or desperately rowing, until as they scudded to safety on the other side the bowsman threw his paddle into the air in exhilarated triumph, and the soldiers burst into hilarious laughter of relief. They grew fitter, and more skilful, and happier as the weeks passed, rising at dawn and travelling until dusk, and by the end of the adventure the clumsiest rifleman from Winchester or the East End, the flabbiest Toronto real estate agent, was adroitly mending his boat, cooking fresh-caught fish over a campfire, bargaining with Indians for souvenirs, or ranging the forest in search of wild berries. Their uniforms were cheerfully ragged, or patched with biscuit sacking, their faces and arms were burnt nearly black with sun. Not a man fell sick, and always in the van, in a light birch-bark canoe with a crew of sinewy Iroquois, travelled Colonel Garnet Wolseley himself, dapper and undaunted, intermittently moved to sketch book or purple passage by the beauty of the scenery, but dreaming more often, one suspects, of promotions and honours lists to come.

8

On August 21, 1870, the expedition camped for the night upon Elk Island in Lake Winnipeg, twenty-five miles from the mouth of Red River. It was a balmy evening. Camp-fires flickered in the sky, bugles echoed across the water, scaring the duck from the sedgy reeds. Lake Winnipeg was like an inland sea there, with real waves and seagulls, and Elk Island lay close to its eastern shore, thick with spruce and larch. With its white sandy bluffs and its gentle beaches it looked not unlike a Caribbean islet. The air was fragrant with conifer sap and birchwood, the lake water swished in the darkness, and sometimes a strong fresh wind blew off the prairie to the west, to whip up mares' tails on the water.

In this beguiling spot, spoiled only by the unspeakable insects, Wolseley and his officers planned their advance upon Fort Garry. They called it an 'assault', for by now Wolseley was more than ever persuaded that this was war. Riel, he had learnt, had assembled 600 fighting men at the fort—news which 'cheered our men's hearts', for it seemed to mean that he was going to put up a fight. When the expedition set off in the morning, it paddled in battle order into the Red River, six-pounders cleared for action. Up the soldiers resolutely rowed, against the sluggish current of the Red, and as they approached the first farms and churches of the Protestant settlers, church bells rang out to welcome them, and crowds of people ran waving to the river's edge to watch them pass—flags flying, guns ready, Colonel Wolseley proud and eager in the lead. Drama was promised them upstream. It was said that Riel might suddenly ambush their flotilla out of the woods, or that he would blow up the fort with himself inside it, or destroy it with time fuses when the British were already there.

But when they turned the last river-bed, and disembarked below the fort on the morning of August 23, the anti-climax was pathetic. By now it was pelting with rain. The sky was grey, the ground deep in mud, and all the fun went out of the action. Wet through, not quite steady on their legs, the soldiers laboured up the soggy bank pulling their little brass guns behind commandeered Red River carts, whose wheels howled to their curses as they stumbled through the rain. Everything around them looked run-down and deserted, and when they topped the bank and saw the fort in front of them, clustered about by the shuttered dripping village, there was no sign of life. The south gate was open. Two mounted men entered it at full gallop, but nobody fired at them. Riel and all his men, realizing in their innocence what kind of expedition this was, had prudently disappeared. The Union Jack was hoisted above the fort, and a Royal Salute was fired from the guns, in lieu of more exciting fusillades.

9

'Personally I was glad,' wrote Wolseley, 'that Riel did not come out and surrender, as he at one time said he would, for I could not then have hanged him as I might have done had I taken him prisoner while in arms against his sovereign.' But then Wolseley, without the advantages of hindsight or historical perspective, never grasped the true implications of the Red River affair. To such an imperial soldier it was rebellion pure and simple. To contemporary Canadians it was never so straight-forward, if only because it had become infected with the racial and religious rivalries of the nation as a whole. To us it seems sadder still. It was a timeless tragedy, the intuitive protest of a people whose manner of life was doomed by the no less instinctive progress of an empire: a gesture from that older, simpler world, impelled by airier aspirations, and worshipping more fragile gods, which it was so often the destiny of the British Empire to destroy.[1]

Wolseley's expedition effectively ended the Metis resistance. The troops soon returned east, and Wolseley went home to prepare for the later discipline of the Ashanti, the Zulus, and the Sudanese. The village around Fort Garry presently grew into the city of Winnipeg, the principal base from which the Canadians made the west ordinary. It was there that Indian Treaty No 1 was signed, the first of a sequence of agreements which, while sparing Canada the miseries of Indian wars, effectively dampened the fire of Chippewa and Cree, and settled those wastelands for the grain farmers to come.[2] From Winnipeg, too, the first contingent of the North-West Mounted Police rode out in 1873 to police and pacify the more distant west, away to the Rockies and the Pacific coast, arresting the smugglers, keeping the bad men out, checking the flow of guns, demolishing the strongholds of the whiskey smugglers—Forts Whoop-up, Stand-off, Slide-out—and clearing the way for that great artery of imperial authority, the Canadian Pacific Railway. Across the American frontier all was still lawless vigour and excitement: north of the border the British imperial presence made the development of the Canadian west almost decorous.

[1] For parallel cross-purposes, misunderstandings, streaks of pathos and stubborn innocence, I recommend the study of the Welsh nationalist movement in the 1970s.

[2] Besides guaranteeing the signatory chiefs and their descendants a new suit of clothes every three years for ever: in 1969 Chief David Courchene of the Ojibways got a blue serge suit made by prisoners at Kingston gaol in Ontario, with red stripes down each trouser leg, brass buttons, gold braid and a black bowler hat.

Riel had one last try, in 1885. He had escaped over the frontier before Wolseley's approach, had spent some time in a lunatic asylum, and was a much stranger and less stable man than he had been in 1870. Called back to their forlorn leadership by the Metis of Saskatchewan, he allied himself with dissident Indians of the prairies, under Poundmaker and Big Bear, and fought a pitched battle with the Canadian forces—sent there, in sad symbolism, in wagons of the C.P.R. He lost of course, and this time the Empire-builders did not spare him. They put him on trial at Regina, formerly known as Pile o'Bones, and hanged him in the winter of 1885. He was buried in Winnipeg in the churchyard of St Boniface, his coffin being covered with three feet of masonry to deter body-snatchers, and 'no murderer', commented Wolseley, voicing the imperial conviction, 'ever better deserved his fate'.[1]

[1] Frome time to time it is rumoured that Riel's corpse has been removed by vandals—'from over the river', as the St Boniface caretaker told me in 1969, for Winnipeg is still recognizably segregated, most of the French-speakers living on the east bank of the Red, most of the English-speakers on the west. Of the original Fort Garry there remains only a reconstructed gateway beside the railway tracks, but every incident of the Red River rebellion is familiar still to the French Canadian community of Manitoba. Riel, whose execution made him a martyr and eventually destroyed the Canadian Conservative Party, remains one of the few truly striking figures of Canadian history, and arouses passionate controversy to this day.

CHAPTER EIGHTEEN

In the Pacific

STILL the British as a nation were not conscious expansionists. Power for power's sake had not yet seized the public imagination. Painting the world red was not a popular purpose. British industry, commerce and finance remained supreme, and did not seem to need new imperial markets—Free Trade still worked well enough in the British interest, and British investors found plenty of scope in the developing economies of Europe and the United States. Considerations of prudence, of expense and of morality restrained the nation, and made its empire-building still a fitful, unpremeditated and often reluctant process.

In particular we sense this restraint in the Pacific Ocean, where the British were always conscious of another grand dynamic on their flanks or over their shoulders: the growing power, still half-flexed and half-realized, of that incorrigible ex-colony, the United States.

2

To many Englishmen the United States was still hardly a foreign country at all. When the young politician Charles Dilke travelled through the republic in 1866, he thought of it essentially as a projection of England, and all its phenomena, from Manhattan to the Mormons, seemed to him only new extensions of the English genius.[1] The *Illustrated London News*, in its Christmas issue for 1849, said that though the British race would undoubtedly continue to rule the world, it would presently be from the other side of the Atlantic—

[1] As he made clear in his best-seller *Greater Britain*, one of the source-books of late Victorian imperialism, and still excellent reading.

'the genius of our people can exert itself as well on the banks of the Ohio, or the Mississippi, as on the banks of the Thames, and rule the world from the White House at Washington with as much propriety as from the Palace of St James'. Romantics often foresaw a reconciliation between the two peoples, even a reunion, to form an Anglo-Saxon super-power of limitless potential, and if travellers like Dickens or Trollope did not much take to the Americans in practice, British spokesmen generally lauded the American ideal in principle. 'Our American cousins' were frequently buttered up at banquets, or fed with snobbism and Scotch whiskey in Royal Navy wardrooms.

Yet the Great Republic was the chief foreign threat to the well-being of the British Empire—more immediate by far than the Russian bogey which so haunted addicts of the Eastern Question, let alone the impotent rebellions of sepoys and Riels. The Empire remained the hereditary enemy of the United States, and throughout the century good little Americans had been taught, in history book or fireside tale, embroidery sampler or handwriting text, never to forget their revolutionary origins:

> *We love our rude and rocky shore*
> *And here we stand.*
> *Let foreign navies hasten o'er*
> *And on our heads their furies pour*
> *And peal their cannons' loudest roar*
> *And storm our land.*
> *They still shall find our lives are given*
> *To die for home, and leant on Heaven*
> *Our hand.*

Time and again since Victoria's accession the two Powers had quarrelled. They had quarrelled over the sovereignty of Oregon, over British naval supremacy during the American Civil War, repeatedly over Newfoundland fishing rights, incessantly over Canadian frontier issues—Canada sometimes seemed to be nothing *but* frontier, as the Duke of Wellington had expostulated long before. Twice Irish dissidents had invaded Canada from American territory, and often the U.S. cavalry crossed the Canadian line in pursuit of warlike Indians, who knew they were safe on the northern side of the frontier, and called it 'the medicine line'. At the inaugural dinner of the Royal Colonial Society, in London in 1869, the American Ambassador made a distinctly improper joke about Canada's future within the United States, and in Washington the Secretary of State himself, W. H. Seward, declared that 'Nature designs this whole continent, not merely these thirty-six states, shall be, sooner or later, within the magic circle of the American Union'.

The magnetic pull of the United States, too, perpetually disturbed the imperial rotations. Most British emigrants to Canada presently moved on to the States, and even British capital tended to prefer American to colonial investment—the risks might be greater, but so were the profits. Before the abolition of American slavery, the dispossessed slave owners of the Empire looked to the southern States as last exemplars of a crippled civilization, and the American Civil War had drastic effects upon the Empire. Cotton was first planted in Fiji because of it, refugees emigrated to several imperial possessions, and more than once Great Britain came precariously near involvement herself. Lord Palmerston hoped the Confederates would win, so that the united republic would no longer be a threat to the Empire: Gladstone was glad they lost, because he thought a defeated North might grab Canada instead.

Several colonies seemed half-American anyway. The Bahamas, for instance, which lay less than 100 miles from Florida, were very close in spirit to the southern States—easy-going, stylish, corrupt. Any Southern planter would feel at home there still, and the colony's Assembly buildings were actually modelled upon the public buildings at New Bern, in North Carolina—small shuttered buildings of coral limestone, grouped around lawns and palm trees on Bay Street in the centre of Nassau. Down by the shore the Nassau merchants in their wide straws, smoking Havanas and tilting their kitchen chairs outside their office doorways, talked island politics with the authentic rasp of Charleston or Newport News, and the most exciting thing that ever happened to the colony was the Civil War, when the blockade-runners slipped dashingly in and out of harbour, when Lancashire cotton men outbid each other for the Carolina cotton crop, and in the Royal Victoria Hotel, whose buffet was open night and day, Union and Confederate officers eyed each other warily across the lobby, or engaged in enjoyable skull-duggeries of espionage and peculation.

Bermuda, too, which had once been a dependency of Virginia, was strongly American still. Many of its colonists had supported the American Revolution, and their loyalties had been shaken again during the War of 1812. The colony's colour-washed houses had wrought iron lattice-work, like New Orleans, and white jalousies like Charleston, and scattered around the island all the paraphernalia of Puritanism reminded one constantly of the Old Thirteen—the stocks, the pillory, the ducking-stool enclosure at Hamilton.[1] New York was the principal market for Bermuda's spring vegetables, and Americans provided most of the island's tourist trade, the British-ness of the place being a principal attraction—travel brochures assured intending visitors that 'British officers, in all finery, fre-quently attended Social Functions from their Barracks'.

But it was in the Pacific that American power pressed most in-sistently upon the British Empire. The American West had been won by the later 1860s, the Pacific shore from Oregon to southern California was ruled and settled by the Americans: but stolidly north of the Columbia river, and hazily out at sea, the British pre-sence stood, and the two expanding Powers, each with its own style, ethos and method, constantly bumped and circumvented each other in Pacific climes. Let us recreate two episodes, as representative of many more: the reluctant British acquisition of Fiji, the perilous farce of a long-forgotten Anglo-American imbroglio, the Pig War of San Juan.

3

The Pacific was, in imperialist terms, almost virgin territory. It was littered with a thousand islands, many of them rich in copra, bread-fruit or potential labour, many more admirably suited for imperial purposes like sugar plantations, naval bases or penal settlements, and nearly all governed only by picturesque local chiefs of distasteful

---

[1] Dignified in 1970 with a notice hardly less in the American manner:
I am a Park with Feelings
Please do not litter me with Trash and Peelings.

custom. The British had been sailing these waters for a century and more, and the further shores of the Pacific, Hong Kong to New Zealand, had long been familiar with British power. The ocean as a whole, however, seemed destined to become an American preserve. As Dilke wrote in 1868, 'the power of America is now predominant in the Pacific: the Sandwich Islands are all but annexed, Japan is all but ruled by her, while the occupation of British Columbia is but a matter of time, and a Mormon descent upon the Marquesas is already planned'.

To the British the island groups had seemed irrelevant, for they were utterly detached from the great imperial trade routes, and seemed to offer neither threat nor promise to the imperial aspirations. Successive British Governments had declined to assume new responsibilities there, though urged to do so by Australians and New Zealanders, and repeatedly supplicated by island kings and queens. In many parts British missionaries had converted the islanders to Christianity and western civilization, more or less; in many others British traders had been active and influential for generations; but to provide administrations for these remote and infinitesimal communities, to be saddled with the cost of garrisons or the bore of moral responsibility, to take on yet another rivalry with the Americans, was the last thing British Governments had desired. It was not until the late 1860s that a kind of despairing conscience compelled the British Empire towards its first possessions in the American ocean.

The most important island group of Melanesia, and one of the most beautiful, was the archipelago called collectively Fiji. There were at least 300 Fijian islands, about 100 of them inhabited—islands majestic and islands insubstantial, islands deep in forest or bare of all foliage, mountainous islands, flat islands, shimmering half-submerged coral reef islands, islands palm-fringed, surf-washed or soggy with mangrove swamp. A full-blooded sensual beauty was splashed across these scenes, in the evening especially, when the island outlines blurred and melted, when the sea looked an unguent blue and the sun sank in a diffusion of pinks and crimsons; but the rainfall was heavy, too, and Fiji was often steamy and puddly, water dripping from its thatched roofs, gleaming tropical insects crawling through its grasses, and a mouldy fibrous smell emanating, when the sun came out again, from the drying undergrowth of its woods.

Until recently the Fijians had been polygamous cannibals, and fearfully bloodthirsty. They had no central authority, and recognized no sovereign higher than their own tribal leaders. They fought each other constantly, tribe against tribe, island against island, and they sailed about the archipelago in terrible war canoes, and brandished huge clubs, and danced terrifying war dances, and cooked each other with a more than symbolic pleasure—one mid-century chief claimed to have eaten 999 human beings. Their pagan faith was inextricably enmeshed with sorcery, and expressed itself frightfully: unwanted old people might be buried alive, human sacrifice was common, shipwrecked sailors were assumed to have been discarded by the gods, and were accordingly eaten as a matter of course.

Other Pacific islanders stood understandably in awe of this alarming people, and among Europeans too their reputation was horrific —'Feejee, or The Cannibal Islands' is how early navigators habitually described the group. Even so, by the middle of the century a fair number of Europeans had drifted to Fiji. There were peripatetic traders of many nationalities, liberated convicts from Australia, adventurers like the Swede Charles Savage, mercenary commander to the Chief of Mbau, who introduced the Fijians to firearms, or the Irishman Paddy Connell, who was a favourite of the Chief of Rewa, and claimed to have a hundred wives. The first Christian missionaries had arrived in the 1830s ('Ah well,' said one eminent cannibal laconically when they told him about hell-fire, 'it's a fine thing to have a fire when the weather's chilly.') It was they who first put the Fijian language into writing,[1] and in a remarkably short time they had converted almost the entire population to the Christian faith, some of them suffering in the task the most absolute form of martyrdom.[2]

[1] Not altogether successfully, some may think, for their orthography is less than self-explanatory. B is pronounced MB in this gnomic system, Q is pronounced NGG, C is pronounced TH. Nadi, the international airport of Fiji, is pronounced 'Nandi', and Fijian studies are not made easier by the discovery that, for example, Cakobau and Thakombau are one and the same king, or that Beqa and Mbengga are the same island all the time.

[2] My favourite museum caption is to be seen in the Fiji Museum at

All this made for a rag-bag, cosmopolitan society of aliens: a rakish, under-the-counter, no-questions-asked society, a haven for the beachcomber with the forgotten past, the remittance man, the easy-profit trader, the 'blackbirder' supplying plantation labour by methods not very different from slaving—the whole ironically completed by settlements of permanently horrified missionaries, and the by no means incorruptible representatives of the Powers.

Unredeemed squalor characterized the developing conflict between this gallimaufry of foreigners and the confused indigenes. Every kind of venality flourished. Consuls spent half the time making their own fortunes in land speculation, and the other half summoning warships for retributive visits. We read of the American consul drawing up his own land title deeds and officially registering them with himself, of Australians acquiring 200,000 acres of land for £10,000, of kidnapped natives shipped in from the New Hebrides to work European-owned farms, of claims and counter-claims, swindles and double-crosses—all against the habitual Fijian background of inter-tribal conflict and intrigue. One loses count of the punitive expeditions by which the Powers vainly tried to protect their subjects, or more pertinently their stakes, in these tumultuous islands: events obscure enough even in their time, and now to be dimly recalled only by the sub-headings of old history books—*Americans storm the stronghold of the Waya murderers—French corvette seizes prisoner at Levuka—HMS 'Challenger' burns a hostile village up the Rewa river—HMS 'Dodo' restores order at Mbau.*

But in 1867 there arose a Fijian king who claimed authority over most of the 300 islands. Off the coast of Vita Levu, the largest of the group, there lay a far smaller but much more holy islet, Mbau. This was the ancestral home of Cakobau, who had raised himself by war and conspiracy to be the most powerful of the Fijian chiefs, and who now claimed suzerainty over them all. It was a very queer place. No more than two miles round, and densely foliaged, it rose abruptly to a central hill, and was a kind of shrine or ark of Fijiness. The thatched temples of Fiji paganism still towered above its

---

Suva. 'Wooden vessel,' it says of an indefinable sort of artifact, 'which was said to be used for sending portions of Rev. Baker's flesh to nearby chiefs.'

crowded houses and narrow muddy lanes, the great Fiji war-canoes lay ominously upon its beaches, and in the centre of the island stood the ancient killing stone of Mbau, upon which captive enemies of the tribe had traditionally been slaughtered.[1] In this sinister and congested place, abetted by American adventurers and encouraged by dim visions of monarchies far away, Cakobau was proclaimed king. They made a crown for him, tin with gold paper and imitation jewels, and they designed a flag, and they encouraged him to sign his proclamations Cakobau R, and issue his own currencies in the royal name. One may still see in the stamp catalogues the postage stamps issued by his authority, with a big CR on them and a crown, in carmine rose and deep yellow-green.

Cakobau was a Christian, and knew white men very well, but even he could not cope with the complexities of the European incursion—which had brought with it, besides drunkenness, disease, Methodism and gunpowder, an infinity of legal disputes. Among these jostling foreigners Cakobau never knew where he stood. Now the British Consul steps in with a decree, now an American Note demands immediate payment of compensation for an outrage; one day the European community decides to establish its own Assembly, the next a body called the Planters' Protection Society declares itself ready to resist Cakobau's authority by force. While the Fijians clung to their traditional tribal ways, the Europeans arrogantly ruled themselves, refusing to pay taxes. Cakobau was soon in despair. 'If matters remain as they are,' he presciently said, 'Fiji will become like a piece of drift-wood on the sea, and be picked up by the first passer-by.'

The only solution, he was quick to realize, was annexation, or at least protection, by one of the Powers. The question was, which? The Americans were the obvious choice. Not only were they the

[1] It is now the font of a Methodist church on the same site. Though mostly deserted, Mbau is still a peculiar place to visit. It remains the home of the senior Fijian chieftaincy, and approaching it from the mainland by boat, the silence broken only by the swish of the paddles, the squawks of recondite water-fowl, and perhaps the chop of an axe from the hidden recesses of the island, is an experience partly Venetian but mostly Stygian. Cakobau, who died in 1833, is buried with his wife beneath a stone slab on the island summit.

most active in raising Cakobau to his regal eminence, but they had already succeeded in reconciling the monarchical traditions of Hawaii with their own republican ideals. Besides, for years they had been hounding Cakobau for compensation for the burning of their Consulate building, once threatening him with transportation to America, and once claiming three of his islands as collateral for the debt. Who more suitable, then, as protectors? But when Cakobau offered to cede Fiji to the United States *in toto*, the State Department did not even bother to reply.

So the king turned, after a half-hearted attempt to interest Bismarck, to the British. It was in fact the British Consul in Fiji, William Pritchard, who first drew up a petition for cession to the Crown, but at first he got only dusty answers. The British were still deeply reluctant to embroil themselves, particularly as an alternative to the Americans. They were not yet in their imperialist mood, while the chance of Christian duty no longer seemed compelling enough to lure them into new colonial adventures—'the hope of the conversion of a people to Christianity', austerely noted the Duke of Newcastle, Colonial Secretary in Gladstone's first Liberal Government, 'must not be made a reason for an increase in the British dominions'.

But the pressure grew. The Americans on Fiji petitioned Washington for annexation, the Australians, alarmed by the thought that islands so close to home might come under a foreign flag, hinted that they might seize Fiji for themselves. Still the British hesitated. Mr Gladstone had little fellow-feeling for South Sea settlers, and even when, in 1874, the Liberal Government fell and Disraeli came into power, nobody wanted to take the plunge. Commissioners were cautiously sent to Fiji, to inquire further on the spot; and it was only when they reported that British annexation would cause 'general rejoicing among all classes, Black and White', and when the Governor of New South Wales, Sir Hercules Robinson, cabled that Fiji was in 'a state bordering on anarchy', that the British at last agreed to incorporate Fiji within their Empire.

Robinson himself sailed up from Sydney to accept the transfer of power, and Cakobau and all his most powerful chiefs assembled for the ceremony at Levuka, on the island of Ovalau. This was a suitable venue, for Levuka had been the centre of everything most unsavoury and bewildering in the long awakening of Fiji. The town was squeezed on the foreshore facing west, with hills running so abruptly down behind that some of its streets were no more than steep flights of steps, dropping disconcertingly out of the bush. All around the harbour were the artifacts of the foreigners who had so drastically changed the life of the Fijians: the taverns and the wooden warehouses, the stores, the sailmakers, while from its eminence up Mission Hill the Methodist church looked warily down, in figurative pince-nez, upon the skull-duggeries below.

Here it was, on October 10, 1874, that Fiji voluntarily entered the imperial bond, and Great Britain embarked upon an Empire in the central Pacific—presently to include the Cook Islands, the Gilbert and Ellice Islands, the Solomon Islands, Tonga, Ocean Island, and a thousand lesser reefs, atolls and archipelagos. Nobody could call this aggressive empire-building, but even so it eventually made of the southern Pacific not an American preserve, as might have been foreseen, but preeminently a ward of the Raj. To the salute of guns from British warships in the harbour Cakobau's flag was lowered that day, and the Union Jack hoisted in its stead. Sir Hercules, whom we shall briefly meet again in very different imperial circumstances, ceremonially saluted it, and Cakobau, dressed in all the flowered and wreathed magnificence of Fiji chieftainship, handed him his royal warclub with a message to Queen Victoria.

'Before finally ceding his country' (said this declaration, at least in a contemporary British translation) 'the King desires to give Her Majesty the only thing he possesses that may interest her. The King gives Her Majesty his old and favourite war-club, the former, and until lately the only, known law of Fiji. . . . With this emblem of the past he sends his love to Her Majesty, saying that he fully confides in her and in her children, who, succeeding her shall become kings of Fiji, to exercise a watchful control over the welfare of his children and people; and who, having survived the barbaric law and age, are now submitting themselves under Her Majesty's rule, to civilization.'[1]

[1] The club was kept at Windsor Castle until 1932, when King George V returned it to be used as the mace of the Fiji Legislative Council, which it

4

On the eastern shore of the Pacific the British and the Americans confronted each other more sternly. There they had resented each other's presence for years. Ever since the discovery of the Columbia River, entering the Pacific magnificently from its great gorge through the Cascade Mountains, the western end of the U.S.-Canadian frontier had been a cause of bitter contention. It was a rich place—rich in furs and fish, in the prospects of minerals, in farmland and forest. It was also one of the most handsome parts of the temperate globe. The white volcanic peaks of the Cascades provided a stupendous background to the scene, extending like tremendous vertebrae from horizon to horizon, so celestial that the Indians worshipped them, so terrific in their isolation that the first overland immigrants estimated Mount Hood (altitude 11,245 feet) to be at least 18,000 feet high. An American had been the first to glimpse the mouth of the Columbia, but a Briton had been the first to sail up it, and to realize that it provided a highway into the grand interior of America.

The Hudson's Bay Company first administered this marvellous country, and the Company's fur traders and factors were its earliest European explorers. The original Vancouver was a company stockade near the Columbia's mouth, from which the formidable and eccentric John McLoughlin ruled almost single-handed what was then called the Oregon Territory. But once the American overlanders arrived, following the Oregon Trail through the Rockies and Cascades, the British hold on the territory was doomed. Sheer weight of numbers forced them out. The first wagon-teams of pioneers were kindly received by Dr McLoughlin;[1] but almost as

---

still is. In the meantime the British introduced Fiji to the benefits of imperial membership with such effect that by 1945 the Indian population of the islands, imported by the British to provide labour for their sugar estates, outnumbered the indigenes.

[1] Who presently, as it turned out, became an American himself, was dubbed the Father of Oregon, and is still honoured by the preservation of his house in Oregon City as a National Monument. Many visitors to it, its cura-

soon as they formed a majority in the country, they began to clamour for American sovereignty. The Oregon Question, the Anglo-American dispute over ownership of the Pacific north-west, was a perennial of American politics for thirty years, and during the most feverish period of American expansion could be guaranteed to set any political audience aflame: for the possession of Oregon, it seemed, like the acquisition of California, was essential 'to the fulfilment of our national destiny to overspread the continent allotted by Providence for the free development of our yearly multiplying millions'.

Even when, in 1846, the question was peacefully settled by the Treaty of Washington, and the Canadian frontier to the Pacific was demarcated along the line of the 49th parallel, differences remained. The whole of what are now Oregon, Washington and Idaho went to the Americans; the whole of Vancouver Island, which overlapped the parallel, went to the British: but nobody was sure who owned the archipelago that lay in the Strait of San Juan de Fuca, north of Puget Sound, and thirteen years after the settlement of the Oregon Question proper, this petty anomaly almost brought the British Empire and the United States to war.

By then the country on both sides of the frontier was well populated, and each community had developed pronounced characteristics of its own. To the south had grown up a raw American frontier society, one of the toughest communities on the Pacific, exuding a lively disrespect for Queens, Empires and Limies, and a frank belief that one day the whole of the North American continent really would be overspread by those yearly multiplying millions. To the north was the very British colony of British Columbia, recently acquired by the Crown from Hudson's Bay Company. Victoria on Vancouver Island was its capital, with a brand-new legislative building built in a faintly Chinese style on the foreshore, and there was a Royal Navy base at Esquimault, all bugle-calls and admirals' barges, and a formidable Scottish Governor named Sir James Douglas: and

---

tor told me in 1971, still remember how kindly 'Big John' McLoughlin welcomed their forebears on the Oregon Trail, but McLoughlin was soon disillusioned by life in the United States, and died beset by lawsuit and chicanery.

though the colony had its own fair share of adventurers, speculators, wandering negroes and opportunist Chinese, still each year more respectable British settlers arrived, to honour their transplanted loyalties with British institutions and native phlegm.

Between the two communities lay the islands of the Strait. They were not in themselves of much value. Mysteriously wooded, sandy-beached, separated by narrow winding channels, they looked lovely from a distance, but did not invite settlement. Sometimes people landed on one island or another, to chop wood, or fish, but nobody lived there permanently, and when the British and the Americans signed the treaty of 1846, the islands were not mentioned. It was simply agreed that the boundary between Vancouver Island and the American mainland should run 'through the middle of the channel' through the Straits. The trouble was that there were two navigable channels. If the signatories meant the Rosario Channel, nearly all the islands would be British: if they meant the Haro Channel, they would nearly all be American. Since at that time the Strait was very inadequately charted, and nobody much cared about the islands anyway, the issue did not arise for years: but in 1852 the legislature of Oregon Territory, U.S.A., in an expansionist moment, established a county government for the islands of the Haro Archipelago—Island County it was called, and it specifically included San Juan Island, one of the biggest of them all.

The British reacted promptly. They had always assumed the islands to be theirs, and to make the assumption clear in December 1853 the Hudson's Bay Company steamer *Beaver*, the best-known vessel on the whole north-west coast, paddled over to San Juan from Victoria and disembarked 1,300 sheep and a shepherd, Charles Griffin, who built himself a shack at the southern tip of the island, called it the Company Farm, and settled down as the only human inhabitant. The Americans protested. The Company retorted. Sir James Douglas bristled. Officials investigated. A few American settlers defiantly trickled over from Oregon Territory. The name of San Juan Island, hitherto unknown to Foreign Office and State Department alike, made its first fitful appearance in the diplomatic documents.

For the next five years the dispute was held in testy suspense, but in 1859 it unpredictably exploded. By then there were nineteen Americans living on San Juan, and sixteen Britons, including the resilient Mr Griffin. It was scarcely a tranquil island now. The wild Indians of northern British Columbia were in a warlike mood, and now that there was somebody to raid on San Juan, they included the island in the itineraries of their war canoes. The claimant Powers themselves, represented by their respective Governors in these remote dependencies, were only too ready to squabble, and public opinion on both sides of the 49th parallel was inflammatory.

The crisis burst in June. An American farmer called Lyman Cutler had settled near the southern end of the island, and had fenced a small potato plot near the Hudson's Bay farm on Cattle Point. He was not on good terms with the Company. Their cattle and pigs wandered freely around the place, and whenever they damaged his fences he complained. Too bad, he was told, the whole place belonged to the Company anyway, and he must look after his own fences. On the contrary, Cutler retorted, it was American territory, he had every right to be there, and he had been officially assured of American protection and support. The next time he saw a Company pig rooting around his potato patch, he stormed out of his cabin and shot it dead. Its protracted obsequies have been known ever since as the Pig War.

The American military commander in the north-west was General William S. Harney, one of the most extraordinary and difficult men in the U.S. Army. He was a famous Indian fighter, and seems to have been perpetually in a rage. Perhaps he was psychotic. Certainly with his jutting beard and his glaring eyes, his predilections for cruelty and revenge, his constant grievances and sudden impulsive accusations, he was a dangerous man to command the American forces on that touchy frontier. As a young colonel he had invaded Mexico without orders, suffering an ignominious defeat and being court-martialled for his impetuosity. As a general he had placed a number of Irish-American deserters under a wagon with nooses around their necks, obliging them to watch the course of an action against the Mexicans until, the battle won, he gave the order for the wagon to move off, and the prisoners were strangled. Since he had been in the north-west he had quarrelled with nearly everyone—with his own officers, with his civilian colleagues, with Hudson's Bay Company, with his superiors. Some said he had ambitions for the Presidency: others that he was off his head.

The death of Cutler's pig was just his style. He sailed to San Juan almost at once, and decided to occupy it by force, the American settlers obligingly easing his way by formally requesting protection against Indian raids. On July 27 a company of U.S. infantrymen landed at Griffin Bay, at the other end of the island from the Company farm. They were commanded by a protégé of Harney's, Captain George Pickett, who immediately issued a proclamation announcing that 'This being United States Territory, no laws, other than those of the United States, nor courts, except such as are held by virtue of said laws, will be recognized or allowed on this island'. Almost at once a British Justice of the Peace arrived on the island too: Major John de Courcy, who was pointedly empowered to arrest 'all persons who by force or by a display of force' seized lands not their property.

By the end of July the British had landed a force of Royal Marines on San Juan, and all because of a pig the island seemed ready for war. The two little armies, one at each end of the island, flew their flags boldly and greased their guns for action, while at weekends boatloads of sightseers from Victoria cruised expectantly off-shore. Far away in London and Washington nobody had yet heard of Mr Cutler's pig, but on the spot the atmosphere was perilous. In Victoria hotheads demanded the instant expulsion of the Americans: in Fort Vancouver Harney was urged to summon all available American naval forces. In August the Americans landed more men and guns on the island, and Admiral Lambert Baynes, Royal Navy, arrived to take over the British naval command at Esquimault in the great three-decker *Ganges,* eighty-four guns. The *British Colonist,* in Victoria, suggested a pre-emptive war at once, while the odds were in British favour; the American Governor of Washington Territory visited San Juan to be greeted with a salute of cannon from the American camp. General Harney announced that the Indian raids along the coast were instigated by Hudson's Bay Company to scare American settlers off, and observed piously that in occupying San Juan he had merely 'assumed a defensive posture against the encroachments of the British . . . upon the rights, the lives and property of our citizens'.

He really seemed to want a war. Perhaps it was only his native belligerence. Perhaps he thought a quick victory over the traditional enemy would bring him political kudos. Some British theorists supposed him to be obeying secret orders from Washington, intending to neutralize the British fleet at Esquimault as the first step in an attack on British Columbia. Others speculated that he thought a foreign war might avert the impending disaster of the War between the States at home, or alternatively (he came from Tennessee) that it might give the South a better chance to secede. But the British would not play. Governor Douglas held his hand, Admiral Baynes would not shoot, and the soldiers bore themselves with a sensible restraint. In any case both the British and American Governments were preoccupied with more desperate events elsewhere—the British with disquieting shifts of power in Europe, the Americans with the prospect of civil war.

It was ten years before the Pig War was settled. Throughout the 1860s San Juan island, some ten miles long, was occupied by the rival toy armies, one at the north end, one at the south. The Americans consolidated their position above Griffin Bay, a windswept healthy place with a magnificent view over the bay to the Olympic Mountains beyond. They built five or six clapboard huts up there, and surrounded the camp with a neat stockade, and erected an immense white flagstaff for Old Glory. The British, though, on the shore of Garrison Bay in the north, built themselves a station more in the imperial manner. On the beach they erected a blockhouse of wood, with rifle-slits commanding the bay, and behind it they cleared a large parade ground, to keep the Royal Marines up to scratch. For the rest, the encampment had a comfortable, almost a domestic look. Two rows of Douglas firs were planted, in honour of the Governor. Little flower gardens were lovingly tended. The steep wooded hill behind was hacked into limestone terraces for tennis courts and croquet lawns. There was a white clapboard barrack for the men, and the officers did themselves very well with seven-roomed houses among the trees. The commander's house had a ballroom and a billiard room, and in old pictures of the establishment everybody

looks very contented in this improbable outpost of imperial arms—
the soldiers spanking and muscular in immaculate uniforms, the
officers lounging about on verandahs in sporting gear, with gun-dogs
at their feet.

The rival forces grew friendlier as the years passed. Nobody
bothered them much, and the officers often visited each other,
competed at race meetings, or enjoyed picnics together on the beach.
It was not until 1871 that the Governments of Great Britain and the
United States finally submitted the San Juan question for arbitration by the newly-proclaimed Emperor of Germany, Wilhelm I.
His Supreme Highness did not in fact give the matter his closest
personal attention, but referred it to three learned sages, Doctors
Grim, Kiepert and Goldschmidt, who studied the Washington
Treaty in its hydrological, geographic, legal and historic aspects,
and advised the Emperor accordingly. On October 21, the Kaiser
gave his decision: 'The claim of the Government of the United
States, *viz.*, that the line of boundary between the dominions of Her
Britannic Majesty and the United States should be run through the
Canal de Haro, is most in accordance with the true interpretation of
the Treaty. . . .'

Within a fortnight the British garrison had embarked, and even
before they left the Americans had cut down the flagpole at Garrison Bay, and chopped it up for souvenirs.[1]

5

This was still mid-Victorian imperialism. The British Empire could
afford to lose, especially to the Americans, for it was not yet a national infatuation. Convinced of its own merit and generally sure of
its rights, the Empire in the 1860s was not habitually aggressive. Its
wars were, by its own lights, chiefly fought in self-defence, and its
acquisitions were often forced upon it. Not only in the Pacific, but

---

[1] Tourists on San Juan, now a popular resort island, are still guided to the
twin encampments of the Pig War, though the blockhouse on Garrison Bay
is the only surviving building. Many soldiers, both British and American,
settled on the island after their service, and several San Juan families still
trace their ancestries to the murder of Mr Cutler's pig.

everywhere in the world the British were still without envy, for they knew themselves beyond challenge.

But a very different mood was presently to animate the Raj— which, while it fortunately never again came so close to war against the Americans, soon became so obsessed with its own glories, and so freely threw its weight about the rest of the world, that within a couple of decades it had scarcely a friend to call its own, only enemies, rivals or subjects.

PART THREE

The Imperial Obsession
1870–1897

CHAPTER NINETEEN

A Fixed Purpose

IN 1870 an English visionary of the merchant class elevated the imperial idea to the level of faith or art. The sage John Ruskin, art historian, painter, social reformer, the physically impotent master of a gloriously potent prose, had just been appointed Slade Professor of Fine Art at Oxford. There clung to his person, as to his reputation, the charisma of a prophet. He was a born conservative in the stateliest sense. He revered the past for its own sake, thought Gothic architecture the highest expression of human genius, had a taste for the grand, the spacious, the noble, the dedicated, and admired men of imperious decision: Bishop Colenso ('loyal and patiently adamantine'), Herbert Edwardes of the Punjab ('invincible soldiership and loving equity'), Governor Eyre ('honourable performance of duty is more truly just than rigid enforcement of right').

All his views he expressed with a magical conviction, and this was fortunate, for not infrequently he changed them. He was one of the most compelling and popular speakers in Britain, at working men's clubs as at Eton or Oxford, his matter ranging splendidly free—he apologized once when his lecture, announced as being about Crystallography, turned out to be on Cistercian architecture. His style was incomparably majestic, and audiences of every kind hung upon his phrases. He spoke, we are told, 'in a mediaeval way', his pronunciation archaic, his Rs peculiarly rolled, and his words remained in the memory like music. Ruskin talked much nonsense in his time, but when he struck one of his grand themes the effect was unforgettable.

One such theme was Imperial Duty, and this was the subject of his inaugural lecture at Oxford. So many undergraduates had packed the University Museum to hear it that the lecture was adjourned while they all moved along the road to the larger Sheldonian

Theatre. Even there they overflowed the seats, sitting on the floor
and hanging about the doors: and from the high dais of Wren's
little masterpiece, beneath the painted putti on the ceiling, rolling
back their painted tentage to reveal the pale blue sky behind, Ruskin
delivered his call for the ideology of Empire:

*There is a destiny now possible to us, the highest ever set before a nation to be
accepted or refused . . . Will you youths of England make your country
again a royal throne of kings, a sceptred isle, for all the world a source of
light, a centre of peace; mistress of learning and of the Arts, faithful
guardian of time-honoured principles? This is what England must either do or
perish; she must found colonies as fast and as far as she is able, formed of her
most energetic and worthiest men; seizing every piece of fruitful waste
ground she can set her foot on, and there teaching these her colonists that their
chief virtue is to be fidelity to their country, and their first aim is to be to
advance the power of England by land and sea . . . If we can get men, for
little pay, to cast themselves against cannon-mouths for love of England, we
may find men also who will plough and sow for her, who will behave kindly
and righteously for her, and who will bring up their children to love her . . .
You think that an impossible ideal. Be it so; refuse to accept it, if you will;
but see that you form your own in its stead. All that I ask of you is to have a
fixed purpose of some kind for your country and for yourselves, no matter how
restricted, so that it be fixed and unselfish.*

Such a view of the imperial summons placed the Empire in the
very centre of national affairs—a task, Ruskin seemed then to be
saying (for he soon lost interest in the subject), around which the
whole of British life should revolve. Few who heard him that day
could have been unmoved by the appeal, and some we know were
influenced by it for the rest of their lives; for the first time the imperial idea now seemed to satisfy some craving in the British consciousness. Times had greatly changed during the thirty years since
Victoria's accession, when the possession of the Empire had seemed
an irrelevance, or an eighteenth-century anachronism. In those days
the announcement of a debate on imperial matters would almost
certainly empty the House of Commons. The imperial topics were
seldom political issues, the great public was not interested, and during the first half of the century no sensible politician would have

cared to stake his future upon the issue of overseas expansion. Though in fact the Empire had steadily grown throughout the Queen's reign, it seemed to have happened without design or satisfaction—'in a fit of absence of mind', as was said of the process in a famous phrase. Even as late as 1861 a Select Committee of the House of Commons was recommending a complete withdrawal from West Africa, and though many Britons felt a sense of imperial duty, few were yet moved by an imperial enthusiasm.

Between 1837 and 1869, six men had been Prime Ministers of England. Three had been Conservative, three Whig or Liberal, but none could really be described as men of Empire. Melbourne had been a gentlemanly relict of the previous century, Peel a social reformer from the new industrial classes, Derby, Russell and Aberdeen old-school patricians. It occurred to none of them that the destiny of the British might lie primarily not in the British Isles at all, but in distant possessions overseas. Even the fire-eater Palmerston, ready though he was to slap a gunboat up any creek in defence of British interests, did not wish his country to possess the world, believing rather in the power of trade and moral prestige: unable to find a Colonial Secretary, it was said, for one of his ministries, with a sigh he took on the job himself—'Come upstairs with me, H., when the council is over, we will look at the maps and you shall show me where these places are'. At no time in the first half of Victoria's reign was Empire a central preoccupation of British statesmanship. Imperial episodes sometimes captured the centre of the stage—the Afghan tragedy, the Durham Report, the Mutiny— but no politician had tried to give the Empire an ideological meaning, or to convince the small and privileged electorate that theirs must be an imperial future. On the whole the Tory Party was the party of Empire, as the trustees of tradition and pride, while the Liberals were the champions of free trade and liberty: but neither could be described as a party of imperialism—a word which indeed carried for the English distasteful undertones of foreignness.

In the 1870s, however, there were signs that the British conviction of merit was growing into a conviction of command. Ruskin's vision was partly an inspiration, but partly a symptom: and during the next decade two astonishing statesmen forced the issue of imperialism into the forefront of British affairs, capping the Victorian age with its passions. Benjamin Disraeli became the maestro of Empire: William Ewart Gladstone, its confessor.

2

They might have been cast by some divine theatrical agency for their parts in the drama, so exactly suited were they to their roles not merely in manners and morals, but actually in appearance. They represented two complementary impulses in the British political genius: the idealistic impulse, which wished to make Britain the paragon of principle, the urge for glory, which fed upon the exotic, the flamboyant, even the slightly shady. In Victorian politics both these elements thrived, as they thrived too in everyday life, and it was their confrontation at the apex of the century that dictated the final character of Victoria's Empire, setting its style and dictating its reputation for posterity.

Disraeli adopted the imperial cause deliberately. He recognized it for what it was, a sure vote-catcher, especially since the Reform Bill of 1867 had added a million urban labourers to the franchise (as early as 1849 he had suggested giving seats at Westminster to thirty MPs from the colonies, as a means of strengthening the Tory party). It was in June 1872, in a famous speech at the Crystal Palace, that he first presented to the British public his own romantic prospectus of Empire, coupling it with the English Constitution as the foundation of Tory policy. The English, he said, had a choice before them. They could choose to be subjects of 'a comfortable England', insular and ordinary, or of 'a great country, an imperial country, a country where your sons, when they rise, rise to paramount positions, and obtain not merely the esteem of their countrymen, but command the respect of the world'.

Later this conception intermittently coloured all his politics, and guided his statesmanship too. Half-measures of glory were unworthy of such a nation at such a time. 'Money is not to be considered in such matters,' he told the House of Commons when accused of extravagant imperial expenditures, 'success alone is to be thought of.' At home, he accused the Liberal Party of wanting to jettison all the splendours of Empire, and described the English working classes as being 'proud of belonging to an Imperial country'. Abroad he attended the Congress of Berlin in 1878, which settled the fate of south-eastern Europe for the next thirty years (and incidentally gave Britain possession of Cyprus), as the representative not just of a nation, but of an Empire—'an Empire of liberty, truth and of justice'. He believed in the show of things, in prestige, in self-advertisement. Nations like people, he believed, were accepted at their own valuation. When he created Victoria Queen-Empress, or ordered the posting of Indian troops to Malta, or manipulated the Eastern Question to his purposes, he was making fact out of fantasy, and exploiting the world's imagination. To the end of his days he represented, more colourfully than any other great statesman of British history, that latent English taste for the spiced and the half-foreign which was a driving motive of imperialism—after the Mutiny he was widely tipped as the first Viceroy of India, a dazzling prospect unhappily never fulfilled.

Tremendously on the other side stood Gladstone, who distrusted the imperial ethic with fastidious profundity, and made equal political capital out of his opposition to it. Gladstone was at once more explicit in his philosophies, and more diffuse. His every political instinct was for Little England, and for him the true national glory lay in moral superiority—supported of course by commercial good sense, for he was after all the son of a Liverpool West Indian merchant.[1] The central strength of England, he wrote in 1878, lay in England. Those who believed in imperial expansion were the materialists of politics. 'Their faith is in acres, in leagues, in sounding titles and long lists of territories. They forget that the entire fabric of the British Empire was reared and consolidated by the energies of a people which was . . . insignificant in numbers . . . and that if by some vast convulsion our transmarine possessions could all be submerged, the very same energies of that same people would . . . without them in other modes assert its undiminished greatness.'

Gladstone's most celebrated political *tour-de-force* was his

[1] Whose 2,183 West Indian slaves brought him, upon the abolition of slavery, £85,600 in compensation—perhaps £800,000 today.

Midlothian campaign, the whirlwind speaking tour by which, in 1879, he snatched an electoral victory from the Conservatives, and brought the Liberals back to power. This was not only a democratic innovation—the first time a British statesman of his rank had so freely solicited the support of the electorate: it was also a passionate attack upon the idea of Empire. In every corner of the globe, Gladstone cried, British imperialism had come as a pestilence. The Queen's imperial title was theatrical bombast. The current war against the Afghans was a crime against God. In South Africa 10,000 Zulus had been slaughtered 'for no other offence than their attempt to defend against your artillery with their naked bodies, their hearths and homes, their wives and families'. These were false phantoms of glory—mischievous and ruinous misdeeds—a policy in its result disloyal, in its essence thoroughly subversive—a road which plunged into suffering, discredit and dishonour. National pride should not blind a nation to higher dictates of justice. 'Remember the rights of the savage! . . . Remember that the happiness of his humble home, remember that the sanctity of life in the hill villages of Afghanistan, among the winter snows, is as inviolable in the eye of Almighty God as can be your own!'

One could see by the look of them which of these two remarkable rivals stood for Empire. Disraeli the literary Jew, with his black curls, his brilliant eye, his flashy dress, his catchy way with words and notions, his fun, his conceit, his air of worldly scandal—Disraeli the author of *Sybil* and *Tancred* seemed nurtured for sultry enterprise. Temperamentally he was an oriental himself, and he loved pomp and glitter, whether real or spurious. Many of the imperial activists were not altogether British, or stood in some way aside from the British mainstream, and Disraeli was from start to finish a gaudy outsider. The son of a littérateur, he went neither to public school nor to university, and married a widow thirty years his senior, excessively plain but agreeably rich, whom he adored for the rest of his life. He charmed the susceptible Queen, antagonized the conventional gentry, thrust himself into the senior ranks of the Conservative Party by guile and showmanship. His great political successes were managed as *coups de théâtre*, and his debating technique was wonderfully dramatic. He had no evangelical impulse whatsoever, being utterly without religious instinct, and the older he got, the less he cared for orthodoxy of appearance or behaviour. Even the way he talked was intriguing—standard English but with an indefinably foreign gloss.

As he governed, so he lived—with bravura. He revelled in the company of women, captivating them in return with his high spirits and curious fancies—'I am the blank page,' he once declared, 'between the Old Testament and the New.' His house at Beaconsfield, which he dearly loved, was not large, nor even impressive, but was full of delight: a Gothick house, tucked away in a fold in the Chilterns, with a couple of ponds where Disraeli ineptly fished, a dingle running down to the valley in which he loved to plant trees, a pleasant arcaded verandah for writing witty novels on, and a hall full of mementos. The house had an eastern tinge, like a muted cousin of Sezincote, and perhaps it was the Jewishness in Disraeli, the old ineradicable strain of awareness, that made him feel England to be too large for her islands, and sent his eyes so often to the east.

Mr Gladstone preferred chopping trees down, as if in holy judgement. Legend does not see him as a creative man, but as a figure of grave arbitration—a better, grander, wiser man than Disraeli, but less brilliant, and much less fun. He seems to us far older than his rival, but he was really five years younger. Though his father was self-made, Gladstone's background was orthodoxy itself—Liverpool and Jamaica money, Eton and Christ Church education, staunch Anglican religion, Scottish origins, and a profound Victorian belief that all politics, all life itself, could be defined in terms of right and wrong. A self-mortifying Christian faith lay behind his every activity, whether it be his concern with the welfare of the Armenians of Turkey or the nocturnal visits to London prostitutes which so damaged his reputation with Queen and public, but which were really so guileless an expression of kindness. Yet he was a man of disturbing contradictions, self-doubts, inconsistencies—a much odder fish than Disraeli really, and something of an enigma still. He was highly sexed, and in private life a passionate traditionalist—'in everything except essentials', as Arthur Balfour was to say, 'a tremendous old Tory'. Gladstone's wife was once heard to sing with him, their arms entwined around each other's waists,

A ragamuffin husband and a rantipoling wife,
We'll fiddle it and scrape it through the ups and downs of life.

Gladstone's children loved him dearly, treating him with cheerful familiarity and talking to him in a private language. Gladstone's monarch detested him, and showed it so clearly in her neglect that it became one of the sadnesses of Gladstone's life—for he did not possess the knack of charm, and spoke his slightly Lancashire English in such learned convolutions, with such labyrinthine qualifications and subordinate clauses, that it was hard for him to express a simple thought, or bring to the surface the innocent benevolence that lay behind his majesty.

For truly majestic he was—a splendid pale face, a thrilling voice, a flaming eye, and all the presence of greatness.[1] We have already seen him in his political youth, colliding with the Bishop of Paxos: let us visit him finally in his old age at home and at peace in his beloved Flintshire home. One best approaches Hawarden (pronounced 'Harden') from the north, through its wide but gloomy park, dingy with industrial particles, and past the ruins of its mediaeval fortress, restored by Mr Gladstone himself upon a grassy mound. Around this bump the drive proceeds, and there in all its faintly comic dignity stands Hawarden Castle—which came into Gladstone's possession by marriage, but became his spiritual home. Its centre portion is Georgian, but the Victorians have worked enthusiastically upon its wings, and now no building in England is more authentically Gladstonian. High and heavy are its towers, mullioned its innumerable windows, fine old oaks and elms surround it, and its rooms appear to be, from our respectful distance beyond the ha-ha, mahogany-panelled, book-lined, damask-curtained and embellished with busts of philosophers.

From the house a wide lawn with rose beds runs away to the surrounding wall and the playing-field of the Hawarden Cricket Club beyond: and there in the distance upon a deck-chair we may see the Grand Old Man himself, 'The People's William', all in black and white—wispily bearded, leaning back with his right hand thrown sideways as if to catch manna from the elms, and his left hand holding

---

[1] 'Terrifying', Lloyd George found it, perhaps with reason.

before his eyes a small but evidently solemn volume—a recent Homeric commentary, perhaps, a new theory of economic progress, or possibly a re-issue of one of his own scholarly works (for long before his death the entries under his name filled twenty-five pages of the British Museum Catalogue).[1]

3

Both these statesmen knew the potential of the imperial excitement, and both were willy-nilly caught up by it, Disraeli dying triumphant at its apogee, Gladstone surviving sadly to see even his own Liberal Party split by its dynamic. Around their persons the debates of empire were to swirl; the one man would always be identified with patriotic dash, the other with liberal humanity, but both were to find themselves in the end the agents of imperialism.

Disraeli did not of course invent Imperialism as a political philosophy. He merely gave it a new emotional force, and translated into demagoguery the intuitions of seers like Ruskin. He crystallized the idea, dressed it up, gave it a new sheen, and eventually made it part of the Tory political credo. As a word and as a philosophy, imperialism gained a new currency. The Liberals threw it back at Disraeli with contempt—a vogue word, they said, and a vogue doctrine. *The Times* called it 'tawdry', the *Spectator* called it 'despotism coupled with vulgar mass-appeal', and *Punch* dismissed it as cheaply specious:

> *Imperialism! Hang the word! It buzzes on my noddle,*
> *Like bumble-bees in clover time. The talk on't's mostly twaddle.*
> *Yet one would like to fix the thing, as farmer nails up vermin;*
> *Lots o' big words collapse, like blobs, if their sense you once*
> *determine.*

But Disraeli had judged right. The diverse sentiments of Empire, whose development we have traced through war, commerce and

[1] Hawarden is still the home of Gladstones, but Hughenden Manor, Disraeli's house, is now the property of the National Trust, and there pilgrims may inspect such beguiling imperial curios as the Silver Seal of Nana Sahib, or the necklace of King Theodore of Abyssinia, presented to Disraeli by Lord Napier after the latter's punitive expedition to Magdala in 1868.

philanthropy, were coalescing now into grandiloquence and chauvinism. 'What does Imperialism mean?' demanded the philosopher Robert Lowe. 'It means the assertion of absolute force over others . . . if by the menace of overbearing force we can coerce a weaker state to bow before our will, or if, better still, we can by a demonstration of actual force attain the same object, or, best of all, if we can conquer our adversary in open fight, and impose our own conditions at the bayonet's point, then, as Dryden sings, "these are imperial arts and worthy thee".' He was speaking ironically, but in fact he was prophetic. By 1877 Gladstone reckoned that Disraeli's aggressive overseas policies were supported by 'the Clubs, the London Press (in majority), the majority of both Houses, and five-sixths or nine-tenths of the Plutocracy'. Before very long the public as a whole would freely express its approval of imperial braggadocio, even bloodshed: *Punch*, *The Times* and the *Spectator* would all be organs of imperialism; the Poet Laureate of England would not be ashamed to confess that his idea of heaven was to sit on a lawn being brought news alternately of British victories by land, and British victories by sea.

Lord Carnarvon, Disraeli's Colonial Secretary, was nicknamed 'Twitters' and at first found it difficult to understand what imperialism meant. Later he sorted it out in his mind, and cogently explained it to others. There were two kinds of imperialism, he said. There was the false kind—Caesarism, despotism—and there was the British kind—a world-wide trust, keeping the peace, elevating the savage, relieving the hungry, and uniting in loyalty all the British peoples overseas. Imperialism certainly entailed expansion, but it was not bullying expansion, it was merely the extension of British institutions and wholesome influences, if necessary by force. This conception proved irresistible. It became the great popular movement of the late nineteenth century, displacing humanitarianism in the universal approval. It seized in its enthusiasm all classes of the British, and eventually all parties too. Queen Victoria loved it; Lord Salisbury, the greatest of the aristocrats, gave it the sanction of the patricians; chambers of commerce voted in its favour; family generations devoted themselves to its service; churchmen raised collections for it; soldiers and sailors revelled in it; children collected biscuit lids stamped with its emblems; the poor looked to its gaudy stimulations and sang its rumbustious rhythms in music-halls; the rich looked to its dividends, and remembered the blessings of Rand or Broken Hill as they sang the national anthem. 'The British People', Disraeli once wrote, 'being subject to fogs and possessing a powerful Middle Class, require grave statesmen': but they also required excitement. Imperialism gave them, in the last twenty-five years of Victoria's reign, the most exciting, the most astonishing, perhaps, for better or for worse, the most satisfying quarter century in all their modern history.

4

On the surface it was just an urge to glory. 'A nation without glory', wrote Garnet Wolseley once, 'is like a man without courage, a woman without virtue. Those who in youth learn to value it as a holy possession are, as life goes on, inspired by its influence. It becomes eventually a sort of national religion. . . .' The long success of the British, proceeding from triumph to triumph since the end of the Napoleonic wars, had gone to their heads, and given them a new taste for supremacy: like many another nation at the summit of its power, Great Britain in the second half of the nineteenth century was an image of conceit, and brazenly equated glory with strength, wealth and size.

But the sense of duty, too, powerfully contributed to the passions of Empire. It was less a missionary duty now: the idea that the world's natives could be converted to Christian Britishness had lost some of its conviction. But it was still, in its austere way, a philanthropic mission. Justice, security, communications, opportunity—these were the advantages of civilization which the British now diligently if aloofly distributed among their subjects. Indian school textbooks, in the second half of the century, included a short chapter entitled *Angrezi Raj Ki Barkaten—Blessings of the English Raj*. It enumerated law and order, schools, canals, roads and bridges, railways, telegraphs and public health, but made no reference to the ending of evil custom, the reform of society, or the benefits of Christian example. The British had no doubts about the merits of their own civilization, or qualms about their mission to distribute it across the world: but they had come to suppose that not all aspects of it were transplantable.

The profit motive, too, had subtly shifted its emphasis. It was still potent, of course, perhaps preeminent among the imperial urges, but now it had undertones of disquiet. Great Britain was still the supreme industrial, financial and commercial Power of the world, but only just. Rivals were catching up. Economically the 1870s were difficult years for the British, and the financiers of the City of London, the industrialists of the north, began to feel that their preeminence might not last for ever. Germany and America would soon be producing more steel than Britain; most European countries had now completed their own industrial revolutions; in a whole range of new products, chemical dyes to breech-loading guns, British designers and manufacturers lagged behind. The penalties of easy success were beginning to show—complacency, conservatism, even laziness—and the old panacea of Free Trade was losing its effect. Only Empire, it seemed to many businessmen, could restore the proper status quo: with new markets, with new sources of raw material, and with convenient barriers, actual if not explicit, against foreign competition.

Strategically the impulses of the new imperialism were also largely defensive. If the London military planners wished to acquire new territory, it was generally to prevent foreigners acquiring it first, or to protect some existing possession, or guard a threatened trade route. The grand assurance of Waterloo and Trafalgar had waned rather with the years. The Britain of the 1870s was no longer beyond challenge. The Americans, in their civil war, had shown themselves capable of immense military exertion, and had for a few years possessed not merely the most experienced, but actually the largest armies in the world. The Germans, newly federated, proved by their victory over France in 1870 that they were the most formidable military nation in Europe, unlikely to leave the British Empire indefinitely sacrosanct. The French, the Italians, the Germans, the Americans were all building battle fleets. The world was far more complex than it had been in 1837, and Britain's place in it was so much the less serene. Once again, imperialism seemed to provide an answer: not only the means of strategic insurance, but good practice for the armed forces too, and the most awesome possible instrument of warning. Across the world the flag flew, and everywhere it seemed to say 'Hands off!'

5

But to keep its momentum the Empire must grow. By now the British had almost filled the available empty spaces of the world. The half-hearted Empire of 1837 had doubled in population, and tripled in area. The empty wilderness of Canada had been tamed, the desolations of Australia had been explored, Burma, New Guinea, New Zealand, Natal, Hong Kong had all been acquired, since Victoria came to the throne. Flushed with the magnitude of their success, eager to find new outlets for their energy, apprehensive, if only subconsciously, about their future, during the last years of Victoria's reign the British turned to the last unexploited continent. The first part of this book was dominated by India: the last will take us time and again to Africa, for it was there, in a new, headier and seamier series of adventures, that the idea of Empire would find its obsessive fulfilment.

CHAPTER TWENTY

Ashanti

IN Africa stood Ashanti-land. There on a Friday near the beginning of the eighteenth century the sage Okomfu Anokye, fetish priest to Osei Tutu the Asantahene, had received from Heaven the Golden Stool: a mysterious gold-encrusted throne, hung as the centuries passed with talismanic emblems—golden handcuffs, human masks, bells, thongs, images—never to be used as a seat or even allowed to touch the ground, but to be cherished for ever as the dwelling-place of the *sunsum* or national spirit. So, according to legend, the Empire of the Ashanti was born, to become by the middle of the Victorian era one of the most remarkable of the myriad black Powers of Africa.

Until Osei Tutu's time the Ashanti had been no more than a tribe. Their original home was the country around Lake Bosomtwe, a sinister tree-infested mere which intermittently belched gas and mud from its recesses, and was thought by some Africans to be the hole out of which the human race first crawled. It was in the seventeenth century that they first entered history. They then began to display a talent for organization, both civic and military, exceptional in West Africa. Gradually they imposed their suzerainty upon their neighbours until the hereditary Asantahene, the king of the Ashanti, became the most powerful indigenous ruler of the entire region, his writ running in one degree or another from the Black Volta to the sea.

The revelation of the Golden Stool had consolidated this power, providing a supernatural focus of loyalty. Where it really came from, nobody knows. It was a wooden tripod partly sheathed in gold, and according to legend it first appeared from the skies during an assembly of chiefs and people at Kumasi, the Ashanti capital, floating down from the sky in a cloud of dust, to the sound of thunder and the flash of lightning. The Ashanti revered it as the embodiment of their nationhood. So long as it was safe, the kingdom would flourish in unity. The Stool took precedence over the Asantahene himself. It reclined upon its own Chair of State, shaded by its own palanquin and attended by its own acolytes. It provided a constant in the amoebic structure of the Ashanti State, and upon its mystique there rested the whole fabric of Ashanti custom. There can have been few other nations whose soul was embodied in a *thing*: but one might perhaps fancy a similar arcane identification among the jumbled urns and effigies, the hushed inscriptions and the allusive references of Westminster Abbey.

2

Not, however, the Victorian empire-builders, to whom such a suggestion would have seemed not merely ludicrous, but probably sacrilegious. Africa in mid-century appealed to their instinct more than their reason, and brought out the best and worst in them. The best was the long and passionate struggle against the slave trade, still an inspiration to idealism. 'I go back to Africa,' Livingstone told an audience of Cambridge undergraduates in 1857, 'to try to make an open path for commerce and Christianity. Do you carry out the work which I have begun! *I leave it with you!*' The worst was a crude contempt which, in the last decades of Victoria's rule, was progressively to taint the spirit of Empire.

In the common British view Africa possessed no worth-while values of its own. Its people, mostly pagan and almost all illiterate, seemed not far removed from beasts in the Darwinian scale. Its customs sounded childish, meaningless or repulsive. Its languages were so useless or obscure that until the end of the eighteenth century no European bothered to learn any of them. Its art, expressed in the ambiguities of Obo legend, or the stylized grotesqueries of Ife art, appeared downright debased. The imperialists were at once horrified and fascinated by the cruelty of Africa, the sensuality, the shamelessness. It was, they thought, a continent congenitally inferior, a slate upon which the Empire might scrawl what it pleased, compassionate text or raw obscenity.

In Africa white faced black, strangers to each other, and in the confrontation between these two elemental forces no conflict was more telling than that between the empires of Britain and Ashanti— a conflict of fits and starts, in which the white power pressed inexorably upon the frontiers of the black, sometimes by guile, sometimes by force, until in the end it burst into the heart of the black kingdom to violate the Golden Stool itself. This was, to both sides, a conflict of destinies. The Ashanti regarded it as divinely ordered, and so did the British: as Hope Grant wrote in 1874, as he prepared to invade the Ashanti homeland, 'I cannot help thinking that it is willed by the all-powerful Ruler above that Africa shall be opened, and that these savage and inhuman tribes will be brought to reason, and their horrible iniquities put an end to. The poor wretched creatures at present know no better. . . .'

3

By African standards the Ashanti civilization was urbane. Its polytheistic observances were intricate and devout. Its social forms were liberal. The Ashanti were excellent craftsmen in gold, silver and wood, and they had developed an architectural style all their own, with projecting eaves, high-pitched thatched roofs, complicated plaster fretwork and curious ornaments of animals and birds. Early British visitors to Kumasi, in the first years of the nineteenth century, found the capital unexpectedly impressive. In 1817 Edward Bowdich reported a reception by bands of flutes, horns and drums, and by vast companies of warriors, resplendently accoutred with horns, feathers, bells, shells and leopard tails. The city he found well-planned and scrupulously clean, with wide named streets and carefully planted trees. Each house had its lavatory, flushed with boiling water, and rubbish was burnt daily. The royal palace, in the centre of the capital, was a group of interconnecting courtyards covering some five acres, and when Sir William Winniett was entertained to dinner there in 1848 he was given roast sheep, turkey, plum pudding, nuts, ale and wine—'really very nicely served up'.

But the root of Ashanti policy was a lust for power. 'If power is for sale,' ran an Ashanti proverb, 'sell your mother to buy it—you can always buy her back again.' Ashanti nationalism was aggressive and self-confident, and the Ashanti national practice of human sacrifice was ruthless in its scope. When an Asantahene died, scores, sometimes hundreds of people were slaughtered to provide a ghostly retinue for the king. Most of the victims were criminals or war prisoners whose lives had been saved for the occasion, but others were senior officials or royal relatives who had sworn to die with their ruler. Every Ashanti generation knew this communal re-dedication by death, and at times of war or crisis there were often *ad hoc* sacrifices too, of victims doomed on the spur of the moment. Like the Golden Stool, the practice gave cohesion to the nation, binding the past with the present, fate with free will, the decrees of gods with the destinies of humans.

All this the Ashanti veiled in a web of mysticism. They were people of secretive tastes, and their minds worked in elusive bounds and side-steps, very difficult for Europeans to grasp. Ashanti folktales, for example, were extraordinarily opaque. When the duiker told the man called Hate-to-be-Contradicted that his palm nuts were ripe, this is how Hate-to-be-Contradicted replied: 'That is the nature of the palm nut. When they are ripe, three bunches ripen at once. When they are ripe, I cut them down, and when I boil them to extract the oil, they make three water-pots full of oil. Then I take the oil to Akase to buy an Akase old woman. The Akase old woman comes and gives birth to my grandmother who bears my mother, who, in turn, bears me. When Mother bears me, I am already standing there'.

This was unnatural stuff, to readers of Samuel Smiles or Marcus Aurelius. The British Empire had no taste for the avant garde. Glimpsed by the imperialists through the screen of their surrounding forests, the Ashanti seemed a disconcerting people; murderous, queer, alarming, with their fearful orgies of sacrifice, their weird fetish shrines among the trees, their dark sacred lake upon which no boat could sail, their central enigma of the Golden Stool, and this topsy-turvy manner of thought.

4

The British had been on the Gold Coast, the foreshore of Ashanti, for 250 years. Together with the traders of eight other European countries, they had built themselves fortresses on the coast to act first as slave stations, later as entrepôts of more general trade. At first they did not aspire to sovereignty, but when one by one the rival European Powers withdrew from the coast, so their own interest in the country became more political. They were no longer content to be respectful traders on a foreign shore, but wished to control the trade themselves. As the Victorian years passed their trading forts became imperial outposts, the coastal tribes became their wards, and their headquarters at Cape Coast Castle acquired a pro-consular air. It had been built by the Dutch and embellished by the Portuguese, but by the middle of the nineteenth century the British had made it all their own. Its sea-gate gave entrance to a parade ground within the walls; its double staircase led ceremonially to gubernatorial quarters above; bugles sounded from its ramparts; prisoners languished in its gaol. Around its walls an African vassal village had arisen, woodsmoke rising from its mud huts, dried fish stinking in its yards, and the castle stood there like a royal palace above the hovels, gleaming whitewashed in the sun, while the surf beat against its foundations, and the black fishermen paddled their canoes beneath its ramparts.[1]

From this imposing base the British looked inland towards the mysterious recesses of Ashanti. Though they had no coastline of their own, the Ashanti exerted a compelling influence over the Fanti tribes along the shore, and their presence astride the trade routes from the interior powerfully affected prices and supplies. The British had opened relations with them in the 1820s, but never made friends with them. Both sides really wanted mastery of the coast, however

[1] It was based upon the pattern of Elmina Castle, to the north, which was built by the Portuguese in 1482 and was the oldest European building in the tropics. Cape Coast itself, begun in 1682, became the prototype of fortified trading 'factories' in many parts of the British Empire, and was a principal point of call, so my guide there assured me in 1971, during Queen Victoria's well-remembered visit to the Gold Coast.

circumlocutory their diplomacy or nicely served up their plum puddings. There were constant misunderstandings, and intermittent skirmishes. At one time the Ashanti army threatened Cape Coast Castle itself, and in 1824 the British Governor, Sir Charles McCarthy suffered so ignominious a defeat that he killed himself: the Ashanti sent his skull triumphantly to Kumasi, where for years the Asantahene used it as a drinking cup, parading it before the people on ceremonial occasions, and sometimes swearing oaths upon it.

These were sparring contests. It was only in the 1870s, when the British Empire turned its attention to the future of Africa, that the Ashanti learnt the meaning of modern imperialism. In hindsight it appears an unequal conflict, between a European empire approaching the apogee of its power, and an unlettered kingdom of the bush. To the Ashanti at the time it did not seem so unbalanced. If the British were an imperial people, so were they. The Ashanti military record was as proud as the British. The British generals might have their Gatling guns and rocket batteries, but the King of Ashanti went into battle hung all over, head to foot, with infallible ju-jus, forming a kind of spiritual chain mail, and fastened so thickly to his person that his face scarcely showed through the magic tufts and fragments, and when he moved the whole silhouette of his presence menacingly rippled.

These were armies that clashed in ignorance, like Arnold's armies of the night. Neither side remotely understood each other. The Ashanti pagan culture on the one hand, the European Christian civilization on the other, were both movements of immense aggressive assurance, armoured in faith. The Ashanti thought the British perfidious cowards, the British considered the Ashanti superstitious savages. The Ashanti, having little conception of the strength of the forces opposing them, still thought they might drive the white men into the sea. The British, impelled by interests mercantile, evangelical and plain expansionist, were reaching the conclusion that Ashanti must be shackled. The Europeans brooded and bided their time: the Ashantis brooded too, and marched here and there in inconclusive petty wars.

In 1872 the belligerent young Asantahene Kofi Karikari precipitated the issue. The Dutch then decided to withdraw from the

Gold Coast, and sold their fort at Elmina to the British. This the Ashanti resented, because they claimed to own the fort themselves, and they accordingly crossed the River Prah, the traditional frontier of Ashanti proper, to besiege both Elmina and Cape Coast Castle. They were driven off, taking with them European missionaries as hostages; and the British seized the pretext for a crash campaign to settle the fractious Ashanti once and for all, and achieve an imperial stability upon the Gold Coast.

5

Of all the colonial wars of the Victorian era, this was the most classically perfect, a metaphor of the genre. At its head was Lieutenant-General Sir Garnet Wolseley, KCMG, CB, now emerging as the very archetype of the imperial soldier—or as W. S. Gilbert had it, 'the very model of a modern major-general'. He was invited to take complete civil and military charge of the operation, and 'Heavens', he later recalled, 'with what internal joy I did so!' At 40 he was the youngest general in the army, and he now gathered around him the 'Wolseley Ring', that coterie of clever, reformist and socially desirable officers which was to play so large a part in British military affairs for the rest of the century. 'I felt', he wrote, 'that ordinary men could not be good enough for the war I had undertaken', and among the young men who formed his staff were nine who would later become generals themselves, and one future Field-Marshal. Buller was there, from Red River, and William Butler, and a brilliant newcomer, Colonel George Colley, who had just written the article 'Army', sixty pages long, for the ninth edition of the *Encylopaedia Britannica*.[1] They sailed off to the Gold Coast in a spirit of elevated purpose, whiling away the voyage in a careful study of the geography and history of Ashanti. Wolseley himself thought of their mission as a crusade. He intended, he said, to inflict 'such a heavy punishment upon King Koffee, to show him, his people, and all neighbouring nations that no extent of deadly forest could protect them from the British Army'. Right was on his side. To be British was enough. 'Remember', he told his soldiers, 'that

[1] Dropped alas, for reasons which will presently appear, from the tenth.

the black men hold you in superstitious awe: be cool; fire low, fire slow and charge home.'

The black men did not hold them in superstitious awe. On the contrary, it was an old Ashanti dictum that the bush was stronger than the white man's cannon: also they had plenty of firearms themselves, thoughtfully supplied by British traders through French West African ports. The Asantahene was confident in his cause, his traditional tactics, his knowledge of terrain, his jujus and his Golden Stool, and when Wolseley sent him an ultimatum he took no notice. This was a sad rebuff to the Empire and the nineteenth century, for the ultimatum was lordly in its style and was sent by traction engine.[1] The Queen of England had heard with profound concern, it declared, of the Asantahene's recent conduct, but she had sent Sir Garnet to Africa to arrange a lasting peace. Before negotiations could open the Ashanti must withdraw from British protected territories, release all captives, and guarantee compensation. If these terms were satisfied Sir Garnet was ready to meet the Asantahene in a friendly spirit. If not, 'I hereby warn you to expect the full punishment your deeds had merited. . . . Rest assured that power will not be wanting to that end'.

By November, 1873, the power was on the spot: 4,000 first-class British regulars, from the Black Watch and the Rifle Brigade, with a detachment of native artillery, and reserve companies from the Royal Welch Fusiliers and the West India Regiment, fresh from Jamaica. They wore specially-made uniforms of grey homespun, and they were equipped with all the latest devices for tropical warfare—respirators against the heat, veils against the insects, cholera belts and quinine. Three hospital ships lay off Cape Coast Castle, waiting to receive the wounded, and a second army of some 8,500 porters was recruited in support. Diversionary attacks were mounted north and south, but the main force was to advance across the Prah direct to Kumasi, building its own road as it went, and accompanied by a corps of war correspondents that included Henry Stanley the

[1] In the hands of an Ashanti captive, who chugged off into the forest in a hiss of steam, but upon whom, an eye-witness wrote, the experience had little visible effect—'he seems to have regarded the whole operation as a ponderous prelude to his own execution'.

explorer. Sir Garnet was quite certain of victory, but was resigned to the possibility of casualties, soldiers being made to die in action—'and oh! how fortunate they are who do so!'[1]

6

It went like clockwork. The Ashanti fought courageously, using their traditional tactics of envelopment, and sometimes halting the action to make a propitiatory sacrifice: but the shots of their muzzle-loaders as often as not bounced harmlessly off the British, their effective range being about forty yards, and all their magic spells and incantations proved ineffective. Over the wide and soupy Prah the British steadily advanced, into the unmapped forests of Ashanti, with their engineers, their seven-pounders, their rocket projectors, their eager newspapermen and their apprehensive army of porters. They laid their own telegraph as they went, built 237 bridges, and literally cut a path through the monotonous and suffocating foliage of the rain-forest, frondy, brambly, tangled and dense, squelchy underfoot and pendulous overhead. There were frequent skirmishes along the way, as the Highlanders of the advance guard swore and sweated through, and the light-footed Ashanti fell upon them out of the shadows, but the one decisive action of the advance occurred at Ejinasi, a village about half-way to the capital.

There the main body of the Ashanti army lay in wait, deployed along a ridge in horse-shoe formation. There were scouts on each wing, and assembled behind the central force were the stately chiefs with their ceremonial umbrellas, their gold-headed knobkerries and their stools of state. The British were attacked on both flanks as they approached Ejinasi, and there ensued the first major engagement between the British Army and an organized army of Africans. It was a theatrical kind of battle, made vivid for us by the drawings of the war artists. The Ashanti were mostly invisible, being hidden in the thick forest, so that only the flash and smoke of their muskets showed, with an occasional glimpse of shining black, or nodding finery among the foliage. The British, on the other hand, in their

[1] In the event only eighteen had the good luck to be killed, though fifty-five enjoyed the consolation of dying from disease.

pith-helmets and grey cotton, made little attempt at concealment, and within the hollow square of their formation, look in the pictures as though they are fighting some kind of demonstration battle.

There stands the bugler, blowing his commands. There are the orderlies, standing by for messages. There the quartermaster keeps his ammunition tally, the doctors bandage their wounded in the shade of the great mahoganies, the prisoners squat huddled in their corral. All around the perimeter the moustachioed soldiers crouch watchfully at their rifles, sometimes firing through the scrub, and in the very centre of the scene a war correspondent interviews Sir Garnet Wolseley himself, KCMG, chain-smoking cigars as he paces between his soldiers, his staff officers at his heels, receiving messages from the firing line and coolly commenting upon the course of the action. To complete the exhibition effect, through the crash of the rifles and the hiss of the rockets two mysterious sounds answer each other through the forest: from the Ashanti the unnerving howl of a war-cry, from the British the swirl of the Black Watch pipes.

In the end the Ashanti broke, faced by vastly superior fire-power, unshakeable discipline and a confidence equal to their own. On February 3, 1874, the Black Watch, sweeping aside successive Ashanti pickets and ambushes, and once interrupting the act of a human sacrifice, entered the city of Kumasi. For the first time the Ashanti saw a foreign force within the walls of their sacred city: for the first time the British, so used to storming the citadels of Asia, marched as conquerors into a black African capital. It proved a curious denouement. Kofi had abandoned his palace, retreating into the bush beyond, but the people of Kumasi poured unafraid into the streets, shaking hands with the soldiers, and murmuring 'Thank you', the only English words they knew.

Nevertheless the British wandered through Kumasi in a horrified frisson, up and down the wide streets, in and out of the palace, and spending longest of all in the purlieus of Death Grove, where they inspected the remains of the 120,000 victims supposedly sacrificed there. The whole area stank, we are told, from the human blood that saturated the ground, and Wolseley himself did not venture into it, 'hating all horrors', and feeling sickened indeed by the descriptions he could not prevent his colleagues passing on. He did

examine however, with indescribable loathing of course, the great
Death Drum, ornamented with human bones, and the sacred stool
kept permanently wet with the blood of victims.

He had his own ideas about the fate of Kumasi. 'In my heart,'
he later wrote, 'I believed that the absolute destruction of Koomas-
sie with its great palace, the wonder of Western Africa, would be a
much more striking and effective end to the war than any paper
treaty.' He had been at Peking in 1861, when the incomparable
Summer Palace of the Chinese Emperors had been burnt by Lord
Elgin's British force: 'a well-placed blow to Tartar pride', he had
thought it, as the smoke from the great fire drifted over Peking, and
he evidently believed the destruction of the Asantahene's elegant
compound, with its steep thatched roofs and its gilded ornaments,
would be equally salutary to the Ashanti. He wanted to be out of
Kumasi as soon as possible, to save his soldiers from fever, but he
sent a last ultimatum to the Asantahene advising him to come to
terms at once. When no reply came, on February 6, 1874 the old
city of Kumasi was destroyed. Its houses were stacked with tinder,
its Death Grove was cleared for burning, and the engineers placed
mines all around the walls of the royal palace. At seven in the morning the main body of troops marched out of the city; at eight the
fuses were lit by the rearguard; at nine the last men of the Black
Watch, hastening away through the forest to the coast and the
waiting troopships, looked back to see the sacred city disintegrating
into rubble.

Kofi took the point, and sent his messengers of peace hurrying
after the British. At a village called Fomena they submitted, agreeing
to pay an indemnity of impossible value, to release their hostages,
to renounce their claim to Elmina, to recognize the independence
of several vassal tribes, and to do their best to end human
sacrifice. They remembered the war ever after as the Sagrenti War,
after its British commander, and Sir Garnet went home once more in
glory. He was nicknamed 'Britain's Only General', and when people
wanted to describe something supremely well done, neatly wrapped
up like the Ashanti War, they called it 'All Sir Garnet'.

7

The soldiers left Ashanti thoughtfully. It had been their first experience of modern war in Africa, and it had been full of surprises. Wolseley himself thought it a horrible experience, but was impressed by the discipline, courage and high morale of the Ashanti, under their tyrannical militarism, compared with the feckless depravity of the coastal tribes under British suzerainty. He was not, he hastily added in his memoirs, an apostle of military despotism, but the Ashantis had taught him that national pride and contentment came naturally to a people which placed the greatness of the State above the interest of the individual. William Butler, a more subtle observer, found the war a lesson in historical determinism: Africa was the 'real bed-rock school of human nature'. The poor black savages of west Africa had many good traits—patience, honesty, fidelity—and much of what was bad in them was the fault of the British Empire. 'It was our drink, our trade, our greed which had hopelessly demoralized the native African. We had drugged him with our drink; we shot him with our guns; we sold him powder and lead, so that he might shoot and enslave his fellow-black. Those castles along his coast were the monuments of our savage injustice to him.'

Reactions at home were simpler. There the Ashanti War powerfully stoked the fires of imperialism, and excited the public imagination with visions of African glory. At least eight books were written about the campaign: it was the first of the colonial wars to take the popular fancy, and gave to the imperial idea a new aspect of boyish adventure. Wolseley was made a Grand Commander of the Order of St Michael and St George, and given £20,000 by a grateful Parliament, and the Queen herself reviewed his little army on its return, assembled in hollow square in Windsor Great Park. Even Gladstone spoke warmly of the Ashanti triumph in the House of Commons, and the Press was ecstatic.

Yet it was a triumph of ignorance. The causes of the war remained obscure to the British public, its purposes were cloudy, and nobody made any attempt to understand the Ashanti case, to master the baffling Ashanti culture or explore the national history. The real meaning of the campaign, its underlying emotions, its catalytic quality as a clash of convictions—all went unremarked, and it seemed that the war was an end in itself, and that Sir Garnet's masterly little campaign had, like successful surgery, simply cut out a canker once and for all.

This was to be characteristic of the imperial activities in Africa, where the British armies, returning time and again to the attack against the scattered black kingdoms of the continent, seldom understood the nature of their opponents, or reasoned out the significance of their actions. Africa was a brutalizing influence upon the Empire: not because the black peoples were more brutal than others, but because the British thought them so, and behaved accordingly. It was not long before the imperial armies were obliged to return to Kumasi, this time to annexe the Ashanti kingdom to the British Empire: but by then war in Africa was a commonplace, and the Golden Stool of the Ashanti no longer seemed even a mystery to the British, only a tiresome childish geegaw.

CHAPTER TWENTY-ONE

By the Sword

THE Ashanti War was a popular success partly because it was a reassurance. The British had been taken aback by the spectacle of the Prussian armies sweeping so brilliantly into Paris three years before, and they needed to know that British armies too could move with swift decision and efficiency. It was a militarist age in Europe, as the vast standing armies of the continental Powers girded themselves for new struggles, and the British were infected too. A new note of belligerence entered the imperial oratory. What was won by the sword must be kept by the sword. Seldom a martial people, as the century proceeded the British acquired a new, flushed pride in their fleets and armies, now seen not simply as bulwarks against the plots of hostile autocrats, but as instruments of world supremacy. The Indian Mutiny had clearly demonstrated that a sizeable number of Victoria's subjects detested the presence of the Raj, but the British were neither depressed nor disillusioned by this disclosure. It merely confirmed a growing national suspicion that they had been called to terrible but noble duties. They were not made to be loved: they were made to rule the world for its own good.

For the rest of the century this sense of vocation, backed by commercial opportunism and patriotic fervour, was to be based frankly upon military power, and the record of the Empire's progress is all too largely a record of war. The British fleets and armies emerged everywhere as true imperial forces, geared to the requirements and convictions of Empire, and they bore themselves uninhibited. This is how a British subaltern once put down an incipient mutiny among a force of Sikhs and Gurkhas under his command. He knocked down the first mutineer with a blow on the head from his pistol.

He broke his pistol-butt on the head of the second, flooring him with a blow from a second pistol when he tried to resist. He seized a third and gave him 500 lashes there and then. The mutiny failed.

2

The British Army was the striking force of the imperial mission. Though in the second half of the century Indian forces were often used in campaigns overseas, still the Queen's regiments provided the strategic reserve, and it is said that there were only two years during Victoria's reign when the British Army was not somewhere fighting a skirmish—'what in our little army', as Wolseley mock-modestly said, 'we call a battle'. It was all done by volunteers—there was no conscription in Victoria's Empire—and casualties were a running drain upon the nation's young manhood, as though some great catastrophe were to strike the British every year. The cost was enormous too. In the 1860s the Imperial Government withdrew many garrisons from self-governing possessions overseas —'the withdrawal of the legions', as imperial romantics called the process—in the hope of inducing the colonists to assume more of the burden themselves, but the price of imperial defence was still overwhelmingly borne by the British at home, and their soldiers remained scattered in garrisons, fortresses and islands across the world. The army's range of experience was unrivalled. When the Queen elevated to the peerage General Sir Hugh Gough, who had commanded in more general actions than any British officer except Wellington, he adopted, to commemorate highlights of his career, the title Baron Gough of Chingkeang-foo, Maharajpore and the Sutlej.[1]

In some ways the Army had not much changed since we last inspected it, forty years before on the Afghan passes. Socially it was still rigidly caste-ridden. The purchase of commissions had been ended, regimental patrons being bought out at black market prices (£14,000, for example, for the owner of a cavalry regiment), but officers were still for the most part men of means and family, and

---

[1] And lived happily ever after at his family seat, near Booterstown in County Dublin.

the smart regiments remained excruciatingly smart. Most of the private soldiers still joined because they could find nothing better to do, or coveted the anonymity of the military life, and about a quarter of them were still Irish—when the British Army charged with the bayonet, it released a warcry defined by Queen Victoria herself as 'a terrible cry, half British cheer, half Irish hurrah'. Their basic pay was still a shilling a day, and by the time they had paid their dues for rations, rum and cleaning gear, most of them had no money at all, and lived absolutely within the ordered family of their regiment. The gulf between officers and men remained profound, and the one emotion that bound them was not patriotism, nor even loyalty to the queen, but *esprit de corps*.

The temper of the Army was eighteenth century, and its outlook had not been softened by the experience of empire. The drinking was terrific, the whoring insatiable, the looting endemic: 'Mud Wallah Caste', is what the Indians called the worst of the soldiery, and the military memoirists are frank enough about the brutality of the campaigning life. Here an army surgeon in China, finding a Chinese girl who had committed suicide rather than face the barbarians, coolly cuts off her little bound feet for his collection. Here a private soldier discovers a Pathan boy cutting the head off a dead British colour-sergeant, and picking the child up on the point of his bayonet, throws him over a cliff. Here an officer recalls the day when some hostile Sikhs climbed into trees to hide from the British —'great sport for our men, who were firing up at them as at so many rooks . . . down they would come like a bird, head downward, and bleeding most profusely'.

But technically the British Army was much improved. It had been scoured by the traumatic experiences of the Crimean War, and steeled by the Mutiny, and in the 1860s it had been drastically modernized by the reforming zeal of Edward Cardwell, Secretary of State for War in Gladstone's first administration. Privates no longer enlisted for life, so that the average age of soldiers was now much lower. The old numbered infantry regiments had been reorganized on a county basis, a reserve army was formed, flogging was abandoned except in times of war. It was a more professional service now, and it was freed of its last stultifying vestiges of royal control—except one, the immovable Duke of Cambridge still occupying the office of Commander-in-Chief.

It was still essentially an army of Empire, different in kind as in purpose from the great conscript armies of the Continent. Its strength lay in the tight small loyalties of the regimental spirit, in improvization, in the resource and prestige of individual generals. Its speciality had become the small campaign in distant parts against a primitive enemy (though not always *so* primitive—the Sikh armies, for instance, had better artillery than their British opponents). In 1854 Wolseley had likened the army's organization to a steam engine with its boiler in Halifax, its cylinder in China, its other machinery distributed wherever the map was coloured red, and no water, coal, oil or tools. Thirty years later, when the army was preparing an invasion of Egypt, in a few weeks the commissariat had assembled a fleet of seventy-four transports to convey to the Mediterranean a railway from England, mules from the United States, South America, Italy, Greece, wood fuel from Cyprus and troops from Britain, Malta, Gibraltar and India. Some of the army's anachronisms survived because of its imperial role: the hollow square, volley firing, the frontal cavalry charge—all these would be disastrous in a European war, though they were still effective against primitives. On the other hand the imperial commitment tautened the army's organization, gave it an unrivalled expertise in combined operations, and battle-hardened its soldiers.

There was still no general staff, and the War Office remained a warren of interconnecting houses in Pall Mall, all on different levels, and ranging from the backrooms of a draper's shop to a baroque-decorated mansion. In 1871, though, manoeuvres were held for the first time on Salisbury Plain: many of the older generals thought them childish, theatrical and foreign,[1] and so many horses and wagons had to be hired from civilian contractors that the transport was nicknamed Pickford's Irregulars, but even so the event was an earnest of modernity. Since 1854, too, Aldershot, the army headquarters in Hampshire, had been developed as a centre for the whole

---

[1] Like old Sir James Scarlett, who, finding the 'enemy' forces, commanded by a junior general, impertinently winning a battle against him, angrily ordered them to retreat.

of British military life. With direct railway lines from London, and good connections to the south coast port, the little town had become in effect the rear base of all the imperial campaigns. When, at one o'clock precisely each day, the Aldershot time gun was fired electrically from the Royal Observatory at Greenwich, it was like a time-check for the entire Raj—a reminder to all the scattered garrisons of Empire that the price of dominion was spit and polish.

At first no more than a huge collection of huts and tents upon the sombre heath, Aldershot had grown into a complete garrison town—'The Home' as it was ever afterwards to be called, 'of the British Army'. Some of its barracks were immense and gloomy red-brick structures, with first-floor balconies in the Indian manner, and royal crests over ceremonial gateways. Others were tents on permanent foundations, lined in interminable rows across the heath. There was a garrison church rich in monuments of Empire, and blessed with an Ethiopian chalice looted by Lord Napier's expedition to Magdala in 1868. There was an officer's library of books about war. There were five military hospitals. There was a soldiers' newspaper, *Sheldrake's Military Gazette*, founded by a former colour-sergeant of the Coldstream Guards. The town was full of pubs ('Where's the Duke of Cambridge?' asks a staff officer in an old Aldershot joke. 'I don't know, sir. I'm teetotal'), and was famous for its rat-pit, one of the best in the provinces, where the well-known rat-catcher, Mr Jack Black, often showed off his terriers. An act of Parliament had decreed that three members of the local council should be nominated for ever by the Army, giving the little town a municipal status analogous only to the university towns of Oxford and Cambridge.

Aldershot demonstrated the new status of arms in British life—a status that rose with the rise of imperial pride. Prince Albert himself was credited with the idea of it—'if the Army had never had any other good reason to revere his memory', said Wolseley, 'the creation of that camp of instruction should render it dear to us'. Many of the local tradesmen were by Royal Appointment, including it was claimed Mr Black the rat-catcher, who habitually wore a sash emblazoned with a crown, a pair of rats and the letters VR: for since 1855 the royal family had maintained a modest wooden villa, called the Royal Pavilion, on a ridge above the heath, where Her Majesty stayed when she came down for a review (she wore a military habit with a Field-Marshal's insignia, and a plume in her hat). By now her soldiers were more familiar with war than most, and perhaps enjoyed it more. Wolseley, surveying his brother officers as they embarked for a war against the Chinese, said they seemed to think 'the world was specially created for their own wild pleasures, of which, to most of us, war . . . with its maddening excitement was the greatest'. At the Prussian manoeuvres of 1874 a party of British officer-observers, reminiscing jauntily about the atrocities of the Indian Mutiny, found themselves rebuked by the Crown Prince Friedrich Wilhelm himself, who felt obliged to remind them how dreadful war was.

When Hyde Park Corner in London was replanned later in the century, a colossal bronze statue of the Duke of Wellington, by the sculptor Matthew Wyatt, was removed from the top of Constitution Arch and brought by the Queen's command to Aldershot. It was re-erected on a mound behind the garrison church, and there the Iron Duke superbly sat his charger above the Tented Encampment, surveying the busy military scene below, but seeming to extend his gaze much farther too—across the distant Channel to fields of operation far away, to the deserts and velds where the redcoats, sweating, cursing, womanizing and making merry, carried the imperial message to a not always unanimously grateful world.[1]

3

Behind the Army stood the Royal Navy. Everyone knew that *au fond* this was a sea-empire. Maritime supremacy alone enabled the British to throw their armies into action upon the colonial frontiers,

[1] Victorian Aldershot has almost vanished—even the Royal Pavilion was demolished in 1961—but one can still see the great gate of the original cavalry barracks, the garrison church has survived the abolition of compulsory church parades, the officers' library thrives, and the Duke of Wellington, his surroundings sadly unkempt when I was last there, still looks imperiously across the nations.

or warn off the predations of rival Powers. In the years since Trafalgar the Navy had enjoyed a prestige so mystic that its power was taken for granted. It was the genius of the Pax Britannica: its reputation was towering, its size was unequalled, and its complacency was immense.

The Royal Navy had a Nelson fixation. It talked in Nelsonic terms, it practised Nelsonic tactics, it examined every situation through Lord Nelson's blind eye—until 1869 Nelson's *Victory* was still afloat as flagship of the Commander-in-Chief at Portsmouth. Its elderly commanders still lived the spirit of Nelsonic derring-do—like the truculent Sir James Scott, who had joined the service in 1803, was on the active list for sixty-three years, and liked to claim that he had taken part in two general actions and five sieges, had assisted at the capture or storming of one capital city, twenty-three towns, thirty-two batteries and twenty-two forts, and had been present at the capture or cutting out of one line of battleship, five frigates, six sloops of war, twenty-one gunboats, 300 merchant vessels and several privateers.[1]

Most of the Navy's battleships were still heavy wooden three-deckers, full-rigged and rated by the number of their muzzle-loading guns. The accepted naval manoeuvres were still those made classic by Trafalgar. The last great naval expedition, an abortive Baltic enterprise during the Crimean War, had been essentially a sailing-ship affair, and when in 1860 the Navy was required to take an invading army to China, it did so in a fleet of 173 sailing-ships, carrying in their creaking hulls, at five knots through the China Sea, 20,000 soldiers with all their horses, guns, food and *matériel*.[2] All the admirals had grown up in sail, and many of them viewed the arrival of steam with undisguised dislike—for they regarded a warship less as a weapon of war than a floating pageant, or perhaps

---

[1] 'Thou hast girded me with strength unto the battle', says his memorial limply in the crypt of St Paul's, giving full details of this exhausting career.

[2] The first man ashore, through the mud of the Peiho River, was an elderly brigadier in a white helmet, whose shirt-tail flapped beneath his red-serge jacket, and who carried his trousers, socks and boots slung over his sword on his shoulder. At the end of the war the commanding general and his staff hired a P and O steamer, and went over to Japan for a short holiday.

a work of art, not to be risked in battle or even dirtied with gun-smoke.[1]

On board little had greatly changed since Trafalgar. Even in the new ironclads life was tough, stuffy and fearfully noisy, with the primitive reciprocating engines thumping and rattling the entire ship, and the living quarters, encased in metal on the waterline, lit only by smelly tallow candles. Food was generally meagre, water was strictly rationed, pleasures were homespun and often bestial. The young officers, whose professional education had generally consisted of a few months on the old three-decker *Britannia*, moored in the River Dart, went in for practical jokes and horseplay. The ratings loved games like Sling the Monkey, in which a man swinging on a long rope was attacked with rope-ends, or Baste the Bear, in which the victim crawled about the deck on all fours. The bluejackets drank enormously, and nearly all chewed tobacco: when approached by an officer they simultaneously removed the hats from their heads and the wads from their mouths, returning both in a single movement when the officer had passed.

The Navy was full of odd characters, upper and lower deck—eccentrics, runaways, wild younger sons, Irishmen from Cork or Galway, lower-deck inventors, religious fanatics. The sailors were terrific dandies: with their heavily oiled hair, their meticulously trimmed side-whiskers (beards were not allowed before 1870), their wide-brimmed sennet hats of straw or canvas, and the knife-edge creases to their bell-bottoms, they went ashore in Bombay or Singapore cockily ready for anything, and returned in the evening liberty boats, as likely as not, insensible in the stern sheets or sitting on the thwarts singing bawdy songs. Until the 1860s they made most of their own clothes, even to boots, and they still danced horn-pipes, as they had since the Middle Ages, when the boatswain's mate piped all hands to 'dance and skylark'.

[1] An attitude which was long to linger, by the way. 'The highest ideals of grace and power,' wrote an officer of the battlecruiser *Tiger*, completed in 1914, 'had taken form at the bidding of the artist's brain of her designer. No man who ever served in her fails to recall her beauty with pride and thankfulness.' 'It is a thousand pities,' wrote Sir Oscar Parkes of her in 1956, 'that a shifting of her topmast . . . was made necessary—it changed her in the same way that twisted eyebrows would spoil classic beauty.'

Socially the Royal Navy had gone up in the world during Victoria's reign. Its officers, once drawn chiefly from the middle classes, now included many men of title and means, so that even the Queen, who used in her younger days to wonder if it were proper to invite naval officers to the same table as her Guards officers, was now quite taken with the senior service. Naval ratings, too, were men of higher standing now. They were volunteers, pursuing a regular and relatively well-paid career, in a service which became more popular with the public every year. Impressment, though never legally abolished, was in abeyance—the Navy was only half its size in Nelson's day, and there was no shortage of recruits—and flogging too, though it was never formally abolished, petered out in the 1870s.

Now this whole elaborate structure was threatened by the new technology. Steam threatened all—threatened the Navy's status in the world, for now all navies could start from scratch, threatened the style of the service and the well-being of the admirals. Tenaciously the Navy clung to its heritage. In 1859 the last of the wooden three-decker battleships was launched—*Victoria*, the first warship to be named for the Queen.[1] But for her size and armament she was little more than an improved *Victory*, with auxiliary steam engines. Her sides were marked out in the traditional checker of black and white, her great masts were fully-rigged, her bowsprit rose above a splendid gilded figurehead, and from her big square ports protruded the barrels of 120 muzzle-loading guns, with an enormous 68-pounder mounted in the bows for the better pursuit of the French. In such a ship the Royal Navy still felt at home, and Sir James Scott could cheerfully have grappled with the most vicious of privateers.

But she was the last of the old kind, and even as she sailed with a dowager dignity to become flagship of the Mediterranean Fleet, the keel was laid of the first of the new—the original sea-going steam iron-clad, *Warrior*, specifically designed to 'overtake and overwhelm any other warship in existence'.[2] Throughout the 1860s

[1] The only other one, a turret battleship launched in 1890, sank in a collision with the battleship *Camperdown* off the Syrian coast in 1893, with the loss of 359 officers and men. The Navy has never used the name since.

[2] In the event she never saw action, but she is afloat to this day as a hulk at Pembroke Dock in Wales.

and 1870s ideas fell upon the Navy thick and fast, and slowly, creakily, not without magnificence, the Royal Navy adapted to modernity. Sometimes its trust in new methods was severely shaken—by the loss of the battleship *Captain*, for example, a revolutionary new turret ship which capsized on her maiden cruise in 1870, confirming the worst forebodings of the reactionaries. Sometimes it was beset by Navy scares, alarmist reports of French rearmament or American inventiveness. It progressed in a welter of argument, admiral against admiral, newspaper critics against naval spokesman, and if its professional ideas changed slowly, its gnarled, stubborn and ornate style was more resistant still.

Like the Army, it became more and more an imperial force. It was increasingly concerned with the protection of the imperial sea-routes, the suppression of subversion, showing the flag and overawing the natives. Much of its energy was invested in gunboat diplomacy, that ubiquitous instrument of imperial prestige, which required the dispersal of innumerable small vessels in every corner of the world. In 1875, for instance, the Royal Navy had 16 ships on the North American and West Indies station, five on the South American, nine on the South African, 11 on the East Indies, 10 on the Pacific, 11 on the Australian and 20 on the China station. They might be required at any moment for the most diverse duties: shelling recalcitrant tribespeople, embellishing consular fetes, scaring off pirates, rescuing earthquake victims, transporting friendly potentates—tasks which, though not always directly imperialist, contributed to the mosaic of imperial pride, and strengthened the illusion of inescapable British strength.

It *was* partly illusion. The Navy had no war plans, no staff college, very little tactical training, and its attitude to war, as to life, remained incorrigibly conservative—nostalgic even, for the longer ago Trafalgar was, the more romantic Nelson's navy seemed. Its power was none the less real, though, for its element of bluff. As C. J. Napier once observed, 'an English admiral is difficult to reckon up. He may be wise, or he may be otherwise, no man knows, for he dwells not upon the hearth, but away upon the waters: however, all men know that he has a strength of cannon at his back. . . .' Even the Navy's worst enemies admitted the splendour of its traditions and its style, and at home, as the century passed, its legend became almost sanctified. Powerful lobbies arose to press for its well-being and expansion. The Navy League was one of the most insistent pressure groups of the late nineteenth century, and Parliament was seldom without its political admirals. The Empire and the Navy went together, and the very first statue ever erected of Lord Nelson stood not in Trafalgar Square, but in the cobbled New Place in Montreal.[1]

4

And behind the Navy were the bases. Steam power, though it increased the mobility of British power, made the Empire dependent upon coaling stations, and the Royal Navy was tied more than ever to its bases overseas. Fortunately these were everywhere. Almost every strategic island had been acquired by the British at one time or another, and as the distant imperial stakes grew more valuable, so the safety of the shipping routes became the chief preoccupation of the strategists in London, and largely dictated the policies of the Empire. Almost any imperial possession could be justified, it seemed, by naval necessity. When the Ionians were abandoned it became absolutely essential to acquire Cyprus as a substitute, and the British Empire could scarcely survive without Bermuda, covering as it so obviously did the entrance to the Caribbean and the Gulf of New Orleans.[2] Ascension Island, originally acquired as a protective outpost of St Helena, where Napoleon was imprisoned, was now irreplaceable as a coaling station, and St Helena itself, though Napoleon lay harmless in Les Invalides, turned out to be indispensable as a source of watercress for the Fleet.

Sea-power was the basis of Empire, but Empire, it now appeared,

[1] Now Place Jacques Cartier. The statue is still in good condition after 160 years of the Quebec climate, having been made in London of a secretly-formulated substance called Coade Stone—'impervious to FROSTS and DAMPS'.

[2] Despite a lasting reputation for dockyard idleness and thievery. 'Everything gets stolen here', a watchman told me when I visited the old naval installations in 1970, 'except the lavatory seats and the storehouse clock—someone's always sitting on the lavatory, and everybody keeps an eye on the clock.'

was essential to sea-power. It was an imperialist circle. By the 1870s the system was almost complete. The Mediterranean was policed and serviced from Gibraltar, Malta and Cyprus, the Atlantic from Halifax and Bermuda, the Indian Ocean from Bombay and Trincomalee, the Pacific from Hong Kong and Esquimault, the Red Sea from Aden. And linking all these scattered dockyards, deposited everywhere along the shipping routes, the imperial coaling stations offered their mountains of best Welsh steam coal, and their sweating and blackened armies of coolies. Some of these bases and stations were new, but some were very old, and seemed in their Britishness part of some natural sea-order. It seemed organically rather than historically ordained that the Union Jack should fly over the watchposts and cross-roads of the sea. Foreigners for the most part accepted it as a fact of life, and the British scarcely thought about it.

Take for instance the naval base of Simonstown in South Africa. The Cape of Good Hope, the southernmost tip of the African land mass, was one of the most spectacular of the world's headlands: a wild and glorious place, rocky, wind-scoured, where baboons and antelopes roamed the moorland, stormy seabirds of the south whirled in the wind, and below the precipitous cliffs one could see the waters of the Atlantic and Indian oceans mingling in currents of blue and green. Sheltering in the lee of this prodigy was Simonstown. It was one of the snuggest and prettiest places imaginable, and unchangingly British. Trimly around a sheltered inlet clustered its demure villas, its cottages, its sailors' barracks, its steepled church and its esplanade of shops, the whole nicely washed and painted, and built to a happily domestic scale. The dockyard, its gates superbly surmounted by the royal cipher, was embedded so neatly between town and sea that the whole had a family unity, and everything in the place was comfortably Navy: the church memorials to Esteemed Shipmates and Ever-Regretted captains' ladies—the shops selling naval gear, tobacco, homely souvenirs, needles, boot-leathers—the taverns, the smell of rum, the cab-driver's transplanted Portsmouth's slang—or the pleasant Admiral's House at the water's edge, whose gardens were fragrant with trellissed roses, and at the foot of whose private jetty, like a skiff on the Thames, the squadron flagship habitually lay. Simonstown looked as though it had been there for ever, and for ever there would stay—like the great Cape above, or the Royal Navy itself, without which Victoria's world seemed inconceivable.[1]

5

But there was a weak link in this network of strength. Most of the imperial bases were concerned *au fond* with India, the greatest and richest of the British possessions, but in 1869 the position of India in the world was shifted by the opening of the Suez Canal. This was a notably un-British event. The French engineer Ferdinand de Lesseps had built the canal, French capital had largely financed it, the French Empress Eugénie had sailed to Egypt in her royal yacht to open it. At first the British unaccountably failed to grasp its significance. They had always thought a railway across the Isthmus a better proposition, and argued for years that a canal was scientifically unfeasible, if only because the Mediterranean and the Red Sea lay at different levels. When de Lesseps built one anyway, they doubted its effect—most traffic, they thought, would continue to sail around the Cape. Altering as it did the familiar shape of the world, the canal seemed unreal to them, even unnatural, especially as it was not British-made, and they appeared to think that if they scoffed at it for long enough it would dry up again.

Presently, though, they were obliged to take it more seriously, for their attention was repeatedly focussed upon Egypt by the Eastern Question. Disturbed always by the presence of the rival Russian Empire beyond the Hindu Kush, the British were perennially afraid that the western flank of India might be turned. They had fought the disastrous Afghan War of 1839 on this issue, and they went back again to Afghanistan in 1878, when another presumptuous Amir embarked upon a flirtation with the Russians, another

[1] The Royal Navy still uses Simonstown, and has rights still at many another old imperial dockyard, Gibraltar to Hong Kong: its dependence upon bases became so ingrained, even after the evolution of fast tankers and supply ships, that in the second world war the Pacific Fleet found itself without a fleet train, and thus hard put to keep up with the United States Navy.

British Resident was murdered, another British Army was defeated, and another punitive force stormed back to Kabul in revenge. They fought a war against the Persians in 1845, they could be roused to Jingoism by any threat to the Dardanelles, and in 1875 Pendeh, a place in Persia whose existence nobody in Britain had hitherto suspected, became for a month or two a household name, as a near-miss *casus belli* with the Russian Empire.

Many an obscure and dusty fortress, Herat to Kandahar, briefly achieved the eponym 'Key to India', but the master-key was now unquestionably Egypt. Napoleon had recognized this long before, when he called Egypt 'the most important country', and seized it as the principal staging-post of his advance to the east. Now the British belatedly recognized it too, and the future of Egypt became crucial to the Eastern Question. The Khedive of Egypt was theoretically a satrap of the Sultan of Turkey, so that whoever controlled the Dardanelles had a hypothetical control of the Suez isthmus too: when the British armies fought in the Crimea, when the music-hall audiences sang the Jingo song, when the statesmen met at Berlin to hammer out the future of the Balkans, Egypt was always in the wings.

By 1875 even the British had to admit the importance of the Suez Canal, and very galling it was. In the person of Lieutenant Waghorn they themselves had pioneered the Egyptian route to India, and though the Canal Company was a French concern, with the Khedive holding a 40 per cent minority interest, by 1875 more than three-fifths of its traffic flew the British flag, and nearly half the ships that sailed from Britain to India took the Suez route. The P and O company rebuilt its entire fleet in order to operate through the canal, besides abandoning its vast investment in the overland route and in the docks and shipyards that serviced its vessels around the Cape. Via Suez armies could now sail from Europe to India in a month, altering the whole pattern of imperial defence. The canal had become, in effect, an extension of India; for the rest of the century the British would think of Suez and India in the same breath, as part of the same preoccupation, and Suez replaced the Cape of Good Hope as a synonym for the beginning of the east.

Disraeli, who became Prime Minister for the second time in 1874, viewed with concern the spectacle of this organically imperial water-way in alien hands. He liked to say winsomely that the real key to India was London, a conceit he had filched from the Russian Ambassador, but more than any other British statesman he was fascinated by the Eastern Question. The east suited him; the concerns of oriental empire gilded his public image, and enhanced his aura of subtle glitter. Besides, his novelist's imagination made him see the Compagnie Universelle du Canal Maritime de Suez, with its attendant Khedive, as an interloper astride a highway of Empire. Palmerston, it is true, had defined Egypt as no more than an inn on the road to India—all that Britain needed was a well-kept establishment, 'always accessible', and well-supplied with 'mutton chops and post-houses'. To Disraeli, though, foreign control of the canal meant that at any time the inn might be barred and shuttered against British clients, a threat from which the Empire must be released.

In 1875 a promising prospect was reported to him. The profligate Khedive was bankrupt, the interest on his foreign debts being about equal to the national income of his country, and almost his only remaining assets were his shares in the canal. Finding himself in even more appalling straits than usual, he was now disposing of them, and already two French banking groups were in pursuit, one group wanting to buy, one offering a mortgage. Disraeli heard of it all in a characteristically Disraelian way—from his millionaire Foreign Secretary, Lord Derby, who had heard it from the proprietor of the *Pall Mall Gazette*, who had heard it from Henry Oppenheimer the French Jewish banker at a private dinner party.

The Prime Minister's fancy was fired. He instructed the British Consul-General in Cairo to investigate the reports, and to tell the Khedive that 'Her Majesty's Government are disposed to purchase if terms can be arranged'. He told the Queen in his best conspiratorial style: ''Tis an affair of millions, about four at least; but it could give the possessor an immense, not to say preponderating, influence in the management of the Canal'. He threw himself with enthusiasm, if at long range, into the veiled negotiations in Cairo, the comings and going of emissaries, the half-truths and the secret commitments, the proposals and counter-proposals of Nubar Pasha, Sherif Pasha, and many another tasselled eminence of the Egyptian scene. He warned off the French Government with a stiff statement by Lord Derby. And when the Consul-General in Egypt reported that de Lesseps himself had offered 100 million francs for the Khedive's shares, but that the Khedive would prefer to sell them to the British Government, Disraeli instantly agreed. 'The Viceroy's offer is accepted. Her Majesty's Government agree to purchase the 177,646 shares of the Viceroy for four million pounds sterling.' 'It is settled,' the Prime Minister told the Queen. 'You have it, Madam.'

Disraeli raised the purchase price from his friends the Rothschilds. His private secretary, Montague Corry, loved to tell how the Prime Minister had sent him to the office of Baron Edmund de Rothschild to ask for a loan of four million pounds.

Rothschild: When?

Corry: Tomorrow.

Rothschild (pausing to eat a muscatel grape and spit out the skin): What is your security?

Corry: The British Government.

Rothschild: You shall have it.

When the shares were counted they proved to be forty short, and the price was accordingly amended to £3,976,582—doubtless pleasing the thrifty Mr Gladstone, who thought the whole transaction deplorable. The documents were packed in seven zinc boxes, and the troopship *Malabar*, en route to England from Bombay, was ordered to call at Alexandria to 'receive certain cases'. A special train took the cases from Cairo to the coast; an armed guard waited at Portsmouth to receive them; on December 1, 1875, they were deposited in the vaults of the Bank of England.[1]

---

[1] Where they remained until, in 1964, they were burnt in the Bank's printing works: by then they had increased to some 300,000, occupied nine cupboards and weighed about four tons. They had been exchanged anyway in 1958 for shares in the new Compagnie Financiere de Suez, successor to the nationalized Canal Company, which is actively involved in the Channel Tunnel project, which has interests in numerous banks, insurance companies, property firms and industrial groups, and in which the British Government is a 10% shareholder to this day.

6

The British were delighted at this coup. Commercially their control of the company remained vestigial, British Government directors still constituting only one eighth of the Board, and for the rest of the century the conduct of the canal remained a frustration to British shipowners and strategists alike. But the shares did give Britain a permanent and powerful stake in Suez, and to the world at large it seemed, in a vague but suggestive way, to give them possession—Bismarck called the canal the Empire's 'spinal cord'. Disraeli's acquisition of the shares, transmuted into legend over the years, entered the national myth as the acquisition of the canal itself, and in the end that is what it became. Out of a two-fifths commercial share, itself a highly profitable investment, the British evolved complete military control of the canal, so that before long the Compagnie Universelle du Canal Maritime, still preponderantly French in ownership and altogether French in management, was operating under the protection and patronage of the British Empire.

So the seal was set upon British command of the oceans, and thus of the Empire. It was now absolute, and any merchant ship captain sailing the imperial routes in the last decades of the Victorian century found himself moving in effect from one British bastion to another. For two decades after the acquisition of the canal shares, British military supremacy was scarcely tested, and the Royal Navy sailed the world, convoying its expeditionary forces, showing the Queen's flag, as though its admirals owned the oceans. The public responded with growing pride, and for the first and probably the last time in their history, the British people acquired a taste for drums, guns and glory.

CHAPTER TWENTY-TWO

South of the Zambesi

YET there were forebodings. To many the Empire seemed too diffuse an organism, set against taut new Powers like Germany or the United States, and throughout the 1870s and 1880s there were repeated attempts to give it logic. The sloppiness jarred, and imperialist intellectuals applied themselves to the task of binding the Empire more closely, and sharing its responsibilities more rationally among its members. It took some mental readjustment, to think of all the scattered millions of Victoria's subjects, Hindus and Muslims and Buddhists and pagans, black, brown, yellow or white, Sioux or Burmese, Chinese or Ashanti, as fellow-citizens of a single immense super-State: but in the new vision of Empire, often figuratively interpreted in mosaics and bas-reliefs, they stood there shoulder to shoulder in comradely profile, backed by scenes of pastoral prosperity or victorious pride, and gazing trustfully upwards, as often as not, towards the bulk of Her Imperial Majesty. The vaguely formulated ideology of British Imperialism had something in common with Soviet Communism half a century later: an innocent optimism, a facile disregard of unwelcome truths, an instinct to simplify and categorize, and a dreadful taste in propaganda.

How could one rationalize the Empire, which was stuck together more by habit than design, had been acquired piecemeal over the centuries, and was held together by force? Some kind of federalism was the fashionable answer, most forcibly expressed by the historians Sir John Seeley and J. A. Froude, and an eager proponent of this solution was Lord Carnarvon, 'Twitters', Disraeli's Colonial Secretary. Carnarvon thought the first step towards a super-Power should be a grouping of the Empire into larger sub-units, starting with the white self-governing colonies. Canada seemed to offer a successful precedent, and Carnarvon prided himself on having fathered Canadian Confederation in Parliament. Australia, where there were five separate colonies, would doubtless soon be federated too—perhaps with New Zealand, a country which, though separated from Australia by a thousand miles of ocean, seemed to many Whitehall theorists more or less the same place. And the third constituent federacy, Lord Carnarvon thought, to form another pillar of the grander imperial structure, should be established in South Africa, which undeniably needed order or collectivism, and was also very expensive to rule.

2

The South African scene had changed, in the forty odd years since the Great Trek, but had changed predictably. There were now two British colonies, Cape Colony and Natal, and two independent Boer Republics. The Orange Free State, with its capital at Bloemfontein beyond the Orange River, was generally moderate and on friendly terms with the British. The Transvaal republic, called the South African Republic, was the high retreat of everything most doggedly Boer, and was not generally on friendly terms with anyone. Around these four white settlements swirled the black peoples in their diverse tribes, outnumbering the Europeans by twenty to one, generically known to the whites as Kaffirs or Bantus, but possessing ancient tribal loyalties of their own, to the chiefs of Bechuana or Basuto, to the misty divinities of the bushmen or the tremendous feathered kings of Zululand.

In 1875 this magnificent slab of country, ranging from the heavenly wine valleys of the Cape to the arid plateau of the Transvaal, was as usual in tumult. The obdurate Transvaal Boers were constantly at war with the blacks upon their ill-defined frontiers, and were also threatening to cock a snook at the Empire by building a railway to Delagoa Bay, in Portuguese East Africa, to give themselves an independent outlet to the world. The Zulus were in a fighting mood, their young warriors chafing for battle, their elders resentful of Boers and Britons alike. The British had internecine squabbles of their own, and by employing the imperial sleight of

hand to acquire the newly discovered diamond field area in Griqua-
land East, they had gravely offended the Afrikaners of the Orange
Free State.[1]

Over it all, though, the British believed themselves to have
rights of paramountcy, or at least trusteeship, and the whole inflammatory muddle, Carnarvon reasoned, could be cleared if Africa
south of the Zambesi could be amalgamated into a single imperial
unit. In particular the South African Republic of the Transvaal,
which prescient imperialists already foresaw as the future epicentre
of South Africa, must be drawn back into the imperial brotherhood
which its leaders had so stubbornly eluded for so long. The British
would outnumber the Boers in such an association, the blacks
would be subdued by sweet reason, and the imperial authority could
devolve its authority and cut its costs without taking undue risks
(for as a Colonial Office specialist had declared only a few years before the opening of the Suez Canal, the Cape was unquestionably
'the true centre of the Empire', and upon the security of the Simonstown base might depend the whole imperial future).

First Carnarvon tried persuasion, sending out to Durban that
inescapable champion of empire, Major-General Sir Garnet Wolseley,
K.C.B.—ostensibly as Governor of Natal, really as an apostle of
federation. For a time he hoped that a confederation might actually
be convened under the chairmanship of Britain's Only General, but
Wolseley's charm proved less effective with the Boers than with the
susceptible British colonists, and the plan came to nothing. Carnarvon was therefore goaded into a very different tactic. In the spring
of 1877 he ordered, if not explicitly at least between the lines of his
instructions, the annexation of the South African Republic.

3

The Transvaal had this in common with the British Empire, that it

---

[1] Though the President of that republic, Johannes Brand, was actually
British. 'His father is the Speaker of the Cape Assembly,' complained the
British High Commissioner in Cape Town, 'his wife is an Englishwoman,
his eldest son is now studying at the Middle Temple, and he can declare war
on me tomorrow.'

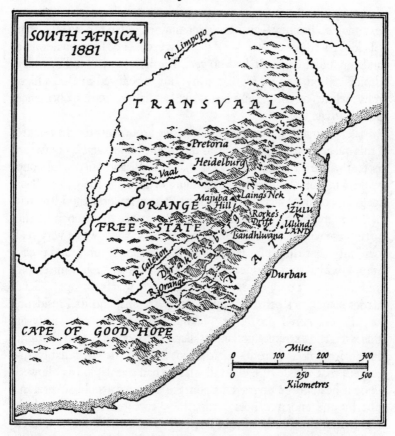

SOUTH AFRICA,
1881

R. Limpopo

TRANSVAAL

Pretoria

Heidelburg

R. Vaal

ORANGE

Majuba
Hill
Laing's Nek

FREE STATE
Rorke's
Drift
Isandhlwana
ZULU
Ulundi
LAND

R. Caledon

Drakensberg

R. Orange

Durban

CAPE OF GOOD HOPE

Miles
0   100   200   300
0   250   500
Kilometres

distinctly lacked system. The Voortrekkers who had pushed across
the Vaal and encamped upon that bitter and remote plateau had
taken with them their own ideas of an acceptable society—one in
which Government interference was limited to the minimum, and
burghers were free to trek where they liked, farm how they liked,
treat their natives as the Bible taught them and their elected rulers
with absolute familiarity. They were an intensely political people,
but parochial. Their little State was racked always with dissension,
and the writ of the Republic ran feebly among the scattered farmsteads of the veld. As always, the Boers wanted only to live the
lekker lewe. For the most part they left commerce to the thousand or
so English settlers in the Republic. They honoured their own ideals

of privacy—farms so big that one could not see the smoke from the next man's chimney—and they maintained a labour system that still looked to foreigners very like slavery. The Transvaal was a fundamentalist State. It had no real frontiers, only a rudimentary administration, and no regular army, but it believed in God's hierarchy: whites on top, blacks below, and an unquestioning obedience to the Mosaic law.

Federation apart, there were persuasive arguments for the seizure of this queer republic. Disraeli was taking the imperialist bit between his teeth, and probably reasoned that a small and successful coup would win votes. There were rumours of gold up there; the Boer treatment of the blacks still stuck in British gullets; the idea that the Boers might be plotting with the Germans, the French or the Portuguese was disturbing to the imperialists; there was a very real possibility that the Zulus might overwhelm the Republic and precipitate a wider war. Besides, the Republic was in such a miserable condition that it only deserved annexation. It was bankrupt, official salaries sometimes being paid in postage stamps, and its President, the mild-mannered predikant Thomas Burgers, was constantly at odds with the extreme fundamentalists, the Doppers, who thought him an irreligious heretic—he did not believe, it was reliably rumoured, that the devil had a tail, and he had sacrilegiously allowed his own head to be engraved upon the Transvaal gold sovereign. Split by the endemic Boer antipathies, threatened by its black neighbours, the South African Republic seemed ripe for Victoria's maternal embrace.

The Empire's agent in the affair was Sir Theophilus Shepstone, one of the best-known Englishmen in South Africa, and a veteran imperialist. Shepstone had spent most of his life in Africa, being the son of a Wesleyan missionary, and his clan was to figure repeatedly throughout the late Victorian history of South Africa. He had been Secretary for Native Affairs in Natal, he spoke Zulu and Xhosa, he was called by the Africans 'Somtseu', or Mighty Hunter, and had no love for the Boers. A silent cunning man, his high brow and dark eyes, set above a large severe mouth and a cleft chin, made him look paradoxically piratical, like an evangelical Disraeli. Shepstone was sent to Pretoria, the Transvaal capital, as

Special Commissioner to the South African Republic, ostensibly to report on the situation there, but with secret instructions to annex the republic if he found that enough Transvaalers wanted it—or for that matter, he was told verbally, if they did not. Such a mission suited his temperament. He was not a very straightforward man. A lifetime of African intrigue had given him an African approach to life and affairs, and he rode into the Transvaal in what might be called a tribal frame of mind.

There he goes along the dusty road to the capital, in many ways the archetype of the British imperialist in Africa—shrewd, calculating, pious, half-educated, overbearing, elated by his recent KCMG and accompanied by his private secretary Rider Haggard ('a leggy-looking youth', as was said at the time, 'who seems the picture of weakness and dullness'). Two or three clerks rode with him, and they were escorted by a troop of mounted policemen. The Boer farmers along the way, lounging outside their farmsteads in their floppy hats and corduroy leggings, smoked their pipes impassively as the little convoy passed; and the British traders whose stores they used for lodgings along the road, when the troopers had fed their horses and His Excellency had retired to his tent for dinner with young Haggard, curiously inquired after the purpose of the mission, and doubtless drew their own conclusions.

After a month's leisurely travel they reached Pretoria. It was the simplest of capitals then. It had not existed at all until 1856, when four squabbling Trekker republics had united, and it was still little more than a village on the veld, flowered and dusty. An avenue of blue gum trees led into town from the south, and trees and gardens were everywhere—fig trees beside every verandah, roses on every trellis, willow-trees to mark the bungalow boundaries, with rows of rich vegetables behind. Along the dirt-streets rumbled the great ox-wagons of the Boers, not much changed since the days of the Trek, their long teams of oxen flicked still by ox-hide whips from wagoners far behind. On the stoeps the burghers comfortably sat, and the women wore clogs and poke bonnets. Sparkling watercourses gave the town vivacity, and all was bathed in the brilliant smokeless light of the high veld, the most exhilarating light on earth.

In the centre of town was Church Square, the heart of the republic, and of Afrikanerdom. There stood the thatched Reform Church, and the Raadsaal with its broad steps, where the burghers of the Volksraad deliberated, and outside whose doors, every three months, the people met in Nachtmaal—half a religious ceremony, half a folk-gathering, when marriages were celebrated, babies were baptized, feuds were consummated and the square was cluttered with market stalls, tents and wagons. Into this symbolic spot, this kraal of the Boers, Sir Theophilus Shepstone confidently rode: and presenting himself to the President, who cautiously welcomed him as 'a friendly adviser', he presently set in train the extinction of the Republic.

Shepstone was soon able to persuade himself that most of the Boers wished to join the Empire again. 'Great majority of Boers,' he cabled Carnarvon, 'welcome change.' This was quite untrue. The vast majority of the Boers had not shifted their views about the British Empire since their forebears first escaped from it forty years before. The Transvaalers were, however, unprepared and divided; President Burgers was sick and weak; on April 12, 1877, the annexation of the South African Republic was declared. Shepstone's mounted policemen paraded smartly in Church Square, and Haggard himself ran the Union Jack up the Raadsaal flagstaff. The Volksraad was suspended. The President was pensioned off. Sir Garnet Wolseley arrived to assume the administration, proclaiming the Queen's will that the Transvaal should continue to be for ever an integral part of her dominions in South Africa—until, he added, warming to his theme, the River Vaal reversed its flow. Two generations after the Great Trek, the British had caught up with the last of the Voortrekkers.

4

At home the Liberals fiercely attacked the annexation. Gladstone, as leader of the Opposition, called the Transvaal a country 'where we have chosen most unwisely, I am tempted to say insanely, to place ourselves in the strange predicament of the free subjects of a monarchy going to coerce the free subjects of a republic'. The public, though, generally approved of the move, and Carnarvon was encouraged to proceed with further plans for federation. He appointed to the Governorship of Cape Colony Sir Bartle Frere, an eminent Anglo-Indian administrator, who would he hoped be the first Governor-General of the confederacy.

Frere was a bold and frank expansionist, and in Cape Town he enjoyed the advantages of remoteness. There was no cable from London yet, and telegrams had to come by steamer from the Cape Verde Islands, taking at least 16 days. The next move in the South African drama was accordingly all his own. Ignoring prohibitions from home, behaving as his dauntless predecessors might, long before in India, in January 1879 he carried things a stage further by ordering a British invasion of Zululand, another awkwardly independent segment in the patchwork of South African sovereignty.

The Zulus were still among the most alarming of the African peoples. Dingaan's grandson Cetewayo was king now: he had been crowned in 1873 by Shepstone himself, as representative of the Great White Queen, with an *ad hoc* crown like Cakobau's in Fiji. He himself was not a very military man, but his armies remained ferocious. Their system was based upon an effective combination of universal military service and obligatory blood-lust. No Zulu was considered to be a man until he had 'washed his spear in blood', and warriors of the Zulu army were compulsorily celibate until they had killed or wounded an enemy, which made for warlike men and sanguinary women. With their terrible feathered panoplies, the inexorable jog-trot of their advance, the scream and eerie hiss of their war-cries, and the massed black immensity of the impis, organized by age-groups and often 20,000 strong, in which they moved shield to shield across the grand landscape of Zululand, they were among the most spectacular of all the theatrical enemies the British empire felt itself obliged to fight. They had very few guns. They relied upon their heavy assegais, and upon simple tactical manoeuvres—in particular a double encircling movement, in which an enemy found itself, half-paralysed with terror like a hypnotized chicken, swamped by the mass of the Zulu frontal force ('the chest') while smaller racing impis ('the horns') swept behind to cut off their retreat.

The Zulus were splendid of appearance and very brave, and

there were Englishmen who swore by their integrity. Bishop Colenso was the most famous of Zuluphiles, but scattered throughout Zululand were English traders and missionaries whose lives were in Cetewayo's hands, and who found themselves treated fairly, even generously. Shepstone, who had lived much of his life among the Zulus, had a high opinion of their abilities: the English trader John Dunn had married into the Zulu royal family and become a Zulu chief himself, ruling over some 10,000 people and maintaining forty-nine wives.[1] But they were inconceivably bloodthirsty. To them as to the Ashanti, or to Speke's lion-stepping king of the Buganda, human life was scarcely sacrosanct. Death was part of the natural order, and could be hastened without degradation. Zulus who broke the kingdom's rigid social laws were ruthlessly tortured or killed, and captured enemies too found themselves lightly chopped about with assegais. The nation was like a vast black predator lurking in its downlands, now pouncing upon the Swazis or the Basutos, now threatening the British or the Boers. Everybody was scared of the Zulus, and the British in particular were nervous that some grand Zulu washing of the spears might trigger off a native rising throughout South Africa.

Frere had early reached the decision that this ferocious people must be subdued, if South Africa was to be ordered. Carnarvon had resigned in 1878, disagreeing with Disraeli's policies towards Russia, and his successor as patron of South Africa federation was Sir Michael Hicks Beach, a remote and ineffectual politician. Frere accordingly followed his own instincts. He used as his *casus belli* an old Boer-Zulu frontier dispute, which had been settled in Cetewayo's favour by a British commission of inquiry. The disputed land would only be handed over, he told the King, if the Zulus would disband their terrible armies, reform their draconian code of justice, and receive a British Resident at their capital, Ulundi. He demanded, in fact, the disbandment of the old Zulu order, and the abdication of

[1] His descendants are numerous in Zululand still, and are classed in the modern South African context as 'coloured'. I met Mr Stanley Dunn, a great-grandson of the original John, at Eshowe in 1970. He is a strikingly handsome man of great courtesy, and works as a mechanic in a Greek-owned bakery.

its military power. Such a demand was, of course, no surprise. Cetewayo must have expected it sooner or later; even Colenso recognized its inevitability, and approved the ultimatum. The Zulus were given thirty days to reply, and when no answer came, in January 1879 three columns of the British Army, 16,000 strong, crossed the northern frontier of Natal, and invaded Zululand.

Lord Chelmsford was the British commander in this, perhaps the best-known of the colonial wars, and many another military figure now familiar to us haunts the background of the drama—Butler, Buller, Colley, the ubiquitous Wolseley. Chelmsford was born Frederick Thesiger, of a family which had emigrated to England from Saxony a century before, and he had enjoyed a conventionally varied imperial career: in Canada, in India, in Ireland, in Abyssinia. He had married the daughter of an Indian Army general, had commanded at Aldershot, and was exceptional among the often choleric commanders of the day for his qualities of reticent tact and sympathy.

But tact and sympathy, alas, were the last qualities needed to crush the merciless Cetewayo, who had 50,000 men under arms, and who had once replied to a mild British protest about the frequency of executions in Zululand: 'Do not consider that I have done anything yet in the way of killing. . . . I have not yet begun; I have yet to kill; it is the custom of our nation and I shall not depart from it'. The fascination of the Zulu War is its confrontation of temperamental opposites, each fighting by their own military standards a war of text-book orthodoxy. If the Ashanti campaign was like an exhibition war, this was like a war in fiction, so wonderfully apposite were its settings, and so faithfully did its shape conform to dramatic unities. There were three memorable battles: each meant something different to the British, and together they composed a pattern of action that was to become almost compulsory in the later campaigns of the British Empire—the opening tragedy, the heroic redemption, the final crushing victory.

5

The tragedy was Isandhlwana. Setting off into the uplands of Zululand in the glorious stimulation of a South African January, Lord

Chelmsford meant to make this a quick war of attrition. He wanted to destroy the impis wherever they were, and with all the paraphernalia of the Victorian wars, the heavy guns and the traction engines and Hale's patent rockets, the great shire horses brought specially from England, the inescapable naval brigade, the customary cloud of locally recruited irregulars or militia-men, the worldly-wise columns of redcoats, he made straight for Ulundi, but hoped to meet and obliterate the main body of the Zulu army on the way. He himself commanded the central column of the force, entering Zululand at a crossing over the Buffalo River called Rorke's Drift, where an Irish farmer had built a store thirty years before, and where there was now a mission house. Ten miles beyond the ford the soldiers reached a level plain among the Nqutu Hills, and there, where the track ascended northwards towards a saddle in the ridge, they pitched camp.

This was Isandhlwana. It was a place of grim magnificence. Above the plain there arose a crook-backed mountain, whose outline was unmistakable, and could be seen crouching tawnily among the low surrounding ridges from far away across the downs. The plain itself, rising gently towards the peak, was enclosed by folded hills, pierced here and there by ravines to the wider flatlands beyond. A shallow stream ran across it, but gave no sparkle to the scene, and there were few trees to be seen—only the brown and shaly ground, the shadowed ridges all around, and the ominous crooked silhouette of the mountain above. Isandhlwana looked just what it proved to be: a killing ground. The British pitched camp there without laagering or entrenching, despite advice they had been given by the Boers, who knew all about Zulu wars. Instead pickets were posted, mounted vedettes were dispatched to the surrounding heights, and a guard was set on the saddle beside the peak, with a view up the track to the north.

There was no sign of the enemy on the night of January 20, but next day a reconnaissance force clashed with an impi to the north-west, and Chelmsford himself, hoping he might have found the main enemy force, marched off over the hill with about half his men. As a result almost all the others died: for while the general was away, on January 22, 1879, the main body of Cetewayo's army did indeed appear—some 20,000 warriors, pouring in a black and feathered mass over the Isandhlwana ridge, sweeping aside pickets and outposts as they advanced upon the plain. Most of the British soldiers had never seen Zulu fighting men before, and the experience was nightmarish. They were like people from another world. They wore ear-flaps of green monkey-skin, otter-skin headbands, high ostrich plumes—they carried shields covered with white hide, or red with white spots—they moved at a horrible changeless trot, rattling their assegais against their shields, hissing between their teeth, and shouting '*Usuthu! Usuthu!*'—Cetewayo's personal war-cry.

It was war of the most bestial kind. Thousands of Zulus died in the British rifle-fire, but nothing could stop them: when they reached the lines they slashed about them indiscriminately with their assegais, while the British fought desperately back with bayonets and rifle-butts. All over the plain isolated groups of redcoats were surrounded, helplessly struggling, by masses of feathered black men. Sometimes the Zulus threw their own dead in front of them to blunt the bayonets; the British, split, shattered and disorganized, fell back in twos and threes to wagons, or tents, or hid terrified among the field kitchens, or fought to the death all alone, bayoneting and bludgeoning to the last. Some ran away out of the camp circuit, stumbling down the track towards Rorke's Drift and safety, but when they crossed the southern ridge they found another force of Zulus waiting for them on the other side, and they were hunted down relentlessly, in and out of gulleys, across streams, crouching in scrub, hounded over cliffs or speared one by one as they fell in exhaustion beside the track.

When Chelmsford returned stunned to Isandhlwana that night, he found the camp a silent smoking ruin—a shamble of burnt wagons, broken tents, rubbish and corpses. The British dead had been disembowelled: most of the Zulus had been dragged away over the hills. Of the Europeans Lord Chelmsford had left in the camp, only fifty-five had escaped, and were now scattered somewhere between the battlefield and the Natal border. Six companies of the 2nd Warwickshire Regiment had been entirely obliterated: in all 858 Britons had died, together with some 470 men of the native levies. It was the worst disaster to British arms since the Afghan tragedy of 1842, and the news of it, reaching England three weeks later, plunged the nation into bewildered mourning. Disraeli took to his bed with depression, and the cause of imperialism suffered a distinct if temporary setback.[1]

6

But it was already a British practice to balance disaster with triumph —losing every battle but the last, it was popularly called. As a sustainer of morale it was wonderfully successful, and as a historic device it made wars much more interesting—Henry Knollys the historian observed of one rather too successful colonial war that 'the exploit was unaccompanied by reverse or blunder, and without these features it is in vain to hope for enthusiasm and interest'. Only a little triumph was necessary, to restore the nation's pride, and indeed no triumph could be much smaller than the second of the Zulu War battles, the defence of Rorke's Drift, which has gone into the language as a synonym of British heroism, and in which rather more than 100 Britons were involved (most of them Welshmen at that). As one contemporary poet wrote of this almost imperceptible success,

> *Her sons in gallant story,*
> *Shall sound old England's fame,*
> *And by fresh deeds of glory*
> *Shall keep alive her name;*
> *And when, above her triumphs,*
> *The golden curtains lift—*
> *Be treasured long, in page and song,*
> *The memory of Rorke's Drift.*

[1] Rider Haggard, still in Pretoria, heard of Isandhlwana strangely. On the morning of January 24 his Hottentot washerwoman told him that Cetewayo the king had killed hundreds of redcoats two days before—'they lie like leaves upon the plain—red winter leaves steeped in blood'. She would not say how she knew, and it was not until twenty hours later that the first messenger from Natal arrived at Pretoria with the news.

While the slaughter was proceeding at Isandhlwana, the post at Rorke's Drift, ten miles to the rear, was held by a company of the 24th Regiment under two subalterns, Lieutenant John Chard and Lieutenant Gonville Bromhead. They heard the gunfire of the battle up the track, and learnt of the disaster when the first terrified refugees arrived at the river bank opposite the little group of buildings —a few to join the Rorke's Drift garrison, the rest to career wildly past without stopping, back to the safety of Natal. It was plain that the impis, when they had obliterated the Isandhlwana camp, buried their dead and licked their wounds, would next fall upon the Drift, and hastily the two subalterns fortified their little command, intended only as a rear-station for Lord Chelmsford's advance, with sandbags, sacks of mealie and biscuit boxes. The three buildings lay in the flank of a hill, the Oskarberg; the Buffalo river ran, out of sight, about 100 yards away; from a short way up the track the silhouette of Isandhlwana mountain could be seen, with a wreath of smoke now rising ominously about it. The whole defensible area was hardly more than 100 yards square, and the garrison included a chaplain, five invalids, and a contingent of African levies.

Late in the afternoon of January 22, the same day as the Isandhlwana battle, lookouts on the Oskarberg saw impis approaching— one wing of the Isandhlwana force, perhaps 4,000 men—led by two chiefs on white horses, and moving in their fatal tireless rhythm towards the post. The Zulus had tactics but no strategy: if they had crossed into Natal they might have created havoc, but their killing instinct directed them blindly towards Rorke's Drift, where there was blood to be drawn. 'Here they come!' one of the British sentries cried as he raced down the hillside—'black as hell and thick as grass!' At their first glimpse of this terrible sight all the African levies abandoned their posts, vaulted the barricades and vanished: the 110 Britons left behind just had time to reorganize themselves around their perimeter when a thousand Zulus appeared around the flank of the Oskarberg and attacked the back of the post, while a moment later 3,000 more charged screaming from the front.

The action was immortalized in Britain in a painting by Elizabeth Butler, William Butler's celebrated wife. It was called *The Defence of Rorke's Drift*, and every Victorian knew it. There we see the little battle as the British public saw it, fact and legend interwoven. To the right is the burning thatched hospital, the core of the defence, through whose flimsy walls the wounded were dragged from room to room as the Zulus battered the doors down. On the left is the parapet of mealie sacks and biscuit tins, with the redcoats lunging with their bayonets into the sea of Zulus beyond, or returning the fire of the black snipers hidden on the Oskarberg above. The ground is littered with tins, helmets, assegais, scraps of material; centre-stage Lieutenant Chard draws attention to a gap in the defence; indefatigably the bearded barehead chaplain distributes comfort and ammunition to the soldiers; in the foreground a young man lies exhausted, or perhaps dead, with his topee pushed to the back of his head. The skyline is silhouetted with raised rifle-butts, bayonets, the outflung arm of a man just shot, the dim shapes of flying spears. The air, dark with gunsmoke, is speckled with sparks from the burning hospital roof. Dimly glimpsed on the left of the picture, like a black inchoate dream, are the contorted faces and brandished shields of the impis, dashing themselves wave after wave upon the post.[1]

All afternoon the Zulus attacked, and late into the night. The hospital was abandoned, and the perimeter contracted until the British, illuminated by the flames, crouched within the last corner of the yard. Then, gradually, the attack tailed off. The sniping ended, the hurled assegais grew fewer, the war-cries less urgent, until by four in the morning, when the hospital fire had burnt itself out and all was dark, silence too had fallen upon Rorke's Drift. When dawn came the British survivors, preparing themselves for their last hopeless stand, found that the impis had gone. Only a few wounded warriors were dragging themselves around the side of the mountain. All about the post the Zulu dead lay in their hundreds, some twitching still, and the area was littered with their eerie ornaments. At seven o'clock the impi briefly re-appeared, squatting. beyond rifle range and taking snuff in the morning sunshine: but the Zulus had suffered terribly in the battle, and presently, rising

---

[1] 'One more picture like this,' Butler told his wife, 'and you will drive me mad.' He was acquiring strongly anti-imperialist views now, and thought a battle between riflemen and spearmen no subject for art.

to their feet in a body, they trotted silently in a wide circle, well away from Rorke's Drift, down to the river and away.

7

Eleven heroes of Rorke's Drift were awarded the Victoria Cross, and the action was acclaimed as having restored the honour of England and saved Natal from invasion. Still the crowning victory was to come. Opinion at home, stunned by Isandhlwana, had been further shocked by the death of the Prince Imperial Louis Bonaparte, son of Napoleon III and a popular exile in Britain, who had gone to Zululand as an observer, and had been killed in an ambush. Disraeli's Government took the orthodox action to redress the situation, and called as if by instinct upon Sir Garnet Wolseley. The 'Only General' had been serving as Governor of Cyprus, recently acquired from the Turks: he was now summoned, like Cincinnatus from the plough, to proceed at once to South Africa as High Commissioner in Natal. Once there he was to take over the command from Lord Chelmsford and win the war.

Lord Chelmsford, however, was determined to win it for himself, and redeem his military reputation. He withdrew all his forces from Zululand for a fresh start, and six months later, just as Wolseley landed at Durban, a second invasion was launched, and Chelmsford was once more on his way to Ulundi. Nothing would stop him this time. His career was at stake, his blood was up, and he carefully sidestepped the instructions which pursued him sternly from the coast. 'I am astonished at not hearing from you', Wolseley told him peremptorily by heliograph. 'Acknowledge receipt of this message at once and flash back your latest moves'. But it was too late. Chelmsford was already on the wide plain outside the royal kraal at Ulundi, and the culminating battle was about to start.

This was the grand set-piece of the war, the all-British victory. The site was wide and dignified, the occasion momentous, the style of battle high-flown and traditional. Everyone was eager for a last settling of accounts—the 17th Lancers and the 1st Dragoon Guards, the 80th and 90th Regiments of Foot, the Frontier Horse, the Transvaal Rangers, the Natal Light Horse—5,000 men in all, including 900 cavalrymen, moving on to the Ulundi plain on the morning of July 4 in the classic British military formation, the hollow square. A band played the regimental marches as they moved. The regimental colours fluttered. Around the flanks the cavalrymen gleamed and jangled. It was a truly imperial spectacle.

The Zulus arose in their thousands from the bush, and attacked the square from all sides. The British fought back in the old way, four deep with fixed bayonets, with guns and Gatlings at each corner of the square. No biscuit tin barricades here, no laagers in the Boer style, no digging in—'they'll only be satisfied', Chelmsford said, thinking of armchair critics far away, 'if we beat them fairly in the open'. It was in fact a victory of symbolic completeness. The Zulus threw themselves suicidally upon the wall of rifle-fire, not a single warrior getting within thirty yards of the redcoats, and when the fury of the impis faltered, Chelmsford let loose the cavalry. Through a gap in the square there moved at a menacing trot the 17th Lancers, pennants streaming from their lances—gradually gaining momentum, to cheers from the square behind them, from a trot to a canter, from a canter to a gallop, into a violent pounding charge, irresistibly driving the Zulus before them, impaling them with lances, savaging them with sabres or simply trampling them underfoot, until not a warrior was left alive upon the open plain, and the way was clear to the sprawling kraal of mud huts, on the rising ground overlooking the battlefield, that was Cetewayo's capital. Lord William Beresford, 9th Lancers, who was on leave from his post as aide-de-camp to the Viceroy of India, galloped away from the field and jumped his horse clear over the surrounding barricade of thorn scrub to be the first Briton in Cetewayo's capital. It was deserted. The soldiers hoped to find hidden treasures among its huts, but all they discovered was a single silver snuff-box, a buried iron chest full of boot-brushes, and the makeshift crown with which, only six years before, Cetewayo had been crowned by Theophilus Shepstone.[1]

---

[1] The British held no grudge against the Zulus, whom they admired for their martial qualities—when Cetewayo visited England in 1882 he was lavishly feted, and inspired some affectionately ironic music-hall verse:

White young dandies, get away, O!
You are now 'neath beauty's ban;

8

Lord Wolseley presently fragmented Zululand into thirteen impotent chieftaincies, all under British suzerainty, and in theory the elimination of the Zulu power might have meant the success of Carnarvon's plans. Except for the quiescent Orange Free State, all South Africa was now under imperial control: and when in 1880 Disraeli's Government fell, to the consternation of the Boers and the surprise of the British electorate Mr Gladstone did nothing to liberate the Transvaal. In opposition he had thundered against annexation, in office he declared that confederation 'eclipses and absorbs every other consideration'. By this time the British administration in Pretoria was well established, at least in its own estimation, and Wolseley had reached the conclusion that the Boers would be reconciled to British rule by the sheer power of *fait accompli*. He devised a new constitution for them, depriving the burghers of any direct representation, and was so confident of success that by 1880 the imperial garrison in the Transvaal consisted only of three battalions—perhaps 3,000 fighting men, in a country larger than Britain.

But of course the more resolute of the Transvaalers were not reconciled to British rule at all. They had gone to the high veld specifically to evade it, and they were unlikely to accept it now. Pre-eminent among the dissidents was the former vice-president of the South African Republic, Paul Kruger. A man of singular power, perhaps of genius, at 55 Kruger was exceedingly ugly. He looked

---

Clear the field for Cetewayo,
He alone's the ladies' man.

The three battlefields of his war against the Empire remain much as they were—Isandhlwana especially, where the peak stands like a grim memorial obelisk, Zulu boys on donkeys tout lead balls and cartridge cases, Zulu women in high hats wander about with goats, and a haunted hush still seems to hang over the scene. At Ulundi a domed monument marks the site of the British square, and the thirteen men killed on the British side are buried on the spot—native auxiliaries well away from the rest.

exactly what he was—a Dopper of the most arid kind, living by the very syllables of the Old Testament, and subscribing to all the most fundamental of fundamentalist texts. As a child he had come northward with the Great Trek, and though by now he was getting fat and slow on his legs, he had been in his day a master of all the frontier crafts. He was a great hunter, horseman, guerilla fighter—it was he who had warned Chelmsford to use the laager system in Zululand, for though he did not love the British, he preferred them to Kaffirs. He had amputated his own thumb after a shooting accident, curing the resultant gangrene by plunging his hand into the warm stomach of a goat. He was a coarse man, a man of spittoons and pipe-smoke, home-spun philosophies on the stoep, religious bigotry: but so absolute were his principles, and so profound his sense of Afrikanerness, that he moved among his people like a prophet.

Kruger had assumed that the fall of Disraeli would mean the restoration of independence to the Transvaal. When Gladstone announced that 'our judgement is that the Queen cannot be allowed to relinquish her sovereignty over the Transvaal', he and his followers rebelled. The Zulu War had removed the danger of attack from Cetewayo; most of Chelmsford's troops had returned to Britain; Wolseley had been succeeded in Pietermaritzburg by a gentler High Commissioner, George Colley, now a knight and a major-general. On December 16, 1880, 4,000 burghers and their wives met at Paardekraal, some forty miles south-west of Pretoria, and ritually reconstituted the South African Republic. In the spirit of the Voortrekkers they elected Kruger and two others as governing triumvirate, and swore to live or die for independence: then one by one, in solemn ceremonial, each threw a stone upon a commemorative cairn—a mighty pile of stones which would stand in perpetual monument to their pledge.[1]

'I don't think,' Colley was told by his representative in Pretoria, 'that we shall have to do much more than show that we are ready and sit quiet.' The Boers were not only 'inflated toads', they were 'incapable of any united action, and . . . mortal cowards, so anything

---

[1] And still does, though the original pile was replaced by a more solid substitute in 1890. It remains one of the sacred sites of Afrikanerdom, standing as it does almost in the centre of the Rand goldfield.

they may do will be but a spark in the pan'. But on Dingaan's Day, 1880, the forty-third anniversary of the Boers' revengeful victory over Dingaan during the Great Trek, the Transvaalers rose to arms. Commandos seized the town of Heidelberg, sixty miles south of Pretoria, as a provisional capital, and besieged all the British forces, scattered as they were in seven impotent garrisons throughout the Transvaal. Four days later blood was shed. Only thirty-six miles from Pretoria a Boer force ambushed a column of the Connaught Rangers, one of the most famous of all imperial regiments. The soldiers were straggling cheerfully along a road eating peaches they had bought at the last halt, their heavy gear in ox-wagons and mule-carts, their colonel benevolent on a white horse, their band playing *Kiss me Mother, kiss your darling daughter*—

> *Lean my head upon your breast,*
> *Fold your loving arms around me,*
> *I am weary, let me rest.* . . .

They marched at ease, many of the soldiers having thrown their rifles into the wagons, and their four mounted scouts ambled beside them, chatting. On the morning of December 20, as they approached a watercourse called Bronkhorst Spruit ('Watercress Creek'), a Boer horseman galloped out of a thicket and handed the colonel a note. It was an ultimatum. The Transvaal was now a Republic again, it said, and the movement of foreign troops was forbidden. If the British column did not within two minutes agree to turn back, they would be attacked. When the colonel rejected the ultimatum, and the regimental band defiantly struck up *God Save The Queen*, a devastating fire was opened upon the column from the rising ground about. In a matter of moments 57 of the British were dead and more than 100 wounded, 20 of them mortally. All the officers were killed or wounded. The average number of wounds was five per man. The Boers, Kruger announced, were 'bowed down in the dust before Almighty God who has stood by them, and with a loss of over 100 of the enemy allowed only two of ours to be killed'. The British were buried where they fell, and the peach stones in their pockets, so it was said, presently grew into a sad line of trees.

9

No retributive British victory was to rescue the imperial prestige in this, the first Boer War. It was ignominy from start to finish. The British troops in the Transvaal were unable to move out of their garrison towns, the British administrators were besieged in Pretoria, and the whole of the rest of the country was soon back in Boer hands. The Boers, who had seemed so cowardly and disunited, and who numbered only 7,000 fighting men, proved to be guerrilla fighters of disconcerting skill: the British Army, facing its first European enemy since the Crimea, blundered on from complacency to despair, never winning a battle. The whole war lasted only three months, and its culminating episode provided one of the saddest and most evocative names of the imperial story: Majuba.

Majuba Hill marked the border between Natal and Transvaal, where the road from Pietermaritzburg to Pretoria wound its way through the Drakensberg over the frontier pass called Laing's Nek. It was most beautiful country, green, fresh and rolling, to the south the lush and fertile plains of Natal, to the north the high veld—country rather like Wales, except for the lizards, the exotic flowers and the piping of unfamiliar birds. The grass grew springy to the foot, the air shone, the light was crystal clear. Against this delectable background Majuba Hill stood unmistakable, as distinctive as Isandhlwana itself. It rose massively flat-topped above the pass, and could be seen from far across the Natal border like a sentry guarding the inner fastness of Afrikanerdom. Majuba was 6,000 feet high, but looked higher, and had a majestic if brooding presence.

Almost as soon as the Transvaal rebellion began, Sir George Colley, who was Commander-in-Chief as well as High Commissioner in South-East Africa, set off from Natal with a scratch army to relieve the beleaguered British garrisons in the Transvaal. He had 1,200 soldiers, mostly young short-service soldiers recruited under Cardwell's system, together with a naval brigade of 120 men drawn from warships that happened to be in Durban harbour, but he never reached the Transvaal. On the Natal side of Laing's Nek his soldiers were twice humiliated by the Boers, using their revolutionary guerilla tactics of individual rifle fire, and by the last week of February the British were bogged down helplessly among the kopjes, having already lost 300 men. There now arrived at the border, however, reinforcements sent from India, and almost at the same time General Colley conceived the idea of capturing the summit of Majuba Hill.

It was a perfect site for epic. It was so symmetrical, its summit so bare and flat, its wide African prospect so magnificent, that it might have been reserved for a spectacle of war: but just why Colley chose to occupy it as a military objective, nobody really knows. Perhaps he thought the mere presence of the British up there would demoralize the Boers around the pass below. Perhaps he thought vaguely of emulating Wolfe's coup at Quebec. Some say he was 'not himself'. He took no guns or rockets with him; he disclosed no plan to his officers; he dug no trenches; he simply took the hill, theatrically, almost as an end in itself.

He was not the apoplectic incompetent later legend would make him. An Anglo-Irishman, he had taught himself Russian, was interested in chemistry, and was widely experienced, having served in the Cape, in China, in the Ashanti war, and as private secretary to the Viceroy of India. But he was also a kind, sensitive and imaginative man, who took his water-colour sketch-book wherever he went, and whose heavily bearded soldier's face was given grandeur by a dreamy look to the eyes. His approach to war was knightly. 'Sir,' he wrote to the Boer commander whose men had lately decimated his own at Laing's Nek, 'I . . . write to offer you medical assistance for your wounded should you not have skilled assistance at hand . . . I can either send a surgeon to any place you name or, if you will send any bad cases into our hospital here or at Newcastle they will receive the same attention and care as our own wounded.' To his soldiers, indeed, he sometimes seemed too nice a man for generalship. 'A more charming and courteous man you could not meet,' one of them wrote of him, 'but he ought not to be trusted with the corporal's guard.'

Colley had a presentiment about Majuba, and perhaps in taking the hill he was pursuing less a tactical than an aesthetic fulfilment.

His little assault force, about 400 strong, climbed the precipitous southern slope of the mountain during the night of February 26, 1881, and when dawn broke on the summit, and veld and mountain, sunshine and cloud were laid in tribute at their feet, so exhilarated were they that they stood silhouetted on the edge of the plateau to jeer at the Boer encampments far below. How right it must have seemed to Colley, with his eye for landscape and occasion! And when, almost effortlessly, the Boers came storming up the northern slope of the mountain, the easy slope, to fall upon the British in broad daylight, how fitting the death of the general himself, a bullet through his head, stretched out there on the mountain grass as though in alabaster!

The scale was very small—the summit plateau of Majuba was perhaps half a mile around. There was no room for manoeuvre, only for advance or retreat. The only cover was provided by shallow folds in the ground and by a slight hollow where the field hospital was established, and where many of the British soldiers, after their exhausting night climb, promptly went to sleep. It was a curious force assembled up there, under the command of that strange and gentle general—who seemed to move, once they were on the summit, in a kind of trance. There was the young Ian Hamilton, a man very much in Colley's mould, who was to become a general himself, and preside over still sadder sequences of British military history. There was poor Hector Macdonald, 'Scotland's Pride', who was to rise from private to general only to shoot himself in a Paris hotel when accused of homosexuality. There were 170 men of the Gordon Highlanders fresh from victories in Afghanistan, 340 more of the 58th and 60th regiments, and sixty-four bluejackets from the cruiser *Boadicea*—men dressed in all the bright panoply of the imperial wars, the scarlet jackets, the kilts, the white tropical helmets, the blue trousers, the pipe-clayed pouches—splashing the green plateau with colour, while the tall figure of the general wandered immaculate and bemused among them.

'All I ask of you', Colley said, 'is that you hold this hill three days', but they only held it until half-past one. The Boers came up that morning. Dismounting from their ponies below the crest of the hill, they climbed up undetected and opened fire at point-blank range.

In little more than half an hour the redcoats, so cock-a-hoop that morning, cracked in disorder. The terrified men on the perimeter, retreating across the plateau, infected the men behind with their panic, until the survivors of the little force threw themselves down the mountain again and ran away. One Boer was killed in this brief action, and five were wounded: 280 Britons were killed, wounded or captured. General Colley, slowly turning to follow his soldiers off the hill, was among the last to die.

It was rumoured that he had killed himself, and perhaps he did. Would he have wanted to live, haunted by such ignominy? Would not a shot in the head, as the catastrophe descended, perfectly have fitted the Wagnerian drama he had directed? Majuba was a kind of abdication from the start. It was a flamboyant admission of failure —for possession of the hill without artillery could really achieve nothing—by a commander without the magic gift of victory. 'Think lovingly and sadly,' Colley had written to his wife the evening before, 'but not too sadly or hopelessly of your affectionate husband.'[1]

10

Majuba proved an abdication in a wider sense, too. The news reached London the following day, by a new submarine cable from the Cape, and the War Office at once resolved to send further reinforcements to South Africa from India, Ceylon, Bermuda and Britain, and to appoint Sir Frederick Roberts, one of the Empire's most successful generals, to succeed Colley. But Gladstone thought otherwise, and in another unpredictable volte-face, he immediately opened peace negotiations with the Boers, to the contempt of the Conservatives and the dismay of the Queen. The first talks were held in O'Neill's Farm, a small farmstead at the foot of Majuba Hill, and there in the shadow of defeat the war was ended, humiliatingly for the British, who had not won a single engagement, triumphantly for the Boers, who understandably reached the conclusion that the

[1] A slab marks the spot where he died, on the summit of the hill, and his soldiers are buried near him. Majuba is the most moving battle-field I know, and its summit can be reached by an agreeable climb up the route the Boers took, from the village of Volksrust—'People's Rest', named for the relief given the Boer people by the victory on the hill.

Empire was much easier to deal with when it had just suffered a bloody nose. It was the only occasion in the history of Victoria's Empire when the British negotiated a peace settlement from the losers' side of the table. The Transvaal recovered its independence, subject only to a debatable reservation called 'the suzerainty of Her Majesty', and three years later the Transvaal Republic was constituted with Kruger as its President. So the Trekker Boers, who had strived so assiduously for half a century to evade the rule of the red-necks, finally established their independence of the British Empire's sometimes arrogant, often complacent, but fundamentally humane system of values.

With the Transvaal went the last hope of voluntary confederation in South Africa. If the mixed bag of colonies, protectorates and Boer Republic were ever to be united now, it would only be by *force majeur*, British or Boer. South Africa lapsed into tawdry opportunism, as the values of the diamond fields, the colonial politicians and the entrepreneurs overwhelmed the ideals of the imperial visionaries: and in 1887 the discovery of gold on the Witwatersrand not only set a seal upon this squalor, but also made Kruger's petty backwoods republic, where the predikants read Ezekiel so gravely on their stoeps, and the President himself was often to be seen sitting on his bench beside the road in Pretoria, one of the most fateful nations on earth.

The story of Britain's efforts to master South Africa was not ended yet: but a few seers already understood that the ultimate conflict down there, the true meaning of the Great Trek, Ulundi and Majuba Hill alike, was not mere imperialism, but was a more passionate, profound and terrible dispute between the white man and the coloured—the very dispute which, in the long run, was to shatter the precarious logic of Empire itself.

CHAPTER TWENTY-THREE

The End of the Tasmanians

EMPIRE *was* Race. For an illustration of this truth at its cruellest and most poignant, let us see what happened to the aboriginal people of Tasmania, when they fell beneath the aegis of Victoria's Empire.

For many years after the European discovery of Australia, nobody realized that Tasmania was an island. To the early navigators it seemed only a protrusion from the south-east corner of the continent, and it was assumed that its flora and fauna would be more or less the same as the rest. Yet it was in many ways a particularly insular island, with a character all its own: a hilly island, about the size of Ceylon, covered in dense forests of pine, beech and eucalyptus, sometimes so thickly interwoven with creepers that a man could walk suspended on a web of foliage far above the ground. In the east there was fine rolling downland, in the west impenetrable forests fell away from the central mountains in gorges and fjords to the sea. The climate was wet but fresh, rather like Britain's: and there were some corners of the island that looked astonishingly like northern Europe—Ireland especially, in the fertile but somehow melancholy spaces of upland, or the empty coves along the eastern shore.

Most of the weird marsupials of the Australian mainland were present in Tasmania: kangaroos and wallabies in countless herds, duck-billed platypi, the black swans which, loitering strangely in the creeks of the south-east, sometimes gave the landscape an inverted look, like a photographic negative. But there were also creatures found nowhere else. There was the Tasmanian mountain shrimp, which lived only in the high mountain pools of the island, and the huge Tasmanian crayfish, and the minute Tasmanian pigmy opossum, and the Tasmanian water-hen, and the Tasmanian yellow wattle bird. There was the Tasmanian Devil, which looked like a venomous long-haired bear, and the Tasmanian Tiger, which looked like a great striped dog, walked on its toes, made a noise half-way between a bark and a miaow, carried its babies backwards in a pouch beneath its stomach, and could open its jaws so wide that at full stretch they formed almost a straight line top to bottom.

And strangest of all there existed, shadowy among the ferns and gum-trees, a race of human beings altogether unique, different ethnically and culturally from the aboriginals of the Australian mainland, and living, in their secluded forest encampments, or crouched over wood-fires on shellfish shores, lives unaffected by contact with any other men and women than themselves. From the moment these people first set eyes upon an Englishman, they were doomed.

2

Natural Selection had been a popular thesis among the English long before Darwin, for the idea of being a superior people was deeply ingrained in their history. Familiarity with the Scots, the Welsh and the Irish had long bolstered their sense of specialness, and their insular status, their religion, their continuity and their success all went to confirm it. As long before as the 1640s, it is said, a New England assembly of overseas Britons had passed the following resolutions: (1) The Earth is the Lord's and the fullness thereof. *Voted*. (2) The Lord has given the earth or any part of it to his chosen people. *Voted*. (3) We are his chosen people. *Voted*. By mid-Victorian times these assumptions, warped by the theories of racialists like the Comte de Gobineau, and apparently supported by the hazily understood principles of Darwinism, were most virulently translated into colour prejudice: 'the contempt and aversion', as Sir James Stephen had described it, 'with which the European races everywhere regard the black races'.

At heart, by now, nearly every Briton considered as his organic inferior everyone who was not white—the less white, the more inferior. Even educated people seldom bothered to hide their racial prejudices, and soldiers and working men expressed their views frankly enough in bawdy song or disrespectful nickname.[1] The British in India scornfully assessed half-castes in monetary terms—eight annas in the rupee, or ten annas in the rupee. The British in Hong Kong talked to all Chinese in a kind of baby-talk—'Here, boy, take piecey mississy one piecy bag topside'.[2] If a coloured man was ever honoured by the British, or even treated as an equal, it was because he was notorious (like Cetewayo) or very rich (like the Indian maharajahs) or a credit to the Empire (like the black Bishop Crowther of West Africa).

The British were not often physically cruel. They were more generally unsympathetic, or misunderstanding, or contemptuous, while the experience of the Mutiny made them congenitally suspicious.[3] They were also terribly aloof, sometimes deliberately, sometimes through shyness, even those who took a scholarly interest in the subject peoples generally inspecting them with a strictly anthropological detachment.[4] These attitudes were not, it seemed, a matter of personal choice, but of national destiny, to which even other white peoples could not equally aspire. Both the King of Prussia and the King of the Belgians had offered troops to help

[1] Of which my favourite is 'Beetle-fuck', the East Indiamen's nickname for the Arabian coffee town of Bait-al-Fakih. Other agreeable examples are 'Sam Coilinson', which is what the soldiers called the Chinese general San-ko-lin-sin in the China war of 1860—a predecessor of the well-known Soviet general Tim O'Shenko—and 'Mr Radish and Mr Gooseberry', the Hudson's Bay Company's eponyms for the French explorers Radisson and Groseilliers. When a Bombay plutocrat named Radah Moonee erected a public drinking fountain in Regent's Park, London, the grateful British public neatly christened him Mr Ready Money.

[2] But the Chinese in particular sometimes answered in kind. 'The dispatch written on this occasion,' declared the Chinese authorities in answer to a British ultimatum in 1860, 'is in most of its language too insubordinate and extravagent for the Council to discuss its propositions more than superficially. For the future the British Minister must not be so wanting in decorum. . . .'

[3] 'I never did hold with foreigners,' Harold Nicolson's housekeeper told him in 1940, complaining about aliens sheltering in the London underground during the blitz. 'My father was an Indian Mutiny veteran and always warned me against them since I was a child.'

[4] It was only in 1911 that the India Museum, now part of the Victoria and Albert Museum, first acquired an Indian artifact for its artistic merit.

suppress the Indian Mutiny, and Napoleon III had suggested that British reinforcements for India might travel through French territory, but all three offers Lord Palmerston had rejected, for he believed it was a British duty, a British privilege perhaps, to settle the account of 'those dark coloured Miscreants'.

Only the humanitarians of Empire tried to believe that the races were fundamentally equal, and even they had sometimes to admit that, in God's mysterious way, the evidence was against them. The British were approaching their apogee as a nation—as a Race, they liked to say. They went critical, so to speak: and though the whole world was to sense the fall-out of this event, the heaviest radiation fell upon the black, brown and yellow peoples, who now seemed to the British more than ever humans of the second class.

3

Nobody knows how many of the original Tasmanians existed when, in 1642, Abel Tasman discovered the island. There were probably not more than a few thousand, and since they were nomadic hunters, there were no permanent settlements at all. The Tasmanians never built a village, let alone a town: generally the only traces they left of themselves were the middens to be found here and there along their hunting-routes.

Equally nobody knows where they had come from in the first place. Victorian anthropologists much enjoyed 'the Tasman problem', and spent many happy evenings debating possible migratory routes, or ethnic progenitors. Since the Tasmanians were unquestionably distinct from the mainland natives, it was assumed that they had originated somewhere in the north or central Pacific, and had worked their way southwards over the millennia. They were smallish but long-legged people, red-brown rather than black, with beetle-brows, wide mouths, broad noses, and very deep-set brown eyes. The men had rich beards and whiskers, and the women were hirsute too, often developing incipient moustaches. Many Europeans found them unattractive. Mrs Augustus Prinsep, writing in 1833, thought they all had a 'most hideous expression of countenance', and George Lloyd, thirty years later, found the women 'repulsively ugly'. To modern tastes, if we are to judge by surviving photographs, they might not seem so disagreeable: they look homely, but oddly wistful, like elves, or perhaps hobbits—there is something very endearing to their squashed-up crinkled faces, which never seem actually to be smiling, but look suggestively amused all the same.

The Tasmanians did not by and large wear any clothes, except for loose cloaks of kangaroo skin, but they smeared their bodies with red ochre, and wore necklaces of shells or human bones. They slept in caves or hollow trees, or beneath rough windbreaks of sticks and fronds, and their staple foods were kangaroos and wallabies, supplemented by shellfish, roots and berries, fungi, lizards, snakes, penguins, herons, parrots and the eggs of ants and emus. Physically they seem to have lacked stamina: their senses were uncannily acute, and they were adept at running on all fours, but they were not very strong, nor very fast, nor even particularly agile. They made crude boats of bark or log, but never ventured far out to sea: instead they roamed incessantly, pursuing the fugitive marsupials, through the dense bush forests of their island, over its wide downlands, or down to the shingle shore to eat oysters.

A touching sadness surrounds them, from our distance of time. They seem an insubstantial people. Polygamous by custom, they were affectionate by disposition, and merry, singing in a sweet Doric harmony, and dancing strenuous, hilarious and frequently lascivious animal dances. But living down there on the edge of the world, they seem to have been on the edge of reality too. Their small tribal bands seldom strayed outside their own hunting circuits, and they inhabited a little inconstant world of a few families. If they met another tribe they generally fought it, but the moment a man on either side was killed, the battle ended. If they had a religion at all, it was concerned only with local sprites and goblins: few had any conception of an after-life. Some were apparently able to count up to five, others never went further than two. Their only system of government seems to have been a patriarchal authority tacitly invested in the head of a family, or the bravest hunter of a tribe. Their only visual art consisted of rings chipped out of boulders, and striped patterns in red ochre. Even their language was rudimentary, being a series of disconnected words with no grammar.

This is one of their dancing-songs, in a Victorian missionary translation:

> *It's wattle blossom time,*
> *It's spring-time.*
> *Bird whistle.*
> *The birds are whistling.*
> *Spring come,*
> *Spring has come.*
> *Cloud sun,*
> *The clouds are all sunny.*
> *Bird whistle,*
> *The birds are whistling.*
> *Dance.*
> *Everything is dancing.*
> *Spring-time.*
> *Because it's spring-time.*
> *Dance.*
> *Everything is dancing.*
> *Luggarato, Luggarato, Luggarato*
> *—Spring, Spring, Spring.*
> *Because it's spring-time.*

Luggarato, Luggarato, Luggarato! There was a haunting naïvety to the Tasmanians. They lived all by themselves, like children in the woods, and they seem to have thought of life as essentially provisional. The old and the sick they often abandoned, when they moved on to new hunting grounds. When somebody died he was usually cremated without ceremony, the tribe seldom staying to watch him burn: or he was placed upright inside a hollow tree, with a spear through his neck to keep him there.

And when a man was gone, he was gone. His name was never mentioned again. It was as though, having lived his short hard life of wandering, having fathered his sons and eaten his feasts of parrot or emu egg—having appeared briefly upon the foreshore of the world, his life had been expunged retrospectively, and he had never existed at all.

4

Once it was realized that Tasmania was an island, it acquired a peculiar usefulness to the British. It would form a convenient out-station, they thought, to their penal settlements on the Australian mainland, so sending a group of convicts and soldiers to the south-east corner of the island, in 1803 they had claimed it all for the Crown. By the 1820s there were European settlements at both ends of the island, called in those days Van Diemen's Land, and by 1840 there were more free settlers than convicts. A fine road connected Cornwall in the north with Buckingham in the south, by way of Melton Mowbray, Bagdad and Mangalore, and many free settlers were living in distinctly gentlemanly style in those substantial country houses we have already visited. Yet the basis of its society was punitive: this was a place of exile, a criminal island, and its life was organized around the fulcrum of its penal purpose. In a sug-gestive way it remained so throughout the century. Though trans-portation to Tasmania ended in 1853, much the most compelling sight in the island remained the celebrated penal settlement of Port Arthur, on the Tasman Peninsula in the south.

This had never been the severest of the several prisons. The worst, abandoned in 1832, had been at Macquarie Harbour, on the in-accessible west coast, where the prison buildings stood on a reef unapproachable by land except at low tide, and recalcitrant convicts were sometimes confined alone for weeks at a time on uninhabited rocks in the estuary: the hinterland there was so terrible that of the 112 prisoners who ever escaped from Macquarie Harbour, 62 died of starvation in the bush and nine were eaten by their comrades. Port Arthur, though, was much larger and better-known, and was a famous sight almost from the start—a railway used to take official visitors part of the way down the peninsula from Hobart, the capital, its trucks being pushed along by manacled convicts.

The first thing one saw was the square English tower of the inter-denominational church, looking rooky and rural, surrounded by English elms and oaks, and by the neat verandahed houses of the Governor and his assistants. Just around the corner, however, beyond a discreet stretch of green with an ornamental fountain, the granite buildings of the prison were grouped with a terrible dignity beside their harbour. Here was the watchtower, around whose ramparts the sentries perpetually tramped, and here the flogging-wall, and here the lunatic asylum. In the building called the Model Prison were practised the latest techniques of criminal reform, imported direct from Pentonville: notably the silence system—a system so absolute that the warders wore felt slippers, and prisoners were held in such utter lonely silence that even in church they wore masks to preserve their isolation from humankind, and worshipped in single shuttered cubicles. All the buildings were grey, and a grey suspense hung over the scene like a vapour, even on a bright summer morning, when the visitors walked bonneted and cotton-frocked from block to block, led by an attentive officer.

Port Arthur was starkly insulated from the rest of Tasmania, guard posts with dogs watching the narrow spit, Eaglehawk Neck, which was the only land approach to the peninsula; but the very presence of the settlement there, with its hundreds of helpless men numbed or animalized in despair, pervaded the whole of the island, and doubtless made society everywhere else coarser by the experience of it. Many of the settlers outside were themselves emancipated convicts—very few of those freed in the Australian settlements ever went back to Britain. Nearly all the others employed convict servants. When food ran short in the early days of the settlement, convicts were allowed to go into the bush to forage for themselves: some became bush-rangers or bandits, founded a desperado tradition, and graduated often enough to be the romantic heroes of local legend. They lived with the symptoms of imprisonment—the chain gangs and the clank of irons, the terrible rumours of torture, insanity and suicide: in Hobart convict women could sometimes be seen wearing iron collars padlocked around their necks, with long iron prongs protruding each side like the horns of cattle. Society was polarized between an authoritarian establishment on the one hand and a huge criminal population on the other, and at either extreme was instinct with violence. A coat of arms suggested for the colony in 1852 was defined in rhyming heraldics as 'Two posts standant, One beam crossant, One rope pendant, One knave on the end on't', and sensitive visitors to Tasmanian homes were sometimes chilled to remember, as they sat among the samplers, the Chelsea figures, the auntly water-colours and the grand-fatherly cricket groups, that men in chains built those amiable English houses, prisoners milked the cows in those fresh white-washed dairies, and that the little daughters of the family, demure in pantaloons and hair-ribbons, were growing up in the intimate knowledge of whip and manacle.

5

Inevitably this harsh community, gradually spreading from its seashore settlements, came into contact with the elusive aboriginals of the forest. It was known from the start that they were there. When Tasman, the island's discoverer, arrived off the south-east coast in 1642, his crew heard 'certain human sounds' and 'sounds resembling the music of a trump or small gong'. In 1777 Captain Cook found the natives trustful and unafraid, while the Frenchmen of Nicholas Baudin's expedition, in 1802, seem to have been enchanted by them. 'The gentle confidence of the people in us, the affectionate evidences of benevolence which they never ceased to manifest towards us, the sincerity of their demonstrations, the frankness of their manners, the touching ingenuousness of their caresses, all concurred to excite within us sentiments of the tenderest interest'. The Europeans felt no threat from such guileless primitives: the aborigines thought the peculiar pale strangers might be the ghosts of their own dead, and perhaps welcomed their appearance as a break in the immemorial monotony of hunt, sex and corroboree.

But when the British settled in Tasmania, the relationship changed. Almost at once the original Tasmanians were defined as enemies, actual or potential, and found themselves treated more and more as predators or vermin. The free settlers wanted land, and ruthlessly drove the nomads from their seasonal hunting-grounds. The shifting riff-raff of bushrangers and sealers used the black people as they pleased, for pleasure or for bondage. By the 1820s horrible things were happening in Tasmania. Sometimes the black people were hunted just for fun, on foot or on horseback. Sometimes they were raped in passing, or abducted as mistresses, or as slaves. The sealers of the Bass Strait islands established a slave society of their own, with harems of women, employing the well-tried disciplines of slavery—clubbing, stringing up from trees, or flogging with kangaroo-gut whips. We hear of children kidnapped as pets or servants, of a woman chained up like an animal in a shepherd's hut, of men castrated to keep them off their own women. In one foray seventy aboriginals were killed, the men shot, the women and children dragged from crevices in the rocks to have their brains dashed out. Bushrangers used to catch aborigines in man-traps, and use them for target practice. A man called Carrotts, desiring a native woman, decapitated her aboriginal husband, hung his head around her neck, and drove her home to his shack.

It is true of course that these horrors were committed by white men of the lowest sort, many of them criminals. Even so, it was not long before almost the entire European community behaved little better towards the aborigines. The black people, in their turn, understandably responded with violence. Gone were those sentiments of tender interest. 'I well know that these undiscriminating savages,' wrote Governor Collins in a report to his superior on one fracas, 'will consider every white man their Enemy.' He was right. Despised, debased and brutalized themselves, their numbers precipitously declining, now they were often the aggressors. Stockmen were murdered. Cattle were speared. Farms were burnt. In 1827 the natives actually raided Launceston, the second town of the island.

It did not take long for the white community to convince itself that the Europeans were the aggrieved party, and soon the classic settler-native syndrome was far advanced. The gentlemen in their country houses, the rich merchants in their Hobart mansions, the local administrators preoccupied with penal affairs and orderly government—all were reaching the conclusion that life in Tasmania would be much happier if there were no Tasmanians. In language the decrees of Authority remained irreproachable, and frequently warned the colonists that they must not mistreat the natives. In intent they became ever less tolerant. The Reverend Thomas Atkins, after a visit to Van Diemen's Land in 1837, usefully rationalized the attitude in Christian terms. It was a universal law in the Divine Government, he explained, that when savage tribes came into collision with civilized races of men, the savages disappeared. This was because they had not complied with the divine conditions for survival—'For God blessed them, and God said unto them, "Be fruitful and multiply, and replenish the earth and subdue it". '

6

Authority could not sanction the extermination of the natives. Public opinion in England would never stomach genocide. As one Whitehall directive observed, 'the adoption of any line of conduct having for its avowed or for its secret object the extinction of the native race could not fail to leave an indelible stain on the character of the British Government'. Anyway, God would doubtless arrange such a consummation in his own time—'it is not unreasonable to apprehend that the whole race of these people may at no distant period become extinct'. Meanwhile, what could be arranged with a clear conscience was the removal of the entire race somewhere else. There were several suitable lesser islands around the Tasmanian coast, and extensive unsettled tracts of mainland too. 'Really it is high time', remarked the *Launceston Adviser* one day, 'they were either removed out of the Island, or driven by force of arms to the uninhabited districts"

But first they had to be found. By now they could be counted in hundreds rather than thousands, but they were a slippery will-of-the-wisp people, moving dappled through the eucalyptus groves, or blending indistinguishably with the seashore rocks. Unsuccessful attempts were made to lure them into Hobart and the paternal arms of Government: in 1830 it was decided that they must be flushed, like game upon some vast estate, methodically from their nests, and beaten before an inescapable cordon mile by mile down the length of the island into the Tasman peninsula at the bottom. There they would be rounded up and taken away to convenient reservations for ever.

Colonel George Arthur, the Governor, himself assumed command of the operation, and planned the cordon—'the Black Line'— on the most orthodox military principles. He called upon every farm to send an able-bodied volunteer, he conscripted ticket-of-leave men, and he mustered the three regiments of redcoats available on the island. In all some 2,500 men were engaged. In case the settlers took the operation too frivolously—some of them were after all accustomed to chase aboriginals in innocent blood-sport—the Government publicly warned the participants that it was 'not a matter of amusement or recreation, but a cause of the most important and serious kind, in which the lives and property of the whole community are more or less at stake'. Martial law was proclaimed against the native population, and Arthur himself, ordering his charger saddled, rode away from Hobart to lead his soldiers into action.

It was perhaps the most farcical campaign in the whole history of British imperial arms. The plan called for a steady advance on a front that began by being 120 miles wide, but would narrow in the course of the action until its two flanks were united like a noose in the peninsula. No man was to be farther than sixty yards from his neighbour, and strict military precepts prevailed. Dispatches were sent back to Hobart by equerry; requisitions were signed for ammunition, food, clothing and 300 pairs of manacles; when a sceptical civilian expressed doubts to one officer about the scheme, 'Oh', the colonel replied, 'this is an entirely military manoeuvre, which you as a civilian would not understand'.

Sometimes they did see an aborigine—once they briefly glimpsed a party of forty. More often they mistook clumps of trees, or black swans, or the rustle of leaves, or kangaroos, for the presence of the black people. For seven weeks the Black Line struggled down the island in increasing confusion, soaked through by incessant rains, its clothes wet and torn, its rations inadequate, its whereabouts distinctly uncertain, its soldiers and volunteers chiefly interested, after a week or two of this discomfort, in getting themselves dry, fed and settled at the next bivouac. When at last they closed upon Eaglehawk Neck, assuming that a mass of black fugitives must be moving somewhere before them into the trap of the peninsula, they found nobody there at all. Not a single aboriginal had crossed the Neck. Like ghosts the black people had slipped through the cordon, crouching in brambles while the soldiers stumbled past, or scuttling away on all fours into the shadows. The final assessment of the operation showed that while four British soldiers had been accidentally killed in the course of it, only two of the original Tasmanians had been caught. One was a small boy, and the other very soon escaped.

7

Now there enters our story a resolute evangelical, George Augustus Robinson, 'The Conciliator', whose destiny it was to organize, when all else had failed, the disappearance of the Tasmanian race from the face of the earth.

Robinson was a Londoner, a non-conformist builder who had emigrated to Van Diemen's Land with his wife and seven children, and become well-known for his good works on the Hobart waterfront. He was in all ways a man of his time, a Dickensian figure transplanted from *Hard Times* or *Dombey and Son* to these incongruous environments. He was infinitely pious, humourless and indefatigable—a thick-set, red-haired, florid man, whom one can imagine running some particularly grim and improving school for indigent waifs on the outskirts of Manchester, or perhaps supervising, with Mrs Robinson of course, a reformatory for London harlots. He was an uneducated man and correspondingly dogmatic, and his bent was for redemption.

He had entered the Government service as an intermediary with the natives. Out he would go into the bush, with his couple of servants, his Bible pack, and a tame native woman, Black Moll, dressed up in gay ribbons to attract attention—they called her Robinson's decoy duck. He learnt the aboriginal language, and over many months of wanderings throughout the island he had made contact with most of the surviving tribes, and gained the confidence of many. He approached the natives kindly, often entertaining them upon his flute, and sometimes spending weeks at a time in their company: for he knew that God had called him to save them from their sinful ways, and lead them towards the truth.

This was the man to whom a baffled Government, after the fiasco of the Black Line, turned for an alternative solution. Robinson willingly accepted the charge. He undertook to persuade all the surviving Tasmanians out of the bush and into Government control, and almost single-handed he succeeded. For five years he came and went, sometimes by boat around the coast, generally on foot with a little band of native helpers—notably Truganini, a redeemed sealer's mistress, who was to become the most celebrated Tasmanian of all. Each year he brought out a few more aboriginals—63 in 1832, 42 in 1833, 28 in 1834—until at last there were none left in the bush at all, and the whole Tasmanian population, an entire race of human beings, was safely in the care of authority.

Robinson had approved for their final destination Flinders Island, in the Bass Strait, some forty miles north of Tasmania, and in January 1832 the first of the expatriates were shipped there. The *Hobart Town Courier*, whose reporter watched one party embark, declared that the aboriginals showed themselves delighted at the idea of going to the island, 'where they would enjoy peace and plenty uninterrupted', and their removal would greatly benefit Tasmania too. 'The large tracts of pasture that have so long been deserted owing to their murderous attacks on the shepherds and stock huts will now be available, and a very sensible relief will be afforded to the flocks of sheep that had been withdrawn from them and pent up in inadequate ranges of pasture—a circumstance which indeed has tended materially to . . . keep up the price of butcher's meat.'

Flinders was, as it happened, a singularly beautiful island, at least to northern tastes. It was a place of windswept silence, bare on its central hills but thick with aromatic foliage along its shores—like an amalgam of Orkney and Corsica. The flies and mosquitoes were troublesome, as in so many otherwise idyllic corners of Empire, but there were many butterflies, too, and bright tropic birds, and wallabies, and a constantly changing southern light. To the aboriginals, though, it looked desolate and depressing. They may have seemed happy as they boarded their ship at Hobart, smiling their child-like smiles and 'going through feats of their wonderful dexterity', but eye-witness accounts of their arrival at Flinders read very differently. 'When they saw from shipboard the splendid country which they were promised, they betrayed the greatest agitation, gazing with strained eyes at the sterile shore, uttering melancholy moans, and, with arms hanging beside them, trembling with convulsive feeling. The winds were violent and cold, the rain and sleet

were penetrating and miserable . . . and this added to their foreboding that they were taken there to die.'

So they were. Authority would not admit the fact, even to itself,
but like unwanted old relatives consigned to an institution, the
aboriginals were taken to Flinders Island to expire. After a couple of
false starts they were housed in a settlement on the southern
shore, named for them Wybalenna—Black Man's Houses. It was set
on the neck of a promontory: from the heights above it, which looked
like stretches of English downland, one could see the sea on either
side, and on a clear day even make out the hills of Tasmania itself.
Wybalenna had its own jetty, convenient for the Bishops and Governors who occasionally came to observe the progress of the natives'
salvation, and its own chapel, and naturally its own cemetery.
The aborigines lived in an L-shaped terrace of cottages, the staff in
houses nearby.

Some 200 Tasmanians were sent to Wybalenna, and there, slowly,
far away and out of sight, forgotten by the settlers, guarded by
second-rate officials and homesick soldiers, the race wasted away in
tedium. At first the aboriginals seemed cheerful enough—they were
pleased with the warm clothing the Government gave them, and
the hot food: but gradually they sank into apathy. They needed to
wander, and pined for the limitless forests and beaches of their larger
island. They died by the dozen from chest complaints, stomach
troubles and plain home-sickness: there was nothing for them to do
but to brood, forlornly dance and sing, listlessly look for opossums
and kangaroos, or dig potatoes in their garden patch.

Presently Robinson himself, having rounded up every last
aboriginal, arrived at Flinders Island to preside over their decay,
and added to other causes of death a sort of sacred insemination.
In his Wesleyan zeal he wanted to reform them still. He dressed them
in European clothes. He forbade their corroborees. He was helped
by a catechist named Robert Clark, who had declared it among the
dearest objects of his life to disseminate moral and spiritual light
among the natives, and the two of them worked assiduously to
explain the ways of God to those benighted agnostics, Robinson
at the same time recommending to the Lieutenant Governor the
construction of a lock-up.

Now a Wybalenna Sunday became a day full of purpose. 'There is no strolling about, all are expected to attend the divine service, none are exempt except through illness, such is the way the Sabbath is kept since I have had the honour to command.' Well though he knew his charges, Robinson remained appalled at their religious indifference. Their mental darkness was truly shocking. Some actually thought they had been created by their own mothers, and one woman believed her brother had done it. As for the afterlife, the aboriginals were now inclined to suppose that when a black man died his soul went to England, where it 'jumped up whitefellow'. A Sunday school was founded to correct these misconceptions, and a visitor who attended one of Mr Clark's addresses thought it 'very evident from the anxious and searching looks of these people that they were really yearning to know and to feel that there is a God and that God is something powerful'. Soon seven natives knew the Lord's Prayer by heart, decorum reigned at Wybalenna, and the 'yells and monotonous chanting which at one time . . . frequently hurt the repose of the white inhabitants is no longer heard'.

Here is an extract from one of Robinson's sermons, in his own English version of it:

'*One good God. One good God. Native good, native dead, go up in sky. God up. Bad native dead, goes down, evil spirit fire stops. Native cry, cry. Good native stops God sky, no sick, no hungering.*'

And here are some of the questions, with the prescribed answers, from a Wybalenna catechism class:

Q   *What will God do to this world by and by?*
A   *Burn it.*
Q   *Who are in heaven?*
A   *God, angels, good men and Jesus Christ.*
Q   *What sort of country is heaven?*
A   *A fine place.*
Q   *What sort of place is hell?*
A   *A place of torment.*
Q   *What do you mean by a place of torment?*
A   *Burning for ever and ever.*

Robinson also inculcated in his wards, dependent during the past few millennia entirely upon the hunt and the scavenge, a more suitable sense of property. He put English copper coin into circulation, stamped on one side 'F.I.' for Flinders Island, and he made the aboriginals pay for their European clothes and comforts, to teach them the meaning of money. He started a weekly market, every Tuesday at 11, at which they could sell the game they caught or the few poor artifacts they made, and buy in return pipes, tea caddies, crockery, fishing rods or straw hats.

But despite it all they wasted, declined to have babies, and grew thinner, and more morose, and more helplessly melancholic. The Tasmanians were literally losing heart. Even the Conciliator now complained of their feckless indolence, and Mr Clark sometimes found it necessary to flog girls, 'in religious anger at their moral offences'. By 1850 there were only forty-four aboriginals left alive, and the Government, deciding them to be no longer a danger to the European community, abandoned Wybalenna and shipped the hang-dog survivors back across the Strait to die in Tasmania. Having thus arranged all things to the divine satisfaction, Mr Robinson took his family home to Bath, where he died in genteel circumstances in a hill-top villa overlooking the city: he was 78, and his death certificate, in the column headed 'Occupation', described him simply as 'Late Protector of the Aboriginees, Tasmania'.[1]

8

Now the end was near for the Tasmanian race. The survivors—

[1] Wybalenna soon crumbled into dereliction, and wistfully derelict it remains. Robinson's house there is now a farm, and washing flutters in its garden on Mondays, but the only other sign of human habitation is an old black car, abandoned on the hillside above. The chapel is now used as a shearing shed, and beside it are the overgrown remains of the aborigines' living quarters. Nearby is the cemetery, but the bones of its native corpses, so a persistent local tradition says, were dug up years ago and sent to England hidden in bales of wool for the edification of anatomists.

When I searched out Robinson's Bath villa in 1971, I found it occupied by Mr Arnold Haskell, the authority on ballet, who was unaware of his dour predecessor there, and used the house I fear a great deal more elegantly.

twelve men, twenty-two women, ten young people—were taken to a disused penal settlement at Oyster Cove, twenty-five miles from Hobart, and only fifteen miles from the spot where, two centuries before, Tasman's sailors had first heard those 'certain human sounds'. There they lingered for a last decade. They no longer posed a threat to anyone, nor even provided hopeful material for the evangelicals, for they were generally drunk and shamelessly immoral. Sometimes people went to look at them, and itinerant anthropologists, recognizing them as ultimate specimens, measured their spines and estimated their brain capacities. By 1855 only sixteen Tasmanians were still alive, and all attempts to redeem them had been abandoned. By 1859 Oyster Cove was a slum, the handful of survivors camping in verminous filth among the derelict buildings, and sharing their food with their dogs.

A few were adopted by settlers, as pets or curiosities. One pretty girl, almost the last of the young aboriginals, was befriended by Lady Franklin, whose husband Sir John, after great adventures in the Arctic, had come to Hobart as Lieutenant-Governor. Gaily dressed in European clothes, Mathinna went everywhere with her patroness, high-spirited in her carriage on afternoon drives, cosseted by ambitious aides at Government House balls. But when the time came for the Franklins to go home, Lady Franklin was advised that the change of climate might kill her favourite, so Mathinna was placed in an institution called the Queen's Asylum. There the young men at Government House did not habitually call, and the other inmates teased and taunted her: so in the end, since she seemed to be wasting away, they kindly returned her to her inebriate and syphilitic relatives at Oyster Cove. We do not hear that Lady Franklin ever wrote to her there, and she soon picked up the local habits, drank heavily, prostituted herself with the timber-workers of the surrounding woods, and was eventually found drowned in a creek.

The last male Tasmanian was an alcoholic whaling seaman, 'King Billy' Lanney, who became a public spectacle in his later years, was shown off at Government functions, photographed by scientists, and introduced to Queen Victoria's son Alfred when the prince visited Hobart in 1868. When King Billy died in 1869, of chronic diarrhoea in the Dog and Partridge, he was carried to his grave by four comrades from his old ship, with the ship's flag, an old opossum rug and a clutter of native weapons placed upon the coffin: during the night, though, the grave was re-opened and the skull snatched—probably at the instigation of the Royal Society of Tasmania, whose savants badly wanted the skull for their collection.

The last of all was Truganini, Robinson's faithful follower, whose association with the imperial culture had been long and varied. Her mother had been shot by a soldier. Her sister was kidnapped by sealers. Her intended husband was drowned by two Europeans in her presence, while his murderers raped her. In 1839 she was one of a group of natives taken by Robinson to New South Wales: there she, two other aboriginal women and two men were charged with the murder of two Europeans, the men being found guilty and publicly hanged, the women acquitted and returned to Tasmania.

Long after the end of Oyster Cove Truganini (whose name meant 'sea-weed') clung to life, the very last of her people. For nearly twenty years she lived with a kindly European family in Hobart, and she became a well-known and popular figure in the capital. Short and stout, with staring eyes and a hairy chin, she liked to wear bright red turbans, and loved a good chat, a glass of beer and a pipe of tobacco. She was terrified that, like King Billy before her, she would be exhumed and dissected after burial. 'Don't let them cut me up', she pleaded on her death-bed. 'Bury me behind the mountains.' So when, 73 years old, she died in May, 1876, her body was taken secretly, in a shoe-blacked pauper's coffin on a cart, through the night to the Cascades Female Factory— the women's reformatory, that is—in a cleft in the hills behind Hobart. There she was buried to the tolling of the reformatory bell, wrapped in a red blanket, in the presence of the Tasmanian Premier (for in the course of these events Tasmania had graduated to self-government). 'I regret the death of the last of the Tasmanian aborigines,' wrote a correspondent in the Hobart *Mercury* next day, 'but I know that it is the result of the *fiat* that the black shall everywhere give place to the white.'

Truganini's life had exactly spanned, to the year, the association between Europeans and Tasmanians. In her own time her people, confronted by the strange white newcomers from over the sea, had been humiliated, degraded and finally utterly extinguished. They buried her within the reformatory compound: but before very long she was dug up anyway, and her skeleton, strung upon wires and upright in a box, became for many years the most popular exhibit in the Tasmanian Museum.[1]

9

'The sad and untimely destruction of this interesting primitive race,' wrote the ethnologist H. Long Roth, 'is one of the greatest losses Anthropology has suffered.' But though the majority of the Empire-builders viewed their coloured subjects with something less than fraternity, throughout the Victorian century, even in the most ferocious episodes of Empire, there were honourable exceptions—men to whom race really was irrelevant, and colour added only variety to the human scene. Some were practising Christians. Many more were just people of decent instinct—sometimes tempered, especially in Irishmen, Scotsmen, and Welshmen, by hereditary experiences of their own. In Hong Kong the poor Chinese called the maverick John Pope-Hennessy, Governor of the colony in the 1870s, 'Number One Good Friend'. In Bermuda the black people were still using the Well of the Black Watch, beneath its little wooden shelter beside the sea, which was 'sunk by some soldiers of the 1st Battalion . . . for the sake of the poor and their cattle in the long drought'. When Cetewayo was imprisoned in Cape Town Castle after the Zulu war, he pined for the green rush mats he had always slept upon: William Butler, of Wolseley's Ring, made a special journey from Natal to take him some, reducing the king to tears of gratitude—'it was the same', said Butler, 'as putting a bit of green

---

[1] Though now only displayed, I was told in 1971, to visitors of genuine scientific purpose, for in recent years the fate of the aboriginals has become a popular protestors' issue in Tasmania, and Truganini's bones have been removed to the museum basement. A more accessible relic is 'Shiney', a Tasman's mummified head in the possession of the Royal College of Surgeons in Dublin. This macabre object has been in Ireland since the 1840's, but though it is familiar to every Dublin medical student, when I inspected it in 1973 I was said to be the first outsider to ask for it in 25 years.

sod into the cage of a lark'. And this is how Arabi Pasha, the
Egyptian nationalist overthrown and deported by the British in
1882, wrote to his Welsh gaoler, Major Baldwin Evans:

*In the name of God, the Merciful and the Compassionate, my good and
Honourable Friend, Mr Evans: I beg to offer you my devotion for the great
zeal and trouble you have taken on our behalf during the examination of our
case, and also for your frequent visits to us in our prison cell. I pray God to
reward you for your great kindness to us in our hours of grief and darkness,
and we beg of you to accept our most grateful thanks. I have done this in my
own hand to be a remembrance and a lasting sign of the great esteem and
friendship I have for you.*

Ahmed Arabi, The Egyptian[1]

[1] Major Evans came from Rhuddlan in Flintshire—where, as it happened,
in 1277 Edward I of England imposed his harsh terms upon the conquered
Welsh.

CHAPTER TWENTY-FOUR

The Rebel Prince

THROUGH all these years Ireland festered. Drained of vitality by famine and emigration, alternately conciliated and coerced by its imperial masters, pitifully derelict and neglected, in the decades since the Great Famine the island had not reconciled itself to subjection. Sometimes years had gone by without trouble, and the country lay in stagnant trance. At other times it flamed into violence. Ireland remained the most baleful, in some ways the most alien of all the British possessions, and though the old Gaelic language had retreated to the remoter corners of the countryside, still the sense of Catholic Irishness was as deep and as emotional as ever. All over the island work still stopped in the fields and peat bogs when the Angelus rang, and in the shanty-churches of the west the priests still cheerfully splashed holy water over their congregations with a mop out of a zinc bucket. Wherever they went, Irishmen remained the most virulent enemies of British rule. An Irish priest was one of Riel's closest advisers. An Irish labourer tried to kill Prince Alfred during his visit to Australia. The militant Governor of Montana during the worst period of Anglo-American rivalry in the west was an Irishman educated in the prisons of Tasmania. An Irish free-lance, Alfred Aylward, alias Murphy, was an influential adviser to the Boer command in the Transvaal war. Far more than most emigrants, the Irish abroad retained their sense of nationhood and ancestral grievance. '*Good Health!*' ran a well-known toast of their *diaspora*,

> *Health and long life to you,*
> *Land without rent to you,*
> *A child every year to you,*
> *And may you die in Ireland.*

468

Within Ireland the groundswell of discontent was now embodied in two very different movements. The Fenians were people of violence, who believed in the overthrow of British rule by force, and who had powerful friends among the Irish emigrants in America and Australia: mostly working-class men, they had launched an unsuccessful rebellion in 1867, besides mounting two ludicrously abortive invasions of Canada from the United States. The Irish Home Rule movement, on the other hand, fought its cause constitutionally, and demanded only autonomy for Ireland within a federal system. Founded in 1870 by a Protestant barrister, Isaac Butt, many of its members were Anglo-Irishmen of the professional classes, and everything about it was moderate. Its leaders were moderate. Its demands were moderate. Its abilities were moderate. Butt's personality, though colourful in a stagey way, expressed the spirit of reasonableness, aggrieved rather than furious: and doggedly his supporters soldiered on, year after year in the House of Commons, against the apathy of Tories and Liberals alike—for as yet few people in Britain took Ireland's passions very seriously, believing as they generally did that Irishmen were only an inferior and misguided sub-variety of Englishmen.[1]

For years these two liberation movements, as different in texture as in velocity, flowed along in separate streams—the ferociously anti-British Fenians, the restrained Home Rulers, each representing in such different styles a common irrepressible instinct. But in 1875 there appeared in the House of Commons a new Irish member of such dazzling originality that in his person both factions could find their champion, to make him the spokesman of all Ireland's aspirations, and for one tumultuous decade the uncrowned king of his people.

2

Avondale, in County Wicklow, was the family home of Charles

[1] When Elizabeth Butler exhibited a sad painting of an Irish eviction at the Royal Academy, Lord Salisbury, who lived in the ancestral palace of the Cecils at Hatfield, said in his speech at the opening banquet that the scene looked so bright and breezy that he almost wished he could take part in an eviction himself.

Stewart Parnell—whose name was pronounced with the emphasis on the first syllable, and whose family divided their time between their town house in Dublin and this delectable estate. It was a paradigm of Anglo-Ireland. The square Georgian house stood well away from the road, wide-eaved and comfortable, not unlike those misery-built mansions of Tasmania: sheltered by silver firs, attended by pleasant gardens, with woods all around for children's adventuring, well-built stables for hunters and carriage horses, and lawns running gently towards the river below. Here there grew up the most memorable of all the Irish patriots, whose cause was the cause of all the bog-Irish, the dispossessed illiterate villagers, the superstitious Catholic townsmen and the Fenian fanatics.

Parnell's father was an unobtrusive Anglo-Irish country gentleman, but his mother was the stridently opinionated daughter of an American naval officer. From this mixed background Parnell derived a curious magic of personality, and a bigot streak. There was said to be madness in his father's family, and all his life Parnell was the slave of eccentric fancies and taboos. He hated the colour green, and blamed the greenness of a floor carpet when he had a sore throat. He was afraid of October, of Fridays, of three candles, and thought cobwebs good for the treatment of cuts. Moody, silent, an animal lover, a devoted reader of *Alice in Wonderland* who found nothing in it to make him smile, nobody who met him in his prime ever forgot his presence. Some found him evil, some thought him a kind of saint, none seemed quite able to isolate his fascination. It was like a spell.

He was a strikingly handsome man, high-browed, trimly whiskered, with a sense of powerful self-control—indifference, some critics called it. His breeding was part of his appeal, for it struck piquantly on the ear to hear this urbane Protestant, captain of the Wicklow cricket team, proclaiming the revolutionary cause of Ireland, and his power came from his combination of latent ferocity and languid, mannered elegance. Butt called him 'an ugly customer, though he is a damned good-looking fellow', and Gladstone called him 'a genius —a genius of an uncommon order'. As an orator he was *sui generis*. He was not a natural speaker—his repartee sounds laboured and un-rhythmic, perhaps because he had no ear for music—but even so he could enthrall the House of Commons as easily as he could arouse a crowd of Irish peasants to ecstasy. Parnell was the antithesis of the political dilettante: in his early years at least he wanted neither office, nor popularity, nor even perhaps fame for himself, but only the freedom of Ireland. He detested England. He despised the Parliament he sat in, as he despised his beery Irish colleagues there. He was, first to last, an unreconcilable enemy of the British Empire.

Yet it was to Avondale, with all its measured delights of the Ascendancy, its gentle sounds and merry pleasures, that this strange rebel returned for solace or stimulation. His career was full of troubled ironies, and perhaps the old life in County Wicklow touched some suppressed emotion in his heart. He loved the place all his life. 'There is no place like Avondale, Jack', he used to tell his brother.[1]

3

The Anglo-Irish, whom we last saw in perplexed disarray during the Great Famine, had now reached their corporate maturity—passed it, perhaps, for they were eighteenth century people at heart. They had lost little of their confidence during the century, and 'Ascendancy' was a weak word for their status in the land. They still owned most of it, they still governed their peasantry absolutely, they could still evict at will, set their own rents and choose their own tenants. They were a ruling class by inheritance, by instinct and by nature. The economic gulf between landlords and peasants had perhaps narrowed since 1848—by 1871 there were only 40,000 single-room mud cabins in Ireland—but the improved roads and railways had enriched the social lives of the Anglo-Irish gentry, and had made them more than ever an alien elite. Some were rich, and lived with plentiful servants and lordly horses. Many more were poor or spendthrift, and cheerfully scratched along in big draughty houses where the rats ran wild. Hygiene was not their forte, hardship did not dismay them: until 1875 even Pakenham Hall, the vast country house of the Pakenham family, employing at least twenty indoor servants

[1] It is now a State forestry school, but has not much changed since Parnell's day. 'I sometimes see him walking out,' a man once told me there, 'but it's only an illusion.'

and engaging the affection of earls, possessed only one bathroom. Yet whatever their circumstances, all were *special* people, born to authority, feeling themselves to stand by right as by heredity in the position of noblemen.

Their self-esteem had increased with the extension of Empire, for if they provided a ruling class for Ireland, they formed an imperial caste too. For its private soldiers the British Army depended still upon Irish Catholic recruits, for its leadership it relied to an astonishing degree upon the Anglo-Irish, and the Irish regiments of the Crown were among the cockiest and most formidable of them all:

> *You may talk about your Guards, boys,*
> *Your Lancers and Hussars, boys,*
> *Your Fusiliers and Royal Artillerie—without the guns!*
> *The girls we drive them crazy, the foe we bate them aizy,*
> *The Rangers from Old Connaught—*yarrgh!
> *The land across the sea.*

Many of the imperial activists who have appeared in these pages sprang from the Protestant Ascendancy: Macnaghten of Kabul, Napier of Sind, the Lawrence brothers, John Nicholson, Burton the explorer, Garnet Wolseley, William and Elizabeth Butler, Colley of Majuba. 'Getting the old man's Irish out', subordinates used to say when one of these leaders was especially stimulated, and the Empire was engraved with their deeds, quirks and excesses. Wherever they went the Anglo-Irish behaved larger than life, and their high spirits, their touch of brogue, their good looks and their habitual irreverence gave to their English colleagues a very misleading impression of life in Ireland. They looked at the Empire in their own way, for they had grown up with the miseries of the Great Famine and the Fenian troubles, the conflicts of Irish patriotism and imperial sentiment, the alternate clenching and relaxing of British resolve in Ireland. They knew imperialism from both sides, and perhaps understanding its dilemmas more clearly than most, threw themselves into the imperial adventure with an extra gusto or sense of involvement.

Yet they had inner conflicts of their own: for though they formed an occupying caste in their homeland, foreign to its working people and commonly hated by them, still they often loved the island with a tortured intensity.

4

The Anglo-Irish still lived separately. If to visiting Englishmen they seemed archetypically Irish, to the indigenes they seemed inalienably English. They often resented this anomalous condition—those whose families had been in the island for a couple of centuries felt themselves to be as truly Irish as any hut-peasant of the west—but they could never quite escape it.

Nobody was more shut off from the life of the country than the Viceroy or Lord-Lieutenant, the head of the Irish Government and the Queen's representative. By the 1870s his office was a political appointment, and he was generally a member of the British Cabinet, but he lived in Dublin in a state of royalty. His headquarters and official residence was Dublin Castle, a weird conglomeration of structures in the heart of the capital. Armed sentries stood at its gates, beneath the gilded crests of monarchy, and it seemed to stand withdrawn or sequestered from the life of the city about it. Within its confused perimeter it was like a municipality of its own. A great parade ground was its centre, and around it an irregular jumble of buildings represented the imperial continuity, all ages, all styles, all purposes. There were classical porticos and colonades. There was a round tower like Windsor's. The Chapel Royal was whimsical Gothick, the Bedford Tower was based upon a design for Whitehall by Inigo Jones. The yard was lit by tall gas-lamps, and high above its ornamental archways stood lead figures of Mars, with attendant lion, and Justice, holding her scales with a dubious air.

Through their State apartments here the Viceroys and their ladies ornately moved, the focus of Irish social life, at whose balls and levees appeared not only the grandees of the Ascendancy, but numbers of Catholic gentry too.[1] The great hall of St Patrick was

[1] 'The occupancy of an exalted, though fictitious, social position,' the future Lord Crewe satirically described the job, when appointed to it in 1892, 'with a purpose of rendering everybody within reach (including the occupant) as grotesque as possible.'

hung with the banners of the Knights of St Patrick, the Ascendancy's own order of chivalry, and decorated with apposite paintings—*The Beneficent Government of George III*, or *Henry II Receiving the Submission of the Irish Chieftains*. The presence chamber above, with its canopied throne in red velvet, was thick with the mystique of monarchy, and over the yard in the Chapel Royal Viceroy and Primate sat each in his private pew surrounded by the names, dates and arms of his predecessors. It was a powerful presence, Dublin Castle, but it had a defensive air, as though its occupants had constantly expected to discover, during the long centuries of their authority, that the Irish Chieftains had not submitted after all, but were hammering at the gates with shillelaghs.

In the country the Anglo-Irish style was easier, but scarcely less introspective. Perhaps the most striking enclave of all, where the Ascendancy seemed to be most neatly encapsulated, was the well-known village of Castletownshend in County Cork. This was one of the prettiest places in Ireland, and one of the few in which the Anglo-Irish chose to live in community. It stood only a few miles from Skibbereen and Schull, whose miseries were glimpsed during the years of the Great Famine, but it was far from emaciated itself. Its single main street, with a clump of trees in the middle, led gently downhill to the harbour (the haven, as they called it in Ireland), with the castle and the Protestant church at one end, and substantial family houses scattered throughout: and it formed, in its pleasant way, as solid a block of Anglo-Irish values and memories as Dublin Castle itself. Two closely connected families, the Somervilles and the Townshends, dominated the place. They had repeatedly intermarried, they were always in each other's houses, and they had made Castletownshend, tucked away at the water's edge, almost a private colony of their own.

The Anglican church, trimly stacked against rising ground above the sea, was plastered with memorials to the two families. One could read of Somervilles and Townshends fighting the imperial wars, administering the imperial justice, governing territories of hideous remoteness, sitting on Admiralty courts or being Anglican bishops. Here was a Townshend who had commanded the 14th Light Dragoons under Wellington, and here a Coghill, a lateral branch of the Somervilles, who had won a posthumous VC saving the regimental colours of the 24th Regiment after Isandhlwana. The Townshends, who had come to Ireland in the seventeenth century, lived in their waterside castle surrounded by family portraits and mementos, beneath ceilings elaborately painted by the Italian craftsmen who used to travel around Ireland catering to the Ascendancy. The Somerville headquarters was the house called Drishane at the top of the village, a comfortable, rectory-like place, shingled all over, with cedars in the garden and ivy on the walls. Between these two homes sundry ancillary Somervilles flourished, and lesser Townshends thrived.

The two clans lived in happy intimacy, hunting, dancing, marrying, the boys going off to the University, the Army or the Navy, and all growing up together, living and dying, with a sense of private permaner ce. They were neither rich nor poor; their houses were verminous, cold, and often needed a lick of paint: but they enjoyed the happy assurance of inherited privilege, not much blunted by feelings of guilt or self-doubt, and they very much enjoyed themselves.[1]

5

It was in 1879 that Parnell, determined to break the hegemony of this imperial caste, came into his own as leader of the Irish. He was already famous on both sides of the Irish Sea, because he had perfected in the House of Commons a technique of obstruction. Fiercer and more incisive than his leader Butt, he had lost patience with the plodding constitutionalists, and reached the conclusion that the British could not be reasoned into generosity, only goaded—'we will

[1] Castletownshend remains, I think, the most telling single monument to the Anglo-Irish way of life. Townshends and Somervilles still dominated the village when I visited it in 1970, a Mrs Salter-Townshend occupied the castle, and I actually heard a Townshend hail a Somerville in the village street with the Cranfordian greeting 'Morning, Cousin Robert!' It was in his house at Castletownshend that Admiral Boyle Somerville, Royal Navy, was murdered, apparently for political reasons, in 1936: and Edith Somerville of the literary partnership Somerville and Ross, though born as we know in Corfu, spent much of her life in the village.

never gain anything from England', he told an Irish audience in Lancashire, 'unless we tread upon her toes—we will never gain a single sixpenny-worth by conciliation'. He declared open war, so he wrote, 'against Ministers, Imperial Parliament and English public opinion', and he fought that war excitingly and infuriatingly upon the floor of the House. His tactics made him immensely popular in Ireland—wherever he went vast crowds escorted him in triumphal progresses—and gradually the Irish members of Parliament, scenting the shift of the wind, swung into line behind him. He became the voice of Ireland, The Chief, the first Irishman who had ever succeeded in catching the English ear.

The technique was simple. It was literally to prevent Parliament doing any work at all until the British Government conceded Home Rule for Ireland. Whatever the subject of debate, Parnell and his colleagues would talk about it so endlessly, in such indefatigable relays, that the House of Commons was stagnated. Sometimes they just read hour after hour from Blue Books. Once a Joseph Biggar, the member for Cavan, told by the Speaker after three hours of filibuster that he must stop talking because his tired throat made him inaudible, picked up his papers and a glass of water, moved closer to the Chair, and said 'As you have not heard me, Mr Speaker, perhaps I had better begin all over again'.

Parnell became the most hated man in the House—perhaps the most hated member Parliament had ever known. Whenever he stood to speak the House broke into jeers and howls, sometimes keeping him standing there for half an hour before he could open his mouth. Time and again he was expelled for obstruction, and the picture papers portray him escorted by Black Rod down the floor of the House in an attitude of suave disdain, one hand in his pocket, while from the Tory benches bearded, monocled or be-whiskered Conservatives shake their fists or wave their tophats in fury. Parnell did not appear to care, for he was over-awed by nobody: when Gladstone once quoted an inflammatory speech of his, Parnell accosted the Grand Old Man, whom he had never met before, in the lobby outside. 'I wonder, sir, if I could see that portion of the speech at Sligo, that you read aloud?' Gladstone handed it to him, and pointing to one passage Parnell said without rancour: 'That is inaccurate. I never said it. Thank you, sir'.[1] This maddening new kind of revolutionary accepted the abuse of the House with steely calm, infuriating his enemies by the imperturbable Britishness of his responses. He was every inch a gentleman, which made it all the worse.

In all this Parnell enjoyed the support of the Fenians, and in 1879 he capped his preeminence by becoming president of a new body, the Irish National Land League, concerned with the rural grievances of Ireland. The winter of 1878 had been brutal for the peasantry—heavy rains, crop failures, falling prices. Thousands had gone bankrupt. Thousands more had lost their homes. The eviction of peasants had been a commonplace of Irish life since the beginnings of English rule, but this was the period in which the image of Irish eviction impressed itself upon the imagination of the world. There we can see it all still, in faded sepia: the shabby whitewashed cottage behind, with its tufted thatch and tumble-down outbuildings, and the bowler-hatted landlord's agent with his stick, and the helmeted constables lounging with rifles behind walls, as though about to take part in street fighting. There is no sign of the unfortunate tenants themselves, but a few pathetic scraps of furniture have been thrown out through the open door, and one policeman thoughtfully looks through the window, suggesting melancholy despairs inside. Through the Land League Parnell ruthlessly exploited the symbolism of the classic scene, and made the pathos of the Irish countryside the permanent backdrop of his drama.

The Irish had recovered some of their spirit since the demoralizing years of the Famine, and the 'Land War' now became a mass movement. For the first time the tenant-farmers as a class dared defy the Anglo-Irish. When a tenant was evicted, huge crowds of Irishmen gathered at his cottage to demonstrate in his support, and take his family off to shelter. Nobody would move into his farm, and the offending land agent was sent to Coventry—it was the terrible ostracization of Captain Charles Boycott, Lord Erne's haughty agent in County Mayo, which gave his name to the English language.[2]

[1] He never did say it, either, as Gladstone later confirmed.

[2] And to many others too—*boicottare*, *boicotear*, *boycotter*, *boikittirovat* in Basque, *bojkot* in Croatian, *boykot* in Turkish, *boicotio* in Welsh.

The Land League became almost a rival Government, setting up its own courts and making its own laws, and half Ireland was in a tumult of agitation. 'Captain Moonlight' made his terrifying appearance as agent of the Irish revenge, and landlords everywhere received threatening letters—'Yo will be treated like a mad dog that is quartered and Berried under ground and that is the death yo must get'—'the time has come that by God we don't care for man or the divil'—'we are the lads that dis not feare to do you. . . .' There were nineteen separate attempts upon the life of W. E. ('Buckshot') Forster, Chief Secretary of Ireland, and crime of every sort stalked the island horribly.

Parnell threw himself into this campaign with his usual ambiguous grace. He apparently welcomed a degree of violence—not enough to bring the full power of the Empire storming into Ireland, but enough to convince Westminster that Ireland could not be ruled by coercion. 'Hold the harvest!' the Land League exhorted the peasants, urging them not to hand over their crops to the landlords, and in Massachusetts Parnell's eldest sister Fanny interpreted the phrase in a stirring nationalist poem, published in the Boston *Pilot*, an old enemy of Empire, and soon immensely popular among Irishmen all over the world:

> *Oh by the God Who made us all, the seigneur and the serf,*
> *Rise up and swear this day to hold your own green Irish turf.*
> *Rise up and plant your feet as men where now you crawl as slaves,*
> *And make your harvest fields your camp, or make of them your graves.*

6

When, in 1868, a telegram arriving at Hawarden had told Gladstone he was to be Prime Minister for the first time, he was cutting down a tree in the park: and pausing for a moment from his work, he remarked to his companion: 'My mission is to pacify Ireland'. In 1880, when he was called to office for the second time, he was still preoccupied with the island. First, he was persuaded, he must restore law and order there, and within a few months he had introduced severe measures of coercion. In particular, he suspended *habeas corpus* so that the Land League agitators including Parnell, could be imprisoned without trial—for no Irish jury would have convicted The Chief, whatever the charge.

This led to the most spectacular of all Parnell's Parliamentary displays. So incessant and relentless was the opposition of the Irish members that it took 46 hours of unbroken debate to force the coercion bill through. Parnell's men filibustered in relays, taking it in turns to snatch a few hours' sleep in the lobby, and constantly nagged by their leader to go back and keep talking—hour after hour, day after day, to the impotent frustration of Liberals and Tories alike. The House was baffled by this culminating impertinence. The principle of free speech seemed to be at stake—the English constitution turned topsy-turvy in the interests of Irish separatism. After forty hours of it the House presented a scene of squalid exhaustion. The dishevelled members sat about pale and testy, some of them in rumpled evening clothes from the night before last. The galleries were packed by successions of visitors. The Irishmen were all alone on one side of the house, about 100 Englishmen generally sat on the other. Every speech was interrupted by abuse, jeering and sarcasm, until at last, at nine in the morning of the third day, the Speaker interrupted the debate. He was Henry Brand, second son of the 21st Baron Dacre, who was no man to be trifled with by enemies of England. Since the days of Oliver Cromwell no single man had ever arbitrarily closed a debate in the House, and it was disputable whether the Speaker had a right to: but choosing a moment when Parnell was out of the chamber, and reading from a paper which trembled visibly in his hand, Brand now declared on his own responsibility, in defiance of the ancient customs of the House, that the debate must end.

It did. The British members cheered with relief. The Irish members, nonplussed in the absence of Parnell, walked out of the House in a body, shouting 'Privilege! Privilege!' as the Parliamentarians had cried it when Charles I invaded the Commons. The Coercion Bill was carried, and Gladstone now felt the decks clear for progress. He had Parnell and most of his principal lieutenants arrested, and locked up on suspicion of subversion in Kilmainham Jail—a grim old fortress above the Liffey in Dublin which was the traditional place of incarceration for Irish patriots. Having proved his readiness to quell violence by force, he promptly put through a grandly conciliatory land reform bill, assuring the Irish tenants fair rents and fixed tenures.

Then, in a political act of great imagination, he persuaded the imprisoned Parnell to help him implement these reforms. 'The Chief' was offered his release if he would use his influence to calm the country, and see the Land Act safely through. Agreement was surreptitiously reached through intermediaries, and in March 1882 Parnell and his colleagues were released under the so-called Kilmainham Treaty. The first reactions were predictable—the Irish extremists accused Parnell of selling out to the English, the English reactionaries accused Gladstone of compromising with traitors. 'Buckshot' Forster resigned in protest, and the Queen herself was inexpressibly shocked. But the anger died, Parnell seemed ready to honour his word, the Land Act went ahead, and Gladstone's favourite nephew, Lord Frederick Cavendish, sailed over to Dublin as a new and more liberal Chief Secretary and a precursor of better times. Barring unforeseeable setbacks, it seemed, the way to Home Rule in Ireland was open at last.

But as usual in Ireland, the unforeseeable almost immediately occurred.

7

The Viceregal Lodge, the Viceroy's second residence, was a pleasant Georgian mansion surrounded by gardens and a ha-ha in the middle of Phoenix Park, one of the most beautiful parks in Europe. From his upstairs window the Viceroy could look across the grand green expanse of the park—1,750 acres, seven miles around, like a slab of open country on the flank of the capital—to the distant chequered pattern of the Wicklow mountains, generally blurred and hazy in the soft Irish light. Horsemen rode in the morning across the downlands of this paradise; street urchins threw sticks for conkers in the long lush avenues of horse-chestnuts; on Sunday afternoons music echoed faintly from The Hollow, where the St James Brass and Reed Band, the Father Mathew Band, or the heavily escorted Glencree

Reformatory Band, played boisterous marches to huge jolly audiences. Away to the left Robert Smirke's immense monument to the greatest Anglo-Irishman, the Duke of Wellington, was embellished with iron sculptures made from the metal of captured cannon.

On the evening of May 6, 1882, the Viceroy, Lord Spencer, who had just returned to Dublin for a second term, was looking at this fine view out of his window. He had been sworn in that morning in the customary ornate ceremonies at the Castle, with his Chief Secretary, Lord Frederick Cavendish. Now he was awaiting the arrival of Cavendish as his dinner guest, together with Thomas Burke the Under-Secretary. They had already spent the afternoon together, discussing Gladstone's plans for Ireland: Spencer had returned to the Lodge by carriage, his guests were following on foot. They would make an odd dinner trio. Spencer was a hospitable man who owned 26,000 acres of the English Midlands, but who had been an active politician all his life, and was known as the Red Earl because of his flaming beard. Cavendish was the second son of the Duke of Devonshire, a diligent but unexciting man, who had been Gladstone's private secretary, had married the Prime Minister's niece, and had risen steadily in the Liberal ranks. Burke, from Galway, had spent his life in the Irish administration: he was a Catholic, a nephew of Cardinal Wiseman, but was a stern law-and-order man, and was particularly loathed by the extreme nationalists. The three men were doubtless expecting a sombre business dinner. Times were crucial in Ireland, Spencer and Cavendish had assumed office at an especially demanding moment, Burke would probably find his brains picked all evening.

From his window, then, Lord Spencer looked out into the evening—a summer Saturday evening, warm, with a polo match in progress on the green, and the park full of strollers, picnickers and cyclists: and he noticed on the Grand Avenue, the thoroughfare which ran beyond the Viceregal ha-ha, what appeared to be a scuffle among a few men on the pavement. Drunks, he thought, and turned his attention elsewhere. Others assumed it to be one of the impromptu pavement wrestling matches to which Irishmen were addicted, and two cyclists rode by without taking a second look. What in fact was happening, though, was that Lord Spencer's dinner guests were being murdered. They were stabbed to death by seven members of a secret revolutionary society, the Invincibles, as they walked the last hundred yards to their dinner. Burke was the planned victim, and the murderers did not know who Cavendish was: but they cut both men's throats anyway, as they lay dying from their stab wounds, before vanishing from Phoenix Park into the city.

8

Gladstone was not deterred from his grand design. 'Be assured it will not be in vain,' he told Lady Frederick Cavendish, and she responded in kind: 'across all my agony,' she wrote in her journal, 'there fell a bright ray of hope, and I saw in a vision Ireland at peace, and my darling's life blood accepted as a sacrifice. . . .' Assured still of Parnell's support, Gladstone proceeded from land reform towards Home Rule—domestic autonomy, that is, within a federal arrangement. Though he was briefly out of office in 1885, in 1886 he was returned again, and presented his first Home Rule Bill to Parliament. It split the nation.[1] Conservatives declared it a gross betrayal of the Anglo-Irish, especially the Protestant majority of Ulster in the north—'essentially like the English people', cried Lord Randolph Churchill, 'a dominant, imperial caste. . . . It is only Mr Gladstone who would imagine for a moment that the Protestants of Ireland could recognize the power or satisfy the demands of a Parliament in Dublin'. The idea of separating the home islands seemed to stand against the trend of the times, the growing awareness of Empire and the rising aspiration towards imperial unity. Disraeli was dead, but Gladstone was more than ever the *bête noire* of the imperialists, and most of the London Press, now half-way to an imperialist conversion, was vehemently against the bill. Even the intellectuals opposed it, and its defeat became inevitable when Gladstone was deserted by the most brilliant of his younger lieutenants, Joseph Chamberlain—the very man who had, by his negotiations with Parnell in Kilmainham Jail, made the bill a political possibility.

[1] Robert Blake (*Disraeli*, London 1966) sees it rivalled only by the repeal of the Corn Laws in 1846 and Munich in 1938 as the bitterest issue in British political history.

Chamberlain, who was presently to be the grand entrepreneur of the imperial climax, clearly sensed the coming blaze of Empire, and decided to warm his hands at it. He also coveted the leadership of the Liberal Party. He defected to the Opposition with enough fellow-Liberals to defeat the bill and bring down the Government. At the ensuing general election the Tories came back with a new title, the Conservative and Unionist Party—with a new group of allies, the Liberal-Unionists under Chamberlain—and with a new Irish policy, based upon Churchill's perception that the close-knit Protestant community of Ulster was the strongest justification for British rule in Ireland. 'Ulster will fight,' ran the new slogan, 'and Ulster will be right—Home Rule is Rome Rule.'

Now Parnell's position in Parliament was more equivocal than ever. He was equivocal about Home Rule, for he might never have accepted the limitations of Gladstone's bill. He was equivocal about his relationship with the Liberals. Above all he was equivocal about violence—'the English', he once said, 'murder and plunder all over the earth and they howl when somebody is killed in Ireland'. Five men had been hanged for the Phoenix Park murders, but still a slight haze of suspicion connected The Chief himself with the tragedy.[1] Publicly he had condemned it, but when openly accused of complicity in the Commons, he scornfully declined to defend himself. On the whole, perhaps, most of the country believed in his innocence. The Liberal Party clearly still did, as did Mr Gladstone himself. There was no hard evidence against him, only a miasma of distrust.

But in the same month as the presentation of the Home Rule Bill, April 1886, a young Irishman named Edward Houston presented himself at the office of *The Times*, in the tiny private courtyard which the paper then occupied at Blackfriars in the City. *The Times* was at the apogee of its power, and Printing House Square was rather like a very worldly Oxford college, with its elegant dining-room, its wine waiter, its discreet but intimate contacts with the

---

[1] A sixth man, having turned Queen's Evidence, was smuggled out of the country to South Africa, but was himself murdered at sea on board the *Kinross Castle*: a grateful memorial to *his* assassin stands in Glaslevin cemetery, Dublin, paid for by a ladies' committee in New York.

sources of power, and its traditions of gentlemanly scholarship and enterprise. Into this dignified milieu Houston cast a sensational proposition. He was in a position to prove, he told the Editor, that Parnell was directly connected with the Phoenix Park murders; and asking merely for his own expenses, for he was, he said, concerned only for the well-being and good name of his country, he produced a series of ten letters, five of them apparently from Parnell, which seemed to show that the Land League had financed the murders, and that The Chief had personally approved of them. Here is the most damning of the letters, No 2:

Dear Sir, I am not surprised at your friend's offer, but he and you should know that to denounce the murders was the only course open to us. To do that promptly was plainly the only course and our best policy. But you can tell him, and all others concerned, that though I regret the accident of Lord F. Cavendish's death I cannot refuse to admit that Burke got no more than his deserts. You are at liberty to show him this, and others who you can trust also, but let not my address be known. He can write to the House of Commons. Yours very truly, Chas. S. Parnell.

Only the signature was apparently in Parnell's handwriting, and *The Times* responded cautiously. The paper was fiercely opposed to Home Rule, but decided to fly a legal kite by publishing first a series of articles, *Parnellism and Crime*, implying in general terms that the Irish Nationalist Party and the Land League were implicated in Irish violence. When no writs followed, on April 18, 1887, the paper published letter No 2. Never in the history of *The Times* had a scoop been launched with such drama. For the first time the newspaper carried a double-column headline; beneath it the letter was reproduced in facsimile, in the centre of the editorial page. On the streets posters appeared bearing in enormous letters the words: '*The Phoenix Park Murders: Facsimile of a Letter from Mr Parnell Excusing His Public Condemnation of the Crime.*' *The Times* was satisfied, said an editorial, that the evidence was 'quite authentic . . . we invite Mr Parnell to explain how his signature has become attached to such a letter'.

It was four years since the murders in the park, but the public reaction was intense. A Special Commission of Inquiry was set up to investigate the whole question of collusion in Irish violence. This was in effect a State Trial of Parnell. The three judges of the Commission were all well-known opponents of Home Rule, and all the resources of the State were applied to the exposure of Parnell and his colleagues. But it proved an astonishing triumph for The Chief. After months of inquiries, some 150,000 questions, and 445 witnesses there appeared in the stand a disreputable Irish journalist named Richard Piggott, described as having 'the general appearance of a coarsely composed and rather cheapened Father Christmas', who was very soon forced into the admission that he had forged the Parnell letters. Parnell was cleared absolutely. Piggott went to Paris and killed himself.

9

Parnell's mercurial career thus reached a climax of unexampled success. He was 42, and a hero not only in Ireland, where people often fell to their knees in his presence, but in England too. The Liberals fulsomely made amends for public suspicions—when Parnell entered the Commons for the first time after his vindication, the Liberal members rose to their feet, and Mr Gladstone bowed. He was elected a life member of the Liberal Club, publicly shook hands with Lord Spencer the Lord Lieutenant, was fêted at soirées and waved at by doting progressive ladies. Gladstone's daughter Mary, thought he exhibited 'all the fruits of the Spirit, love, patience, gentleness, forebearance, long-suffering meekness. His personality takes hold of one, the refined delicate face, illuminating smile, fire-darting eyes . . . Loved Parnell's spiritual face, only one's heart ached over his awfully delicate frame and looks'.

We are told that he accepted it all sceptically. 'Isn't it wonderful?' somebody said to him after his return to the House. 'Yes wonderful,' he replied, 'but how much more pleased they would have been if the forgery had proved genuine!' But he attached the greatest importance to his alliance with Gladstone, and as the 1880s passed, and the Liberals regained their strength in opposition, so it seemed that these two extraordinary men, backed by the combined energies of English liberalism and Irish patriotism, would in the end achieve the autonomy of Ireland. 'Think not for the moment',

Gladstone had told the House when he presented his Home Rule Bill, 'but for the years that are to come': an election was due in 1892, and this time, it seemed, Home Rule for Ireland was almost a certainty.

But now the last catastrophe occurred. In the culminating irony of Parnell's ironic life, at the threshold of his greatest triumph, he was ruined. He had never married, but for years he had enjoyed a mistress, Katherine O'Shea, who was the wife of one of Parnell's own followers, Captain William O'Shea, MP for Galway. O'Shea was a feckless adventurer, formerly of the 18th Hussars, who had survived phases of bankruptcy, been a mine manager in Spain and a stud farmer in Hertfordshire, and had virtually forced his Parliamentary nomination out of Parnell's gift, in return for Kitty's favours. Throughout the dramatic fluctuations of Parnell's political fortune, this poignant affair had nagged at his emotions. Mrs O'Shea was his only lover, and he was faithful to her for life. He had loved her at first sight: a rose she accidentally dropped in 1880 was found among his papers when he died, and was placed over his heart in his coffin. He called her 'Queenie' or 'Wifie', and she bore him at least two children. If he was away from her for more than two days, he sent her two telegrams daily, and one letter.

Yet this child-like love affair was, by the conventions of the time, wrapped up in squalor. Many people knew about it, perhaps including Gladstone himself, yet it was made sordid with furtive deceit. For Parnell it became a crippling obsession, more important even than the future of Ireland, so that his friends accused him of neglect, and his enemies of hypocrisy. In December 1889, Captain O'Shea treacherously brought it into the open by suing for divorce, and instantly Parnell's career was shattered. Gladstone himself, obeying the nonconformist conscience of his party, demanded Parnell's immediate resignation from the leadership of the Irish Nationalists, and the whole tentative structure of Irish emancipation evolved so painstakingly out of the Kilmainham Treaty, was ignominiously demolished. Some say O'Shea sued for divorce at the instigation of Chamberlain, who foresaw in the affair the defeat of Home Rule and the end of the Liberal Party. Certainly Gladstone had little choice but to disown Parnell, for the news of the divorce horrified most of his own supporters, and he threatened to resign himself from the leadership of the Liberals if the Irish Nationalists would not renounce Parnell.

For a week, in December 1890, the Irish members debated the issue in Committee Room 15 at Westminster. The debate, even the number of the room, has gone into Irish history. If the party had unanimously decided to keep Parnell as its leader, Ireland would have followed a very different path to freedom, and the whole course of Empire might have been altered: if it had unanimously asked Parnell to resign, Home Rule might have come thirty years earlier than it did. Parnell presided over the meeting himself, and used all his well-tried tactics of obstruction to delay a conclusion. But the magic had gone. Dazed perhaps by the suddenness of events, uncertain of loyalties and resentful of betrayals, quibbled at by party factions, excoriated by rivals, unsure even of the support of the Irish people, to whom the idea of divorce, and divorce of a prince at that, was still anathema—deprived of his own sure touch, he seemed bewildered, perhaps even a little mad. His fascination remained, but it had become a more peculiar allure, haggard and bizarre—he was like a poet, one of his colleagues wrote, 'plunged in some divine anguish, or a mad scientist mourning over the fate of some forlorn invention'. After days of sad acrimony, the debate came to a ragged conclusion when forty-six members of the party left Room 15 in silence, thereby renouncing Parnell's leadership, to leave only twenty-seven at his side.

He flatly refused to resign and let the furore die—'Resign— Marry—Return', as Cecil Rhodes the imperialist financier succinctly advised by cable from South Africa. Instead he issued a manifesto to the Irish people, denouncing Gladstone's conception of Home Rule as a feeble half-measure, and thus ending his alliance with the Liberals on a note of sour desperation. 'Blot out his name!' wrote Mary Gladstone now, and the Queen was appalled. 'Not only a man of very bad character,' she wrote, 'but a liar and devoid of all sense of honour or any sort of principle.' The Home Rule cause was discredited. When Gladstone in due time returned to power, and introduced his second Home Rule Bill in 1893, it scraped through the Commons but was contemptuously rejected by the Lords.

Gladstone, old, deaf, half-blind and discouraged, retired from public life, offering a despondent valediction to the perennial Irish debate: 'There can be no more melancholy, nor in the last result, no more degrading spectacle on earth than the spectacle of oppression, or of wrong in whatever form, inflicted by the deliberate act of a nation upon another nation, especially by the deliberate act of such a country as Great Britain upon such a country as Ireland'.

10

As for Parnell, desolately he wandered Ireland looking for friends. He was the lost leader. He married his Kitty, but this only did him harm—'the climax of brazened horrors', declared the Bishop of Raphoe. Rejected by the Liberals, disowned by most of his own party, in Ireland he was abused for immorality or scorned by those who thought of mere Home Rule as supine surrender. The virtue had left him. 'Our general has betrayed us', wrote Archbishop Croke. 'For his own miserable gratification he has sold the pass, preferring an ignoble and licentious life in London to the liberation and advancement of his too confiding countrymen.' Even the poor people, who had worshipped him, now refused to listen. In Kilkenny they pelted him with mud, and jeered at his passing. At Mallow they ripped the doors off his carriage, while a priest cried 'Down with libertinism!' Though Parnell still regularly took his seat in Parliament, and campaigned tirelessly throughout Ireland, still he was broken, and in his unlucky month of October, 1891, 45 years old, he died at Katherine's side in their house at Brighton.

His memory was to remain ambivalent. Was he true or false, a patriot or an opportunist? Was he ever playing fair with Gladstone, or would he have denounced home rule as soon as he had achieved it? The English generally thought the worst of him, agreeing with Queen Victoria. The Irish, however harshly they treated him in his last years, knew him at least for a genius, as Gladstone did, and never forgot his charisma. When his funeral procession drove up Sackville Street towards Glasnevin cemetery, past the pillar with Nelson on the top, immense silent crowds of Irishmen watched it pass. The air was charged with a special quality of Ireland, familiar to Parnell all his life—a mingled quality of bitterness, sorrow, conspiracy and pride. British soldiers marched with the procession, and among the onlookers was the imperial commander-in-chief in Ireland, Garnet Wolseley. It was, he later wrote, the only crowd he was ever afraid of.

CHAPTER TWENTY-FIVE

The Martyr of Empire

WE are approaching the imperial climax. Now the great searchlight of the imperial mission seemed to sweep the world incessantly, here playing upon an Irish funeral, there peering into kraal or heathen temple. The horizons of the British marvellously widened, as the scope of their power and responsibilities dawned upon them, and for the first time ordinary people, as Disraeli had foreseen, began to take a pride in the British Empire. How glorious it was, when one thought about it, to see so much of the map painted the imperial red! What giants there were about! How majestic, Britain's providential stance at the summit of the world!

In fact Britain's comparative status, financial and military, was weakening still: but this was not yet apparent to the public, least of all to that newly coherent public, literate for the first time, enfranchised for the first time, and given a window on the world by the new penny Press, which was to provide the chorus of *fin de siècle* imperialism. To its members Britain was never so unchallengeable; and to more educated Britons too the nation's right to exert its power in the world, and extend its beneficent sway over less fortunate peoples, admitted of no doubt.

It was a destiny passionately accepted, for good reasons as for bad, watered by tears as it was emblazoned by triumph, noble as well as squalid: and the more fragile the British supremacy became in reality, the more emotional became the idea of Empire. The Raj was growing plumper now, full-blown almost, and since the British themselves habitually saw their Empire in anthropomorphic terms, Britannia with her sceptre or full-whiskered redcoats in sentinel poses, we too may legitimately imagine it a little maudlin in its developing prime, coarsened rather, bosomy. This was an age of

hero-worship, and the Empire idolized its own, showering its protagonists with medals, ribbons and indulgence.

In 1885 all this heightening of emotions, this port-and-ginger
sentiment, this beat of drum and heaving of corsage, reached a
supreme expression in the death of General Charles Gordon, Commander of the Bath, Royal Engineers, whom Queen Victoria herself
described as 'dear, heroic, noble', and for whom Lord Tennyson
wrote the nation's epitaph:

> *Warrior of God, man's friend, and tyrant's foe*
> *Now somewhere dead far in the waste Soudan,*
> *Thou livest in all hearts, for all men know*
> *This earth has never borne a nobler man.*

2

Gordon, than whom in fact the earth has seldom borne a more
complicated man, entered the saga of Empire obliquely, at a tangent
on the River Nile. Since the geography of that river had been eluci-
dated in the 1860s, the British had felt a possessive interest in it. For
one thing they realized that control of the terrible African slave
trade, still an issue close to their hearts, lay in the control of the
Nile's headwaters. For another they hazily conceived that the security
of India was dependent upon command of the Nile: the Nile
governed Egypt, it was reasoned, Egypt contained the Suez Canal,
the Suez Canal was the spine of Empire.[1]

The British repeatedly claimed that they had no designs on
Egypt, but nobody believed them for long. Once Disraeli had acquired the Suez Canal shares, Britain's physical presence on the
Nile seemed only a matter of time. The Egyptian State was still in
theory a dependency of the Ottoman Empire, with the Khedive as
the Sultan's Viceroy, and its financial condition was so chaotic and

---

[1] A dangerous strategic principle, as Gladstone presciently foresaw. If
Britain felt she had special rights along all her strategic communications, it
was tantamount to claiming 'a veto upon all the political arrangements of all
the countries and seas which can possibly contribute any one of the routes
between England and the East, between two extremities, or nearly such, of
the world'.

corrupt that the Western Powers had already intervened to control its economy and protect their own interests. When in 1882 an idealist Egyptian Army officer, Arabi Pasha, launched an insurrection to rid the country of all such foreign interference, the moment had come for an imperial occupation. Unsuccessfully inviting the French and the Italians to join them in the enterprise, the British sent an invasion army to Port Said under General Sir Garnet Wolseley, G.C.M.G.—who, swiftly defeating Arabi at the battle of Tel-el-Kebir, and displaying his organizational talents at their most brilliant, in two days occupied Cairo and ran up the Union Jack above Saladin's citadel.[1] This was not, the British declared, an annexation. It was merely a temporary occupation, intended to restore order and stability to Egypt.

In fact everything about it was anomalous. It never became explicit. The Khedive remained Khedive, the Sultan far away remained the theoretical head of State, in whose name firmans were issued and dignitaries elevated. The British did not provide a Government exactly, they merely supplied compulsory advisers: though their soldiers controlled Egypt, and their officials soon came to run the country, they did not appoint a Governor or even a Resident, their senior representative holding the innocuous rank of Agent-General.

What was more, it was never made clear whether the British, in assuming responsibility for Egypt, also took on the burden of the Sudan, the next territory to the south, which had been for 60 years a dependency of Cairo. A million square miles of desert, its African inhabitants Islamicized and half Arabized, this forbidding country meant nothing whatever to the British public, and not much more to the British authorities in Cairo, but the imperial expansionists were already arguing that without its possession slavery would never be ended and Suez would never be safe. Unfortunately it was in a state of endemic rebellion; its inhabitants, under a magnetic and mysterious Muslim holy man called simply the Mahdi—the

---

[1] Not much of a war, thought William Butler, who naturally went with Wolseley, 'but the soldier of today must be content with what he can get'. Wolseley himself called it 'the tidiest war in British history', though his army included a general for every 900 men.

Leader—had risen in arms against the inefficient and impious Egyptian Government. The British thus had a Sudanese problem on their hands almost before they knew where the Sudan was. Should they, as the new suzerains of Egypt, intervene to put the rebellion down? Gladstone, having astonishingly committed the British Empire to the invasion of Eygpt itself, vehemently thought not. There was still an Egyptian Government, he argued, and an Egyptian army in the Sudan. The British were not the rulers of Egypt, only the temporary occupiers, and the Sudan was none of their business. So an Egyptian force it was, though under a British mercenary commander, Colonel Hicks, which marched off in the summer of 1883 to put down the revolt in the name of the Khedive.

The expedition, 10,000 strong, was fallen upon by 50,000 Sudanese in the desert near El Obeid, and annihilated. Hicks and his British staff were never seen again, and only a few hundred Egyptians straggled away from the battlefield. The Mahdi thus became supreme in the southern Sudan, only a few isolated Egyptian garrisons remained in the country, and the scene was set for the appearance on the imperial stage of General Gordon.

3

The Egyptians had ruled the Sudan with the help of free-lance employees from Europe, men of several nationalities and disparate styles, who frequently rose abruptly from obscurity to be the Governors of vast remote provinces. The most remarkable of them had been Gordon. After a varied career in or around the British Army, including an adventurous time in China which earned him the life-long sobriquet 'Chinese' Gordon, in 1874 he had accepted an Egyptian invitation to be Governor of Equatoria, the southernmost province of the Sudan, in succession to Sir Samuel Baker the explorer. He had seen the task as a Christian call. The Sudan was in the grip of the slave traders, often in corrupt alliance with Egyptian administrators, and for five years Gordon strenuously fought them, making enemies and admirers in equal numbers, upsetting the conventions of generations, prodding his Egyptian masters into action and opening the country to trade and government almost to the Great Lakes themselves. His work had been much publicized at home as an example of the muscular Christianity then in vogue, and Gordon had persuaded himself that he had achieved some arcane ascendancy over the tribespeople, but his success had really been limited. The Egyptian administrators remained irreformably corrupt, the Egyptian soldiers were cruel racialists, the Khedive himself, though publicly committed to the abolition of the slave trade, could do little about it because several of his most powerful subjects were engaged in it. If Gordon did bring a momentary degree of order to the Sudan, the country soon relapsed into its habitual misery. Gordon resigned once, in 1876, but was persuaded back as Governor-General in Khartoum: in 1879 he resigned again, and this time it seemed he would never return to the Nile.

His Chinese and African adventures, his lofty Christian ideals, had made him a legend in England already, but he loitered the years away. Once he accepted the job of private secretary to the Viceroy of India, only to change his mind before his ship reached Bombay. Once he went to China again, to persuade the Chinese against war with Russia. He was in Ireland for a time, briefly commanded the Royal Engineers in Mauritius, went to South Africa as commandant of the colonial forces in the Cape, spent a year in Palestine investigating the sites of the Holy Places, and was about to resign his commission and take employment with the King of the Belgians when, in January 1884, he was summoned to London by telegram for an interview with Mr Gladstone's Cabinet.

More than ever, after the catastrophe at El Obeid, the British Government wanted nothing to do with the Sudan. Gladstone was not only unwilling to send an imperial expedition to avenge Hicks and reconquer the country for Egypt, he also insisted that the Khedive should withdraw all the Egyptian garrisons and trading communities left in the Sudan, abandoning the country in effect to the Mahdi. While this was, in its anti-expansionist aspects, a properly Gladstonian decision, in other ways it was uncharacteristic of the Grand Old Man. To many of his supporters it seemed unworthy, to most of his opponents it seemed feeble. It was abandoning the work of civilization. It was leaving the field to slavers and Muslim fanatics. It was a betrayal of all that Gordon and his colleagues had achieved, not to speak of Livingstone and the missionaries of central Africa. There was a growing public agitation to do something about the Sudan—just what, nobody was quite certain—and the man most often mentioned for the job was Gordon, a hero unemployed.

So on January 18 Gordon presented himself at the War Office in Pall Mall, chaperoned by the Adjutant-General of the British Army, Baron Wolseley of Cairo and Wolseley—so old a friend that the two men, we are told, remembered each other nightly in their prayers. Gladstone was ill at home, but his senior Cabinet colleagues were present, and most of them were more Empire-minded than he was himself: Lord Hartington the War Minister ('Harty-Tarty'), Lord Granville the Foreign Minister ('weak as water', in the Queen's opinion), Lord Northbrooke the First Lord of the Admiralty, Sir Charles Dilke of *Greater Britain* fame. Did they know what they were doing? Did they really wish, as Dilke perhaps wished, to acquire the Sudan for the British Empire? Or did they hope, as Gladstone more probably hoped, that General Gordon would simply settle the Sudan himself, in his own inimitable way, and enable them to forget it? We can never be sure. They commissioned Gordon only to report on the prospects of evacuating the Egyptian garrisons from the Sudan—instructions vaguely worded, and perhaps imprecisely meant. Gladstone, away in his bed at Hawarden, limply telegraphed his acquiescence, and Gordon agreed to leave upon this nebulous mission that very evening, by the night train to Paris and Brindisi which connected with a P. and O. steam packet to Alexandria.

Lord Granville, Lord Wolseley and the Duke of Cambridge, Commander-in-Chief of the British Army, all went to Charing Cross to see him off. Wolseley, finding that the hero had no money in his pockets, gave him the cash from his own wallet, together with his watch and chain. The Duke of Cambridge opened the carriage door for him. Removing their top hats in farewell, holding their kid gloves in their hands, the three great men watched the train crossing the Thames into South London's murky dusk, before returning to their carriages and dinner. They had, as Gladstone later said, let loose a genie from a bottle: or more pertinently, launched to his apotheosis an imperial martyr.

4

Here are a few facts about Charles Gordon, who was 51 in 1884, unmarried, a passionate Christian fundamentalist, and who was shortly to become, for a few months, the most celebrated man alive. He was a slight man of 5′ 5″, with brown curly hair, a smile of great sweetness, and eyes of a piercing cold blue—unnaturally bright eyes, magical eyes some people thought, 'filled with the beauty of holiness', 'an eye and expression that might have lived a thousand years', 'eyes with a depth like that of reason', or as a Sudanese child once put it, 'eyes very blue, very bright, and I frighted when I see eyes'. It was said that he could see in the dark: certainly he was so colour-blind that he could tell one postage stamp from another only by the number on it.

Gordon had been a zealous evangelist since being stationed as an engineer officer at Gravesend, when he used to stick tracts on walls or trees, and throw them out of train windows. He loved boys, with a love apparently innocuous but nonetheless intense, running a youth club at Gravesend, and curiously describing his efforts to evangelize its members as 'adventures with Royalty'. He was also an indefatigable visitor to the sick and the old: in Gravesend, where dying people often asked for him instead of the doctor, one sometimes saw the graffito 'God Bless the Kernel' on the walls of slums. He believed implicitly in Heaven, though perhaps not in Hell, and regarded death as a triumphant release, to be coveted all through life —'the glorious gate of eternity, of glory and joy unmixed with a taint of sorrow'. 'I went to Polly's', he recorded of one death-bed visit, 'and saw her off to the Golden City. She left at ten minutes to 12, very happily and beautifully. "What are those bands playing for?" she said just before her departure. It was the Harpers with their harps, harping. . . .'

At the same time he was a mystic of a weirder kind. He believed the earth to be enclosed in a hollow globe, the firmament, with God's throne resting upon it immediately above the altar of burnt offering in the temple at Jerusalem. When God spoke at the creation, he maintained, the devil fled to the point in the hemisphere of darkness farthest from God's throne—latitude 31° 47' South, he estimated, 144° 5' West, which was not far from Pitcairn Island in the South Pacific. As for the Garden of Eden, it was on the bed of the sea near the Seychelles, the forbidden fruit being really the *coco de mer*. Gordon had pronounced theories too about the Holy Places in Jerusalem, vigorously denying the authenticity of most accepted sites, and confidently identifying alternatives of his own.[1]

He was obviously eccentric: he was also notoriously undisciplined. Wherever he went he made disciples, but he nearly always quarrelled too. He was the very antithesis of the good regimental soldier: he spent most of his life on independent missions, generally in command, and almost the most compelling thing about him was his air of absolute self-reliance. He gave the impression of *knowing*— knowing the tribes, the terrain, the enemy intentions, the inner reasons for a development or its unrevealed results. He liked to be alone, preferably in a position of uninterruptable power, and from his commanding isolation he looked out upon the world with a caustic but not humourless fatalism, tinged with bitterness sometimes, but more often with a sense of the transient or the ludicrous.

Gordon's influence on those he met was generally stunning, though not always permanent. It was the eyes that did it, with the conviction, and a modesty which, while in retrospect it often seems specious, was clearly persuasive at the time. The Archdeacon of Mauritius, for instance, used to record with reverence that Gordon, as commanding engineer on the island, liked to sit at the back of the church with the native Mauritians. 'But one day, on some official church ceremonial, Gordon had to attend in full uniform and take his place in the front pew. The chest of the great soldier was blazing with medals. But every time he stood up during the service Gordon picked up his helmet and held it in front of his chest . . . to hide (them).'

Garnet Wolseley called Gordon 'God's friend'—one of the few men among his acquaintances, as the Only General cautiously added, 'who came up to my estimate of the Christian hero'. Gladstone too thought him 'a hero, and a hero of heroes'. William Butler, that

---

[1] Which a few faithful followers accept to this day: Gordon's sites are still shown to visitors in Jerusalem.

invaluable chronicler of imperial reactions, called him 'the noblest knight among us all'. Richard Burton described him as 'a man whose perfect truthfulness and integrity . . . made him a phenomenon in the nineteenth century'. A Sudanese steamer captain, remembering him after his death, called him 'not a man but a God'. Among the public at large these impressions were wildly magnified. Gordon could do no wrong. He was the greatest guerilla leader in the world. He was a saint. He was a living legend of perfection.

Gladstone and his colleagues were not always so sure. Nor was Evelyn Baring, the cool and able ex-soldier who, as British Agent-General in Cairo, dubiously awaited the arrival of this contradictory paragon. Nor for that matter was Gordon himself—'talk of two natures in one!' he wrote of himself. 'I have a hundred, and none think alike and all want to rule.' Which nature was required on this particular mission, nobody was sure, for nobody quite knew what the mission was. By the time Gordon reached Egypt, his original instructions to 'report' had become a mandate to organize the withdrawal of the garrisons, and he had been appointed Governor-General of the Sudan once more. Even so his purposes were interpreted according to taste. The British Government apparently wanted him to withdraw the garrisons and abandon the country to the Mahdi. The expansionists wanted him either to annex the Sudan to the British Empire, or reorganize it as a dependency of Egypt—the puppet of a puppet. The anti-imperialists wanted him to establish a truly independent Sudan, presumably under the Mahdi. The soldiers were concerned about the security of Egypt and of the Sudanese ports on the Red Sea. The evangelicals thought Mahdism might mean a resurgence of Islamic power throughout Africa, and certainly new life for the slave trade. Some people hoped Gordon would establish his own personal regime in the Sudan, as the buccaneering James Brooke had made himself the beneficent ruler of Sarawak earlier in the century.

As for Gordon himself, one can only say that his purposes did *not* embrace the abandonment of the Sudan, as Gladstone intended. 'Stand fast,' he cabled Khartoum, 'I am coming, you are men, not women.' He was not an imperialist himself—'I have never been able to answer the query in what way we would lose, if we failed to keep

[India]'—and was unlikely to want to seize the Sudan for the Crown of England, let alone for the tinsel coronet of Egypt. Nor was he, for all his Christian fervour, altogether hostile to the Mahdi, who was certainly more admirable than the unspeakable Egyptians he was rebelling against. Perhaps he himself had no very clear notion why he was going to Khartoum, but merely wished to be back there, exerting his magical ascendancy over the people, occupying the centre of the stage, and making all things right. This was, too, the vague but comforting feeling of the British public. As the *Pall Mall Gazette* put it, 'he will have full and undivided responsibility for affairs in the Sudan. Whether we evacuate the country or retain it, as soon as Gordon takes command and for as long as Gordon's command holds, England is directly responsible for whatever is done in the name of the Egyptian Government between the Third Cataract and the Equatorial Lakes'.

With such hyperbole ringing in his ears, and perhaps playing through his mind, did the peculiar Major-General, chain-smoking and dictating incessant telegraphic messages, leave Cairo for Khartoum. He took with him a military assistant, Colonel J. D. Stewart, and a young *Times* correspondent, Frank Power, and he left behind him an anxious Baring, a bewildered Government and a doting British public.

5

On February 18, 1884, he reached Khartoum. It was not a very beautiful place in those days. Its *raison d'être* was the river junction at which, mingling symbolically in the sunshine, the White and Blue Niles joined their streams. For the rest it was unremarkable. It stood along the bank of the Blue Nile, littered with the masts and felucca sails of the river craft, and extended perhaps a mile inland in a hot straggle of mud brick. Its houses were mostly grey single-storey structures, interspersed with gardens and palm groves, with the domes and minarets of a few shabby mosques, and narrow dusty streets criss-crossing the city from wall to wall. There was a small dockyard near the river junction, with its own settlement of dockyard workers in huts and shanties by the water, and here one could see the spindly funnels and white upper-works of the Government paddle steamers which ran downstream to Berber. Behind it were the sleazy streets of the red-light district, geared so habitually to the demands of the Egyptian civic authorities that the Sudanese called it Salamat-al-Pasha—Pasha Town. At the north end of the city were the barracks of the Egyptian garrison, with an arsenal nearby, and there was an Austrian Catholic mission, and an Austrian Consulate in a date grove, and a handful of substantial houses built by the few European traders in the place, and a Coptic church with three domes.

Beyond Tuti Island the main stream of the united river slowly passed, dun-coloured itself, a mile across, with the open desert extending as far as the eye could see on the other side, and only the small village of Omdurman, with its clumps of palms, to break the monotonous silhouette. Khartoum was horribly isolated. There was a telegraph line to Cairo, but the mail, like nearly everything else, had to come by camel over immense tracts of desert, or in boats warped laboriously over the Nile cataracts. The average day-time heat varied from 90° in January to 170° in May; the rainfall ran from nothing at all during five months of the year to about 3″ in August; the city smelt of dust and dung, and heavily on its air hung hot African sounds—the exhausted barking of pi-dogs, the chuff of steam machinery at the dockyard, quavering muezzins in the morning, the rattle of cartwheels and the slow flabby thud of camel-hoofs on the way to market.

'I am glad to see you', Gordon told the people of this stifling African city, arriving there by camel-back with his companions. 'It is four years since I was here, and the Sudan is miserable, and I am miserable, and I want your help to put it right. I have come here alone without troops and we must ask Allah to look after the Sudan if no one else can.' He moved at once into the Governor-General's palace, on the bank of the Blue Nile in the centre of town. This was a dingy building of two stories, grey with green sunblinds, likened in one sufficiently macabre comparison to an Egyptian boarding house. In front, across the open quay, was its private landing-stage; behind, enclosed by single-storey wings, there was a courtyard with a pond, a fountain and a vine-trellis; behind that again, a garden, shaded by palms and watered by a steam-pump. At first Gordon shared this unprepossessing edifice with Stewart and Power, later he lived there all alone; the upper floor, built as a harem, he used as his private quarters, downstairs were his offices.

For nearly a year he stayed there. Exactly why, nobody could be sure, for he confided in nobody, and though he sent a constant stream of telegrams to Baring in Cairo, he never really defined his intentions. As to instructions from London, he simply took no notice of them, first to last. He did not long pretend that he was simply there to evacuate the garrisons, making indeed no attempt to do anything of the kind. Instead he implied that he was chiefly concerned with the future stability of the Sudan. He toyed with the idea of negotiating peace with the Mahdi, and suggested that as an agent of authority the Government should send to Khartoum a notorious former slave-trader, Zubeir Pasha, who had once been Gordon's bitter enemy, but towards whom he had lately developed, he said, 'a mystical feeling'. The very name of Zubeir was anathema to the English evangelicals, and Gordon's quixotic demand for his services was the British public's first intimation that queer things were likely to happen in Khartoum—his employment, said the Anti-Slavery Society, would be 'a degradation for England, a scandal to Europe'.

Next Gordon began to hint that perhaps after all the Sudan should be reconquered by British arms, if only to guarantee the security of Egypt. 'If Egypt is to be kept quiet the Mahdi must be smashed up. Mahdi is most unpopular and with care and time could be smashed . . . evacuation is possible, but you will feel effect in Egypt and will be forced into a far more serious affair in order to guard Egypt. At present it would be comparatively easy to destroy Mahdi.' Within Khartoum Gordon exuded confidence and calm. In his cables to the world outside, he seemed in a perpetual state of irritable dither, constantly changing his mind: telegrams reached Baring in Cairo almost every day, so full of ideas and counter-ideas, at once so exuberant and so inconsistent, sometimes so eminently sensible, sometimes so ridiculous, that poor Baring understandably concluded General Gordon to be 'half-cracked'.

In March the situation abruptly changed. A message from the

Mahdi put paid to any hope of negotiated settlement: if Gordon surrendered he would save himself and his supporters, 'otherwise you shall perish with them and your sins and theirs shall be on your head'. Now the tribes to the north of Khartoum, hitherto quiescent, rose in support of the Mahdi. The rebels invested Khartoum itself, and the telegraph line to Cairo was cut. Gordon's communications with Baring were reduced to messages on scraps of paper, sent out by runner, and Khartoum became a city under siege.

Now at least Gordon was explicit. When the British Government got a message through asking why he seemed to be making no attempt to leave Khartoum with the garrison, as instructed, his reply was tart. 'You ask me to state cause and intention in staying in Khartoum knowing Government means to abandon Sudan, and in answer I say, I stay at Khartoum because Arabs have shut us up and will not let us out.' This was not true. He could still fight his way out of Khartoum, but he had never tried to do so, and gradually, as the summer of 1884 dragged by, it became dimly apparent to Mr Gladstone's Government that Gordon was blackmailing them. He had no intention either of withdrawing the garrisons, or even escaping himself: he wanted the British to reconquer the Sudan by force of arms, and he was staking his own person as hostage. If the British public baulked at Zubeir, despised the Egyptians, was not very interested in the future of the Sudan and had little idea where Khartoum was, it would certainly not be prepared to let 'Chinese' Gordon, the perfect Christian gentleman, die abandoned and friendless in the heart of Africa.

By the middle of September Gordon was almost the only European in Khartoum. Power and Stewart had tried to get away by steamer, only to be caught and slaughtered by Arabs downstream. The city was closely invested now, very few messages arrived from Cairo, and our only reliable account of Gordon's circumstances comes from his own journal, which he sent to Egypt on board the steamer *Bordeen*, the last to leave Khartoum. He was an impulsive diarist, erratic but enthralling in this as in all else, and his chronicle is jumpy, tense, sometimes a little paranoiac, decorated with thickly-shaded pen sketches and cartoons, and informed always with a bitter humour. Rumours had reached Gordon of a relief expedition being prepared in Egypt to rescue him, and the knowledge of that distant army, so reluctantly it seemed coming to his support, sours many of his entries, and moves him to an often unconvincing sarcasm. He apparently wanted the army to come, if only to restore order to the Sudan, and to embarrass the pacifist Gladstone, already embarrassed enough by the conquest of Egypt: but he only half wanted to be rescued. His journal is full of the death wish, for he shared with the Mahdi and his warriors the conviction that death in battle was the quickest way to God.

He wrote his journal in his stifling upstairs bedroom. He had refused to have its windows sandbagged against blast or rifle-fire: the fierce sun came slanting through its slats all day, the dust dancing on its shafts, while at night candles burnt defiantly at the open window. Gordon wrote at first on ruled account paper, neatly and methodically. Later he used very thin tissue paper, on which the ink often messily blotted, and when this ran out he wrote on old cable forms, headed *Administration des Télégraphes Egyptiens du Sudan*, and generally slipped into his journal upside-down. His writing is cramped but clear—he uses the eighteenth century 's'—and at first he evidently intended the journal to be published: 'N.B. This journal will want *pruning out*, if thought necessary, to publish'. Later the diary grew moodier, crankier, more careless, as his chances of survival retreated, and his health and confidence declined. The whole work is an extraordinary performance. The journals are strangely punctuated, sometimes strikingly phrased, sometimes blandly fatalist, sometimes piously orthodox, and their range of subjects, emotions, and allusions extends far beyond the state of the siege or the condition of the Sudan.

Sometimes Gordon does philosophize about the Sudanese ('decidedly slave-huntingly inclined'), sometimes he reflects upon his own part in the drama: 'A MP in one of our last received papers, asked "whether officers were not supposed to go where ordered?" I quite agree with his view, but it cannot be said I was ordered to go, the subject was too complex for any order, it was "Will you go and try?" and my answer was, "only too delighted".' Almost as often, though, he writes about officialdom in general, or throws in a *Punch* parody, or an anecdote of local life. Here he considers polygamy:

'It is really amusing to find (when one can scarcely call one's life one's own) one's servant, *already* with one wife (which most men find is enough), coming and asking for leave for three days in order to take another wife. . . .' Here he muses upon the British bureaucracy: 'I must say I do not love our F.O. or diplomatists, as a whole (and I can fancy the turning up of noses, at my venturing to express an opinion of them, I mean in their *official* attire, for, personally, the few I know are most agreeable (and I specially except Alston the Chief Clerk, and Weller the Hall Porter, (who has, of late years, become quite amiable))'. Here he talks about the conventional bravery—he was *always* afraid himself, he used to say: 'Some accounts in *Gazette*, describing reasons for giving Victoria Cross are really astounding, such as a man who, with another, was out on a reconnaissance, this other was wounded, and his companion waited for him and took him on his horse, saving his life! What would we have said, had he left his companion!'

Once he sends a mock-address to the Lord Mayor's banquet in London. Once he echoes Jeremiah:[1] '*Cursed is he, of the Lord*, who hopes by any arrangement of forces, or by exterior help, to be relieved from the position we are in'. Once he writes R.I.P. for a donkey blown up by a mine, having strong views about the souls of animals. Sometimes he bursts into contumely; on Africa, for example: 'a "beast" to our country, as one of Dickens characters called it'; on a former Italian lieutenant: 'I expect he is a vile traitor, like all Italians I ever met'; on Egyptian troops: 'A more contemptible soldier than the Egyptian never existed'. Sometimes he pulls himself together, after a splurge of irritable complaint, with a biblical quotation or a striking comparison: 'That I have had to undergo a tithe of what any nurse has to undergo, who is attached to a querulous invalid, is absurd, and ought to be weighed together'.[2]

[1] 17.v.: 'Cursed be the man that trusteth in man . . . for he shall be like the heath in the desert, and shall not see when good cometh; but shall inhabit the parched places in the wilderness. . . .'

[2] Gordon's Journal, whose wayward punctuation I have reproduced exactly, is now in the British Museum. Reading it in the original, its pages still stained with the ink-marks and browned with the sunshine of Khartoum long ago, seemed to me one of the most evocative and moving of all historical experiences.

6

'A drum beats—tup! tup! tup! It comes into a dream, but after a few minutes one becomes more awake, and it is in the brain that *one is in Khartoum.* The next query is, where is this tup, tupping going on. A hope arises that it will die away. No, it goes on, and increases in intensity. The thought strikes one, "Have they enough ammunition?" (the excuse of bad soldiers). One exerts oneself. At last, it is no use, up one must get, and go on to the roof of the Palace; then telegrams, orders, swearing, and cursing goes on till 9 a.m.'

For all his oddities and inconsistencies, Gordon was a great commander, and throughout 1884 he was in himself the defence of Khartoum. He had able Sudanese lieutenants, some of them French-trained,[1] but without his own presence the city would doubtless have fallen to the Mahdi without resistance. As it was, Khartoum held out with spirit for ten months. 'As safe as Kensington Park,' Gordon had declared it upon his arrival, and miraculously he had sustained this illusion as the forces of Mahdism assembled all around. Elsewhere in the Sudan the last Egyptian garrisons had long since surrendered. Some of the provincial Governors, most of them old colleagues of Gordon, had been killed: some like Slatin Pasha, the Austrian-born Governor of Darfur, had theoretically accepted Islam, and were spared as prisoners in the Mahdi's camp. Khartoum was an island in enemy territory—not an island of Christianity, for nearly all its inhabitants were Muslim, certainly not an island of Empire, for the Queen's Government claimed no suzerainty over it, but really no more than the island of one man's commanding presence.

Though Gordon's military intelligence was negligible, and his ignorance of the enemy almost wilful, his defence was indefatigable. He used every ruse and device to keep the enemy at bay, and his people's spirits up. He fortified the town with wire entanglements and home-made mines. He sent armed paddle-steamers up and down

[1] They had formed part of an international force sent by Napoleon III to put down a rebellion in Mexico in 1862.

the Nile on patrol, having specialized in the use of gunboats since his China days, and had a new boat built in the Government dock-yard (he called it *Zubeir*).[1] He inspired the arsenal to produce hundreds of thousands of rounds of ammunition. He cast his own medals, inscribed 'The Siege of Khartoum, 1884'—silver for senior officers, tin for everyone else. He sustained morale with band con-certs, hopeful proclamations, even false messages from the relieving army. He showed himself in the streets of Khartoum as confident as ever, and he assiduously cultivated his own super-human legend: 'When God was portioning out fear to all the people in the world,' he once told a Khartoum merchant, 'at last it came to my turn, and there was no fear left to give me; go, tell all the people in Khartoum that Gordon fears nothing, for God has created him without fear.'

Even so, as the weeks passed without sign of relief, as the mes-sages from Egypt became rarer and finally ceased, as food ran short in the capital, and the siege became ever more intense, Gordon's resistance was sustained only by desperate bluff. When the Mahdi sent him a call to surrender, he replied: 'I am here, like iron, and hope to see the newly-arrived English'. When the public spirit sagged, he spread rumours of imminent relief, or set labourers to work on moorings for the relieving army's steamers, or rented houses for the incoming English officers. Sometimes he dispatched runners bearing messages of false assurance, hoping they would be intercepted by the enemy—'Khartoum all right. 12.12.84', or 'Khartoum is all right. Could hold out for years. C. G. Gordon. 29. 12. 84'.

He spent much of his time on the roof of his palace. He had picked up a telescope in the bazaar, 'the best glass I ever had', and through it he kept his eye on the outpost sentries, or watched enemy move-ments on the far bank of the river. From that high watchpost he could see the funnels of his steamers at the dockyard, and look down the line of the Blue Nile quays, and away in the distance, if he could not see the mainstream of the Nile itself, week after week he hoped to sight the flags and upperworks of the relieving steamers sliding past Tuti island.

[1] One of the steamers he used at Khartoum may still be seen there, moored near the Palace as a yacht club.

The heat up there was stunning, especially for a European dressed, as Gordon generally was, in the florid uniform of an Egyptian government official, with a high braided collar and a tarboosh on his head. But it was an heroic prospect, all the same, and it is hard to escape the feeling that 'Chinese' Gordon enjoyed the last weeks of his siege. We can sense from his journals the perverse satisfaction he derived from self-laceration and recrimination; those scurrilous cartoons he drew, those hilariously waspish denunciations of Baring or Gladstone, were, like furious but unposted letters to the editor of *The Times*, obviously fun to compose. He admired his Mahdist enemies, he enjoyed war and responsibility, and if he despised his Egyptian soldiers, he was indubitably attracted by the stalwart Sudanese—the British always were. From his rooftop he could observe the whole grand cycle of the Nile, the very number of whose cataracts held a mystic meaning for him, the rise and fall of its waters, the grand flow of its stream, the movements of the pelicans and great maribou storks that haunted those equatorial reaches. The purposes of his heroism may sometimes have seemed unclear to him, as they do to us, but he must have known that his relief would only have been a sad anti-climax—an ignominious rescue from failure, for brave and skilful though his defence had been, he had really achieved nothing.

He was terribly alone. He had no intimate friend in the city—he spoke little Arabic, nobody else spoke English. Yet he never sounds unhappy. He had, like so many of the Victorian imperial heroes, like Napier, like Hodson, like Colley, a vivid sense of theatre: and there in the throttling heat of his palace roof he was playing the most splendid of all tragic roles, to the best of all audiences. He made sure it was all recorded for posterity, and he did not fail to stage manage the last curtain to legendary effect.

For on Monday, January 26, 1885, at three in the morning, the Mahdi's soldiers burst into Khartoum at last, slaughtering everybody they saw. They reached the palace before dawn, and Gordon went to the roof to see what was happening. Some people say he then changed into his white ceremonial uniform, picked up a sword and a revolver, and went to the head of the palace stairs, where he awaited his death with a saintly scorn, and was speared to death just before the sun came up. Other versions have him fighting desperately to the death—from the roof, on the stairs, into the garden. Yet another says that Gordon was leaning over the balcony shouting in his crude Arabic 'Kill them! Hit them!' when a spear hit him, spun him round, and held him for an instant balanced on the top of the stairs, before he toppled down and was cut to pieces. However it happened, Gordon's death was to be imprinted for ever upon the minds of his wondering audience far away, and for his own generation the perfect archetype of the imperial hero was to remain this fanatic, disobedient and unpredictable original.

7

'Who,' asked Ruskin once at the beginning of this affair, 'is the Sudan?' By now he was sure to know, for the predicament of General Gordon in Khartoum had become the principal preoccupation not merely of the British, but of the world. Almost from the start Gladstone realized what a terrible mistake he had made in sending Gordon to Africa at all. Whether he had been deceived by more imperially-minded colleagues, or duped by Gordon himself, a mission that had begun as mere reportage had fatally changed its character, and the genie had left its bottle with a vengeance. Already deep in a quagmire of imperial adventure and domestic reform, Gladstone now found his worst nightmare coming true: a true-blue British hero, sent by a Liberal Government to do a desperately dangerous task surrounded by savages in an inconceivably hot and distant land, was at large in Africa, inspiring the public to adulatory hero-worship, and summoning all those false phantoms of glory which the Prime Minister most detested. Empire all too often followed trade, as Mr Gladstone knew, and sometimes (more beneficially) followed the missionaries, and occasionally (such was the inscrutability of that Providence which, as history confirmed more explicitly each year, could only be Divine) followed the armies. Here it seemed horribly likely to follow the Hero. If the Grand Old Man obeyed the call of glory, he would be betraying his own principles: if he ignored it, he would soon be out of office.

To everybody else but Gladstone the idea of abandoning General

Gordon seemed almost unimaginable, and his Cabinet knew that to do so would be political suicide. The Press, the clergy, the army, the Queen herself as emotionally as anyone—all demanded the dispatch of an army to rescue the general. Yet for weeks the Prime Minister temporized. He was understandably exasperated by Gordon's behaviour—'turning upside down and inside out every idea and intention with which he had left England, and for which he had obtained our approval'. He was reluctant to embark upon a war against the Sudanese, 'a people struggling to be free', as he assured the House of Commons—'yes, those people are struggling to be free, and they are rightly struggling to be free!' Besides, he thought Gordon's predicament exaggerated. To send an expedition 'would be to act in the teeth of evidence which, however imperfect, is far from being trivial, and would be a grave and dangerous error'. It was possibly true that Khartoum was hemmed in, 'that is to say, that there are bodies of hostile troops in the neighbourhood forming more or less of a chain around it', but 'I draw a distinction between that and the town being surrounded, which would bear technically a very different meaning'.

Nevertheless he knew himself to be both hemmed in and surrounded. His Government depended upon the fate of General Gordon, who had, Gladstone now began to think, deliberately arranged things to manoeuvre him into this quandary. 'The cause,' he told Lord Granville, looking back upon it all, 'was insufficient knowledge of our man.' Everybody now pressed him to mount a relief expedition, even Granville himself. Public feeling was fierce. Crowds hissed him for the delay. Mass meetings protested against the 'betrayal' of Gordon. White feathers were stuck on cards and called 'Gladstone primroses'. It is true that Lord Tennyson sent him a poem, rich in Nilotic imagery, which began with these lines:

> *Steersman, be not precipitous in thy act*
> *Of steering, for the river here, my friend,*
> *Parts in two channels, moving to one end.*
> *This goes straight forward to the cataract,*
> *That streams about the bend;*
> *But tho' the cataract seem the nearer way,*

Whatever the crowd on either bank may say,
Take thou the bend, 'twill save thee many a day.

It was, however, only a Freudian slip of metaphor, for the Poet
Laureate was referring not to the cataracts of Africa at all, but to
the hazards of a wider enfranchisement.

In the Autumn Gladstone capitulated, and asked the House of
Commons for a grant of £300,000 'to enable operations to be undertaken for the relief of General Gordon, should they become neces-
say'. It was, he said, 'a most distressing and perplexing affair', and
was likely in the long run to put twopence on the income-tax.

8

It was like a parable: Gordon the half-mad hero in Khartoum, Gladstone the embattled man of conscience at Westminster, Victoria the
Queen-Empress furiously underlining her diary entries at Windsor.
Of course the only man to lead the rescuing armies up the Nile was
Lord Wolseley. Among all the figures of the fable, it seems, he alone
knew his purpose throughout: one suspects he foresaw it all, under-
stood exactly the character of Gordon, and realized that his presence
in Khartoum would lead inevitably, in the end, to a British invasion
of the Sudan. He was already the conqueror of Egypt, the first since
Napoleon. Now he would take the British power majestically where
Napoleon never penetrated, upstream towards the headwaters of the
Nile—for 'I don't wish', as he had pointedly observed in a memorandum to the Cabinet, 'to share the responsibility of leaving Charlie
Gordon to his fate'.

All the true Wolseleyan touches marked the preparation of the
expedition. All the Ring were there, or at least all those who survived: Buller, Butler—'the grandest and noblest work of war in my
time'—and many another veteran of Red River, Ashanti and South
Africa. Even the *voyageurs* who had, so many years before, taken
Wolseley with songs and high spirits to Fort Garry, were recruited
again to navigate the British Army through the cataracts—supplemented this time by Kroomen from West Africa, and by advice upon
the use of river boats by that old African hand, Henry Stanley. Every-

body wished to share in the great enterprise. The Prince of Wales volunteered to go, but was forbidden by his mother, and all the grandest regiments wanted to join the army, drawn from garrisons in Britain, India, Malta and Gibraltar, which Wolseley assembled for the campaign: even its *ad hoc* camel corps was recruited exclusively from the Household Cavalry, the cavalry regiments of the line, the Foot Guards, the Rifle Brigade and the Royal Marines.[1] There was a Naval Brigade too, of course, and a marvellous assortment of adventurers from all over the world attached themselves to the colours in Egypt. William Butler's personal boat crew comprised two Canadian voyageurs, six Kroomen, an Arab guide, a Syrian interpreter and an English servant, and he wrote a song to keep their spirits up:

> *Row, my boys, row away,*
> *Cowards behind may stay,*
> *Bend to the strain, man!*
> *Miles, as they rise and sink,*
> *Knock off another link,*
> *From Gordon's chain, man!*

Carefully and efficiently Lord Wolseley, having safely assembled this heterogeneous force in Egypt, travelled up the course of the Nile, supplied with coal, rations and river steamers by Thomas Cook the travel agents. By November, 1884, they were through the first and second cataracts. By December they were at Korti, and the New Year saw them crossing the Bayuda desert. On January 17 they defeated a Mahdist army at Abu Klea, 100 miles from the Capital, and on January 28, 1885, the crew of the leading armed steamer sighted the distant silhouette of Khartoum itself. It was

---

[1] *I've rode in a ship, I've rode in a boat,*
I've rode on a railway train.
I've rode in a coach, I've rode a moke,
And I hope to ride one again.
But I'm riding now an animal
A Marine never rode before,
Rigged up in spurs and pantaloons,
As one of the Camel Corps.
—Sergeant Eagle, R.M., 1884.

one of the great moments of the imperial story, and to dramatize it further still twenty men on board the ship were dressed in scarlet—the last British soldiers ever to wear the red coat of Empire into battle.

It was a year to the day since Gordon's departure from Cairo, and the relieving force had no idea whether he was dead or alive. Rifle fire spattered against the little steamer as it paddled up the river, shells splashed all around, its engine thumped and its flags fluttered, until at last its crew could see, away to the east across the parched blank expanse of Tuti Island, the outline of the palace against the palms. No flag flew from the roof, and on the sandy spit below the river bank hundreds of Sudanese were gathered beneath the banners of the Mahdi. The British were, as they later discovered, just three days too late.

9

Too late! Too late to save him,
In vain, in vain they tried.
His life was England's glory,
His death was England's pride.

So the anti-climax was avoided, and the British Empire achieved its moment of sacrament. The nation was stricken. Society put on its blackest silk, in a hundred cartoons, broadsheets and popular songs Britannia mourned her champion's death. Not only in London, but in Paris, Berlin and New York too, black-draped portraits of Gordon appeared in shop windows.

At Windsor, when the news reached her, Queen Victoria stalked all in black into the cottage of her lady-in-waiting, Mary Ponsonby, to proclaim sepulchrally '*Gordon is dead!*' In South Africa Cecil Rhodes said over and over again 'I'm sorry I was not with him! I'm sorry I was not with him!' And in the Mahdi's camp at Omdurman the apostate Rudolf Slatin, sitting in chains outside his tent, was approached by three black soldiers carrying something wrapped up in a cloth, and followed by a crowd of people. Unwrapping the cloth with a mocking air, they revealed to Slatin the head of General Gordon. His famous blue eyes were half open still. His hair was almost white. 'Is not this the head of your uncle the unbeliever?' they said. 'What of it?' Slatin replied, at least in reminiscence. 'A brave soldier who fell at his post; happy is he to have fallen; his sufferings are over'.[1]

[1] Though Wolseley failed in this, his greatest adventure, and for the rest of his life believed it to mark a turn in his fortunes, still his imperial ambitions for the Sudan were satisfied thirteen years later when Kitchener conquered the country and annexed it, in fact if not in theory, to the Empire. Gordon's presence in Khartoum may still be tellingly evoked by a visit to the roof of the palace, now the home of the President of the Sudanese People's Republic, which has been rebuilt on the same site, commands the same dun view of Tuti, Omdurman and the Nile, and is still, as it happens, and for similar reasons, fortified with sandbags against attack. Gordon's memory remains vivid in the city, too. Until Sudanese independence in 1956 a camel-back statue of the hero stood in the main cross-roads of the capital (it is now at the Gordon Boys' School near Woking in Surrey). A favourite Anglo-Sudanese anecdote concerned the English boy taken by his father every Sunday after morning service to pay homage at this shrine. After several weeks of reverent pilgrimage he ventured to ask his father a question. 'Who is the man,' he inquired, 'on Gordon's back?'

CHAPTER TWENTY-SIX

Scramble for Africa

IN the last week of December, 1895, a curious military force was
assembled at a place called Pitsani, in the Bechuanaland Protectorate just across the frontier from the Transvaal Republic—
where President Paul Kruger now ruled the destinies of a State
transformed by the discovery of gold on the Witwatersrand. Pitsani
stood on the Missionary Road, the old highway into central Africa
from the south, and was now on the route of the railway line being
built northwards from Cape Colony. The country around was
magnificent open veld, vast and daunting, covered with stubbly
rough grass, littered with huge boulders, with the occasional thorn
tree in silhouette against the horizon, and the shadows of gulleys
here and there. A few small kopjes broke the flat immensity of the
scene, and patches of blue and yellow wild flowers lay like stains
upon the dun.

Pitsani was 4,400 feet up on the veld. The air was tingling, and
was scented only by a faint dry smell of dust. In the daytime the
sky was often banked tremendously with white rolling clouds, and
the light was so clear that miles away across the plain one could see
the distant slow movements of tribespeople with their cattle. At
night the sky was tremendous with unfamiliar constellations, and
smudged with the mysterious Magellanic Clouds, and through the
silence crickets chafed and night-birds abruptly whooped. It was a
place for simple romanticism, schoolboy thoughts of fate and infinity, glorious impulses and heady self-delusions.

The commander of the force was not a soldier at all, but a well-
known colonial physician, Dr Leander Starr Jameson. He was best
known to the world as an intimate of Cecil Rhodes, who was now not
only Premier of Cape Colony, but had created his own eponymous

British colony, Rhodesia, north of the Transvaal. But the doctor was remarkable enough in his own right. A small, elfin sort of man, with big brown eyes and a disturbing wistfulness of expression, he had graduated from medicine to be Administrator of Rhodesia, and was now, in his tent upon a Pitsani kopje, about to embark upon one of the most fateful of all the imperial adventures. A lifelong gambler, he was soon to stake not merely his own reputation, but the good name of the entire British Empire, upon a once-and-for-all, hit-or-miss stroke of piracy. He hoped to achieve what the British had, during the past half-century of Victoria's reign, so signally failed to arrange: the inclusion within the Empire of those most resilient of its opponents, the Voortrekker Boers.

By now the Transvaal Republic, though still arguably subject to the suzerainty of the Queen, was defiantly independent once more. In the years since Majuba Hill its circumstances had greatly changed, for thanks to the gold strikes it was now immensely rich. It was also ironically cosmopolitan. Thousands of adventurers, mostly British but representing every nationality under the sun, had poured across its frontiers to the Rand diggings, and they had created in its principal mining centre, Johannesburg, one of the toughest and wildest towns in Africa. It was mostly a shanty town still, and it teemed with every kind of opportunist: peripatetic miners, wandering from gold strike to diamond rush across the world, specialists in land speculation or mineral assay, shady lawyers, ill-defined agents, saloon keepers, prostitutes, remittance men, money-lenders from many countries in top hats and muddied gaiters, even itinerant actors, musicians and portrait painters. There were able and distinguished men among them, too, most of them living in a kind of enclave at Doorfontein, the most respectable quarter of town. These included English gentlemen-adventurers, well-known Jewish financiers and mining engineers of international standing, and they formed a closely-knit inner community of their own, their houses set in gardens side by side, precisely like the management of some foreign concession.

For though it was set in the innermost keep of the Afrikaner fortress-land, Jo'burg (as even its inhabitants called it) was scarcely a Boer town at all. Its foreigners were known to the Volk simply as Uitlanders, and were looked upon with distaste not unmixed with envy. While they were clearly ungodly, they were also indispensable, for without their skills and enterprises the great gold reef could never be exploited at all. From the stoep of his home in Pretoria, forty miles to the north,[1] Kruger looked upon Johannesburg as a more fallible Moses might have looked upon the Golden Calf. He was not prepared to compromise with stiff-necked idolaters, but he was reluctant to destroy the device which had so transformed his indigent pastoral State. He treated Johannesburg as though it were some transient evil from which good might come, but lest it should prove in the end yet another British device to drag the Voortrekkers into the Empire, he assiduously sought friends abroad—the Portuguese, whose African colonies marched with the Transvaal, the Dutch, with whom the Boers still felt a faint and misguided affinity, and the Germans, who had African ambitions of their own.

The Uitlanders were understandably dissatisfied. Though they had created the gold industry of the Rand, and certainly had no intention of fading away again, they had no say in the conduct of the State's affairs, and felt themselves exploited, oppressed and ostracized. A revolutionary movement came into being in Johannesburg, calling itself simply the Reform Movement, ostensibly committed to gaining the franchise for the Uitlanders, but really hoping to rid the Rand of what was now generally called, for convenience as for camouflage, Krugerdom. It was this vestigial movement, centred upon the Doorfontein enclave, which Dr Jameson now hoped to fire. Surreptitiously backed by Rhodes at Cape Town, conspiratorially awaited by the Reformers in Johannesburg, confident of the tacit approval of the imperial Government in London, he proposed to invade the Transvaal from across the Bechuana frontier: with a hard-riding, straight-shooting, reckless handful of true-blue Britons, he would storm into Johannesburg in the best Elizabethan style, subvert Kruger and his dour government of predikants, and make the whole of southern Africa British at last.

This was something new to Victoria's Empire. The aim was

[1] Now open to the public, but 'Natives and Coloured Persons Not Allowed on Sundays'.

brasher. The means were more dishonest. There were hints of falsehood in high places which would have repelled Disraeli as much as they would have horrified Gladstone. Big business of a distasteful kind was concerned with the adventure. The evangelical instinct of Empire played no part in it, and the profit motive was blatant. They were not even imperial forces which were camped at Pitsani that December, but were a scratch company of colonial policemen, supplemented by miscellaneous freebooters and led by not very intelligent English gentry. There was no dignity to this gamble. If it succeeded, it would be a triumph of a vulgar kind: if it failed it would be ignominy.

In all this Jameson's Raid would prove a figure of its time. The imperial theme had now reached its ostentatious climax, and Disraeli's imperial instinct was fulfilled. British Governments might still be intermittently hesitant about the rights, the values, above all the costs of imperial expansion, but by now the great British public had few reservations. Empire was the grand excitement of the day, bringing into every household, almost every week, intoxicating tales of triumph or heroic disaster. The years since Ruskin's Oxford lecture had been perhaps the most consistently dramatic in the whole of British history. Wars against the Ashanti, the Afghans, the Boers, the Zulus—the Suez coup—the invasion of Egypt—the Phoenix Park murders—the death of Gordon—the epic of Stanley and Livingstone—the tragedy of Parnell—the great Disraeli-Gladstone duel—all these marvellous events, occurring one after another month after month through the decades, had sustained the British people in a condition of flush, and helped to keep their minds off drabber circumstances at home. It was like one long and thrilling piece of theatre, with scarcely a flat moment, and a scenario of brilliant daring.

This was the New Imperialism, a craze of *fin-de-siècle*. Backed by its truculent exuberance, the British Empire had embarked upon its climactic enterprise, the scramble for Africa, of which the Jameson Raid was to be at once the epitome and the disillusionment.

2

Empires were fashionable everywhere now. There was little moral opposition to the imperial idea, and the lavish success of the British, who seemed despite economic setbacks to be unquestionably the richest and most virile of the nations, made rival peoples suppose that imperial expansion must be the *sine qua non* of greatness. Empire was good for a people, it appeared, not just because it made them rich, but because it provided an arena for their best energies— adventure for their manhood, challenge for their skills, action for their ideals and aspirations. Even the Americans sometimes pined for empire now, and did not resent it when the poet Rudyard Kipling advised them to share in the civilizing mission:

> *Take up the White Man's Burden—*
> *Have done with childish days—*
> *The lightly proffered laurel,*
> *The easy, ungrudged, praise.*

The last great field for imperial expansion was Africa. The British were the chief imperial Power in the continent, but they were not unchallenged. The French were active in the north and west, the Germans had a foothold in Tanganyika, the King of the Belgians had a stake in the Congo, the Portuguese had old colonies on both the east and west coasts, and the Italians were in possession of Eritrea—though their attempt to acquire Ethiopia too had been less than successful, many of then soldiers being killed, many castrated and the rest running away. Large tracts of the continent, nevertheless, were still governed by indigenous chiefs and princes, ranging from the resplendent Sultan of Zanzibar, or the mysterious Asantahene, to myriad tufted, beaded and be-fetished petty potentates of the interior. Africa was racked still by its own incessant wars, rivalries and predations—tribe against tribe, trader against slave, Arab against negro, warrior against pastoralist. There were spoils still to come, civilizing duties yet to be fulfilled, and activists in all the imperial countries eyed the continent hungrily, some imagining its map swathed with green from coast to coast, some envisaging slabs of Prussian blue, and many conceiving one long strip of British red, veld to delta, Cape to Cairo.

Sometimes the Powers seemed likely to clash, as their traders, missionaries or troops advanced into the continent, and often diplomatic exchanges between the chanceries of Europe were prompted by episodes on distant reaches of tropic rivers, or in steamy unmapped banyan swamps: but in 1884 Bismarck, Chancellor of the new Federal Germany, perhaps foreseeing the inflammatory properties of Africa, invited all the leading nations of the world to confer in Berlin about its future. Twenty-four nations were invited. Fifteen accepted. No Africans were asked.

In Berlin the rules were laid for the final partition of Africa. It was tacitly agreed there that the civilized Powers had a right to seize, govern and civilize any part of Africa not already imperialized. Powers which held strips of African coastline were specifically authorized to control the relevant hinterland—a word which, taken from the German, entered the English language in the African context ('a very modern doctrine', the *Daily News* called it approvingly in 1891). Views were exchanged, too, on another convenient political conception, the 'sphere of influence', and it was sportingly agreed that claims to new acquisitions in Africa should be reported to other interested Powers—for African potentates not uncommonly ceded their territories to several European contenders at the same time.[1]

The Berlin Conference gave legitimacy to the scramble for Africa. It did not control the process, but it recognized the reality of this new Great Game, and made it internationally respectable, more or less. At Berlin the Powers agreed that Africans were not exactly people; though they passed some pious resolutions about the slave trade, they made it clear that the kings and nations of the continent were not kings and nations in a true, contemporary sense, bound by treaties like the nations of Europe, and entitled to rights of their own. African desires were not considered at the Berlin Conference. Imperial policies were the issue, and even they were reduced to a less than lofty scale. Richer trade and grander prestige were the aims of the diplomats, together with political success at home, and

[1] 'An inconvenient flaw', as Lord Salisbury once observed.

the tone of the conference was cynical. 'The whole colonial business is a swindle,' was Bismarck's private view, 'but we need it for the election.'

3

This was *nouveau-riche* imperialism. It was a far cry from the great days of imperial trusteeship, when British Prime Ministers saw themselves as friends and protectors to the simpler people of the world, and Empire-builders wished their story to be written, as Raffles had said, 'in characters of light'. Sir James Stephen, Colonial Under-Secretary in the brave days of evangelical imperialism, had been nicknamed 'Mr Mother-Country'. Lord Knutsford, Colonial Secretary now, was known as 'Peter Woggy'—the Wog Man.

The idea of Empire was becoming vulgarized, like some fastidious sport cheapened by arrivistes. It had often been brutal in the past, and often misguided, but it had seldom been mean. Even in hypocrisy its aspirations were at least grand, and it had been ennobled always by the lingering vision of the evangelicals. Even in moments of vindictive frenzy its furies could be interpreted as divine, and most of Victoria's imperialists genuinely believed the British Empire to be an instrument for the general good of the world.

Africa and the New Imperialism tainted this conception. There were still visionaries genuinely concerned with the betterment of the Africans, who saw the humiliation of tribes and ancient kingdoms only as sad means towards honourable ends. Generally, though, the African scramble was a chronicle of squalor—chiefs gulled, tribes dispossessed, vast inheritances signed away with a thumb-print or a shaky cross. One by one the African nations were absorbed: after the Zulus the Matabele, the Mashonas, the kingdoms of Niger, the Islamic principalities of Kano and Zanzibar, the Dinkas and the Masai, the Sudanese Muslims, Benin and Bechuana—all, one by one, in one measure or another, deprived of their sovereignty and made subject to the Great White Queen across the oceans. We see tawdry scenes of this enthusiasm: officers of the Royal Horse Guards, for instance, swaggering in full dress uniform into the kraal of King Lobengula of Matabeleland, to prepare him in the Queen's name for his swift and utter dispossession; or Charles Goldie of the Niger

Company, in his rooms off the Strand, sighting his newly-acquired Gatling gun across the Thames in preparation for trade expansion in West Africa. There was no style to it all. It was second-rate glory.

African expansionism was not the deliberate intention of power-crazed British Governments. 'Terribly have I been puzzled and perplexed', wrote poor Mr Gladstone once, 'on finding a group of the soberest men among us to have concocted a scheme such as that touching the mountain country behind Zanzibar with an unrememberable name. There *must* somewhere or other be reasons for it which have not come before me.' During the most competitive years of the African scramble the conservative Lord Salisbury was both Prime Minister and Foreign Secretary, and he was by no means a frenzied imperialist—indeed he was debatably an imperialist at all. It was he who defined British policy as drifting lazily downstream, occasionally putting out a boathook to prevent a collision, and he viewed the African imbroglio with fastidious detachment. Behind him, though, forces more strident and grasping were forcing the imperial frontiers deeper into the continent. Once the barriers were breached, the process was inevitable, so great was the gulf between the technically advanced countries, whose exemplar was Britain, and the pre-industrial societies of Africa. Many kinds of Briton urged it on. There were merchants looking for new customers, and industrialists looking for raw materials, and financiers looking for investments, and strategists arguing about India or the Nile, and soldiers coveting glory of one kind, and missionaries hoping for glory of another, and Chambers of Commerce in Liverpool or Bristol, and patriotic newspapers, and behind them all, like an intoxicated crowd at an immense spectator sport, the British public itself, now insatiably imperialist. In 1895 Joseph Chamberlain joined Salisbury's administration: he was given a choice of portfolios, and nobody was surprised when, astute politician that he was—'the People's Joe'—he chose the Colonial Office.

Avarice was the most obvious motive of the scramble, and it was only proper that as an instrument of their Empire in Africa the British should revive the idea of the Chartered Company, dormant since the abolition of the East India Company and the dispossession of Hudson's Bay. A Chartered Company, incorporated by the

Queen's authority, could raise its own armies, devise its own administrations, build its own cities, settle its own pioneers, not merely without a charge upon Treasury funds, but with luck actually at a profit for its shareholders. The new examples seemed to the British a satisfying return to form, for they combined business enterprise and political loyalty with a detectable element of swashbuckle—like the Honourable Adventurers of old, the newspapers thought, or the fighting traders who created the Indian Empire. Goldie's Niger Company conquered, ruled and successfully developed the Niger Basin in the west, and hoped to expand eastward to the Indian Ocean.[1] Rhodes's British South Africa Company was the constituted Government of Rhodesia, and hoped to expand northwards to Egypt. The Imperial East Africa Company brought Kenya and Uganda under the Crown, and hoped chiefly to make money. It was like farming out an Empire to private industry, or handing over the care of several million souls to a board of company directors, and it reduced the imperial mission to something less than Rhodes's cynical formula—'philanthropy plus five per cent'. As a perceptive West African chieftain once observed, 'One time we tink Englishman almost same as God Almighty. Now we tink he be same as other white men—all same as we.'

4

To observe the New Imperialism in the field let us station ourselves one day in December, 1890, upon a hilltop in Uganda called Kampala, almost within sight of Lake Victoria. The hill is scarcely more than a grassy knoll, with a flat summit and a few trees, but the prospect from it is splendid, and is full of meaning: for it overlooks the ancient capital of the kings of Buganda, the Kabakas, whose incumbent thirty years before Speke had found walking tiptoe like a lion. His palace stands there still on the hill called Mengo about a mile to

---

[1] Goldie's admirers wanted to call the consequent dominion 'Goldesia'. Goldie himself, who claimed to be able to hypnotize people, and carried a phial of poison in his pocket in case he was suddenly struck with an incurable illness, disclaimed all such ambitions, and regarded the scramble for Africa as 'a game of chess'.

the south, and a fine sight it is. The slopes of Mengo are covered with neatly compounded thatched huts, large and well-kept, separated by walls of grass thatch, and busy all day with the movements of men, women and animals—tethered dogs, wandering goats, cattle, armed guards, turbanned page-boys hastening from hut to hut, clutching their long skin robes around them. At the top stands the royal audience chamber, a superb round hut of intricate construction, and from it a fine broad avenue runs like a king's command down the hill to the town below.

There is a small market on the west side of Kampala hill, all white-robed bustle and bargaining, and half-hidden among the foliage are the huts and places of worship of the religious missions to Buganda—the mosque, the Roman Catholic church, the thatched Anglican cathedral. But the scene is dominated by the presence of the Kabaka, Mwanga. Strange sounds drift across the banana groves from his palace, the beating of drums, the firing of random shots, the tinkling of harps, the blare of sudden trumpets. Sometimes bands of armed men can be seen marching down the avenue into town. Fires burn at night all over the flank of Mengo, and around the corner may be seen the dark and eerie expanse of the Kabaka's sacred lake, which dries up when the king is in danger, and is loud with the screeching of egrets, and haunted by flickering black dragon-flies, and infested by bilharzia snails.

Astonishing African things have been happening in Buganda during the past few years. Plot has succeeded plot. The Catholic missions have conspired against the Anglicans. The Muslims have fought against the Christians. Mwanga has been deposed, and fought his way back to the throne again. Karl Peters, the German explorer, has made a treaty with the Kabaka later repudiated by his own Government. James Hannington, sent from London to be the first Anglican bishop in East Africa, has been murdered at Mwanga's command. Scores of Christian converts, refusing to recant their faith, have been burnt alive on pyres outside the city. Bewildered by coup and counter-coup, torn by religious dissension, presided over by the half-mad sodomite Kabaka, Buganda seems to exist in a state of nightmare uncertainty, liable at any moment to burst into bloodshed.

Yet for the British, into whose agreed sphere of influence it falls, it is the key to East Africa. To the Imperial East Africa Company, with its headquarters at Mombasa on the coast, it seems a promising field for trade and perhaps settlement. To the evangelists it is a paradigm of the African misery, only awaiting redemption. To the stragetists it promises command of the Nile headwaters, and would form a vital link in the cherished chain of British properties from Cairo to the Cape. The Company, as the agent of British power in East Africa, has already tried unsuccessfully to conclude a treaty with Mwanga. Now, in the last month of 1890, it has sent to Buganda the most promising of its adventurous young men, Frederick Lugard, to settle the matter.

Lugard is a former Indian Army officer, and seems on the face of it the antithesis of your New Imperialist—small, sensitive, erect, alert like a bantam cock, he is always good to his Africans, generally treats the tribal chiefs with respect, and views the imperial mission with an idealist fervour. Yet he is, in 1890, the agent of a simple grab. He may not think it himself, but he is: for though the Company is more interested in trade than conquest, and is at one level genuinely concerned with African welfare, still the deeper truth is that history is compelling the British inexorably towards the control of Uganda, and Lugard is its agent. No niceties of protocol or morality will deter him. He is caught up in the standards of his time, and he behaves accordingly. Here he comes now through the bush, his bright eyes blazing, his long moustaches drooped with sweat, leading a raggle-taggle army from the coast—a couple of British officers, seventy Sudanese askaris, a few Somali scouts and the usual muddle of porters. They are armed with elderly Snider rifles and with a solitary Maxim gun—which, having already crossed Africa with Henry Stanley, is no longer at its best; and led by the askaris in their best blue jerseys and white pants, on December 3, 1890, they march into the Kabaka's capital pursued by jostling crowds of sightseers.

Lugard has not been invited, and he behaves more like a conqueror than a guest. He refuses two proffered camping sites ('damp and dirty') and instead, climbing to the top of Kampala Hill, with its commanding prospect all around, he pitches his camp upon its summit. 'I have since heard that it is not etiquette to camp on top of a hill, only the King does that . . . but my own idea is that it is better to show Mwanga that we do not intend to be fooled, and that we come like men that are not afraid.'

'*Men that are not afraid.*' Lugard's position is precarious. His intentions are strictly dishonourable, and there are many people in Buganda all too willing to murder him and his little army. Yet he is utterly brazen. When, next day, he marches over to Mengo to see the Kabaka, he does so arrogantly. He wears a flannel pyjama jacket with brass buttons, and takes his own chair—for he has heard that European supplicants at the Kabaka's court are normally expected to kneel upon the ground. He takes a stalwart Sudanese bodyguard, too, and when, at the door of the royal hut, the Kabaka's minstrels strike up a welcome, beating their drums, blowing their flutes and ivory trumpets, and strumming violently upon their xylophones, the askaris reply with a fanfare of bugles. 'I was my own master, and of course tho' I have taken this somewhat independent attitude, I have been at great pains to show that it does not arise from insolence, disrespect, or a wish to wound the sensibilities of the king, but merely that I am an officer of the English army, and an accredited Envoy from the Company and do not mean to be ordered about, and treated as an inferior at the beck and call of Mwanga.'

In no time at all Lugard's status in Buganda is properly imperial. Up on the hill his newly-washed tents gleam white above the town. The more tents the better is Lugard's view—'I don't want it to look *small* here'. The track through the camp is hoed and trim, the soldiers are kept busy with spit and polish, and when Lugard goes through the town he is escorted by his huge Sudanese with fixed bayonets. A constant crowd of Baganda comes to stare at these arrangements, or wonder at the Maxim gun greased and gleaming upon its tripod, and though the whole country is still in a condition of imminent catastrophe, nobody dares challenge this magnificent affront (though once the atmosphere is so ominous, Lugard admits in his diary, 'that I looked up the book about the Maxim gun, and looked over the gun too').

So with seventy soldiers and the effrontery of the New Imperialism, Lugard conquers a nation without a shot. By Christmas he is ready to present a draft treaty to the Kabaka. 'Much discussion and even uproar arose at times but I scowled and looked as fierce as I could and insisted on reading it right through.' In return for the Company's benevolent protection, it demands that British jurisdictional rights in Buganda shall be exerted by a Resident—in other words, as the Kabaka will shortly discover, that the British shall have complete authority over the affairs of his country. Mwanga, lying on a mat, stalls for a few moments, but Lugard thrusts the treaty paper before him, and insists that he make his mark. 'He did it with a bad grace, just dashing the pen at the paper and making a blot, but I made him go at it again and make a cross, and on the 2nd copy he made a proper cross.' The thing is done. Lugard signs as 'an officer of the army of Her Majesty Victoria, Queen of Great Britain, Empress of India, etc', and the marks are appended of Apollo the Chief Minister, Kimbugwe the Chief Admiral of Canoes, Mjusi the Head of the Army and Kauta the Lord Chief Cook. The Kabaka of Buganda signs away his independence, and the British Empire acquires a promising new Protectorate (another up-to-date term, devised in its imperial context at the Berlin Conference).

5

Such was the Scramble, which brought out the bully in most imperialists, and lent itself fatally to double-dealing and self-delusion. It was a patchwork process, a muddle of aims good and bad, a huge charade of Mwangas and Lugards, Sniders and ceremonial xylophones, exchange quotations and diplomatic initiatives, and one man more than any other summed it up in his person: Cecil Rhodes, the Colossus of the Cape.

Rhodes was an enigma because he seemed to embrace within himself such widely disparate standards and motives. He was all contradictions. He was a vicar's son from Bishop's Stortford, but he looked like a Jewish millionaire of sporting habits. He adored Oxford and all it stood for, yet his abiding passion was the pursuit of material power. In some ways his notion of Empire was crass, in others it was truly noble, in others again half-crazy: 'I walked between earth and sky and when I looked down I said—"this earth shall be English" and when I looked up I said—"the English shall rule this earth".'

It was less than twenty years since, with some unlovely financial partners, he had made his fortune on the Kimberley diamond field, yet by 1895 he was the most powerful man in Africa, and one of the richest in the world. He was Premier of the Cape, he was virtual dictator of Rhodesia, and his British South Africa Company was much the most powerful of the new chartered companies. When Queen Victoria once asked him conversationally what he had been doing lately, he replied with perfect truth 'Adding two provinces to your Majesty's dominions'.

If the official view of Africa seemed diffuse, as Lord Salisbury drifted so urbanely down the stream of time, Rhodes had a more exact vision of the Empire's African destiny. He saw the entire continent dominated by British authority. Financed by the limitless treasures of South Africa, British power would extend in a spinal column north and south through the continent, from Egypt to the Cape. Along the central corridor a railway would run the entire length of Africa, its windows consecrated by the spray of the Victoria Falls,[1] and feeder lines would link it to British colonies on both coasts of the continent, like rivers from a watershed. Other Powers might have footholds here and there in Africa, but this over-riding pattern of suzerainty and communication would mean that in effect the continent would be as British as India. It would be a complete organism. The cycle would begin with the digging of wealth from the seams of the Witwatersrand, and it would end with the imposition of British civilized standards upon the whole African world—'equal rights', as Rhodes saw it, 'for all civilized men'.[2]

Step by step towards *fin de siècle* the British Empire approached the fulfilment of this dream. From the south British suzerainty advanced from South Africa across the Limpopo to the Zambezi. From the north, as General Kitchener embarked at last upon the reconquest of the Sudan, conveniently financed by the Egyptians,

[1] Which Rhodes never set eyes on.
[2] Rhodes was not the first to foresee a British Cape-to-Cairo corridor. Gladstone himself direly predicted it, five years before Tel-el-Kebir, as an inevitable consequence of intervention in Egypt—'be it by larceny or be it by emption'.

the Empire marched towards the headwaters of the Nile. The Cape-Cairo railway had reached Wadi Halfa in the north, Rhodesia in the south, and the first of the feeder lines was already being built between Uganda and the coast. Only a narrow strip of German territory in Tanganyika interrupted the all-British corridor from Egypt to South Africa. On the African flanks Nigeria, the Gold Coast, the Gambia, Sierra Leone, Somaliland, Uganda, Kenya and Zanzibar were all safely under the flag, importing their guns, cloths and iron goods from Manchester and Birmingham, sending to Britain their cloves, cocoa, ivory, coconuts and coffee. It was not yet a very profitable estate, but it had great promise, and to the imperial seers it seemed almost a new empire, the India of the coming century.[1]

Yet like an infuriating particle of grit in the gears of this great machine, the infinitesimal republic of the Transvaal still resisted the British Empire. Now that it possessed within its frontiers the world's principal source of gold, its independence seemed more than ever an impertinence to history. Never did a destiny seem more manifest, than the Transvaal's eventual inclusion within the British pattern for Africa. It is true that to the east the republic was bordered by Portuguese Mozambique, and that a railway line now linked Johannesburg with the Portuguese port of Delagoa Bay, enabling the Boers to send their exports abroad without crossing British territory at all. But with the Empire north, south and west of them, with British capital financing their industries, and British expertise extracting their gold, with Queen Victoria still hazily suzerain to their State, the extinction of the republic appeared inevitable in the end. This was the last decade of the nineteenth century: no time for anachronisms.

Even in the 1890s the British were not prepared to indulge in naked aggression against white people, and once more they approached the Transvaal problem deviously. A kind of half-tacit conspiracy was fostered. It was well-known that the Reform Move-

---

[1] In fact the British north-south corridor was not achieved until after the first world war, when Tanganyika became a British mandated territory, and the Cape-to-Cairo railway was never completed. Nor, except within South Africa, did the British ever control an east-west corridor across Africa.

ment in Johannesburg was fitfully considering an armed rising. Joseph Chamberlain, the Colonial Secretary in London, now authorized Sir Hercules Robinson, British High Commissioner in the Cape,[1] to intervene in Johannesburg if such a rising occurred—not of course to seize the country, but merely to restore order as representative of the suzerain Power. At the same time Rhodes, Premier of the Cape, and Jameson his chief assistant, went a stage further, and conspired with the Reformers to support their revolution: the moment the word came, they would send in a force to overthrow Kruger and establish a new Government, either independently British, or as a colony of the Empire. How far all the conspirators knew each other's minds has never been made clear. Perhaps they did not want to know. It was an unwritten, unspecified arrangement. Nothing was spelt out. Much was left, in the true spirit of the African Scramble, to a wink and a crooked nod.

In 1895 the British in South Africa, hoping to circumvent the Boer railway to Delagoa Bay, removed the customs controls on their frontier with the Transvaal, so that trade could come their way again. Kruger immediately responded by closing the drifts or fords by which the roads out of Pretoria and Johannesburg crossed into British territory. This was a slap in the imperial face, and it was an obvious signal for the rebellion of the Uitlanders. The conspirators moved. Jameson and his force went to Pitsani. A flow of coded messages streamed from Johannesburg to Cape Town, from Cape Town to Pitsani, from Cape Town to London. The South African air hummed with rumour. There were false alarms, second thoughts, cancellations, misunderstandings. The rising was planned for tomorrow, for the day after, it was cancelled, it was postponed. On December 30 Rhodes, learning from Johannesburg that the Reformers were once again postponing the rising, cabled Jameson to hold his hand. But it was too late. On December 29, 1895, at dawn, the little force at Pitsani had saddled its horses, struck its tents, ridden away from the kopjes and crossed the unmarked frontier into the Transvaal Republic.

[1] Whom we last met hoisting the flag in Fiji and accepting Cakobau's war-club for the Queen.

6

The Jameson Raid was the summation of the scramble for Africa, and a turning-point in the story of the British Empire. It was like a poor parody of the imperial process. It was underhand, it was mean, and it failed. It was the beginning of the end of that grand confidence which had sustained Victoria's Empire through so many hazards, always to emerge victorious in the end. The Empire never quite recovered from the ignominy of Jameson's Raid: it was as though a bubble had been pricked, or some great exotic blossom, grown glorious in the sunshine of a long summer, had reached its amplitude at last and begun to shed its petals.

Jameson's men were mostly very young, and foolish. There was Sir John ('Johnny') Willoughby, and the Honourable Major Bobby White, and there was J. B. Stacey-Clitheroe. There were the 470 troopers of the British South Africa Company police, well-mounted, sensibly dressed in grey, with wide-brimmed 'smasher' hats and dark blue puttees. They had a 12-pounder gun and five Maxims, and they seemed to be well enough organized for a dash into the Rand. Stores and remounts had been surreptitiously arranged for them along the route. The telegraph wires would be cut. The Reformers had promised to send out a body of horse to meet them as they approached Johannesburg. Jameson's own brother was one of the Doorfontein plotters; so was Rhodes's brother Frank; it was a conspiracy of intimates.

Jameson had been ready to ride since the beginning of December, and he was already primed with a *casus belli*—an undated letter from the Reform Committee, to be cabled to *The Times* in London at the right moment, allegedly appealing for help against Boer oppression. Week after week, as the rising was repeatedly postponed, Jameson and his men fretted in the Pitsani heat, until on Boxing Day Jameson heard direct from his brother Sam in the city: 'Absolutely necessary to postpone flotation. . . . We will endeavour to meet your wishes as regards December but you must not move until you have received instructions to'. Something seemed to crack inside the Doctor, when he read this. The Uitlanders would never rebel, he told himself, unless he made them. Two messengers arrived from Johannesburg telling him on no account to move, but by December 28 his mind was made up. 'Shall leave tonight for the Transvaal', he cabled Cape Town, and summoning his young soldiers to parade, he read them the letter of appeal from the Reformers, and assured them (or so it was later sworn) that the Imperial authorities supported their adventure. They cheered, sang the National Anthem, and led by Dr Jameson on a black horse, crossed the frontier at Burman's Drift at five in the morning.

Nothing went right. Not all the telegraph wires were cut, so that the Boers knew of the invasion almost at once. The remounts could not be caught. Two messengers overtook the raiders to order them back in the name of the British Government—'Her Majesty's Government', said the second directive, 'entirely disapprove your conduct in invading Transvaal with armed force. Your action has been repudiated. You are ordered to retire at once from the country and you will be held personally responsible for the consequences of your unauthorized and most improper proceeding'. Another message told Jameson that the rising in Johannesburg had fizzled out with an armistice between the Reformers and Kruger, so that the entire enterprise was aborted anyway.

Still the Raid continued, in a spirit one feels more of boyish bravado than of power-politics. The horsemen had to cross 190 miles of rough country to reach the outskirts of Johannesburg. At first it was splendid easy going, as the Raid itself perhaps seemed to its protagonists—fine open downland, almost treeless, with wooded ravines and cactus bushes: but when they reached the Rand itself the flavour of the country, as of the adventure, subtly changed. Now the landscape was corrugated with ridges and valleys, tracks twisted here and there, gulleys interrupted every downland gallop, and the points of the compass were never easy to grasp. The conviction of the enterprise faltered, like the pace. The guides lost their way. The troopers were tired and hungry. The horses were worn out. The first Boer horsemen appeared like shadows on the hillsides, following the raiders silently at a distance. When the first shots were fired, on the afternoon of New Year's Day, 1896, the raiders were only some thirty miles from Johannesburg, but they hardly had a hope. Skilfully the Boers forced them north-west around the perimeter of the city, skirmishing all the way, until at a place called Doornkop, almost within sight of the gold mines, they found themselves surrounded. They fought back bravely enough. Their Maxims were fired until they jammed, their 12-pounder was almost out of ammunition, when on the morning of January 2 they ran up the white flag and limply surrendered. The grand slam had failed. The rising in Johannesburg had never happened. The British Government had publicly condemned the raid. Rhodes in Cape Town was shattered and disgraced: 'poor old Jameson', was all he could say, 'twenty years we have been friends, and now he goes in and ruins me'.[1]

7

It did not at once break the spirit of the New Imperialism. Though Jameson was tried in England and imprisoned for treason, and though Rhodes was driven from office and never really recovered from the disaster, and though the Kaiser sent President Kruger a warm congratulatory telegram, still the British public on the whole did not disapprove of the venture. They thought it a dashing piece of buccaneering, and were sorry it failed. They admired rather than resented the British Government's part in the conspiracy—for though Chamberlain was cleared of complicity by a Select Committee, few really believed it, and some thought the Queen herself privy to the plot. They considered that Kruger deserved to be overthrown, that the Uitlanders were unfairly oppressed, and that Jameson was in trouble only because he did not succeed. The amorality of the adventure did not shock them. A celebratory poem by the new Poet Laureate, Alfred Austin, exactly reflected the general mood:

[1] Nowadays one may follow the route of Jameson's raid fairly exactly by car, the cross-road stores one sees often being the sites of his secret supply depots—in those days most of the store-keepers were British. At Pitsani a pair of kopjes are still named for Rhodes and Jameson, and in 1970 the Pakistanis who ran the store were able to take me in their pickup to the site of the raiders' camp. As for the Transvaalers, bitterly though they remember most aspects of their long struggle with the British Empire, Dr Jameson they seem largely to have forgotten.

Wrong! Is it wrong? Well, may be;
  But I'm going just the same,
Do they think me a Burgher's baby,
  To be scared by a scolding name?
They may argue and prate and order;
  Go tell them to save their breath:
Then, over the Transvaal border,
  And gallop for life or death!

Let lawyers and statesmen addle
  Their pates over points of law;
If sound be our sword, and saddle,
  And gun-gear, who cares one straw?
When men of our own blood pray us
  To ride to their kinsfolk's aid,
Not Heaven itself shall stay us,
  From the rescue they call a raid.

There spoke the spirit of the Scramble, the last rationale of the will to rule. The British people, in the last years of Victoria's century, believed the Empire must be its own judge. When Kruger seemed likely to visit London shortly after the raid, even Lord Salisbury said he hoped he would be drowned in turtle soup. The young politician Winston Churchill thought similarly at the time, and considered Jameson's adventure no more than a bold attempt to avenge Majuba. Later he came to change his opinion, and looking back upon the Raid through the tragedies that were presently to befall the British Empire, saw in that crude filibuster a different and darker meaning. 'I date the beginning of these violent times', he wrote then, 'from the Jameson Raid.'

CHAPTER TWENTY-SEVEN

An Imperial Fulfilment

'I EXPRESS to you my sincere congratulations,' said the Kaiser's telegram to President Kruger, 'that without calling on the aid of friendly Powers you and your people, by your own energy against the armed bands which have broken into your country as disturbers of the peace, have succeeded in re-establishing peace, and defending the independence of the country against attack from without.'

He was premature in his satisfaction. The failure of the Jameson Raid was an omen, no more, and the British had not yet lost their imperial resolution. Against such insolence from a foreign ruler, they instantly closed their ranks: Chamberlain was cleared, Jameson was glorified, Rhodes was forgiven.[1] In fact the British were only now reaching the apogee of their public complacency, and when in 1897 good old Queen Victoria celebrated the sixtieth anniversary of her accession to the throne, the nation made it gaudily and joyously a celebration of Empire. Never had the people been more united in pride, and more champagne was imported that year than ever before in British history.[2] What a century it had been for them all! How far the kingdom had come since that distant day when Emily Eden, hearing upon the Ganges bank of the young Queen's accession, had thought it so charming an invention! What a marvellous drama it had offered the people, now tragic, now exuberant, now uplifting, always rich in colour, and pathos, and laughter, and the glow of patriotism! In 1897 Britain stood alone among the Powers, and to most Britons this isolated splendour was specifically the product of

[1] And by 1899 the Kaiser was cabling Rhodes to congratulate *him* upon the successful defence of Kimberley against Kruger's forces in the second Boer war.

[2] Or since—9·5 million bottles, compared with 7·37 million in 1971.

Empire. Empire was the fount of pride. Empire was the panacea. Empire was God's gift to the British race, and dominion was their destiny.[1]

2

In some ways it was true. The possession of Empire, and particularly of India, kept Great Britain in the forefront of the Powers. There was a good deal of bluff to it, and much self-deception too, but the universal presence of the British flag made the island kingdom a force to be reckoned with everywhere. Britain's resources of man-power far exceeded her own paltry population. Her world-wide systems of commerce and intelligence were unrivalled. While it was true that the strategic burden of Empire was heavy, it was also true that Britain could exert pressure around the flank of every other Power—on Russia's south-east frontiers, on America's northern frontiers, on the European States from her bases in the Mediterranean.

Besides, the very splendour of the Empire was in itself an asset. If it was not in fact impregnable, it certainly looked it, and its assurance gave it authority. Just as the Royal Navy remained supreme largely by virtue of its own swagger, so the proclamation of Empire possessed the virtue of a decree, and made people think it must be binding. The mystique of it all, the legend of blood, crown, sacrifice, formed a sort of ju-ju. The red looked ingrained on the map, as though it had been stained there in some arcane ritual, and the vast spaces of Greater Britain were like a field of perpetual youth, where future generations of Britons would for ever be regenerated.

Whether it had made the British rich was always to remain debatable. Rich they undoubtedly were, and the pound sterling was the basis of the whole world economy, but how much of this wealth came from the Empire, nobody really knew. There were pros and

---

[1] A view of the English heritage shared, 25 years later, by Adolf Hitler, who identified the causes of English supremacy in the world as patriotism, racial segregation and masterful behaviour in the colonies. For a fuller picture of the climactic Empire, its motives, its emotions and its manners, perhaps I may be forgiven for suggesting the central volume of this trilogy, *Pax Britannica* (London and New York, 1968).

cons. On the one hand was India, which had for many generations provided a flow of specie, and during Victoria's reign had offered an almost limitless field for investment. On the other was the terrible cost of maintaining the vast and ramshackle imperial structure, with its garrisons in every continent, its enormous patrolling fleets, its consumption of talent and energy that might have found more immediate productive uses at home. One could point to the immense flow of trade within the Empire, but equally one could argue that the most profitable British overseas investments were in foreign countries. There was no single year in Victoria's reign in which Britain's exports were more valuable than her imports; but she always enjoyed a handsome balance of payments, because of the City of London, the financial and insurance capital of the world, whose pre-eminence had little to do with Empire. Nobody could really strike a balance: but if economists sometimes argued for less elaborate ways of keeping the nation prosperous, the man in the London street in 1897 had little doubt that the cash in his pocket, like the pride in his spirit and the grand excitement of Jubilee, sprang from the success of Empire, the national vocation.

3

By now the effects of imperial possession, scattered and particular in 1837, were diffused throughout Great Britain, and formed a familiar part of life's pattern. There were no longer specific ports, like Bristol or Liverpool, which were imperial gateways: the whole island was a gateway of Empire now, and the imperial products and merchandise flowed through every seaport. Nabobs no longer came home to build their Sezincotes, but there was scarcely a gentleman's house in the country which was not in some way enriched by the imperial experience, whether by the existence of a bank account stuffed with the profits of colonial trade, or just by the Maori carvings, Benares trays or Sioux beadwork which gave a lick of the exotic to the drawing-room.

London was littered now with imperial statuary, heroes of the Mutiny, great pro-consuls, C. J. Napier in Trafalgar Square, Gordon like a mystical vicar on his plinth. Colonial outfitters, colonial agents, colonial bankers, the makers of colonial inks, beers, pianofortes, camp beds, portable baths were inescapable in the streets and directories of the kingdom. Whole industries of Birmingham or Lancashire thrived upon the colonial trade. High on its bleak hill in Easter Ross Sir Hector Munro's gates of Negapatam still intermittently showed through the mist, but by now the trophies and emblems of Empire were generally less theatrical, more accessible, and were beginning to form a homely part of the national heritage.

Not far from Henley-on-Thames, for instance, at the village of Ipsden in Oxfordshire, there stood the Maharajah's Well, with its attendant orchard. It was covered with a dome of cast iron, and it had been given to the village by His Highness the Maharajah of Benares, in token of his attachment to the British Empire. A charitable trust ensured that the villagers of Ipsden should have free water from the well for ever; a warden lived on the spot, in a pretty circular cottage; an orchard was planted with cherry trees, to provide for the maintenance of the well. Nearby a pleasure garden was created, for the enjoyment of the fortunate villagers: it contained a pond shaped like a fish, the Maharajah's personal symbol, a mound called Prubhoo Teela, and an ornamental ravine called Saya Khood. The whole was called Ishree Bagh, and around the dome of the well were inscribed in iron letters the words 'His Highness The Maharajah of Benares, India, Gave This Well'.[1]

4

Not many people doubted the rightness of Empire—'any question of abstract justice in the matter', wrote Trollope, 'seems to have been thrown altogether to the winds'. The British knew that theirs was not a wicked nation, as nations went, and if they were insensitive to the hypocrisies, deceits and brutalities of Empire, they believed genuinely in its civilizing mission. They had no doubt that British rule was best, especially for heathens or primitives, and they had

---

[1] Which is spick and span to this day, under the care of the same charitable trust. Though Ishree Bagh is fenced and overgrown, there is still a caretaker in the circular cottage, and cherries flourish in the orchard. The well was the first of several commissioned by emulative Maharajahs.

faith in their own good intentions. In this heyday of their power they were behaving below their own best standards, but they remained as a whole a good-natured people. Their chauvinism was not generally cruel. Their racialism was more ignorant than malicious. Their militarism was skin-deep. Their passion for imperial grandeur was to prove transient and superficial, and was more love of show than love of power. They had grown up in an era of unrivalled national success, and they were displaying the all too human conceit of achievement.

Nor were they ever without their self-critics. Liberalism was out of fashion in the 1890s, and the dying Gladstone was distressed to see politicians of every shade subscribing to the imperial heresy: but there had always been voices of restraint or modesty in England, men who pleaded for gentler values, or plainer ambitions, or who believed in the true equality of all peoples, or wondered if the British Empire really was constituted by divine appointment. Even in 1897 there were dissentients—men like Edward Fairfield of the Colonial Office, who was said to 'look down upon the British Empire as a profound mistake', or the poet Wilfrid Blunt, who fought the Empire vehemently on every front, or General William Butler of the Ring, by now a passionate anti-imperialist. The nation was never unanimous about anything, and although at the time of the Diamond Jubilee the New Imperialists had it all their own way, many a dissenting argument was in the formative stage, and Gladstone's ideals, if discredited, were far from dead.

There were forebodings, too, even then. The British looked all-confident to the world outside, but the very frenzy of the imperial climax was revealing. For all her pomp and circumstance, Britain was more vulnerable than ever before: her population had doubled since 1837, and she was now dependent upon imported food for her survival. A few political scientists sensed that an Empire based upon autocratic resolution sat uneasily upon a democratic foundation. A few maverick economists were arguing that Empire was more trouble than it was worth, and that Britain would be in better condition if she had no overseas possessions at all. There were repeated attempts to give the Empire a tauter meaning: conferences of colonial premiers, proposals for common defence arrangements, institutions like the Colonial Society, the Imperial Institute, the Empire League. There was a trace of disquiet to it all, as though the imperialists knew by some unadmitted instinct that, however momentous the occasion and unexampled the glory, time was running short.

5

Still, it was a grand moment of history, and the world recognized it without rancour. Mark Twain, surveying the many-coloured pageant of imperial troops that poured into London for the commemorative parade, called it 'a sort of suggestion of the Last Day'. During the sixty years of Victoria's reign the Empire had grown by more than ten times, from a scatter of disregarded possessions to a quarter of the land mass of the earth, and a third of its population. It had changed the face of the continents with its cities, its railways, its churches, its myriad cantonments, and it had changed the manner of life of entire peoples, stamping its own values upon civilizations from the Cree to the Burmese, besides creating several fully-fledged new nations of its own. There had never been such an Empire since history began, and the Powers of the world, envious of its splendour, respectfully if reluctantly acknowledged its supremacy. Even the Kaiser congratulated his grandmother upon her glorious jubilee. Even Kruger released two English prisoners to mark the occasion. Even the *New York Times* conceded that the United States, that incorrigible republic of rebels, was really part of Greater Britain all the time.

Before she set out on her Jubilee procession, on the morning of June 22, 1897, Queen Victoria went to the telegraph room at Buckingham Palace, wearing a dress of black moire with panels of pigeon grey, embroidered all over with silver roses, shamrocks and thistles. She pressed an electric button; an impulse was transmitted to the Central Telegraph Office in St Martin's le Grand; in a matter of seconds her Jubilee message was on its way to every corner of the Empire. '*From my heart I thank my beloved people,*' it said, speeding through the cables to Ottawa and Calcutta, Lagos and the Cape, Sydney and Christchurch, the fortress islands of the Mediterranean and the old slave colonies—to Lucknow where the flag still flew above the shattered Residency, to Winnipeg where Riel lay beneath his stone-clamped tomb, to Truganini's Hobart, to Cakobau's Fiji, to Eyre's shabby Spanish Town, to Ashanti and Zululand and Dublin and Kampala—*'From my heart I thank my beloved people. May God bless them.'*

ACKNOWLEDGEMENTS

The following friends and colleagues most kindly read parts of my manuscript for me, saving me from many errors and stupidities: Mrs Mildred Archer, Mrs Joan Craig, Professor John Gallagher, Mr J. G. Links, Professor Christopher Lloyd, Major-General James Lunt, Miss Mary Lutyens, Professor F. S. L. Lyons, Mr Leo Marquard, Dame Margery Perham, Mr L. T. C. Rolt, Professor A. G. L. Shaw, Professor Jack Simmons and Sir Ronald Wingate. Finally Mr Donald Simpson, librarian of the Royal Commonwealth Society, read the whole book in proof, placing me greatly in his debt.

Mr Denys Baker, as usual, drew the maps. Mr Julian Bach, as always, made possible the necessary travel. The Editors of *Horizon*, New York, and *Encounter*, London, have allowed me to reproduce passages first published in their magazines. It is entirely due to my indulgent publishers, on both sides of the Atlantic, that I have been able to devote so much time to the imperial subject. I must acknowledge too the pleasure of getting books from the London Library and pictures from the Mansell Collection.

In a later volume I plan to include a bibliography covering the whole range of my trilogy, 1837 to 1965. As to original research, it has mostly been confined to the quest of the wanderer's eye.

Index

After Oxford and a Harkness Fellowship in the United States, James Morris spent ten years as a foreign correspondent for the London *Times* and *The Guardian*, an experience that led to Morris's historic coverage of the 1953 Everest expedition and subsequent ventures to cover wars, revolutions, trials, elections, and political crises on every continent. The recipient of the George Polk Memorial Award for Journalism in America for 1961 and the Heinemann Award of the Royal Society of Literature in England for the same year, Morris left newspaper work in 1961 to write books. In 1972, James Morris became Jan Morris; *Farewell the Trumpets* was the last of her works to appear under her original name. Morris has lived in America, Venice, the French Alps, Egypt, Spain, and Wales, where she is now settled.